POVERTY
IN THE UNITED STATES

An Encyclopedia of History, Politics, and Policy

POVERTY IN THE UNITED STATES

An Encyclopedia of History, Politics, and Policy

VOLUME 1 A–K

edited by Gwendolyn Mink and Alice O'Connor

ABC CLIO

Santa Barbara, California • Denver, Colorado • Oxford, England

Library of Congress Cataloging-in-Publication Data
Poverty in the United States : an encyclopedia of history, politics, and policy / Gwendolyn Mink and Alice O'Connor, editors.
p. cm.
Includes bibliographical references and index.
ISBN 1-57607-597-4 (hardback : alk. paper) — ISBN 1-57607-608-3 (e-book)
1. Poverty—United States—Encyclopedias. 2. Poor—United States—Encyclopedias. 3. Public welfare—United States—Encyclopedias.
I. Mink, Gwendolyn, 1952– II. O'Connor, Alice, 1958–
HC110.P6P598 2004
339.4'6'097303—dc22
2004017618

08 07 06 05 04 / 10 9 8 7 6 5 4 3 2 1

This book is also available on the World Wide Web as an eBook.
Visit abc-clio.com for details.

ABC-CLIO, Inc.
130 Cremona Drive, P.O. Box 1911
Santa Barbara, California 93116-1911

This book is printed on acid-free paper.
Manufactured in the United States of America

Contents

VOLUME 1

VOLUME 2

Contributors

Emily K. Abel
University of California, Los Angeles
School of Public Health
Los Angeles, California

W. Andrew Achenbaum
University of Houston
Graduate School of Social Work
Houston, Texas

Martha Ackelsberg
Smith College
Department of Government and Women's Studies Program
Northampton, Massachusetts

Vivyan C. Adair
Hamilton College
Department of Women's Studies
Clinton, New York

Randy Albelda
University of Massachusetts Boston
Economics Department
Boston, Massachusetts

Ruth M. Alexander
Colorado State University
Department of History
Fort Collins, Colorado

Rebecca A. Allahyari
School of American Research
Santa Fe, New Mexico

Barbara Bair
Library of Congress
Washington, D.C.

John Baranski
Fort Lewis College
Department of History
Durango, Colorado

Lucy G. Barber
California State Archives
Sacramento, California

Rosalyn Baxandall
State University of New York, Old Westbury
Chair and Professor of American Studies
New York, New York

Daniel E. Bender
University of Waterloo
History Department
Waterloo, Ontario, Canada

Jared Bernstein
Economic Policy Institute
Washington, D.C.

Dwight B. Billings
University of Kentucky
Department of Sociology
Lexington, Kentucky

Elizabeth Blackmar
Columbia University
Department of History
New York, New York

Fred Block
University of California, Davis
Department of Sociology
Davis, California

Charles C. Bolton
University of Southern Mississippi
Department of History
Hattiesburg, Mississippi

Eileen Boris
University of California, Santa Barbara
Women's Studies Program
Santa Barbara, California

Heather Boushey
Center for Economic and Policy Research
Economist
Washington, D.C.

Rose M. Brewer
University of Minnesota–Twin Cities
Department of African American and African Studies
Minneapolis, Minnesota

Evelyn Z. Brodkin
University of Chicago
School of Social Service Administration
Chicago, Illinois

Dorothea Browder
University of Wisconsin–Madison
History Department
Madison, Wisconsin

Michael K. Brown
University of California, Santa Cruz
Department of Politics
Santa Cruz, California

Lisa D. Brush
University of Pittsburgh
Department of Sociology
Pittsburgh, Pennsylvania

Heather E. Bullock
University of California, Santa Cruz
Psychology Department
Santa Cruz, California

Steven B. Burg
Shippensburg University of Pennsylvania
Assistant Professor of History
Shippensburg, Pennsylvania

Jay Carlander
University of California, Santa Barbara
Department of History
Santa Barbara, California

Mina Carson
Oregon State University
Department of History
Corvallis, Oregon

Sarah Case
Independent Scholar
Santa Barbara, California

Nancy K. Cauthen
Columbia University
National Center for Children in Poverty
New York, New York

Noel A. Cazenave
University of Connecticut
Department of Sociology
Storrs, Connecticut

Grace Chang
University of California, Santa Barbara
Women's Studies Program
Santa Barbara, California

Christine N. Cimini
University of Denver
College of Law
Denver, Colorado

Aixa Cintron
Russell Sage Foundation
New York, New York

Elisabeth S. Clemens
University of Chicago
Department of Sociology
Chicago, Illinois

Daniel M. Cobb
D'Arcy McNickle Center for American Indian History
The Newberry Library
Chicago, Illinois

Sheila D. Collins
William Paterson University
Political Science Department
Wayne, New Jersey

Susan A. Comerford
The University of Vermont
College of Education and Social Services
Burlington, Vermont

Ruth Crocker
Auburn University
Department of History/Women's Studies
Auburn, Alabama

Lisa A. Crooms
Howard University
School of Law
Washington, D.C.

Martha F. Davis
Northeastern University
School of Law
Boston, Massachusetts

Ronald L. F. Davis
California State University, Northridge
Professor of History
Northridge, California

Adela de la Torre
University of California, Davis
Chicana/o Studies Program
Davis, California

Maritza De La Trinidad
University of Arizona
Department of History
Tucson, Arizona

Mary Jo Deegan
University of Nebraska–Lincoln
Department of Sociology
Lincoln, Nebraska

Karen deVries
University of California, Santa Cruz
History of Consciousness
Santa Cruz, California

Bonnie Thornton Dill
University of Maryland
Department of Women's Studies
College Park, Maryland

Matthew Diller
Fordham University
School of Law
New York, New York

Diane Dujon
Massachusetts Welfare Rights Union; Survivors, Inc.
University of Massachusetts/Boston
Boston, Massachusetts

Cynthia M. Duncan
The University of New Hampshire
Director, The Carsey Institute
Durham, New Hampshire

Peter Edelman
Georgetown University
Law Center
Washington, D.C.

Anne B. W. Effland
Economic Research Service
U.S. Department of Agriculture
Washington, D.C.

Peter Eisinger
Wayne State University
College of Urban, Labor, and Metropolitan Affairs
Detroit, Michigan

Ronald D. Eller
University of Kentucky
Department of History
Lexington, Kentucky

Jennifer L. Erkulwater
University of Richmond
Political Science Department
Richmond, Virginia

Carol Faulkner
State University of New York, College at Geneseo
Department of History
Geneseo, New York

Cara A. Finnegan
University of Illinois at Urbana-Champaign
Department of Speech Communication
Urbana, Illinois

Gordon M. Fisher
U.S. Department of Health and Human Services
Office of the Assistant Secretary for Planning and Evaluation
Washington, D.C.

Sheldon Friedman
AFL-CIO
Department of Public Policy
Washington, D.C.

Jennifer Frost
University of Auckland
Department of History
Auckland, New Zealand

Lynn H. Fujiwara
University of Oregon
Women's and Gender Studies Program
Eugene, Oregon

Mary O. Furner
University of California, Santa Barbara
Department of History
Santa Barbara, California

Herbert J. Gans
Columbia University
Department of Sociology
New York, New York

Kent B. Germany
University of Virginia
Miller Center of Public Affairs
Charlottesville, Virginia

Michele Estrin Gilman
University of Baltimore
School of Law
Baltimore, Maryland

Daniel P. Gitterman
University of North Carolina at Chapel Hill
Assistant Professor of Public Policy
Chapel Hill, North Carolina

John M. Glen
Ball State University
Department of History
Muncie, Indiana

Jonathan A. Glickstein
University of California, Santa Barbara
Department of History
Santa Barbara, California

Gertrude Schaffner Goldberg
Director, Doctoral Program, School of Social Work
Adelphi University
Garden City, New York

Michael Goldfield
Wayne State University
College of Urban, Labor, and Metropolitan Affairs
Detroit, Michigan

Joanne L. Goodwin
University of Nevada, Las Vegas
Department of History
Las Vegas, Nevada

Linda Gordon
New York University
Professor of History
New York, New York

Dawn M. Greeley
Independent Scholar
Silver Spring, Maryland

James N. Gregory
University of Washington
Department of History
Seattle, Washington

Timothy A. Hacsi
University of Massachusetts Boston
Department of History
Boston, Massachusetts

Jonathan L. Hafetz
Gibbons, Del Deo, Dolan, Griffinger & Vecchione
John J. Gibbons Fellow in Public Interest and Constitutional Law
New York, New York

David E. Hamilton
University of Kentucky
Department of History
Lexington, Kentucky

Joel F. Handler
University of California, Los Angeles
Richard C. Maxwell Professor of Law and Professor of Policy Studies
Los Angeles, California

Bradley A. Hansen
Mary Washington College
Department of Economics
Fredericksburg, Virginia

Susan B. Hansen
University of Pittsburgh
Department of Political Science
Pittsburgh, Pennsylvania

Cynthia Harrison
George Washington University
History Department/Women's Studies Program
Washington, D.C.

Heidi Hartmann
Institute for Women's Policy Research
Washington, D.C.

R. Allen Hays
University of Northern Iowa
Director, Graduate Program in Public Policy
Cedar Falls, Iowa

Kara Heffernan
Center for Neighborhood Technology
Chicago, Illinois

G. Mark Hendrickson
University of California, Santa Barbara
Department of History
Santa Barbara, California

Ruth Wallis Herndon
University of Toledo
Department of History
Toledo, Ohio

Frank Tobias Higbie
The Newberry Library
Dr. William M. Scholl Center for Family and Community History
Chicago, Illinois

Thomas M. Hilbink
University of Massachusetts Amherst
Department of Legal Studies
Amherst, Massachusetts

Christine Firer Hinze
Marquette University
Associate Professor, Christian Ethics
Milwaukee, Wisconsin

Beatrix Hoffman
Northern Illinois University
Department of History
DeKalb, Illinois

Elizabeth Cobbs Hoffman
San Diego State University
Department of History
San Diego, California

Douglas Imig
University of Memphis
Hooks Institute of Political Science
Memphis, Tennessee

Maurice Isserman
Hamilton College
Department of History
Clinton, New York

Thomas F. Jackson
University of North Carolina at Greensboro
History Department
Greensboro, North Carolina

Dolores E. Janiewski
Victoria University of Wellington/Te Whare
School of History, Philosophy, Politics, and International Relations
Wellington, New Zealand

Volker Janssen
University of California, San Diego
Department of History
San Diego, California

Laura S. Jensen
University of Massachusetts Amherst
Department of Political Science
Amherst, Massachusetts

Ollie A. Johnson III
Alfred University
Department of African American Studies/Social Sciences
Alfred, New York

Julia S. Jordan-Zachery
Howard University
Department of Political Science
Washington, D.C.

Michael B. Kahan
Stanford University
Program on Urban Studies and the History Department
Stanford, California

Elif Kale-Lostuvali
University of California, Berkeley
Department of Sociology
Berkeley, California

Devesh Kapur
Harvard University
Department of Government
Cambridge, Massachusetts

Michael B. Katz
University of Pennsylvania
History Department
Philadelphia, Pennsylvania

Lisa A. Keister
The Ohio State University
Department of Sociology
Columbus, Ohio

Grant H. Kester
University of California, San Diego
Department of Visual Arts
San Diego, California

Jennifer Klein
Yale University
Department of History
New Haven, Connecticut

Eric Klinenberg
New York University
Department of Sociology
New York, New York

Anne Kornhauser
Princeton University
New York, New York

Robert Korstad
Duke University
Sanford Institute of Public Policy
Durham, North Carolina

Isaac Kramnick
Cornell University
Department of Government
Ithaca, New York

John Krinsky
The City College of the City University of New York
Department of Political Science
New York, New York

Kenneth L. Kusmer
Temple University
Department of History
Philadelphia, Pennsylvania

Robert J. Lacey
University of Massachusetts Amherst
Political Science Department
Amherst, Massachusetts

Molly Ladd-Taylor
York University
Department of History
Toronto, Ontario, Canada

Leslie Leighninger
Arizona State University
School of Social Work
Tempe, Arizona

Sherry Leiwant
Legal Momentum
NOW Legal Defense
Senior Attorney
New York, New York

Lisa Levenstein
University of North Carolina at Greensboro
History Department
Greensboro, North Carolina

Nelson Lichtenstein
University of California, Santa Barbara
Department of History
Santa Barbara, California

Ann Chih Lin
University of Michigan
Gerald R. Ford School of Public Policy and Department of Political Science
Ann Arbor, Michigan

Kriste Lindenmeyer
University of Maryland, Baltimore County
Department of History
Baltimore, Maryland

Diane Lindstrom
University of Wisconsin–Madison
Department of History
Madison, Wisconsin

Kathryn Lofton
University of North Carolina at Chapel Hill
Department of Religious Studies
Chapel Hill, North Carolina

Theodore J. Lowi
Cornell University
Government Department
Ithaca, New York

Kristin Luker
University of California, Berkeley
Sociology and the Program in Jurisprudence and Social Policy, Boalt Hall School of Law
Berkeley, California

Nancy MacLean
Northwestern University
Department of History
Evanston, Illinois

Lisa Magaña
Arizona State University
Department of Chicana/o Studies
Tempe, Arizona

Lawrence H. Mamiya
Vassar College
Religion Department and Africana Studies Program
Poughkeepsie, New York

Anne M. Manuel
University of Michigan
Political Science Department
Ann Arbor, Michigan

Jason D. Martinek
Carnegie Mellon University
Department of History
Pittsburgh, Pennsylvania

Carol Mattingly
University of Louisville
Department of English
Louisville, Kentucky

Leslie McCall
Rutgers University
Department of Sociology and Department of Women's and Gender Studies
New Brunswick, New Jersey

Carole R. McCann
University of Maryland, Baltimore County
Women's Studies Program
Baltimore, Maryland

Martha T. McCluskey
State University of New York, Buffalo
Law School
Buffalo, New York

Elaine McCrate
University of Vermont
Economics Department and Women's Studies Department
Burlington, Vermont

Richard W. McHugh
National Employment Law Project
Staff Attorney
Dexter, Michigan

Amy E. McLaughlin
University of Maryland
Consortium on Race, Gender, and Ethnicity
College Park, Maryland

Suzanne Mettler
Maxwell School of Citizenship and Public Affairs, Syracuse University
Department of Political Science
Syracuse, New York

Sonya Michel
University of Maryland
Department of American Studies and Department of History
College Park, Maryland

Cheryl M. Miller
University of Maryland, Baltimore County
Department of Public Policy
Baltimore, Maryland

Jennifer Mittelstadt
Brooklyn College
Brooklyn, New York

Sandra Morgen
University of Oregon
Center for the Study of Women in Society and Department of Anthropology
Eugene, Oregon

Andrew Morris
Union College
Department of History
Schenectady, New York

Robyn Muncy
University of Maryland
Department of History
College Park, Maryland

Premilla Nadasen
Queens College, City University of New York
History Department
Flushing, New York

Nancy A. Naples
University of Connecticut
Sociology/Women's Studies
Hartford, Connecticut

Immanuel Ness
Brooklyn College, City University of New York
Department of Political Science
New York, New York

Kenneth J. Neubeck
University of Connecticut
Professor Emeritus of Sociology
Storrs, Connecticut

Julie A. Nice
University of Denver
College of Law
Denver, Colorado

Carl H. Nightingale
University of Massachusetts Amherst
Associate Professor of History
Amherst, Massachusetts

Erin O'Brien
Kent State University
Department of Political Science
Kent, Ohio

Ruth O'Brien
The City University of New York
Political Science Program, the Graduate Center and Government Department, John Jay College of Criminal Justice
New York, New York

Edward T. O'Donnell
College of the Holy Cross
Department of History
Worcester, Massachusetts

Margaret Pugh O'Mara
Stanford University
Department of History
Stanford, California

Laury Oaks
University of California, Santa Barbara
Women's Studies Program
Santa Barbara, California

Acela Minerva Ojeda
University of California, Riverside
Sociology Department
Riverside, California

Paul Ong
University of California, Los Angeles
School of Public Policy and Social Research
Los Angeles, California

Richard Parker
Harvard University
John F. Kennedy School of Government
Cambridge, Massachusetts

Jacqueline K. Payne
Assistant Director of Government Relations
Planned Parenthood Federation of America
Washington, D.C.

Diana M. Pearce
University of Washington
School of Social Work
Seattle, Washington

Jamie Peck
University of Wisconsin–Madison
Department of Geography
Madison, Wisconsin

Stephen Pimpare
Yeshiva University
New York, New York

Frances Fox Piven
The City University of New York
The Graduate Center
New York, New York

Anthony M. Platt
California State University, Sacramento
Division of Social Work
Sacramento, California

Janet E. Poppendieck
Hunter College, City University of New York
Department of Sociology
New York, New York

Steven Pressman
Monmouth University
Department of Economics and Finance
West Long Branch, New Jersey

Wendell E. Pritchett
University of Pennsylvania
Law School
Philadelphia, Pennsylvania

Karen Quintiliani
California State University, Long Beach
Department of Anthropology
Long Beach, California

Ellen Reese
University of California, Riverside
Department of Sociology
Riverside, California

Belinda I. Reyes
University of California, Merced
Merced, California

Ann M. Robbart
University of Massachusetts Boston
Public Policy/McCormack Graduate School of Policy Studies
Boston, Massachusetts

Dorothy E. Roberts
Northwestern University
School of Law
Chicago, Illinois

David Brian Robertson
University of Missouri, St. Louis
Department of Political Science
St. Louis, Missouri

David A. Rochefort
Northeastern University
Department of Political Science
Boston, Massachusetts

Rebecca K. Root
University of Massachusetts Amherst
Political Science Department
Amherst, Massachusetts

David Rosner
Columbia University, Mailman School of Public Health
Departments of History and Sociomedical Sciences
New York, New York

Elizabeth Sanders
Cornell University
Department of Government
Ithaca, New York

Sanford F. Schram
Bryn Mawr College
Graduate School of Social Work and Social Research
Bryn Mawr, Pennsylvania

Bruce J. Schulman
Boston University
Department of History
Boston, Massachusetts

Danielle S. Seiden
University of California, Los Angeles
Center for Community Health
Los Angeles, California

Amanda I. Seligman
University of Wisconsin–Milwaukee
Department of History
Milwaukee, Wisconsin

Andrea Y. Simpson
University of Richmond
Department of Political Science
Richmond, Virginia

Peter Siskind
Princeton University
History Department
Princeton, New Jersey

Anna Marie Smith
Cornell University
Government Department
Ithaca, New York

Jason Scott Smith
Harvard University
Harvard-Newcomen Fellow
Boston, Massachusetts

Steven Rathgeb Smith
University of Washington
Daniel J. Evans School of Public Affairs
Seattle, Washington

Rickie Solinger
Independent Scholar
New Paltz, New York

Joe Soss
University of Wisconsin–Madison
Department of Political Science
Madison, Wisconsin

Mark J. Stern
University of Pennsylvania
Department of Social Work/Department of History
Philadelphia, Pennsylvania

Landon R. Y. Storrs
University of Houston
Department of History
Houston, Texas

Dara Z. Strolovitch
University of Minnesota
Department of Political Science
Minneapolis, Minnesota

Matthew A. Sutton
University of California, Santa Barbara
Department of History
Santa Barbara, California

Heidi J. Swarts
Syracuse University
Department of Political Science
Syracuse, New York

Dana Takagi
University of California, Santa Cruz
Department of Sociology
Santa Cruz, California

Lorrin R. Thomas
Rutgers University
Department of History
Camden, New Jersey

Ann R. Tickamyer
Ohio University
Department of Sociology/Anthropology
Athens, Ohio

Chris Tilly
University of Massachusetts Lowell
Department of Regional Economic and Social Development
Lowell, Massachusetts

David Torres-Rouff
University of California, Santa Barbara
Department of History
Santa Barbara, California

Joe William Trotter Jr.
Carnegie Mellon University
Department of History
Pittsburgh, Pennsylvania

Laura Tuennerman-Kaplan
California University of Pennsylvania
Department of History and Political Science
California, Pennsylvania

Lauri Umansky
Suffolk University
Department of History
Boston, Massachusetts

Abel Valenzuela Jr.
University of California, Los Angeles
Cesar E. Chavez Center for Interdisciplinary Instruction in Chicana/o Studies and Department of Urban Planning
Los Angeles, California

Dennis J. Ventry Jr.
New York University
School of Law
New York, New York

Udaya Wagle
University of Massachusetts Boston
McCormack Graduate School of Policy Studies
Boston, Massachusetts

Mark R. Warren
Harvard University
Graduate School of Education
Cambridge, Massachusetts

Jeffrey B. Wenger
University of Georgia
Department of Public Administration and Policy, School of Public and International Affairs
Athens, Georgia

Robert Whaples
Wake Forest University
Department of Economics
Winston-Salem, North Carolina

Diane Winston
University of Southern California
Annenberg School for Communication
Los Angeles, California

Ann Withorn
University of Massachusetts Boston
College of Public and Community Service
Brookline, Massachusetts

Preface

Understanding the history of poverty in the United States necessarily takes us to many facets of the American past. Central, of course, are the diverse experiences of the many people who have lived in and struggled against poverty. But also important are the economic transformations, the social movements, the competing ideas and ideologies, and the political debates and policy decisions that have made poverty—and the struggle against it—integral parts of the broader American experience since the colonial era. The history of poverty, then, is about the rise of laissez-faire capitalism and efforts to tame and redress its inequities. It is about the divisions of power and prejudice that have systematically denied opportunity to people of color, women, and the unorganized working classes—and the ongoing efforts of civil rights, feminist, welfare rights, and labor activists to challenge those divisions through legislation, litigation, and grassroots political organizing. It is about the creation and evolution of a national system of government-subsidized social welfare in the twentieth century, backed by a combination of reform coalitions, social scientific ideas, and shifting value commitments. And it is about such critical historical developments as the Great Depression of the 1930s, the War on Poverty of the 1960s, and the so-called end of welfare of the 1990s, which have brought issues of poverty and social welfare—however momentarily—to the top of the nation's political agenda.

In *Poverty in the United States: An Encyclopedia of History, Politics, and Policy*, we offer the elements of such a multifaceted perspective, presenting the dynamics of poverty and social welfare in broad historical context while providing information about more specific political, social, and policy developments. The encyclopedia opens with a series of chronologically organized essays, written by leading historians of their respective eras, that discuss the occurrence, perceptions of, and changing political and moral responses to poverty as part of the broad sweep of American history. It then turns to more topical, alphabetically organized entries that identify, describe, and interpret the core issues, events, debates, concepts, social and political movements, legislative developments, and social experiences that have shaped poverty and social welfare historically and that continue to influence policy debates in the twenty-first century. Drawing on the expertise of historians, political scientists, economists, legal scholars, and social welfare practitioners, these entries illustrate the value of interdisciplinary analysis and interpretation. Interspersed throughout are excerpts from key primary source documents, including speeches, congressional testimony, court decisions, and photographs, that both illustrate and influence changing popular perceptions of poverty and the poor.

We are fortunate to have had guidance from editorial advisers Frances Fox Piven and Eileen Boris in conceptualizing and compiling this encyclopedia. Their advice, along with the knowledge of our many contributors, has been instrumental in making *Poverty in the United States* both a comprehensive resource and a gateway to deeper inquiry about issues of enduring historical and contemporary significance.

Gwendolyn Mink and Alice O'Connor

A Chronological Introduction in Five Essays

Colonial Period through the Early Republic

The history of poverty and social welfare in the United States dates back to the country's origins and has been deeply ingrained in the American experience ever since. Indeed, poverty and social welfare are closely linked to the major political, economic, and social developments that shaped the nation throughout its history.

In early American history, poverty grew out of the processes of immigration, conquest, and enforced labor that accompanied the European settlement of North America and the founding of the United States. At the same time, and even as the experience of poverty became more widespread, this period laid the groundwork for the idea of America as a "land of plenty" and the home of a revolutionary ideology. Future generations would invoke that ideology to protest enduring social and economic inequalities and the poverty conditions they produced.

In retrospect, colonial America sometimes appears to have been a golden era, when communities were marked principally by hope and opportunity. Colonial promoters in sixteenth- and seventeenth-century Europe certainly strove to give that impression. In his *Discourse on Western Planting* ([1584] 1877), English social theorist Richard Hakluyt argued for colonizing North America in part to provide a place where the children of "the wandering beggars of England" might be "unladen" and "better bred up . . . to their own more happy state." In his *Historical and Geographical Account of the Province and Country of Pensilvania* (1698), Gabriel Thomas described the newly established colony as a place where "poor people (both men and women) of all kinds, can here get three times the wages for their labour they can in England or Wales"; furthermore, he noted, food was plentiful and cheap, children were born "beautiful to behold," and inhabitants "live friendly and well together." The hopeful image persisted. In 1773, American printer John Greenleaf produced a one-volume abridgment of *Burn's Justice of the Peace and Parish Officer,* an English legal manual for local magistrates. For his American version, Greenleaf eliminated all the information "of no possible use or importance to us in *America,*" including the entire 250-page entry on "The Poor."

Greenleaf had seriously miscalculated what might be useful to American officials, for the American colonies never knew a time without poverty. In every seventeenth- and eighteenth-century European-American community, officials were elected or appointed to oversee the poor. In fact, when Greenleaf printed his abridged volume, poverty was on the rise everywhere in North America, most especially in Greenleaf's town of Boston (Nash 1979,

312–338). Philadelphia, too, was overwhelmed; one scholar has estimated that during the latter part of the 1700s, at least 15 percent of Philadelphia's inhabitants were unable to provide themselves with the necessities of life (Alexander 1980, 9). Certainly, many colonists did realize the promise of prosperity in the expanding economy of North America, but many others saw no part of it. Poverty and poor relief wore familiar faces.

Poverty came to colonial America in different forms. Some immigrants, desperate to leave behind the problems of their European hometowns, spent all they had to cross the ocean, hoping to eke out a living in a new place. Often the pioneering settlers faced starvation in the first years; the mortality rate would have been even higher if the Native Americans had not assisted these fledgling communities with food and instructions in living off the land. Many Europeans who could not otherwise afford the journey sold themselves into indentured servitude in exchange for ocean passage; some were actually kidnapped and forced into bondage. Still other immigrants were African captives, forcibly transported across the Atlantic by European slave traders and subjected to poverty conditions as slaves in colonial America; these unwilling arrivals constituted a majority of *all* North American immigrants in the eighteenth century. Further, many of the original Native American inhabitants were impoverished by European settlement. Decimated by warfare and disease and surrounded by European houses, farms, and fences, surviving Native people were forced to abandon traditional occupations of hunting, fishing, and agriculture. In a story repeated many times over, Native people living "behind the frontier" struggled to feed their families and eventually resorted to menial labor in the households of European colonists or peddled traditional craft items door to door.

As European settlement expanded and colonies matured, poverty increased. Acquiring land—the most reliable way of achieving economic independence in a predominantly agrarian society—became harder and harder, both for new immigrants and for the original settlers' grandchildren and great-grandchildren trying to farm successively smaller inheritances, and some of them migrated to more-populous towns in search of a living. At the same time, voluntary European immigrants streamed into port towns in North America seeking work. Accordingly, poverty became concentrated in such places as Boston, New York City, Philadelphia, and Charleston. As poverty grew over the course of the eighteenth century, so did the gap between rich and poor: While wealthier colonists purchased material goods as evidence of their rising prosperity and elevated social standing, the low status of the poor became ever more noticeable and was marked by their lack of material goods.

An early American dictionary (1789) defined the poor as "those who are in the lowest rank of the community, those who cannot subsist but by the charity of others" (quoted in Alexander 1980, 8). A thin line separated these charity-dependent poor from those commonly referred to as "the poorer sort"—independent laboring people who barely scraped by and whose conditions of life would today be considered below the poverty level. The poorer sort lived in an insecure environment where menial jobs brought little hope for advancement and where wages seldom stretched to provide "competent" food, clothing, rent, firewood, and medical care. An otherwise minor misfortune could instigate a crisis for these "near poor" and prompt a desperate application for public relief. Relief provided the necessities of life, but it also brought the humiliation of official oversight; the poor had "overseers," much as servants and slaves did. Being poor meant social and economic dependence.

In terms of occupations, "the poorer sort" and "the poor" tended to be tenants of small or unproductive farms; skilled artisans such as shoemakers, tailors, and coopers; unskilled laborers, such as seasonal farmhands, domestic day servants, washerwomen, and woodcutters; sailors; bound servants; and slaves. The last two groups are usually considered a separate category of unfree labor, but even though masters were obligated to provide the essentials of life, many servants and slaves experienced daily life much as the poor did: owning no property, living in straitened material circumstances, and having no expectations of future advancement.

Certain groups were particularly at risk of becoming impoverished: African Americans, Native Americans, women without spouses or partners, children, the elderly. These people were especially vulnerable to outside forces—economic downturns, weather disasters, poor harvests, wars, disease epidemics—and had few resources to cope with such personal difficulties as disabling injuries, handicaps, chronic illnesses, alcoholism, death or desertion of spouse or parent, or the birth of a child out of wedlock.

Recent scholarship has demonstrated that race and gender were key factors in early American poverty. African slavery and the military conquest of Native America stripped people of color of property and effectively barred them from receiving training in skilled labor, the two main avenues of economic advancement. Women, too, were economically disadvantaged. Work was highly gendered in seventeenth- and eighteenth-century America, and male tasks were valued significantly more than were female tasks. Women customarily received half to two-thirds what men did for an equivalent amount of work. The legal principle of coverture diminished married women's property rights by transferring control of the property to their husbands. In addition, pregnancy and child rearing complicated women's work lives; having babies made women vulnerable as wage earners precisely when they needed extra income to feed extra mouths. Widows with young children and mothers of "bastard" children swelled the relief lists in every community and were especially overrepresented among the poor in colonial Philadelphia (Wulf 2000, 153–179).

Poverty was a grinding experience in early America. Although charity or relief was available to some on a limited basis, most had to work or starve. They worked at the most tedious and grueling tasks—the jobs that no one else wanted to do—in their neighbors' households, fields, workshops, and wharves. Poor women helped with the grain harvest and picked fruits and vegetables in agrarian areas; in every community, they did the unpleasant "housewifery" tasks such as spinning thread, cleaning chamber pots, and nursing the sick. Poor men chopped wood, mended equipment, swept streets, and carried loads. Their hard labor often resulted in injury or illness, but they had no emergency funds to tide them over when ill health, bad weather, or the capriciousness of employers halted their labors.

The scanty wages such labor earned were never enough to provide a "sufficiency" of life's essentials. The poor lived in rented houses or rooms within other people's homes, in quarters that were often small, cramped, in bad repair, and sparsely furnished. There was seldom enough firewood for adequate cooking and heating. Meals were frequently thin, unsatisfying, and less than regular. The make and material of their clothing and shoes (if they had them) effectively communicated their low status. Their possessions were few and unremarkable.

Such bleak conditions—overwork, inferior housing, inadequate food and clothing—made the poor vulnerable to illness. Unsanitary living conditions and poor hygiene resulted in infections and chronic problems such as worms. Living in close quarters in cramped housing spurred the spread of contagious diseases like smallpox, which periodically swept through North America in the 1700s, and yellow fever, which arrived in port cities in the 1790s. The search for work also put the poor at a disadvantage, since such migrations exposed them to different disease environments. Working in wet and icy weather in insufficient shoes and clothing increased the risk of respiratory ailments, frozen feet and fingers, and broken bones from falls. In eighteenth-century Philadelphia, the poor were far more likely than the upper classes to fall ill and die (Smith 1990, 55–56).

Given all these disadvantages, it is not surprising that the family lives of the poor were often as fragile as their jobs and their health. The search for work divided spouses from each other and parents from their children. A high mortality rate left holes in family units. Conflict and violence were not uncommon in financially struggling households. Wives were abandoned by their husbands; children were deserted by their parents. The grim realities of living in poverty in the seventeenth and eighteenth centuries stand in stark contrast to the hopeful predictions of colonial promoters and to Greenleaf's cheerful assumption that laws governing the poor were of "no possible use or importance" in colonial America.

Just as poverty had many faces, so social welfare took many forms in colonial America. Family offered the first line of defense against poverty, and in most cases relatives would naturally turn to each other for support. Reluctant kin—particularly negligent adult children of elderly parents—were prodded along by magistrates, who were empowered by colonial laws to require parents and grandparents (if they had the ability) to take care of their children and grandchildren. Beyond family, friends and neighbors might assist a struggling household, providing necessities and services in moments of distress. Religious groups often assisted the poor in their number: The Jewish community in colonial Newport had a synagogue charity fund to help members in distress; Dutch Reformed congregations in New York maintained alms chests; the Philadelphia Society of Friends opened an almshouse for needy Quakers in 1713; itinerant Anglican minister George Whitefield established the Bethesda Orphanage for Boys in Savannah, Georgia, in 1740. In the most populous communities, charities and mutual aid societies also sprang up in the eighteenth century: The Philadelphia Hospital was opened in 1751, expressly to minister to the poor who were ill.

Public support was the last resort, both by custom and as a matter of law. Every colony had some system of social welfare that was fashioned after English law and precedent. English parliamentary legislation during the seventeenth and eighteenth centuries (referred to collectively as the "poor laws") codified and regularized the patchwork of relief that had sprung up after the dissolution of the manors, monasteries, and guilds that had formerly given aid to those in distress. These poor laws made local government responsible for poor relief—to be funded out of the general tax or by means of a special poor tax—and theoretically ensured that all inhabitants would receive the necessities of life in times of crisis. The poor laws equipped magistrates with three principal ways to address poverty: Warning out removed needy people who legally "belonged" to another community. Orphan or pauper apprenticeship placed poor children in labor contracts with masters who provided daily maintenance in exchange for work. Poor relief (sometimes termed "outdoor relief") gave money, goods, and services directly to poor people or placed such persons with caretakers who were repaid out of the public purse.

No common system of relief existed in colonial America. Rather, each British North American colony enacted legislation that made poor relief a local (town or county) matter. In 1642, Plymouth colony enacted a series of statutes that provided for the "poore" in the towns where they resided. English colonists fashioned a poor-relief system in New York as soon as they took control of the colony from the Netherlands in 1664; by 1696, they had opened a hospital for ailing paupers. South Carolina passed its first poor-relief act in 1695; Pennsylvania, in 1706; and North Carolina, in 1749. Colonial legislation also stipulated who would be responsible for the poor. Sometimes specially appointed or elected overseers, guardians, or wardens of the poor took on this task separately; other times it was part of the larger responsibilities of selectmen, aldermen, church wardens, vestrymen, or justices of the peace, depending on the political and judicial structure of the colony.

Official managers of the poor stepped in when all other supports failed. In some cases, the tax assessors might "consider the poor" and grant exemptions to struggling widows, for example. In other cases, the poor were allowed to graze a cow or plant a vegetable garden on public land. When such indirect support proved insufficient, officials arranged for the direct supply of necessities such as rent money, firewood, food, blankets, or even a small stipend.

As the practice of warning out indicates, receipt of relief hinged on whether the needy person had a legal settlement in the community and was entitled to public tax money. If poor people moved about in search of work, they would have to return to their place of legal residence for help when they fell into need. Some of the warned out were too ill or too recalcitrant to leave on their own and had to be removed by constables. Countless poor people were moved from one local jurisdiction to another in colonial America; those whose place of residence could not be identified were usually put to work in a labor contract or in a workhouse. The time and money officials invested in this sorting and transporting was considered to be worth the effort, since communities thereby avoided the greater cost of supporting dependent people over the long term. The system of warning out or removal was practiced everywhere in colonial America, but with special vigor in New England during the eighteenth century. It fell particularly hard on people of color and on women without spouses, who constituted the majority of those removed (Herndon 2001, 16–20).

Binding out poor children in apprenticeship indentures was the most common method local authorities employed to address the widespread problem of child poverty. As early as the 1630s, orphan courts in Maryland, for example, began binding out unfortunate youngsters. Every colony followed suit. In orphan or pauper apprenticeship, illegitimate and destitute children—as well as orphans—were taken from their surviving parents and raised to adulthood (usually defined as twenty-one for boys and eighteen for girls) in more-prosperous households. Town or county magistrates negotiated terms with potential masters. Generally, the master was bound to provide the child with all the necessities of life as well as basic literacy education and training in some manual skill; the child was bound to live with, obey, and labor for the master. Work training was the form education took for most children in colonial America and constituted practical preparation for adulthood. A master who would stand in the role of parents and see that a child learned basic husbandry (boys) or housewifery (girls) skills, as well as reading and writing, effectively removed that child from the list of the town's poor and saved the taxpayers a considerable sum.

Warning out and binding out cost the community something in the way of fees to administrators and constables, but most poor-relief funds were spent for "outdoor relief"—money, goods, and services that went directly to the poor or to those responsible for keeping them. Although outdoor relief sometimes involved direct payment, it was also paid to people who served as individual keepers or caretakers by boarding or providing goods and services to the poor. A wide network of local citizens usually participated in this enterprise. Some were paid for making clothes and shoes for the poor, others for providing food or firewood, repairing their houses, nursing them when they fell ill, and digging their graves. Most often, such third-party payments went to those who took in the poor as lodgers, daily providing food, shelter, and heat and making the poor person part of the household.

Group institutions for the poor appeared quickly in colonial America, though only in the most populous towns and only tentatively in the early years. Boston had its first almshouse in 1660 and opened its first workhouse in 1739. New York City had a poorhouse by 1700 and constructed a municipal almshouse in 1735. Philadelphia tried a series of group institutions in the early 1700s and finally constructed a "bettering house"—a combined workhouse and almshouse—in 1766. Charleston built a workhouse in 1734 and opened an orphan house—the first municipal orphanage in the country—in 1792. Even where workhouses or almshouses were constructed, however, a secondary system of outdoor relief continued to exist. For the most part, the poor were treated on a case-by-case basis and according to the needs and interests of the community throughout the colonial and Revolutionary eras.

Because each case was addressed individually, receipt of support depended in part on the way the needy person presented himself or herself to those authorities who would judge the circumstances. In most places, colonial magistrates distinguished between the "worthy" and "unworthy" or the "deserving" and "undeserving" poor. A person was more likely to merit support if he or she displayed an attitude of deference toward authorities. Those who received relief were expected to be grateful and submissive toward their betters.

Overseers (the "betters") desired that the provision of relief be as brief as possible, that it be as cheap as possible, and that recipients contribute to their support through their own labor. Most relief was intended as a temporary measure to deal with temporary circumstances: a laborer sidelined by a broken leg; an unmarried mother unable to work during the final stage of pregnancy and the "lying-in" after delivery. Long-term, continuous support of individuals—usually because of totally disabling injury or handicap—was much less common. Public relief was also meager, designed to provide only the absolute essentials. Officials were constantly on the lookout for less-expensive ways to keep the poor. Sometimes poor people were moved from one caretaker to another as overseers struck a better bargain. In Charleston in the early 1700s, potential caretakers publicly bid against each other for the business of taking in the sick poor; the lowest bidder won (Bellows 1993, 5). Later in the century, many New England communities turned to similar publicly held "poor auctions" to dispose of indigent persons to the keeper who offered the cheapest rate.

As such public "shows" indicate, being on relief was not a private matter. Taxpayers expected an accounting of how their money was being spent, and in most colonies before the Revolutionary era, those receiving relief were required to wear on their clothing a special badge bearing the letter *P* or some other symbol (*NY* in New York). Even though it was not private, however, relief was very personal. The names and faces of the poor were usually known to magistrates in agrarian communities; in more-populous towns, magistrates sometimes required an endorsement of relief applications so that the poor person could demonstrate a personal link to the community.

Over the course of the seventeenth and eighteenth centuries, poverty steadily rose in North America. As the American economy expanded and became more industrialized, wealth became increasingly stratified and poverty became more obvious and more entrenched, particularly in the most populous towns. Accordingly, poor-relief costs climbed throughout the eighteenth century. This was particularly evident in such places as Boston, New York, Philadelphia, and Charleston, but even in the countryside—where poverty and vagrancy were considerably less frequent—poor relief rose over the course of the 1700s. During the pinched years following the Revolutionary War, taxpayers urged officials to find cheaper methods of caring for the poor, and numerous agrarian communities experimented with workhouses and poorhouses. Not until the nineteenth century did poor farms and almshouses come to dominate the landscape, but the shift had already begun decades before.

As poverty and poor relief changed, so did attitudes toward the poor. In some regions, the language that officials used to distinguish among the poor underwent its own transformation: from "worthy" versus "unworthy" poor to "industrious" versus "idle" poor or "respectable" versus "improper" poor. Increasingly, the idea that the poor were dangerous and prone to vice and crime crept into the language of the overseers of the poor.

Whatever benefits the Revolution brought to the middling sort, it did little for the material or even the political standing of the poor. Everywhere, overseers began to characterize the poor less often as unfortunate neighbors and more often as an undifferentiated mass of strangers with dangerous tendencies. The early decades of the nineteenth century saw efforts to crack down on or even to eliminate poor relief in many localities, to limit the sense of community responsibility for the needy, and to restrict assistance to the "deserving" poor. Simultaneously, treatment of the poor became increasingly racialized. Children of color were more likely than white children to be bound out in post-Revolutionary Rhode Island, Maryland, and Virginia, for example, and the contracts for children of color in all regions promised them less-adequate work training, literacy education, and eventual payment for labor. Adults of color were disproportionately subjected to warning out and removal in New England, especially after the Revolutionary War. Separate systems of charity and public relief for people of color were put in place: Charleston's Orphan House, for example, admitted only white children (Bellows 1993, 121). In the northern states, gradual emancipation laws and the forces of Revolutionary ideology prompted many masters to free their slaves, but people of color left slavery with no resources to establish themselves and found themselves relegated to the lowest rungs of society. The colonial economic system that had put women and people of color at a disadvantage intensified during the Revolutionary era. The Revolution did not improve the lot of the poor; rather, it cemented them as an integral part of American society. And yet, even as poverty grew more visible and widespread during the early nineteenth century, the Revolution left an ideological legacy of individual rights and social equality that would fuel labor, civil rights, women's rights, and antipoverty activism for generations to come.

Much work remains to be done to uncover the experience of the poor in early America. We know more about poverty in the largest towns than in the rural areas, especially in the southern colonies. Further, despite the concerted efforts of recent scholarship to tell the story of the "inarticulate," we still know more about poor-relief administrators and caretakers than we do about those who lived in poverty. This is largely a problem of sources. The well-to-do and the powerful were the most literate colonists and had the greatest opportunity to leave a written record. The poor and the powerless, far less literate, had little opportunity to tell their side of the story. Nevertheless, it is sometimes possible to reconstruct the lives of the poor by carefully piecing together public and private records, and such research promises exciting results. It will give us a much needed "underside" perspective on the relationship between established communities and the poor and help us find the answers to some elusive questions. Who were the poor in different communities? Did women dominate relief lists in the countryside? Were the poor treated differently from one town to another? Could they expect greater humanity in one place and greater brutality in another? Were relief officials motivated primarily by economic concerns? Overall, was poor relief in early America a relatively benign or a relatively pernicious system? The stories of individual poor people will help us gain a more balanced perspective on these important questions.

Ruth Wallis Herndon

See also: Deserving/Undeserving Poor; Indentured Servitude; Poor Laws; Poorhouse/Almshouse; Relief;

Slavery; Vagrancy Laws/Settlement Laws/Residency Requirements

References and Further Reading

Alexander, John K. 1980. *Render Them Submissive: Responses to Poverty in Philadelphia, 1760–1800*. Amherst: University of Massachusetts Press.

Bellows, Barbara L. 1993. *Benevolence among Slaveholders: Assisting the Poor in Charleston, 1670–1860*. Baton Rouge: Louisiana State University Press.

Cray, Robert E., Jr. 1988. *Paupers and Poor Relief in New York City and Its Rural Environs, 1700–1830*. Philadelphia: Temple University Press.

Greenleaf, Joseph. 1773. *An Abridgement of Burn's Justice of the Peace and Parish Officers*. Boston: Joseph L. Greenleaf.

Hakluyt, Richard. [1584] 1877. *A Discourse on Western Planting, Written in the Year 1584*. Cambridge, MA: Press of J. Wilson and Son.

Herndon, Ruth Wallis. 2001. *Unwelcome Americans: Living on the Margin in Early New England*. Philadelphia: University of Pennsylvania Press.

Nash, Gary B. 1979. *The Urban Crucible: Social Change, Political Consciousness, and the Origins of the American Revolution*. Cambridge, MA: Harvard University Press.

Smith, Billy G. 1990. *The "Lower Sort": Philadelphia's Laboring People, 1750–1800*. Ithaca, NY: Cornell University Press.

Smith, Billy G. 2004. *Down and Out in Early America*. University Park: Penn State University Press.

Thomas, Gabriel. 1698. *An Historical and Geographical Account of the Province and Country of Pensilvania*. London: A. Baldwin.

Wulf, Karin A. 2000. *Not All Wives: Women of Colonial Philadelphia*. Ithaca, NY: Cornell University Press.

An Inquiry into the Nature and Causes of the Wealth of Nations, Adam Smith

Every individual is continually exerting himself to find out the most advantageous employment for whatever capital he can command. It is his own advantage, indeed, and not that of society, which he has in view. But the study of his own advantage naturally, or rather necessarily leads him to prefer that employment which is most advantageous to the society.

Every individual necessarily labours to render the annual revenue of the society as great as he can. He generally, indeed, neither intends to promote the public interest, nor knows how much he is promoting it. . . . He intends only his own gain, and he is in this, as in many other cases, led by an invisible hand to promote an end which was no part of his intention.

Source: Adam Smith, *An Inquiry into the Nature and Causes of the Wealth of Nations* (1776), Book 4, Chapter 2.

Nineteenth Century

The history of poverty and inequality in the United States during the nineteenth century can be approached through thinking contextually of four key writings—both emblematic and consequential—that flanked the century like conceptual bookends. At the start, reaching back to the era of the American Revolution, are Thomas Jefferson's Declaration of Independence and Adam Smith's *Wealth of Nations* (1776). At the end, providing traction both on what had gone before and on what lay ahead, are the Omaha Platform of the People's Party (1892) and a volume of economic theory called *The Distribution of Wealth*, written by a Columbia University economics professor, John Bates Clark, in 1899.

The Declaration of Independence announced political commitments that inspired protests against poverty and inequality throughout the nineteenth century: the "self-evident" truths that all humans are created equal, that they are endowed with "inalienable" rights to liberty and property. In republicanism, the dominant political language of the late eighteenth and nineteenth centuries, the link between liberty and property was a core value. Drawing as well on a

Omaha Platform of the People's Party of America, July 4, 1892

In addition to the following ringing declaration, the Omaha Platform of the National People's Party endorsed a series of reforms, including the progressive income tax, direct election of senators, the secret ballot, and the eight-hour workday—all eventually legislated, albeit after years of political organizing and struggle.

Assembled upon the 116th anniversary of the Declaration of Independence, the People's Party of America, in their first national convention, invoking upon their action the blessing of Almighty God, puts forth in the name and on behalf of the people of this country, the following preamble and declaration of principles:—

The conditions which surround us best justify our co-operation; we meet in the midst of a nation brought to the verge of moral, political, and material ruin. Corruption dominates the ballot-box, the Legislatures, the Congress, and touches even the ermine of the bench. The people are demoralized; most of the States have been compelled to isolate the voters at the polling places to prevent universal intimidation and bribery. The newspapers are largely subsidized or muzzled, public opinion silenced, business prostrated, homes covered with mortgages, labor impoverished, and the land concentrating in the hands of the capitalists. The urban workmen are denied the right to organize for self-protection, imported pauperized labor beats down their wages, a hireling standing army, unrecognized by our laws, is established to shoot them down, and they are rapidly degenerating into European conditions. The fruits of the toil of millions are boldly stolen to build up the fortunes for a few, unprecedented in the history of mankind. . . . From the same prolific womb of governmental injustice we breed the two great classes—tramps and millionaires.

Assembled on the anniversary of the birthday of the nation, and filled with the spirit of the grand general and chief who established our independence, we seek to restore the government of the Republic to the hands of "the plain people," with which class it originated. We assert our purposes to be identical with the purposes of the National Constitution, "to form a more perfect union and establish justice, insure domestic tranquility, provide for the common defense, promote the general welfare, and secure the blessings of liberty for ourselves and our posterity." We declare that this Republic can only endure as a free government while built upon the love of the whole people for each other and for the nation; that it cannot be pinned together by bayonets; that the civil war is over, and that every passion and resentment which grew out of it must die with it, and that we must be in fact, as we are in name, one united brotherhood of free men.

Source: As reprinted on the Web site History Matters.

liberal principle most clearly outlined by John Locke, that humans were entitled to mingle their labor with nature and take possession of its fruits, this linkage of liberty and property expressed a broad consensus among nineteenth-century Americans that labor created all value and that the preservation of political liberty would depend, if not upon a precise distributive equality, then at least upon a very wide dispersal of small holdings of property in the form of shops and farms and upon the rejection of monopoly and privilege (Huston 1998).

Just as the Declaration of Independence attacked monarchical society and the corruption it fostered, so Smith's *Wealth of Nations* attacked mercantilism (policies that limited what colonies could trade and produce, aimed at maintaining a favorable balance of trade for the mother country) for stifling initiative. Smith offered economic liberty—including what today would be referred to as "free trade"—as a far better route to individual and national wealth. This founding text of modern liberalism drew together Scottish Enlightenment strands of reasoning that endowed men with acquisitive instincts and imagined a modern world in which competition would remain the norm. The government it described would be restrained by laissez-faire, but through improvements such as roads and harbors and institutions such as the rule of law and widely accessible education, it would nevertheless provide the wherewithal for those lower down the social order to participate in accumulation. There was an undeniable and politically fruitful tension between Smith's *Wealth of Nations* and the Declaration of Independence and between their visions of a good society. Over time, the Declaration of Independence was imitated by disenfranchised women, indebted or landless farmers, exploited workers, and oppressed people of color in countless petitions against the denial of their liberty, whereas Smith's *Wealth of Nations* became (with some injustice) the bible of nineteenth-century antistatist individualists. Yet the two documents together captured the promise of the Enlightenment in America for the downtrodden poor.

Inequality and poverty persisted throughout the entire colonial period, most acutely for the earliest settlers and for those in various categories of unfree labor (indentured servants and slaves, who made up about one-fourth of the non-Native population, and married white women), who were legally barred from claiming the fruits of their toil. Though poverty was increasing in the major seaboard cities immediately prior to the Revolution, most white immigrants to the American colonies almost certainly escaped worse privation and significantly greater inequality in Europe (Williamson and Lindert 1980). During the framing of the Constitution, the Founding Fathers were pressed by the "people out of doors" to remember not only the "ladies" but urban wage workers in places such as Boston and Philadelphia. Victorious in the early political debates, Jeffersonians and Madisonians overcame both foreign and domestic opposition to implement policies intended to provide the material basis for liberty and for their distinctive version of a republic: a youthful society in which industrious white males could become proprietors, whereas the "dark satanic mills" would remain in old Europe. Success for this republican vision would preclude the most pernicious European forms of lifelong poverty, but for whites only and excluding "servants" and women, groups who—not coincidentally—were also excluded from politics. Sustaining a virtuous citizenry required opportunity, the rationale for buying Louisiana in 1803. And in the early decades of the nineteenth century, Jeffersonian Republicans such as Albert Gallatin, National Republicans such as John Quincy Adams, and Whigs such as Henry Clay did not hesitate to recommend lavish government programs to build up the infrastructure for (white, male) liberty (McCoy 1980).

We lack an adequate statistical basis for hard generalizations about the precise extent of poverty in the nineteenth century. Only late in the century did public and private social investigators begin to produce reliable studies of household budgets and to estimate how much income a family needed to rise above poverty—about $800 a year at the turn of the twentieth century. Nevertheless, historians have been able to locate major ideological shifts and key turning points in political economy that altered the character, extent, and cultural construction of poverty. Of the ideological shifts, the most important were (1) a powerful tendency in the early decades of the century to picture poverty as a product of individual moral failings, and (2) as part of the emergence of the "social question" late in the century, a multilayered reframing of the poverty problem in historical, environmental, and structural terms.

Rooted in Puritan moralism, the Protestant work ethic in the early and mid-nineteenth century defined earthly success as evidence of

God's favor—the product of industry, good character, and thrift—and poverty, by contrast, as the result of laziness and sin. Help for the poor, provided largely by churches or by community-based private charities, thus concentrated largely on minimally meeting paupers' most immediate needs for food and shelter, while "friendly visitors" saw to their moral improvement. Although this view of poverty was an improvement on the centuries-old view that "the poor would always be with us," it typically framed the poor as "other" and often invoked moral language to justify enormous wealth. Toward the end of the nineteenth century, Andrew Carnegie still preached a "Gospel of Wealth" that claimed the biblical role of "good stewards" for wealthy philanthropists, whom he insisted would make better use of the profits of industry than average Americans could do for themselves (Ward 1989; Cawelti 1965).

The success myth did not go unchallenged. A populist countercurrent criticizing the moneyed class as predatory monopolizers was always present, nourished by a sturdy republican distrust of concentrated wealth that culminated in the populist movement of the 1890s (McMath 1993; Kazin 1998). In the final decades of the century, the Social Gospel movement and the new social sciences redefined the worsening urban poverty of the Gilded Age as the product of environmental factors. They cited as causes of urban poverty overcrowding, poor sanitation, bad housing, filthy streets, unhealthy and dangerous workplaces, and a consequent loss of adult workers' wages to sickness and disability, which also blighted childhood by sending thousands of children into factories. These evils could be remedied not mainly through moral reform, they argued—though that would help—but through market regulation and through a new social contract based on a heightened sense of social solidarity. A major catalyst for this new view came with the building up of a "New Liberalism" by social investigators and social scientists in the 1880s and 1890s to replace key principles of classical, laissez-faire, Smithian liberalism. Exploitation of labor, rising class conflict, and devastating business depressions made it difficult to defend classical teachings about the beneficence of competition, a natural harmony of interests between capital and labor, and a natural equilibrium between supply and demand. Rather than blaming poverty on failings of the poor, these social theorists cited several structural problems of capitalism, particularly the cyclical economy, chronic unemployment, low wages, and barriers to effective working-class organization, as the most persistent causes of poverty, more significant even than the selfishness condoned in Social Darwinism (Furner 1993; O'Connor 2001).

In the nineteenth-century American political economy, three critical turning points dramatically affected the character, numbers, and status of the poor: (1) the Market Revolution of the 1820s–1850s, (2) a major episode of "capital deepening" (that is, vastly more investment capital was accumulated and applied to production) following the Civil War, and (3) a series of cyclical depressions—1873–1877, 1884–1886, 1893–1897—that threw as much as 40 percent of workers in numerous industries and cities out of work, all within a long deflationary period in the U.S. economy during the Gilded Age.

The Market Revolution

The first of these turning points was the Market Revolution, which arrived along with political democracy in America. Not an instantaneous thing, this "revolution" was, rather, an elongated process of eliminating older cultural and economic strategies that had privileged family and community subsistence over production of goods for sale, and of pulling ever-greater numbers of Americans into producing for the market—a process that continued both before and after the Civil War as the "Transportation Revolution" reached ever-remoter regions, annihilating the barriers of time and distance. Improvements in transportation and communication, technological advances, and wider availability of credit all accelerated the rise of manufacturing known as the Industrial Revolution. Trends in U.S. wealth accumulation and poverty rates during this period appear to coincide with what is predicted by the famous Kuznets hypothesis: There will be less inequality in the early stages of industrialization, rising inequality in the middle segment of a modernization process, and declining inequality during later stages of growth. Yet neither the Market Revolution nor the Industrial Revolution, whose early stages in the United States came in the early nineteenth century, should be taken as components of an *inevitable* modernization process (Sellers 1991; Kuznets 1989).

Rather, both these "movements"—and the decades-long increases in poverty and inequality they engendered—should be seen largely as complex outcomes of deliberately chosen policies and of laws and institutions designed to implement these policies. By eliminating imprisonment for debt, easing bankruptcy, lifting common-law tests for intrinsic fairness in contracts, and shifting many of the costs of development from entrepreneurs to the quiet members of the community, the legal system in the early republic encouraged speculation and protected wealth accumulation. Although the social and ideological sources of Jacksonian political economy were more democratic, its consequences tended to reinforce this entrepreneurial bias in the law. Jacksonian Democrats, holding slim majorities through most of the late antebellum years, organized a political reaction against more-interventionist and more communally oriented approaches to achieving the public good represented by National Republicanism and Whiggery, which were thought by their plebeian critics to favor elites and to promote monopoly. Reacting as well to a depression in the 1830s that forced several state governments to default on bonds they had sold to invest in canals and railroads, the states withdrew from investing in "internal improvements." A number of policy innovations—most important among them, President Andrew Jackson's veto of a major national road project, general incorporation, tariff reduction, elimination of the Second Bank of the United States, and removal of Native Americans remaining east of the Mississippi—inaugurated what became the closest thing to a laissez-faire era the United States had yet known (Horwitz 1977).

Though the Declaration of Independence had pronounced the right to life, liberty, and property *inalienable*, the realities of the Market Revolution were otherwise. By definition, a market society is one in which all the factors of production—capital, land, and labor—are for sale. The one glaring exception—recognized by the Constitution and protected by major sectional compromises—was slavery, which was rapidly disappearing in the North but was thriving in the South even after the slave trade ended in 1808. In slavery, it was the laborer as chattel who was for sale. In the case of wage workers, it was their labor time that was for sale to the highest bidder: Beyond the small protection provided by journeymen's associations and the few antebellum labor unions, the price of labor was determined by supply and demand. To the extent that yeoman culture survived in rural America, it retained the labor of farm women and children within a system of rural patriarchy. Otherwise, every factor of production, including most particularly the labor of the working poor, was in fact alienable.

Although the Jacksonian "era of the common man" provided new opportunities for young men on the make, it was not an easy time for the poor. Industrialists seeking to control the moral environment of factory towns and a massive religious revival shifted attitudes toward poverty, as we have seen, blaming individual failings and stigmatizing the poor. Americans paid close attention to the English poor law debates of the 1830s that led to repeal of the Speenhamland system, in which local governments gave relief to their own local poor to supplement low wages. Critics had charged that this poor law was holding workers in the countryside where they were no longer needed and keeping wages low. Changes in U.S. poor laws also weakened social provision, forcing more of those on public relief either to obtain aid in county poorhouses rather than "out of doors" or to depart for the cities. These changes in attitude and policy ushered in what historians have called "the era of the poorhouse." Those most likely to be poor were children, women alone, and those of either sex too old or ill to work. A cult of domesticity that prescribed a separate sphere of home and family for respectable women did not apply to the growing numbers of single and married women who worked outside the home, in factories or as domestic servants. As craftsmen's workplaces shifted away from the home to factories and shops, the unpaid household labor of women was devalued. Many immigrants, including more than 2 million of the Irish poor, arrived in the United States between 1815 and 1850, in time to build the canals and railroads that fed the Market Revolution (Johnson 1978; Boydston 1990).

For white males, including these immigrants, "free labor" ideology expressed the republican ideal of propertied independence as the basis of political liberty from the American Revolution through the antebellum era. Abraham Lincoln, speaking in 1858 to the Wisconsin State Agricultural Society on the eve of the Civil War, rejected what he called the "mudsill theory" that most men were doomed to labor for others all their lives as either hirelings or slaves. In America, Lincoln insisted,

> the prudent, penniless beginner in the world labors for wages awhile, saves a surplus with which to buy tools or land for himself, then labors on his own account another while, and at length hires another beginner to help him. This, say its advocates, is *free* labor—the just and generous and prosperous system which opens the way for all, gives hope to all, and energy and progress and improvement of condition to all. (Lincoln [1858] 1953, 478–479)

Lincoln's moving expression captured the social and cultural aspirations of northerners before the Civil War, and the democratization of American free society did indeed give (healthy, white) males a larger measure of control over their economic, political, and social lives than similarly situated men anywhere else.

Yet this reality was complicated by a growing concentration of income and wealth and by barriers to opportunity and mobility based on gender, ethnicity, race, and class. In large northeastern cities, for example, the top 1 percent of the population owned one-fourth of the wealth in 1820, and by 1850 that same top 1 percent held more than half the total wealth. Inequality varied by region, and adult males had a better chance to acquire in rural America than in the cities. Women were denied not only the vote but equal access to education and the professions. Married women lost their legal identities under a legal principle known as coverture, which awarded their property (including wages they earned) and full control of children to husbands, conditions protested in the Seneca Falls Declaration of 1848 (which recognized as self-evident "that all men *and women* are created equal"). Women working in northeastern textile factories became strikers against wage cuts. Only one-fourth of southern whites owned slaves, but the mudsill formed by slavery had economic and psychological value for many whites. Slaves were whipped, penned, sexually exploited, and sold at auction like animals, protected somewhat from even worse treatment by their growing market value. Historians have debated the political economy of slavery without agreeing on how much slaves received of what their labor produced. But although some were allowed to keep their own gardens or to hire out for wages, it seems quite certain that most lived only a little above subsistence level. With the hardening of slavery between the 1830s and 1850s, conditions worsened for the vast majority of African Americans, not only slaves but free Blacks. Expansion of slavery, especially in the prosperous 1850s, produced a massive forced internal migration of Blacks torn from their families, away from the seaboard states, into the Deep South and Texas. Conditions for slaves in rice and sugar culture and in the breaking of new lands for cotton were exceptionally hard (Pessen 1990; Roediger 1999).

Ironically, as antislavery hardened into abolitionism in the 1830s–1850s, it narrowed the meaning of freedom for working-class whites as well by defining the difference between liberty and slavery as the right to sell one's labor. This reframing of true freedom as freedom of contract, which carried over into the Reconstruction after the Civil War for Blacks as well as whites, represented quite a different vision from the ideal of free laborer as independent proprietor held by Jefferson and Lincoln. Indeed, it offered some superficial credence to an antebellum southern critique of the northern capitalist labor system by slavery apologists such as George Fitzhugh: that wage labor was in fact a pernicious form of "wage slavery," in which there was no security in illness or old age.

Capital Deepening and Industrial Transformation in Post–Civil War America

The second major turning point in the nineteenth-century history of poverty was the Civil War, which had vast implications for the future not only of freed Blacks but of white wage workers and farmers and which spurred changes in the political economy that led to a period of rapid industrialization in the war's aftermath. In political power at last after years of minority status, a Whig, nationalist, development-oriented component of the Republican Party implemented policies that significantly advanced the mechanization of production for a national mass consumer market. These measures included funding the war through bonds and greenbacks, creating a national bank that drew savings away from the countryside and into major money centers, returning to a policy of high tariff protection that prevailed until the end of the century, and granting massive subsidies for transcontinental railroad construction that—along with a liberal land distribution policy through the Homestead Act—encouraged (mostly white) settlement of the trans-Mississippi West and the final removal of the Plains Indians. Crucially, shortly after the war, the Treasury redeemed war bonds at full face value, in gold, including large numbers of bonds that the original owners had resold at depreciated prices to wealthy investors. This windfall profit to the investor class sparked an extraordinary twenty-year period of capital deepening that drastically altered power relations in the United States. Outstripping all competitors, U.S. capital formation as a percentage of gross national product (GNP) doubled between the 1850s and the 1880s—a onetime event in U.S. history, bringing the United States from fourth to first place in industrial production by the turn of the century (Williamson and Lindert 1980).

The victory achieved by the Republican Party and the growth that followed put two crucial elements of the economy, southern plantation agriculture and northern manufacturing, into play. Power and poverty are always related, as was certainly true in the South following the war. Newly freed African Americans sought land of their own, as a fulfillment of the promise of emancipation, and wanted to work as "free labor," whereas planters, who retained almost all of their landholdings, wanted to return Blacks to the land in gangs, now as wage labor. Black resistance and determination to work as family units, the devotion of the Radical Republicans to a fuller meaning of "liberty," and intervention by the Freedmen's Bureau provided some assistance in resettling Blacks and forcing planters to sign labor contracts. Indeed, the Freedmen's Bureau, which also helped displaced whites, can be seen as an early U.S. experiment in social provision, and as such it was attacked by both southern and northern conservatives and was soon terminated. As long as southern state legislatures—some with numerous Black members—were in Republican hands, they shifted taxation in ways that aided poor white farmers and spent more on education and infrastructure, raising the social wage a bit. Radicals in Congress such as Thaddeus Stevens clearly intended a major social and political reconstituting of the South that would make each southern state a genuine republic. But Stevens's plan—which envisioned confiscating and redistributing the largest rebel-owned plantations as a way of breaking planter power and empowering a biracial class of poor and middling southern yeomen—was not enacted. When the Republican Party finally abandoned Reconstruction in the 1870s, Blacks were left to wonder what kind of freedom they had achieved. For most, it was not freedom but peonage, a status little better than slavery in which Black sharecroppers and tenant farmers were tied to the land by debt. Most southerners were poorer for decades after the Civil War. Cotton production did not return to prewar levels until the turn of the century. For white and Black farmers generally, rates of tenancy rose well into the twentieth century, whereas diets deteriorated and diseases such as hookworm and pellagra became common among the rural poor (Foner 1990).

Conditions in the South well illustrate the extent to which poverty and dependency were created by law and politics. The same was true for other groups in postbellum American society. Politics and policy had a good deal to do with turning four other groups of Americans into poor people in the Gilded Age. Mark Twain and Charles Dudley Warner coined this term for the period running from the 1870s through 1900, when great fortunes were made in the expanding urban-industrial economy. During these years, law and policy coincided to turn Indians, immigrants, unskilled male and female workers, and many children into poor people. Western Indians, largely nomadic, were herded onto reservations where they were expected to take up farming—alien to their culture—without adequate supplies of fertile land, seed, machinery, tools, and education. The goal of even their friends among whites was to convert them from tribalism to liberal individualism. The 1887 Dawes Severalty Act aimed to accomplish this by dividing tribal lands into individual allotments, most of which in short order passed into the hands of white settlers. Lacking skills (and, like Blacks in schools such as Booker T. Washington's Tuskegee Institute, taught skills that were increasingly irrelevant to the machine age), most Indians ended up in poverty.

The poverty of a large fraction of European immigrants, virtually the entire immigrant class after adoption of policies that excluded nearly all Asians, was also in significant part the result of policy. The era's trade unions typically called for immigration restriction. Gilded Age capitalists, engaged in recruiting and disciplining an industrial workforce, favored and obtained virtually unrestricted immigration. To be sure, unrestricted immigration was modulated by the business cycle, but it was generally productive of a surplus pool of unskilled labor willing to begin work for wages at close to subsistence level. For whites who were not labeled in some way as demonstrably criminal or "defective," the United States had essentially open borders until the 1920s. Though the American standard of wages was higher than what comparable work earned in urban-industrial Europe, for most of the "new immigrants" from southern and eastern European peasant backgrounds, this was hardly a relevant comparison. Unions in some cases succeeded in artificially restricting the labor supply by using work rules or job actions to control hiring. Against such efforts at "worker control," capitalists implemented, if not the entire package of scientific management outlined in the 1890s by Frederick Taylor, at least the part that involved relentless de-skilling. In the Chicago meatpacking industry, for example, the labor of a skilled butcher was subdivided into seventy separate tasks, easily taught to raw immigrants standing each day outside the factory gates. Courts and police assisted an aggressive policy of union busting that drastically weakened worker power between the 1880s and the turn of the century. Strikes and class violence in those years were typically about wage cuts (for example, the Great Railroad Strike of 1877 and the Pullman Strike of 1894), working hours (for example, the eight-hour movement that provided the context for the bombing in Haymarket Square in Chicago and the subsequent execution of four anarchists), or abrogation of a wage contract (for example, Carnegie Steel's contract abrogation leading up to the Homestead Lockout of 1892), or they were called in sympathy with other strikers (for example, the Pullman Strike led by Eugene V. Debs). Judges used a new version of the equity injunction to stop 4,300 strikes between 1880 and the passage of the Norris–LaGuardia Act in 1932. Little wonder that the most powerful union, the American Federation of Labor, saw little hope in government regulation. Gilded Age courts struck down sixty labor laws, including laws regulating sweatshops, in which women, children, and entire families labored in the most dangerous and unsanitary conditions in an effort to produce a "family wage." By this time, the frontier, officially closed in 1890, no longer provided a safety valve (Montgomery 1979; Barrett 1987).

Law, policy, and culture divided the rural poor and the urban working classes, preventing them from forming a united, class-based "poor people's party" in the Gilded Age. At a time when farmers were pummeled by falling prices for staple crops, high-cost credit, and monopoly prices for shipping and machinery, consistently deflationary Republican monetary policies produced an unexpected gain in real wages for steadily employed skilled workers. (Wages tend to be "sticky," falling or rising more slowly than prices.) In the 1880s, organized skilled workers were able to deprive capitalists of profits they had expected to reap from capital deepening—thus the escalation of union busting, and particularly the capitalist assault in the 1890s against industrial unions.

Capitalist Crisis and the Making of the "Social Question"

Capitalists were also periodically caught in overproduction crises, the root cause of the recurrent depressions, and they turned for relief toward various forms of combination into ever-bigger firms in the core industries, culminating with the Great Merger Movement of 1898–1902. For students of poverty in the nineteenth century, overproduction is also a major part of the explanation of a very high incidence of desperate poverty despite rising real wages, middle-class affluence, and a burgeoning consumer culture. Industrial workers were constantly victims of unemployment and underemployment. With little public social provision for unemployment or injury, loss of wages threw many families into poverty. Social provision remained insufficient, a matter largely for private charities organized along religious and ethnic lines, which attempted in the scientific charity movement to apply means and morals testing as a condition of relief but which also tried to improve the administration of relief and to provide a better knowledge base for it (Katz 1983; Ward 1989).

For most Americans, the most striking and frightening social patterns of the Gilded Age were the rise of monopoly, the worsening of conditions in urban slums, and the increasing frequency and violence of clashes between workers and capital. The existing two-party system seemed unable to cope with these issues, calling forth efforts on the part of groups outside the system of courts and parties to understand and resolve them. Conceiving it broadly, Social Gospelers, social workers, social investigators, social theorists, academic social scientists, critical journalists, realist writers, settlement house workers, female reformers, and eventually progressive political leaders began to address what—lumping all these issues together—was called the "social question." Social Gospelers such as Walter Rauschenbusch led a movement that accused the churches of being too soft on capitalists and doing too little to help the poor, who should not be blamed as individuals for their poverty. Henry George turned the American gaze toward the way speculators skimmed off socially created wealth, and Edward Bellamy's *Looking Backward* charted the route to a utopian cooperative commonwealth. By the final decades of the century, intellectual, social, and political movements had begun to address this social question, with consequences that remind us of the cultural strains reflected in the tensions between the Declaration of Independence and Smith's *Wealth of Nations*.

Beginning in the 1880s, reformist new liberals aggressively took on the task of charting the nature of the new economy. A platform text (one that sets the terms for subsequent discussions) of the 1880s, Henry Carter Adams's "Relation of the State to Industrial Action," zeroed in on ways the classical liberal reliance on competition could no longer be trusted as a sure guide to policy. First, Adams pointed to the appearance of a new kind of monopoly, the product not of favoritism and fraud, as had been the case in the era of the American Revolution, but, rather, of efficiencies—economies of scale—that could be gained by very large business firms in so-called natural monopolies. More important for the study of poverty, Adams also pointed to the tendency for increased competition to push wages and working conditions—what he called the "moral plane of competition"—down to the lowest level. In this sense, Adams was in touch with the moral emphasis of the Social Gospel, which shifted the onus of immorality from the worker to the capitalist. Along with the mounting evidence of blameless poverty conveyed by other means, this text provided a mandate for regulation to enforce a standard of protection for workers in accord with the evolving moral sense of the community.

Work by another brilliant political economist, Thorstein Veblen, helped explain the increasingly severe and frequent depressions in business and employment that impoverished millions. Veblen's analysis traced this structural pattern of advanced capitalism to the increased use of credit in the form of loans that could not be serviced or shares that plummeted in value during periods of slack demand. In this analysis, overproduction was intrinsic to unregulated capitalism. Capitalism does not merely have cycles, Veblen contended; it *is* cycles.

Rejecting these rationales for increased government regulation, another group of thinkers preferred to seek stabilization of business and improved relations between bosses and workers through self-regulation by business, amendments to the Sherman Anti-Trust Act permitting combination into even larger enterprises to reduce competition, and recognition of the conservative goals of organized labor. Historians refer to these people as "corporate liberals." Progressive reformers campaigned for limitations on women's working hours and child labor, for protections for unions, and for comprehensive social insurance. Yet, then as now, regulation remained controversial, particularly for Americans who placed their faith in "the market" (Furner 1993).

The market was always, of course, a social and political creation, and its meaning—indeed, the reality of it in any recognizable Smithian sense—was highly contested. For the poor farmers and workers and for men and women in the middle classes who heard their message, the Omaha Platform of the People's Party expressed the hard-won conclusion, learned in a decade of efforts to climb out of poverty by mobilizing producers' cooperatives and politics, that the free market was an illusion. Populism targeted monopoly capitalism as a new economic formation that organized the industrial, financial, and transportation core of the economy and that was able to extract value above a subsistence level from workers and from farmers, who labored in the economy's competitive periphery along with small-time capitalists. What were the People's Party's solutions to this failure of the market—this failure of competition—whose outcome had been monopoly? The People's Party program was a republican one of regulation, government credit and currency, public ownership of financial and infrastructural industries (railroads, grain elevators, and the like) that denied fair-market access to many small producers, and protection for workers and unions.

Almost simultaneously and under heavy pressure from mounting criticisms of existing theories, neoclassical economists were closing in on a major revision of Smithian economics that mounted a vigorous defense of an altered conception of what was going on in the capitalist market. The clearest statement of the new paradigm appeared in John Bates Clark's *Distribution of Wealth*. This work, and the international movement toward neoclassical economics generally, offered a crucial reframing in value theory. As we have seen, the labor theory of value had been central to both republican and traditional liberal philosophies throughout the nineteenth century, providing a potent moral basis for indicting a system that left in poverty people who worked and played by the rules. In Clark's economics and subsequently in neoclassicism, the value (or the price) of things was the result of their "utility," or their capacity to satisfy wants. This is a demand-side rather than a supply-side judgment made by consumers. The way Clark figured it, every factor of production—every individual unit of labor, land, and capital—would get exactly the value it produced, so long as there was full and effective competition. Apparently unmoved by the Great Merger Movement going on around him at the turn of the century and by heavy criticism from Veblen, among others, Clark claimed that the forces suppressing competition—monopoly, problems in the money supply, excess immigration—were only temporary; like waves made by blowing on the surface of a tub of water, they would disappear.

Juxtaposing these emblematic texts suggests a good deal for the subsequent history of poverty and social provision. Americans have oscillated between the visions captured by the Omaha Platform and by Clark's *Distribution of Wealth*, unable to make a lasting commitment to either. These tensions were evident in the limited though significant reforms achieved during the Progressive Era. In the United States, between the turn of the twentieth century and its final decades, welfare economics and a potent social democratic tradition that accounted for poverty in institutional and structural terms heavily contested the neoclassical endorsement of the market. In the most recent period, since the 1970s, neoclassical economics has largely triumphed, giving increased authority to a hedonistic view of the human person as rational maximizer, to "rational choice" as a politics and economics that can be applied to nearly every situation, and to supply-side, tax-cutting, budget-cutting policies that have impoverished the public sector, dramatically reducing the capacity of national, state, and city governments to provide for health, education, and infrastructure and to maintain incomes. Meanwhile, complicated now by the shift of massive numbers of manufacturing jobs offshore and by the rapid growth of a low-wage service sector, poverty is still more than anything else lack of sufficient work opportunities and low wages.

Mary O. Furner

See also: Agrarian Movements; Capitalism; Charity; Charity Organization Societies; Coxey's Army; Economic Depression; Freedmen's Aid; "Gospel of Wealth"; Immigrants and Immigration; Industrialization; Liberalism; Poor Laws; Poorhouse/Almshouse; Poverty Research; *Progress and Poverty*; Relief; Republicanism; Slavery; Speenhamland; Sweatshop; Work Ethic

References and Further Reading

Barrett, James. 1987. *Work and Community in the Jungle: Chicago's Packinghouse Workers, 1894–1922*. Urbana: University of Illinois Press.

Boydston, Jeanne. 1990. *Home and Work: Housework, Wages, and the Ideology of Labor in the Early Republic*. New York: Oxford University Press.

Bremner, Robert H. 1992. *The Discovery of Poverty in the United States*. New Brunswick, NJ: Transaction Books.

Cawelti, John. 1965. *Apostles of the Self-Made Man*. Chicago: University of Chicago Press.

Foner, Eric. 1990. *A Short History of Reconstruction*. New York: Harper and Row.

Foner, Eric. 1995. *Free Soil, Free Labor, Free Men: The Ideology of the Republican Party before the Civil War*. New York: Oxford University Press.

Furner, Mary O. 1993. "The Republican Tradition and the New Liberalism: Social Investigation, State Building, and Social Learning in the Gilded Age." In *The State and Social Investigation in Britain and the United States*, ed. Michael J. Lacey and Mary O. Furner, 171–241. Cambridge: Cambridge University Press.

Horwitz, Morton J. 1977. *The Transformation of American Law, 1780–1860*. Cambridge, MA: Harvard University Press.

Huston, James L. 1998. *Securing the Fruits of Labor: The American Concept of Wealth Distribution, 1765–1900*. Baton Rouge: Louisiana State University Press.

Johnson, Paul. 1978. *A Shopkeeper's Millennium: Society and Revivals in Rochester, New York, 1815–1837*. New York: Hill and Wang.

Katz, Michael B. 1983. *Poverty and Policy in American History*. New York: Academic Press.

Kazin, Michael. 1998. *The Populist Persuasion*. Ithaca, NY: Cornell University Press.

Kuznets, Simon. 1989. *Economic Development, the Family, and Income Distribution*. Cambridge: Cambridge University Press.

Lincoln, Abraham. [1858] 1953. "Address before the Wisconsin State Agricultural Society, Milwaukee, Wisconsin." In *The Collected Works of Abraham Lincoln*, vol. 3, ed. Roy P. Basler, 471–482. New Brunswick, NJ: Rutgers University Press.

McCoy, Drew R. 1980. *The Elusive Republic: Political Economy in Jeffersonian America*. Chapel Hill: University of North Carolina Press.

McMath, Robert C. 1993. *American Populism: A Social History, 1877–1898*. New York: Hill and Wang.

Montgomery, David. 1979. *Workers' Control in America: Studies in the History of Work, Technology, and Labor Struggles*. New York: Cambridge University Press.

O'Connor, Alice. 2001. *Poverty Knowledge: Social Science, Social Policy, and the Poor in Twentieth-Century U.S. History*. Princeton: Princeton University Press.

Pessen, Edward. 1990. *Riches, Class, and Power: America before the Civil War*. New Brunswick, NJ: Transaction Books.

Roediger, David R. 1999. *The Wages of Whiteness: Race and the Making of the American Working Class*. London and New York: Verso.

Sellers, Charles. 1991. *The Market Revolution: Jacksonian America, 1815–1846*. New York and Oxford: Oxford University Press.

Ward, David. 1989. *Poverty, Ethnicity, and the American City, 1840–1925: Changing Conceptions of the Slum and the Ghetto*. Cambridge: Cambridge University Press.

Williamson, Jeffrey G., and Peter Lindert. 1980. *American Inequality: A Macroeconomic History*. New York: Academic Press.

Progressive Era and 1920s

The period from the turn of the twentieth century through the 1920s marked an important turning point in the way Americans thought about and responded to poverty and related problems. Known as the Progressive Era for the great number of progressive reforms implemented at the time, the years from roughly 1900 to 1920 introduced new ideas, institutions, and knowledge into public debate, which became the basis for more-modest expansions in social protection during the 1920s. Although a great deal of conflict and frequent setbacks accompanied these debates, on the whole this was a period of intellectual and political ferment about the role and obligations of government and about the relationship between capitalism and democracy. New approaches to poverty broke away from the nineteenth century's emphasis on the failure of individuals and began to examine poverty in terms of the political economy and social environment. The idea that charity should reform the individual was challenged by the idea that public social welfare should mitigate the effects of industrial capitalism, especially the conditions of labor and living in the rapidly growing, increasingly immigrant industrial city.

Poverty and charity had developed along with the nation. U.S. ideas about the causes of and cures for poverty initially came from England during the colonial period. The new nation embedded colonial poor laws into U.S. legal codes and into the national culture. The tenets of voluntary (private) charity, limited government, and laissez-faire economics shaped the social welfare infrastructure throughout the nineteenth century. Just as important, these tenets were entwined with such cultural values of good citizenship as personal responsibility, independence, and self-support. To receive assistance meant to accept willingly the designation of "dependent," a status reserved for those outside the economic mainstream: the very young, the very old, women, slaves, the chronically ill, and the disabled.

Private charities dominated the infrastructure of social welfare until the Progressive Era, but they usually provided assistance selectively to their own constituents. A survey of private groups in the 1890s would have revealed listings such as the Catholic Charities, Norwegian Lutheran Home and Hospital, Associated Jewish Charities, and the Bohemian Charitable Association. Maintaining a distinct group of beneficiaries retained national, cultural, or religious ties. However, this privatized method of distributing aid produced an inequitable system of assistance based not on the need of individuals or families but on the ability of a particular group to raise funds and deliver services. Small groups on the margins of economic prosperity could not take care of their own people as well as better-situated groups could.

During the nineteenth century, public resources for the poor were local and limited. Counties provided "indoor relief" through their poorhouses and "outdoor relief" through in-kind aid to families. Individual states funded institutions for the aged, mentally ill, orphans, and tuberculosis victims. The sole example of federally funded assistance in this era was pensions for military service. Although military pensions helped alleviate poverty for the aged or injured veteran and his wife, it was considered less a charity than an entitlement for service, a view that retained the status of independence for the former soldier. In fact, the fear of fostering dependence, pauperism, or irresponsibility found its way into most arguments against expanding aid to the poor.

At the end of the nineteenth century, when the wealth and power of some corporations surpassed that of state governments, Americans began to view poverty as a by-product of social and economic processes. This change in perspective laid the groundwork for a greater public role in social provision during the 1920s. Massive immigration, unregulated industrial expansion, and the rapid growth of urban areas made the breadth and depth of poverty more visible. These trends also revealed the inadequacy of arguments that blamed individual behaviors for the cause of poverty. Some feared that the economic and social changes threatened democracy itself. Others called for businesses to take greater responsibility for the social problems they created.

Reformers proposed solutions to poverty and market insecurity that imagined a role for government in attenuating the effects of industrial capitalism. Advocates of publicly funded social welfare made modest advances at the local level. New programs for workers and widowed mothers joined older relief programs for the aged and ill. These initial forays into social provision created a rudimentary welfare state, albeit one that was fragmented and local.

The social policy debates and innovations of the first two decades of the twentieth century departed from older traditions of more-individualized and more-privatized prescriptions for poverty. Yet the new ideas, which helped earn this period its name, also reflected social struggles and visions already in play. Among the many recent European immigrants that made up the industrial working class, for example, several were familiar with Karl Marx's ideas about class relations and the value of labor. They chose new strategies—socialism and unionism, for example—to rebalance worker-manager power relations. Progressive reformers supported many of the workers' demands for improved working conditions and for unions. They also argued that government needed to mediate between individuals and businesses to preserve democracy and the health and welfare of its citizens. Progressives further worked to deepen understanding of the causes and cures for poverty. In the tradition of progressivism—investigate, educate, and legislate—reformers placed their trust in empirical research and social policy.

The expanding administration of private charity organization societies and public poor-relief offices also sought better information. In the early stages of professionalization, public and private charities needed to train and educate their practitioners. Professional conferences like the National Conference of Charities and Corrections (later the National Conference of Social Work) offered state and national venues in which to share research and debate new policies.

Several major empirical studies that explored the extent of poverty were published between 1890 and 1910. Inspired by British social survey methods and by new analyses incorporating social science data, Americans embarked on a fact-finding era in hopes of understanding how the poor became poor. Congress commissioned the first comparative study of poverty in several large cities. The resulting book, *The Slums of Baltimore, Chicago, New York, and Philadelphia*, produced by Carroll D. Wright, the commissioner of labor, provided the single greatest accumulation of data available until then when it was published in 1894. Robert Hunter's *Poverty* (1904) was less empirical but was perhaps more widely read as a treatise on the subject of poverty in the United States. The nineteen-volume *Report on Condition of Woman and Child Wage-Earners in the United States*, published by the Department of Commerce and Labor between 1910 and 1913, provided extensive documentation of the correlation between sex and job segregation, low wages, and job crowding, all of which contributed to poverty for female wage earners. Studies by W. E. B. Du Bois examined the impact of industrialization, migration, and race on the high rates of poverty among African Americans. These few examples represent a fraction of the book-length studies on poverty, yet they defined the populations most likely to be poor.

Research showed that unemployment, illness, and injury of the male head of the family could bring an otherwise self-sustaining family to the brink of poverty. Without savings, family resources, or other private aid, such a family would become desperately poor until the job market improved or until other family members found jobs. In addition, people who were structurally and ascriptively marginal to the workforce were also vulnerable to poverty: the elderly, the very young, and mother-only families. People of color, whose wages were low because of job segregation and discrimination, experienced a double exposure to poverty. Consequently, families of color (as well as recent immigrant families) sent wives and children into the workforce to supplement the family income.

Among the dozens of innovations designed to address the problems of poverty and urban life, two deserve special mention: settlement houses and the National Urban League. Settlement houses were largely an urban phenomenon, although a few existed in rural communities. Their novelty came from the premise that providers of social services needed to live as neighbors among those they served so they could thereby better understand the circumstances of the poor. Inspired by London's Toynbee Hall, predominately native-born, middle-class, white Protestants volunteered. Educated women found settlement house work to be an excellent opportunity to move into semiprofessional work. Indeed, within the country's most progressive settlements, women such as Jane Addams, Florence Kelley, Edith Abbott, and Lillian D. Wald learned vital lessons about politics and poverty that they would use in policy work. Furthermore, the applied research conducted by settlements contributed to the newly emerging field of social work.

Hull House, a settlement located on Chicago's West Side, led in innovative social programs. Founded in 1889 by Jane Addams and Ellen Gates Starr, Hull House played an important role in the creation of the nation's first juvenile court in Chicago, maternal and infant health clinics, day nurseries, and mothers' pensions. Residents participated in the 1893 survey of slums in large cities (noted above), conducted studies on nationalities and housing, and provided recreation and meeting spaces for neighbors. Several of the Hull House residents who began their research as advocates of private initiative discovered the limits of that approach. Increasingly, they recognized the need to mix private and public responsibility. A few settlements served African American neighborhoods, but the Black community created its own distinctive service organization.

The National Urban League, founded in 1911, had chapters in major cities outside the South. It incorporated numerous small self-help organizations into one coordinated effort to provide services to African Americans. Rather than providing charity, the National Urban League saw its mission as assisting African Americans to be self-supporting. Men and women made use of the League's employment services. But hiring practices that discriminated on the basis of race created additional hurdles for Black workers that employment services alone could not overcome.

Although employment was perceived as the primary weapon against poverty, the vast changes in the workplace wrought by industrial capitalism left workers vulnerable to poverty in new ways. Furthermore, new workers in the industrial workforce—children, women, immigrants, and people of color—faced occupational segregation and lower wages. Even the efforts of workers to organize for leverage against employers became stratified and marked by sex and race when male trade unionists linked their rights to earn a "family wage" to their self-definition as white "American" men, citizens, and breadwinners. All of these issues became part of the debates surrounding labor laws during the era.

Industrialism exposed the legal fiction inherent in the presumed equality of worker and employer that underpinned the vaunted "liberty of contract" for individual workers. Two court cases raised this issue but answered it differently for male and female workers. In *Lochner v. New York* (198 U.S. 45 [1905]) the U.S. Supreme Court invalidated a state law that limited the number of hours bakers could work. Yet a few years later, in *Muller v. Oregon* (208 U.S. 412 [1908]), the maximum hours of labor was set at ten hours, but only for women workers. The Brandeis Brief used extensive evidence from medical studies and factory reports to argue that long work hours damaged women's reproductive system and consequently threatened the best interests of the nation.

Once employed, workers still could have difficulty maintaining a basic standard of living. Trade unionists could negotiate wages in contracts with employers, but only a minority of workers had unions to represent them. The Women's Trade Union League not only helped women workers organize but also conducted research on the issues of wages and standards of living. Employed women generally were paid too little to earn a living wage, leading some reformers to call for a minimum wage to help eliminate poverty among this group of workers. Several industrial states discussed minimum-wage legislation, reviewed the evidence, and heard the testimony of workers. Massachusetts passed the first minimum-wage law for women and children in 1912. Unlike legislation setting maximum hours, a minimum wage for women proved far more difficult to achieve. In 1923, the U.S. Supreme Court struck down a minimum-wage policy for women in *Adkins v. Children's Hospital* (261 U.S. 525). Legislation on hours and wages would wait for passage until the 1930s, when it received support for both men and women workers.

Although the above-mentioned legislation were officially color-blind, several factors combined to deny people of color the benefits of new policies. African Americans, Asian Americans, and Latinos worked predominately in agriculture and domestic service during this period. Neither of these job sectors was covered by hours laws. In addition, racial prejudice applied different cultural assumptions to African American, Asian American, and Latina women than to white women. They and their children were perceived by whites to be *more able to work* than similarly situated white women and children. Consequently, these families remained underserved by Progressive-Era social welfare measures.

The most extensive developments in public social welfare during the Progressive Era were in the field of child welfare. The incarceration of young people with adults inspired the juvenile court movement and different treatments for people of different ages. The presence of children in the poorhouses of the late nineteenth century led to advocacy for aid to dependent children and measures to keep families in their own homes. The number of young children (under age fourteen) found in factories, fields, and mills created a groundswell of support for child labor laws. Each measure required a greater role for government. At the federal level, leadership emerged in a limited capacity. In 1909, the White House sponsored the first of several decennial conferences on the health and welfare of the youngest citizens in the United States. The establishment of the U.S. Children's Bureau in 1912 and the Women's Bureau in 1920 extended federal responsibility to conduct research, provide educational materials, and contribute to nonpartisan policymaking regarding children.

The line between child welfare and family welfare was often blurred, as in the case of the first so-called maternalist legislation: mothers' pensions. Illinois passed the first statewide legislation enabling mothers' pensions in 1911, which allowed counties to set aside revenue to support families with young children in their own homes. The idea spread rapidly across the states. The U.S. Children's Bureau took a major role coordinating information about state mothers' pension laws and providing information to other states that wanted to explore similar legislation. They also conducted numerous studies on the impact of the laws upon the health and welfare of children in mother-only families. Mothers' pensions set the prototype at the state level for a social policy that aimed to support women so they could stay home and care for their children. But from its earliest days, approximately half the mothers receiving pensions had to supplement their stipends with earnings. When the New Deal established a safety net for mother-only families, it adapted state-level mothers' pension laws to create Aid to Dependent Children (later Aid to Families with Dependent Children, AFDC) as Title IV of the Social Security Act (1935).

Workmen's compensation, another state-level program, sought to provide some measure of insurance for workers' families to protect them from poverty in the event of a disabling accident or death on the job. Initially, organized labor resisted the intrusion of government into benefits they believed should be negotiated between unions and management. Nevertheless, unions supported the state-level plans for workers' compensation laws. Between 1910 and 1917, all of the industrial states passed some form of workmen's compensation law to provide for workers who were either killed or terribly injured at work and for their survivors.

The experimentation in social welfare stalled during and after World War I. All suggestions for reform that relied on centralization or that enhanced state authority or taxpayer revenues were compared to socialism. The existing programs in child welfare, old-age pensions, workmen's compensation, and mothers' pensions continued to be state-level programs, implemented, if at all, at the county level. Looking broadly across the nation during the 1920s, one would find state laws on the books and perhaps even a state infrastructure to operate a program, but inadequate resources within the counties to adequately serve the program's mission. Similarly, retaining local authority over eligibility prolonged discriminatory operations of programs. For example, agricultural counties in the South and West that depended upon the labor of fieldworkers found ways to remove children and mothers from public relief when laborers were needed in the fields. In areas where fieldworkers were largely Hispanic or African American, the results were race based.

Maternalist legislation received a boost with the Sheppard-Towner Act (1921) for maternal and infant health. Riding high on a wave of support following passage of the Nineteenth Amendment, a coalition of women's organizations lobbied Congress for this public health measure. The act intended to reduce the high rates of mortality in childbirth and in infancy through federal funding of health care for mothers and infants. Although it was not specifically designed for the poor, it certainly had a great impact upon them because they were the least able to afford health care. Supporters hailed the law as visionary while detractors tagged it a socialist invention. Every two years, the act came before Congress for refunding authorization. By 1925, its opponents had gathered significant support. By 1927, its budget was cut, and by 1929, its funding was ended. Maternal and infant care lost support during the 1920s, as did the minimum-wage campaign and the child labor amendment.

The real area of growth in social welfare during the 1920s could be found in the infrastructure of social provision: training schools, professional organizations, and new government agencies. Schools of social work formalized their curriculum of accepted practices, taught the history of social welfare, and shepherded the research of graduate students. The profession developed established standards, procedures, and ethical guidelines and then attempted to get agencies to hire their trained graduates. Over the next two decades, graduates of social work schools were hired across the country as administrators of bureaus of public welfare as well as of private charities. A further transformation came in the state coordination of welfare practices. Though still small relative to contemporary bureaucracies, the state departments of welfare would become the coordinating body for aid programs. Yet the public sector did not take over social provision. Rather, it merged its responsibilities with that of the private sector.

The relationship between citizens and their government began to change during the first thirty years of the twentieth century. State and federal governing bodies assumed responsibilities that had once belonged only to families and communities, and the size of public administration grew to accommodate those changes. Americans did not embrace big government, nor did the concept of pauperism lose any of its stigma, but the principles of laissez-faire economics found vigorous competition from the principles of social democracy. These ideas and the experiments they fostered provided a blueprint for the social welfare policies initiated during the New Deal. Further, they began a process in which U.S. citizens came to expect their government to take some responsibility for their economic security.

Joanne L. Goodwin

See also: Aid to Families with Dependent Children (ADC/AFDC); Charity Organization Societies; Child Welfare; Citizenship; Dependency; Family Structure; Maternalist Policy; National Urban League; Settlement Houses; Trade/Industrial Unions; U.S. Children's Bureau; Welfare State

References and Further Reading

Berkowitz, Edward D., and Kim McQuaid. 1980. *Creating the Welfare State: The Political Economy of Twentieth-Century Reform*. New York: Praeger.

Goodwin, Joanne L. 1997. *Gender and the Politics of Welfare Reform: Mothers' Pensions in Chicago, 1911–1929*. Chicago: University of Chicago Press.

Gordon, Linda. 1994. *Pitied but Not Entitled: Single Mothers and the History of Welfare, 1890–1935*. New York: Free Press.

Katz, Michael. 1986. *In the Shadow of the Poorhouse: A Social History of Welfare in America*. New York: Basic Books.

Koven, Seth, and Sonya Michel, eds. 1993. *Mothers of a New World: Maternalist Politics and the Origins of Welfare States*. New York: Routledge.

Lemann, Nicholas. 1991. *Promised Land: The Great Black Migration and How It Changed America*. New York: Knopf.

Orloff, Ann Shola. 1993. *The Politics of Pensions: A Comparative Analysis of Britain, Canada, and the United States*. Madison: University of Wisconsin Press.

Patterson, James T. 1986. *America's Struggle against Poverty, 1900–1985*. Cambridge, MA: Harvard University Press.

Piven, Frances Fox, and Richard O. Cloward. 1971. *Regulating the Poor: the Functions of Public Welfare*. New York: Pantheon Books.

Shaw, Stephanie. 1996. *What a Woman Ought to Be and to Do: Black Professional Women Workers during the Jim Crow Era*. Chicago: University of Chicago Press.

Skocpol, Theda. 1992. *Protecting Soldiers and Mothers: The Political Origins of Social Policy in the United States*. Cambridge, MA: Belknap Press/Harvard University Press.

Great Depression and New Deal

"We in America today are nearer to the final triumph over poverty than ever before in the history of any land," Herbert Hoover boasted in accepting the 1928 Republican presidential nomination (Singer 1976, 33). A little over a year later, the deepest economic crisis in U.S. history, the Great Depression, mocked his confidence. The hunger, homelessness, and poverty that long had preoccupied at least a third of the nation in slums and on farms now became a specter haunting the lives of the more prosperous. The Wall Street crash of October 1929 wiped out three-quarters of the stock market's worth. Without adequate government spending to inhibit the downward spiral in 1930 and 1931, construction halted, automobile sales plummeted, and machine tool orders stopped. With rapid economic and social disintegration discrediting empty reassurances that recovery was just around the corner and with Hoover's reliance on voluntary action to jump-start the economy failing, the nation in 1932 elected Democrat Franklin D. Roosevelt as its next president. Through innovative government programs, Roosevelt's New Deal sought to alleviate distress, promote recovery, and reform the structural conditions that had precipitated the collapse.

The New Deal first attempted to shore up the nation's financial system and its productive and distributional capabilities in both industry and agriculture. It also concentrated on the immediate needs of the unemployed through a variety of work-relief programs. Only then did it initiate more structural approaches to poverty and social welfare. It established mechanisms to protect collective bargaining and labor standards that were key to its work-centered agenda. The limited welfare state that emerged relied on concepts of social insurance that privileged full-time employment in the core sectors of the economy over those who labored, often without a wage, in homes, on farms, or for the family. The white male industrial worker and his dependents gained a modicum of security, but men and women of color and white women found themselves inadequately covered by the law and subject to discrimination.

The crash exposed the human consequences of poverty. Resulting inadequate diets meant more cases of dysentery, pellagra, and chronic illness. Starving children picked over garbage. Homelessness soared, while those fortunate enough to have shelter shivered through the winter, unable to purchase fuel. Shantytowns, nicknamed "Hoovervilles," skirted the perimeters of cities. At the Depression's nadir in 1933, unemployment reached nearly 25 percent and double that for African Americans and other racial minorities. Anglos now displaced Mexicans and African Americans from low-wage agricultural and service jobs that they had previously rejected as beneath them. Millions worked reduced hours. Real income dropped 30 percent below its 1929 peak, while the gross national product was cut in half. With net receipts rapidly falling, foreclosures on farms numbered in the hundreds of thousands; everywhere, families defaulted on their mortgages. When 5,000 banks collapsed, 9 million Americans lost savings. Couples postponed marriage and pregnancy; no longer the breadwinners, more men deserted their families. Searching for work, a quarter of a million teenagers left home. The labor force participation of married women jumped by 50 percent, leading to complaints that they had no right to take jobs away from single persons or married men. Governments dismissed married female employees, leading some to divorce their husbands in order to keep jobs. By 1932, families seemed to be disintegrating.

Income inequalities, along with an unstable banking system and questionable investment practices, precipitated the Depression; the resulting lack of demand, or underconsumption, assured its depth and length. The 1920s had "roared" only for some Americans; 60 percent of families actually had only enough income for basic necessities (Badger 1989, 23). Northern textile workers, midwestern farmers, southern sharecroppers, and minority racial and ethnic groups throughout the nation already faced economic hardship. Only 2 percent of Native Americans, for example, earned over $500 a year (Badger 1989, 28). Natural disasters—the boll weevil, the 1927 Mississippi flood, and then drought—exacerbated the instability of cotton farmers reeling from a crisis of overproduction. Facing debt as well, about a quarter of all farmers lived in depressed conditions during the 1920s (Lichtenstein, Strasser, and Rosenzweig 2000, 344). So too did workers in ailing industries, some of whom faced technological displacement; those in the coal, shoe, and textile industries saw wages drop and jobs disappear or move to lower-paid regions, such as the South or Puerto Rico. Unskilled laborers in most sectors experienced wage declines and irregular employment. Although the overall standard of living grew during the 1920s, the gap between rich and poor widened. In 1929, the income of the 36,000 wealthiest households equaled that of the 12 million poorest, while only 200 companies received half of all corporate wealth (Lichtenstein, Strasser, and Rosenzweig 2000, 326).

Monetary and trade policy only intensified the economic crisis. The Federal Reserve Board's low interest rates had encouraged speculation during the 1920s. When stocks declined, investors who had bought on margin lost all, intensifying the drop in value. Instead of slashing rates, the Fed raised them, destabilizing the banking system when customers of rural banks and ethnic savings and loans could no longer receive credit or repay loans. Many uninsured and undercapitalized financial institutions collapsed. The 1930 Smoot-Hawley Tariff stymied international commerce, while the Federal Reserve Board raised interest rates in response to European abandonment of the gold standard in 1931. Further depressing the economy was the German default on reparations to Britain and France, which resulted in European bank collapses. Foreign trade nearly stopped; the worth of U.S. goods exported abroad plunged from $5 billion to $1 billion between 1929 and 1932.

A combination of declining tax revenues and the rising cost of public assistance bankrupted state and city governments. Out of desperation, Chicago and Detroit issued IOUs instead of paying teachers, firemen, and other employees. Spending $1 million a month in 1931, Philadelphia coordinated a model program with private groups, like the United Way. But the distress was so great that even though Philadelphia offered amounts of relief below the sustenance level, it ran out of funds within eighteen months, leaving 57,000 families without resources. Local relief agencies elsewhere looked for reasons not to aid individuals, whose very need for assistance marked them as unworthy. Instead of cash, agencies distributed food orders or organized soup kitchens, and, even then, three-quarters of the unemployed received no aid during the early 1930s. In Chicago and Detroit, relief bureaus also instigated repatriation campaigns that pushed Mexican American steel and automobile workers across the Mexican border. Around 500,000 migrants returned to Mexico, mostly before 1933, taking their U.S.-born citizen children with them.

At least 2 million unemployed persons marched for relief and jobs, meeting resistance from public authorities and private security guards. Street violence erupted on March 6, 1930, at the Communist-organized International Unemployment Day in New York. Two years later, during a hunger march on Ford's River Rouge plant in Dearborn, Michigan, four people died and over sixty sustained wounds after the police fired into the retreating crowd. Although some people bartered goods and services and others looted surplus commodities, Communist and Socialist Unemployment Councils defended the right to relief in confrontations with welfare officials in Chicago, Detroit, New York, Saint Louis, and elsewhere. They blocked evictions on Chicago's Southside, moving families' possessions back into apartments. These "eviction riots" forced the city to issue cash so the unemployed could pay rent. Similarly, in Iowa and South Dakota, farmers disrupted auctions, leading legislators to prohibit the sale of farms to cover taxes or other debt.

Police retaliation in the South was worse. Landlords attempted to reduce costs by kicking tenants off the land; some even refused to advance food or other supplies. In July 1931, the sheriff of Tallapoosa County, Alabama, violently broke up a meeting of the Black Sharecroppers' Union, one of many Communist-led groups that protested landlord actions. When 20,000 veterans, some joined by their families, marched on Washington, D.C., a year later demanding immediate payment of cash bonuses, the U.S. Army, under Gen. Douglas MacArthur, brutally destroyed their encampment.

Hoover sought to coordinate state, local, and private responses. He encouraged voluntary cooperation among businessmen, but despite attempts to maintain employment, firms were unable to sustain spending or production. Many followed U.S. Steel's lead in cutting wages 10 percent in 1931. When Hoover advocated billions of dollars for the Reconstruction Finance Corporation to aid failing businesses and banks, funds went to the healthiest among them. Under his philosophy of self-help and fiscal caution, public works projects were to pay for themselves, while farm relief fed livestock rather than the families of farmers. Relief, Hoover argued, was a local rather than a national responsibility, even though only eight states had legislated unemployment benefits.

Pledging to put the nation back to work, Roosevelt entered office at the lowest point of the Depression, facing bank closures in forty states. A more effective politician than Hoover, he gained success for fiscal measures that did not radically depart from those of his predecessor. Immediately declaring a national "bank holiday," Roosevelt had Congress pass legislation to restore confidence in the financial system by loaning funds, reorganizing troubled institutions, and certifying solvency. The Glass-Steagall Banking Act of 1933 established the Federal Deposit Insurance Corporation, which protected savings accounts. In April, Roosevelt removed the country from the gold standard. Securities acts in 1933 and 1934 created the Securities and Exchange Commission.

In an initial attempt to raise production, end unemployment, and stabilize industry, the National Industrial Recovery Act (NIRA) legalized employer cartels. Under the resulting National Recovery Administration (NRA), industries drew up codes of fair competition to regulate themselves through tripartite governing boards representing business, labor, and government. Section 7(a) of the act mandated that the codes include labor standards (minimum wages and maximum hours) and collective bargaining. Consumers were to do their part by purchasing only from companies displaying the "Blue Eagle," an emblem that business earned for complying with the NRA. Before the U.S. Supreme Court ruled it unconstitutional in 1935 as undue federal regulation of intrastate commerce, the NRA had approved over 1,000 codes. But many of these contained wage differentials that either directly (as with women) or indirectly (as with Blacks and other racial minorities, the young, and the homebound) discriminated against certain categories of workers by allowing lower rates in the South and for trainees and homeworkers.

Though employers dominated the code authorities and hampered enforcement in unorganized industries, such as southern textiles, trade unionists—notably John L. Lewis of the United Mine Workers (UMW)—regarded the NRA as their emancipation proclamation. Black leaders were more dubious, referring to the NRA as "Negroes Ruined Again" because it did nothing to stop racial exclusions. Numerous groups of white men—Toledo autoworkers, Minneapolis truckers, and West Coast longshoremen and seamen—sought to enforce 7(a) through massive picketing and strike action during 1934. Some unions, such as the UMW, recovered membership lost to Depression layoffs, while collective bargaining flourished in highly competitive sectors, such as the garment industry. But organizing drives hit mass-production industries with mixed results. Automobile companies resisted weak unions, which were unable to win concessions during the code-making process.

Unaware that the NRA excluded agriculture, unionizing Pennsylvania farmworkers, Massachusetts cranberry harvesters, California cotton growers, and Florida citrus pickers also found inspiration in the NRA. But rather than aiding farmworker organization, government actually stymied it by excluding agriculture from all labor legislation. Instead, agriculture came under the Agricultural Adjustment Administration (AAA), which the Supreme Court in 1936 also struck down as an overextension of federal powers. In an attempt to raise the price of basic commodities and to improve rural purchasing power, AAA paid farmers to reduce crop acreage; food processors were taxed to finance the program, and they in turn passed on the cost to consumers. Within three years, gross farm income had grown by 50 percent, though by 1939 farm income still fell 20 percent short of "parity," the ratio of farm to industrial prices set during World War I (Lichtenstein, Strasser, and Rosenzweig 2000, 399; Badger 1989, 168). Meanwhile, to enhance productivity and improve daily life, the Rural Electrification Administration brought power to farms.

Some farmers plowed up crops and slaughtered livestock to receive cash subsidies. Others evicted tenants rather than share government checks with Black, Mexican, and poor Anglo families. Landlords also replaced Anglo tenants with African Americans and Mexicans, whom they forced to sign away payments as a condition of tenancy. Such labor practices not only intensified the racialization of farm labor and lowered standards of living but also further increased the anti-immigration and anti-Black sentiments of whites in the South and Southwest. The Southern Tenant Farmers Union organized the displaced into roadside encampments but failed to reverse evictions. After purging radical staff, the Department of Agriculture responded to the mounting crisis by creating the poorly funded Farm Resettlement Agency (FRA) in 1935.

This represented a halfhearted attempt to provide loans for those displaced by agribusiness. The Farm Security Administration (FSA), which coordinated rural programs beginning in 1937, established over ninety "permanent" camps that provided welfare services, like health care and work relief, to migrants until World War II shifted its purpose to raising farm output.

At his second inauguration, Roosevelt pledged to eradicate the plight of "one-third of a nation ill-housed, ill-clad, ill-nourished" (Kennedy 1999, 287). The South, he judged, was "the Nation's No. 1 economic problem" (Carlton and Coclanis 1996, 42). The 1938 *Report on Economic Conditions of the South* called for increasing the purchasing power of a region underdeveloped by culture and cultivation. While the progressive Southern Conference for Human Welfare sought federal aid to eliminate poverty, Roosevelt remained hampered by entrenched southern Democrats in Congress, whom he failed to dislodge during the 1938 midterm elections. The New Deal lacked the political will to challenge the poll tax, lynching, and the South's entire Jim Crow system, despite the advocacy of first lady Eleanor Roosevelt. Still, it did open federal programs elsewhere to African Americans. This inclusion began the shift of African Americans into the Democratic Party.

Relief for the dispossessed expanded during the New Deal. Early in 1933, Congress appropriated $500 million for direct relief. By 1936, the Federal Emergency Relief Administration (FERA) had distributed roughly $1 billion a year, about 2 percent of the national income. But by requiring matching funds from the states, FERA exacerbated inequality. The national average relief payment was around fifteen dollars a month, but Mississippi paid less than four dollars, and some states refused to supplement federal monies with their own. Even when southern African Americans managed to obtain aid, they received less than did white recipients. Localism encouraged favoritism and politicization, leading relief czar Harry Hopkins to federalize operations in six states. He also sent journalist Lorena Hickok to tour the nation and report back on the conditions of ordinary people.

Congress approved a number of innovative programs in which the unemployed received cash for labor, maintaining an ideological link between individual self-worth and the work ethic that Roosevelt himself feared would be undermined by the dole. Administered by the army, the Civilian Conservation Corps (CCC) engaged some 3,000 young men in conservation and recreation construction projects. Though its 2,000 forest camps were segregated, with most serving whites, the CCC nonetheless paid Black men equal wages. A similar program for women was smaller (housing only 5,000 in ninety camps), lasted for less time, and offered some education, healthy food, and medical care but no wages. The National Youth Administration (NYA), funded in 1935, gave employment to 4.5 million young people, mostly students; it had a separate Office of Negro Affairs, run by the unofficial leader of Roosevelt's Black cabinet, Mary McLeod Bethune.

Hopkins established the Civil Works Administration (CWA) for the winter of 1933–1934, which reached 4.2 million people and pegged wages to jobs performed rather than to assets or personal characteristics of the worker. Although 95 percent of projects—such as road construction and building repair—required manual labor, 10 percent of employees were white-collar and professional men and women, who taught literacy, surveyed buildings, and painted murals. Southern employers, in particular, complained that CWA rates, which were higher than wages in textiles or agriculture, caused a labor shortage, undermining their racial caste system. However, the actual number of African Americans employed under CWA was small.

Considered too costly, the CWA was short-lived; nonetheless, it foreshadowed the creative arts projects that were a controversial component of the Works Progress Administration (later

Work Projects Administration) (WPA), launched in 1935. A means-tested program, the WPA focused on the able-bodied unemployed. It represented a massive shift in policy to temporary work relief made concurrently with the establishment of Social Security for those defined as unable to labor. Receiving for their labors double what emergency relief programs had provided, the unemployed under WPA viewed themselves as workers rather than as welfare recipients. They formed unions, demanded higher wages, went on strike, and lobbied Congress for continued funding under the leadership of the Communist-influenced Workers' Alliance, which claimed 600,000 members in forty-three states in 1936 (Badger 1989, 202). By the WPA's end in 1943, 8 million men and women, a fifth of the workforce, had improved the nation's infrastructure, beautified cities, and spread the arts. They built 2,500 hospitals, 5,900 schools, 1,000 airports, and 13,000 playgrounds (Lichtenstein, Strasser, and Rosenzweig 2000, 426; Badger 1989, 203). The Women's and Professional Division employed teachers, nurses, and librarians, though more than half of all women, especially in rural areas, worked on sewing projects. Between 300,000 and 400,000 women labored in WPA jobs, less than 20 percent of the total but more than in any previous work-relief program (Badger 1989, 205).

Under the Federal Art Project, 6,000 painters, muralists, and sculptors, 90 percent of whom qualified for relief, decorated public buildings. Thousands of white-collar unemployed joined the Federal Writers' Project to document the nation's past and its people through state guidebooks, collections of folk songs, and interviews with former slaves. Music and theater projects brought symphony orchestras and live performances to remote areas. Actors performed in Yiddish and Spanish, while all-Black ensembles gave new meaning to Shakespeare. With works of social commentary like the *Living Newspaper*, the Federal Theatre Project generated heated criticism from conservative politicians, such as New Deal opponent Martin Dies and his House Un-American Activities Committee in 1939.

The 1935 Social Security Act further protected against unemployment by offering benefits to those who had worked and assistance to those unable to labor due to age, disability, or motherhood. Workers in the industrial sectors of the economy participated in contributory social insurance—Old Age Insurance (OAI) and Unemployment Insurance (UI). By basing security on the employment relation, the act relegated those with irregular work histories, part-time hours, or jobs in marginal sectors (like service and agriculture)—disproportionately women of all races and men of color—to means-tested assistance programs such as Old Age Assistance (OAA) and Aid to Dependent Children (ADC). These programs subjected nonworkers to personal scrutiny, stigmatizing them as less deserving than those who qualified for benefits through paycheck deductions, touted as worker contributions, or through employer contributions paid in the form of taxes on payrolls.

Social Security emerged in response to more-radical calls for a social wage, such as Louisiana governor Huey Long's "Share Our Wealth" plan. Its old-age provisions sought to deflect the popular Townsend movement, which demanded a generous monthly pension of $200 for all persons over age sixty without criminal records who were not employed, provided that they spent the money within thirty days. Social Security also offered a moderate alternative to the more universal unemployment, old age, and social insurance sections of the unsuccessful Workers' or Lundeen Bill of 1934 and 1935, which covered farm, domestic, and professional workers as well as industrial labor and included maternity disability payments.

Despite centralized administration through a quasi-independent board with appointed experts, Social Security consisted of programs that were hardly uniform in their rules or structure. The percentage of federal financing varied. The states could establish their own benefit levels and eligibility criteria for OAA and ADC. Only OAI had national standards and existed as a right of all qualified wage earners. But it based benefits on earnings, rewarding those who had gained higher wages rather than those with lesser resources.

UI also helped regulate the economy and maintain a skilled workforce. Funded by a combination of state monies and payroll taxes, UI left implementation to the states, which led to variations dependent on local conditions. It rewarded large firms who could maintain employment levels by reducing their taxes. Because it covered only those businesses with eight or more employees, it excluded the most vulnerable workers: 98 percent of those on farms and 90 percent of those in households, as well as 46 percent of those in trade and wholesale. Workers laid off from qualified jobs had to meet a threshold of earnings and hours, had to be actively searching for new work, and had to have lost their job due to employer action. The vagueness of criteria allowed arbitrary personalism, as well as race and sex discrimination, to creep into eligibility evaluations.

Social Security reinforced gender inequalities. Among those laborers unable to qualify for UI were housewives and women temporarily out of work due to maternity. Amendments enacted in 1939 to Social Security responded to the problem of female dependency by providing for the wives of socially insured men. The housewife gained her own old-age insurance, equal to half of her husband's. During a time when a majority of wives lacked sustained labor force participation, this amendment both subsidized female domesticity and provided real gains for some women. Under Survivors' Insurance, widows with children under eighteen received three-fourths of their late husband's pension (unless they remarried or entered the workforce); the divorced or never married remained in the more arbitrary ADC program. This system doubly disadvantaged the vast majority of African American, Mexican American, and immigrant women (especially Asians restricted from citizenship), whose husbands were not included in the social insurance system and whose own labor histories were outside the system as well.

ADC superseded state-level mothers' pensions. It promised security to mothers without other means, requiring states to offer the program in all jurisdictions as a condition for receiving federal funds. But lack of federal oversight meant that states could impose residency and citizenship requirements, limit benefits by marital status, link eligibility to morals tests, and force work outside the home. Despite sentimentalized paeans to mother care of children, lawmakers provided no caregiver's grant, and thus mothers had to obtain additional funds to make ends meet. From the start, southern states assumed that Black women would go out to service or into the fields. Beginning with Louisiana in 1943, states adopted "employable mother" rules to compel would-be recipients into the labor market without the rights others had gained as workers.

The 1935 Wagner Act had enhanced worker freedoms, increased their purchasing power, and alleviated industrial unrest by establishing for wage earners the right to collective bargaining through representatives of their own choosing. This labor law system nourished and was made possible by the rise of industrial unionism and the Congress of Industrial Organizations (CIO), marked by victories at General Motors and U.S. Steel in 1937. Decisions by the National Labor Relations Board (NLRB), however, created a maze of bureaucratic rules that contained workplace activism. These procedural requirements, while advancing the rights of those in mass-production industries, did nothing for workers outside of NLRB jurisdiction who labored in fields, offices, schools, and homes. The 1938 Fair Labor Standards Act (FLSA) federalized wage and hour laws in a race- and gender-neutral manner. But it also excluded from coverage most jobs dominated by women, especially those

"An Economic Bill of Rights," President Franklin D. Roosevelt, Campaign Speech, October 28, 1944

In his January 1944 State of the Union address, Franklin D. Roosevelt spoke of "economic truths [that] have become accepted as self-evident" and challenged Congress to implement them on the home front in anticipation of victory in World War II. FDR's "Economic Bill of Rights" soon became a stock feature in his final campaign for the presidency in 1944, where he used it to attack those who would dismantle his New Deal reform program and to assert an expanded role for government in assuring social well-being.

. . . The American people are prepared to meet the problems of peace in the same bold way that they have met the problems of war.

For the American people are resolved that when our men and women return home from this war, they shall come back to the best possible place on the face of this earth—to a place where all persons, regardless of race, color, creed or place of birth, can live in peace, honor and human dignity—free to speak, and pray as they wish—free from want—and free from fear.

Last January, in my Message to the Congress on the state of the Union, I outlined an Economic Bill of Rights on which "a new basis of security and prosperity can be established for all—regardless of station, race or creed":

I repeat them now:

"The right to a useful and remunerative job in the industries, or shops or farms or mines of the nation;

"The right to earn enough to provide adequate food and clothing and recreation;

"The right of every farmer to raise and sell his products at a return which will give him and his family a decent living;

"The right of every business man, large and small, to trade in an atmosphere of freedom from unfair competition and domination by monopolies at home or abroad;

"The right of every family to a decent home;

"The right to adequate medical care and the opportunity to achieve and enjoy good health;

"The right to adequate protection from the economic fears of old age, sickness, accident and unemployment;

"The right to a good education.

"All of these rights spell security. And after this war is won we must be prepared to move forward, in the implementation of these rights, to new goals of human happiness and well-being."

Some people have sneered at these ideals as well as the ideals of the Atlantic Charter and the Four Freedoms—saying they were the dreams of starry-eyed New Dealers—that it's silly to talk of them because we cannot attain these ideals tomorrow or the next day.

The American people have greater faith than that. I know that they agree with those objectives—that they demand them—that they are determined to get them—and that they are going to get them.

The American people have a habit of going right ahead and accomplishing the impossible. . . .

This Economic Bill of Rights is the recognition of the simple fact that, in America, the future of the worker and farmer lies in the well-being of private enterprise; and that the future of private enterprise lies in the well-being of the worker and farmer.

The well-being of the Nation as a whole is synonymous with the well-being of each and every one of its citizens.

held by African Americans, as well as jobs that employed most men of color. For covered workers, the act set minimum wages and required time-and-a-half overtime after the forty-hour week; it also ended child labor under age sixteen. Treading on terrain similar to that covered by the NRA, which had been struck down by the Supreme Court, the FLSA limited its reach to those workers engaged in interstate commerce. This overcame previous Supreme Court objections to federal regulation of the labor contract, and following an abortive attempt to pack the Supreme Court after Roosevelt's 1936 landslide reelection, the justices upheld the FLSA and other New Deal measures.

The 1937 "Roosevelt Recession" revealed that the New Deal had mitigated rather than ended the Depression. Only the massive deficit spending of World War II revamped the economy. But the New Deal stabilized the banking, agricultural, and industrial relations systems. Its labor law and welfare regime promised a caring state. Poverty again became an item for national action. Nonetheless, Roosevelt recognized before his death in 1944 that the nation required a "Second Bill of Rights" to guarantee its citizens "economic security, social security, moral security" (Lichtenstein 2002, 30).

Eileen Boris

See also: Aid to Families with Dependent Children (ADC/AFDC); Civilian Conservation Corps (CCC); Deserving/Undeserving Poor; End Poverty in California (EPIC); Fair Labor Standards Act (FLSA); Public Works Administration; Share Our Wealth; Social Security; Social Security Act of 1935; Townsend Movement; Wagner Act; Welfare Policy/Welfare Reform; Welfare State; Works Progress Administration (WPA)

References and Further Reading

Badger, Anthony J. 1989. *The New Deal: The Depression Years, 1933–1940*. New York: Hill and Wang.

Carlton, David L., and Peter A. Coclanis. 1996. *Confronting Southern Poverty in the Great Depression: The Report on Economic Conditions of the South with Related Documents*. Boston: Bedford Books.

Cohen, Lizabeth. 1990. *Making a New Deal: Industrial Workers in Chicago, 1919–1939*. New York: Cambridge University Press.

Edsforth, Ronald. 2000. *The New Deal: America's Response to the Great Depression*. Malden, MA: Blackwell.

Gordon, Linda. 1994. *Pitied but Not Entitled: Single Mothers and the History of Welfare*. Cambridge, MA: Harvard University Press.

Kennedy, David M. 1999. *Freedom from Fear: The American People in Depression and War, 1929–1945*. New York: Oxford University Press.

Kessler-Harris, Alice. 2001. *In Pursuit of Equity: Women, Men, and the Quest for Economic Citizenship in 20th-Century America*. New York: Oxford University Press.

Lichtenstein, Nelson. 2002. *State of the Union: A Century of American Labor*. Princeton: Princeton University Press.

Lichtenstein, Nelson, Susan Strasser, and Roy Rosenzweig. 2000. *Who Built America? Working People and the Nation's Economy, Politics, Culture, and Society*. Vol. 2, *Since 1877*. New York: Worth Publishers.

Mink, Gwendolyn. 1995. *The Wages of Motherhood: Inequality in the Welfare State, 1917–1942*. Ithaca, NY: Cornell University Press.

Patterson, James T. 2000. *America's Struggle against Poverty in the Twentieth Century*. Cambridge, MA: Harvard University Press.

Singer, Aaron. 1976. *Campaign Speeches of American Presidential Candidates, 1928–1972*. New York: Ungar.

1940s to Present

In 1940, no one knew how many poor people there were in America. Public officials lacked both the technical capacity and the will to count them. In fact, it would be two decades before the nation acquired an official poverty line. Few, however, would have denied that poverty was widespread, not only among the old, widows, and single parents but among working families as well. Public programs did little to reduce this pervasive poverty. Indeed, insofar as they addressed the condition of the poor, government focused more on their survival—their immediate need for food, shelter, and medical care—than on their potential prosperity.

All this changed in the decades that followed. The prevalence of poverty dropped dramatically, if unevenly, among all groups, and for the first time, in the 1960s, its eradication became a stated goal of public policy. However, the 1970s and 1980s brought the end of the liberal politics, economic growth, and expansive social policies that had sustained the nation's assault on poverty since the New Deal. As public priorities changed and the energy of antipoverty initiatives dissipated, income inequality grew and poverty actually increased. At the end of the twentieth century, it was not poverty but so-called dependency on public assistance that policymakers targeted as the main enemy. More and more, poverty was accepted as a "normal" condition for millions of Americans.

Defining Poverty

In the United States, there was no official definition of poverty until the 1960s, when the necessity of measuring the impact of antipoverty programs forced the issue. The ambiguities surrounding poverty were papered over by an official measure, known as the poverty line, which rested on the assumption that food consumed about a third of a family's income. Government statisticians determined the cost of a thrifty food budget for families of various sizes and multiplied that by three. Households with incomes below that amount were officially in poverty (Orshansky 1977). With modifications, this definition has persisted, largely because any definition that is more adequate will raise the number of people in poverty, a result no government wants.

Despite its widely recognized flaws as an assessment of how much families actually need to get by, the official poverty line provides a useful if crude standard against which to measure trends in poverty over time, and it is the measure used here. Because official poverty statistics are not available before 1960, this entry uses cost-of-living studies to determine a poverty line for 1940 and 1950 roughly comparable to the government's official one for later years. It also follows the convention of basing poverty rates on post-transfer income, that is, income that takes account of government cash benefits. But it will disaggregate the sources of income as well, comparing the extent to which families have been able to surmount poverty on their own to their ability to do so with the contribution of public programs.

Trends in Poverty

The massive reduction in post-transfer poverty among all groups since 1940 is the first major story in the modern history of poverty. In 1939, the year whose experience was captured by the 1940 census, poverty was widespread because wages were low, unemployment was high, and the economy was stuck in the Depression. Men, excluding the self-employed, averaged an annual income of $1,006, and women averaged $592. Manufacturing operatives earned $824 and laborers $571, at a time when the poverty threshold was $925 for a nonfarm family of four composed of two children and a household head under sixty-five years of age. Although only service workers (largely women) and laborers had average earnings less than the poverty line, other blue-collar incomes remained uncomfortably close, frequently falling below it. Overall, 40 percent of households whose wage earners were under the age of sixty-five made poverty wages—a figure that rises to 53 percent with the inclusion of households with adults over sixty-five and those not working in the paid labor force. Nor were nonmanual workers immune from poverty: The incomes of 18 percent of male professionals, 12 percent of male managers, 18 percent of male clerical workers, and 21 percent of male sales workers put them below the poverty line. Within the manual working

Table 1

Percent of working household heads under the age of 65 with earnings lower than their family's poverty threshold, by occupation and gender, United States, 1939

	Male	*Female*	*Total*
Professionals	18.2	10.4	16.8
Farmers	83.8	100.0	84.3
Managers	12.2	34.8	12.8
Clerical workers	18.0	24.3	19.1
Sales workers	20.8	44.8	22.5
Construction workers	53.0	100.0	53.1
Other craft workers	21.7	40.0	21.8
Manufacturing operatives	35.9	70.8	39.4
Other operators	41.9	72.0	42.8
Service workers	46.7	81.3	58.6
Laborers	73.4	70.0	73.3
Government white collar	15.9	15.8	15.9
Government blue collar	30.9	72.8	32.0
No occupation	42.7	100.0	50.0
Working householders under 65	39.1	54.9	40.3
All householders	46.5	84.0	53.0

Source: U.S. Census, 1940. Author's calculations from Ruggles and Sobek (2003).

class, aside from skilled workers in industries other than construction, the proportion of householders with earnings below the poverty threshold ranged from 22 percent among craftworkers to 73 percent among laborers. (See Table 1.)

The rates for female householders—who earned lower wages than men within the same occupations and clustered in low-wage work—were 40 percent higher than the rates for men.

Poverty also related closely to age. Although working-class men's earnings rose during their twenties and thirties, these increases were outstripped by the consumption needs of large families. Thus, in 1940, 65 percent of working men in their early thirties could support their family on their wages alone, and this proportion declined for older age groups. Thanks to the contributions of other family members, however, poverty rates fell among families whose adults were in their thirties or forties before rising among those in their fifties and sixties.

The period of economic growth, expanding workforce participation, and social change that accompanied and followed World War II rearranged these long-standing contours of poverty. Nevertheless, the benefits of postwar prosperity were not universally shared. Although the 1950s may have seemed prosperous compared to previous decades, in that year one-quarter of factory operatives, 37 percent of those in service occupations, and 18 percent of craftworkers lived in poverty. In 1950, two-thirds of farmers lived in poverty, at a time when the highest rate among urban occupations was for laborers, at 41 percent. Poverty, clearly, remained the lot of a very large share of Americans.

During the next thirty years, the decline in poverty was extraordinary. At the end of the 1930s, nearly half the households in America had incomes below the poverty line; by the end of the twentieth century, that number had been reduced by nearly three-quarters. Farmers' poverty rate had fallen to 16 percent, still high compared to other occupations but a dramatic improvement from fifty years earlier, and only service workers and laborers had poverty rates higher than 10 percent. Among all those in the labor force, poverty had fallen from 27 percent in 1950 to 7 percent five decades later. Among all households, poverty declined from 44 percent in 1939 to 12 percent in 1999 (Danziger and Weinberg 1995, 18–50).

This impressive achievement, however, did not happen evenly across the decades. The poverty rate dropped 27 percent in the 1940s, 36 percent in the 1950s, 29 percent in the 1960s, 20 percent in the 1970s, and not at all in the 1980s. Although poverty has always varied with age, its relation to life's stages reversed during the late twentieth century. Earlier, it appeared among families under the greatest economic strain—when parents were in their thirties and their children were too young to work—but it was most pervasive among the elderly, a majority of whom lived in poverty. By late in the century, this pattern had turned 180 degrees: The elderly were the least likely of any age group to be poor, and children—nearly one of five of whom were poor—were the most likely to find themselves below the poverty line. The numbers are stunning: In 1940, 54 percent of children under the age of ten and 62 percent of adults age sixty-five and over were poor. By 1999, child poverty had dropped to 19 percent and poverty among the elderly to 10 percent (see Figure 1). Despite this decline, at the start of the twenty-first century, America had the highest rate of child poverty among industrial democracies.

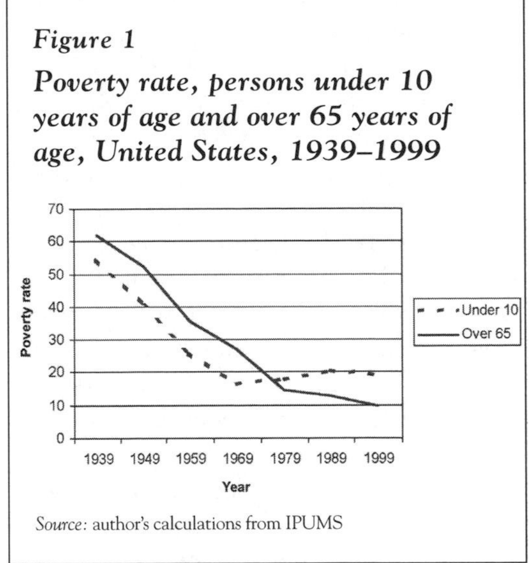

Figure 1

Poverty rate, persons under 10 years of age and over 65 years of age, United States, 1939–1999

Source: author's calculations from IPUMS

Another way to think about the relation of age to poverty is to examine the age composition of the poor. Here we use an indicator—an index of representativeness—that shows whether a group was over- or underrepresented among the poverty population. A score of 100 means that the number in poverty was proportional to the group's share of the total population. The change is striking: The overrepresentation of children under the age of ten among the poor decreased from 127 in 1939 to 120 in 1969 and then rose to 150 in 1999. (The scores for young people between ten and nineteen followed a similar trajectory.) The scores for those over sixty-five moved in the opposite direction: In 1939 and 1959, they were the most overrepresented group among the poor, with index scores of 146 and 167. Thereafter, their relative position improved until, by 1999, with a score of 80, they were underrepresented. (See Table 2.)

Trends in Poverty by Race, Ethnicity, Gender, and Region

Although absolute poverty rates plummeted for all groups, the disparities—the degrees of difference—among races and among men and women remained strikingly durable, testimony to enduring inequities. Among African Americans, poverty rates have been much higher than among whites, even though after World War II poverty among them fell with the Great Migration from the South to northern and midwestern cities. Although African American poverty decreased dramatically between 1939 and 1999—from 71 percent to 24 percent—its distance from the white rate widened. In 1939, the ratio of African American to white poverty was 195; in 1999 it was 274. In 1999, African Americans made up 13 percent of the population but 25 percent of the poor, for an index score of 199 compared to 177 sixty years earlier. The 1999 score, however, did register a decline from the peak year, 1969, when it had climbed to 262. (See Table 3.)

Poverty among Latinos followed a different trajectory, reflecting the increased immigration of recent decades. In 1949, Latino poverty—58 percent—was 14 percent lower than the figure for African Americans. By 1999, following the arrival of millions of poor Mexicans and others of Hispanic origin, it was 5 percent lower than Blacks'. In the same years, poverty among Asians also reflected the rhythms of immigration. The 37 percent poverty rate among the small Asian and Pacific Islander population in 1939 plummeted to 12 percent in 1969 and then, after

Table 2

Poverty rate and index of representativeness, by age, United States, 1939–1999

Year	Under 10	10–19	20–29	30–39	40–49	50–59	60–64	Over 65	Total
Poverty rate									
1939	54.2	49.8	34.4	33.3	32.7	36.9	46.5	61.9	42.5
1949	40.4	43.4	29.0	27.2	27.1	28.2	35.9	52.2	34.9
1959	25.6	24.2	17.9	14.5	13.9	16.4	22.6	35.6	21.3
1969	16.3	15.0	10.3	9.4	8.1	8.9	14.5	27.0	13.6
1979	17.7	15.0	12.0	8.8	7.3	7.6	10.8	14.4	12.2
1989	20.4	17.7	15.0	10.1	7.5	8.2	9.2	12.6	13.3
1999	19.7	16.9	17.5	10.7	8.5	7.9	10.1	10.5	13.1
Index of representativeness									
1939	127	117	81	78	77	87	109	146	100
1949	116	124	83	78	78	81	103	149	100
1959	120	114	84	68	65	77	106	167	100
1969	120	110	76	69	59	65	106	198	100
1979	145	123	99	72	60	63	88	118	100
1989	154	134	113	76	57	62	69	95	100
1999	150	130	134	82	65	60	78	80	100

Source: author's calculations from IPUMS

Table 3

Poverty rate and index of representativeness, by ethnicity, 1939–1999

Census year	Nonhispanic white	Nonhispanic Black	Latino	Asian, Pacific Islander	Other	Total	Black/white ratio
Poverty rates							
1939	38.6	75.4	69.6	36.8	88.8	42.5	195
1949	30.3	72.0	58.1	40.3	85.0	34.9	238
1959	16.5	54.9	43.2	14.3	47.4	21.3	334
1969	10.3	35.7	25.9	12.0	32.9	13.6	345
1979	8.7	29.2	23.1	13.2	27.2	12.2	337
1989	9.1	31.3	24.0	14.8	30.7	13.3	344
1999	9.5	26.0	21.1	13.1	24.3	13.1	274
Index of representativeness (total population =100)							
1939	91	177	164	86	209	100	
1949	87	206	167	115	243	100	
1959	77	258	203	67	223	100	
1969	76	262	190	88	241	100	
1979	71	239	189	108	223	100	
1989	69	236	181	111	231	100	
1999	72	199	162	100	186	100	

Source: author's calculations from IPUMS

Asian immigration resumed and the United States accepted many refugees, began to increase, reaching 15 percent in 1989 and falling to 13 percent in 1999. (See Table 3.)

Until the late twentieth century, the combination of limited job opportunities, low wages, labor market discrimination, and household responsibilities kept most women from earning their way out of poverty. For much the same reason, families headed by women have historically been poor more often than families headed by men. Compounding these labor market disparities is the fact that women heading households are far more likely to be single parents and reliant on the earnings of only one breadwinner or on inadequate public assistance. Thus, the combination of lower earning power, scant welfare benefits, and changing family patterns are reflected in a demographic reality that underlines what some writers have labeled the "feminization of poverty" (Pearce 1978, 28–36). Although poverty among women declined over the post–World War II period, the male/female disparities widened. As a result, women made up a much greater proportion of the poverty population. The index score for adult women (age twenty-one and over) was 108 in 1939 and 137 in 1999 (a slight decline from their peak, 153, in 1969). (See Table 4.)

Table 4

Poverty rate, by gender, persons over the age of 21, United States, 1939–1999

Census year	*Male*	*Female*	*Female/ Male ratio*
1939	36.3	38.9	108
1949	29.9	32.5	109
1959	16.6	20.8	125
1969	9.6	14.7	153
1979	8.1	11.9	147
1989	8.5	12.6	148
1999	9.0	12.3	137

Source: author's calculations from IPUMS

Similarly, the steep decline in poverty among female-headed households—from 62 percent to 21 percent—between 1939 and 1999, a decline of 66 percent, was much less than the drop in poverty in households headed by men, bringing the poverty ratio of female- to male-headed households from 169 to 263. As a result, the proportion of all poor people who lived in female-headed households increased from 18 percent in 1950 to 55 percent in 1999.

Comparisons among ethnic groups reveal the degree to which gender disparities are compounded by race: Households headed by Black and Latina women have historically been poor more often than those headed by white women, and they remain so today. In 1999, 33 percent of Black and 32 percent of Latina female-headed households remained in poverty—compared to 17 percent of whites.

Poverty rates have varied geographically as well as by race, ethnicity, gender, age, and occupation. Indeed, they have traced the shifting economic fortunes of the nation's regions and the changing balance between city, suburb, and countryside. Early in the twentieth century, the South was the most impoverished region, and the cities were the engines of prosperity, with poverty rates lower than those of the countryside. In fact, it was Appalachian poverty, not the poverty of cities, that first inspired the War on Poverty of the 1960s (Patterson 1981, 134). In 1939, central-city poverty was 30 percent, compared to 29 percent in the suburbs and 59 percent in rural America. By the last decade of the century, with city economies decimated and economic growth transferred to suburbs, the central-city poverty rate had dropped by less than half whereas the suburban poverty rate had plunged by more than two-thirds and the rural rate had fallen below that for the central cities. The 1990s saw some small relative improvement for central cities and rural areas. The poverty rate of central cities fell from 19 to 17 percent during the decade while the rate in nonmetropolitan areas fell from 18 to 14 percent. The shifting central city–suburban balance in poverty rates appears even more vividly in the case of individual metropolitan regions. For instance, in 1939 the poverty rate in the city of Saint Louis, Missouri, was 29 percent; that of its suburbs was 31 percent. By 1980, however, city and suburbs had become two nations. Twenty-two percent of Saint Louis's urban residents were poor, compared to only 7 percent of those in the suburbs. In the same years, economic growth in the Sun Belt erased much of the distinction in prosperity between North and South. And yet everywhere, race, gender, and low wages trumped geography. No longer highly concentrated by region, poverty had been nationalized.

Wages, Inequality, and Deindustrialization

A very large number of families have always had to find ways to close the distance between the inadequate wages of their principal earners and the incomes needed to lift them out of poverty. In 1940, families still survived, or found their way out of poverty, through strategies that had been practiced within the working class for a very long time. These were of four types: help from other family members, household extensions, informal social relations, and public benefits. Children often contributed significantly to family incomes. In all, child labor lifted 7 percent of families out of poverty. But this help was skewed toward older families with working-age children. By contrast, household heads in their thirties, whose children were young, often found themselves in acute distress (National Center for Children in Poverty 1999). The increase in work among married women also helped some families escape poverty. Although only 6 percent of families left poverty as a result of women's work, in instances where women were employed, 40 percent of otherwise-poor families added enough income to move above the line. Wives helped, too, by looking after boarders and relatives who added to the family income by paying rent. The practice of taking in household extensions remained common: 19 percent of households contained a relative and 10 percent had at least one boarder. These additional household members most often lived with economically vulnerable families (Sobek 1997, 162–168).

Poor families in 1940 also survived with the help of informal social relations, which are impossible to quantify. They turned to kin and friends for donations of food, clothes, small amounts of money, and temporary housing. They were sustained by credit from landlords and local grocers. They found help when sick in free dispensaries and hospitals. And they turned to the network of private charities and mutual aid societies. None of these sources of aid lifted families out of poverty. That was not their purpose; their mission, instead, was to assure survival (Katz 1995, 144–172). The same can be said of the work programs of the New Deal, especially the Works Progress Administration, and of Aid to Dependent Children, Old Age Assistance, and Unemployment Insurance, all introduced as part of the Economic Security Act (later to be called the Social Security Act) in 1935. (Social Security had not yet started to pay benefits; although workers first paid Social Security payroll taxes in 1937, no retirees collected benefits until 1940.) Aid to Dependent Children paid benefits to about 1.2 million Americans in 1940, but the average benefit was $32 a month, or $384 a year at a time when the poverty threshold for a family of three was $1,000. Old Age Assistance helped about 2 million people with an average individual grant of $240 a year, which meant that it moved a couple about half the distance toward the poverty line of $840. Unemployment insurance paid benefits to about 1 million workers each week, or about 5 million at some point during the year. Its average benefit was $10.56 a week. A worker who exhausted his twenty-six weeks of benefits (unemployment insurance was skewed toward employed males) would have collected $275, or about one-sixth of the amount necessary to keep a family of five above the

Table 5

Percent of population whose household head earned more than the poverty threshold and the percent of population that escaped poverty because of the earnings of other family members, primary families whose head is under 65 years of age, United States, 1939–1999

	Householder under 65 years of age		*All primary families*	
Year	*Householder with earnings above poverty threshold*	*Escaped poverty through earnings of other family members*	*Householder with earnings above poverty threshold*	*Escaped poverty through earnings of other family members*
1939	47.4	11.3	43.7	12.8
1949	57.6	7.2	53.6	8.1
1959	70.0	8.0	64.5	9.3
1969	79.1	6.3	72.1	7.5
1979	75.5	8.3	67.3	9.3
1989	72.6	10.8	63.5	11.7
1999	71.0	11.3	62.3	12.1

Source: author's calculations from IPUMS

poverty line (Katz 2001). Unemployment insurance did make a notable difference for relatively well-paid workers—such as those in the automobile industry—periodically out of work for short periods. There was, however, one other strategy frequently used by working-class families who anticipated the poverty accompanying old age: buying a house. Poor families, interestingly, did not own property at an appreciably lower rate than others. But ownership was sharply skewed by age: As families aged and lost earning capacity, their rate of ownership increased. Clearly, they used income from working-age children to assure they would have a place to call home when their earning capacity declined with advancing years (Byington [1910] 1974, 126).

With time, poor families exchanged the paid labor of children for that of wives, shed household extensions, and began to rely on transfer payments from government. Thus, since 1940, the sources of poverty reduction have been divided roughly into three sources: increased earnings of household heads, earnings of secondary workers (mainly wives), and government transfer payments.

These strategies proved necessary because a shifting but substantial fraction of household heads earned too little to keep their families out of poverty. In 1939, only a little more than four of ten household heads earned enough to boost their families over the poverty threshold—a number that increased by about 10 percentage points during the next decade. In 1969, 72 percent of the population—the highest proportion recorded—lived in households whose heads earned more than poverty wages. Between 1969 and 1989, this proportion fell to 63 percent (see Table 5). The expansion of women's work, however, compensated for this trend. In each decade between 1940 and 1990, the labor force participation of adult women increased by about 10 percentage points, with the rate for white married women soaring (Goldin 2000, 577). Thus, in 1969, the earnings of other family members pulled 7 percent of the population out of poverty; in 1999, the proportion had increased to 12 percent. Earnings from spouses did not just compensate for the low wages of household heads; they also replaced some of the income once derived from boarders and lodgers, whose share among households declined from 4.6 percent in 1950 to 1.5 percent in 1990. Even with most married women working, between 1993 and 2000, the proportion of poor families with at least one full-time worker increased 20 percent—from 45 percent to 54 percent (U.S. Census Bureau 2000). At the century's end, the term "working poor" was not an oxymoron but a troubling reminder of stalled progress in wage growth and equality.

The shifting earning capacity of household heads tracked macroeconomic changes. Indeed, after World War II, the federal government, which viewed poverty as a consequence of unemployment, focused on full employment rather than on antipoverty policies, expecting that economic expansion would increase jobs and income. At first, experience seemed to support these assumptions. Real wages of manufacturing workers, which had increased on the average by 1.43 percent between 1900 and 1929, declined slightly during the Great Depression of the 1930s and spiked during the labor shortages of World War II. Then, between 1948 and 1973, they grew at a stunning annual average of 2.35 percent, supplemented by increasing employee benefits, which rose from 0.01 percent of compensation in 1929 to 0.17 percent in 1980. In the same years, poverty declined.

The 1973 oil embargo fueled inflation and recession, abruptly ending the postwar expansion and halting the decline in poverty rates. After 1973, manufacturing wages stagnated, growing only 0.46 percent annually (Goldin 2000, 565, 570), while unemployment increased and inequality widened. Between 1949 and 1969, real median family income rose by 99.3 percent; between 1973 and 1991, growth was just 3.4 percent (Danziger and Gottschalk 1995, 46). When recession ended in the early 1980s, the seven-year expansion that followed benefited only a minority of the population. In the 1980s and 1990s, income grew rapidly among the wealthiest Americans but remained stagnant among the middle and working classes and declined among the most disadvantaged groups: less-educated workers, single-parent families, Blacks, and Hispanics (Danziger and Gottschalk 1995, 3–5). Even though unemployment fell, millions of families failed to gain income, and poverty rates did not go down. Official unemployment rates for Black men remained more than double those for whites, and Hispanics fared only slightly better (Blank 1995, 171). Labor force participation rates were even worse: A great many young Black men remained chronically out of the regular labor market. In the 1980s and 1990s, soaring incarceration rates as well as chronic unemployment removed African American men from the labor force.

Despite the increasingly widespread experience of declining wages and unstable employment, the problems of an unemployed "underclass" of African American men drew a great deal of attention in the media and among policy analysts in the 1980s and 1990s. Social scientists frequently trace the chronic unemployment of Black men, as well as the overall decline in wages, to the deindustrialization of American cities. The model on which this argument rests, however, fits only a minority of cities, notably Chicago and Detroit. Elsewhere, Blacks did not find extensive employment in manufacturing; indeed, they were denied the best jobs in the industrial economy. Even in cities where Black industrial work was common, service jobs remained the core of Black urban employment. In 1949, in Saint Louis, to take one city, 26 percent of whites and 4 percent of Blacks held skilled and semiskilled jobs. In 1949, the largest category of work among African Americans—30 percent—was service (barbers, caterers, cooks, maids) rather than industrial jobs, and a decade later, more African Americans still worked in service jobs than in industrial jobs. Nor did Black industrial workers fare better than African Americans who worked in other kinds of jobs; they neither earned higher wages nor worked more steadily. In 1949 in Detroit, for example, 43 percent of African Americans employed in industrial jobs, compared to 67 percent of whites, earned a living wage and had steady employment. In a sample of fifteen representative cities, Buffalo, New York, had the highest share of Black industrial workers after Detroit. But Buffalo's Black poverty rate was among the highest. Atlanta, Boston, San Francisco, and Washington, D.C., by contrast, had the lowest Black poverty rates, and relatively few African Americans in those cities worked in industrial jobs. (See Figure 2.) Among those cities, there was, in fact, no statistically significant relationship between poverty rates and the share of the African American population in industrial work (Stern 1999).

Figure 2

Correlation of African American poverty rate with manufacturing operatives as percent of African American labor force, selected metropolitan areas, 1950

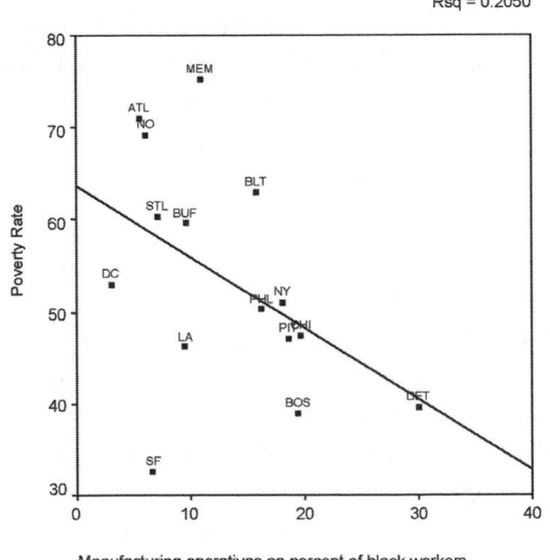

Key: ATL: Atlanta, BOS: Boston, BLT: Baltimore, BUF: Buffalo, CHI: Chicago, DC: Washington, DC, DET: Detroit, MEM: Memphis, LA: Los Angeles, NO: New Orleans, NY: New York City, PHL: Philadelphia, PIT: Pittsburgh, SF: San Francisco, STL: St. Louis

Source: author's calculations from IPUMS

What correlated most directly with different rates of urban Black poverty was the incorporation of African Americans into local political structures, a process that translated into government jobs and expanded welfare benefits. Politics and public service held the key to lower Black poverty rates. After World War II, the Great Migration of Blacks to northern and midwestern cities registered in increased political power and public jobs. This was the work that proved steadiest and paid best. In 1949, when only 32 percent of African Americans held steady jobs that paid a living wage, 75 percent of African American white-collar government employees earned more than poverty wages. Blue-collar government jobs did not pay as well, but at least they were steady. Government employment proved the best predictor of Black poverty rates. In four cities with more than 10 percent of Black household heads in government work in 1949 (Boston, Los Angeles, San Francisco, and Washington, D.C.), Black poverty rates were below 50 percent; cities with the lowest numbers of Blacks in public employment (Atlanta, Detroit, Philadelphia, Pittsburgh, and Saint Louis) had the highest rates of Black poverty. (See Figure 3.) In all, public employment explained more than 60 percent of the variance in Black poverty rates across the fifteen cities.

At the same time, county boards administered the public transfer programs that served Blacks directly—the categorical programs in the Social Security Act (Old Age Assistance, Aid to Dependent Children, Aid to the Blind) and state general assistance. Where Blacks had some standing in local bureaucracies that determined eligibility and administered aid, they eased the access of poor African Americans to these programs (Kleppner 1985; Grimshaw 1992). This is why the effectiveness of transfer programs in helping Blacks to escape poverty correlated highly with Black public employment. In 1949, it was in cities with the highest levels of public employment that the most African Americans

Figure 3

Relationship of African American poverty to government employees as percent of African American labor force, selected U.S. metropolitan areas, 1950

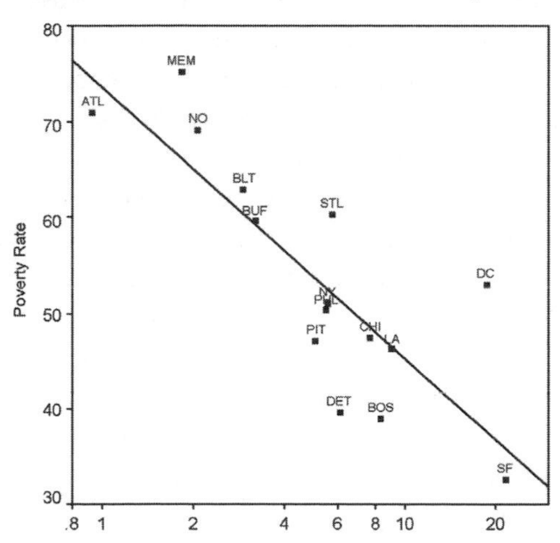

Key: ATL: Atlanta, BOS: Boston, BLT: Baltimore, BUF: Buffalo, CHI: Chicago, DC: Washington, DC, DET: Detroit, MEM: Memphis, LA: Los Angeles, NO: New Orleans, NY: New York City, PHL: Philadelphia, PIT: Pittsburgh, SF: San Francisco, STL: St. Louis

Source: author's calculations from IPUMS

escaped poverty because of public transfers (Sterner 1973; Lieberman 1998). The size of Black public employment explained 33 percent of the effectiveness of a city's public assistance payments.

In the 1970s and 1980s, attacks on transfer programs led to cuts in public assistance, unemployment insurance, and disability payments, and these cuts reduced Black family incomes. In addition, a number of cities responded to the fiscal crises of these decades by cutting their workforces—actions that affected African Americans severely and disproportionately. Together, reduced public benefits and public-sector layoffs pushed up the Black poverty rate. By the late 1980s, Black public employment had fallen from its high of 9 percent to 7 percent. The decline registered in the economic health of Black communities, where incomes from government jobs were dispersed widely, sustaining many families and businesses. Indeed, the correlation between the African American poverty rate and African American government employment was –0.7 (Stern 1999).

Family, Race, and Public Policy

Conservative writers on social policy have argued that most of the reduction in poverty predated the expansion of government transfer programs and that social welfare programs, in fact, unwittingly made poverty worse by reducing incentives to work (Murray 1984). This argument misreads the history of poverty and badly underestimates the importance of government. Indeed, it masks the relatively constant rate of pretransfer poverty. Ever since income has been measured, the national economy has generated about the same amount of poverty, although poverty has been distributed differently. In 1967, for instance, the pretransfer poverty rate for "nonelderly male-headed families" was 11.5 percent; although it declined between 1969 and 1979, in 1990 it was 11.4 percent. For "nonelderly female-headed households," the 1967 and 1990 rates were 58.8 percent and 54.5 percent; for the elderly, they were 58.3 percent and 51.0 percent (Danziger and Weinberg 1995, 46). The story of poverty's uneven decline, therefore, is much more than a tale of economic growth and rising real wages. It is, even more, a narrative about the effects of public policy.

The conservative narrative also misses the erosion of the iron link that had joined poverty to work. Before the 1950s, poverty remained largely a market phenomenon; in the 1950s, expanded government programs began to partially insulate select groups from the market. As a result, among the more fortunate, low wages—or the absence of earned income—no longer automatically meant poverty. Nor is there credible evidence that the generosity of welfare payments intensified poverty by dampening incentives for work. In the years when welfare rolls grew most rapidly, the real value of public assistance benefits dropped steeply (Schwarz 1983; Stern 1993).

In the 1950s, unemployment insurance, expanded Social Security coverage and increased benefits, and the introduction of disability insurance began to reduce poverty. However, they proved more effective among whites than among Blacks, Latinos, and other minorities, who at the time were heavily employed in occupations that had been deliberately excluded from benefits that most workers had come to take for granted. For similar reasons, these programs also benefited men more than women. Indeed, the reference point for early U.S. social insurance programs was the two-parent family supported by a husband/father employed in the regular labor market.

In the 1960s and early 1970s, for the first time, government mounted programs aimed directly at reducing poverty. The War on Poverty and Great Society rejected the ancient assumption that widespread poverty was normal and inevitable. Instead, they rested on the radical assumption that public programs combined with economic growth could erase poverty from the nation. Unfortunately, public spending and program design proved unequal to the objective. Nonetheless, the era could count a number of major accomplishments. Indeed, the liberalization of public assistance, the expansion of food stamps, the introduction of Supplemental Security Income, and the further expansion of Social Security finally helped minority as well as white families raise their incomes and began to push the benefits of the welfare state beyond the male-breadwinner model. In 1979, for instance, public transfer programs reduced poverty among the partially employed from 24 percent to 17 percent and among those who did not work from 65 percent to 30 percent.

The most effective public antipoverty program has been Social Security. Increased in size and indexed for inflation, Social Security benefits in the 1970s reduced the poverty rate among elderly householders from 26 percent to 17 percent in one decade. Of the elderly at risk in 1979, two-thirds avoided poverty because of government transfer payments. Today, because of public benefits, the poverty rate among the elderly is the lowest for any age group.

The question, then, is why public programs proved so successful at reducing poverty among some groups and not others. Many whites escaped or avoided poverty through the accumulation of assets—notably, real estate—as well as through income. In this, they received preferential help from government. Federal mortgage programs underwrote home ownership in suburbs, from which Blacks and other minorities were excluded, and refused to lend in the inner city and other heavily minority neighborhoods. In various other ways, public programs subsidized the acquisition of appreciating property assets by whites; the result is that, today, vast differences separate the wealth of Blacks and whites of similar incomes (Oliver and Shapiro 1995; Conley 1999). As a practical matter, this means that African Americans and other minorities often cannot turn to a home equity loan to tide them over temporary economic trouble or to finance a comfortable old age. Lacking an economic cushion, they remain more vulnerable than whites, more prone to fall into poverty in moments of crisis.

At the same time, old distinctions between the "deserving" and "undeserving" poor launched policies along different trajectories. Social insurance programs, the most effective public antipoverty measures, serve groups considered to be the "deserving" poor, notably the elderly and workers who have lost jobs in the regular labor market. Indexed for inflation since the 1970s,

Social Security spending increased while spending on public assistance (income-based programs directed at the "undeserving" poor) stagnated. Indeed, while Social Security benefits grew in real dollars, the value of Aid to Families with Dependent Children (AFDC) payments fell by about half between 1973 and the 1990s (Blank 1995, 179–180). By 1995, Social Security alone cost five times as much as AFDC, food stamps, and Supplemental Security Income (SSI) combined (Katz 2001, 11). General assistance programs, that is, state-level public assistance, also were eliminated or slashed in the 1980s along with other public programs that served the poor.

"Dependency"—defined in political debates as the inability to support oneself through work on account of moral or personal failings—has always been the official hallmark of the "undeserving" poor. But in the 1990s, this definition ran up against a troubling fact: For millions of Americans, work in the regular labor market no longer guaranteed escape from poverty. To resolve this contradiction between work and reward—to "make work pay"—Congress relied on the third branch of the public welfare state, taxation, and, prodded by the administration of President Bill Clinton, expanded the Earned Income Tax Credit. This tax benefit lifted many family incomes close to or over the poverty line. It did almost nothing, however, for those not employed in the regular labor force (Katz 2001, 293–298; Howard 1997, 69, 74).

Indeed, public policy aggressively attacked the "dependency" of the presumably "nonworking" poor, particularly single mothers who relied on public benefits. This attack culminated in the 1996 welfare reform bill, which replaced AFDC with Temporary Assistance for Needy Families (TANF). TANF ended the entitlement to public assistance, put time limits on welfare, mandated work for welfare recipients, and turned the administration and design of welfare programs over to the states in the form of block grants. It also withdrew benefits from many immigrants. In the latter half of the 1990s, a combination of factors—the boom economy, tax changes, and the new legislation—resulted in a massive reduction in the welfare rolls, which dropped by about half within five years. At any one time, roughly six of ten former welfare recipients were employed. But they worked mainly at low-wage jobs with few benefits. Most of them, in fact, remained in poverty (Cancian, Kaplan, and Meyer 1999). The fates of those who were not employed remained unclear, but reports of increased hunger and homelessness surfaced around the country.

Women newly excluded from welfare benefits were disproportionately African American and Puerto Rican and had not graduated from high school. Eighty-three percent of them worked, mostly full-time. But less than half earned enough to lift their families out of poverty. Like the poor of the past, they looked outside the labor market for help: 7 percent escaped poverty because of other family members' earnings; another 4 percent because of private unearned income (private charity and gifts); and a slim 3 percent because of other government aid. For them, as for the poor of a half century earlier, poverty was the rule, not the exception. During the great economic expansion of the late 1990s, 39 percent of families that once would have received welfare lived below the poverty line.

In effect, welfare reform had moved many former welfare recipients into the ranks of the working poor. That consequence troubled remarkably few commentators or legislators, who hailed welfare reform as a great success. Poverty once again had become an accepted feature of the national landscape, regrettable but normal, not, as it had been for a brief time in the 1960s and early 1970s, an anomalous and unnecessary disgrace.

Michael B. Katz and Mark J. Stern

See also: Child Welfare; Crime Policy; Dependency;

Feminization of Poverty; Globalization and Deindustrialization; New Right; Old Age; Poverty, Statistical Measurement of; Poverty Line; Privatization; "Underclass"; War on Poverty; Wealth; Welfare Policy/Welfare Reform; "Working Poor"

References and Further Reading

Berlin, Gordon L. 2000. "What Works in Welfare Reform: Evidence and Lessons to Guide TANF Reauthorization." Manpower Demonstration Research Corporation. http://www.mdrc.org/reports2002/TANF/TANF-introduction.htm.

Blank, Rebecca M. 1995. "The Employment Strategy: Public Policies to Increase Work and Earnings." In *Confronting Poverty: Prescriptions for Change*, ed. Sheldon Danziger, Gary D. Sandefur, and Daniel H. Weinberg, 168–204. Cambridge, MA: Harvard University Press.

Byington, Margaret F. [1910] 1974. *Homestead: The Households of a Mill Town*. Pittsburgh: University of Pittsburgh Press. Originally published New York: Russell Sage Foundation.

Cancian, Maria, Thomas Kaplan, and Daniel R. Meyer. 1999. "Outcomes for Low-Income Families under the Wisconsin AFDC Programs: Understanding the Baseline So That We Can Estimate the Effects of Welfare Reform." Institute for Research on Poverty, special report 76. July. http://www.ssc.wisc.edu/irp/sr/sr76.pdf.

Conley, Dalton T. 1999. *Being Black, Living in the Red: Race, Wealth, and Social Policy in America*. Berkeley and Los Angeles: University of California Press.

Danziger, Sheldon, and Peter Gottschalk. 1995. *America Unequal*. New York: Russell Sage Foundation. Cambridge, MA: Harvard University Press.

Danziger, Sheldon, and Daniel H. Weinberg. 1995. "The Historical Record: Trends in Family Income, Inequality, and Poverty." In *Confronting Poverty: Prescriptions for Change*, ed. Sheldon Danziger, Gary D. Sandefur, and Daniel H. Weinberg, 18–50. Cambridge, MA: Harvard University Press.

Edin, Kathryn, and Laura Lein. 1997. *Making Ends Meet: How Single Mothers Survive Welfare and Low-Wage Work*. New York: Russell Sage Foundation.

Goldin, Claudia. 2000. "Labor Markets in the Twentieth Century." In *The Cambridge Economic History of the United States*, vol. 3, *The Twentieth Century*, ed. Stanley L. Engerman and Robert E. Gallman, 549–624. Cambridge and New York: Cambridge University Press.

Grimshaw, William J. 1992. *Bitter Fruit: Black Politics and the Chicago Machine*. Chicago: University of Chicago Press.

Howard, Christopher. 1997. *The Hidden Welfare State: Tax Expenditures and Social Policy in the United States*. Princeton: Princeton University Press.

Katz, Michael B. 1995. *Improving Poor People: The Welfare State, the "Underclass," and Urban Schools as History*. Princeton: Princeton University Press.

Katz, Michael B. 2001. *The Price of Citizenship: Redefining the American Welfare State*. New York: Metropolitan Books.

Kleppner, Paul. 1985. *Chicago Divided: The Making of a Black Mayor*. DeKalb: Northern Illinois University Press.

Lieberman, Robert C. 1998. *Shifting the Color Line: Race and the American Welfare State*. Cambridge, MA: Harvard University Press.

Murray, Charles. 1984. *Losing Ground: American Social Policy, 1950–1980*. New York: Basic Books.

National Center for Children in Poverty. 1999. "Young Children in Poverty Fact Sheet." http://www.nccp.org/media/ycp99-text.pdf.

Oliver, Melvin L., and Thomas M. Shapiro. 1995. *Black Wealth/White Wealth: A New Perspective on Racial Inequality*. New York: Routledge.

Ornati, Oscar. 1966. *Poverty amid Affluence*. New York: Twentieth Century Fund.

Orshansky, Mollie. 1977. *The Measure of Poverty: Technical Paper I, Documentation of Background Information and Rationale for Current Poverty Matrix*. Washington, DC: GPO.

Patterson, James T. 1981. *America's Struggle against Poverty 1900–1980*. Cambridge, MA: Harvard University Press.

Pearce, Diana. 1978. "The Feminization of Poverty: Women, Work, and Welfare." *Urban and Social Change Review* 10: 28–36.

Ruggles, Steven, Matthew Sobek, et al. 2003. Integrated Public Use Microdata Series: Version 3.0. Minneapolis: Historical Census Projects, University of Minnesota. http://www.ipums.umn.edu.

Schwarz, John E. 1983. *America's Hidden Success: A Reassessment of Twenty Years of Public Policy*. New York: Norton.

Sobek, Matthew Joseph. 1997. "A Century of Work: Gender Labor Force Participation, and Occupational Attainment in the United States, 1880–1990." Ph.D. diss., University of Minnesota.

Stern, Mark J. 1991. "Poverty and the Life-Cycle, 1940–1960." *Journal of Social History* 24, no. 3 (Spring): 521–540.

Stern, Mark J. 1993. "Poverty and Family Composition since 1940." In *The "Underclass" Debate: Views from History*, ed. Michael B. Katz, 220–253. Princeton: Princeton University Press.

Stern, Mark J. 1999. "The Management of African-American Poverty." Unpublished paper. Available from author.

Sterner, Richard. 1973. *The Negro's Share: A Study of Income, Consumption, Housing, and Public Assistance*. New York: Harper and Brothers.

U.S. Census Bureau. 2000. "Poverty: 2000 Highlights," Table C. http://www.census.gov/hhes/poverty/poverty00/tablec.pdf.

Abbott, Edith

See Aid to Families with Dependent Children (ADC/AFDC); Maternalist Policy; Social Security Act of 1935

Abbott, Grace

See Aid to Families with Dependent Children (ADC/AFDC); Maternalist Policy; Social Security Act of 1935; *Social Service Review*

Addams, Jane

See Hull House; Progressive Era and 1920s; Settlement Houses; *Twenty Years at Hull-House*

Adolescent Pregnancy

Adolescent pregnancy as a symbol for why poor Americans tend to have poor children became common in public debate during the early 1970s. At the end of the 1980s public opinion polls and governmental action alike demonstrated that many Americans believed that teenagers having babies was a serious and troubling social problem, one that created what was referred to as a "cycle of poverty."

This was not the first time that Americans had worried about young people and their babies. Over the course of the nineteenth century, as informal family and community control over marriage and childbearing began to weaken, public policy and legal doctrine stepped in to fill the gap. In the Progressive Era, the growing acceptance of eugenic thought among both liberals and conservatives alike led to more regulation of the entry into marriage than had been the case previously and more-draconian policies aimed at those individuals thought too young or too poor to have children and at those who produced "illegitimate" births. Such measures as age-of-consent laws, marriage licenses, the institutionalization of the "unfit," and eventually compulsory sterilization were implemented during this period as measures to improve the "fitness" of the American population.

By the 1950s, however, teenage childbearing had become both common and accepted; American teenagers had more babies and were marrying at younger ages than in any other industrialized country. Although some commentators bewailed youthful marriage and motherhood (and fatherhood), the nation as a whole was experiencing a postwar return to what Betty Friedan would later call the "feminine mystique," and few worried about "teenage pregnancy," although there were more pregnant teenagers than there had ever been (or would be again).

Ironically, teenage birth rates were declining from the high rates of the baby boom as American policymakers came to be concerned with the new problem of adolescent pregnancy in the 1970s. Several factors crystallized concern in the face of an actual drop in teenage births. First, the legalization of abortion in 1973 and ensuing political controversy over it made preventing pregnancy and hence abortion an attractive policy option across the political spectrum. Young women just entering their reproductive years, like older women just leaving them, have a disproportionate number of abortions. Because of their youth, they became a focus of public concern and were targeted for education and other interventions.

At the same time, American women (like women in all of the industrialized nations) were beginning to bear children while unmarried. This trend was first visible among young women, particularly African Americans, but became increasingly common among women of all ages, races, and ethnicities, creating growing concerns about the future of marriage.

Finally, national surveys showed that young Americans were increasing their rates of premarital sexual activity. During the 1970s and subsequently, the rates of premarital sexual activity began to converge among young men and young women, among members of minority and majority populations, and among the affluent and the less well-to-do.

As sexual activity increased among all groups, so did pregnancy rates, but birthrates did not. What was obscured in much of the debate was that although increasing numbers of affluent, white, and female teenagers were becoming sexually active, they were more likely than their minority and poor peers to use birth control and substantially more likely to use abortion in order to prevent an adolescent pregnancy from becoming an adolescent birth.

The differences in class and ethnicity between affluent and poor teens was noticed; an extremely influential report published by the Alan Guttmacher Institute in 1976 argued that public policy should acknowledge the class and racial differences between teen mothers and nonmothers (young men virtually disappear from the debate) and move affirmatively to redress the imbalance. In the service of pursuing more reproductive autonomy on the part of poor and minority teens, the Alan Guttmacher Institute in effect proclaimed a causal connection between teen motherhood and poverty, suggesting that teen motherhood makes young women poorer than they would otherwise be.

A growing body of data suggests that the correlation between giving birth at a young age and subsequent poverty of mother or child is, to say the least, overstated. Sexual activity at young ages, failure to use contraception, the decision not to have an abortion, and the decision not to marry all serve as filters, sorting in such a way that a young person who started sex at an early age, did not use contraception at all or effectively, did not seek an abortion, and did not get married is probably *already* poorer, having more trouble in school, and more discouraged than the larger pool of sexually active teens, or even the pool of teens who become pregnant.

In the 1990s, a discourse of "predatory" older males emerged, serving to legitimate even more paternalistic and ultimately punitive policies toward pregnant teenagers. (Since most teen mothers are in their late teens, and since most women have relationships with men on average two years older, it is not terribly surprising that eighteen- and nineteen-year-olds are likely to have partners in their early twenties.) Growing alarm about "illegitimacy" and about "babies having babies" also fueled support for policies that singled out teenagers for discipline and regulation. Culminating these policies was the 1996 Personal Responsibility and Work Opportunity Reconciliation Act, popularly known as "welfare reform," which severely limits welfare participation by unmarried teenagers (on the grounds that the availability of welfare contributed to teen out-of-wedlock birthrates), calls for criminalizing consenting sexual behavior among adolescents, promotes abstinence before marriage or economic "self-sufficiency," and encourages marriage as the normatively expected behavior for poor women (this in a context in which virtually all first world nations are seeing a dramatic decrease in marriage itself and a dramatic increase in childbearing outside of marriage).

The idea that young women can rescue themselves from poverty by using welfare only as a last resort and even then only under adult supervision, by being sexually abstinent until marriage and "self-sufficiency," and by becoming and remaining married is an attractive idea to many Americans—especially those who are troubled by changes in gender roles since the mid-1970s. But none of these strategies address the preexisting poverty that constrain poor teenagers' choices; nor do they cure the economic deprivation and inequality that keep teenage mothers poor.

Kristin Luker

See also: Adoption; Birth Control; Child Care; Child-Saving; Foster Care; Orphanages; Reproductive Rights; Welfare Policy/Welfare Reform

References and Further Reading

Geronimus, Arline T., and Sanders Korenman. 1993. "The Socioeconomic Costs of Teenage Childbearing: Evidence and Interpretation," *Demography* 30, no. 2 (May): 281–290.

Hofferth, Sandra L., and Cheryl D. Hayes, eds. 1987. *Risking the Future: Adolescent Sexuality, Pregnancy, and Childbearing.* Report of the U.S. National Research Council. Panel on Adolescent Pregnancy and Childbearing. Washington, DC: National Academy Press.

Luker, Kristin. 1996. *Dubious Conceptions: The Politics of Teenage Pregnancy.* Cambridge, MA: Harvard University Press.

Murray, David W. 1994. "Poor Suffering Bastards: An Anthropologist Looks at Illegitimacy." *Policy Review,* Spring: 9.

Nathanson, C. A. 1991. *Dangerous Passage: The Social Control of Sexuality in Women's Adolescence.* Philadelphia: Temple University Press.

Adoption

In the United States, adoption has always been associated with transferring children born to resourceless women into families with resources. Before the late 1940s, adoption was not a common practice in this country. In the nineteenth century, urban, church-related child welfare organizations, such as the Children's Aid Society in New York, transported small groups of "orphans" usually immigrant children defined by "child rescue" workers as insufficiently and improperly supervised by their impoverished immigrant mothers—to farm families in the West. These children were sometimes formally adopted and often provided their new households with much-needed farm labor.

Generally, however, poor women, even unwed mothers, kept and raised their own children, often within supportive, if shamed, kin networks. During the late nineteenth and early twentieth centuries, eugenicists and other mainstream social commentators associated both white and African American unwed mothers with biological inferiority. These females, the experts said, were products of depraved upbringings, alcoholic parents, and slum living and had subnormal intelligence. Such women were unlikely to produce babies desirable to better-off families.

After World War II, meanings associated with nonconforming childbearing became thoroughly racialized in the United States. Experts now defined white girls and women (but not females of other races) who had babies outside of marriage as psychologically disturbed rather than as biologically inferior. Child welfare professionals and others announced in this era that the babies of these women were born untainted and should be removed from unwed women who proved, by having a child but no husband, that they were not fit mothers.

Between approximately 1945 and 1973, in part drawing on this theory of white illegitimate pregnancy, social workers, psychologists and teachers, clergy, and other community authorities oversaw the construction and functioning of an adoption mandate as the solution to unmarried sex and pregnancy of hundreds of thousands of deeply shamed white young women in the United States. The white babies of these women became super-valuable commodities for the new, burgeoning adoption market. The biological mothers of these babies were generally not from resourceless families, though often, in the context of the adoption mandate, parents threatened to withhold all support from a daughter who refused to surrender her illegitimate child for adoption. Also in this era, white, unwed mothers, like other young women, had few opportunities to earn a living wage, and they often had no knowledge of the welfare system, whose benefits might have helped them keep their children if they so chose. Decades after the adoption mandate collapsed, adoptees, unaware of the coercive context of relinquishment, typically believe that they were abandoned by selfish, unloving women unwilling to be mothers.

It is notable that in this era, as white babies became valuable commodities, social commentators and policymakers continued to construe African American and other babies of color born outside marriage as tainted products of biologically inferior mothers and as valueless, not marketable.

The national legalization of abortion in 1973 yielded a startling and unexpected consequence regarding adoption. Thousands of young women began to resist the adoption mandate after the U.S. Supreme Court's decision in *Roe v. Wade* (410 U.S. 113 [1973]), insisting to parents, social workers, and community experts that if they could decide whether or not to stay pregnant, surely they could decide whether or not to be mothers to the child they gave birth to. Also by the 1970s, young women had access to a larger number of jobs and careers that paid living wages. These factors, coupled with the legalization of abortion, caused the number of white babies available for adoption to fall precipitously and the number of never-married single-mother-headed households to rise rapidly.

Persons seeking babies to adopt now largely had to rely on agencies and direct marketing strategies targeting the poorest, most vulnerable and resourceless young women in the United States and on agencies developing baby-transfer networks in the poorest countries in the world. Many potential adopters have looked abroad for babies before or instead of adopting homeless children of color in the United States.

For the most part, families of color (for decades formally and informally shut out of adoption agency services as both suppliers and seekers of babies) moved children around within kin networks when parents were unable to provide care. In the second half of the twentieth century, as the kin networks of very poor women and of the working poor became attenuated, the state placed many poor and minority children whose mothers were variously incapacitated into foster care. This child rescue system was devised to provide temporary care for children who could in time return home or who would eventually be adopted. Social workers' lack of confidence in family preservation has combined with a lack of resources to undermine permanent placement of children in families, however. This, along with the persistence of poverty in many minority communities and the relatively small number of persons willing or able to adopt children of color—especially those who are no longer infants or who are disabled—has caused a long-term crisis in the foster care system. In 1972, an organization of Black social workers issued a manifesto calling for an end to the practice, inspired by the civil rights era, of white families' adopting children of color. Government officials have since repudiated this call and mandated, instead, "color-blind" and "culturally blind" adoption in the United States.

In the last decades of the twentieth century and continuing in the twenty-first century, conservative public policy experts have defined adoption as the solution to the abortion problem and as a solution to illegitimate motherhood among poor women. In both cases, adoption is promoted as a child rescue operation, though one that thoroughly discounts the status and the experiences of pregnant women and mothers.

Some feminist scholars define adoption as a feminist issue not on the basis of "essentialist" claims that all women want to have children or that all women want to mother the children they give birth to. Rather, these feminists argue that the recognition that almost all babies available for adoption were born to poor and otherwise resourceless women raises important questions about which women in the United States and around the world get to be the mothers of their own children and which do not. Traditionally, considerations of adoption have focused on the child's "best interests" and on "child rescue" while effacing the mother entirely. Understanding the circumstances that push particular women to surrender their children illuminates the centrality of women's poverty and vulnerability to both the enterprise of adoption and to definitions of legitimate motherhood.

Rickie Solinger

See also: Child Welfare; Child-Saving; Foster Care; Maternalism; Orphanages; Reproductive Rights

References and Further Reading

Berebitsky, Julie. 2000. *Like Our Very Own: Adoption and the Changing Culture of Motherhood, 1851–1950*, Lawrence: University Press of Kansas.

Perry, Twila. 1998. "Transracial and International Adoption: Mothers, Hierarchy, Race, and Feminist Legal Theory." *Yale Journal of Law and Feminism* 10, no. 101.

Solinger, Rickie. 2001. *Beggars and Choosers: How the Politics of Choice Shapes Adoption, Abortion, and Welfare in the United States*. New York: Hill and Wang.

Affirmative Action

"Affirmative action" is an umbrella term for an assortment of measures designed to break down segregation in employment and education and ensure equal access for members of groups historically excluded from full citizenship. A key demand of the Black civil rights movement since the early 1960s, affirmative action has since been embraced as a strategy for inclusion by other groups, most prominently women and Chicanos. It was first applied to jobs and later broadened to education. Plans may be voluntary, adopted in conciliation with government agencies such as the Equal Employment Opportunity Commission (EEOC), or imposed by the courts; some have been promoted by labor unions in collective bargaining agreements. The programs vary. Most contain "soft" affirmative action measures: wider and more-active recruitment of minorities and women, for example, or training provisions for those who have the ability but not the specific skills needed. Some programs include "hard" measures, such as numerical goals and timetables for hiring or admitting the underrepresented, or more rarely—in cases of well-documented discrimination—specific quotas. The phrase "affirmative action" comes from the 1935 Wagner Act. It was first used in association with racial justice by President John F. Kennedy in a 1961 executive order and was then extended by the presidencies of Lyndon B. Johnson and Richard M. Nixon in later executive orders broadening the mandate of the Office of Federal Contract Compliance (OFCC) for oversight of hiring practices on federal contracts. Most important, the employment section of the Civil Rights Act of 1964, Title VII, empowered courts to order such "affirmative action as may be appropriate" to remedy discrimination. In doing so, the courts have built up an important body of case law defining discrimination and equal access.

These policies arose from the recognition that simply announcing equal opportunity would not dislodge deep-rooted patterns of institutional discrimination based on race, gender, and national origin. Some reformers also argued for affirmative action as a form of compensation for the cumulative damage of past as well as ongoing discrimination and as reparations for slavery and Jim Crow. Martin Luther King Jr., in his 1963 *Why We Can't Wait*, himself made the case for "some compensatory consideration for the handicaps" Blacks had "inherited from the past." The burden of that history and ongoing discrimination placed Blacks at a disadvantage. "It is impossible to create a formula for the future which does not take into account that our society has been doing something special *against* the Negro for hundreds of years," reasoned King. "How then can he be absorbed into the mainstream of American life if we do not do something *for* him now, in order to balance the equation and equip him to compete on a just and equal basis?" Fairness demanded "more" than formal equality (King 1963, 134).

Affirmative action became widely embraced in the mid-1960s because it addressed ongoing problems of employment discrimination, poverty, and growing unrest fed by chronic unemployment and underemployment among African Americans. Job segregation by race was as old as slavery in the United States. It was upheld by law in much of the South until 1964 and by entrenched practice throughout the country. Even unions perpetuated segregation through nepotism in the crafts and separate seniority lines for whites and Blacks in industry. The new affirmative action policy offered a way to break down the racial division of labor at a time when protests against employment discrimination were sweeping the nation's urban centers, particularly at government-funded city construction projects but also at private businesses large and small. At the same time, affirmative action promised to reduce Black poverty rates just as the mechanization of southern cotton farming and the move of much northern industry to the suburbs were concentrating poverty in urban ghettos. Politically, the policy appealed to middle-class African Americans expecting the better jobs for which their training had prepared them, to working-class Blacks shut out of higher-paying blue-collar and white-collar jobs, to white policymakers juggling many urgent problems tied to low incomes, and even to large employers seeking protection from costly lawsuits for discrimination.

Affirmative action was also a political response to several decades of struggle mounted by civil rights groups against workplace discrimination: the "Don't buy where you can't work" boycotts of the Depression years, the March on Washington movement during World War II that prompted the creation of the short-lived federal Fair Employment Practices Commission, and Left-led trade union efforts in the 1940s and 1950s to combat racial injustice on the job that fell victim to McCarthyism. By the early 1960s, the goal of full economic inclusion for Black Americans had gained stronger backing through such organizing as the 1963 March on Washington *for Jobs* and Freedom, the National Urban League's campaign for a domestic Marshall Plan, a decade of struggles for employment access waged by the Congress of Racial Equality (CORE) and the National Association for the Advancement of Colored People, and the movement for a Freedom Budget, which proposed a $100 billion plan to achieve "freedom from want" in ten years.

Affirmative action plans had barely come into effect for Blacks before members of other long-excluded groups demanded coverage. The largest and most vocal group was women. The National Organization for Women (NOW), soon the nation's best-known feminist group, came into being out of anger over the EEOC's early refusal to take sex discrimination seriously even though two in every five complaints came from women. Mexican Americans also mobilized at the outset. They filed the lion's share of "national origin" complaints under Title VII and remained in the forefront of Hispanic organizing for affirmative action thereafter. Since

A young boy demonstrating for affirmative action holds a sign reading "Equal Opportunity is a BIRTH RIGHT!" at the University of California, Berkeley. Students and families are protesting to keep affirmative action during a demonstration outside a Board of Regents meeting. (David Butow/Corbis SABA)

the late 1970s, some Asian American organizations have pressed for inclusion in affirmative action programs. In recent years, however, some conservative Asian Americans have opposed such programs, particularly in California, arguing that special efforts to include Blacks in the state's flagship universities in effect exclude accomplished students of Asian descent, an argument the nation's leading Jewish organizations began making in the early 1970s when affirmative action came to colleges, universities, and professional schools.

Since it was first developed, affirmative action has been used in countless institutions with varying levels of commitment. Social scientists have found measuring its distinctive impact a challenge when so many other variables are in play. In general, however, the consensus among economists (who have analyzed the issue with the most methodological rigor) is that the policies had a limited but significant impact in improving employment and reducing poverty in the heyday of their application in the 1970s, and especially in government employment. For various reasons, Blacks made great headway with these policies in some industries, such as textiles, while other industries, including construction and the uniform trades, proved much harder to change. Three things have subsequently undercut progress, however. First, economic restructuring produced job loss in the industries where working-class Blacks had scored the greatest gains after 1965, textiles, steel, and auto among them. Second, affirmative action's efficacy declined markedly in the Reagan era due to much-reduced federal enforcement. Third, antidiscrimination efforts have also been weakened by the chronic underfunding of the EEOC by Congress and by the unwillingness of the OFCC to cancel large contracts under its jurisdiction even for egregious discrimination.

As such halfhearted enforcement might suggest, the struggle to open employment and education has been contentious in the United States, in part because exclusion runs so deep in the nation's history. Affirmative action has also been subject to fierce opposition and backlash from several quarters. Most conservatives fought affirmative action from the beginning. Yet they had also opposed the Civil Rights Act and *any* government action that treated discrimination as a social problem worthy of public energy. Millions of whites felt the same way: In the late 1950s and early 1960s, they rejected measures to ensure fair treatment for Blacks in hiring and defended employers' "right" to discriminate if they so chose. Many whites—pluralities in some opinion polls—saw even simple equal opportunity as "special treatment" for minorities and a threat to their own customary privileges. Conservative political groups, playing upon this sentiment, labored in print, speech, and litigation to change the terms of debate, depicting whites and men as the victims of so-called reverse discrimination and men of color and women as grasping, illegitimate claimants of unfair advantage.

Ironically, though, the group that may have most turned the tide on affirmative action was a vocal subset of liberals, most of them white male academics and writers who mobilized when higher education faculties came into the policy's catchment after 1970 due to pressure from white women. Although some continued to support "soft" affirmative action, their arguments provided conservatives with a winning language they had hitherto lacked. Denouncing affirmative action as "quotas" and "discrimination" that violated "equal rights for all," they charged that the policy violated the spirit of the civil rights movement and the principle of colorblind opportunity. The troubled economy of the mid-1970s and early 1980s then enhanced the appeal of zero-sum politics that treated any gain for Blacks or women as a loss for whites or men. The presidencies of Ronald Reagan and George H. W. Bush aggressively reoriented the Justice Department and the EEOC toward narrow interpretations of discrimination (focused on conscious intent and individual cases rather than on patterns resulting from unintentional institutional practices) and more-formalistic standards of equal opportunity. The Clinton era slowed but did not reverse this shift in practice. It is doubtful that affirmative action programs will again be as ambitious as in the 1970s, and it is likely that they will be scaled back further in court challenges now pending.

Affirmative action's standing today is paradoxical. On the one hand, it has become a veritable epithet among many white Americans, who interpret it as "quotas" that grant undeserved rewards to the less qualified, violate fair play, and deprive whites, especially white men, of opportunities that would otherwise be theirs. (Some social scientists report that mere mention of the phrase evokes hostility that brings rancor to subsequent topics.) On the other hand, partly through affirmative action, "diversity" has become an ideal in American public life as never before; it influences even conservative Republicans in their staffing choices.

Nancy MacLean

See also: Civil Rights Acts, 1964 and 1991; Civil Rights Movement; Racism

References and Further Reading

Bergmann, Barbara. 1996. *In Defense of Affirmative Action*. New York: Basic Books.

Graham, Hugh Davis. 1990. *The Civil Rights Era: The Origins and Development of National Policy*. New York: Oxford University Press.

King, Martin Luther, Jr. 1963. *Why We Can't Wait*. New York: New American Library.

Robinson, Jo Ann Ooiman, ed. 2001. *Affirmative Action: A Documentary History*. Westport, CT: Greenwood Press.

Skrentny, John D. 1996. *The Ironies of Affirmative Action: Politics, Culture, and Justice in America*. Chicago: University of Chicago Press.

The Affluent Society, *John Kenneth Galbraith*

John Kenneth Galbraith (1908–) has been America's best-known economist since the 1950s, and throughout his career he was deeply involved in issues of poverty and development.

His prominence in America's poverty debates dates from *The Affluent Society* (1958), in which he critiqued fellow economists and fellow liberals for their preoccupation with economic growth. Arguing that by midcentury, America had moved to a new level of affluence, he decried the country's excessive worship of materialism and its systematic underfunding of public goods and services, leaving well-fed and well-dressed citizens to drive their immense, chrome-plated and gas-guzzling cars through blighted cities and polluted countrysides. In making his central case, however, he remarked that poverty was "more nearly an afterthought," a phrase he came to regret (he meant a comparison to the Great Depression); the book's actual discussion of poverty made clear that extensive antipoverty funding was a high priority. In a widely read debate with economist Leon Keyserling in the *New Republic* and in subsequent editions of *The Affluent Society*, he made his views much clearer.

Galbraith in fact was acutely familiar with American and global poverty. Born into a progressive, politically active farm family in Ontario, Canada, he graduated from Ontario Agricultural College (B.S., 1931) and in agricultural economics from the University of California, Berkeley (M.S., 1933; Ph.D., 1934). He worked as a Harvard economics instructor and a New Deal adviser on agricultural policy (specializing in land use policy, agricultural credit, and price support systems) to relieve rural poverty during the 1930s, and he coauthored a quite liberal book on economic planning. During World War II, as deputy head of the Office of Price Administration, he became intimately familiar with both consumer prices and issues of household income and wealth distribution, and he advocated wartime economic policies that favored the poor, working, and middle classes. Then, as a director of the Strategic Bombing Survey, he meticulously examined the wartime German economy, knowledge he put to important use immediately after the war as the State Department's director of economic recovery planning for both Germany and Japan. Back at Harvard by the late 1940s (after several years spent introducing Keynesianism to corporate CEOs as economics editor at *Fortune*), he pioneered the university's first courses in economic development. In the 1950s, he also served as an economic consultant to the governments of Puerto Rico and India.

Galbraith had become a Keynesian in the late 1930s, shortly after the appearance of *The General Theory of Employment, Interest, and Money* (1936) by British political economist John Maynard Keynes. By the 1950s, he had developed his own powerful critiques of both orthodox neoclassical economics and the newly emerging "mainstream" Keynesian synthesis that viewed permanent full-employment growth as its macroeconomic summum bonum. In the case of American poverty, he was a roughly a "structuralist" who believed that aggregate growth per se was doing—and would do—too little to address the "special" conditions of the poor, especially in geographic "pockets of poverty" such as Appalachia and the inner cities or when men and women were poor in part because of racial discrimination, age and gender, health, or addiction.

Appointed ambassador to India by President John F. Kennedy, he managed to remain involved in the administration's domestic policy debates as a powerful advocate for increased public spending, with a particular emphasis on antipoverty programs, as an alternative to the tax-cut strategy favored by Kennedy's Council of Economic Advisors. Abroad, he was a vocal advocate of increased economic development aid, and in particular of investment in education and public infrastructures designed to relieve poverty. After Kennedy's death, President Lyndon B. Johnson appointed him to the planning board that created the Office of Economic Opportunity, where he was actively involved in shaping several of its early programs (and where he criticized attempts to apply Policy-Planning-Budgeting methods borrowed from the Defense Department as "too narrow and insensitive"). After breaking with Johnson over the Vietnam War and becoming a prominent antiwar figure, he continued campaigning for major increases in antipoverty spending, especially in his work with the presidential campaigns of Eugene McCarthy (1968) and George McGovern (1972). Elected president of the American Economic Association in 1971, he focused the group's annual convention on poverty and tied the issue to overarching problems of income maldistribution, arms spending, and racial and sexual discrimination. The author of nearly four dozen books and hundreds of articles, he has always insisted on linking economic theory and policy to democratic politics, arguing that the elimination of poverty (as part of the broader and conscious design of a good society) is a matter of political choice that electoral majorities must make, despite the opposition of the well-to-do and vested economic interests.

Richard Parker

See also: Economic Theories; Labor Markets; War on Poverty

References and Further Reading

Galbraith, John Kenneth. [1958] 1983. *The Affluent Society*. New York: Houghton Mifflin.

———. 1967. *The New Industrial State*. New York: Houghton Mifflin.

———. 1972. *Economics and the Public Purpose*. New York: Houghton Mifflin.

———. 1979. *The Nature of Mass Poverty*. Cambridge, MA: Harvard University Press.

———. 1996. *The Good Society: The Humane*. Boston: Houghton Mifflin.

Parker, Richard. 2005. *John Kenneth Galbraith and the Making of American Economics*. New York: Farrar, Strauss and Giroux.

Waligorski, Conrad. 1997. *Liberal Economics and Democracy: Keynes, Galbraith, Thurow, and Reich*. Lawrence: University Press of Kansas.

African American Migration

The migration of African Americans from the South to the northern, midwestern, and western parts of the country was one of the most significant developments of the twentieth-century United States, with major implications for the history of poverty and social welfare. Although there had been some out-migration before then, African Americans remained overwhelmingly concentrated in the southern states, primarily in rural areas, at the start of the twentieth century. By the 1970s, after decades of continuous migration interrupted only by the Great Depression of the 1930s, African Americans were a highly urbanized, increasingly visible presence throughout the country, and especially in the large industrial cities of the North and Midwest. Known as the Great Migration because of its transformative influence on American society and culture, this massive population shift reshaped the economic prospects for African Americans, bringing considerable opportunity and upward mobility but also establishing new patterns of poverty in racially segregated urban ghettos. It also left an indelible mark on popular perceptions of poverty, which became more and more distorted by racial fears and stereotypes as Black poverty became more urbanized and visible. By the late 1970s and early 1980s, a variety of scholars, policy experts, and journalists had adopted the notion of "underclass" to describe and explain increases in Black urban poverty. According to these analysts, the urban underclass—defined as those families and individuals who existed outside the mainstream of the American occupational structure—was a new phenomenon that signaled a shift from relatively low levels of unemployment and social disorder before the 1960s to a new era of widespread joblessness, crime, and welfare dependency thereafter. What "underclass" theorists failed to acknowledge, however, was that such urban problems were not entirely new. They had characterized earlier Black life and were rooted in the older dynamics of class, racial, and geographic inequality that African Americans encountered under the impact of mass urbanization, shifts in industrial capitalism, and enduring racism outside as well as within the South.

During World War I, an estimated 700,000 to 1 million Blacks left the South. Another 800,000 to 1 million left during the 1920s. Whereas the pre–World War I migrants had moved to southern cities, including Atlanta, Birmingham, Louisville, and Norfolk, and to a few northern cities, such as Chicago, New York, and Philadelphia, Blacks after the war moved throughout the urban North and West. Moreover, whereas upper South and border states had been the chief sources of out-migration before World War I, Deep South states dominated the migration stream to northern and western cities. Blacks born in Alabama, Georgia, Louisiana, Mississippi, and South Carolina, for example, made up over 60 percent of the Black population increase in all of Illinois as well as in the city of Chicago between 1910 and 1920. At the same time, whereas Black women migrants had outnumbered men before the war, men migrants now outnumbered women. In the rapidly industrializing cities of Cleveland, Detroit, and Milwaukee, for example, the sex ratio ranged between 120 and 140 men to every 100 women during the war years.

A variety of factors underlay Black population movement. African Americans sought an alternative to sharecropping, disenfranchisement, and racial injustice in the South. In 1917, the *African Methodist Episcopal Church Review* articulated the forces that propelled Blacks outward from the South. "Neither character, the accumulation of property, the fostering of the Church, the schools and a better and higher standard of the home" had made a difference in the status of Black southerners. "Confidence in the sense of justice, humanity and fair play of the white South is gone," the paper concluded (quoted in Grossman 1989, 34). One migrant articulated the same mood in verse:

> "An' let one race have all de South
> Where color lines are drawn
> For "Hagar's child" done [stem] de tide
> Farewell
> we're good and gone."
> (Marks 1989, v)

African Americans were also attracted by the pull of opportunities in the North. The labor demands of northern industries, legislation restricting immigration, and greater access to their rights as citizens (including the franchise) all encouraged the movement of Blacks into northern cities. Wages in northern industries usually ranged from $3.00 to $5.00 per eight-hour day, compared to as little as 75 cents to $1.00 per day in southern agriculture and no more than $2.50 for a nine-hour day in southern industries. Moreover, between 1915 and 1925, the average wages of domestics in some northern cities doubled. Northern cities also promised access to better health care, schools, and the vote.

African Americans often viewed the Great Migration to northern cities in glowing terms: "The Promised Land," the "Flight out of Egypt," and "Going into Canaan." One Black man wrote back to his southern home, "The (Col.) men are making good. [The job] never pays less than $3.00 per day for (10) hours." In her letter home, a Black female related, "I am well and thankful to say I am doing well. . . . I work in Swifts Packing Company." "Up here," another migrant said, "our people are in a different light." Over and over again, African Americans confirmed that up here, a man can "feel more like a man" (Drake and Cayton [1945] 1993, 99). As one southern Black man wrote home from the North, "I should have been here twenty years ago. . . .

I just begin to feel like a man. . . . My children are going to the same school with the whites and I don't have to humble to no one. I have registered. Will vote in the next election and there isn't any yes Sir or no Sir. It's all yes and no, Sam and Bill" (Grossman 1989, 90).

The Great Migration was by no means a simple move from southern agriculture to northern cities. It had specific regional and subregional components. More Blacks migrated to southern cities between 1900 and 1920 than to northern ones. Moreover, African Americans frequently made up from 25 to 50 percent of the total number of migrants in southern cities, compared to little more than 10 percent in northern cities. Before moving to northern cities like Boston, New York, and Philadelphia, for example, rural migrants first moved to southern cities like Birmingham, Charleston, Jacksonville, Memphis, New Orleans, and Savannah. The Jefferson County cities of Birmingham and Bessemer, with extensive rail connections, served as the major distribution points for Blacks going north from Alabama. The Southern, Louisville, and Nashville railroad, the Saint Louis and San Francisco railroad, and the Illinois Central railroads all traveled northward from Birmingham and Bessemer. In Georgia, cities like Albany, Americus, and Columbus served as distribution points for Blacks leaving from west Georgia and east Alabama, while Brunswick, Savannah, Valdosta, and Waycross served as distribution centers for Blacks leaving the depressed agricultural counties of southern and southeastern Georgia. To Blacks moving up from Alabama, Arkansas, Louisiana, Mississippi, and Texas, Chicago was the logical destination, whereas cities in Pennsylvania, New Jersey, New York, and the New England states attracted Blacks from Florida, Georgia, South Carolina, and Virginia. Upon arrival in northern cities, Black population movement usually developed secondary streams. As one contemporary observer noted, "All of the arrivals here [Chicago] did not stay. . . . They were only temporary guests awaiting the opportunity to proceed further and settle in surrounding cities and towns" (Scott 1920, 106, 134).

Southern Blacks helped organize their own movement into the urban North. They developed an extensive communications network, which included railroad employees who traveled back and forth between northern and southern cities, northern Black weeklies like the *Chicago Defender* and the *Pittsburgh Courier,* and an expanding chain of kin and friends. Using their networks of families and friends, African Americans learned about transportation, jobs, and housing before moving. In a variety of settings—including barber shops and grocery stores—their conversations soon established a litany of reasons for leaving. Also fueling the migration process were the letters, money, and testimonies of migrants who returned to visit. As one South Carolina migrant to Pittsburgh recalled,

> I was plowing in the field and it was real hot. And I stayed with some of the boys who would leave home and [come] back . . . and would have money, and they had clothes. I didn't have that. We all grew up together. And I said, "Well, as long as I stay here I'm going to get nowhere." And I tied that mule to a tree and caught a train. (Gottlieb 1987, 43)

Other migrants formed migration clubs, pooled their resources, and moved in groups. Deeply enmeshed in Black kin and friendship networks, Black women played a conspicuous role in helping organize the Black migration. As recent scholarship suggests, women were the "primary kinkeepers" (quoted in Trotter 1991, 33). Moreover, they often had their own gender-specific reasons for leaving the rural South. African American women resented stereotyped images of the Black mammy, who presumably placed loyalty to white families above loyalty to her own. Black women's migration reinforced the notion that lifting the race and improving the image of Black women were compatible goals.

As Blacks moved into northern cities in

growing numbers, a Black industrial working class emerged. Southern Black sharecroppers, farm laborers, sawmill hands, dockworkers, and railroad hands all moved into new positions in the urban economy. In Cleveland, Detroit, Milwaukee, and Pittsburgh, the percentage of Black men employed in industrial jobs increased from an estimated 10–20 percent of the Black labor force in 1910 to about 60–70 percent in 1920 and 1930. Black women also entered industrial jobs, although their gains were far less than those of Black men. In Chicago, the number of Black women in manufacturing trades increased from less than 1,000 in 1910 to over 3,000 in 1920. Industrial jobs now made up 15 percent of the jobs held by Black women, compared to less than 7 percent in 1910 (Spear 1967, 32–33, 152–153).

Although labor agents initially helped recruit Black workers for jobs in meatpacking, auto, steel, and other mass-production industries, these agents were soon supplanted by the expansion of Black familial and communal networks. Employers testified that, "'After the initial group movement by agents, Negroes kept going by twos and threes. These were drawn by letters, and by actual advances of money, from Negroes who had already settled in the North.' . . . 'every Negro that makes good in the North and writes back to his friends starts off a new group'" (Trotter 1996, 1783).

African Americans improved their lot by taking jobs in urban industries. Nonetheless, they entered the industrial economy on the lowest rungs of the occupational ladder. Racial barriers blocked their ascent up the job ladder, leaving them more vulnerable to poverty than were whites. Moreover, as their numbers increased in northern and western cities, they faced growing restrictions on where they could stay, educate their children, and gain access to much-needed social services and public accommodations. Racially motivated riots erupted in Chicago, East Saint Louis, Philadelphia, and Pittsburgh during the era of the Great Migration and especially during the years immediately after the end of World War I, when fears of economic downturn and residential overcrowding exacerbated the racist attitudes and beliefs with which many white residents—including some immigrants who themselves had suffered discrimination—greeted the urban "newcomers." Such riots not only helped reinforce residential segregation in northern cities but also highlighted the spread of African American poverty from rural to urban America.

Although the incidence of poverty depended on a variety of factors (including up- and downswings in the business cycle), African Americans experienced greater levels of poverty than did their white counterparts. In the 1920s, for example, the average Harlem family earned $1,300, compared to $1,570 for a typical white family. According to an intensive health study of the area, the Black death rate from all causes was 42 percent higher than the city's rate; infant mortality was 111 per 1,000 births, compared to 64.5 for the city as a whole; and tuberculosis deaths were two and a half times the city rate. Although Blacks had fewer young children than the city average (17.5 percent for Blacks, compared to 24.5 percent for the city in 1930), their cases before the juvenile authorities rose from 2.8 percent of all cases in 1914 to 11.7 percent of all cases in 1930 (Trotter 1993, 74).

Not only was urban Black poverty disproportionate to that of whites, but it became more spatially concentrated within the urban environment. Under the impact of World War I and the 1920s, the size and number of racially segregated neighborhoods increased, and the relationship between ghettoization, proletarianization, and poverty intensified. Between 1920 and 1930, residential segregation increased in all major cities. The "index of dissimilarity"—a standard measure of segregation—rose from 66.8 to 85.2 percent in Chicago; 60.6 to 85.0 percent in Cleveland; 64.1 to 77.9 percent in Boston; and 46.0 to 63.0 percent in Philadelphia (Taeuber and Taeuber 1965, 54).

Poverty increased not only within the Black community but also within certain neighborhoods. In his studies of Chicago and New York City, sociologist E. Franklin Frazier demonstrated the division of the Black urban community along socioeconomic lines. Each city contained significant areas of interclass mixing, but poverty increasingly characterized specific sections of the ghetto. In Chicago, based on the records of the city's United Charities, Frazier found "under normal conditions" between 8 and 9 percent of the families in the poorer areas "dependent upon charity." Rates of dependency declined "in the successive zones," so that only 1 percent of Black families depended on charity in the highest socioeconomic zone. Spousal desertion and nonsupport, crime, and educational and skill levels also varied from zone to zone.

African Americans responded to the impact of poverty and class and racial restrictions on their lives by intensifying their institution-building, cultural, political, economic, and civil rights activities. They built churches, mutual aid societies, fraternal orders, and social clubs; established a range of new business and professional services; and launched diverse labor, civil rights, and political organizations. These activities culminated in the rise of the "New Negro" movement during World War I and its florescence during the 1920s, a decade that saw the rise of the Black nationalist movement led by Marcus Garvey, the cultural renaissance in Harlem and other African American enclaves, the growing militance of the National Association for the Advancement of Colored People (NAACP), the spread of the National Urban League (NUL) movement, and the emergence of the Brotherhood of Sleeping Car Porters (BSCP). While voicing the demands and sensibilities of increasingly urban working- and middle-class migrants, such organizations developed programs designed to counteract the impact of urban poverty on the lives of African Americans.

The African American struggle against poverty also included the unique contributions and strategies of the poor themselves. Although some of these strategies had analogues among whites, others, like the use of blues songs to articulate reactions to poverty, reflected the unique culture of African Americans. One song, for example, begins, "Ain't yer heard of my po' story? / Den listen to me." The blues singer William Lee "Big Bill" Conley recorded many of these songs from the mid-1920s through the 1940s. In one song, "Looking Up at Down," he said, "Yeah, I'm down so low, baby. . . . lord, I declare I'm looking up to down." In 1938, another bluesman, John Lee "Sonny Boy" Williamson, recorded "Moonshine." The song captured the debilitating impact of alcohol and efforts to overcome it:

> Now and it's moon shine
> Moon shine have harmed many men
> Now moon shine will make you shoot dice
> Make you want to fight . . .
> Now that is the reason why
> I believe I'll make a change.
> (Sackheim 1969, 416; Dixon and Goodrich, 1982, 74–82, 846–847)

Another song captured the pain of tuberculosis, often called the "scourge of the Negro race" during the period:

> T.B. is all right to have
> But your friends treat you so low down: you will ask them for a favor
> And they will even stop coming 'round.
> (Sackheim 1969, 416; Dixon and Goodrich 1982, 74–82, 846–847)

Describing his movement from city to city, one migrant stated, "We sing songs as we ride [on railroad boxcars] and when we stopped we sing them" (this and the remaining quotations in Trotter 1993, 79). Songs not only enabled the Black poor to articulate their reactions to poverty; they helped them endure.

Unable to earn enough to buy food and pay

rent, some Blacks participated in the illegal underground economy. Numerous poor Blacks played what was known as the policy game: They placed small bets amounting to as little as one cent and received relatively good returns if they "hit" the lucky number. Policy became a major business and employer of the unemployed. During the Depression, one South Side Chicago Black tried to visualize the city without policy: "7,000 people would be unemployed and business in general would be crippled, especially taverns and even groceries, shoe stores, and many other business enterprises who depend on the buying power of the South side." At the same time, a Harlem resident called numbers the Black man's "stock market." Moreover, gambling establishments often represented a source of direct aid to the poor. As one interviewee stated, "Well, the Christians would always give me good advice but that was all, so I just got so I wouldn't bother with them and whenever I wanted anything I used to make it to the gamblers."

Others turned to prostitution. As one New York City woman stated,

> I don't play the street—I mean I don't lay every pair of pants that comes along. I look 'em over first, I'm strictly a Packard broad. I only grab a drunk that looks like his pockets are loaded. If they get rough my man [pimp] kick 'em out. When they're drunk they shoot the works. I've gotten over two hundred dollars, and so help me, the bastard didn't even touch me. He got happy just lookin at me.

Still others turned to theft and wound up in the penitentiary or jail, but even incarceration sometimes helped: "I have stole small things. I don't reckon I would care if I was turned over to officers, because I would have a place to stay. You see I don't have any particular place to go and stay, so I could stay there. I'd just have a place to stay."

As the nation entered the Depression and then World War II, the Great Migration continued to transform both Black and white America. After diminishing during the economic downturn of the 1930s, migration out of the rural South resumed at an even faster pace, bringing more than 3 million African Americans to the cities of the North, Midwest, and, increasingly, the West, where the booming wartime and postwar economy once again offered the promise of better-paying industrial jobs, educational opportunities, and hoped-for improvements in race relations. The technological revolution in southern agriculture, the emergence of the New Deal welfare state, and the militant modern civil rights and Black power movements of the 1950s and 1960s all helped complete the long-term transformation of Blacks from a predominantly rural to a predominantly urban people. By the 1970s, African Americans, once the most rural of Americans, had become the most urbanized segment of the U.S. population.

Like their predecessors in the Great Migration, however, the postwar migrants experienced varied and changing economic fortunes along with enduring barriers of racial and class exclusion. Although many were able to establish a foothold in the blue-collar or professional workforce, Blacks still faced discrimination in hiring and promotion that kept them underrepresented in better-paying jobs. Equally significant, even as African Americans (and other people of color) were arriving in record numbers, two related developments were transforming the large industrial cities they had looked to as the land of hope. One was the vast migration of white middle- and working-class residents to rapidly expanding, racially exclusive suburbs—with substantial assistance from federal government subsidies denied to nonwhite urban dwellers. Second, and related, was the migration of industrial jobs to the suburbs, to low-paying southern states, and, increasingly, to other parts of the globe. Meanwhile, while work opportunities were diminishing in the cities, persistent residential segregation was helping assure that Blacks would remain a heavily urbanized group—a pattern that has only recently and gradually begun to change. As the nation increasingly shifted from a goods-producing to a service-producing economy during the 1980s and 1990s, African Americans also faced new forms of urban poverty, characterized by long-term unemployment and rapid disinvestments in urban neighborhoods amid middle-class flight. By then, poverty had been widely identified as a "Black" problem, with consequences reflected in the diminishing support for antipoverty and welfare programs. In this and other ways, although the idea of an urban "underclass" camouflaged past forms of urban poverty, its focus on a highly stigmatized form of poverty did underscore the reconfigurations of urban, and African American, poverty over time.

Joe William Trotter Jr.

See also: Housing Policy; Racial Segregation; Racism; "Underclass"; Urban Poverty; Urban Renewal

References and Further Reading

Dixon, Robert M. W., and John Goodrich, eds. 1982. *Blues and Gospel Records, 1902–1943*. Essex, England: Storyville Publications.

Drake, St. Clair, and Horace R. Cayton. [1945] 1993. *Black Metropolis: A Study of Negro Life in a Northern City*. Chicago: University of Chicago Press.

Gottlieb, Peter. 1987. *Making Their Own Way: Southern Blacks' Migration to Pittsburgh, 1916–30*. Urbana: University of Illinois Press.

Grossman, James R. 1989. *Land of Hope: Chicago, Black Southerners, and the Great Migration*. Chicago: University of Chicago Press.

Harrison, Alferdteen. 1991. *Black Exodus: The Great Migration from the American South*. Jackson: University of Mississippi Press.

Katz, Michael B., ed. 1993. *The "Underclass" Debate: Views from History*. Princeton: Princeton University Press.

Lemann, Nicholas. 1991. *The Promised Land: The Great Black Migration and How It Changed America*. New York: Knopf.

Marks, Carole. 1989. *Farewell—We're Good and Gone: The Great Migration*. Bloomington: Indiana University Press.

Painter, Nell Irvin. 1976. *Exodusters: Black Migration to Kansas after Reconstruction*. Reprint: Lawrence: University of Kansas Press, 1986.

Sackheim, Eric, ed. 1969. *The Blues Line: A Collection of Blues Lyrics*. New York: Grossman Publishers, a Mushinsha Book

Scott, Emmett J. 1920. *Negro Migration: Changes in Rural Organization and Population of the Cotton Belt*. New York: W. D. Gray.

Spear, Allan H. 1967. *Black Chicago: The Making of a Negro Ghetto, 1890–1920*. Chicago: University of Chicago Press.

Taeuber, Karl, and Alma Taeuber. 1965. *Negroes in Cities: Residential Segregation and Neighborhood Change*. Chicago: Aldine.

Trotter, Joe William, Jr. 1985. *Black Milwaukee: The Making of an Industrial Proletariat, 1915–45*. Urbana: University of Illinois Press.

Trotter, Joe William, Jr., ed. 1991. *The Great Migration in Historical Perspective: New Dimensions of Race, Class, and Gender*. Bloomington: Indiana University Press.

Trotter, Joe William, Jr. 1993. "Blacks in the Urban North: The Underclass Question in Historical Perspective." In *The "Underclass" Debate: Views from History*, ed. Michael B. Katz, 55–81. Princeton: Princeton University Press.

Trotter, Joe William, Jr. 1996. "African American Migration and Population Development." In *Encyclopedia of African American Culture and History*, ed. Jack Salzman, 1779–1786. New York: Macmillan.

Trotter, Joe William, Jr. 2001. *The African American Experience*. Boston: Houghton Mifflin Company.

African Americans

African Americans' relationship to social welfare policy has been shaped by slavery and its lasting impacts. African Americans are disproportionately represented among the poor, the less educated, the more imprisoned, and the medically underserved. These experiences and circumstances arise from the distinctive poverty of a people whose legal status as property under slavery gave rise to a host of legal, political, and economic disabilities even after Emancipation. Any exploration of African Americans and social welfare must consider the political regime of segregation, discrimination, and inequality that succeeded the institution of slavery in the late nineteenth century. Supported by state and national laws until the mid-twentieth century, this regime governed African Americans' relationship to the education system, the labor market, housing, and health care. Although officially repudiated by federal judicial and legislative action, the regime of discrimination and inequality continues to animate important social policies, especially welfare.

Overwhelmingly, African Americans are residentially segregated in urban areas. This pattern of segregation followed African Americans even as millions moved out of the South during the first half of the twentieth century. Segregation resulted from deliberately discriminatory housing policies, such as restrictive covenants. Even as formal segregation measures were repealed, informal practices such as mortgage discrimination continued to hinder African Americans' residential mobility. Notwithstanding the achievement of legal equality, individual and government-sponsored discriminatory practices have led to a situation in which African Americans find themselves poorer, dying younger, more unemployed, less protected by health insurance, and less educated in comparison to their white counterparts.

In 2002, African Americans experienced a poverty rate of 24.1 percent overall (U.S. Census Bureau 2002). For children under the age of eighteen, the poverty rate for African Americans was 30 percent in 2001, compared with a rate of 10 percent for whites (U.S. Census Bureau 2002). There is also a disparity in income levels between African American and white adults. In 2001, the median earnings of African Americans was 64 percent that of comparable non-Hispanic whites, or $29,470 annual earnings for African Americans compared to $46,305 for non-Hispanic whites (U.S. Census Bureau 2001). Earnings disparities reflect both wage discrimination and occupational segregation: African Americans tend to be concentrated in service jobs and are less likely to work in managerial or professional specialties. In addition, the Black unemployment rate is often double that of whites. In 2002, the unemployment rate of African Americans was 11 percent, more than double the 5 percent experienced among whites (U.S. Census Bureau 2002). Concentration of poor African Americans in urban America has culminated in the image of the urban "underclass." The image of the urban "underclass" is often employed to epitomize poverty in American society.

Despite their disproportionate poverty, African Americans have at times been systematically excluded from the social welfare system. State-level mothers' pension programs, among the earliest forms of social welfare policy, systematically excluded African American women and their children from receiving assistance. President Franklin D. Roosevelt's New Deal program, like earlier mothers' pension programs, was not racially inclusive. By excluding agricultural and domestic workers from social insurance coverage, the Social Security Act of 1935 created and enforced a bifurcated system, relegating disproportionate numbers of African Americans to public assistance, or welfare, while male-headed white families enjoyed pensions from the Social Security system. The modern civil rights movement of the 1960s, along with the welfare rights movement, challenged the treatment of public assistance recipients and called for more-reliable and more-adequate benefits in a system that recognized recipients' rights.

The federal government responded to the civil rights movement with a War on Poverty and various new civil rights laws and initiatives. Targeting urban America, the War on Poverty took direct aim at the problem of racial segregation and its consequences for educational and employment opportunity. The legislative program included (1) the Housing and Urban Development Act of 1965, (2) the Economic Opportunity Act of 1964, (3) the Elementary and Secondary Education Act of 1965, and (4) the Demonstration Cities and Metropolitan

Development Act of 1966, better known as the Model Cities program. Combined, these various acts were designed to eliminate racial discrimination in employment and to equalize economic opportunity.

Since the passage of the civil rights legislation of the 1960s, African Americans have made some gains. One such gain was the growth of the Black middle class, signaling improved economic opportunities for some African Americans. However, racial backlash has undermined many of these gains, feeding opposition to programs that have aided African Americans. Some opponents have called for dismantling antipoverty programs altogether. This has been especially true for welfare policy, the public assistance program that provides income primarily to single mothers and their children. Stigmatizing African Americans for the structural poverty they experience, the media, policymakers, and many in the public often attribute the use of welfare to a kind of racial misbehavior. This racialized backlash against welfare drove the welfare reform efforts of the 1990s, which led to the replacement of Aid to Families with Dependent Children with the Temporary Assistance for Needy Families program.

Although antiwelfare forces have declared an end to welfare, the need for income support, for job creation, and for other effective antipoverty programs remains undiminished in many African American communities. Cities and the urban poor continue to suffer from a decline in manufacturing and other blue-collar jobs; inadequate, segregated, and inequitable public schools; various public health crises, including AIDS; an inadequate tax base and diminishing resources; homelessness; and an increasingly impoverished population.

Racial backlash against the civil rights legislation of the 1960s, especially against attempts to make welfare policies racially inclusive, have not abated in the early twenty-first century. Whether inflamed by the media or by antiwelfare politicians, the association of poverty with African Americans still stokes popular hostility toward programs to mitigate poverty. As a result, disparities in the economic opportunity and well-being of Black and white America persist.

Julia S. Jordan-Zachery

See also: Affirmative Action; African American Migration; Aid to Families with Dependent Children (ADC/AFDC); Civil Rights Acts, 1964 and 1991; Civil Rights Movement; Racial Segregation; Racism; Slavery; Social Security Act of 1935; "Underclass"; Urban Poverty; War on Poverty; Welfare Policy/Welfare Reform

References and Further Reading

Gilens, Martin. 1999. *Why Americans Hate Welfare: Race, Media, and the Politics of Antipoverty Policy.* Chicago and London: University of Chicago Press.

Neubeck, Kenneth J., and Noel A. Cazenave. 2001. *Welfare Racism: Playing the Race Card against America's Poor.* New York: Routledge.

Quadagno, Jill. 1994. *The Color of Welfare: How Racism Undermined the War on Poverty.* New York: Oxford University Press.

Schram, Sanford, Joe Soss, and Richard Fording, eds. 2003. *Race and the Politics of Welfare Reform.* Ann Arbor, Michigan: University of Michigan Press.

U.S. Census Bureau. 2001. "Income 2001." http://www.census.gov/hhes/income/income01/inctab1.html.

———. 2002. "The Black Population in the United States." March. http://www.census.gov./hhes/poverty02/r&dtable5.html.

Agee, James

See Let Us Now Praise Famous Men

Ageism

Ageism—prejudice or discrimination against people on the basis of age—has been a contributing factor of old-age unemployment, underemployment, and poverty in the United States. Negative stereotypes of old age take many forms, including assumptions that older individuals suffer from poor health, physical disabilities, and mental decline. These assumptions have led employers to discriminate against older job applicants and to judge their senior employees by their age rather than by their ability to perform their work, resulting in unfair treatment such as restricted duties, missed raises, denied promotions, forced early retirement, and termination. Employers have also fired senior workers to reduce costs or to avoid paying pensions. Older women have faced workplace discrimination due to attitudes favoring the appearance of younger women for public roles such as flight attendants, secretaries, and sales clerks.

Although negative attitudes toward the aged have been present since the nation's founding, employment discrimination against older workers became more prevalent with the rise of industrialization and the premium that mechanized industries placed on younger workers' speed and endurance. Twentieth-century popular culture reinforced the prejudices against old age by celebrating the vigor and freedom of youth while often denigrating old people's appearance and values. The economic and cultural stigma of old age found expression in corporate policies that often explicitly banned the hiring of older workers, limited them to certain jobs, or required their mandatory retirement. Though such policies remained legal and widespread into the 1960s, such discriminatory practices varied in their severity depending on the labor needs of the economy.

Pressure from such senior citizen organizations as the Gray Panthers, the American Association of Retired Persons, and the National Council of Senior Citizens helped win passage of the Age Discrimination in Employment Act (ADEA) in 1967. The law offered protection to workers over the age of forty employed by state and local governments, employment agencies, labor organizations, and private businesses with more than twenty employees (a U.S. Supreme Court decision in 2000 removed state employees from coverage). Between 1992 and 2000, an average of 17,000 workers per year filed ADEA discrimination charges with the Equal Employment Opportunity Commission (U.S. Equal Employment Opportunity Commission 2001). Another federal law, the Age Discrimination Act of 1975, extended protection to all participants in programs receiving federal funding. Although these laws, combined with state and local initiatives, have provided some legal recourse, ageism continues to hinder the ability of many older Americans to find and retain suitable employment.

Steven B. Burg

See also: Old Age; Social Security; Social Security Act of 1935; Townsend Movement

References and Further Reading

Achenbaum, W. Andrew. 1983. *Shades of Gray: Old Age, American Values, and Federal Policies since 1920*. Boston: Little, Brown.

Falk, Ursula, and Gerhard Falk. 1997. *Ageism, the Aged, and Aging in America: On Being Old in an Alienated Society*. Springfield, IL: Charles C. Thomas.

Fischer, David Hackett. 1977. *Growing Old in America*. New York: Oxford University Press.

U.S. Equal Employment Opportunity Commission. 2001. "Age Discrimination in Employment Act (ADEA) Charges, FY 1992–2000." http://www.eeoc.gov/stats/notable/adea.html.

Agrarian Movements

From the mid-nineteenth through the first three decades of the twentieth century, social movements of farmers were a major force for democratization and the development of government institutions to deal with problems associated with a nationalizing, industrializing economy. A sequence of agrarian movements—the Grange, antimonopoly, and greenback movements, the Farmers' Alliance, Wheel, Populists, and Farmers' Union—brought democratic demands onto the agenda of national politics.

These movements radicalized the economic program of the Democratic Party and saw many of their demands incorporated into law in the period from the mid-1880s to World War I. Their legacy was also evident in farm, labor, monetary, and regulatory legislation of the New Deal era. Farmers in the United States played the role taken by industrial workers in other Western societies, providing the bulk of early support for public control of corporations and a national government more responsive to the needs of the working population (or "producers," in agrarian rhetoric, a term often contrasted with "plutocrats").

Why farmers? For one thing, there were so many farmers, and they were always committed to politics. The country had vast fertile lands, and public policy strongly encouraged settlement by yeoman farmers who owned the land they worked. And in a nation where universal male suffrage was achieved very early (before rapid industrialization began in the 1840s), farmers voted in large numbers. Farmers were always a major force in both parties and were the largest interest group in the post–Civil War Democratic Party.

Farmer movements repeatedly reached out to workers (their putative "producer" allies) but found them unreliable coalition partners. Industrial workers and miners tilted toward the Republican high-tariff platform when they voted. But a system with opposing national parties controlled by farmers on the one hand and capitalists on the other provided an unsatisfactory set of political choices for labor. Some turned to socialist parties, but the poor prospects of third parties, the recent immigrant status of many workers, and the determined nonpartisan and anti-Populist stances of most labor leaders weakened labor's commitment to the proffered alliance with farmers.

Just after the Civil War, farmers went on an organizing binge. Oliver H. Kelley, a Minnesota farmer who later worked in the U.S. Department of Agriculture, received a grant from the department to travel through the southern states in 1866, surveying the state of agriculture in the war-devastated region. A few years later, with the help of friends and relatives, he organized the Patrons of Husbandry, a fraternal order of (white) men and women devoted to education, self-help, and the promotion of agriculture generally. Its local organizations were known then, as they are now, as "granges." By the mid-1870s, the Grange movement had achieved unprecedented penetration into the farm sector, with more than 11 percent of the male and female agricultural population over ten years old claimed as members. At its peak in 1875, the Patrons of Husbandry had about 760,000 members in nearly 19,000 granges, most in the north-central and south-central states.

Originally nonpartisan, the Patrons of Husbandry ("Grange") always encouraged its members to be politically active. Grangers flocked to the mass meetings triggered by the 1873 financial panic and clamored for government regulation of the railroads and of their exploitative and discriminatory rate structures. Without the official endorsement of the Grange, farmers mounted widespread protests against conservative state governments in the North and South and joined independent and "antimonopoly" parties (whose main targets were railroads, warehouses, and grain elevators). They have been credited with the passage of "granger laws" establishing railroad and warehouse regulation by state governments in the Midwest in the 1870s and with the agitation that led to passage of the national Interstate Commerce Act in 1887.

The Grange was the first large-scale, nationally organized reform organization in the United States, and it strongly influenced later farm and labor movements (both in their fondness for fraternal society rituals and in their reformist political passions). Its legacy also endured in enthusiasm for producer and consumer cooperatives, perceived by grangers and other farmer and worker organizations as key mechanisms for gaining some independence from the snares of monopolists and middlemen in the new industrial economy. But the Grange itself came to be seen as too timid for late-nineteenth-century conditions. It was overtaken by a more dynamic farm organization, the Farmers' Alliance, and by the greenback movement.

The federal government's post–Civil War deflation policy brought sharply lower commodity prices and higher debt loads for farmers. Labor organizations and small manufacturers were the first groups to endorse the notion that a contraction in the volume of circulating currency produced business failures and unemployment. By the late 1870s, farmers too—mainly wheat, corn, cotton, and tobacco farmers in the Midwest and South—joined the chorus of inflationists. In 1877–1878, small farmers in the cash-starved South, many of them grangers, joined independent political movements that favored repudiating state debts contracted by corrupt or incompetent conservative governments. They also demanded railroad regulation (and an end to land grants to railroads), better public schools, and laws easing the financial burdens of sharecroppers and workers.

The greenback movement of 1876–1880 emerged in a period of deflation, wage cutting, and agricultural depression. Its central demand, quite radical for the times, was that the national government, not private banks, should control money creation and should supply sufficient currency to accommodate a growing population and economy. Having taken the position that the national government should assume an active role in the economy, the greenbackers inevitably moved on to other political demands on behalf of farmers and workers.

With a platform drawing on principles of the Grange, antimonopoly parties, and labor organizations, the National Greenback Party ran strongly (for a third party) in both farm and labor districts in 1878 and elected fifteen congressmen. In 1880, the Greenback platform called for a host of radical reforms in labor law and in the conditions of industrial workers, as well as an expanding, government-controlled money supply, regulation of railroads, a national income tax, and universal suffrage. It also expressed its opposition to standing armies and militia laws that threatened labor. The party's candidate, James B. Weaver of Iowa, conducted the nation's first popular presidential campaign. However, despite its broad reform platform, Greenback Party support was predominantly agrarian, concentrated in the Midwest and Southwest.

As the Greenback Party waned, the Southern Farmers' Alliance emerged in an area of north-central Texas that was a hotbed of greenback agitation. An organization of small farmers drawing on the social bonds of rural churches, granges, and reform politics, the Alliance recruited farmers and farmworkers and accepted local professionals like ministers, teachers, and physicians (the dynamic Texas State Alliance leader Charles Macune was both a Methodist minister and a self-educated doctor). Bankers, lawyers, and merchants were excluded from membership.

The Alliance, like the Grange before it, organized both men and women. It did not, however, accept Blacks, though a few of its leaders helped to organize a Colored Farmers' Alliance, and Black farmers were permitted (encouraged in some states) to participate in Alliance cooperatives. The organization grew rapidly in the mid-1880s, thanks to its ambitious cooperative program and its system of itinerant education through "lecturers." The lecturers were farmers and rural professionals who, though often possessing little formal education, carried the Alliance message of cooperative economy and political action to dusty farms, schoolhouse meetings, and open-air gatherings where speeches, singing, eating, and political discussion drew large crowds.

In 1886, after bitter debate, the organization began to put more emphasis on politics and to collaborate with the Knights of Labor (KOL), the ascendant labor organization of the period. The "Cleburne Demands" issued by the 1886 state convention incorporated previous Grange, antimonopoly, greenback, and KOL principles and presaged the later platforms of the Populist Party.

In 1887–1888, the Alliance merged with another fast-growing and even more militant farmers' organization, the Arkansas Wheel, which had established branches in eight other southern states. The amalgamated movement called itself the Farmers' and Laborers' Union of America (FLUA), another announcement of its outreach to workers. In 1889, the FLUA held a joint convention in Saint Louis, Missouri, with the smaller, somewhat more conservative Northwestern Farmers' Alliance, but was unable to effect a merger of the two movements. However, the more radical South Dakota and Kansas chapters of the northern Alliance broke away from their parent organization to join the southerners.

The new biregional organization, with a membership of 1 million–1.5 million persons, was renamed the National Farmers' Alliance and Industrial Union (NFA&IU). Representatives of the Knights of Labor, whose organization was now on the decline, added their endorsement to a platform calling for monetary and land reforms and for nationalization of communication and transportation services. The two organizations also agreed to work together in their Washington, D.C., congressional lobbying efforts.

The main obstacles to a broader merger of midwestern and southern farm organizations at Saint Louis were partisan and product-based policy differences, as well as the southern organization's secrecy and rituals (which were typical of fraternal organizations of the times but which were viewed with great skepticism by religious leaders), its exclusion of Blacks, and its championing of Charles Macune's radical "subtreasury" plan.

Macune's plan, which would later inspire New Deal agricultural policy, proposed the creation of government-owned warehouses where farmers could store their crops and secure government loans for 80 percent of crop value. This would enable farmers to escape the snares of crooked private warehouses and the crop-lien system through which so many had lost their farms and become tenants or sharecroppers to the merchants and landlords who controlled scarce agricultural credit.

Macune promoted the subtreasury plan through the Alliance newspaper, the *National Economist*, which he founded and edited (he also started a National Reform Press Association to link the Farmers' Alliance to other reformers). The network of Alliance lecturers carried Macune's explanation of the plan to all the local sub-Alliances, and Alliance members pressed congressional and other candidates to endorse the subtreasury in return for their votes. But disappointment with the performance of Alliance-endorsed candidates and a cascade of failures among financially pressed Alliance stores ("exchanges") and crop-bulking cooperatives seemed to call for a new political strategy.

The People's Party was tentatively launched at an 1891 convention of Alliance members, greenbackers, prohibitionists, advocates of women's suffrage, and hundreds of other diverse reformers. In February 1892, the NFA&IU convened about 800 delegates in a "conference of industrial organizations" in Saint Louis. After lively debate and much agonizing about a third-party strategy, the delegates adopted a reform manifesto based on Alliance principles but postponed final action until the summer. Macune and many other southern Alliance leaders were particularly reluctant to break definitively with the Democratic Party. But third-party advocates in Alabama, Arkansas, Georgia, North Carolina, and Texas worked to rally white and Black farmers and industrial workers to the People's Party. Though backers of the independent political party hoped to preserve the Farmers' Alliance, the all-out political strategy inevitably sapped the energies of the farmers' organization.

In July 1892, advocates of the new party met in Omaha to nominate former Greenbacker James Weaver for president and to condemn the "vast conspiracy against mankind" by economic and political elites. The People's (Populist) Party platform called for "union of labor forces" to "restore the Government of the Republic to the hands of the 'plain people.'" Its first demand was for monetary reform: a single, nationally standardized, federal government–issued currency with an increase in circulation to fifty dollars per capita; free coinage of silver and gold at the ratio of 16 to 1; and the subtreasury plan of the Farmers' Alliance "or a better system." In addition, the People's Party demanded a graduated income tax; government ownership of railroad, telephone, and telegraph companies; postal savings banks; an end to speculative and foreign land ownership; and reclamation of unused railroad and corporate lands for actual settlers. For labor, it demanded the eight-hour day, an end to the use of Pinkerton "mercenaries" against workers, immigration restrictions, and enforcement of contract labor laws. There were also calls for a free and secret ballot, direct election of senators, and a limit of one four-year term for the president.

The People's Party candidate won just over a million votes in 1892, 8.5 percent of the total. The party was strongest in the mountain and plains states, along with Alabama, Oregon, and Texas. In the South, massive vote fraud by Democrats defeated Populist (as affiliates of the People's Party came to be known) candidates. Though the party's vote improved by 50 percent in the 1894 elections, the limitations of a third-party strategy—exaggerated by the impact of massive economic depression—were clear. Loyalties to the two major parties were too entrenched, and the dream of winning labor support for an independent farmers' party had proved ephemeral. When the Democrats repudiated their conservative, antilabor, hard-money president and nominated William Jennings Bryan in 1896, the Populists saw no better alternative than to make him their own nominee.

Bryan and fusion politics implanted Alliance/Populist principles in the Democratic Party, which became, in effect, the leading national farmers' organization. But not until the alienation of western and midwestern farmers from the Republican Party allowed Democrats to capture Congress and the presidency in 1912 did the old agrarian movement's agenda begin to bear fruit. An outpouring of regulation, labor, income tax, trade, education, and monetary reform laws in 1913–1917 may thus be seen as the belated legacy of the Farmers' Alliance and populism.

So, too, was the formation of a new farmers' organization in the old Texas Alliance heartland. The Farmers' Union, founded in 1902, carried on many of the same battles and took credit for many of the reforms passed in the Progressive Era. Later, in the 1940s and 1950s, it fought for progressive causes and farmer-labor politics against a newer, much more conservative organization, the Farm Bureau. Today, the Farmers' Union has only about a third the membership of the old Farmers' Alliance at its peak, but it can still be found at congressional hearings arguing for laws to protect the family farm and to oppose tight money and monopoly.

Likewise, the National Grange, revived in the Progressive Era, continues to champion rural, education, and family farm interests that resonate with the old Patrons of Husbandry platforms. But these two farm organizations, with roughly 300,000 members each, are too small to constitute major political forces in the twenty-first century.

Elizabeth Sanders

See also: Agricultural and Farm Labor Organizing; New Deal Farm Policy; Nineteenth Century; Rural Poverty; Trade/Industrial Unions

References and Further Reading

Bensel, Richard. 2000. *The Political Economy of American Industrialization*. New York: Cambridge University Press.

Goodwyn, Lawrence. 1976. *The Democratic Promise*. New York: Oxford University Press.

McMath, Robert. 1975. *Populist Vanguard*. Chapel Hill: University of North Carolina Press.

Palmer, Bruce. 1980. *Man over Money*. Chapel Hill: University of North Carolina Press.

Sanders, Elizabeth. 1999. *Roots of Reform*. Chicago: University of Chicago Press.

Agricultural Adjustment Act

See New Deal Farm Policy

Agricultural and Farm Labor Organizing

Agricultural and farm labor organizing arose in the United States in response to the characteristically low wages, intermittent employment, and poor working and living conditions generated by large-scale agriculture. For more than a century, agricultural workers have banded together to demand improvements through spontaneous and planned strikes and other forms of resistance, but a unified, long-lasting farm labor movement has been elusive. Organizing has generally occurred independently in different regions and in the production of different commodities and has often remained localized. Farmworker transience and poverty have made even local organizing difficult to sustain, and the exclusion of farmworkers from the 1935 National Labor Relations Act that recognizes the right of other workers to form unions and bargain collectively has added further impediments. Farm labor organizing and strike activity peaked during the 1930s and again in the 1960s–1970s, both periods of widespread social unrest during which a sympathetic public supported the farm labor movement by exerting economic and political pressure on behalf of workers. Federal and state governments have frequently responded to such pressure with regulation and assistance programs, which have brought better conditions and access to services. But conflict persists, as growers try to reduce production costs in the face of increasing pressures from global competition and workers try to protect the gains they have made in wages, working and living conditions, and organizing.

Local groups of cowboys and sheep shearers created the earliest organizations of hired agricultural labor during the 1880s and 1890s. About the same time, immigrant workers formed mutual aid associations, which operated as both social support groups and labor organizations. During the 1920s and 1930s, Mexican, Filipino, and Japanese farmworkers formed their own trade unions, but these unions also worked closely with other organizing campaigns. The Industrial Workers of the World (IWW), a national labor syndicate espousing the idea of a single union for all workers, began the first nationally directed agricultural organizing campaign among itinerant laborers, who migrated seasonally from city to countryside for employment. In California, the IWW led the 1913 Wheatland strike, in which hop pickers demonstrated against desperate living conditions, low wages, and lack of food and supplies. The strike ended in violence and the organizers' imprisonment, but the IWW reappeared among seasonal wheat harvest workers in the Midwest in 1915. The union successfully influenced wages and working conditions in the wheat harvest for the next two years but declined in the face of internal jurisdictional disputes and active suppression of radical organizations during World War I.

The Dust Bowl and Depression of the 1930s reenergized the farm labor movement as farmworkers sought to secure the same rights as President Franklin D. Roosevelt's New Deal offered industrial workers. Nationally directed organizations of the period included the Cannery and Agricultural Workers Industrial Union (CAWIU) in the early years of the decade, followed by the United Cannery, Agricultural, Packing, and Allied Workers of America (UCAPAWA). Both organized primarily in California and Arizona, among Mexican and other long-established groups and among new migrants from the drought-stricken southern plains. In 1933, CAWIU's most successful year, estimates

People attending a meeting for African American and foreign-born members of the Agricultural and Cannery Workers Union. Bridgeton, New Jersey, 1936. (Corbis)

put the number of workers on strike at over 47,000 in cropwide actions against growers of peas, berries, sugarbeets, apricots, pears, peaches, lettuce, grapes, and cotton. Of the twenty-five actions led by CAWIU, only four were lost (Jamieson 1945, 87). Among the most dramatic, the 1933 San Joaquin Valley cotton pickers' strike, led by CAWIU with strong support from the Mexican and other ethnic unions, succeeded in raising wages through a federally mediated settlement. UCAPAWA found less success later in the decade, losing a similar 1939 cotton pickers' strike in 1939, in part because of a change in public sympathy for federal intervention on behalf of workers. UCAPAWA turned to organizing processing workers, whose higher wages and more stable working conditions offered a better prospect for effective organizing.

In the Southeast during the 1930s, the Southern Tenant Farmers Union (STFU), an outgrowth of earlier sharecropper and farm labor organizations in the region, became the primary representative of sharecroppers and tenant farmers facing eviction and of day laborers facing falling wages and unemployment. The STFU openly organized without regard to race or tenure status and led both strikes and demonstrations to dramatize the conditions of displaced workers and tenants. Although most STFU actions failed to achieve their explicit goals, the publicity surrounding them forced federal intervention against the worst antistrike violence and brought relief and resettlement to some of the participants. The United Citrus Workers in Florida recruited field and processing workers, as well as mechanics, carpenters, and other wage laborers in an effort to achieve an industry-wide organization. The union led a number of strikes for higher wages and union recognition, but it eventually succumbed in the mid-1930s to powerful employer opposition. In New Jersey, the eastern counterpart of CAWIU, the Agricultural and Cannery Workers Union, led a strike in early 1934 at Seabrook Farms, one of only a few large-scale agricultural enterprises in the region. Workers won increased wages, overtime pay, and union recognition, but the gains were quickly rescinded. A violent second strike later in the year ended with federal mediation that reestablished the wage gains and appointed a board of worker, grower, and government representatives to oversee labor relations but that did not recognize the union.

During and after World War II, foreign farm labor supply programs left little leverage with which to press employers. Rather than continuing to try to organize, the National Farm Labor Union (NFLU), led by H. L. Mitchell, former head of the STFU, focused its energies on opposing the Bracero Program, the Mexican farm labor supply program that lasted until 1964. The NFLU, which became the National Agricultural Workers Union in 1952, quickly disappeared with the appearance of the Agricultural Workers Organizing Committee (AWOC), affiliated with the AFL-CIO. AWOC, however, remained relatively inactive until reenergized by the rise of a more militant, democratic farmworker movement.

Led by Cesar Chavez, the new farmworker movement was consciously connected to the civil rights and poor people's movements of the 1960s. Chavez and fellow leaders Dolores Huerta and Gilbert Padilla shared years of community organizing experience. The National Farm Workers Association (NFWA) used these community organizing techniques, rather than traditional workplace organizing, and adopted the civil rights movement's strategies of nonviolence and cultivation of public sympathy. Alliances with other activists, especially students, proved to be a valuable source of committed volunteer staff members and a powerful channel for raising public awareness of job actions.

NFWA's first strike, the 1965 Delano Area grape strike, pioneered the public marches and hunger strikes that came to characterize Chavez's leadership and launched the first of the highly successful grape boycotts that brought union recognition. Out of the strike arose the United Farmworkers Organizing Committee (UFWOC), modeled on the democratic design of the NFWA and joined by the remaining local chapters of AWOC. The UFWOC, which became the United Farm Workers (UFW) in 1972, had 10,000 members and contracts with 150 growers covering 20,000 jobs and 85 percent of the table grapes grown in California by 1970 (Mooney and Majka 1995, 164). The union had secured a wide array of benefits, ranging from higher wages, union control of hiring, seniority rights, grievance procedures, pesticide controls, health clinics, and economic assistance for disabled and displaced workers to drinking water, toilets, and rest periods in the fields.

Agricultural employers in California quickly organized in opposition, concerned by the UFW's ability to disrupt the critical timing of the harvesting of perishable crops. They lobbied state government, and in order to undermine the growing power of the UFW, they signed collective bargaining agreements with the Teamsters Union, which represented agricultural processing workers in the area and had long-standing jurisdictional and political differences with the

UFW leadership. New legislation restricted the use of boycotts, required cooling-off periods before strikes, and prohibited collective bargaining over pesticide use and mechanization. As violent confrontations erupted between UFW pickets and Teamsters Union members working with growers to disrupt strikes, the UFW launched a new national grape boycott in 1973 to force recognition of farmworkers' right to be represented by the union of their choice. In 1975, the California Agricultural Labor Relations Act created the Agricultural Labor Relations Board (ALRB), which functioned to protect UFW organizing and collective bargaining rights in California for the next eight years. When the political leadership of the state changed in 1983, however, the membership and orientation of the ALRB also changed. Grievances and enforcement requests by labor were frequently delayed, dismissed, or overturned, and the ALRB declined to intervene when employers resisted organizing drives and contract negotiations. Without ALRB support and stressed by internal disagreements, UFW organizing activity declined rapidly. Although the union experienced a resurgence following the death of Chavez in 1993, the global restructuring of agricultural production has introduced new challenges, including an influx of farmworkers, often undocumented, with only temporary ties to the United States.

In the Midwest, the Farm Labor Organizing Committee (FLOC), led by Baldemar Velásquez, began organizing tomato and cucumber workers in Illinois, Indiana, Michigan, and Ohio, in 1967. Initially adopting tactics similar to those of the UFW, FLOC won some localized strikes in the late 1960s and early 1970s. Unlike in California, however, most specialty crop growers in the Midwest contracted directly with processing companies for their entire crop at an agreed price for the season, leaving growers with limited flexibility to increase wages. In light of this arrangement, by the late 1970s, the union embarked on a new strategy, unique in the American labor movement, to bring the processing companies into three-way negotiations with workers and growers. The Campbell Soup Company, which held contracts for processing tomatoes, became the first target and responded by requiring its contract growers to mechanize their tomato harvests. FLOC initiated a consumer boycott against Campbell Soup in 1979, modeled on the successful UFW grape boycott, but by 1984, FLOC had developed an additional strategy of public demonstrations and boycott threats against corporations with close ties to Campbell to encourage them to pressure the company to negotiate. The negative publicity from both campaigns led to contract talks in 1985. Other large processing corporations, including the H. J. Heinz Company and Vlasic, also signed contracts providing higher wages, benefits, and improved working conditions. In subsequent contracts, the union also negotiated an end to the practice among cucumber pickle growers of declaring farmworkers to be independent contractors, which had kept them from coverage under workers' compensation, Social Security, and child labor laws.

FLOC continues to organize in the Texas and Florida home bases of many Midwest migrants, as well as in other areas of the Southeast. In addition to FLOC and the UFW, small local and regional unions also demonstrate and negotiate to improve the working and living conditions of agricultural labor, as they have for more than a century. The unions are complemented by the continuing work of farmworker advocacy organizations, a legacy of the allied activism of the 1960s and 1970s. These groups focus on securing the legal assistance, health care, housing, education, and other services farmworkers often cannot find or afford on their own.

Anne B. W. Effland

[The views expressed are those of the author and do not necessarily reflect those of the U.S. Department of Agriculture.]

See also: Agrarian Movements; Bracero Program; Chicana/o Movement; Dust Bowl Migration; *Factories in the Field; The Grapes of Wrath; Harvest of Shame;* Migrant Labor/Farm Labor; New Deal Farm Policy; Rural Poverty; Sharecropping; Trade/Industrial Unions

References and Further Reading

Edid, Maralyn. 1994. *Farm Labor Organizing: Trends and Prospects*. Ithaca, NY: ILR Press.

Hahamovitch, Cindy. 1997. *The Fruits of Their Labor: Atlantic Coast Farmworkers and the Making of Migrant Poverty, 1870–1945*. Chapel Hill: University of North Carolina Press.

Jamieson, Stuart Marshall. 1945. *Labor Unionism in American Agriculture*. U.S. Department of Labor, Bureau of Labor Statistics, bulletin no. 836. Reprint, New York: Arno, 1975.

Martin, Philip L. 1996. *Promises to Keep: Collective Bargaining in California Agriculture*. Ames: Iowa State University Press.

Mooney, Patrick H., and Theo J. Majka. 1995. *Farmers' and Farm Workers' Movements: Social Protest in American Agriculture*. New York: Twayne.

Weber, Devra. 1994. *Dark Sweat, White Gold: California Farm Workers, Cotton, and the New Deal*. Berkeley and Los Angeles: University of California Press.

Aid to Families with Dependent Children (ADC/AFDC)

Between 1935 and 1996, Aid to Dependent Children (ADC)/Aid to Families with Dependent Children (AFDC)—Title IV of the Social Security Act of 1935—provided basic income support for millions of poor women and their children. Commonly known as "welfare," the program was funded jointly by the federal government and the states and was administered by the states under supervision of various federal agencies, the latest of which was the Administration for Children and Families of the U.S. Department of Health and Human Services. Aid to Dependent Children (subsequently renamed Aid to Families with Dependent Children), although deficient in a number of respects, provided these poor mothers with an alternative to hunger and to having to take any job at any wage. Moreover, it was a major refuge for minority families rendered economically dependent by discrimination, low wages, and chronic unemployment and underemployment. The program, however, was always controversial, and its history is one of continuous attempts to "reform" it. This article summarizes the history of ADC/AFDC, its eligibility conditions, the adequacy of its benefit levels, its changing assumptions about women's roles, the AFDC-labor market interface, and the process known as welfare "reform" that culminated in the repeal of welfare.

ADC was hardly noticed at the time of its enactment in the midst of the Great Depression, and it did not generate nearly the same level of debate and controversy as did the other parts of the Social Security Act of 1935. In a time of many social movements, there were none for or by poor women and their families. The chief advocates for ADC were social welfare leaders, including Grace Abbott, and administrators of the U.S. Children's Bureau Katharine Lenroot and Martha Eliot, who as professional staff of the bureau were principally responsible for drafting the bill. Many of these advocates were part of the network of maternalist reformers who had been actively promoting aid to mothers and children since the Progressive Era. Basing their recommendations on state mothers' aid or widows' pension programs, the bureau's leaders prepared a report on which the ADC legislation was based.

Although modeled on state programs, ADC departed from them in significant ways. In contrast to its predecessors, ADC was partly funded by the federal government, was available in all jurisdictions of participating states, and was at least nominally subject to federal supervision and minimal standards. In time, ADC came to serve many more women of color, never-married, and divorced or separated mothers than did the orig-

U.S. House of Representatives, Committee on Ways and Means, Hearings on the Economic Security Act Statement of Miss Grace Abbott, Member, Advisory Council on Economic Security and Former Chief of U.S. Children's Bureau, January 30, 1935

Grace Abbott, longtime social welfare activist, head of the U.S. Children's Bureau from 1921 to 1934, and leading child welfare expert, was one of the architects of the Aid to Dependent Children program in her capacity as a member of the President's Advisory Council on Economic Security in 1934–1935. In her testimony before the House Ways and Means Committee about the proposed Economic Security Act (later retitled and passed as the Social Security Act of 1935), Abbott endorsed the act's provisions for the care of dependent children, emphasizing their essential continuity with the state-run mothers' pension programs while pointing out the need for a stronger federal role. Abbott did take issue, however, with the legislation's failure to house the program's administration in the U.S. Children's Bureau, which by the mid-1930s had built up considerable expertise on the implementation of mothers' pensions and the overall well-being of children.

The whole idea of mothers' pensions is that it should be enough to care for the children adequately, to keep the mother at home and thus give some security in the home. . . .

It is not only the best but the cheapest method of taking care of children—much cheaper than taking care of them in an institution or in somebody else's home. And it does preserve the relationship of the mother and the child.

This type of legislation, then, has been tested. Its value is not challenged but it is impossible to expect to make State and local governments take over the whole load that is now being carried on relief without some assistance. If the Federal Government assists, and encourages the State to make a larger contribution, the gain will be very great.

It seems to me of very great importance. The types of families that are not now receiving mothers' pensions resemble those of 25 years ago. We have been making a study of the families that are on the waiting list for the mothers' pension in the juvenile court and also of those on relief in Chicago. We find the same discouraging type of situation that we used to find before the mothers' pension was granted.

A widowed mother, with a large number of children or a small number, is usually quite unable to take care of them. For instance, here is one case of a mother whose husband died at 30. She has 3 children, 2 boys of 5 and 12, and a girl of 8. At the time of her husband's death they owned a home, but about a year later the mortgage was foreclosed. With the $500 that she received at the time of the foreclosure, she rented a basement flat in which they now live and turned the front room into a store, stocking it with candies and cigars, things of that sort. She has one other room where the family lives. She keeps the shop open all day and into the night, until about 10 or 11 o'clock. But she does not make enough to pay the rent and take care of the family, even though all of them live in the one rear room. They are very inadequately fed, and very inadequately clothed. This woman has been on the mothers' pension waiting list for 2 years. She expects to be evicted almost any time.

In one case that I have here, the mother has put the children in an orphanage, although the children want to get out and she wants to get them out. The most she has been able to earn is $7.50 a week, and she cannot take care of them and herself on that wage. So she is doing the best she can by contributing somewhat to their support and keeping in touch with them.

. . . [O]ne could go on and on with instances of that sort. Usually the children are really nice children and the families are nice families, if they could just be put on a permanent basis of knowing that the money was coming, and plan for it. It would make a great difference in the security of these families.

I am sorry that the administration of this grant in aid program is not given to the Children's Bureau. I think it belongs in a permanent bureau instead of an emergency bureau, and the Children's Bureau has worked for 21 or 22 years on this problem with the States.

inal state programs. Nevertheless, both were based on the assumption that mothers were nurturers, not breadwinners—an approach consonant with the Depression-era policy of removing women from the labor force as a solution to mass unemployment. Particularly in its formative years, ADC continued another mothers' aid policy, making moral worthiness a criterion of eligibility.

Despite ADC's maternalist approach, many poor mothers were forced to work outside their homes. Eager to protect the low-wage economy of their region, southern senators removed from the draft of the Social Security Act the requirement that monthly benefits provide "a reasonable subsistence compatible with decency and health." Consequently, many states paid very low benefits throughout the history of ADC and AFDC. When AFDC was terminated, all state allowances, plus the cash value of food stamps, were on average below the meager U.S. poverty standard of $12,516 for a family of three in 1996 (U.S. House of Representatives, Committee on Ways and Means 1996, 437–438). Many poor families whose incomes exceeded their state's paltry cutoff levels were ineligible for assistance, leaving them no recourse but low-wage employment. Minimal benefits also led some mothers to combine work and welfare, often not reporting some or all of their income to welfare officials in order to maintain their benefits (Edin and Lein 1997).

Two other policies kept families off the rolls, particularly before the 1960s. First, some states periodically cut families from assistance when more laborers, such as field hands, were needed (Bell 1965). Second, many mothers whose behavior was deemed "unsuitable" (usually interpreted as having children out of wedlock) were also deemed ineligible and denied assistance. Since unmarried motherhood was much higher among African Americans than among whites, this policy was only thinly veiled racism (Bell 1965). Thus, while ADC became an entitlement in 1950, meaning that everyone who met eligibility requirements would receive benefits, many poor, single-mother families failed to meet these conditions.

In still another respect, ADC/AFDC was not an entitlement for *all* poor children. Planners of the Social Security Act assumed that single-mother families were without breadwinners, but they did not so regard two-parent families where the parents were unemployed but ineligible for the program. They expected that the economy would either accommodate most unemployed men or that the federal government would continue to employ them in work programs like those initiated during the Great Depression (Goldberg and Collins 2001, 39). Neither hope was realized.

Nevertheless, overall employment conditions did have an important impact on welfare. As a by-product of waging World War II, the nation experienced full employment, and during that brief interval, the welfare rolls fell, despite changes that would otherwise have expanded the rolls (for example, modest benefit increases). Between 1942 and 1945, the number of ADC recipients per 1,000 population under the age of eighteen fell by more than one-third (Alling 1948, 13). Despite its demonstrated benefits, Congress defeated full-employment legislation in 1945. For most of the postwar period, however, millions of men and women, particularly minorities, faced chronic unemployment and underemployment in unstable, low-paying labor markets while remaining ineligible for public assistance. Although families with two unemployed parents became eligible for AFDC in some states in the 1960s, unemployment was defined so narrowly that few two-parent families actually qualified. Feminist scholars have maintained that AFDC regulated poor women and rewarded those who upheld the family ethic (Abramovitz 1996). Yet AFDC denied benefits to most women in poor, two-parent families, women who were adhering to the family ethic of marriage.

In the postwar years, increases in divorce,

unmarried motherhood, and unemployment (except during the Korean War) increased the need for public assistance. Another source of increasing need was the high unemployment rate of African American men and women who migrated from rural areas to northern and southern cities. Yet restrictive eligibility conditions, including moral worthiness and residence requirements, as well as social stigma, kept many families off the rolls who should have been on them.

During the 1950s, rising costs and numbers of caseloads troubled politicians on both sides of the aisle, even though the number served fell far short of the number who needed help. Increasing numbers of African Americans on the rolls were another source of unpopularity. In 1961, national attention focused on Newburgh, New York, whose conservative mayor responded to the "coloring" of the town's caseload with measures that violated New York State welfare laws; for example, benefits were denied to unwed mothers and to those who voluntarily left their jobs. Yet the mayor's crackdown included many devices that were being used around the country to reduce caseloads and costs (Goldberg and Collins 2001, 51–52).

In 1962, President John F. Kennedy's administration responded to Newburgh with amendments to the Social Security Act aimed at reducing the welfare rolls by means of rehabilitative services. The assumption was that the causes of poverty were more social than economic. In proposing the legislation, Kennedy observed that "many women now on assistance rolls could become self-supporting if daycare programs for their children were available" (Kennedy 1962, 10). Accordingly, the administration proposed not only federal funds for day care but a break with the policy of reducing benefits by the same amount as earnings. The emphasis on self-support in the labor market broke with the earlier maternalist policy and was coincident with the increasing participation of women in the paid labor force. Kennedy also initiated the Unemployed Parent program (AFDC-UP), which provided benefits to some two-parent families with an unemployed parent, and the program was renamed Aid to Families with Dependent Children. The Social Services Amendments of 1962, however, failed to reduce need or to trim the welfare rolls, largely because they were aimed at changing the behavior of poor people rather than addressing the problems of low-wage work, unemployment, discrimination, inadequate opportunities, and other conditions driving the need for assistance (Goldberg and Collins 2001, 77–78).

The seeming paradox of welfare in the 1960s is that the rolls exploded in a time of low unemployment and unparalleled prosperity. This is not to say that labor market disadvantage had disappeared. Quite a few observers, including some high government officials, recognized that Black unemployment and subemployment—a composite measure including involuntary part-time employment and wages below the poverty level—remained at crisis levels, as documented by the U.S. Department of Labor and the Joint Economic Committee (Goldberg and Collins, 2001, 89–91).

But labor market conditions were not the only factor driving welfare enrollments, which also respond to family composition, changes in public opinion, attitudes and assertiveness of prospective relief recipients, and judicial, legislative, and administrative policies. All of these, with the probable exception of changes in public opinion, were at play in the 1960s. The two most important, however, were mutually reinforcing: the much higher proportion of those in need who actually applied for welfare and their higher rate of acceptance into aid programs. Both of these developments reflected broader social and political changes that tended somewhat to loosen the historically stringent regulations and deliberately limited reach of welfare. Thus, the post–World War II migrations that brought African Americans to the cities of the North, Midwest, and West also made welfare more of an option than it had been in the overtly racist, comparatively restrictive rural and small-town South. At the same time, more of the poor claimed the benefits to which they were entitled, and relief officials accepted a higher rate of applications, in part as a result of an era of "rights consciousness" (Patterson 1996, 673). Moreover, the poor got considerable support in asserting their rights from a combination of government and voluntary sources. President Lyndon B. Johnson's antipoverty program contributed community organizers and lawyers through its Community Action Program (CAP) and Legal Services unit. With government and voluntary resources, much of it from church bodies, AFDC gained an organized constituency, the most visible of which was the National Welfare Rights Organization, established in 1966 by welfare mothers influenced by the civil rights movement and antipoverty activism. Legal service lawyers not only represented welfare clients in their individual grievances but successfully challenged restrictive welfare laws and administrative procedures through class-action suits. U.S. Supreme Court decisions in 1968–1970 outlawed residence requirements and other restrictive eligibility conditions and contributed, in turn, to rising welfare rolls.

Johnson billed his War on Poverty as "a hand up instead of a handout"; nevertheless, his program contributed to the expansion of so-called handouts. One reason for this seeming paradox is that the increased provision of relief was an answer to the civil unrest, notably the urban riots in a number of U.S. cities, that began in 1963 (Piven and Cloward 1993). Expanding welfare required no new laws, was a shared expense of federal and state governments, and was both cheaper and more acceptable to the business community than the strategy of major job creation favored by some administration officials and later recommended by the Kerner Commission, the presidential commission investigating the riots (*Report of the National Advisory Commission* 1968; Goldberg and Collins 2001).

Together, the combination of enduring labor market disadvantage, migration, social activism, and shifting government policy contributed to the changing composition as well as the size of the welfare rolls. By the end of the 1960s, the number of people on AFDC had more than doubled. The number of whites receiving assistance increased, but the proportion of Blacks on the rolls also rose. A program already stigmatized by race became even more so. Indeed, it came to be seen as a "Black" program even though African Americans were always a minority of the recipients (U.S. House of Representatives, Committee on Ways and Means 1996, 474).

Policymakers interpreted rapidly rising welfare rolls in a time of unparalleled prosperity as a "crisis" and as a sign of family breakdown rather than as the result of meeting neglected need. Thus, efforts to "reform"—that is, restrict—welfare overlapped the expansion of the rolls. The welfare expansion continued until the early 1970s, but in 1967, Congress took aim at escalating relief rolls and targeted another proxy for African American women, "illegitimacy." The 1967 amendments to the Social Security Act included a freeze on federal matching funds for increased costs related to "illegitimacy" and desertion as well as incentives and coercion to encourage welfare recipients (and potential welfare recipients) to work. Although the freeze was not implemented, it was a signal to single mothers that Congress could get tough with them. Since there were not enough training slots, there was little bite to these initial work requirements. Anticipating subsequent rounds of welfare "reform," later versions of this Work Incentive Program (WIN) put more emphasis on immediate employment than on training. The fact that job availability was a missing ingredient in welfare "reform" was occasionally pointed out but was officially ignored.

During the 1970s, Presidents Richard M. Nixon and Jimmy Carter attempted to reform welfare by providing a modest federal guaranteed income for all families with children—not only single mothers—and a liberalization of the tax on earnings. Both proposed reforms would have given family welfare important political advantages: Welfare would no longer be confined to a stigmatized, single-mother clientele; the income guarantee would unite the interests of welfare recipients and the working poor and would increase the proportion of white recipients, thereby reducing family welfare's racial characterization. The Nixon plan, known as the Family Assistance Plan, was opposed by conservatives who feared the loss of a cheap labor supply (Burke and Burke 1974, 2; Moynihan 1973, 378) and by liberals who considered the guarantee too low and opposed its mild work requirement. In the end, Nixon lost interest because, among other things, he considered the program too expensive (Goldberg and Collins 2001, 145–146). Carter failed to push hard for his Program for Better Jobs and Income, which would have combined a small guaranteed income with work requirements and job creation. The program ran into some of the same political dynamics, however, and was seriously undermined by the political climate of tax revolt. In the wake of the defeat of Nixon's Family Assistance Plan, some of its opponents successfully advocated a refundable tax credit, the Earned Income Tax Credit (EITC), to offset the burden of payroll taxes on low-wage workers. Twenty years later, the EITC was spending more federal funds than AFDC. This decade of failed welfare reform also saw the highest unemployment rates since the Great Depression and responses that were either temporary or ineffective; the first government work programs since the Great Depression (terminated even as unemployment was rising under President Ronald Reagan's administration); and a second attempt to guarantee jobs, the Humphrey-Hawkins Full Employment and Balanced Growth Act of 1978, which achieved neither of its goals.

The election of Reagan in 1980 brought to power a conservative movement aimed at reducing the size of the welfare state, eroding the political clout of labor and advocates for the poor, and restoring power to corporations. Unable to reduce Social Security due to its powerful senior lobby, Republicans instead focused on the politically more vulnerable means-tested programs like AFDC (Goldberg and Collins 2001, 169–170). Never a popular program, AFDC became a stand-in for so-called big government and its attendant evils. Conservative social theorists such as Charles Murray (1984) provided policymakers with rationales for reducing aid to the poor by asserting that programs like AFDC were responsible for poverty, dependency, and social dysfunction. What welfare recipients needed, they claimed, was a policy of "tough love," involving lower benefits and much more stringent work requirements, or even the elimination of welfare altogether.

Budget cuts and changes in eligibility rules, along with state-level retrenchment and the failure to index welfare payments to inflation, are estimated to have cost 500,000 families access to income support in the 1980s (Pierson 1994, 118–119). In addition, states were given waivers from federal rules to create programs that required recipients to engage in work experience programs in exchange for their welfare checks. To be truly effective, such programs would have to spend more money—on training and education, job creation, day care, and the like—but in the economic climate of the 1980s, states were neither willing nor prepared to make this commitment. By 1987, as many as forty states were exercising the work option.

The opening of Reagan's second term began another round of efforts to "reform" welfare at the national level, with Congress, governors, and liberal social welfare institutions all participating. This renewed interest in "reforming" welfare represented a gathering consensus among policy elites that the breakdown of the family and inadequate inner-city educational systems were generating a permanently dependent "underclass," that a reformed system should be based on the concept of reciprocal responsibilities between

Special Message to the Congress on Reform of the Nation's Welfare System, President Richard M. Nixon, August 11, 1969

Several months after assuming office in January 1969, President Richard M. Nixon announced an ambitious proposal to reform the nation's welfare system. Known as the Family Assistance Plan (FAP), the proposal envisioned collapsing federal cash-assistance programs into a single federally administered income guarantee covering most working-age families as well as the elderly, blind, and disabled, coupled with a work requirement for the able-boded and exempting mothers of children under six. In promoting the plan, the administration appealed to liberals by emphasizing the fact that it would eliminate some of welfare's major inequities—establishing a federal floor beneath benefits that varied widely across states and making aid to two-parent families a federal rather than a state-by-state provision. At the same time, FAP proponents promised conservatives a work requirement, along with a reduction in the social services bureaucracy and government "red tape." After several rounds of revision and negotiation and after twice gaining approval from the House Ways and Means Committee, the administration failed to satisfy any major constituency, and the plan was defeated in the Senate—with the exception of proposed improvements in assistance for the low-income elderly, blind, and disabled, which were met through the creation of the Supplemental Security Income (SSI) program. Moreover, by pitching its appeal to two-parent, "working poor" families, the administration played off of the distorted, heavily racialized imagery of Black welfare mothers that eventually helped to steer welfare "reform" away from public income supports and federal standards and toward the work requirements, "devolution," and marriage promotion that currently prevail in welfare policy.

To the Congress of the United States:

A measure of the greatness of a powerful nation is the character of the life it creates for those who are powerless to make ends meet.

If we do not find the way to become a working nation that properly cares for the dependent, we shall become a Welfare State that undermines the incentives of the working man.

The present welfare system has failed us—it has fostered family breakup, has provided very little help in many States and has even deepened dependency by all too often making it more attractive to go on welfare than to go to work.

I propose a new approach. . . .

I propose that the Federal government pay a basic income to those American families who cannot care for themselves in whichever State they live.

I propose that dependent families receiving such income be given good reason to go to work by making the first sixty dollars a month they earn completely their own, with no deduction from their benefits.

government and the welfare recipient, and that states should be given greater discretion over certain aspects of welfare policy.

The Family Support Act (FSA) of 1988 was the result of this latest wave of "reform." The legislation expanded federal requirements that states move their welfare caseloads into work-related programs and increased the states' discretion in designing them. The centerpiece was the Job Opportunities and Basic Skills (JOBS) training program, requiring states to provide assessment, training, education, and work experience or job-search assistance to welfare recipients. It sought to "make work pay" by requiring states to provide child care and Medicaid for up to one year for families leaving the welfare rolls for paid work, by raising the amount of earnings that are disregarded in calculating welfare benefits, and by mandating educational activities as appropriate. While requiring poor family heads

I propose that we make available an addition to the incomes of the "working poor," to encourage them to go on working and to eliminate the possibility of making more from welfare than from wages.

I propose that these payments be made upon certification of income, with demeaning and costly investigations replaced by simplified reviews and spot checks and with no eligibility requirements that the household be without a father. That present requirement in many States has the effect of breaking up families and contributes to delinquency and violence.

I propose that all employable persons who choose to accept these payments be required to register for work or job training and be required to accept that work or training, provided suitable jobs are available either locally or if transportation is provided. Adequate and convenient day care would be provided children wherever necessary to enable a parent to train or work. The only exception to this work requirement would be mothers of preschool children.

I propose a major expansion of job training and day care facilities, so that current welfare recipients able to work can be set on the road to self-reliance.

I propose that we also provide uniform Federal payment minimums for the present three categories of welfare aid to adults—the aged, the blind and the disabled.

This would be total welfare reform—the transformation of a system frozen in failure and frustration into a system that would work and would encourage people to work. . . .

This would be the effect of the transformation of welfare into "workfare," a new work-rewarding system:

For the first time, all dependent families with children in America, regardless of where they live, would be assured of minimum standard payments based upon uniform and single eligibility standards.

For the first time, the more than two million families who make up the "working poor" would be helped toward self-sufficiency and away from future welfare dependency.

For the first time, training and work opportunity with effective incentives would be given millions of families who would otherwise be locked into a welfare system for generations.

For the first time, the Federal government would make a strong contribution toward relieving the financial burden of welfare payments from State governments.

For the first time, the family in America would be encouraged to stay together, free from economic pressure to split apart.

These are far-reaching effects. They cannot be purchased cheaply, or by piecemeal efforts. This total reform looks in a new direction; it requires new thinking, a new spirit and a fresh dedication to reverse the downhill course of welfare. . . .

We have it in our power to raise the standard of living and the realizable hopes of millions of our fellow citizens. By providing an equal chance at the starting line, we can reinforce the traditional American spirit of self-reliance and self-respect.

to engage in work or work-related activity under threat of penalty, it exempted mothers with young children from the work requirements. Perhaps bowing to conservative claims that AFDC created disincentives to marriage, the FSA required all states to provide time-limited welfare payments to poor two-parent families whose "principal earner" was unemployed, requiring that at least one of the parents participate in a work program. (Still, very few two-parent families were served, even in the last years of the program.) The FSA also required states to establish paternity and to garnish the wages of noncustodial parents.

The FSA, however, was destined to be short-lived. The Reagan administration's debt burden, perhaps deliberately created, guaranteed that federal funds, which states would need to move their welfare clients into education, training, or work-experience programs, would not be adequate. Moreover, few states put any effort into job creation, a requisite for moving welfare recipients into the labor market.

Recession in 1991 brought rising welfare rolls and reduced state budgets, pushing states to reduce programs that assisted low-income households. In 1991 and 1992, 78 percent of the states froze or cut welfare benefits and made cuts in other low-income programs, and a majority of states failed to draw down their full federal allocations (Goldberg and Collins 2001, 178). Capitalizing on the public perception of welfare recipients as "immoral" and "irresponsible," many Republican governors requested waivers from federal regulators allowing them to develop programs that were more punitive than the FSA. Shifting from an earlier focus on education and training, states began to emphasize rapid job placement, usually in low-wage, low-quality jobs with no benefits. Although several states sought to loosen federal restrictions, which had made it difficult to move welfare recipients into the labor force, over half imposed stricter penalties for failure to comply with program rules, time limits, and work requirements, as well as penalties for additional childbearing.

Campaigning for the presidency in 1992 as a "New Democrat," Bill Clinton declared his intention to "end welfare as we know it" and hinted at a two-year time limit on welfare support, thus profoundly altering the terms of the debate. Republicans now in control of Congress ran with the slogan, and in 1996 succeeded in passing the Personal Responsibility and Work Opportunity Reconciliation Act with the consent of half the Democrats in Congress. This legislation consolidated several categorical aid programs into block grants. AFDC was repealed and replaced by Temporary Assistance for Needy Families (TANF), an annual block grant given to the states for a six-year period. TANF gave states broad discretion to design welfare programs but set a five-year lifetime limit on government support for families, mandated work requirements, mandated minimum penalties to compel recipient mothers to establish paternity and cooperate with child support enforcement, and limited support for education and training. An entitlement to government support for single-mother families, however limited, was now effectively abolished.

Sheila D. Collins and
Gertrude Schaffner Goldberg

See also: African American Migration; African Americans; Dependency; Earned Income Tax Credit (EITC); Employment Policy; Feminisms; Food Stamps; Kerner Commission Report; Legal Aid/Legal Services; Maternalism; Maternalist Policy; Means Testing and Universalism; Poverty, Statistical Measure of; Poverty Law; Poverty Line; Racism; Social Security Act of 1935; Unemployment; U.S. Children's Bureau; U.S. Department of Health and Human Services; War on Poverty; Welfare Policy/Welfare Reform; Welfare Rights Movement; Welfare State; Workfare; see also the extracts from the following court cases (in sidebars to the entry Poverty Law): *King v. Smith* (1968); *Shapiro, Commissioner of Welfare of Connecticut, v. Thompson* (1969); *Goldberg v. Kelly* (1970); *Dandridge v. Williams* (1970); *Saenz v. Roe* (1999)

References and Further Reading

Abramovitz, Mimi. 1996. *Regulating the Lives of Women: Social Welfare Policy from Colonial Times to the Present*. Rev. ed. Boston: South End Press.

Alling, Elizabeth T. 1948. "Trends in Recipient Rates for Aid to Dependent Children." *Social Security Bulletin* 11 (November): 12–15.

Bell, Winifred. 1965. *Aid to Dependent Children*. New York: Columbia University Press.

Burke, Vincent J., and Vee Burke. 1974. *Nixon's Good Deed: Welfare Reform*. New York: Columbia University Press.

Edin, Kathryn, and Laura Lein. 1997. *Making Ends Meet: How Welfare Mothers Survive Welfare and Low-Wage Work*. New York: Russell Sage Foundation.

Goldberg, Gertrude Schaffner, and Sheila D. Collins. 2001. *Washington's New Poor Law: Welfare Reform and the Roads Not Taken, 1935 to the Present*. New York: Apex Press.

Kennedy, John F. 1962. "Text of President's Message to Congress Seeking Reforms in Welfare." *New York Times*, February 2.

Moynihan, Daniel P. 1973. *The Politics of a Guaranteed Income*. New York: Random House.

Murray, Charles. 1984. *Losing Ground: American Social Policy, 1950–1980*. New York: Basic Books.

Patterson, James T. 1996. *Great Expectations: The United States, 1945–1974*. New York: Oxford University Press.

Pierson, Paul. 1994. *Dismantling the Welfare State: Reagan, Thatcher, and the Politics of Retrenchment*. Cambridge: Cambridge University Press.

Piven, Frances Fox, and Richard A. Cloward. 1993. *Regulating the Poor: The Functions of Public Welfare*. Updated ed. New York: Vintage Books.

Report of the National Advisory Commission on Civil Disorders. 1968. Washington, DC: Author, March 1.

U.S. House of Representatives, Committee on Ways and Means. 1996. *1996 Green Book: Background Material and Data on Programs within the Jurisdiction of the Committee on Ways and Means*. Washington, DC: GPO.

Alaska Natives

The term "Alaska Natives" refers to peoples indigenous to the present-day state of Alaska. Like the tribes located within the contiguous United States, they are linguistically, socioeconomically, and culturally diverse.

Alaska has the highest percentage of Native Americans relative to its total population of any state in the nation. According to the 2000 U.S. census, Alaska Natives and members of American Indian tribes numbered 119,241, or 19 percent of the total population of the state. Concentrated in the northern and western parts of the region, the largest tribal groups were Yup'ik (22,671), Inupiat Eskimo (17, 016), Alaskan Athabascan (14,546), and Tlingit-Haida (12,523) (U.S. Census Bureau 2000).

Despite their diversity and distinctive cultures, contemporary Alaska Natives share much in common with other indigenous peoples in North America. The ratio of males to females is nearly equal but, as is the case with American Indians generally, Alaska Natives are young. The median age for Alaska Natives is 23.6 years, versus 35.3 years for the total U.S. population. They also have high indices of poverty in comparison to the population at large. The poverty rate, according to the U.S. Census Bureau, was 25.7 percent in 2000. That well exceeds the 17.8 percent for all Americans and 9.8 percent for Alaskans of all races. Life expectancy, at 69.4 years, is significantly lower than the 76.7 years for the general population in the United States (Indian Health Service 2000).

Poverty among Alaska Natives must be understood in the context of a complicated political and legal relationship with the United States. First contact with whites began with the Russians during the mid-eighteenth century and continued into the nineteenth century. In 1867, the Treaty of Cession transferred claims to present-day Alaska to the United States. Alaska Natives did not recognize this transaction as valid but found themselves quickly on the defensive. By the late nineteenth century, the extension of civilian rule in the territory was accompanied by an onslaught of settlers and gold seekers. Having been deprived of legal protection under Indian or territorial law, Alaska Natives had no recourse against a devastating process of encroachment and expropriation that continued into the twentieth century. With a population ravaged by disease and with the ability to subsist through hunting and fishing almost completely stripped from them, Alaska Natives pressed hard for the recognition of their aboriginal land claims.

The Alaska Statehood Act of 1958 accelerated the struggle. Although the state was allowed to lay claim to 108 million of the 375 million acres of land in the area, preexisting aboriginal land claims had yet to be resolved. Not surprisingly, this land was the vital hunting and fishing grounds upon which indigenous peoples relied. In October 1966, the Alaska Federation of Natives was formed to serve as a vehicle for defending aboriginal claims to their homelands and to hunting and fishing rights. They rested their argument, in part, on the language of the Organic Act of 1884, which declared, "Indians or other persons in said district shall not be disturbed in the possession of any lands actually in their use or occupation or now claimed by them but the terms under which such persons may acquire title to such lands is reserved for future legislation by Congress" (quoted in Maas 1996, 10). In late 1966, due partially to the pressure placed on the federal government by the Alaska Federation of Natives, Interior Secretary Stewart Udall placed a freeze on the state assumption of any additional land and the issuance of mineral leases.

Congress enacted the Alaska Native Claims Settlement Act (ANCSA) in 1971 to resolve the nettlesome question of aboriginal land claims. It was the culmination of multiple interests, many of them revolving around the discovery of oil on the North Slope in 1968. Both Alaska Natives who sought to defend their land and private corporations that wanted to exploit the valuable resource agreed that a definitive settlement was needed. ANCSA recognized aboriginal land claims and issued fee simple title to individual Alaska Natives. They, in turn, were members of twelve regional and 200 village profit-making business corporations that were charged with managing the property. In all, the United States recognized aboriginal claims to 44 million acres and provided $962.5 million in compensation (Worl 1996, 276).

Present-day economic indicators suggest that the millions of acres of land and hundreds of millions of dollars did not prove to be the boon one might expect. Indeed, far more land went to private corporations for the development of oil and gas pipelines and was set aside as national parks and wildlife refuges than went to aboriginal claims. Indeed, by the early 1990s, the state of Alaska itself had collected some $32 billion from the development of the North Slope oil fields alone (Maas 1996, 12). But even more significant, ANCSA has not provided a means for Alaska Natives to maintain their traditional ways of life or exercise sovereignty. This, in addition to the expropriation of aboriginal lands and resources, has contributed to the persistence of poverty among Alaska Natives.

Daniel M. Cobb

See also: Native Hawaiians; Native Americans/American Indians

References and Further Reading

Colt, Stephen. 1996. "Alaska Native Regional Corporations." *Native America in the Twentieth Century: An Encyclopedia*, ed. Mary B. Davis, 13–17. New York: Garland Publishing.

Haycox, Stephen W. 2002. *Alaska: An American Colony*. Seattle: University of Washington Press.

Indian Health Service. 2000. Division of Planning, Evaluation, and Health Statistics. "Special Reports: Key Facts—Alaska Natives." http://www.ihs.gov/FacilitiesServices/AreaOffices/Alaska/dpehs/ak-dpehs-sp-ak-natives.asp.

Maas, David C. 1996. "Alaska Native Claims Settlement Act." In *Native America in the Twentieth Century: An Encyclopedia*, ed. Mary B. Davis, 10–13. New York: Garland Publishing.

Ogunwole, Stella U. 2002. "The American Indian and Alaska Native Population: 2000." U.S. Census 2000. http://*www.census.gov/prod/2002pubs/c2kbr01–15.pdf*.

U.S. Census Bureau. 2000. "American Indian and Alaska Native Tribes in Alaska: 2000." PHC-T-18. http://www.census.gov/population/www/cen2000/phc-t18.html.

Worl, Rosita. 1996. "Indian-White Relations in Alaska." In *Encyclopedia of North American Indians: Native American History, Culture, and Life from Paleo-Indians to the Present*, ed. Frederick E. Hoxie, 273–277. Boston: Houghton Mifflin.

American Association for Labor Legislation

The American Association for Labor Legislation (AALL) was one of the most prominent social reform organizations of the Progressive Era. Dominated by elite academics, the AALL was unique in its emphasis on labor legislation as the solution to the nation's economic and social ills. AALL leaders opposed direct relief, favoring instead laws that would provide American workers with basic security. The AALL achieved historic success with some of its occupational safety and health initiatives, most notably the creation of workers' compensation. Yet its campaign for compulsory health insurance benefits failed disastrously, demarcating the limits of the American welfare state.

Economists Richard Ely and Henry Farnam founded the AALL in 1906 as the American branch of the Geneva-based International Association for Labor Legislation. John R. Commons, a well-known labor economist at the University of Wisconsin, became the organization's first secretary. National membership never grew to much more than 3,000, but the AALL's journal, *American Labor Legislation Review,* was widely circulated and cited as the major source of information on labor laws throughout the Progressive Era. The association's board was unusually varied; its members ranged from settlement house workers and labor union leaders to physicians and insurance executives. This diversity of interests would sometimes prove to be the organization's strength, but it was also often its weakness.

The AALL's concerns represented the anxieties of the Progressive-Era middle class, torn between sympathy for the masses and fears of a worker uprising. The organization did not advocate socialism; instead, it sought to preserve the capitalist system by curtailing its abuses and protecting American workers from its worst excesses. The AALL viewed government as an instrument of expert-led regulation, not of redistribution. And AALL leaders viewed themselves as disinterested mediators between labor and capital. Labor laws, they argued, would benefit employers as well as workers by improving efficiency and morale.

In its fight against poverty, the AALL advocated European-style social insurance, which would protect workers against injury, sickness, unemployment, and old age. The emphasis on social insurance reflected a preference for prevention rather than relief. The AALL leaders shared the common conception that relief was charity and thus damaging to individual morality and self-respect. Social insurance avoided these pitfalls since workers would contribute from their own paychecks. The AALL's single-minded pursuit of the insurance model led to an exclusive emphasis on the problems of the industrial workforce; agricultural, service, and domestic workers, as well as the chronically unemployed, fell outside the AALL's vision of security.

The AALL achieved its greatest successes and suffered its most stunning failures under the leadership of John B. Andrews, an economist who had studied under Commons. In 1909, Andrews, along with his wife Irene Osgood Andrews, launched an investigation of the gruesome disease known as "phossy jaw" suffered by match-factory workers. By 1912, the AALL had won a federal law eliminating the use of poisonous phosphorus in matches. The organization's next campaign, social insurance in the form of workmen's compensation laws for on-the-job injuries, also bore fruit. Workmen's compensation illustrated two central tenets of AALL philosophy: It would benefit employers as well as workers by replacing the employers' liability system with predictable premium payments, and it would prevent injuries by giving employers a financial incentive to improve workplace safety. Thanks in large part to the AALL's leadership, thirty-eight states and the federal government (for federal employees) created workers' compensation systems between 1911 and 1918.

Believing that compulsory health insurance, another pillar of European worker protection, would follow easily upon the heels of workmen's compensation, reformers were unprepared for a difficult and ultimately futile battle. The AALL's model health insurance bill of 1915 included medical care and sick pay for workers who lost time due to illness, and a small death benefit, to be paid for by equal contributions from workers, employers, and the state. But early support from the medical profession quickly eroded as physicians decried the loss of control over their incomes and practices that health insurance supposedly would entail. The American Medical Association and state medical societies joined with employers, insurance companies, and conservative labor unions to defeat the AALL's health insurance bills in California and New York in 1917 and 1919. The AALL conceded defeat, and compulsory health insurance vanished from public discussion until the New Deal.

Attempts to establish unemployment insurance met a similar fate during the 1920s. The AALL helped introduce unemployment insurance bills repeatedly in several industrial states throughout the decade, but it faced the same stubborn opposition from employers and insurers. Commons and his followers had better luck in their efforts to strengthen state workmen's compensation laws. During the Great Depression, the AALL suffered an ideological divide when Commons and Andrews pushed for an unemployment insurance model, known as the "Wisconsin Plan," that was based on employer contributions and that was more conservative than the federal system advocated by former AALL supporters Isaac Rubinow and Abraham Epstein. The Wisconsin model proved to be more influential in creating the nation's unemployment insurance system.

With the conspicuous exception of health insurance, AALL reformers saw most of their vision realized during the New Deal. As historian David Moss wrote, "The ideas and political activities of the AALL reformers during the progressive period helped to set the subsequent trajectory of U.S. social welfare policy" (Moss 1996, 171). The AALL's activities laid the foundation for a system of protection against injury, old age, and unemployment while reinforcing the system's neglect of nonindustrial workers, its elite-driven policymaking, and its stigmatization of direct relief.

Beatrix Hoffman

See also: Health Policy; Social Security Act of 1935; Unemployment Insurance; Workers' Compensation

References and Further Reading

Hoffman, Beatrix. 2001. *The Wages of Sickness: The Politics of Health Insurance in Progressive America*. Chapel Hill: University of North Carolina Press.

Lubove, Roy. 1968. *The Struggle for Social Security, 1900–1935*. Cambridge, MA: Harvard University Press.

Moss, David, 1996. *Socializing Security: Progressive-Era Economists and the Origins of American Social Policy*. Cambridge, MA: Harvard University Press.

Americanization Movement

Between the 1890s and the 1920s, middle-class reformers, intellectuals, and industrialists promoted the rapid assimilation of immigrants from Europe, Mexico, and Asia in order to alleviate poverty and ease their transition to life in the United States. Started in urban settlement houses and championed by Patriotic Societies and industry after the turn of the century, the Americanization movement aimed to accelerate the process of assimilation and to control its outcome. Over the next fifteen years, it gained some adherents who held genuine humanitarian interests and others who, fearing cultural heterogeneity, desired social control. Private organizations, federal agencies, state and local governments, industrial corporations, and educators turned their attention to making "immigrants" into "Americans" in terms of language, habits, and values. This included establishing public and private policy regarding instruction in the English language, civics and government, hygiene, and manual and domestic arts. Americanization took on ideological and practical dimensions, as Americanizers worked to instill "American" culture while providing essential skills for social, political, and economic participation in the United States.

The movement intensified during World War I and peaked during the subsequent Red Scare of 1919–1920. As Americanizers went on the offensive against perceived immigrant tendencies toward bolshevism, humanitarian elements gave way to outright hostility toward newcomers. Programs and propaganda increasingly highlighted and criticized differences between immigrants and old-stock citizens. However, in the Red Scare's wake, national organizations dissolved; federal, state, and local governments withdrew; most corporations eliminated their programs; and the movement dissolved. Many Americanizers came to regard assimilation as impossible and advocated immigration restriction instead.

After 1920, the Americanization movement endured primarily in education, as sociologists, educators, and industrialists targeted children, hoping to achieve assimilation for the next generation. Yet school-based programs clearly revealed fundamental contradictions. Ostensibly utilitarian curricula, focused on industrial discipline and manual labor, ignored academic training and never stressed economic mobility or political empowerment. This discrete assimilation offered little more than second-class citizenship and demonstrated the Americanization movement's deepest flaw: It never intended to make immigrants first-class U.S. citizens.

Because they attempted to moderate immigrants' transition to life in the United States and to mediate their assimilation, social and settlement house workers took one path toward Americanization. Influenced by firsthand experience and the University of Chicago's sociologists, they were the most humanitarian of their ilk and rarely encouraged immigrants to detach themselves completely from their home cultures and traditions. A lawyer and sociologist by training, Frances Kellor, the most active of these reformers, wrote muckraking essays, served on the New York Commission on Immigration, and founded or directed several private organizations, including the North American Civic League for Immigrants and the Committee for Immigrants in America, which later became the National Americanization Committee. Especially in the early years, Kellor and her Progressive colleagues prioritized immigrants' social welfare and uplift.

Concurrently, patriotic societies, such as the Daughters of the American Revolution and the American Legion, developed their own brand of Americanization, "100 percent Americanism." These zealots saw immigration as a threat to specific values, and they targeted adult males for instruction in English, U.S. history, and proper habits. These included regular voting, submission to U.S. laws, and loyalty to their new nation. In addition to demanding conformity, 100 percent Americanists fostered an intense nationalism among their adherents and their audience.

As the Americanization movement gained momentum, businesses, government agencies, and educators increased their participation. For industrialists who saw their immigrant employees as refugees from a preindustrial world, Americanization programs provided a template for training loyal, disciplined workers who respected the clock and valued hard work. Ford and others instituted mandatory English-language and citizenship naturalization classes at their largest factories and in company towns. The federal Education Bureau and Naturalization Bureau both dabbled in Americanization. Following New York's lead, several states established commissions to address immigrant issues. Numerous school systems initiated adult education programs with the same goals and began emphasizing language skills for immigrant children, while businesses worked with local school boards to develop vocational training programs.

Although still concerned with social welfare, the Americanization movement flourished during World War I as a remedy to disunity and disloyalty. Motivated in part by fear, and complimented by the 100 percenters' nationalism, even humanitarian Americanizers advocated national defense and "America First" in broad-based propaganda campaigns. Liberal approaches lost favor during the war. When the Red Scare gripped the nation on the heels of the war, 100 percenters became the movement's leaders, and its humanitarian elements receded. Securing national unity and immigrant loyalty became paramount, conformity and obedience became mandatory, and the impetus toward policy innovation and immigrant assistance evaporated. Yet even in this extreme phase, the Americanization movement relied on persuasion rather than legislation, for most state laws failed to withstand constitutional scrutiny.

During the Red Scare, expedience superseded organization, and the recession of 1920 left the movement bereft of economic support. More generally, in abandoning all pretense to immigrant aid and social welfare, Americanization had lost much of its sustaining spirit. Many Progressive Americanizers turned their attention elsewhere, while 100 percenters joined the push for total immigration restriction. The Americanization programs that survived in elementary schools and adult education classes during the 1920s and 1930s proved truly destructive. Children were taught that their parents' culture was inferior, creating significant generational tensions at home. By emphasizing instruction in vocational, manual, and decorative arts rather than academic subjects, Americanization in the schools relegated students to lives of industrial and domestic labor without offering support for socioeconomic mobility. Finally, the ongoing assertion of essential difference supported efforts to segregate Mexican and Asian schoolchildren in the Southwest and West.

David Torres-Rouff

See also: Hull House; *Hull-House Maps and Papers;* Immigrants and Immigration; Immigration Policy; Progressive Era and 1920s; Settlement Houses; Social Surveys; Social Work; *Twenty Years at Hull-House;* Vocational Education; Welfare Capitalism

References and Further Reading

Higham, John. 1994. *Strangers in the Land: Patterns of American Nativism, 1860–1925.* New Brunswick, NJ: Rutgers University Press.

Kazal, Russell. 1995. "Revisiting Assimilation: The Rise, Fall, and Reappraisal of a Concept in American Ethnic History." *American Historical Review* 100, no. 2: 437–471.

Tamura, Eileen H. 1994. *Americanization, Acculturation, and Ethnic Identity: The Nisei Generation in Hawaii.* Urbana: University of Illinois Press.

AmeriCorps

In 1993, President Bill Clinton signed the National and Community Service Trust Act, thereby establishing the Corporation for National Service. This corporation oversees three major projects: Learn and Serve America, the National Senior Service Corps, and AmeriCorps. AmeriCorps brought together two preexisting federal community service programs, Volunteers in Service to America (VISTA, created in 1964 by the Economic Opportunity Act) and the National Civilian Community Corps (NCCC, created in 1992 as part of a defense appropriations bill amendment), with the new AmeriCorps State and National Project. Since its creation in 1993, AmeriCorps has allowed more than 250,000 men and women to provide needed assistance to both rural and urban communities. Working through a nationwide network of over 2,100 nonprofit organizations, public agencies, and faith-based initiatives, AmeriCorps volunteers have infused such programs with a vital flow of dedicated and trained individuals to meet diverse needs in the areas of health, public safety, education, and the environment. Major projects have included tutoring youth, teaching computer skills in disadvantaged communities, building affordable housing, disaster response, and cleaning up public parks.

AmeriCorps volunteers serve between twenty and forty hours each week, usually for one year. In exchange, they receive an education award to pay back student loans or to fund future college education. Approximately half also receive a small living stipend and health benefits. Largely decentralized in organization, AmeriCorps relies on states and nonprofit organizations to exercise primary control over resource allocations and volunteer placements. Three-fourths of the program's grant funding is controlled by governor-appointed state commissions, which then pass funds on to selected nonprofit organizations. The remaining funding is directly granted to regional and national organizations who apply for such grants. Habitat for Humanity, the American Red Cross, Big Brothers/Big Sisters, Teach for America, and many smaller organizations have taken advantage of such access to federal resources.

After the terrorist attacks of September 11, 2001, President George W. Bush proposed a major expansion of AmeriCorps programs in public safety, public health, and disaster relief as part of his larger homeland security agenda. Throughout the 1990s, AmeriCorps members worked in the area of disaster relief, often in conjunction with the Federal Emergency Management Agency and the Red Cross. In 2002, Bush created the USA Freedom Corps to promote volunteerism and "expand and strengthen federal service programs like the Peace Corps, Citizen Corps, AmeriCorps, and Senior Corps" (USA Freedom Corps). However, as of early 2004, plans to drastically increase the size and funding of AmeriCorps had stalled, despite a sizable increase in enrollment applications of those wishing to contribute their time and energy to this and other service organizations.

Rebecca K. Root

See also: Peace Corps; Volunteers in Service to America (VISTA)

References and Further Reading

USA Freedom Corps. Web site. http://www.usafreedomcorps.gov.

What Is AmeriCorps? 1994. Washington, DC: Corporation for National Service.

Antihunger Coalitions

Antihunger groups have historically focused on problems of hunger and poor nutrition as a way of drawing attention to larger problems of poverty and social injustice, since the 1980s coordinating with other groups to form a "hunger lobby" on behalf of the poor.

Since the War on Poverty, antihunger and social justice campaigns in the United States have shifted from a focus on welfare rights, to a focus on hunger, then to homelessness, and more recently to impoverished children and to the attempt to establish the roles of individuals and communities—as well as government—in alleviating hunger and poverty.

Following the model of the civil rights movement, antipoverty lawyers during the late 1960s advanced the notion of a constitutional "right to live" that would guarantee a minimum income to all citizens. After achieving an initial string of successes, the welfare rights argument was ultimately rejected by the courts. Growing public opposition to the notion of welfare rights, along with the defeat of guaranteed-income proposals in Congress and the demise of the welfare rights movement, led advocates to move away from the welfare rights litigation strategy in the early 1970s.

Although welfare rights activists lost ground in both the courts and in Congress, a loose coalition of public interest groups, churches, labor unions, and physicians and nutritionists coalesced in the early 1970s in order to document—and fight—hunger in America. Prominent among the national organizations was the Food Research and Action Center (FRAC), which was established in 1970 as a public interest law firm and which has subsequently become a leading research, policy analysis, and advocacy organization serving a nationwide constituency of antihunger and antipoverty organizations. The coalition that formed around FRAC and other groups rapidly gained ground in their attempts to increase federal spending on the poor—principally through expansions in the food stamp program. Between 1970 and 1977, real annual growth in food stamps averaged more than 15 percent—five times the growth rate for the gross national product and twice the growth rate for government as a whole. Supported by private foundations and the Community Services Administration (CSA) and Legal Services Corporation (LSC), the hunger lobby gained support from the media and from key members of Congress and their staffs. It spearheaded the drive to create the Select Committee on Nutrition and Human Needs and gained allies on the House Agriculture Committee. But, again, this period of gains proved short-lived. By 1980, a series of congressional limitations on food stamps along with cuts in federal funding to nonprofit organizations effectively ended the gains of the hunger lobby.

The push by President Ronald Reagan's administration to limit the scope of the federal government represented another challenge to the hunger lobby. Based on his years as governor of California, Reagan and his staff were well aware of the ability of advocates for the poor to harass and challenge efforts to limit welfare. The White House preempted these moves by undercutting federal funding to organizations that opposed the Reagan agenda.

But even as federal support for advocacy was slashed, rates of homelessness in the United States began to rise. Deinstitutionalization of the mentally ill combined with the recession of the early 1980s led to rapidly escalating numbers of homeless Americans, which prompted a growing nationwide mobilization against homelessness. At the forefront of this movement were social movement organizations such as the Association of Community Organizations for Reform Now (ACORN), the National Union for the Homeless, and the Community for Creative Non-Violence (CCNV).

During the 1980s, these activists garnered media coverage through direct action campaigns protesting hunger and homelessness. They built tent city "Reaganvilles" and soup kitchens on the Capitol steps, and they held mass rallies and sit-ins across the country. At the peak of this campaign, CCNV's Mitch Snyder embarked on a fifty-one-day hunger fast, which inspired a made-for-television movie and led to direct negotiations with the White House. This activism, and the media attention it drew, led to congressional hearings on homelessness and to the passage of the McKinney Homeless Assistance Act. Though the ultimate size of allocations for McKinney was fairly small, its adoption in 1987 represented the first expansion in federal social welfare spending since the cuts of 1981. But passage of the McKinney Act also largely diffused efforts to mobilize by and for the homeless.

During the 1990s, antipoverty activists faced a very different set of opportunities and constraints. Poverty rates persisted despite the economic recovery of the late 1980s, leading academics and journalists to write about the lasting implications of a rising economic tide that was failing to lift all Americans out of poverty. Most disconcerting was the persistence of child poverty. Activists thought they had gained a powerful ally in the fight against child poverty in the incoming Clinton administration. The long association of President Bill Clinton and Hillary Rodham Clinton with children's issues and with the Children's Defense Fund offered hope of a renewed federal commitment to alleviating poverty and hunger—particularly among children. But while the children's lobby made several significant gains during the 1990s, particularly in terms of federal support for better child care and family support policies, their principal successes were in holding more serious cuts at bay.

The subsequent conservative realignment of Congress led to the 1996 Personal Responsibility and Work Opportunity Reconciliation Act (PRWORA), which ended the federal entitlement to support for the poorest citizens. The effects of the lifetime caps on eligibility for assistance implemented as part of the Temporary Assistance for Needy Families (TANF) program are still to be determined. Only now is the first wave of recipients coming up against the cap.

The health of the economy through the 1990s resulted in extremely low rates of unemployment, and the PRWORA returned still more of the authority for structuring welfare and assistance programs to individual states. There have been widespread indicators, however—including survey results and record demands on local food banks—showing a rise in the number of families who cannot meet their basic nutritional needs. In addition, many low-income families have been cut off from food assistance as a result of restrictions on the eligibility of legal immigrants.

Currently, there are two frontiers of antipoverty/antihunger activism in this country. There is a strand of "old-style" activism working to mobilize massive public support on behalf of progressive social policy. But probably the dominant strain of antipoverty activism today is based on data-driven policy analysis. Advocates who argue from this base concede that fiscal constraints and tepid political will impose limitations on what government can do, and they argue that there are roles for individuals and communities as well as for governments to play in combating poverty and hunger.

Douglas Imig

See also: Food Banks; Food Stamps; Hunger; Nutrition and Food Assistance

References and Further Reading

Imig, Doug. 1996. *Poverty and Power: The Political Representation of Poor Americans*. Lincoln: University of Nebraska Press.

Melnick, R. Shep. 1994. *Between the Lines*. Washington, DC: Brookings Institution.

Appalachia

Appalachia is commonly identified as an American region of widespread and persistent poverty. Defined by the federal government as consisting of 410 mountainous counties in twelve states from New York to Mississippi, 15.4 percent of its 23 million people were identified as impoverished by federal economic criteria in 1990, in comparison to 13.1 percent of the U.S. population. Poverty rates varied that year from a low of 10.2 percent in Appalachian Georgia to a high of 29 percent in Appalachian Kentucky. With a poverty rate 221 percent higher than the national average, Appalachian Kentucky manifests the region's greatest poverty (Appalachian Regional Commission). Indeed, in 1990, 10 percent of the poorest counties in the United States were in Kentucky, almost all of them in Appalachian Kentucky. Of the twenty-five counties with the lowest per capita income in the United States in 1990, six were in Appalachian Kentucky (Billings and Blee 2000, 4). Although the twelve-state Appalachian region is culturally, economically, and demographically diverse, poverty has commonly been used to define (and stigmatize) the region as a whole since the late nineteenth century, when Appalachia was first identified (wrongly) as a culturally distinct region. Appalachia has been rediscovered (and forgotten) many times since, especially during the Great Depression and in the 1960s. Each of these periods generated competing explanations and remedies for Appalachian poverty, as well as internal movements for social and economic justice.

Appalachia was first imagined to be a coherent region with a homogeneous culture in the last third of the nineteenth century amid the rapid growth of Appalachian railroad building, timber extraction, and coal mining. Alongside the mine operators, land agents, lawyers, and engineers, novelists, home missionaries, educators, and social workers descended upon and narrated the region. Despite rapid industrialization of the countryside, what most fascinated these diverse agents of economic and cultural intervention was what they imagined to be Appalachia's isolation and poverty, factors that seemed to constitute a zone of rural backwardness. Thus imagined, Appalachia served to authenticate, by its exception, the norm of American urban and industrial progress.

Appalachia at that time was commonly described as a strange land and a peculiar people by popular writers, but it was a Kentucky writer, John Fox Jr., who, more than anyone else, popularized the stereotypes of impoverished mountain people in such widely read novels as *The Trail of the Lonesome Pine* (1908) and *The Little Shepherd of Kingdom Come* (1903).

Late-nineteenth- and early-twentieth-century stereotypes portrayed poor Appalachians in both positive and negative terms. Although slaveholding was not uncommon in the mountain South and support for the Union during the American Civil War had been mixed, the postbellum builders of Appalachian schools and settlement houses portrayed mountain people to northern benefactors as being loyal Unionists, the descendants of pioneer America upon whom charity would not be wasted. In the context of middle-class fears about ethnic immigration and despite the region's ethnic and racial diversity, they also pictured Appalachia as a homeland reservoir of worthy, white, Anglo-Saxon Protestants who were in need of educational uplift but who were nonetheless capable of balancing the influx of Catholic, Jewish, and eastern European populations in urban areas. On the other hand, advocates for railroad, mining, and timber industries, as well as apologists for child labor (who portrayed employment in southern cotton mills as being healthier for children than life on impoverished mountain farms), described Appalachian life as degraded and degenerate. Imperialist writings, not unlike those of colonizing regimes in Africa, Asia, or Latin America, depicted mountain people as ignorant and violent obstacles to economic development in order to justify the expropriation of Appalachia's vast timber and mineral resources. In this context, John C. Campbell, secretary of the Southern Highland Division of the Russell Sage Foundation, argued that perhaps no region of the United States was more misunderstood. In 1921, he published the first systematic survey of social conditions in Appalachia, *The Southern Highlander and His Homeland*, and at about the same time, he helped establish the Southern Mountain Workers' Conference, later known as the Council of the Southern Mountains, which became one of the most important early social reform organizations in Appalachia.

Although early Appalachia has been depicted as almost completely isolated geographically and economically, research shows that prior to the twentieth-century development of coal mining, it was more economically diverse and far less isolated than popularly imagined. One study of commerce and industry in antebellum Appalachia, for instance, identified thousands of small manufacturing enterprises, many based on slave labor, that helped link the mountain South to extraregional markets; so, too, did the sale of Appalachian slaves to Deep South planters. Far from being the homespun, egalitarian society of stereotype, nineteenth-century Appalachia was characterized by roughly the same degree of social inequality as the rest of the South. Commercial entrepreneurs (and slave-owning elites in the antebellum period) dominated political life and local government. Unable to generate enough capital on their own to build the transportation infrastructure that modern industrialization required, they became the lawyers, land agents, and junior partners of the outside capitalists who built the railroad, coal, and timber industries that developed the region. Local elites defended the interests of corporate investors, kept taxes on absentee-owned properties low, and used their control of local government to pacify supporters through patronage benefits, including jobs in schools, welfare provisioning, and highway construction and maintenance. They frequently opposed local reform and often co-opted antipoverty programs designed to aid the poor in Appalachia.

Despite the greater prevalence of economic markets than commonly acknowledged, many rural Appalachians lived relatively independently of commerce in the nineteenth century by relying on subsistence farming, open-range livestock grazing, home manufacturing, family labor, and interhousehold exchange to meet their economic needs. Surplus crops and livestock were sold, but farm production was primarily geared to use rather than exchange. For several generations after settlement, these practices provided abundant livelihoods for the Appalachian population, but eventually population increase and the subdivision of farms across generations led to declining farm size and yield, reduced levels of wealth, and increased landlessness and economic hardship. The social origins of Appalachian poverty preceded twentieth-century industrialization, but industrialization nevertheless put severe strain on the farming society by placing additional demands on the land. Farmers sold timber and mineral rights to defend their economic independence, and many turned to employment, at low wage levels, in the region's expanding industries to meet their needs.

Attracted to Appalachia by abundant supplies of high-quality coal and cheap labor, industrialists bought up vast amounts of mountain land, built large mining communities almost overnight in sparsely populated areas, and employed hundreds of thousands of workers in the early decades of the twentieth century. African Americans from the South and immigrants from eastern Europe augmented wage laborers from Appalachia. Employers in the highly competitive coal industry paid low wages (often in scrip redeemable only at company stores), used violent means to resist unionization, restricted civil liberties in tightly controlled company towns, and minimized investments in health and safety. Only the two world wars brought about more American deaths in the twentieth century than did American coal mines, and more nonfatal injuries occurred in U.S. mines than in all the nation's wars from the Revolution through the Vietnam War (Stewart 1996, 99). In the 1920s, mechanization brought the pick-and-shovel era in mining to a close, and 200,000 Appalachian miners lost their jobs.

The nation rediscovered Appalachia in the 1930s when several representations of Appalachian poverty competed for authority. With national policy focused on the threat of underconsumption, the U.S. Department of Agriculture issued the first federally sponsored survey of economic conditions in Appalachia. It described the region as the largest zone of noncommercial ("unproductive") agriculture in the United States and urged the emigration of Appalachia's "underemployed" rural population. At the same time, new disciplinary regimes of economic development, such as the Tennessee Valley Authority (TVA), were established. The TVA flooded mountain farms and whole communities to provide cheap power for southern economic development and forced numerous mountain farmers into the waged workforce. It was also then that the iconic image of the lazy "hillbilly" was standardized in national cartoons. The hillbilly's reputed disregard for economic success expressed a mixture of dread and envy during this time of acute national crisis and served both to call attention to and explain Appalachian poverty.

Other Depression-era reformers advanced alternative representations. Women active in the settlement house movement, for instance, created the Southern Highland Handicraft Guild to preserve their preferred versions of "mountain culture" and to provide economic relief by organizing and marketing women's homemade products. The guild rationalized craft production by supplying standardized materials and design patterns (sometimes of European origin) for commodities that, despite their contrived nature, were marketed as authentic mountain crafts. This approach was opposed by other reformers in the Women's Bureau of the U.S. Department of Labor who attempted to define women artisans as exploited, full-time, low-wage laborers, rather than part-time domestic workers, and to regulate their wages and working conditions (Becker 1998).

Finally, some members of the American Left

represented Appalachia during the Depression as a symbol of capitalist exploitation and imminent proletarian revolution. In this, they were inspired by the mass insurgency of 10,000 armed coal miners who had marched from Charleston, West Virginia, in the 1920s to overthrow the thug-dominated government of Logan County, and by the Communist-led strike of blacklisted miners in Harlan County, Kentucky, in the 1930s. For many on the Left, such events lent credence to the picture of Appalachia as a zone of spontaneous class militancy. Most notably, novelist Theodore Dreiser and his National Committee for the Defense of Political Prisoners took Kentucky mountain folksinger Aunt Molly Jackson to New York City to represent in song Appalachian miners' plight, poverty, and determination.

By the 1960s, the heroic era of class conflict in Appalachia seemingly had passed. Federal laws passed during the New Deal that guaranteed workers' rights to organize aided the unionization of the Appalachian coalfields. The demand for coal shrank after World War II, however, as other fuels began to replace coal use in railroads and home heating. The now-powerful United Mine Workers of America supported further mechanization of the coal industry and the elimination of marginal firms by allying with large producers organized as the Bituminous Coal Operators Association. It exchanged industry-wide contracts and no-strike clauses in the 1950s and 1960s for tonnage royalties used to create pension funds for retired miners and much-needed health care benefits for both working and retired miners and their families (including a chain of hospitals). But mechanization caused many Appalachian miners to lose their jobs and pushed others into low-wage, nonunion mines. Mechanization, along with further agricultural decline, led to the permanent or temporary migration of as many as 7 million people from Appalachia in the three decades after World War II (Philliber 1981). Although many found new jobs in the industrial cities of the Midwest, others ended up living in slum neighborhoods in cities like Chicago, Cincinnati, and Cleveland, where they were stigmatized as "hillbillies" or Appalachian "poor whites" and otherwise experienced prejudice and discrimination. In response, some of these neighborhoods saw the emergence of urban Appalachian identity centers, set up to provide needed social services to poor migrants and to nurture self-respect and group identity.

Mother and child in Page County, Virginia. Images like this were used to stir public sympathy for poor people in Appalachia during the early 1960s, in the years leading up to President Lyndon B. Johnson's declaration of war on poverty. (Wally McNamee/Corbis)

By 1960, it was not uncommon to find counties in West Virginia and Kentucky with federally defined poverty rates over 50 percent. The publication of Michael Harrington's *Other America* (1962) and Harry Caudill's *Night Comes to the*

Cumberlands (1963), John F. Kennedy's widely televised battle for the Democratic presidential nomination in West Virginia in 1959, Kennedy's 1963 appointment of a presidential commission on Appalachian poverty, and President Lyndon B. Johnson's War on Poverty (announced by the president in 1964 from the home of an impoverished Appalachian Kentucky family)—each brought Appalachian poverty to national attention. Sociologists portrayed Appalachia as a regionwide culture of poverty, while mainstream economists—blind to the very factors that had led to crisis—described Appalachia as a region apart that lacked integration with the wider economy. A new regime of economic development, the Appalachian Regional Commission, promised to integrate Appalachia into the national free-enterprise system by investing in highways, sewers, industrial parks, urban growth centers, and training, while the Office of Economic Opportunity sought to overcome the hypothetical alienation of a culture of poverty in Appalachia by encouraging community action by the poor.

When those who tried to advance community action ran up against the obdurate resistance of established power structures, however, they began to describe Appalachia as the third world of the United States. Rather than a culture of poverty, Appalachia was a colony. Its connection to, rather than isolation from, corporate capitalism came to be viewed as the source of Appalachian poverty. Although scholars no longer accept internal colonialism as a useful way of thinking about Appalachian poverty, the trope of Appalachia as a colony helped mobilize movements for social and economic justice in Appalachia that continue today, making it one of the most activist regions in the United States. These movements include efforts to defend welfare rights, democratize communities, reform and strengthen unions, improve occupational health and safety, defend the environment, tax absentee land and mineral owners more equitably, pay living wages, and support sustainable, nonexploitative forms of economic development.

Dwight B. Billings

See also: Area Redevelopment Act; Community Development; Great Depression and New Deal; Highlander; *Night Comes to the Cumberlands; The Other America;* Poverty Research; Rural Poverty; Tennessee Valley Authority; War on Poverty

References and Further Reading

Appalachian Regional Commission. "County Economic Status in Appalachia." http://www.arc.gov/images/programs/distress/04statmap2.pdf.

Becker, Jane. 1998. *Selling Tradition: Appalachia and the Construction of an American Folk, 1930–1940*. Chapel Hill: University of North Carolina Press.

Billings, Dwight B., and Kathleen M. Blee. 2000. *The Road to Poverty: The Making of Wealth and Hardship in Appalachia*. New York: Cambridge University Press.

Eller, Ronald D. 1982. *Miners, Millhands, and Mountaineers: Industrialization of the Appalachian South, 1880–1930*. Knoxville: University of Tennessee Press.

Fisher, Stephen L., ed. 1993. *Fighting Back in Appalachia: Traditions of Resistance and Change*. Philadelphia: Temple University Press.

Halperin, Rhoda. 1994. *The Livelihood of Kin: Making Ends Meet "the Kentucky Way."* Austin: University of Texas Press.

Philliber, William W. 1981. *Appalachian Migrants in Urban America: Cultural Conflict or Ethnic Group Formation?* New York: Praeger.

Shapiro, Henry. 1978. *Appalachia on Our Minds: The Southern Mountains and Mountaineers in American Consciousness, 1870–1920*. Chapel Hill: University of North Carolina Press.

Stewart, Kathleen. 1996. *A Space on the Side of the Road: Cultural Poetics in an "Other" America*. Princeton: Princeton University Press.

Applied Research Center

The Applied Research Center (ARC) is devoted to investigative research on public policy. Its particular and distinctive mission is to develop the information and analyses that support grassroots organizations working to reduce racial and economic injustice.

ARC was founded in 1980 under the leadership of Gary Delgado, who had earlier helped establish the Center for Third World Organizing (CTWO), an organization that itself grew out of the welfare rights movement. A recent ARC publication captures the orientation of the Center at its founding: "Information is not neutral; like most commodities in the public arena, research benefits certain interests. Most of the applied research conducted by institutions such as the Stanford Research Institute, the Brookings Institution, and most universities directly services public and private bureaucracies. Independent grassroots organizations have no comparable analytical arm that would allow for proactive policy development" (Applied Research Center 2003, 2).

Based in Oakland, California, ARC now has a permanent staff of about twenty and recently opened branch offices in Chicago and New York. Consistent with its distinctive mission, ARC has ongoing working relationships with more than 100 grassroots, advocacy, and policy groups across the country. It also continues to work in partnership with CTWO. Together, they helped convene and staff a fledgling network of welfare rights groups known as Grassroots Organizing for Welfare Leadership (GROWL).

ARC is proudest of its efforts in the area of race. It works to keep race issues at the forefront of community organizing efforts. In 2000, it established the Welfare Advocacy and Research Project, which, in cooperation with grassroots welfare recipient groups, collected data documenting racial, gender, and language discrimination in welfare policy. The resulting report, *Cruel and Unusual: How Welfare "Reform" Punishes Poor People*, circulates widely among advocacy and welfare recipient groups.

The organization's other publications include *Beyond the Politics of Place; Sex, Lies, and Politics; Confronting the New Racisms;* and *From Poverty to Punishment*. The quarterly magazine launched by ARC and CTWO in 1998, *Color Lines*, covers racial issues in a wide range of policy areas and also regularly reports on ongoing community organizing efforts. The magazine has already received a number of journalism awards, and its readership has climbed to 30,000.

Frances Fox Piven

See also: Community Organizing; Poverty Research; Welfare Rights Movement

References and Further Reading

Applied Research Center. 2003. *Annual Report*.

Bobo, Kimberly, Jackie Kendall, and Steve Max. 2001. *Organizing for Social Change: Midwest Academy Manual for Activists*. Santa Ana, CA: Seven Locks Press.

Sen, Rinku. 2003. *Stir It Up: Lessons on Community Organizing and Advocacy*. San Francisco: Jossey-Bass.

Arab Americans

Arab Americans are Americans whose ancestral heritage derives from the Arabic-speaking cultures of the Middle East and North Africa. The Arab American community in the United States is estimated at 1 million to 3 million individuals (Arab American Institute 2000). Arab immigration to the United States is divided into three waves: a first wave, roughly toward the latter part of the nineteenth century; a second wave, from World War I to the mid-1960s; and a third wave, after the 1967 Arab-Israeli War. Diverse in religion (Christian and Muslim), economic class, and political affiliation, Arab Americans struggle against stereotypes that link them to terrorism and obscure their long history in the United States.

Most of the immigrants in the first wave of migration were Christian Syrians and Lebanese, who came in response to economic opportunity rather than political discrimination. Ninety percent of these immigrants worked, at least briefly, as traveling peddlers, with women and children participating as both peddlers and manufacturers of products (Naff 1983, 15). Like their southern European counterparts, they faced hostility, including from Protestant and Catholic institutions that did not recognize their Eastern Rite or Orthodox rituals and customs. But their Christianity also assisted their assimilation, as did an ethnic network that both employed the new migrants as peddlers and supported them with services, products to sell, and settlements.

Second-wave immigrants fled to the United States in response to the political turmoil caused by decolonization in the Middle East, as well as for education and postwar economic opportunities. Muslims began to join Christian immigrants in this period. The first substantial emigration of professionals also arrived, many after completing higher education in their own countries or Europe. Chain migration and expanding industrial opportunities continued to bring in working-class immigrants, including many who worked in the automobile plants in and around Detroit.

Third-wave immigrants came in response to the Arab-Israeli conflict and from a region undergoing a rebirth of nationalism and pan-Arab sentiment. The 1967 Arab-Israeli War, the Lebanese civil war in the 1970s, and the 1982 Israeli invasion of southern Lebanon all created streams of migrants. Although valuing the freedoms and economic opportunities of their new country, many of these immigrants saw America's role in their homelands as imperialist and anti-Arab, and their skepticism was strengthened by the political ferment and resurgence of ethnic identification in the 1960s and 1970s in the United States. Muslim migration also began to outpace Christian migration in this period, leading to the establishment of mosques and community centers, Islamic parochial schools, and Muslim associations.

Arab Americans in the United States face a variety of economic and social conditions. Among the most impoverished are Iraqi Sh'ia refugees who fled after the 1991 Gulf War; most had very little education before leaving Iraq and had lived in camps in Saudi Arabia for years before resettlement. At the other end of the income scale are doctors, engineers, and businessmen; about 36 percent of Arab Americans, compared to 18 percent of Americans nationwide, have bachelor's or graduate degrees (U.S. Census Bureau 1994, 1998). The largest communities of Arab Americans nationwide live in four metropolitan areas: Los Angeles, Detroit, New York, and Washington, D.C.

Arab American identities constantly undergo reexamination. Early migrants identified with their religious rite (such as Melkite or Maronite) or their nationality rather than as "Arab." A series of court cases in the early twentieth century debated whether Arabs should be considered "white," and thus eligible for citizenship, or "Asiatic," and thus ineligible (Samhain 1999). However, prejudice against Arabs and self-identification as Arab American became more salient at the end of the twentieth century. The Gulf War and consequent sanctions against Iraq, continuing conflict between Israelis and Palestinians, the attacks of September 11, 2001, and the war to oust Saddam Hussein made Arab Americans more visible to themselves and to others. Some leaders responded by calling on Arab Americans to put aside regional, national, and sectarian identifications in favor of the pan-ethnic "Arab American" label. Groups like the Arab American Institute (AAI) and the American Arab Anti-Discrimination Committee (ADC) worked to have "Arab" listed as an official race on the U.S. census. These groups have also provided information to political leaders and advocates, filed lawsuits, and sponsored many activities to create more awareness of the Arab American community.

Other leaders have promoted "Muslim American" as an identity that could unite East Asian, South Asian, African, and Arab Americans. The post-1965 period saw increasing waves of Muslim migration from all over the world, and many Islamic institutions, especially those serving more-settled immigrants and their children, acquired a pan-ethnic character in response. Prominent Muslim-American groups, including the Center for American-Islamic Relations (CAIR), the Islamic Society of North America (ISNA) and the Muslim Student Association (MSA), have taken active roles in providing support and establishing institutions for Muslims and in fighting discrimination against Islam and its practices. The American-born children of the second and third waves of Arab migration are also shaping these developments, as they rediscover, adopt, and adapt religious practices that their parents discarded or never had at all.

Ann Chih Lin

See also: Americanization Movement; Asian Americans; Catholic Church; Citizenship; Immigrants and Immigration; Immigration Policy; Islam; Protestant Denominations; Racism

References and Further Reading

Abraham, Nabeel, and Andrew Shryock. 2000. *Arab Detroit: From Margin to Mainstream*. Detroit, MI: Wayne State University Press.

Arab American Institute. 2000. *Demographics*. http://www.aaiusa.org/demographics.htm.

Aswad, Barbara, and Barbara Bilge. 1996. *Family and Gender among American Muslims*. Philadelphia: Temple University Press.

Haddad, Yvonne, and John L. Esposito, eds. 1998. *Muslims on the Americanization Path?* Atlanta: Scholars Press.

Naff, Alixa. 1983. "Arabs in America: A Historical Overview." In *Arabs in the New World: Studies on Arab American Communities*, ed. Sameer Y. Abraham and Nabeel Abraham. Detroit: Wayne State University, Center for Urban Studies.

Samhain, Helen Hateb. 1999. "Not Quite White: Race Classification and the Arab-American Experience." In *Arabs in America*, ed. Michael W. Suleiman, 209–226. Philadelphia: Temple University Press.

U.S. Census Bureau. 1994. *1990 Census of Population: Education in the United States*. Washington, DC: GPO.

U.S. Census Bureau. 1998. "Selected Characteristics for Persons of Arab Ancestry, 1990." http://www.census.gov/population/socdemo/ancestry/Arab.txt.

Area Redevelopment Act

The Area Redevelopment Act of 1961 established a program of geographically targeted federal grants and loans aimed at relieving unemployment and industrial stagnation in economically distressed urban and rural areas. Although short-lived, the program was an early and important component of the Kennedy administration's domestic economic strategy, and its geographic targeting of resources to needy cities and regions set a precedent for later "place-based" federal economic development programs. The act was also notable in that federal support of private capital investment was central to the program, making it a departure from earlier federal economic development strategies that had focused solely on public works projects. Between 1961 and 1964, the Area Redevelopment Administration (ARA) established by this act provided about $300 million to "labor surplus" communities through business loans ($170 million), public facility improvements ($90 million), and a smaller amount of technical assistance and workforce training (Patterson 1994, 127). In marked contrast to many of the antipoverty programs that followed it, the ARA focused on rebuilding economic and physical infrastructure rather than improving worker skills and education. The program did not seek to redress the economic discrimination faced by particular groups of *people*, such as racial minorities, but instead focused on distressed *places* that had been left behind by the industrial shifts and technological advances of the postwar period.

Although the program is often identified with President Kennedy's efforts to improve Appalachia, it had its origins in congressional concerns about Midwestern and northeastern rural areas particularly hard-hit by the economic contraction of heavy industry and mining. The most important actor in the design and creation of the area redevelopment program was Illinois Democratic Senator Paul H. Douglas, who first proposed area redevelopment legislation in 1955. The proposal reflected Douglas's and other Rust Belt–area legislators' worries that parts of their region were bypassed by the postwar economic boom, as well as their growing frustration at the disproportionate regional allocation of federal defense spending to Sunbelt states like California. This legislation and subsequent measures introduced by Douglas and others during the late 1950s and early 1960s failed due to partisan disagreements about the scope and administration of such a program. Despite voicing support for geographically targeted measures to reduce unemployment and poverty, President Eisenhower vetoed area redevelopment legislation twice, in 1958 and in 1960.

The repeated failure of area redevelopment bills to become law, combined with a short recession that had increased the number and visibility of high-unemployment "labor surplus" areas, made area redevelopment a high-profile political issue in the 1960 presidential campaign. Democratic nominee John F. Kennedy seized upon this issue and drew attention to the plight of poor communities and regions through campaign events and speeches. The importance of West Virginia to Kennedy's electoral prospects helped to shift the emphasis of his campaign rhetoric toward the economic problems of Appalachia, and through campaign events and speeches Kennedy made the economic distress of this region a national political concern. After his election, Kennedy created a task force on high-unemployment areas and appointed Douglas as its chair. The task force submitted a report to the President in January 1961 recommending that a multibillion-dollar program for area redevelopment be the centerpiece of Kennedy's national unemployment-fighting strategy. In the subsequent Congress, Douglas's area redevelopment bill passed quickly and was signed into law by Kennedy in May 1961.

Despite its high political visibility as the first major product of the President's "New Frontier" domestic agenda, the ARA had difficulties realizing its grand objectives from the start. In order to win broad congressional support for the program, eligibility had been extended to a large number of communities, all of which had to share in a relatively small amount of funding. Under these criteria, the ARA designated nearly 900 urban and rural counties as eligible for assistance; these areas contained more than one-sixth of the U.S. population (Levitan 1964, 64). The lingering national recession meant that a large number of areas were experiencing high rates of blue-collar unemployment, conditions that increased interregional competition for firms and jobs and further disadvantaged the highly distressed areas targeted by the ARA. In addition, rather than becoming the independent agency that its original advocates had envisioned, the ARA became a small subagency of Commerce. As such, the ARA had limited physical space and staffing capacity, and its political effectiveness became hobbled by its location within an inattentive bureaucracy.

The ARA thus had limited resources with which to implement a broad and ambitious mandate to revitalize deeply and chronically poor communities. Lacking both a powerful central administration and a comprehensive and coherent field structure, the program rapidly devolved into "pork-barrel" spending patterns that channeled support in response to political pressure rather than pure economic need. Congress soon realized that the ARA was not working as intended, and congressional debate reopened on how best to help depressed areas. Rather than reauthorizing the ARA upon the act's expiration in 1965, Congress replaced it with more broadly based economic assistance legislation, the Public Works and Economic Development Act (PWEDA). The new program offered a similar combination of public facilities grants and private-sector loans, but it emphasized multicounty and regional economic development efforts rather than the fragmented single-county revitalization schemes funded by the ARA.

Margaret Pugh O'Mara

See also: Community Development; Globalization and Deindustrialization; Rural Poverty; Urban Poverty; War on Poverty

References and Further Reading

Dillon, Conley H. 1964. *The Area Redevelopment Administration: New Patterns in Developmental Administration*. College Park: University of Maryland Press.

Levitan, Sar A. 1964. *Federal Aid to Depressed Areas: An Evaluation of the Area Redevelopment Administration*. Baltimore: Johns Hopkins University Press.

Patterson, James T. 1994. *America's Struggle against Poverty, 1900–1994*. Cambridge, MA: Harvard University Press.

Weir, Margaret. 1992. *Politics and Jobs: The Boundaries of Employment Policy in the United States*. Princeton: Princeton University Press.

Asian Americans

The history of Asian American poverty is inseparable from the history of immigration. Both the timing and context of Asian immigration to the United States and the response of settled Americans to Asian immigrants have conditioned economic opportunities and economic security. Racism and nativism generated discrimination against Asian Americans, while differences of language and culture impaired Asian immigrants' access to many educational opportunities. As a result, many Asian immigrants have been relegated to exploitative low-wage jobs. Poverty among Asian Americans has also been shaped by changing public policies toward immigrants and immigration: for example, immigration and naturalization policy, which restricted Asian migration to the United States and prohibited their naturalization during the first half of the twentieth century; refugee policy, which opened doors to migrants from Asian Communist countries during the second half of the twentieth century; and current U.S. social welfare policies that restrict immigrant participation in social programs.

From the onset of racially restrictive immigration laws in the 1880s, Asians were singled out as "undesirable," and when not excluded altogether, they were barred from citizenship and, in some states, denied access to education, certain categories of jobs, basic legal protections, and property rights. These laws were principally aimed at Chinese and Japanese immigrants—until recent decades the largest proportion of Asian immigrants—and justified through racist ideas about their "devious" or "disloyal" character. The Immigration Reform Act of 1965 finally ended racially biased quotas and instituted a preference for family reunification in immigration, which in turn dramatically increased the absolute and relative numbers coming from Asia. In the decade of the 1950s, 153,000 Asians made up only 6 percent of the incoming immigrants, but 1.59 million Asians made up 35 percent of the incoming immigrants of the 1970s. Refugees augmented the inflow, pushing up the number of incoming Asians to 2.74 million in the 1980s, a level that was maintained through the 1990s. With renewed large-scale immigration, the Asian American population grew from less than a million in 1960 to nearly 12 million in 2000. The growth was accompanied by a shift in composition by nativity. Over two out of three Asian Americans in 1960 were born in the United States, and the proportion fell to less than one out of three in 1990. Although that proportion has gone up slightly, immigrants still make up a large majority of Asian Americans (Ong and Leung 2003).

Post-1965 Asian immigrants are incredibly diverse in terms of socioeconomic background. The largest segment of the population is composed of those who entered the United States through family reunification, and the group that initially benefited the most had family members in the United States prior to 1965. This group included individuals with considerable human capital and individuals with very limited marketable skills. Another important segment is made up of those who entered through occupational preferences and their families. Occupational preferences are designed to attract workers with technical skills, high educational attainment, and exceptional talent. This selective screening has contributed to a remarkable expansion of the middle and professional classes among Asian Americans. Finally, there are the political refugees, made up primarily of those who fled Southeast Asia after the end of the Vietnam War. A disproportionately high number of this group have very limited formal education and few marketable skills. The net result of this mix of immigrants is a population that is overrepresented at both the top and bottom end of the labor market.

The bimodal distribution has altered the poverty rate for Asian Americans relative to the rate for non-Hispanic whites. In 1960, the two rates were comparable, slightly under 18 percent. Economic growth in the 1960s lowered the rate for both groups (to about 10 percent for non-Hispanic whites and 11 percent for Asian Americans in 1970), but since then, the two groups have gone in different directions. By 1990, there was a noticeable disparity: The poverty rate was over 14 percent for Asian Americans and under 9 percent for non-Hispanic whites. The technology-driven business boom of the 1990s has narrowed the gap only slightly. By the latter part of the decade, the average poverty rate for Asian Americans was 12.6 percent, more than 4 percentage points higher than the rate for non-Hispanic whites (Ong and McConville 2004).

Variations in immigration patterns produce ethnic differences in the level of poverty. Japanese Americans are the least affected by contemporary immigration, and two out of three Japanese Americans are at least second generation. As a well-established and highly assimilated group, they have a low poverty rate, only 10 percent in 2000, half the rate for all Asian Americans. The other Asian ethnic populations are all predominantly immigrant groups, but despite this commonality, their poverty rates vary tremendously. Filipinos and Asian Indians have benefited the most from selective occupational migration, and their poverty rates are lower than average (6 percent and 10 percent in 2000, respectively). At the other end are the Southeast Asian refugees. Although the population includes the pre-1975 elite from that region of the world, the typical person has less than a high school education, does not speak English, and has limited work experience relevant to an advanced economy. The lack of human capital translates into high levels of poverty: 16 percent for Vietnamese, 29 percent for Cambodians, and 29 percent for Hmongs (U.S. Census Bureau 2000).

Asian American poverty is concentrated in two types of inner-city enclaves. The first is revitalized Chinatowns, which have been transformed by immigration into working-poor neighborhoods. The highly visible part of the enclave economy is based on tourism, but the hidden half is based on sweatshops, especially in the garment industry. Regardless of sector, the jobs pay low wages and offer few benefits, and many of the working poor are only a paycheck away from falling into poverty. Chinatowns also have a sizable low-income elderly population, many of whom do not have pensions or Social Security.

The second type of enclave is communities that were established since the mid-1970s. Some of these neighborhoods, such as southern California's Little Saigon, are not low-income neighborhoods. Others, such as New Phnom Penh, in Long Beach, California, are extremely economically depressed. Adults in well over a third of the households are jobless, and their main source of income is welfare benefits. The reliance on public assistance is due to both a lack of marketable skills and a failure of refugee policy and programs to integrate this group into the economic mainstream. Welfare reform of the late 1990s is adding to the economic problems of these communities and their residents. The 1996 Personal Responsibility and Work Opportunity Reconciliation Act erects high new hurdles to participation by noncitizen immigrants in social programs from welfare to food stamps to Medicaid. Without access to the social safety net, poverty can be devastating for Asian immigrants.

Unfortunately, Asian American poverty has not received adequate attention. Because of the enormous ethnic diversity among Asian Americans, the underlying causes and the barriers to achieving economic self-sufficiency are complex and numerous. Each ethnic population in poverty has unique and distinct programmatic needs, but designing and implementing appropriate services are difficult because each group is relatively small. The diverse needs and a lack of economies of scale prevent Asian Americans from receiving culturally and linguistically appropriate help. Their small numbers place the groups in a weak political position, which makes it difficult for them to garner a fair share of the available resources. Equally important, poor Asian Americans are overlooked because the prevailing stereotype is one of high educational and occupational achievement. One cannot and should not deny the accomplishments of Asian Americans, but, tragically, that success is masking the economic hardships of 1 million Asian Americans.

Paul Ong

See also: Aid to Families with Dependent Children (ADC/AFDC); Asian Law Caucus/Asian Law Alliance; Immigrants and Immigration; Immigration Policy; Refugee Policy; Sweatshop; Welfare Policy/Welfare Reform; "Working Poor"

References and Further Reading

Hing, Bill Ong. 1994. *The Making and Remaking of the Asian American Community through Immigration Policy, 1860–1980*. Stanford, CA: Stanford University Press.

Ong, Paul M., Dennise Arguelles, Susan Castro, Bruce Chow, Chanchanit Hirunpidok, Tarry Hum, Winnie Louie, Erich Nakano, and Roderick Ramos. 1999. *Beyond Asian American Poverty: Community Economic Development Policies and Strategies*. Los Angeles: Asian Pacific American Public Policy Institute, LEAP. Originally published 1993.

Ong, Paul M., and Loh-Sze Leung. 2003. "Asian Pacific American Demographics: Past, Present, and Future." In *The New Face of Asian Pacific America*, ed. Eric Lai and Dennie Arguelles, 7–16. Los Angeles: AsianWeek and UCLA American Studies Center.

Ong, Paul M., and Shannon McConville. 2004. "The Trajectory of Poor Neighborhoods in Los Angeles." In *California Policy Options 2004*, ed. Daniel J. B. Mitchell. Los Angeles: UCLA School of Public Policy.

U.S. Census Bureau. 2000. Summary File 3 for 2000 Census. Washington, DC: GPO.

Zhou, Min, and James V. Gatewood, eds. 2000. *Contemporary Asian America: A Multidisciplinary Reader*. New York: New York University Press.

Asian Law Caucus/ Asian Law Alliance

The Asian Law Caucus and the Asian Law Alliance are nonprofit, community-based legal organizations that focus on the economic needs, legal services, and civil rights of low-income Asian Pacific Americans (APAs). These law offices work to fight against discrimination and for the empowerment of underrepresented Asian Pacific Americans, of whom immigrants and refugees make up the vast majority. Both organizations incorporate educational programs and community organizing with litigation and policy advocacy.

Founded in 1972, the Asian Law Caucus (ALC) is the first and oldest organization of its kind. First located in Oakland, California, the ALC started as a small storefront operation, staffed largely by volunteers. It then moved to Market Street in San Francisco and now operates with a staff of more than twenty persons and a budget of nearly $1 million. Influenced by the civil rights, Asian American, and other social movements, the ALC founders were motivated to create a community law office for those who have historically had little or no access to adequate legal services or remedies for discriminatory practices. Dale Minami, the cofounder and first managing attorney of the ALC, wrote in 1975, "We wanted to provide free and low-cost legal services for Asian Americans, initiate broad suits attacking institutional racism, forge close ties with community groups, participate in community struggles, . . . and create a model to encourage others to join in community law practice" (Asian Law Caucus 1997).

Since its inception, the ALC has focused on an extensive range of issues that have had widespread impact. Most notable was the critical ALC participation in overturning the wartime convictions for curfew violations imposed against Japanese Americans in *Korematsu v. United States* ([584 F. Supp. 1406]; 1984 U.S. Dist. 1984). This legal victory influenced the passage of the Civil Liberties Act of 1988, resulting in the redress and reparations for Japanese Americans interned during World War II. The ALC won its earliest victory in *Chann v. Scott* (1972), a class-action lawsuit against the San Francisco Police Department for practicing racially discriminatory dragnet arrests of Chinatown youths. In 1972, the ALC successfully settled the first major class-action lawsuit for employment discrimination against Asian Americans in the case of *Salazar v. Blue Shield. Ha, et al. v. T & W Fashions* (1983) was a significant victory, winning a settlement against a major garment contractor and manufacturer, and in 1993, *Chen, et al. v. Ocean Garment Manufacturing, et al.* was the first case to hold the manufacturer liable for labor violations committed by a subcontractor. The ALC continues to use litigation, public education, and organizing to reform the garment industry, and it is a leading member of Sweatshop Watch, a California-wide coalition committed to the elimination of sweatshop conditions in the garment industry.

The Asian Law Alliance (ALA), inspired and modeled after the ALC, was formally established in 1977 to provide legal services to the growing APA community of Santa Clara County of California. Since its beginning, the ALA has assisted tens of thousands of people in obtaining decent housing, justice in the immigration process, and access to basic human and legal rights. Providing legal services particularly for those who are limited in English and who cannot afford legal fees, the ALA provides free or low-cost services in APA languages and conducts extensive outreach and education about basic legal rights.

Campaigns engaged by the ALA have included participation in the redress campaign for Japanese Americans incarcerated during World War II, a joint lawsuit to preserve multilingual services in the Santa Clara County Department of Social Services, assistance with the larger Santa Clara County campaign to oppose discriminatory immigration legislation, and efforts within various Asian language groups to address the problem of domestic violence within APA families.

Housing discrimination has remained a central focus for the ALC and the ALA. The ALC joined the legal defense team in the tenant battle against the eviction of mostly low-income elderly Filipinos from the International Hotel in San Francisco's Chinatown, a landmark struggle of the 1970s for housing rights. In the 1990s, the ALC successfully litigated cases with the San Francisco Housing Authority to remedy unsafe and violent conditions for Asian residents, and in March 2000, the ALC was instrumental in preventing the eviction of residents from a residential hotel on Clay Street in San Francisco's Chinatown.

The ALA has addressed affordable housing and housing discrimination issues in Silicon Valley, where a highly exploited immigrant labor pool must find housing in a high-cost area. With the Fair Housing Consortium and the San Jose Residents for Rent Relief, the ALA has been essential in the formation of tenant associations and has mounted community education classes. In collaboration with other legal organizations, the ALA represented low-income residents in a lawsuit filed against their landlord after they had endured years of nearly uninhabitable living conditions.

A persistent challenge for immigrants has been gaining fair access to welfare benefits, particularly after the 1996 welfare reform complicated requirements for noncitizens. From 1979 to 1981, hundreds of elderly Asian immigrants were prevented by the Immigration and Naturalization Service from reentering the United States after short visits abroad because they received Supplemental Security Income (SSI) and were subject to Public Charge provisions. Their passports and green cards were confiscated because they had received public assistance. The ALC successfully defended many of these immigrants, preserving their immigration status and allowing them to remain on SSI. In 1994, California passed the Save-Our-State initiative, or Proposition 187, which required schools, medical clinics, and public social service providers to deny education and services to undocumented persons. The ALC joined the legal team in *Gregoria T. v. Wilson*, which succeeded in halting implementation of Proposition 187. Both the ALC and the ALA were central to the community organizing efforts that challenged the constitutionality of Proposition 187, as well as to the legal effort.

The 1996 Personal Responsibility and Work Opportunity Reconciliation Act (PRWORA) has had far-reaching consequences for the APA immigrants and refugees living in poverty. The change in eligibility requirements for legal permanent residents resulted in the loss of SSI and food stamps for thousands of legal permanent residents. The ALC, the ALA, and countless other community-based organizations responded to widespread panic and confusion through massive public education campaigns, naturalization drives, and state and local organizing efforts to challenge anti-immigrant provisions.

In addition to assisting individual immigrants reclaim lost benefits, both the ALC and the ALA, along with other community organizations, provided language- and culture-sensitive naturalization programs to encourage preparation for the citizenship test. Also, recognizing that citizenship is the one sure way for immigrants to regain eligibility for SSI and food stamps, staff attorneys and community volunteers worked directly with thousands of immigrants to navigate circumstances that could jeopardize their naturalization.

Immediately following the implementation of food stamp cuts for most immigrants, the ALC and other attorneys filed over 3,500 appeals on behalf of Hmong immigrants who had participated in U.S. military efforts in Laos during the war in Southeast Asia but who were excluded from veteran status due to imprecise wording of the 1996 welfare law. As a result of the flood of cases and a simultaneous visibility campaign, the Agricultural Research Act of 1998 restored food stamps to certain immigrant children, as well as to certain elderly and disabled immigrants. It also allowed members of the Hmong and other highland Laos tribes and their spouses, widows, and children to qualify.

To address the effects of the 1996 welfare reform on immigrants and refugees at the national level, the ALC, along with the National Asian Pacific American Legal Consortium (of which the ALC is a founding member) submitted an amicus brief in *Sinelnikov v. Shalala*, Seventh Circuit (189 F.3d 598 1999 U.S. App), a case that challenged the constitutionality of the 1996 immigrant provisions. Immigrant access to food stamps and other social assistance remains a top priority for ALC and ALA, especially as hunger in immigrant families rises under the impact of the harsh exclusions of 1996 legislation.

Lynn H. Fujiwara

See also: Asian Americans; Food Stamps; Immigrants and Immigration; Immigration Policy; Supplemental Security Income; Sweatshop; Welfare Policy/Welfare Reform

References and Further Reading

Asian Law Alliance. 2001. "Working for Justice,

Dignity, and Equality." http://www.asianlawalliance-ala.org/. July 14.
Asian Law Caucus. 1997. *25 Years in Defense of Civil Rights*. 25th Anniversary Program, San Francisco, California, April 26.
Asian Law Caucus. "In Defense of Civil Rights." http://www.asianlawcaucus.org/. July 14.
Fujiwara, Lynn. 1999. "Sanctioning Immigrants: Asian Immigrant and Refugee Women and the Racial Politics of Welfare Reform." Ph.D. diss., University of California, Santa Cruz.
Kochiyama, Eddie. 1997. "After 25 Years, Asian Law Caucus Still Serves the People." *Rafu Shimpo*, April 19.

Association of Community Organizations for Reform Now (ACORN)

The Association of Community Organizations for Reform Now (ACORN) is one of the country's largest, best-organized, and most-effective grassroots antipoverty organizations. Founded in 1970 as a community organizing project of the Little Rock, Arkansas, chapter of the National Welfare Rights Organization, ACORN has since spawned chapters in fifty-five cities in twenty-four states. ACORN has pioneered grassroots struggles in almost every aspect of antipoverty work, including working for living-wage legislation, workfare workers' rights, public housing tenant unions, and against predatory lending practices by banks and other lenders. ACORN has also created innovative programs to protect and develop low-income housing, has led campaigns against the privatization of public schools, and has sponsored its own public schools. ACORN has helped organize service employee unions and has generated a voter-registration organization and alternative progressive political parties. Chapters conduct multiple, simultaneous campaigns, relying on a committed senior staff, an energetic junior staff of organizers, and grassroots leaders drawn from their membership (150,000 households nationwide). ACORN chapters rely on members' dues for 50–80 percent of their funding, with the balance coming from private foundations (ACORN 2004).

ACORN emphasizes direct action and membership building. It seeks to maintain a strong base of dues-paying members, from which it draws leaders and foot-soldiers for its many campaigns, organizing staff, and governance for the organization. Though guided by national staff and by an elected national board, ACORN chapters are largely autonomous. At the local level, member-leaders and staff steer the organization. Regular meetings keep leaders and staff closely accountable and responsive to active members, even as they educate the members and shape their views on the issues at hand.

Though based loosely on Saul Alinsky's principles of community organizing, ACORN does not organize large coalitions of existing neighborhood institutions. Rather, it builds its own membership. ACORN has often found it difficult to balance the compromises of coalition work with the more deliberative decision-making processes required of membership-based organizations. Stubborn about steering agendas to reflect its members' wishes, it has gained a reputation among other organizations for being a difficult and turf-oriented coalition partner. In spite of these tensions, ACORN has worked in coalitions on nearly every one of its major campaigns for nearly two decades.

ACORN campaigns build their power by focusing on often-divisive issues, such as institutionalized racism in public education or banking, that nevertheless unite their mainly low-income members. ACORN's direct action tactics are backed by campaign-oriented research and tempered by a willingness to negotiate with adversaries. The long-term commitment (and institutional memory) of much of ACORN's senior staff and leadership, along with the renewable outrage and energy generated by its membership, have enabled ACORN to be sophisticated and effective while retaining a militancy unusual among contemporary antipoverty organizations.

John Krinsky

See also: Community Development; Community Organizing; Industrial Areas Foundation (IAF); Living-Wage Campaigns; Welfare Rights Movement; Workfare

References and Further Reading

ACORN. 2004. http://www.acorn.org/index.php?id=2.

Delgado, Gary. 1985. *Organizing the Movement: The Roots and Growth of ACORN*. Philadelphia: Temple University Press.

Reese, Ellen. 2002. "Resisting the Workfare State: ACORN's Campaign to Improve General Relief in Los Angeles." *Race, Gender, and Class* 9, no. 1: 72–95.

Stein, Arlene. 1986. "Between Organization and Movement: ACORN and the Alinsky Model of Community Organizing." *Berkeley Journal of Sociology* 31: 93–115.

Bakke, E. Wight

See The Unemployed Worker and *Citizens without Work*

Birth Control

Birth control encompasses practices that prevent conception. Contraception was first referred to as "birth control" by Margaret Sanger in 1914 as part of her efforts to inaugurate a social movement to overturn laws that had banned the devices in the 1870s. Although Americans may take the right to contraception for granted today, the legal status of contraception has shifted over the course of the nation's history. Public demand for contraceptives in the mid-nineteenth century spurred a booming patent medicine industry and raised concerns that middle-class Americans were shirking their duty to become parents. These fears led, in the 1870s, to federal and state laws that made it a crime to distribute contraceptive information and devices. Throughout U.S. history, elitist prejudices linking poverty to poor planning abilities and to excessive sensuality have provoked anxiety about childbearing among poorer Americans and have inspired efforts to restrict their fertility. Those prejudices were very apparent in the drive to secure compulsory-sterilization laws in twenty-eight states between 1907 and 1931 and in the 1927 *Buck v. Bell* (274 U.S. 200) U.S. Supreme Court decision upholding those laws. The individual's right to make fertility decisions was only established in the mid-twentieth century in two key U.S. Supreme Court cases: the 1942 *Skinner v. Oklahoma* (316 U.S. 535) decision, which limited some sterilization laws and defined the right to procreate as a fundamental; and the 1965 *Griswold v. Connecticut* (381 U.S. 479) decision, which defined the use of contraception to be constitutionally protected by the right to privacy. Even with these decisions supporting individual reproductive choice, fears about the kind of people having children continue to influence state interventions into family planning and into poor women's access to birth control.

Despite its shifting legal status, people practiced birth control throughout U.S. history. Prolonged breast-feeding, withdrawal, and marital abstinence were some of the earliest methods used. Douches, vaginal suppositories, condoms, and other barrier methods were sold commercially in the mid-1800s. And recipe books contained instructions for homemade herbal concoctions. The twentieth century commercial contraceptive market continued to grow, especially with the hard times of the Depression in the 1930s. Massengill and Lysol both advertised their products as douching agents. A wide variety of foams, tablets, and suppositories were also available. Condom manufacturers developed new latex models and expanded their marketing to gas stations and restaurants. Contraceptive manufacturing was unregulated, however, and the reliability and effectiveness of products varied widely. As the twentieth century progressed, women turned more and more to doctor-prescribed contraceptive methods. Clinics sponsored by the birth control movement supported the initial development of spermicides, diaphragms, intrauterine devices (IUDs), and the pill. The 1960 introduction of the pill seemed to promise women a medical method that was almost 100 percent effective. Although the pill is often credited with causing the great decline in fertility since the 1960s, sterilization is actually the leading form of birth control in the United States, with 28 percent of women relying on female sterilization and another 11 percent relying on vasectomies of their male partners (Alan Guttmacher Institute). These surveys do not distinguish between voluntary and coerced sterilizations. Before age thirty-five, poor women, African American women, and women with less than a college education are far more likely to rely on female sterilization than are other women. Given that Medicaid and health insurers often cover only the full costs of permanent birth control methods, this differential pattern reflects, at least in part, the very different reproductive "choices" of poor women of color (Tone 2001).

The first sustained challenge to the legal ban on contraceptives passed in the 1870s came in the wake of Sanger's activism. A participant in radical and socialist politics in New York, Sanger shifted her full attention to birth control in 1914. That year, she was arrested for writing about abortion and contraception in her magazine, *The Woman Rebel*. She also wrote and distributed *Family Limitation*, a pamphlet that provided detailed descriptions of various contraceptive methods. The first pamphlet of its kind, it was widely distributed through socialist and anarchist political circles. In 1916, she and two other women opened the first U.S. birth control clinic in Brooklyn. Sanger chose the Brownsville community as the site for the clinic, in part because of its strong working-class community. And Brownsville's women flocked to the clinic in large numbers in the ten days before the police shut it down. Sanger and her compatriots spent thirty days in jail for their actions and inspired groups around the country to open clinics and challenge laws. Sanger opened her second clinic in New York City in 1923 and helped establish a national network of clinics that joined together as Planned Parenthood in 1942. These clinics provided services to all married women regardless of their ability to pay. Because of the sexual controversy that birth control embodied, the movement was largely disconnected from other female-led social welfare movements of the period.

At the same time that the birth control movement was trying to secure the individual right to contraception, a national movement for compulsory sterilization sought laws to prevent reproduction among "the unfit." Grounded in eugenics, which claimed to apply scientific principles of heredity to human reproduction, this movement helped pass laws in twenty-eight states that required the sterilization of institutionalized, retarded, and insane persons and of convicts. Thus, the first birth control technique actually legalized in the twentieth century was surgical sterilization imposed by court order. In practice, the application of sterilization law fell most heavily on poor women. The standards for fitness used by advocates of sterilization laws embodied class-based and gender prejudices. By the twentieth century, middle-class common sense, derived from Thomas Malthus, held that families should only have as many children as they could afford to support. Following the myth that through hard work and thrift every American could prosper, couples were expected to delay marriage and childbearing until they had secured a stable economic position. In addition, girls, especially, were expected to refrain from sex until they married. Thus only thriftlessness and inherent irresponsibility could explain why poor families had (too many) children and why young women gave birth out of wedlock. Eugenics, which argued that pauperism was hereditary, suggested that those children would necessarily become burdens to society. Such beliefs were widely shared. So for instance, while Sanger criticized the arrogance of the eugenicists' claim to be able to determine a person's fitness, she also expressed disappointment in working-class and poor women when their fertility rates did not decline as quickly as middle-class standards dictated.

In upholding the Virginia sterilization laws in its 1927 *Buck v. Bell* decision, the U.S. Supreme Court enshrined elitist and eugenic prejudices. Ruling that "in order to prevent our being swamped with incompetence," compulsory sterilization was justified. The Court held "it was better" if society could "prevent those who are manifestly unfit from reproducing their kind" (quoted in Reilly 1991). The decision covered only those who were confined in government facilities. However, teenage girls from poor and working-class families who became sexually active before marriage were often placed in such facilities precisely to secure their sterilization. The *Buck* case itself involved such a situation: Carrie Buck, a seventeen-year-old unwed mother and the daughter of an unwed mother, was ordered to be sterilized. Poor young men were most likely to run afoul of compulsory sterilization laws if they were incarcerated for juvenile offenses. In its 1942 ruling in *Skinner v. Oklahoma*, the Court limited the circumstances in which states could compel sterilization. In this case, the Court ruled that Oklahoma's law requiring the sterilization of habitual criminals was subject to class bias because it excluded many kinds of crimes likely to be committed by middle-class persons. Thus, embezzlers would not be subject to the law whereas petty thieves were. The Court ruled that the law violated the equal protection clause. In its ruling, it recognized for the first time that the decision to have children is a fundamental right.

The *Skinner* decision did not end government's role in fertility control. In the 1950s and 1960s, with concern about rising proportions of racial minorities on the welfare rolls, the focus of sterilizations shifted to poor Black, Hispanic, and Native American women. After the *Griswold v. Connecticut* decision legalized contraception, the federal government began funding federal family programs directed at limiting poor women's fertility. Those programs initially increased the practice of compelling poor women to submit to permanent sterilization. In 1978, as a result of activism by a coalition of welfare rights, civil rights, and feminist organizations to end sterilization abuse, the government issued guidelines for Medicaid-covered sterilization. Although forced permanent sterilizations declined, during the 1990s, some state governments pushed the distribution of two long-acting contraceptives, Norplant and Depo Provera, in hopes of preventing conception among poor women, especially teenagers, and thereby reducing welfare rolls. In addition, the federal government incorporated abstinence-only education provisions in the 1996 welfare law, urging unmarried women to practice abstinence until they have achieved economic self-sufficiency. Thus, the eugenic idea that excess fertility causes poverty and that preventing conception is the solution continues to inform much of the current social policy (Roberts 1997).

Carole McCann

See also: Eugenics; Feminisms; Reproductive Rights; Welfare Policy/Welfare Reform

References and Further Reading

Alan Guttmacher Institute. Web site. http://www.agi-usa.org.

Brodie, Janet Farrell. 1994. *Contraception and Abortion in Nineteenth Century America*. Ithaca, NY: Cornell University Press.

Luker, Kristin. 1996. *Dubious Conceptions: The Politics of Teenage Pregnancy*. Cambridge, MA: Harvard University Press.

McCann, Carole. 1994. *Birth Control Politics in the United States, 1916–1945*. Ithaca, NY: Cornell University Press.

Reilly, Philip. 1991. *The Surgical Solution: A History of Involuntary Sterilization in the United States*. Baltimore: Johns Hopkins University Press.

Roberts, Dorothy. 1997. *Killing the Black Body: Race, Reproduction, and the Meaning of Liberty*. New York: Pantheon Books.

Tone, Andrea. 2001. *Devices and Desires: A History of Contraceptives in America*. New York: Hill and Wang.

Black Churches

Throughout a history marred by economic and political oppression, Black churches have served their communities as the primary source for financial, social, and moral uplift. Many historians refer to Black religion in the United States as the "nation within a nation."

For over 300 years, African American churches (and mosques, synagogues, and temples) were the only Black institutions permitted by white authorities. Although categorized as "slaves" and "laborers" in white America, within their religious institutions, African Americans were able to cultivate independence and individual authority. Church buildings were the only place available for African American public meetings, and positions within church bureaucracies for many years provided one of the few opportunities for Black leadership. Thus, with their formal membership, headquarters, publications, and regularly scheduled gatherings, Black churches have historically served as a source of information, management skills, and political mobilization to a people relegated to the margins of American public life—exemplifying the degree to which African Americans have mastered political and economic tactics both within *and* outside of mainstream political processes. African Americans have utilized their churches to organize boycotts, protest marches, and local economic ministries to counter the trends of a culture historically organized against their race.

It would be mistaken, however, to understand the experience of African Americans or Black churches as discrete or unitary. African American religion is as multidimensional and diverse as every Black individual in America. What unifies these disparate believers (and nonbelievers) is the continuing struggle to manage the consequences of racial segregation and oppression. Disproportionately impoverished and persistently prohibited from political participation, African Americans sought and built organizational change and individual economic uplift from the most stable institution within their communities.

Some scholars suggest that the first political act of African American religion was its survival within the dehumanizing system of slavery. As the "invisible institution," the Black churches of the slave era supplied hope and communal encouragement in a context of extreme oppression. Although many studies suggest that the introduction of Christianity by Anglican, Baptist, and Methodist missionaries was a furthering of white social control, it is impossible to deny the empowering and supportive role of religion during the era of slavery (1630–1863). During the antebellum era, the majority of the active Black abolitionists were ministers of independent Black Christian churches, like David Walker, author of *An Appeal to the Coloured Citizens of the World* (1829), and Henry Highland Garnet, a prominent speaker at the antebellum Negro Conventions. The Underground Railroad was managed in part by African American religious leadership and networking; slave preachers (Gabriel Prosser in 1800, Denmark Vesey in 1822, and Nat Turner in 1831) led the three largest slave revolts.

During the first half of the nineteenth century, independent African American churches emerged from the religious syncretism of African survivals, Islamic traditions, and Christian missionary efforts. These churches inevitably sought to provide not only spiritual but also economic and social nourishment for their free and bonded parishioners. Mutual aid societies were often the result. In 1787, Richard Allen and Absalom Jones founded one of the earliest mutual aid societies, called the Free African Society. Out of that society, in 1794, Allen organized the Mother Bethel AME Church of Philadelphia. Throughout the nineteenth century, Black religious institutions and their related mutual aid societies would provide a feeding ground for Black economic development, including the formation of the first African American bank (Freedman's Savings and Trust Company in 1874) and insurance agency (North Carolina Mutual in 1898). Not only were churches the spawning ground for Black enterprises, but they were also themselves economic institutions that provided financial aid to the downtrodden and endorsements to political causes.

The Civil Rights Act of 1866 (effectively revoked by President Rutherford B. Hayes in 1877) brought a brief moment of franchise to the former slaves of the South and to Black people in the North. During a ten-year period, twenty Black congressmen and two Black senators were elected to Congress, the majority of them ministers or lay leaders in Black churches. For example, an African Methodist Episcopal (AME) clergyman, Hiram Revels of Mississippi, became in 1870 the first Black citizen and first Black senator elected to Congress. But even nonelected leadership wielded power in late-nineteenth-century African American culture. The most radical political voice of this era was Henry McNeil Turner, a bishop in the AME Church. Turner wielded a nationalist liberation theology to call for slave reparations and mass emigration to Africa. His position was largely determined by his belief that economic conditions, regardless of the growing financial prowess of Black churches, would never improve for Blacks in America.

The 1896 *Plessy v. Ferguson* decision (163 U.S. 537) effectively ratified Jim Crow segregation in the southern states. Until the passage of the Voting Rights Act of 1965, Black churches became the main arena for Black political activity. During this period, Black America experienced a major demographic shift as hundreds of thousands of African Americans migrated to northern cities, escaping the long-term decline of sharecropping and segregation with the hope of economic mobility in northern industries. Although a great deal of financial advancement was made among these new northerners, racism and residential segregation were pervasive. High rates of poverty, unemployment, and underemployment were common among urban Blacks and were accompanied by poor housing, substandard schools, hunger, and high rates of infant mortality. Black churches began to hire on-site social workers, and secular coalitions, such as the National Association for the Advancement of Colored People and the National Urban League, were formed from religious leadership to fight for broad-based political action in Black communities.

The situation in northern cities encouraged a diverse array of religious ideologies that attempted to answer the economic strife experienced by African Americans. Marcus Garvey (1887–1940) founded the Universal Negro Improvement Association (UNIA) in 1914, advocating Black business ownership and political independence. Major Jealous Divine (1880?–1965), known as Father Divine, was committed to a strict moral code and communitarian ethos with his Peace Mission movement of the 1920s and 1930s, providing housing, food, and spiritual comfort to all those suffering from sickness and poverty. Finally, Wallace D. Fard (Master Fard Muhammad) (c. 1877–1934), founder of the Nation of Islam in 1930, and Elijah Muhammad (1897–1975), his chief follower, attracted a strong following with their message of personal discipline, economic independence, and Black racial supremacy. Perhaps the most famous African American Muslim, Malcolm X (1925–1965), emphasized a nationalist sensibility in order to uplift African Americans from grinding poverty and cultural alienation.

Malcolm X's prominence symbolized a new era for Black churches. The rise of a mass media culture coincided with the civil rights movement, a social effort that confirmed the central role of the Black church in African American life and pressed many individual African Americans into the national spotlight. Black churches were the major points of mobilization for mass meetings and demonstrations, and most of the local Black people who marched and worked in the demonstrations were there as a result of religious campaigns to motivate political activism. It is estimated that several hundred churches in the South were bombed, burned, or attacked during the civil rights years, with ninety-three of the bombings occurring between 1962 and 1965, tragically underscoring white awareness of the power these buildings had within the Black community. The members of the Southern Christian Leadership Conference (SCLC), headed by Martin Luther King Jr. (1929–1968), worked to demolish the structural constraints on African American life. Although at first King emphasized the need for political franchise, he eventually sought to overhaul a culture that stratified classes along racial lines. Through the many movements of the civil rights era, countless food, shelter, and job programs were initiated to abate the economic suffering of African Americans.

Following the civil rights movement, African American religious life has continued to diversify and multiply, following trends across the racial religious spectrum. African American churches persist as financial and political centers in their communities. Contemporary politicians, Black and white, attend national denominational conventions and Sunday luncheons to garner support from the African American electorate. Black churches continue to fund antipoverty programs throughout the country, providing local ministry and political clout to continue the fight against institutional oppression and economic disparity.

Kathryn Lofton

See also: African American Migration; African Americans; Civil Rights Movement; Islam; Mutual Aid; Nation of Islam; Slavery

References and Further Reading

Cox, Arthur J., ed. 1984. *A Black Perspective on the American Social Service System: A Book of Readings*. Carbondale: Southern Illinois University.

Harris, Frederick C. 1999. *Something Within: Religion in African-American Political Activism*. New York: Oxford University Press.

Lincoln, C. Eric, and Lawrence H. Mamiya. 1990. *The Black Church in the African American Experience*. Durham, NC: Duke University Press.

Ross, Edyth L., ed. 1978. *Black Heritage in Social Welfare, 1860–1930*. Metuchen, NJ: Scarecrow Press.

Turner, Richard. 1997. *Islam in the African-American Experience*. Bloomington: Indiana University Press.

Wald, Kenneth D. 1987. *Religion and Politics in the United States*. New York: St. Martin's Press.

Wilmore, Gayraud S. 1973. *Black Religion and Black Radicalism*. New York: Doubleday.

Black Panther Party

The Black Panther Party was one of the most prominent political groups of the 1960s and 1970s fighting for racial equality, social justice, and an end to discrimination against African Americans. The party used bold and provocative tactics to mobilize Blacks to fight for their freedom and democracy. Founded by Huey P. Newton and Bobby Seale in Oakland, California, in October 1966, the party's activities were developed to achieve the organization's Ten Point Platform and Program. The founders demanded full employment for Blacks, an end to capitalist exploitation, decent housing, relevant education, free health care, an end to police brutality, an end to the government's racist and aggressive wars, release of all persons unfairly imprisoned, and fair legal treatment. Moreover, the party advocated Black self-determination or control over all institutions within Black communities.

Beginning with very limited resources, the early Panthers focused their activities on challenging one of the most visible problems in the Black community: police brutality. Arming themselves with guns and law books, the Panthers monitored police interaction with Blacks and promptly intervened when they observed illegal or unwarranted activity directed toward Black citizens. This practice led to numerous confrontations with police officers, who were unaccustomed to having their behavior evaluated and contested. However, the Panthers had reviewed the law and were prepared to use their weapons when the police attempted to harm Blacks or illegally confiscate their weapons. Many Black communities in Oakland and the San Francisco Bay Area saw the Black Panther Party as fearless and courageous. But the party was indisputably controversial. Conservative lawmakers, especially, disapproved of the Panthers and in 1967 proposed legislation aimed at the Panthers making it illegal for most California citizens to carry loaded weapons.

In May 1967, armed party members led by Seale protested this legislation in the state capital, Sacramento. They were arrested following their protest. The news coverage made the Panthers known state- and nationwide. Five months later, the Panthers again gained national media attention when Newton was accused of killing a police officer. The party used Newton's imprisonment and indictment for murder as a rallying cry to raise funds for his legal defense and to build the party across the country. The strategy worked. Newton, although imprisoned for three years, was acquitted of murder in 1970. During this period, the party gained thousands of new members around the country. Many were young Black men and women, including college and high school students, military veterans, and workers.

Although fighting to get Newton out of prison, the party began creating specific programs addressing poverty and the difficult socio-

Eldridge Cleaver was among the most prominent members of the Black Panther Party. Following a period of exile, he reemerged as an outspoken and conservative Christian. (Library of Congress)

economic conditions facing Blacks. The most famous was the free breakfast program for kids. Concerned that Black children were not achieving in school because they were literally hungry, the Panthers engaged churches, businesses, organizations, and individuals within the Black community to donate resources to feed the children. The response was overwhelmingly positive, and free breakfast programs emerged in many cities around the country. Their success led the party to implement more programs. National Panther leaders who witnessed this process included Elridge Cleaver, Kathleen Cleaver, David Hilliard, Erika Huggins, Landon Williams, Audrea Jones, and Elaine Brown.

Between 1968 and 1971, Panther state chapters and local branches created health clinics, food programs, transportation programs, clothing and shoe programs, prison visitation programs, and liberation schools. These programs, among others, addressed specific needs and concerns within Black communities in direct and creative ways. To implement their programs, Panthers requested assistance from diverse sectors of the Black community, including nurses, doctors, medical students, lawyers, law students, professionals, teachers, religious leaders, and the unemployed. In contrast to some Black Power groups, the party worked publicly with progressive white, Latino, Asian American, Native American, and other non-Black groups. The party successfully publicized its work through its national newspaper, *The Black Panther*.

At the same time, there was a growing divide within the party between those members who wanted to emphasize the various social service programs and those who wanted to challenge the government's domestic and foreign policies in more direct and militant ways. This disagreement culminated in 1971 in violent clashes between party members, followed by the expulsion by Newton and the central committee of the more radical forces from the party. The FBI and state and local police generally conspired to sabotage the party and exacerbate its internal differences. These police actions led to the imprisonment of many Panthers and to death and self-exile for some.

In 1972, all Panthers were called to California to work on the electoral campaigns of Bobby Seale for mayor of Oakland, Elaine Brown for city council, and others for lesser offices. The process of consolidating all party resources in Oakland reinvigorated the party there but dismantled it as a national organization. Ultimately, Seale and Brown lost their campaigns, and the party was left exhausted. Newton engaged in increasingly violent and bizarre behavior, such as humiliating and brutalizing party members. Seale and other leaders resigned from the party in 1974. In the same year, Newton went into exile to avoid new murder charges.

Elaine Brown assumed leadership of the party in 1974 and revitalized its few remaining local programs. She also engaged in questionable disciplinary activities against party members and left the party in 1977. Newton returned from exile in 1977 and was acquitted of the charges against him. However, he continued his dubious behavior, and the remaining party members gradually abandoned him. The party ended with the official closing of its one remaining school in 1982.

Ollie A. Johnson III

See also: Civil Rights Movement

References and Further Reading

Cleaver, Kathleen, and George Katsiaficas, eds. 2001. *Liberation, Imagination, and the Black Panther Party: A New Look at the Black Panthers and Their Legacy*. New York: Routledge.

Jones, Charles E., ed. 1998. *The Black Panther Party Reconsidered*. Baltimore: Black Classic Press.

Newton, Huey P. 1973. *Revolutionary Suicide*. New York: Harcourt Brace Jovanovich.

Seize, Bobby. [1970] 1991. *Seize the Time: The Story of the Black Panther Party and Huey P. Newton*. Baltimore: Black Classic Press.

Block Grants

See Federalism

Bonus Army

In 1932, around 40,000 veterans of World War I, members of what became known as the Bonus Army, came to and camped in Washington, D.C., in an effort to persuade Congress to issue the payment—often called a bonus—promised them for their military service. In 1919, Congress had issued these veterans certificates—good for a payment based on time served—rather than paying the veterans directly. To reduce the immediate cost of the program, the certificates were to be paid out in the future, like insurance policies: They were due upon the death of the veteran or in 1945. But in 1932, amid deepening economic depression, these unemployed veterans argued that they, as good citizens, deserved the money immediately. From late May until July 28, 1932, the Bonus Army marched in Washington and lobbied members

Some of the 40,000 war veterans composing the Bonus Army are shown here upon their arrival at the Capitol, following their march up Pennsylvania Avenue from the Washington Monument, Washington, D.C., July 4, 1932. (Bettmann/Corbis)

of Congress for some response. On July 28, after a series of legislative defeats of the veterans' proposal, local city officials appealed to the U.S. Army for help in clearing some of the veterans out of central Washington. After President Herbert Hoover approved, General Douglas MacArthur led the forces, which exceeded the initial scope of the order and forced all the Bonus marchers from the city. Though the Bonus Army did not get their demands met in 1932, their appeal generated a wide-ranging debate about what response the federal government should make to the crisis of the Great Depression.

The forceful expulsion of the veterans accentuated the sympathy many Americans felt for their methods. The veterans remained peaceful during their months in Washington. Their makeshift camps in city parks or abandoned buildings were highly visible versions of the shantytowns developing across the country. Most of the participants emphasized their loyalty to their country by eschewing support from communists. And though many of the marchers were single men, those with families highlighted the way their need affected their wives and children. When Americans saw the photographs and newsreels of deserving veterans being driven out of the capital by soldiers with bayonets, many expressed deep dismay.

But sympathy did not translate into support for the marchers' demands. Legislators and reformers urging the passage of a comprehensive system of relief rejected the demands because they would benefit veterans, not all of whom were among the most needy Americans. Leaders already anxious about the prospect of huge federal relief programs, including Hoover, believed that paying the bonus would be too costly during a time when government revenues were already falling short. Franklin D. Roosevelt, straddling these two positions, also refused to endorse the "bonus" payments, preferring instead to give veterans preferential treatment in work programs. By 1936, however, sentiment across the country had shifted enough that the veterans did finally win immediate payment of their certificates.

Lucy Barber

See also: Communist Party; Economic Depression; Federalism; Relief; Unemployment; Veterans' Assistance; Works Progress Administration (WPA)

References and Further Reading

Barber, Lucy G. 2002. *Marching on Washington: The Forging of American Political Tradition*. Berkeley and Los Angeles: University of California Press.

Daniels, Roger. 1971. *The Bonus March: An Episode of the Great Depression*. Westport, CT: Greenwood Press.

Lisio, Donald J. 1994. *The President and Protest: Hoover, MacArthur, and the Bonus Riot*. New York: Fordham University Press.

Brace, Charles Loring

See Child-Saving; *The Dangerous Classes of New York*; Urban Poverty

Bracero Program

The Bracero Program was a binational agreement between the United States and Mexico that authorized the importation of contracted agricultural workers under the auspices of the Mexican Farm Labor Program Agreement (Public Law 45 [1942]). In Spanish, the term *bracero* means a worker who works with his hands and arms. The measure allowed for the legal recruitment of Mexican workers who were contracted in their homeland and brought to the United States to meet the domestic employment demands brought by World War II. The war had ushered in a robust economy, with women and men employed at all-time highs in war machinery and other production. Unable to meet the demand for farm products, the agricultural industry was forced to search for cheap and readily available labor. The Bracero Program filled this gap, and between the program's start in 1942 and its termination in 1964, more than 4.5 million braceros entered the United States. After its implementation, the program was extended through various acts and lasted twenty-two years, until it was finally terminated after pressure from unions and labor activists concerned with the systematic exploitation of the workers. The Bracero Program also supplied temporary agricultural and railroad workers during the Korean War.

The Bracero Program made general provisions that were meant to protect the workers. For example, the braceros could not engage in any military service, and the legislation prohibited discriminatory acts of any kind. Under the terms of the agreement, Mexicans entering the United States were supposed to enjoy guarantees of transportation, living expenses, adequate housing and sanitary conditions, and health provisions. The agreement also guaranteed a minimum wage of thirty cents an hour. Finally, hiring was to be done on the basis of a written contract between the worker and the employer.

Mexican workers were not to enjoy the benefits of citizenship, however. Specifically designated as temporary workers, braceros were subject to repatriation once their contracts were up, and they could be used merely to fill gaps in agri-

A Mexican family leaves to cross the border during World War II to fill wartime labor shortages as part of the U.S./Mexican Bracero Program, ca. 1944. (Corbis)

cultural or railroad labor, not to displace U.S. workers. Moreover, although the U.S. government formally guaranteed the protections in the agreement, the reality was far more bleak for the workers. Many workers experienced discrimination from their employers and local communities. The program was widely criticized for failing to protect workers from such abuses as wretched living and working conditions, prejudice, ill treatment, and poor wages. Yet many of these workers resisted discrimination, ill treatment, and poor working conditions by striking, demanding repatriation before their contracts were up, or deserting or through other forms of protest. Many of the original braceros never returned to Mexico, and after the end of the program, the number of illegal immigrants in the United States probably increased as workers became firmly implanted through home ownership, employment, and schooling for their children.

Abel Valenzuela Jr.

See also: Agricultural and Farm Labor Organizing; Day Labor; *Factories in the Field;* Migrant Labor/Farm Labor

References and Further Reading

Craig, Richard B. 1971. *The Bracero Program: Interest Groups and Foreign Policy*. Austin: University of Texas Press.

Galarza, Ernesto. 1964. *Merchants of Labor: The Mexican Bracero Story*. Charlotte, CA: McNally and Loftin.

Gamboa, Erasmo. 1990. *Mexican Labor and World War II: Braceros in the Pacific Northwest, 1942–1947*. Austin: University of Texas Press.

Buddhism

Buddhist practice originated in India about 500 years before Christ. Currently, many different kinds of Buddhist practice can be found in the United States, but these different practices, although they have different emphases, share an overarching set of beliefs. Among the most basic are the "four noble truths": (1) Suffering is a part of life. (2) Suffering is caused by our desires or cravings for objects and beings outside of ourselves for personal fulfillment. (3) The end of suffering is located in overcoming our cravings. (4) The way to overcome our cravings is through the eightfold path. Or, as Dogen, the founder of Japanese Zen, noted, "If you cannot find the truth where you are, where do you expect to find it?"

Does Buddhist practice constitute a faith-based approach to poverty and welfare? Yes, although when President George W. Bush extols the virtues of faith-based politics, he is referring primarily to such Christian groups as the Catholic Charities and the Salvation Army. When the Christian Coalition, President Bush, and the Republican Party talk about the importance of "faith" in America, they are probably not thinking about monks in robes. But even though Buddhism falls below the radar screen of faith-based discourses, there are noteworthy efforts by Buddhists to address poverty, inequality, and welfare in America.

It is important to point out that Buddhist approaches to poverty and welfare are very different from those of many of the better-known Christian-sponsored efforts. First, contrary to a common misconception, Buddha is not the "God" of Buddhism. Buddhists do not worship Buddha as Christians do God; rather, Buddhists practice the dharma (the teachings). And the dharma, in turn, is not an inflexible practicum for "sixteen steps to enlightenment." An oft-heard teaching is "When you meet the Buddha, kill the Buddha," which is a way of cautioning against treating the dharma as a set of prohibitions.

A second key difference is that certain Christian groups, such as Catholic Charities and Lutheran Social Services, have, for some time now, had a formal relationship with the government. The government, in a kind of subcontracting relationship with these groups, funds their activities as long as the groups operate separately from the churches they are affiliated with, do not proselytize, and do not discriminate on the basis of religion. Buddhist groups that provide social services, on the other hand, are not commissioned to do so by the government.

A third distinctive aspect of Buddhist antipoverty work follows from the Buddhist understanding of the suffering of *all* people. Such activities as the provision of food for the needy are part of a broad vision that sees suffering wherever it exists and whatever its causes, including suffering as a result of disregard for the environment, the suffering of prisoners who have committed crimes, and the suffering of those with terminal illnesses, such as AIDS and other diseases. But in addition to widely understood charitable activities, such as feeding the hungry, Buddhist social engagement may also "bear witness" to the suffering produced by state violence and war—for example, the Holocaust, the Vietnam War, the Gulf War, and, most recently, the bombing of Afghanistan and the war against Iraq. In short, Buddhist approaches to social activism are different from others' since "witnessing"—an activity that might be viewed as inherently critical of government's neglect or violence—is as much a part of Buddhist social engagement as is feeding the hungry.

After its beginning in India, over many subsequent generations, Buddhism spread across the East, notably to China and Japan. Though many Asian immigrants to the United States in the nineteenth century were Buddhist, there was little interest in Buddhism outside the immigrant communities. But since the 1960s, a trickle of interest in Buddhist meditation and philosophy has grown into a mountain of opportunities for practice. Of the many kinds of Buddhist practice in the United States, four very common "styles" of practice are Zen, Vipassana, Insight, and Tibetan, different practices embracing many teachings.

There are between 2.5 and 4 million Buddhists in America (or approximately 1.6 percent of the total population), which includes both Asian immigrants as well as American converts—although it is important to note that estimates vary considerably (Seager 1999). These estimates should be used with caution since there is no single umbrella organization that oversees Buddhism in the West. The Pluralism Project at Harvard University, a research group that studies religion and diversity in America, found that an incomplete list includes over 1,000 Buddhist centers in the United States as of 2002. One of the difficulties in counting the number of Buddhists in America is that a large and growing number of Americans are interested in various forms of Buddhist meditation as a relaxation technique, for health and medical reasons, or as a means of sitting through difficult times. Also, some people practicing meditation also attend services at Christian churches or at synagogues. One can even earn a master's degree in socially engaged Buddhism at the Naropa Institute. The point here is not that the high or low estimate of the number of Buddhists is the more accurate but, rather, as the Pluralism Project notes citing anecdotal evidence, that Americans from "all walks of life" are "embracing dharma" (Pluralism Project 2004).

"For the benefit of all beings," a saying that is a cornerstone of Buddhist teachings, means that the well-being and the suffering of others are interdependent with our own. This belief is an extension of one of Buddhism's most basic teachings about the relationship of the self to the world. This teaching, known as nondualism or, alternately, codependent origination, is that the self, or the "I," is inextricably identified with the world, or "they." In Buddhism, when one deeply recognizes this teaching, one cannot but feel empathy and compassion for others—whether they are friend, foe, or stranger. For Buddhists, the practice of faith is the practice of mindfulness of our irreducible connection with others.

For many Buddhists, mindfulness of another's poverty, despair, and hunger means *acting* on it. In Buddhism, the principle of *acting* on a social issue is not the same as political action. Buddhists feed the homeless not to make political commentary about homelessness but simply because homeless people are hungry. In general, the Buddhist understanding of activism emphasizes compassionate action as opposed to political action. Buddhist social action, or "socially engaged" Buddhism, a phrase coined by Thich Nhat Han, takes many forms. There are socially engaged Buddhist projects that address war, hunger, poverty, violence, environmental issues, sexual orientation, race, health care, prisons, and schools. A partial list of some of the better-known Buddhist approaches to poverty and welfare include the Buddhist Peacemaker Order founded by Roshi Bernie Glassman; the Order of InterBeing founded by Thich Nhat Han; the Buddhist Peace Fellowship, Fellowship of Reconciliation, and Buddhist Alliance for Social Engagement associated with Roshi Robert Aitken; and the many Buddhist hospice and soup kitchen projects across the nation. Robert Queens, a prominent contributor on engaged Buddhism, suggests that in addition to the above, "mindfulness" workshops—for example, like those developed by Jon Kabat-Zinn, the author of *Full Catastrophe Living*—should also be included in the list of Buddhist approaches to suffering.

What is it that Buddhists do as a part of their approach to poverty and welfare? The characteristic Buddhist response to poverty is to provide services to fulfill needs, such as feeding the hungry, or to provide community services through tutoring, day care, and the like. For example, the San Francisco Zen Center organizes a bag lunch program for homeless people, sponsors recreational and tutoring activities for homeless families, and teaches mindfulness meditation to interested inmates. Similarly, the Buddhist Alliance for Social Engagement (BASE), an outgrowth of the Buddhist Peace Fellowship, developed a training and internship program that is modeled, at least in organization, on the Catholic Volunteer Corps model, for social workers and service providers. BASE, operating in a number of locations across the country—from Berkeley to Boston—integrates participants' work experiences with the Buddhist practice of "engaging with suffering." Another exemplary organization, the Zen Peacemaker Order headed by Roshi Bernie Glassman, fosters a kind of "street" engagement with homelessness and poverty. At Glassman's initiative, the Peacemaker Order set up shop in Yonkers, New York. Among the many enterprises operated by Peacemaker Order is a for-profit bakery (the proceeds support the order), a construction company that trains workers, co-op housing, and AIDS hospices. Following in Glassman's steps, Claude Tenshin Anderson, a Vietnam veteran turned Buddhist priest, runs street retreats with young people across the United States and abroad to raise their awareness about violence in society.

Though the specific activities of socially engaged Buddhist projects vary considerably—from providing services to small enterprise to training—there is a common feature: to engage with suffering in an intimate way and to work for the benefit of all.

Dana Takagi

See also: Asian Americans

References and Further Reading

Eppsteiner, Fred, ed. 1985. *The Path of Compassion: Writings on Socially Engaged Buddhism*. Berkeley: Buddhist Peace Fellowship.

Glassman, Bernie. 1998. *Bearing Witness: A Zen Master's Lessons in Making Peace*. New York: Bell Tower.

Pluralism Project. Web site. 2004. http://www.fas.harvard.edu/~pluralsm/index.html.

Queen, Christopher S., ed. 2000. *Engaged Buddhism in the West*. Boston: Wisdom Publications.

Seager, Richard. 1999. *Buddhism in America*. New York: Columbia University Press.

Snyder, Gary. 1990. *The Practice of the Wild*. San Francisco: North Point Press.

Turning Wheel. Journal of the Buddhist Peace Fellowship. Berkeley, California.

Capitalism

Capitalism is a broadly encompassing economic and social system that is based on principles of private ownership, production for profit, and market exchange. Its historical development has rested on an ever-evolving combination of technological innovation, ideological and political commitment, institutional support, and fiercely contested struggle that has played out differently in different national settings. In the United States, where the notion of "free market," or "laissez-faire," has been most forcefully embraced, capitalism has evolved within a context of relatively limited government regulation and considerable policy support in the form of laws, institutions, tax treatment, and public subsidies for infrastructure building favorable to its growth. Even as it has produced average standards of living higher than in previous epochs (as measured by gross domestic product or per capita income), capitalism has produced higher rates of inequality and poverty in the United States than in other advanced industrialized economies. Millions are unable to meet their basic needs. Nearly 44 million Americans are without health insurance, and millions go without necessary medical care. Infant mortality in some parts of the United States, particularly urban areas, rivals that of many less-developed economies. Poverty in the United States is deeper and traps individuals for longer periods of time than in other advanced economies because government policies to moderate capitalism's reach and even out its cycles have been less effective compared to those of other developed countries.

Although national governments have historically played an important role in shaping capitalism and its impact on social well-being, capitalism also transcends national boundaries. Capitalism is a global phenomenon, and its generation of un- and underdevelopment is also global. Wealth inequalities within developed countries parallel wealth inequalities between developed and undeveloped countries, driven by the same desire to reduce costs of production at the global level. Although capitalists benefit from the advocacy of international financial institutions and from government policies to promote "free trade," the global structures defending the interests of working and poor people and the environment are relatively few and comparatively weak.

Capitalism as an Economic System

Capitalism is a mode of production whereby private firms produce goods and services for profit. Key features of capitalism are that workers are free to sell their labor to private firms, that the capitalist—the owner of the firm or his or her agents—controls the labor process, and that the dynamics of the system entail competition among firms, which generates un- and underemployment. This is because the profit motive and dynamics of capitalist competition lead firms to innovate and adopt increasingly efficient techniques in order to reduce costs. Often, this takes the form of labor-saving technology that increases the firm's productivity and reduces the amount of labor or number of workers employed. This dynamic creates conditions for a permanent pool of unemployed workers while placing limits on wage growth for the employed. Both of these processes establish the potential for unemployment and underemployment, which are leading causes of poverty. Some governments have been able to mitigate capitalism's negative features through social welfare policies that provide insurance and income support during periods of unemployment and by providing public goods that are not adequately supplied through the private market, such as health care and education. Other governments have found their ability to shape capitalism limited by external factors, such as obligations to pay off debts to rich countries, too few or the wrong kind of resources, or social structures inherited from previous modes of production.

There is widespread agreement that the origins of capitalism can be traced back to sometime between the 1500s and the late 1700s in Europe. In Europe, capitalism emerged out of a feudal economic system, in which the individuals who provided most of the labor power were not free to relocate or even choose their employer. The origins of capitalism are to be found in the transformation from this mode of production into one based on the private ownership of the means of production, that is, private ownership of the tools, equipment, and raw materials—capital—necessary to produce goods and services. Governments made this reassignment of property rights possible by creating legal systems that recognize land deeds, labor and financial contracts, and titles to other implements of production. In the United States, founded after the emergence of capitalism and in revolt against feudal traditions, capitalism was anchored in an ideological tradition that linked political liberty to property rights—albeit under conditions in which property was broadly distributed across the (white, male) population and not concentrated in the hands of an aristocratic elite. Indeed, the question of whether those rights should be invoked to protect corporations and large powerful property holders as well as laborers and small proprietors has been a persistent source of conflict and policy shifts throughout U.S. history.

A profound difference between capitalism and other economic systems is that under capitalism, goods and services are produced by private firms for sale and profit rather than for use or simple exchange. Production for profit provided the underpinnings for capitalism's prodigious growth, compelling entrepreneurs to invest in producing goods and services. In the view of classical political economy, if individual capitalists were unable to reap these rewards, it is unlikely that they would continue to invest and thus create economic growth in the way we now know it. Adam Smith, a Scottish political economist writing in the late eighteenth century, referred to this process as the "invisible hand": Individual actors rationally following their own interest in profit were part of a system that would generate employment while producing goods and services. Although some have used this notion of the invisible hand to argue that capitalism grows and produces well-being of its own accord (and thus needs no regulation), subsequent history has demonstrated that the profit motive is often in conflict with the social good and that overall economic growth rests as crucially on public policy as on the economic activities of individual entrepreneurs.

There are clear demarcations between capitalism and other economic systems. The most critical is that under previous economic systems, individuals were not "workers" in that they were generally not free to engage in labor contracts. Individuals were often tied to the land, as in the case of serfdom, or held as slaves. Thus, Karl Marx, author of the three-volume work *Capital,* which exposed the nature of capitalism, referred to the origin of capitalism as the moment when labor was "freed" from both the land and from outside ownership of the means of production. Workers became "workers" when they had to sell their labor power to survive because they no longer had access to subsistence farming and they did not have sufficient capital to go into business for themselves.

Using money as the universal (or nearly universal) medium of exchange is another prerequisite for capitalism. Monetary exchange facilitates the accumulation of profits. In a nonmonetary economy, individuals must barter over goods and services. Without a medium in which individuals can hold assets, capitalists would be unable to time investments to maximize potential sales and profitability. Further, money allows investors—capitalists—to borrow funds for production. Here again, government plays a supportive role, whether by printing this money itself or by coordinating among the private financial institutions that do. Governments have also played an important role in the rise and evolution of capitalism by regulating the supply, or availability, of money and credit. In most advanced industrialized economies, the overall supply of money is under the control of a central bank; in the United States, that bank is the Federal Reserve (established in 1913). The first U.S. Central Bank, chartered in 1791, generated tremendous political controversy that would be echoed in future debates over bank policy and practices. Farmers, artisans, populists, labor, and antipoverty activists are among those who have historically opposed the influence of financial interests and corporate capitalists in central banking policy.

Under capitalism, the capitalist enjoys control over the production process. Control of production by an elite class is common in many kinds of economic systems; however, under capitalism, this control is more precise in that the capitalist controls the entire labor process, from the worker's smallest movement to the structure of the workday. This distinguishes capitalism from economic systems in which small producers maintain control over their own production process and schedule, as well as from socialist forms of production, in which government-owned enterprises or cooperatives make all decisions about resource allocation. The control over the choice of technique and the structure of the workday is fundamental to how work is generally conducted under capitalism and is at the core of productivity gains. For example, much has been made of the innovations made by Henry Ford in his auto-production plants in the early 1900s in the United States. He had efficiency experts analyze the production process down to the tiniest movements of each member of his production team in order to limit all extraneous movements and facilitate the highest possible productivity. This kind of capitalist control over production allows the firm to "speed up" production, through anything from a faster-moving assembly line to an increase in the number of calls taken per hour in a call center. It also allows the firm to use the most productive techniques, increasing efficiency, outputs, and profitability.

Efficient production is at the core of capitalism and is kept at the forefront of the process through the dynamics of capitalist competition. Competition among firms keeps the actors in the system constantly innovating and encourages entrepreneurship. This competition, in turn, pushes individual firms to produce using the best available technology to keep the costs of production as low as possible. Competition means that the firm with the lowest-cost production method can offer goods or services for sale at the lowest price, thereby undercutting its competitors while still being able to earn profits. In order to stay in business, firms with higher costs must increase productivity (output per worker). Competition, however, often leads to unemployment as workers are replaced by labor-saving technologies.

Inherent Contradictions: Capitalism's Tendency to Create Unemployment

Capitalism's reliance on technological innovation and competition produces what Marx called a "reserve army of labor"—a pool of unemployed and partially employed labor generated by the dynamics of capital accumulation itself. In historical terms, the reserve army of labor first developed when peasants were pushed off their common land in the long transition from a feudal, more agricultural and subsistence economy to an increasingly industrialized capitalist economy. Left with no means of supporting themselves without selling their labor, these workers were subject to the shifting demands and standards of a labor market in which a surplus, or overabundance, of workers would drive wages down and unemployment up. In the modern era, as the economy grows, firms hire more and more workers to facilitate increased output. This leads to falling unemployment as all those who want jobs are able to find them. Lower unemployment is associated with higher wages; workers are freer to bargain over their wages and firms are more desperate to hire and maintain employees. Neoclassical economists refer to this as "efficiency wages" (Shapiro and Stiglitz 1984). To keep costs down, firms look to new, labor-saving technologies or move production to locations that have cheaper labor. This brings on a new round of higher unemployment and, as newly unnecessary workers are let go, creates the reserve army of labor. A simple, concrete example of this can be found in the production of banking services. In the 1980s, many banks moved toward the introduction of automated teller machines, replacing bank tellers by machines, which were more cost-effective. Thus, competition among banks led to the unemployment of bank tellers over time as firms adopted labor-saving technologies. Aggregated to the level of the macroeconomy, this creates the reserve army.

The reserve army of labor and capitalist competition affect wage setting under capitalism. In the macroeconomy, higher unemployment places downward pressure on wages. The macrodynamics of wages and unemployment are evident in capitalist economies around the world, as recently documented by David Blanchflower and Andrew Oswald (1994), who showed that higher unemployment is associated with lower wages, all else being equal. This inverse relationship between unemployment and wages was evident in the United States during the economic boom of the 1990s. Between 1995 and 2000, unemployment averaged 4.8 percent—relatively low by recent historical standards—and average annual wages rose at an annual rate of 2.5 percent, significantly higher than during the previous two decades when higher unemployment had been the norm (author's analysis of Center for Economic and Policy Research 2003).

Capitalism is also prone to recurring economic crises: recessions and depressions. As accumulation proceeds, each firm works to lower its production costs in order to be more competitive. This generates a tendency for the rate of profit to fall as each firm tries to undercut its competitors' sale prices. Capitalist economies are subject to short-term business cycles, which are often caused by overproduction, in which firms are unable to sell all their inventories and see no reason to invest in more production. As this occurs, weaker and perhaps less cost-effective firms may be driven out of business, and because economic crises generate higher unemployment, the power of labor to bargain for higher wages is weakened.

Capitalism does not conform to national boundaries in its search for profits or in the way the dynamics of competition play out. As capitalism expands, firms seek new markets and new pools of labor from which to hire. Over the past few decades, the reach of capital seems

"The Socialist Party and the Working Class," Eugene Debs, September 1, 1904

Criticism of unbridled capitalism reached a height in the late nineteenth and early twentieth centuries, amid the great wave of mergers and monopolistic practices that concentrated immense economic and political power in the hands of corporate capitalists and polarized the extremes of poverty and wealth. Labor activist and five-time Socialist Party candidate for president Eugene Debs drew on this growing discontent in campaigns that would eventually (in 1912) garner as much as 6 percent of the popular vote.

The capitalist system is no longer adapted to the needs of modern society. It is outgrown and fetters the forces of progress. Industrial and commercial competition are largely of the past. The handwriting blazes on the wall. Centralization and combination are the modern forces in industrial and commercial life. Competition is breaking down and co-operation is supplanting it.

The hand tools of early times are used no more. Mammoth machines have taken their places. A few thousand capitalists own them and many millions of workingmen use them.

All the wealth the vast army of labor produces above its subsistence is taken by the machine owning capitalists, who also own the land and the mills, the factories, railroads and mines, the forests and fields and all other means of production and transportation. . . .

The overthrow of capitalism is the object of the Socialist party. . . .

The Socialist party comprehends the magnitude of its task and has the patience of preliminary defeat and the faith of ultimate victory.

The working class must be emancipated by the working class.

Woman must be given her true place in society by the working class.

Child labor must be abolished by the working class.

Society must be reconstructed by the working class.

The working class must be employed by the working class.

The fruits of labor must be enjoyed by the working class.

War, bloody war, must be ended by the working class.

These are the principles and objects of the Socialist party and we fearlessly proclaim them to our fellowmen.

We know our cause is just and that it must prevail.

With faith and hope and courage we hold our heads erect and with dauntless spirit marshal the working class for the march from Capitalism to Socialism, from Slavery to Freedom, from Barbarism to Civilization.

Source: Eugene Debs, "The Socialist Party and the Working Class," opening speech delivered as candidate of the Socialist Party for president, at Indianapolis, Indiana, September 1, 1904. Reprinted in *Debs: His Life, Writings, and Speeches, with Department of Appreciations*, ed. Bruce Rogers (Girard, KS: Appeal to Reason, 1908), 371, 373.

especially widespread across the globe as many states have deregulated their financial and commodity markets. However, capital has always had a global reach, as we see in the history of colonization of less-developed countries by imperial powers, which often perpetuated those countries' relative underdevelopment. Individual firms often exploit these gaps in economic development in order to find locations where they can produce at a lower cost. Firms anywhere in the world are increasingly expected to compete using the same global production techniques.

Thus, if firms in South Korea produce steel at the lowest cost, then consumers of steel around the world will purchase their steel from South Korea rather than higher-priced steel produced in their home countries. This pits workers in developed and less-developed countries against each other and against themselves in the fight for adequate employment. For example, virtually all U.S. textile firms now produce overseas because the cost of employing U.S. workers is so much higher than the cost of employing workers in these other countries. Thus, it is fair to say that the reserve army of labor is now also global.

Capitalism as a Social System

Capitalism's dynamics compel it not only to look outward for new markets and labor pools but also to look internally as well, pulling more aspects of social life into its realm. Thus, as capitalism develops, social life is increasingly commodified—that is, brought under the influence of the market. For example, much of the caring labor and home production that was historically provided by unpaid women in the home, even in the early phases of capitalism, has now been commodified. Caring labor, such as child care and home health care, was provided in the home until after the middle of the twentieth century. Now, most families purchase this as a commodity by hiring (often low-paid) care workers. Over time, American families have continued to cut down on home production through the widespread purchase of fast food and pre-prepared meals. Capitalists now earn a profit on these products, whereas decades ago, they did not. This generates growth for the economy overall, but it also has profound consequences for the organization of social life and the level of social well-being.

Greater commodification of social life means that greater numbers of individuals are dependent on firms for their livelihood. In times of economic crisis, millions can end up unemployed and impoverished. With more families needing two incomes to afford even a basic standard of living, the unemployment of one partner in a two-parent family can spell devastation, while single-parent families are under constant economic stress even when the household head is employed. This dynamic also occurs in economies as they move from a traditional mode of production into capitalism. Once families leave subsistence farming (and lose their land), they are then permanent participants in the capitalist economy and subject to capitalism's recurring economic crises.

Political Responses to Capitalism's Inherent Conflicts

The dynamics of the capitalist economy make it a highly productive system for generating goods and services and often for raising living standards. However, there is an inherent tension between an economic system that generates unemployment and strives to keep wages as low as possible and the workers and natural environment that provide the necessary resources to keep the system going. Much of classical and modern economics focuses on the relationship between capitalism and social welfare. Neoclassical economists present the market as benevolent and believe that allowing the market to exist without government interference will increase the welfare of society as a whole. However, the history of modern governments in capitalist economies exposes this doctrine of market benevolence as a myth. Classical economists, such as Marx, Smith, and David Ricardo, saw that capitalism's inherent dynamics often place this system in opposition to social welfare because society's welfare is not in capitalism's purview. It is not in the interest of any one firm to ensure the safety and survival of the society as a whole.

The contradictions inherent within capitalism have led many to criticize it and work to provide alternatives. In the 1800s, socialists and utopian thinkers developed sophisticated criti-

Trading floor of the New York Stock Exchange. (Gail Mooney/Corbis)

cisms of capitalism's indifference to social welfare and advocated alternative, more humane economic systems, which were often grounded in notions of economic equality. Many argued that the government is merely an agent of the capitalist class and that it thus must be overthrown and replaced by governments of and for workers. Over the course of the twentieth century, revolutionary parties in what became the Communist countries of the Soviet Union, China, Cuba, and elsewhere established "command economies" in which goods and services were produced by the state rather than by private actors. However, these economies were more often than not coupled with dictatorial political systems, which in the long run made them unstable as well as undemocratic and undermined their own claims to egalitarianism.

Within what have become the advanced capitalist economies, reformist movements sprang from these criticisms of capitalism. Historians argue that the development of the specific form of capitalism that is moderated by the social welfare state was a response to the instabilities generated by capitalism's inherent dynamics. Karl Polanyi (1944) argued that the social welfare state was society's reaction to the notion of the self-regulating market. The growth of the market economy was checked by the institutional development of measures to protect society from having to face the unhindered effects of capitalism. Thus, as capitalism tended toward global expansion, it was met by countermovements checking that expansion in particular directions. The forward capitalist movement was "economic liberalism," which, relying on the trading class, sought to establish a self-regulating market with laissez-faire and free trade as its methods. The countermovement was propelled by the working and landed classes, using protective legislation, restrictive association, and other methods to protect society, both people and natural resources, from the unregulated market.

This back-and-forth between the market and regulation in the name of social welfare has been a hallmark of the development of the modern state. The state has often acted to preserve the capitalist system as a whole rather than for the benefit of particular capitalists. This was often seen as necessary for the survival of the state within democracies but also as necessary to maintain a level of social welfare and to mitigate the vagaries of capitalism. The inherent contradictions between capitalism and liberal democracy require some type of accord to maintain social stability in the face of these two coexisting conflictual social structures. Over the course of state transformation, there was not one model of state involvement, but many. The European social democratic states, such as Sweden and Denmark, chose to implement expansive welfare programs, while the liberal governments of the United States, the United Kingdom, and Canada have more-limited social welfare states. In the United States, the New Deal, which vastly expanded the federal role in social welfare provisions, was a direct response to an economic crisis and a means by which federal officials restored social order. During the post–World War II era in the United States, the Keynesian welfare state that grew out of New Deal policies came to be a means of political and economic stabilization. The success of this system was contingent, however, on economic growth and on the ability of the government to manage the economy through fiscal and monetary policy.

Global capitalism is not, however, complemented by a global "state" capable of ensuring global social welfare. Furthermore, over the past few decades, international institutions have hindered the development of social welfare institutions in less-developed countries by requiring them to adopt liberal—or free-market—economic policies oriented toward open trade and capital markets, privatization, and deregulation. These policies have not led to a generalized reduction in poverty or a rise in living standards over the past few decades. The push toward an open global economy will probably further amplify the inherent tension between capitalism and social welfare.

Heather Boushey

See also: Communist Party; Economic Depression; Economic Theories; Globalization and Deindustrialization; Industrialization; Labor Markets; New Right; Property; Socialist Party; Wealth; Welfare Capitalism; Welfare State

References and Further Reading

Blanchflower, David G., and Andrew J. Oswald. 1994. *The Wage Curve*. Cambridge: MIT Press.

Botwinick, Howard. 1993. *Persistent Inequalities: Wage Disparity under Capitalist Competition*. Princeton: Princeton University Press.

Center for Economic and Policy Research. 2003. *Current Population Survey Outgoing Rotation Group Uniform Data Files*, version 0.9. Washington, DC.

Marx, Karl. 1986. *Capital: A Critique of Political Economy*. Moscow: Progress Publishers.

Piven, Frances Fox, and Richard A. Cloward. 1971. *Regulating the Poor*. New York: Vintage Books.

Polanyi, Karl. 1944. *The Great Transformation: The Political and Economic Origins of Our Time*. Boston: Beacon Press.

Shapiro, Carl, and Joseph E. Stiglitz. 1984. "Equilibrium Unemployment as a Worker Discipline Device." *American Economic Review* 74, no. 3: 433–444.

Weisbrot, Mark, Robert Naiman, and Joyce Kim. 2000. *The Emperor Has No Growth: Declining Economic Growth Rates in the Era of Globalization*. Washington, DC: Center for Economic and Policy Research.

Caregiving

See Aid to Families with Dependent Children (ADC/AFDC); Child Care; Domestic Work; Home Health Care Work; Maternalism; Welfare Policy/Welfare Reform

Carnegie, Andrew

See "Gospel of Wealth"; Philanthropy; Wealth

Catholic Church

Catholic agencies are major social welfare providers and policy advocates through the departments of the U.S. Conference of Catholic Bishops, religious communities, lay organizations, and diocese- and parish-based groups. Catholic Charities USA is the nation's largest private network of social service providers, serving over 9.5 million people. In 1994, government sources provided 65 percent of Catholic Charities' nearly $2 billion budget (Brown and McKeown 1997, 9, 194). These charity and antipoverty efforts are rooted in Catholic social teaching on ministering to those in need, following the example of Jesus and his disciples. They are also rooted in the social and historical experience of the Catholic Church in the United States. Catholic benevolent societies of the mid-nineteenth century were organized in response to the demands of poor and working-class Catholic immigrants—mainly from Ireland and Germany and predominantly urban—because Catholic leaders feared that "their own" would be influenced by Protestant social reform and public service programs. The founding of the National Conference of Catholic Charities (later Catholic Charities USA), a lay organization, signaled the beginning of a shift in the focus of Catholic charities away from poverty relief toward social reform through changing social structures. In the 1930s, Catholic leaders were active in national welfare policymaking. Reflecting demographic change, by the 1960s, Catholic charities had moved from "caring for their own" with parish-raised funds to providing services to African Americans, Latinos, "new immigrants" (as those of non-European origin are often called), and non-Catholics through Catholic-raised and government funds.

The religious basis of Catholic commitment to charity is founded in the belief that one's neighbor has been created in the image of God and therefore should be assisted out of the love of God. Gospel parables teach that service to others is service to Jesus, who, along with lay followers, cared for the poor, sick, and defenseless. Current Catholic social teaching stresses charity and justice as essential to the mission of evangelization and salvation of souls.

In the mid-nineteenth century, Catholic philanthropic giving differed by class status and gender. The small, wealthy class contributed to the construction and support of seminaries, while the large working-class supported local direct-assistance projects by donating money or volunteering time. Bishops directed charitable works in their dioceses, and the boards of Catholic charitable organizations were composed of professional men and clergy. Direct charitable work was considered "women's work," to be conducted mainly by nuns in such orders as the Sisters of Charity. To this day, religious communities of Catholic women are characterized by their service to the poor and adherence to voluntary vows of poverty, which symbolize solidarity with the poor. (In 1920, religious orders did 75 percent of Catholic-sponsored charitable work [O'Brien 1996, 147].)

Following the Civil War, Catholic leaders mobilized congregation and lay efforts to support local institutions and programs to serve Catholics, which grew to include schools, hospitals, orphanages, women's shelters, youth probation and recreation services, and home nursing services. These Catholic charities lacked centralized organization or leadership until the next century.

The postwar freedom of enslaved men and women heightened Catholics' attention to their lack of charity among African Americans and also among American Indians. Protestants outpaced Catholics in missions among African Americans, and white sisterhoods continued to turn away African American applicants. The

Oblate Sisters of Providence, established by African American sisters with the assistance of white priests in Baltimore in 1828, received little funding and took in laundry to support themselves. Beginning in the 1880s, the daughters of Philadelphia banker Francis Drexel devoted inheritance funds to support African American Catholic churches and schools and the Sisters of the Blessed Sacrament for Indians and Colored People. However, at the turn of the century, a single meeting of Protestants to raise missionary funds for work among African Americans resulted in more donations than Catholics provided annually to such missions (Oates 1995, 58). Further, Catholic social services refused care to African Americans into the early twentieth century. For example, none of 540 Catholic hospitals listed in the 1922 "Directory of Catholic Charities in the United States" admitted Black patients, yet they did admit white, non-Catholic patients (Oates 1995, 64).

In the early twentieth century, social reformers enhanced the Catholic national presence and the "scientific" nature of Catholic charities by creating the National Conference of Catholic Charities (NCCC) in 1910 to evaluate and coordinate Catholic services. Several Jesuit schools specialized in training social workers. Although some Catholic volunteers and clergy criticized these new, overwhelmingly female professionals for earning money by assisting the poor, their services were in demand.

In the 1920s, progressive reformers within the Catholic charity movement argued against the poverty-relief approach to social services and put forward a social justice approach. The NCCC leadership and the bishops' National Catholic Welfare Conference (established as the National Catholic Welfare Council in 1917 and renamed in 1919) maintained that justice requires a foundation of charity. The economic stance of these organizations was progressive, supporting social security, minimum-wage laws, and workers' insurance, but other Catholic positions were socially conservative. For example, the National Council of Catholic Women campaigned against reformers' work to provide birth control to residents of poor Catholic neighborhoods.

During the Depression and the New Deal era, Catholic social welfare advocates gained national prominence, calling on government agencies to supplement inadequate private funds and lobbying to protect Catholic agencies' care for Catholic children under new Social Security legislation. Catholic social workers found work in public welfare departments, and Catholics gained positions of power in federal social welfare agencies. Taking a different approach from that of national policy advocacy, Dorothy Day and Peter Maurin founded the Catholic Worker movement in New York in 1933, working at the local level to directly assist the poor.

The Second Vatican Council (1962–1965) renewed attention to issues of structural injustice, poverty, and peace as part of the charitable vocation. Simultaneously, demographic and economic transformations that had dramatically changed the makeup of post–World War II cities challenged Catholics to address the needs of a largely non-Catholic urban poor. Of particular importance was the upward mobility of second- and third-generation white immigrants, who were drawn to the heavily segregated suburbs by a combination of government-subsidized mortgages and fear of nonwhite neighbors, leaving urban parishes with an increasingly nonwhite ministry. Although on one level the response was to step up efforts to provide services and education to African Americans and other traditionally non-Catholic clienteles, papal encyclicals also urged action toward social transformation as central to Catholics' evangelization mission. A "crusade against poverty," the Campaign for Human Development (CHD), was launched by the U.S. Conference of Catholic Bishops in 1969 to support community-based projects run by poor groups and to motivate people to understand and act on Catholic social teaching. Through such agencies as Catholic Relief Services, established in 1943 as the bishops' overseas development aid program, this structural emphasis became increasingly globalized.

Liberation theology, with a strong emphasis on the church's role as a catalyst in changing "sinful social structures," emerged during the 1960s, most strongly in Latin America. The controversial concept of a "preferential option for the poor" is derived from Latin American Catholic experience and is associated with liberation theology. It calls attention to individuals' and society's responsibility to build solidarity with the poor in order to effect social change. Opponents of the concept argue that it detracts from the universal mission to preach the Gospel to all people and implies that the church is taking a side in "class struggle." Defenders see the concept expressed in the Bible and urge church engagement in progressive politics.

The church's social policy activity in the United States during and since the 1960s has encompassed a broad range of justice-related issues, including advocacy for a national health care plan; protection of the rights of immigrants, migrants, and refugees; promotion of social and economic justice among American Indians; opposition to interrelated structural racism and economic oppression; and calls for peace and disarmament. Support for a social justice approach to Catholic teaching is voiced by Pope John Paul II (installed in 1978), and a 1986 pastoral letter by the U.S. Conference of Catholic Bishops advocated the concept of "economic justice for all." Catholic leaders and agencies opposed federal welfare cuts in the 1990s, citing statistics from Catholic Charities' service programs on inadequate social welfare funding and relying on the moral authority of church statements about governments' responsibility to act for the common good. Continuing a theme from the early twentieth century, they also combined progressive economic stances with socially conservative positions, particularly on birth control and reproductive rights.

The Catholic Church is committed to a continued active role in social services and welfare policymaking. The U.S. Conference of Catholic Bishops released *In All Things Charity* (1999), calling individuals and the government to assist those in need and to work toward social justice. The statement points to enduring poverty in the United States and globally, and it urges people of goodwill to commit to greater solidarity with the poor. It asks Catholics to pray for justice and peace, to serve the poor through volunteering and charitable donations, and to advocate for public policies that "protect human life, promote human dignity, preserve God's creation, and build peace" (U.S. Conference of Catholic Bishops 1999, 55). In June 2001, the bishops endorsed legislation to implement the Bush administration's proposal for funding faith-based and community initiatives.

Laury Oaks

See also: Catholic Worker Movement; Charity Organization Societies; *Economic Justice for All;* Missionaries

References and Further Reading

Brown, Dorothy M., and Elizabeth McKeown. 1997. *The Poor Belong to Us: Catholic Charities and American Welfare*. Cambridge, MA: Harvard University Press.

Dorr, Donal. 1983. *Option for the Poor: A Hundred Years of Vatican Social Teaching*. Maryknoll, NY: Orbis Books.

Levi, Werner. 1989. *From Alms to Liberation: The Catholic Church, the Theologians, Poverty, and Politics*. New York: Praeger.

Oates, Mary J. 1995. *The Catholic Philanthropic Tradition in America*. Bloomington: Indiana University Press.

O'Brien, David J. 1996. *Public Catholicism*. 2d ed. Maryknoll, NY: Orbis Books.

U.S. Conference of Catholic Bishops. 1999. *In All Things Charity: A Pastoral Challenge for the New Millennium*. Washington, DC: U.S. Catholic Conference.

Catholic Worker Movement

The Catholic Worker movement, founded in New York City in 1933 by Dorothy Day and

Peter Maurin, was a movement both spiritual and political in philosophy and agenda: Committed to anarchism, pacifism, and service to the poor, the Catholic Worker movement would pioneer a style of direct action protest and communal living that would both prefigure and directly influence the protest movements and counterculture of the 1960s.

Dorothy Day, born in Brooklyn in 1897, had a rootless childhood because of her father's peripatetic career as a sportswriter. She was a spiritual wanderer as well: Throughout her childhood and as a young woman, she was strongly if episodically attracted to Christianity, in varying denominational hues. Politics also engaged her interest: As an undergraduate at the University of Illinois she joined the Socialist Party. When she came to New York in 1916, she found employment as a left-wing journalist, and her social circle included many of the founders of the communist movement. In the late 1920s, she formally joined the Catholic Church, but she did not abandon her radical political convictions.

In December 1932, in the depths of the Great Depression, Day had a fateful meeting with a fifty-five-year-old French Catholic immigrant to the United States named Peter Maurin. Like Day, Maurin sought to combine his fervent religious piety with an equally fervent social radicalism. He proposed to Day that the two of them should found a lay Catholic movement, loyal to but independent of the church and devoted to living with and caring for the poor as a practical application of Catholic social teachings. Through Maurin's influence, Day became familiar with the writings of reform-minded European Catholics, like the French philosopher Jacques Maritain. These European Catholics were developing an outlook, known as "personalism," that emphasized the uniqueness and autonomy of the human self and also the responsibility of individuals to involve themselves in the great social and moral issues of the day. With its emphasis on providing an immediate and individual response to injustice and unmet human needs, personalism represented an alternative both to mass collectivist movements, such as communism and fascism, and to the managerialism of social democratic and liberal welfare states.

Day and Maurin launched their movement by starting a newspaper, the monthly *Catholic Worker*, which sold for a penny. Its first edition appeared on May Day 1933. From an initial press run of 2,500 copies, its circulation rose dramatically in the years that followed, peaking at 185,000 on the eve of World War II. The newspaper was filled with political and devotional essays, book reviews, and some path-breaking journalism about the lives of the poor, labor struggles, and the underside of urban life. Maurin contributed a series of "Easy Essays" to the newspaper outlining his philosophy, but Day soon emerged as the movement's real leader. From early on in the movement's history, people began to regard her as a saint-in-the-making. Michael Harrington, who knew Day in the early 1950s when he was briefly a member of the Catholic Worker movement, described her as having a "severe, almost Slavic, and yet very serene face. With her hair braided around her head and the babushka she sometimes wore, she might have been a peasant or, had the Dostoevsky she read so avidly written of women as he did of monks, a mystic in one of his great novels" (Harrington 1973, 20).

As Harrington's example suggests, the *Catholic Worker* newspaper attracted not only readers but also volunteers eager to put its preaching into action. Soon, the Catholic Worker movement was operating "Houses of Hospitality" in poor neighborhoods in twenty-seven cities and maintaining a dozen farms. The Catholic Worker houses ran soup kitchens and breadlines, provided beds for the homeless (as well as for the middle-class volunteers who were flocking to the movement), and became centers of vibrant and visionary debate. The Catholic Worker's utopianism was regarded by some outside critics as otherworldly and unrealistic. The movement fell on hard times during World War II, which Day opposed on pacifist grounds; many of the Houses of Hospitality closed down in those years. But Day always insisted that her followers, however uncompromising they may sometimes have seemed to outsiders, were very much involved in the here and now of changing the world: "The spiritual works of mercy," she wrote in her autobiography, "include enlightening the ignorant, rebuking the sinner, consoling the afflicted, as well as bearing wrongs patiently, and we have always classed picket lines and the distribution of literature among these works" (Day 1952, 220). It was with this perspective that members of the Catholic Worker movement joined the picket lines of striking workers during the 1930s and pioneered in direct action protests against nuclear testing in the 1950s.

Life in the Catholic Worker houses could be draining, and few volunteers stayed for long. But their lives were often permanently changed by the experience. The Catholic Worker movement trained a generation of dedicated and talented young activists and intellectuals who would go on to play significant roles within the church, the labor movement, and various social reform movements. Catholic priest and antiwar activist Daniel Berrigan would write in 1981 of Day's teachings, "I think of her as one who simply helped us, in a time of self-inflicted blindness, to see." There were any number of individual radical Catholics who had preceded Day, but Catholic radicalism in the United States was largely her invention. She died in 1980, but her movement survived her. The *Catholic Worker* newspaper continues to appear monthly, and at the start of the new millennium, there were over 180 Catholic Worker communities in the United States and abroad. Day was selected by the Catholic Church in 2000 as an official candidate for sainthood.

Maurice Isserman

See also: Catholic Church; *The Other America*

References and Further Reading

Day, Dorothy. 1952. *The Long Loneliness: The Autobiography of Dorothy Day*. New York: Harper and Row.

Harrington, Michael. 1973. *Fragments of the Century*. New York: Saturday Review Press.

Piehl, Mel. 1982. *Breaking Bread: The Catholic Worker and the Origins of Catholic Radicalism in America*. Philadelphia: Temple University Press.

Roberts, Nancy. 1984. *Dorothy Day and the Catholic Worker*. Albany: SUNY Press.

Troester, Rosalie Riegle, ed. 1993. *Voices from the Catholic Worker*. Philadelphia: Temple University Press.

Caudill, Harry

See Appalachia; *Night Comes to the Cumberlands*

Census Bureau

See Poverty, Statistical Measure of; Poverty Line

Center for Community Change

The Center for Community Change, an outgrowth of the Citizens' Crusade against Poverty, was formally inaugurated in 1968 in honor of the memory of the late Senator Robert F. Kennedy. From its inception, the center took as its mission empowering low-income Americans, a preoccupation that characterized the politics of the 1960s. An initial grant from the Ford Foundation of $3.5 million for 2.5 years gave it a stable financial base, and it now has an annual operating budget just short of $4 million, which supports a staff of eighty-six.

The center works on several fronts to help build grassroots organizations in low-income communities. Its staff members work directly with local groups to provide organizer training, organizational and financial advice, and policy expertise in areas that are critical to low-income people, including bank lending, jobs, welfare and employment policy, and housing. Hundreds of organizations across the country have received center assistance in the form of advice and funding.

The center has also initiated a number of special projects, some directed toward strengthening low-income groups by facilitating coalitions among them, such as the Transportation Equity Network, which includes some sixty organizations concerned about inadequate federal funding for public transportation in poor communities. The Neighborhood Revitalization Project works to increase the flow of bank loans to low-income and minority communities. The National Campaign on Jobs and Income Support is a coalition that brings together some 1,000 grassroots groups and advocacy organizations to discuss work and welfare policy issues and to bring grassroots pressure to bear on these issues; the Public Housing Residents National Organizing Campaign similarly brings together resident leaders from public housing. And the Indian and Native American Employment and Training Coalition brings together Indian tribes and off-reservation organizations to exchange information and influence policies that affect Native Americans.

To complement its organizing work, the center also undertakes research on policy issues that affect low-income people, and it has even sponsored initiatives that could become models for public policy reform, such as its Housing Trust Fund Project, which promotes the creation of trust funds dedicated to the construction of low-income housing that draw on public and private sources.

The scope of the center's efforts are suggested by its publication list, which includes action guides in all the policy areas in which it is working as well as such guides to local groups as "How to Tell and Sell Your Story" and "How—and Why—to Influence Public Policy."

Frances Fox Piven

See also: Citizens' Crusade against Poverty (CCAP); Community Development; Community Organizing; Community-Based Organizations; War on Poverty

References and Further Reading

Bobo, Kimberly, Jackie Kendall, and Steve Max. 2001. *Organizing for Social Change: Midwest Academy Manual for Activists*. Santa Ana, CA: Seven Locks Press.

Douglas R. Imig. 1996. *Poverty and Power: The Political Representation of Poor Americans*. Lincoln: University of Nebraska Press.

Osterman, Paul. 2002. *Gathering Power: The Future of Progressive Politics in America*. Boston: Beacon Press.

Piven, Frances Fox, and Richard A. Cloward. 1977. *Poor People's Movements: Why They Succeed, How They Fail*. New York: Pantheon Books.

Center for Law and Social Policy (CLASP)

The Center for Law and Social Policy (CLASP) is a legal and legislative policy organization dedicated to advocacy on welfare, poverty, and family issues at local, state, and federal levels. Staffed by lawyers and policy analysts, CLASP works with legislators, government administrators, and other advocacy groups to formulate, shape, implement, and explain poverty and welfare policy around the nation. Over its lifetime, the group has focused on such issues as women and poverty, tax reform, the provision of free health care, federally funded legal services for the poor, and family policies including child support reform and enforcement, minimum-wage laws, and job training and creation.

CLASP was founded in 1968 by a group of well-credentialed attorneys with experience in federal agencies and elite corporate law firms, with significant financial and substantive assistance from the Ford Foundation and other philanthropic organizations and with backing from the Great Society–era political establishment that had made litigation and legal services a key component of the War on Poverty. CLASP's creators envisioned its original mission as "representing unrepresented interests," and they sought to "build on the considerable expertise and innovative legal strategies that were emerging in poverty and public interest law" (Halpern 1974, 120). And yet, although CLASP formed alliances with activist organizations, its direction was very much removed from those of grassroots social movements. In explicit contrast to work by poverty lawyers at the time, CLASP emphasized that "the poor are not the only people excluded" from governmental policymaking (Halpern 1974, 120). Working in federal courts and administrative agencies, the legal staff and lawyer-led litigation committee worked on such "middle-class" issues as environmental and administrative law as well as on health care and women's rights. By the end of its first decade, CLASP was the nation's largest general practice public interest law firm.

In the 1980s, faced with rapidly declining foundation support (and thus influence), significant staff changes as units of the organization became independent, and a federal government increasingly hostile in every branch to social policy litigation, the organization made a conscious decision to reorganize. The Reagan administration's hostility to welfare and federally funded legal services further influenced CLASP's choice to specialize in poverty matters. Although deemphasizing federal litigation tactics, CLASP's engagement with policy elites remained constant, its focus on expertise intact.

CLASP's Family Policy Initiative sought to develop "comprehensive, rational" policy on the subject (Center for Law and Social Policy 1995, 5). Recognizing child welfare as the most politically acceptable approach to welfare, the group advocated a guaranteed-child-support program along with enforcement and reform of existing laws. To that end, CLASP collaborated with members of Congress and assisted in lobbying efforts by grassroots groups. In the 1990s, CLASP participated in welfare reform efforts, providing testimony, legislative reviews, and data analysis primarily on the impact of proposed welfare reform legislation on questions of child care, child support, and family issues. Following the passage of the Personal Responsibility and Work Opportunity Reconciliation Act of 1996, the group provided guidance to state and local government officials as they implemented the provisions of the act. It also advocated for job training and job-creation projects.

A leading advocate in the increasingly uphill struggle to save the Legal Services Corporation in the 1980s and 1990s, CLASP served as legal counsel to local legal services programs in challenges to onerous restrictions on the types of litigation that attorneys for the poor could undertake. CLASP also developed state projects aimed at bolstering legal services for the poor, building local support for comprehensive legal assistance programs in civil legal matters as national support slowly evaporated.

Thomas M. Hilbink

See also: Legal Aid/Legal Services; Poverty Law; War on Poverty; Welfare Law Center; Welfare Policy/Welfare Reform

References and Further Reading

Center for Law and Social Policy. 1995. *Twenty-Five Years of Change*. Washington, DC: CLASP.

Halpern, C. L. 1974. "Public Interest Law: Its Past and Future." *Judicature* 58: 118–127.

Center on Budget and Policy Priorities

The Center on Budget and Policy Priorities (CBPP) is a public interest advocacy group that promotes policies to alleviate poverty and hunger, improve economic opportunity, expand health coverage, and lessen income disparity both in the United States and abroad. Since its founding twenty years ago, CBPP has become the undisputed leader in what many regard as the most effective current form of social justice advocacy: data-driven policy analysis.

CBPP was founded in 1981 by Robert Greenstein, who had served as director of the federal food stamp program during the Carter administration. Armed with a major grant from the Field Foundation, Greenstein positioned CBPP to contest the Reagan administration's Office of Management and Budget (OMB) analyses of poverty and malnutrition in the United States as well as OMB assertions about the effectiveness of federal food and hunger programs. CBPP's principal weapon in this fight was—and continues to be—a steady production of economic and policy analyses distributed to members of Congress, to the media, and to researchers and social justice advocates. (These analyses are available today through the World Wide Web.)

Challenging the White House's devolutionary initiatives in the 1980s, CBPP prepared budget analyses timed to reach Congress and the advocacy community at the same time as—or even before—OMB projections. In so doing, CBPP eroded the rhetorical advantage of the White House and blunted some of the more draconian welfare cuts. Policy analysis continues to be CBPP's principal weapon: Its research is timely and quantitatively sophisticated and clearly articulates the implications for working people of otherwise dense and complex budget matters. In consequence, CBPP provides compelling hard data to activists in the fight against poverty. CBPP provides ammunition to those who believe government can be a force for good, and its compelling analyses force its opponents to respond. The Heritage Foundation, for example, has subsequently launched a Center for Data Analysis, which devotes much of its time to attempting to rebut CBPP analyses (and doing so in analytic terms that are very much the hallmark of the work done by CBPP). CBPP's leadership in data analysis and in data-driven advocacy has earned it high marks from members of Congress, their staffs, and administration officials.

CBPP is credited with helping make the 1996 welfare reforms more reasonable and humane, with securing expansions in the Earned Income Tax Credit (EITC), and with leading the effort to secure state EITCs. Today, the center continues to produce research and analysis oriented toward federal policymaking, but it has also expanded its work to include a wide range of state-level programs and has also taken on a major new international budget project working with nongovernmental organizations. The center has continued to grow rapidly, and today it enjoys major financial backing from a range of foundations, including the Charles Stewart Mott Foundation, the Annie E. Casey Foundation, and the Ford Foundation.

Douglas Imig

See also: Earned Income Tax Credit (EITC); New Right; Poverty Research

References and Further Reading

Center on Budget and Policy Priorities. Web site. http://www.cbpp.org. Accessed October 6, 2001.

Charitable Choice

The term "charitable choice" refers to laws encouraging state and local governments to contract with faith-based organizations for the delivery of publicly funded social services. The first charitable choice provision was enacted as Section 104 of the Personal Responsibility and Work Opportunity Reconciliation Act of 1996, landmark welfare reform legislation that replaced the Aid to Families with Dependent Children (AFDC) program with Temporary Assistance for Needy Families (TANF). Section 104 requires the states to treat faith-based organizations on an equal basis with other groups when soliciting bids or awarding contracts for the provision of TANF-funded programs for welfare recipients. Whereas inherently or "pervasively" religious organizations were ineligible for public funds prior to 1996, entities such as churches and congregations may now directly receive public monies to provide welfare-related services, subject to certain statutory conditions.

Section 104 explicitly protects the religious

character of faith-based government contractors. They may retain religious art, icons, and symbols in areas where programs take place; use religious concepts in providing services; and employ religious criteria when hiring staff if the criteria are permitted under Title VII of the Civil Rights Act. However, public funds may not be used for sectarian activities such as worship, religious instruction, or proselytization. Faith-based providers may not discriminate against clients on the basis of religion, religious practice, or refusal to participate in religious activities. Clients who object to receiving assistance from faith-based organizations must be provided with equivalent, secular alternatives. Since Section 104's enactment, charitable choice provisions have been added to other major federal grant programs, and a White House Office of Faith-Based and Community Initiatives has been established.

Charitable choice is a major departure from previous law and practice, and it raises significant legal, moral, and practical issues and has sparked much public debate. Advocates claim that faith-based organizations are uniquely effective and cost-efficient and that they are an untapped resource in the fight against poverty and self-destructive behavior. They also argue that faith-based providers historically have encountered barriers to participation and have been pressured by government to downplay or discard their religious emphases. Critics, by contrast, assert that charitable choice poses serious risks for the constitutional rights of needy citizens, for the autonomy of religious organizations, and for America's long-standing commitment to a meaningful separation between church and state.

Laura S. Jensen

See also: Aid to Families with Dependent Children (ADC/AFDC); Welfare Policy/Welfare Reform

References and Further Reading

Bush, George W. 2001. "Rallying the Armies of Compassion." Report. January. http://www.whitehouse.gov/news/reports/faithbased.html.

Farnsley, Arthur E., II. 2001. "Can Faith-Based Organizations Compete?" *Nonprofit and Voluntary Sector Quarterly* 30, no. 1: 99–111.

Monsma, Stephen V. 1996. *When Sacred and Secular Mix: Religious Nonprofit Organizations and Public Money*. Lanham, MD: Rowman and Littlefield.

Press, Eyal. 2001. "Lead Us Not into Temptation." *The American Prospect* 12, no. 6 (April 9): 20–27.

White House Office of Faith-Based and Community Initiatives. 2001. "Unlevel Playing Field: Barriers to Participation by Faith-Based and Community Organizations in Federal Social Service Programs." August. http://www.whitehouse.gov/news/releases/2001/08/unlevelfield.html.

Charity

Charity—although sometimes, particularly in religious writings, held to be a broad sense of love of mankind—can be defined more narrowly to include actions (donations of time or money), public or private, aimed at aiding the poor or needy. American attitudes toward charity have developed over the last two centuries from an emphasis on religious benevolence and local responsibility to a focus on more "scientific" forms of businesslike charity and on more interdependence with the federal government in exercising responsibility for meeting basic social needs. Ironically, while charitable activities have persisted and grown more organized over time, the term "charity" itself has lost favor and is often replaced by "welfare" in the public sphere and "philanthropy" in the private.

American ideas about charity have been strongly rooted in historical precedent. First, from the earliest written records, there is evidence of a human tradition of charity, of aiding kin, friends, and neighbors in times of need. Supplementing those ideas, there is much in the Judeo-Christian and Muslim traditions to encourage charitable behavior toward those of lesser means and to support the rights of the needy to receive. Ideas about mercy, charity, and goodwill toward others infuse the texts of the Torah, the Talmud, the Old Testament, the

New Testament and the Koran, laying the groundwork for the elevation of the idea of charity to the level of virtue, and in many cases, obligation.

Finally, beyond the religious, there were also legal foundations for charity in colonial America and later the United States, based on English common law and encoded in the Elizabethan Poor Law of 1601 that consolidated and rewrote existing poor laws in England. These laws dictated the responsibilities of public charity, helped define the sphere of private giving, and established some of the bedrock principles—including the concepts of "deservingness," personal and familial obligation, and the work ethic—that continue to guide public and private aid to this day.

During colonial times, local support of the needy—based on traditions of charity among family, kin, and neighbors—was the standard. Colonial Americans, often with their congregations, took responsibility for the needy in their communities. With political and religious powers closely allied, charity toward others was part Christian duty, part state-mandated obligation supported through tithes and taxes. Needs were met locally, and "strangers"—those who had no claim on the community—were "warned off."

Although public charity was the norm, private charity organizations increased in number from colonial times on. The Scots Charitable Society (1657) was the first "friendly society" organized in the colonies. Set up by Scotsmen in Boston, this group, like the countless others that would form throughout the nation, aimed to provide "relief to ourselves and any other" as they saw necessary (Trattner 1999, 35). Throughout the colonies and then the nation, individuals banded together both to assure their own security and to donate time and money to benefit a wide variety of needy recipients. The number of private, charitable societies increased greatly in the early nineteenth century, due at least in part to the impacts of the Second Great Awakening and other religious revivals. During the same period, however, many Americans turned from charity to reform—temperance, the asylum movement, and antislavery—foreshadowing that larger move away from almsgiving that would occur at the end of the century.

During the nineteenth century, although there were a few examples of public, federally funded aid programs such as the Freedmen's Bureau (1865–1872), charity remained predominantly a local responsibility, publicly and privately. One key exception was the Civil War–era U.S. Sanitary Commission, which was a national public health organization, funded and run by private charitable donations. The commission was primarily preventative in its focus, aiming to improve conditions and thus eradicate disease rather than to wait and address its effects. Its focus on "sanitary science" also marked the beginning of a major trend toward the encouragement of a more "scientific" charity based not only on goodwill but also on professional training.

Although traditional forms of charity remained strong throughout the nineteenth century, industrialization, immigration, and urbanization were placing strains on existing practices. In view of an expanding and changing American population, trends in charity also reflected a related concern among social elites about the maintenance of social order. In large urban centers, charitable givers often had no first-hand knowledge of those in need; recipients were no longer their neighbors and fellow parishioners. Reflecting this growing distance between donors and recipients, the demand for professional, charitable organizations increased. Exemplified by the growth of the charity organization movement, donors and leaders in the field of charity began to demand better-organized, more-coordinated charitable efforts that aimed to "improve," or reform, the needy rather than focusing on material need alone. Josephine Shaw Lowell, founder of the New York Charity Organization Society and a leading voice in the movement, summed up the concern of many givers: "Almsgiving and dole giving are hurtful—

The New York Association for the Improvement of the Condition of the Poor, Annual Report, 1845

As the experience of mass poverty became a feature of industrializing cities in the nineteenth century, municipalities turned away from earlier practices of poor relief supervised by designated overseers and began to rely on the services of organized charities, which increasingly depended on the services of "friendly visitors"—often women of the upper or middle class—to serve as investigators as well as moral ministers to the poor. The larger aim of such practices, to put charity on a more "scientific," discriminating basis, was realized in groups such as the New York Association for the Improvement of the Condition of the Poor. What follows is an excerpt from the association's 1845 Annual Report.

[The association's] primary object is to discountenance indiscriminate alms-giving, and to put an end to street-begging and vagrancy. Secondly, it proposes to visit the poor at their dwellings, carefully to examine their circumstances, and to extend to them, appropriate relief; and through the friendly intercourse of Visitors, to inculcate among them habits of frugality, temperance, industry, and self-dependence. . . .

The Institution has been instrumental in feeding the hungry, clothing the naked, reclaiming the vicious, and ministering to the sick. And while it has sympathized with man as a responsible and intelligent being,—traversed the narrow lanes and crowded alleys of this metropolis on its errands of kindness,—while it has sat by the side of the wretched in their comfortless hovels, to listen to the tales of their sufferings, to soothe their sorrows, and to extend relief,—yet it has not blindly dispensed its favors, so as to discourage struggling virtue, or to encourage in vicious courses the idle and depraved. On the contrary, it has detected the impostor, and arrested the vagrant, while it has stimulated the inert and desponding, and relieved the distresses of the deserving. Possessing superior facilities for collecting and diffusing information, its action, free from prejudices and preferences, has been liberal and comprehensive. In inculcating temperance, frugality, and industry, it has stood as the hand-maid of Christianity, in its endeavors to meliorate the condition of the indigent.

Source: From *The First Annual Report of the New-York Association for the Improvement of the Condition of the Poor, for the Year 1845* (New York: John F. Trow and Company, 1845), 17, 21–22. Reprinted in *Annual Reports of the New York Association for Improving the Condition of the Poor,* nos. 1–10, 1845–1853 (New York: Arno Press and *New York Times*, 1971), pages as in original.

therefore they are not charitable." Handouts were potentially hurtful to the needy because, she argued, "false hopes are excited, the unhappy recipients of alms become dependent, lose their energy, are rendered incapable of self-support, and what they receive in return for the lost character is quite inadequate to supply their needs" (Lowell [1884] 1971, 89, 90).

Leaders of the charity organization movement believed that rather than aiming at supporting the needy, donations should be used to "raise and help" the poor. Charitable donations should be distributed by professionals, experts who could investigate recipients to determine if they were "deserving" and if the money would be "well spent." According to Lowell, "The fundamental principle is that all charity must tend to raise the character and elevate the moral nature, and so improve the condition of those toward whom it is exercised, and must not tend to injure the character or condition of others" (Lowell [1884] 1971, 94). Charity was not to be just about monetary handouts; it was also about moral and character instruction.

Although a growing population and professionalization spurred changes in the organization of charity, similar changes were occurring in the nature of giving by the very wealthy. In an age of incredible wealth (by 1916, there were more than 40,000 millionaires in the United States), a small number of very wealthy individuals began to consider bringing science and business practices to bear on their own charitable practices, moving from handouts to expertise, policy advocacy, and reform. Although such scientific charity was not the norm even for the very wealthy, a handful of high-profile individuals and their foundations embraced it (Judith Sealander in Friedman and McGarvie 2003, 218–220). Men like John D. Rockefeller "did not want merely to relieve misery; [they] hoped to end it" (Sealander in Friedman and McGarvie 2003, 217–218). To achieve this goal, new charitable foundations focused on more-systematic, research-based giving—giving that would offer solutions to the problems of the world, not temporary relief.

In the 1910s, the desire for more-organized and better-coordinated giving found yet another form, the Community Chest. Here, business leaders could organize not only the distribution of funds but also the collection of donations. Rather than responding to multiple requests for charity, a donor could now make a single donation. The Community Chest would take care of distribution. The end result was both the introduction of major, highly successful, coordinated civic fund-raising campaigns and the further distancing of charitable givers from receivers.

Another notable result of the move toward a new type of charity was the fall from grace of the term "charity" itself. For example, historian Ruth Crocker has pointed out that leaders of the Progressive-Era movement to build settlement houses in poor communities "rejected the term 'charity' altogether, even as they attempted to fill public needs unmet by the state, using private funds and volunteer labor" (Crocker in Friedman and McGarvie 2003, 205). Many givers associated the term "charity" with old-fashioned ideas about almsgiving rather than with new notions about reform, coordination, and professionalization.

Increasingly during the twentieth century, public programs, especially on the federal level, were developed to meet the needs of Americans. The first major wave of such programs came in the form of the New Deal in the 1930s, during the Great Depression, when private charities were unable to meet growing needs. Since that time, public welfare programs have continued to grow, and in some cases contract, alongside private efforts. Nonetheless, even though the terms to describe charitable action have changed and the responsibilities of private giving have been somewhat circumscribed, American charity continues. As of 2002, according to historian Peter D. Hall, there were nearly 1.5 million charitable organizations registered as tax-exempt nonprofit organizations (Hall in Friedman and McGarvie 2003, 363–364). Large foundations and multipurpose organizations flourish alongside faith-based charitable efforts, mutual aid societies, and neighborhood associations. Beyond organized forms of charity, countless individuals continue to help others through direct handouts and by volunteering at local, unincorporated charitable organizations.

There is no question that charity has been an important response to issues of poverty and need in America. Real needs have been met, and in some cases, relationships between the charitable and the needy have been forged. However, there continue to exist questions over who—private individuals or the state—should determine what needs are met in the United States and over how funds are used. Most recently, debates have been raging over whether the federal government should subsidize faith-based charitable institutions by awarding them government contracts and other assistance and over the notion, fostered in conservative policy circles, that "devolving" antipoverty responsibility to the localities and the private sector will foster more and more virtuous charitable giving. The resurgent preference in social policy for private charity over public responsibility has considerable consequences for the poor. Those who contribute money and time often have the strongest voice in how the benefits of charity are distributed. Thus, in the case of private charity, individual volunteers and donors often determine who is "deserving" of assistance as well as who does—and does not—receive aid. Giving, which is often quirky, is also sometimes highly reflective of the interests and beliefs of the givers. On the other hand, in recent years scholars have begun to investigate the power dynamics inherent in charity and have demonstrated the ways receivers also played an active role in charity, both shaping charitable decisions and at times modifying the ways intended gifts are actually used.

Laura Tuennerman-Kaplan

See also: Charitable Choice; Charity Organization Societies; Community Chests; Deserving/Undeserving Poor; Mutual Aid; Nonprofit Sector; Philanthropy; Poor Laws; Voluntarism

References and Further Reading

Bremner, Robert. 1988. *American Philanthropy*. 2d ed. Chicago: University of Chicago Press.

Friedman, Lawrence, and Mark McGarvie, eds. 2003. *Charity, Philanthropy, and Civility in American History*. New York: Cambridge University Press.

Lowell, Josephine Shaw. [1884] 1971. *Public Relief and Private Charity*. New York: Arno Press and *New York Times*.

Trattner, Walter. 1999. *From Poor Law to Welfare State: A History of Social Welfare in America*. 6th ed. New York: Free Press.

Tuennerman-Kaplan, Laura. 2001. *Helping Others, Helping Ourselves: Power, Giving, and Community Identity in Cleveland, Ohio, 1880–1930*. Kent, OH: Kent State University Press.

Charity Organization Societies

Charity organization societies (COSs), private, voluntary agencies, played a central role in delivering services and in shaping social welfare policy and practice in the half century prior to the creation of the federal welfare state. First founded in England in 1869, charity organization societies spread rapidly in the United States between 1877 and 1920. As embodiments of the new theory of scientific charity, these agencies utilized emerging principles of social science to bring order and reform to the complex system of public and private charity that had evolved under the Elizabethan poor laws. Charity organization societies aimed to make charity more efficient and effective by coordinating the efforts of existing charitable agencies in order to prevent fraud and the duplication of services. The ultimate goal of these organizations was not simply to ameliorate want but to identify and treat the underlying causes of "pauperism," or dependency, and thereby to restore individuals to self-support. Through study and investigation of the causes of individual suffering, scientific charity aimed to remove the distribution of relief from the whims of sentimentality and politics and to place it on a rational, scientific footing. Although they wanted to make charity efficient and organized, COS leaders did not intend to make it impersonal or bureaucratic. To the contrary, through their strong commitment to private, voluntary giving, COSs sought to strengthen the bonds between givers and receivers of charity and to heal social divisions.

The charity organization movement was largely a response to the dramatic increases in urban poverty that accompanied industrialization and mass immigration in the latter half of the nineteenth century. Advocates of scientific charity were deeply concerned with growing relief rolls and with the ever-widening gulf between the social classes. To their mind, the problem lay primarily in the charitable system itself: There were too many agencies and individuals granting alms "indiscriminately," without knowing the facts of each case and without knowledge of each other's activities. At best, they argued, this type of giving was ineffective, providing only limited and temporary respite to the poor without addressing the underlying causes of their distress. At worst, it "pauperized" recipients by eroding their self-respect and their will to be self-supporting. To charity organizers, one of the worst examples of indiscriminate aid was public outdoor relief (direct payments to individuals in their homes). Often distributed by urban political machines as a form of patronage, such relief not only encouraged sloth and fraud but also exacerbated social divisions by breeding a sense of entitlement among the poor and resentment among taxpayers. COS leaders lobbied vigorously, and in many cities successfully, to end or reduce outdoor relief. With relief largely in private hands, charity organization societies set out to instruct charitable agencies and individuals in the principles of scientific giving.

As an alternative to indiscriminate giving, charity organization societies promised individualized care that was both scientific and personal. Charitable individuals and organizations were urged to refer alms-seekers to the local COS office before providing aid. A COS agent would investigate, visiting an applicant's home, employer, neighbors, and relatives to unearth the causes of the distress and the extent of the need. Volunteer district committees assessed the facts of each case and recommended a course of action. Charity organization societies were forbidden by their constitutions from maintaining or dispensing relief funds. This prohibition reflected the assumption that ample sources of relief already existed. When relief was necessary, it could be obtained from other sources, preferably from an individual or agency with whom the recipient had some personal connection. The ban on relief giving also reflected the belief that what the poor needed most was not alms but encouragement and guidance. To provide this solace, the COSs relied on "friendly visitors." These volunteers, mostly upper- and middle-class women, were intended to provide a balance to the cold work of investigation and a means of bridging the social gap between rich and poor.

In their desire to avoid the pitfalls of "pauperization," COSs initially placed great emphasis on repressive measures designed to weed out fraud and to suppress begging. Special mendicancy officers secured the arrest of street beggars, and the able-bodied poor were subjected to a "work test" at COS wood yards or laundries, where they earned meager wages for hours of backbreaking labor. Such measures, together with overly intrusive investigations and emphasis on the individual causes of poverty, earned charity organization societies criticism from their contemporary opponents and from modern-day scholars alike. COS policies underwent significant change during the Progressive Era, however. Through their interaction with poor families and through systematic study of social conditions, charity organizers increasingly emphasized the structural causes of poverty and took steps to combat them by operating employment bureaus, day care centers, visiting-nurse services, and savings banks. In recognition of the role that illness, overcrowding, industrial accidents, and unemployment played in creating dependency, charity organization societies supported tenement reform, unemployment insurance, and workmen's compensation, and they led campaigns to combat tuberculosis and other contagious diseases.

Policies on giving relief were also relaxed over time. Despite formal prohibitions against dispensing relief, COS agents and volunteers frequently did so when faced with very needy or very persistent applicants. In recognition of this reality, most societies had by the turn of the century dropped their bans on giving relief, and emphasis shifted from withholding relief to making sure that it was "adequate" to meet applicants' needs. Opposition to public outdoor relief remained strong, however (as evidenced by COS opposition to mothers' pensions), until the 1930s, when widespread unemployment prompted most COS leaders to endorse large-scale public relief and federal intervention.

Though their record is clearly mixed, charity organization societies played a central role in shaping modern social welfare. COS agents pioneered techniques of social casework and laid the foundations of professional social work. These techniques, along with COS methods of investigation, social research, and administration, were disseminated through national publications like the *Survey*, through professional organizations like the National Conference of Social Work, and through training schools like the New York School of Social Work. COS ideals, practices, and personnel found their way into a wide array of public and private social welfare agencies, including criminal and family courts, schools, and departments of public health. Many charity organization societies continued to operate (though usually under different names) as family casework agencies long after the creation of federal welfare programs.

Dawn M. Greeley

See also: Charity; Dependency; Deserving/Undeserving Poor; Malthusianism; Philanthropy; Poor Laws; Poorhouse/Almshouse; Poverty Research; Relief; Social Work

References and Further Reading

Greeley, Dawn. 1995. "Beyond Benevolence: Gender, Class, and the Development of Scientific Charity in New York City, 1882–1935." Ph.D. diss., State University of New York at Stony Brook.

Kusmer, Kenneth. 1973. "The Functions of Organized Charity in the Progressive Era: Chicago as a Case Study." *Journal of American History* 40 (December): 657–678.

Watson, Frank Dekker. 1971. *The Charity Organization Movement in the United States*. New York: Arno Press.

Waugh, Joan. 1997. *Unsentimental Reformer: The Life of Josephine Shaw Lowell*. Cambridge, MA: Harvard University Press.

Chavez, Cesar

See Agricultural and Farm Labor Organizing; Chicana/o Movement; Migrant Labor/Farm Labor

Chicana/o Movement

The Chicana/o movement, like many social movements during the 1960s and 1970s, emerged within the context of the broader civil rights struggles of that era. The civil rights movement, the antiwar movement, and the women's rights movement were all part of the social upheaval taking place in the United States. Like these larger movements, the Chicana/o movement had a direct impact on the future social structure of American society because it became the vehicle for increased political awareness, participation, and leadership on the part of Mexican Americans. In doing so, it paved the way for the development of the first national-level third party formed by an ethnic group (Navarro 2000, 1–13). In 1970, La Raza Unida Party was founded in Texas not only to provide Mexican Americans and other Latinos with an alternative to the two-party system but also to specifically address the political needs of Latino communities in the Southwest and other parts of the United States.

Although the Chicana/o movement is defined variously by different Chicano/a scholars, it is widely understood "as a social movement that emerged in the 1960s to protest the circumstances in which the Mexican American community found itself" (García 1998, 4–7). Enraged by the sustained exclusion that many Mexican Americans experienced in their political, economic, and social lives, self-empowered young Mexican Americans, who called themselves Chicanas/os, engaged in a struggle to change the conditions of their communities. Some of the issues that sparked protest and activism during the multifaceted Chicana/o movement included farmworkers' rights, substandard education, police brutality, land grants, and cultural devaluation.

Although the Chicana/o movement surged in the 1960s, its origins can be traced back to the early twentieth century. For example, some scholars point to Ernesto Galarza's 1929 speech against racism toward Mexican immigrant workers, which he delivered while a student at Stanford University, as the root of student activism. In this view, Galarza, a scholar and labor activist who authored such seminal books as *Spiders in the House and Workers in the Field* and *Merchants of Labor: The Mexican Bracero Story*, is the unsung hero of the Chicano youth movement, the precursor to the Chicana/o movement, and the farm labor movement of the 1960s (Navarro 1995, 45–48; Muñoz 1989, 21–28, 48–49).

The Chicana/o movement became a critical social force between the mid-1960s and the mid-1970s, inspiring the development of organizations such as the Mexican American Youth Organization (MAYO), the Mexican American Student Organization (MASO), the United Mexican American Students (UMAS), the Movimiento Estudiantil Chicano de Aztlán (MEChA), and the Crusade for Justice; encouraging the student strikes ("blowouts"), the farm labor movement, and the Chicano Moratorium; and leading to the emergence of charismatic leaders such as Cesar Chavez, Reies López Tijerina, Rodolfo "Corky" Gonzales, and José Angel Gutiérrez.

Underlying the social relevance of the movement as well as its potential long-term impact was the stark fact of the economic and political exclusion of Mexican Americans in U.S. society before and during the period of the Chicana/o movement. For example, the seminal work *Mexican-American People, the Nation's Second Largest Majority* (1970), by Leo Grebler, Joan W. Moore, and Ralph C. Guzman, used U.S. Census Bureau data to document the gross educational and income inequality suffered by Mexican Americans during the 1950s and 1960s. The accompanying table, extracted from their study, illustrates both the tremendous gap in educational attainment between Hispanic and Anglo residents of the Southwest and the resulting gap in income between these two groups. As Grebler, Moore, and Guzman stated, the most startling observation was that "Mexican Americans had only 47 cents for every dollar of Anglo income, and they were worse off than non-Whites." Furthermore, the study illustrated that although educational attainment was low for Mexican Americans, education alone did not explain this level of income inequality. Residential segregation was also associated with this income disparity (Grebler, Moore, and Guzman 1970, 19, 144).

Table 1

1960 education and economic indicators of Chicana/o inequality in the Southwest

	Anglo	*Hispanic*	*Non-white*
Educational Gap			
0–8 years	25.8%	61.4%	44.9%
9–12	52.1%	32.9%	43.4%
Some College	22.1%	5.6%	11.7%
Economic Gap			
Median Family Income Index (Anglo=100)	100	65	56
Median Individual Income	100	47	51

(Adapted from Grebler, Moore, Guzman 1970, 19, 144)

In addition to the gross economic and educational differences between Mexican Americans and Anglos, another important catalyst for this social movement was the educational segregation and perceived discrimination in the Southwest. In southwestern public schools, the practice of segregating students of Mexican origin was common before the 1960s and can be traced to the late 1890s, before the 1896 ruling in *Plessy v. Ferguson* (163 U.S. 537) that sanctioned the doctrine of "separate but equal." According to historian Gilbert González, the segregation of Mexican children was extensive between 1900 and 1950. He calls this period "the era of *de jure* segregation" of Mexican Americans in public school systems in the Southwest because the segregation of Mexican students was often supported by administrative policies that justified segregating students, either based on language and cultural "deficiencies" or for "Americanization" purposes (González 1990, 13–29). Some school districts, however, simply barred Mexican American children from attending regular public schools because of their ethnicity. In addition, separate schools and classrooms usually meant inferior facilities, equipment, teaching materials, and curricula, leading to a substandard education for segregated students (González 1990; San Miguel 1987). This segregation and perceived lack of equal educational opportunity played an important role in the student strikes of the late 1960s. Between 1968 and 1970, California (in Los Angeles, Delano, and Santa Clara), Texas (San Antonio, Elsa, and Abilene), Arizona (Phoenix), and Colorado (Denver) experienced student strikes, as did some cities in the Midwest (Martínez 2001, 175–177; Acuña 2000, 362–366; Rosales 2000, 331–332; Navarro 1995, 58–60).

In addition to protesting unequal education, the movement also produced social organizations and networks committed to advancing the economic and political participation of Mexican Americans within their communities. New organizations that focused on improving the social conditions for Mexican Americans included La Raza Unida Party, the Mexican American Legal Defense and Education Fund (MALDEF), the Southwest Voter Registration Project, and the National Council of La Raza (NCLR). Each of these expressed the specific regional and national concerns of the Mexican-origin community in the Southwest. Later, two of these groups, MALDEF and NCLR, developed into national pan-Latino, civil rights organizations.

Beyond the social and political organizations that emerged directly from the Chicana/o movement of the 1960s, the movement led to the establishment of Mexican American/Chicano studies programs in colleges and universities throughout the Southwest. These programs served the following purposes: (1) They developed Mexican American/Chicano–centered curricula largely taught by Chicana/o faculty; (2) they provided a respectful intellectual environment for Mexican-origin and other minority students; (3) they facilitated the development of student groups that were interested in maintaining involvement within the Mexican American/Chicano community; (4) they were a critical force in affirmative action with respect to the recruitment, retention, and promotion of Chicana/o faculty; and (5) they provided a psychological space in which Mexican-origin students could negotiate and understand the complexity of their own identities (Muñoz 1989, 191–202).

Although the Chicana/o movement did strive to represent the Mexican American community as a whole, the movement also repeated the gender stratification and differentiation that could be found both in the community and in the larger U.S. society. More often than not, the identified leaders within the movement were men. In many instances, male leaders enjoyed visibility not only because they authentically represented community interests but also because they exhibited unique charismatic qualities that captured the imagination and support of various Chicana/o communities. The best-known charismatic leaders were Cesar Chavez of the United Farm Workers; "Corky" Gonzales, leader of the Crusade for Justice; José Angel Gutiérrez, one of the founders of the national La Raza Unida Party; and Reies López Tijerina, leader of the land-grant movement and of La Alianza Federal de Mercedes (García 1998, 32–34, 61–62).

Although they were less visible as traditional leaders, women were equally important to the success of the Chicana/o movement. During the Chicana/o movement, personal and familial issues propelled many women into community action as structural leaders. This Chicana leadership style often called on a collective identity based on shared community concerns rather than on the individual visibility of one person. This quality of women's leadership was critical in sustaining the organizational structure of many Chicana/o movement groups. Unlike the charismatic male leaders of this period, the grassroots women activists provided the organizational structure that translated the political rhetoric into specific outcomes that addressed community needs. Marta Cotera, a La Raza Unida Party leader, put it this way:

> Everybody had a chance that wanted to do something. These guys might sit around talking and think that we're running the whole show, but they weren't, when it comes right down to it; they were the least important people, dare I say that. The important people were the organizers, and the organizers were very often women. But they were not necessarily the ones running for office, and we needed them to run for office. . . . we needed them because their sensitivity was real important to the organizing and development of the community. (Quoted in Rosales 2000, 391)

Because many women activists had dual responsibilities as mothers and workers, their organizations emphasized immediate concerns for the well-being of their families. An example of this type of organization was Parents Involvement in Community Action (PICA), which was started in east Los Angeles by Rose Lopez, Nellie Bustillos, and other Mexican American women who were concerned with the quality of the education their children were receiving in the local public schools. These Chicanas organized around the issue of parental rights, teacher quality, and funding for public schools—issues closely linked to family concerns. These women used educational and social networking strategies for group empowerment, which allowed for rapid membership growth in many local community organizations; PICA's rapid organizational growth was one example: "PICA was all women. . . . probably about 300, and that's probably a low estimate because . . . there were people coming out of curiosity. . . . each of us went back and told everybody 'Hey, do you know what's happening?' So it got bigger and bigger. . . . that's when we started breaking off chapters" (interview with retired activist Nellie Bustillos, September 24, 2001). Thus, PICA's organizational success in the area of educational reform in east Los Angeles is directly attributable to the leadership skills and style of its main Chicana organizers.

The notable women who led the Chicano/a movement included Dolores Huerta, cofounder of the United Farm Workers; Marta Cotera, Maria Hernandez, and Virginia Musquiz of the La Raza Unida Party, who also formed Mujeres Pro Raza Unida; and Alicia Escalante, founder of the Chicana Welfare Rights Organization (Rosales 2000, 391–393; García 1998, 40–41; Ruíz 1998, 112–113). Unfortunately, there are many more local structural leaders—like Rose Lopez and Nellie Bustillos—who have not yet been recognized for their contributions as leaders in many local communities during this period. The work of all of these women—Chicanas—helped mitigate and fight the political, educational, and economic causes and effects of poverty in Mexican American communities.

Adela de la Torre and
Maritza De La Trinidad

See also: Civil Rights Movement; Community Organizing; Community-Based Organizations; Latino/as; Mexican American Legal Defense and Education Fund (MALDEF); National Council of La Raza; Racial Segregation; Racism

References and Further Reading

Acuña, Rodolfo. 2000. *Occupied America: A History of Chicanos*. New York: Longman.

Bustillos, Nellie. 2001. Interview, Tucson, Arizona. September 24.

García, Ignacio M. 1998. *Chicanismo: The Forging of a Militant Ethos among Mexican Americans*. Tucson: University of Arizona Press.

González, Gilbert G. 1990. *Chicano Education in the*

Era of Segregation. Philadelphia: Balch Institute Press.

Grebler, Leo, Joan W. Moore, and Ralph C. Guzman. 1970. *The Mexican-American People, the Nation's Second Largest Minority*. New York: Free Press.

Martínez, Oscar J. 2001. *Mexican-Origin People in the United States: A Topical History*. Tucson: University of Arizona Press.

Muñoz, Carlos, Jr. 1989. *Youth, Identity, Power: The Chicano Movement*. London and New York: Verso.

Navarro, Armando. 1995. *Mexican American Youth Organization: Avant-Garde of the Chicano Movement in Texas*. Austin: University of Texas Press.

———. 2000. *La Raza Unida Party: A Chicano Challenge to the U.S. Two-Party Dictatorship*. Philadelphia: Temple University Press.

Rosales, F. Arturo. 1996. *Chicano!: The History of the Mexican American Civil Rights Movement*. Houston: Arte Público Press.

———. 2000. *Testimonio: A Documentary History of the Mexican American Struggle for Civil Rights*. Houston: Arte Público Press.

Ruíz, Vicki L. 1998. *From out of the Shadows: Mexican Women in 20th Century America*. New York and Oxford: Oxford University Press.

San Miguel, Guadalupe. 1987. *Let All of Them Take Heed: Mexican Americans and the Campaign for Educational Equality in Texas, 1910–1981*. Austin: University of Texas Press.

Child Care

The term "child care" refers to the regular care of children provided by persons other than their parents, usually while parents are pursuing education, training, or paid employment outside the home. In the United States today, child care provision is divided into two distinct sectors, public and private. In both sectors, several different types of services may be available, ranging from in-home care to child care centers, and the methods of payment differ. In the private sector, middle- and upper-income parents choose and pay for services directly. In the public sector, poor and low-income parents must find child care centers or family day care providers that will accept state-issued vouchers to be reimbursed at fixed rates, or they may, in some instances, receive state reimbursement for individual arrangements with kith or kin. Although the private sector appears to be wholly self-supporting, in fact it too is subsidized indirectly by the federal government through various income tax provisions and incentives to employers who establish child care services.

The division between the public and private systems of providing child care is the outcome of its erratic history in the United States. Over the centuries, child care has taken many forms, including in-home care by other relatives, domestic servants, and baby-sitters; care in institutions variously named crèches, day nurseries, day care centers, and child care centers; and care in institutions designed for other purposes, including summer camps, preschools and nursery schools, and even orphanages. Because of the enduring value placed on "mother care" within American culture, child care by others has come under frequent criticism, and efforts to gain support for public services have met with strong opposition. The federal government has offered inconsistent support for child care: briefly during the New Deal and World War II, and more extensively since the 1960s, as part of its efforts to reform public welfare policy.

Formal child care was rarely needed in the preindustrial societies of North America; both Native Americans and Euro-Americans were able to combine child rearing with other domestic and productive tasks. In these hunting-and-gathering or agrarian economies, adults placed their offspring nearby while they worked, using various devices, including cradle boards and standing stools, to keep very young children out of harm's way. Most care was provided within the household, though during busy seasons, colonial New Englanders might send slightly older children to inexpensive, loosely organized "dame schools" for supervision and rudimentary education. In general, child care was not seen as the exclusive task of mothers but was shared with fathers, older siblings, servants, and neighbors.

These arrangements became strained as market-based demands sped up the pace of production and as factories drew workers out of homes and fields, making it difficult for household members to combine productive and reproductive tasks. At the same time, late-colonial and early-republican ideologies, both patriotic and religious, defined a more distinctively gendered division of labor within families by enshrining motherhood and emphasizing fathers' breadwinning responsibilities. Although the value of women's productive labor declined, their childrearing and homemaking roles expanded and gained new stature. But the realities of life in industrializing America—illness, poverty, unemployment, desertion, early death—often prevented parents from fulfilling these ideals. Women left to maintain households on their own struggled to get by on paltry wages and whatever their children could earn on the streets. Torn between serving as both caretakers and breadwinners, many ended up entering a workhouse or almshouse and giving their children up for indenture.

It was within this context that the first formal child care in the United States developed. In 1793, a group of female Quaker philanthropists in Philadelphia, moved by the plight of dozens of women who had become widowed as the result of a yellow fever epidemic, decided to circumvent the prospect of family breakup by providing mothers with a means of supporting themselves and keeping their children with them. The House of Industry set up by the Female Society for the Relief and Employment of the Poor allowed the majority of women to work at spinning and weaving while their children were supervised in a separate nursery by some of the older widows. This not only provided the mothers with a small income but also kept the children off the streets; at the same time, it gave philanthropists an opportunity to inculcate the children with the "habits and virtues" of an industrious life.

Other female philanthropists in Philadelphia and in other cities across the United States soon followed the Quaker women's lead, but few, if any, of the "day nurseries" they set up seem to have included workrooms. Services were, for the most part, "custodial"; that is, children were fed, clothed, and kept safe, but their routines were highly regimented, and little attention was paid to education. By the 1870s, dozens of day nurseries were in operation, but their capacity was still far too small to accommodate the needs of the thousands of mothers thrown into the workforce by the vicissitudes of the economy and then by the Civil War and its aftermath. Despite the persistence of maternal employment among poor and working-class families, middle-class child care philanthropists continued to present their services as something mothers might turn to not on a regular basis but only when they were in distress. Moreover, many mothers were put off by the moralistic tone that characterized the nurseries.

Some parents were able to find a more hospitable form of child care in one of the many infant schools that were started in cities and villages along the eastern seaboard from the mid-1820s to the late 1840s. Inspired by several British models, including one established by the utopian industrialist Robert Owen in New Lanark, Scotland, the founders of these schools emphasized education as well as supervision and claimed that even very young children could benefit from attendance. Aware that employment was common among the mothers of the lower classes and that older children were often kept out of school to care for younger siblings, they sought to enroll all children on a regular basis, not only when their families were deemed to be in crisis. This, unfortunately, led to the decline of the infant schools, for middle-class parents, imbued with the ideal of mother care, began to fear that their own influence would be supplanted by that of the schools and withdrew their support. After about two decades, the infant school movement died out.

Another form of child care could be found in

the antebellum South, where slaveholding planters regularly assigned slaves who were either too old or too young for heavy labor to care for very young slave children while their mothers worked at other tasks. On larger plantations, a "nuss house" might hold up to 100 African American children. This system was, of course, devised wholly to benefit the planters; it allowed them to maximize both the productive and reproductive labor of their female slaves, while minimizing the need for family ties among the slaves themselves and also controlling the socialization of their children. Ironically, while female slaves were denied the right to nurture their own offspring, they were frequently pressed into service as "mammies" or even wet nurses to slaveholders' children.

After Emancipation, African American women continued to work outside the home in greater numbers than white women, often as domestic servants and caretakers of white children. African American women's organizations like the National Association of Colored Women responded to the ongoing need for child care by founding a number of day nurseries, particularly in the urban South. The Neighborhood Union in Atlanta, for example, founded five free kindergartens between 1905 and 1908. Unlike their white counterparts, Black child care philanthropists regarded maternal employment as a normal (if less than desirable) part of family life and thus sought to create long-term, rather than temporary, services; instead of the wealthy funding child care for the poor, support was spread widely across African American communities.

Throughout the nineteenth century, lone mothers (and sometimes fathers) of all races who were compelled to work but had no alternative form of care sent their children to orphanages for various lengths of time in order to avoid indenture. These parents had no intention of surrendering the children for adoption; indeed, they often paid for the children's room and board. By the second half of the century, the placement of "half orphans" in asylums became so widespread that some critics accused parents of shirking their responsibilities.

Most orphanages refused to admit infants, creating a dilemma for women who had newborn children and who needed to support themselves. To accommodate this group, in 1854, female philanthropists in New York City founded the New York Nursery and Child's Hospital, and in 1873, Philadelphia women followed suit with the Philadelphia Home for Infants. Such institutions offered two options: Mothers could place their children in the nursery and hire themselves out as wet nurses, or they could remain in the hospital and receive room and board while nursing another infant in addition to their own. Unfortunately, the mortality rate in these nurseries was very high owing to the lack of antibiotics and other biomedical remedies and the severe impact of infectious contagion among infants whose resistance was lowered by what later physicians would diagnose as "hospitalism" or "failure to thrive" under institutional conditions.

Throughout this period, parents who had to work outside the home also turned to older children, their own siblings, and other relatives or neighbors for informal care. Reformers deplored situations in which children were either left alone or in the care of "little mothers"—sisters only slightly older than their charges—but they reserved their severest criticism for "baby farms," the term they used for informal caretaking arrangements in poor urban neighborhoods. Although scurrilous newspaper reports and investigations accused these "shady" and "notorious" operations of trafficking in infants or of allowing them to perish through starvation or neglect, later studies suggest that most such caretakers acted responsibly and provided affordable services to low-income mothers who felt more comfortable leaving their children in a familiar environment (often with co-ethnics, an important consideration for minorities and immigrants) rather than in the sterile, rigid surroundings of a charitable day nursery.

At the end of the nineteenth century, then, American child care had come to consist of a range of formal and informal provisions that were generally associated with the poor, minorities, and immigrants and were stigmatized as charitable and custodial. This pattern of practices and institutions provided a weak foundation for building twentieth-century social services. As women's reform efforts picked up steam during the Progressive Era, however, child care became a target for reform and modernization. To draw attention to the need for child care and to demonstrate "approved methods of rearing children from infancy on" (quoted in Michel 1999, 51), a group of prominent New York philanthropists led by Josephine Jewell Dodge set up a Model Day Nursery in the Children's Building at the 1893 World's Columbian Exhibition in Chicago and then went on to found the National Federation of Day Nurseries (NFDN), the first nationwide organization devoted to this issue, in 1898.

The philosophy of the NFDN was somewhat self-contradictory. Bent upon bringing day nurseries up to date by incorporating the methods of the emerging fields of social work and early childhood education, its leaders nevertheless clung to nineteenth-century attitudes toward maternal employment; that is, they continued to regard day care as an emergency stopgap, as not part of normal family life. In keeping with this philosophy, nurseries subjected applicants to strict scrutiny and expelled children once their families were no longer in dire need, regardless of the educational benefits they might be enjoying. As a result of such practices, day nurseries came to be seen as backward and were pushed to the margins of progressive social services.

In the meantime, reformers began to formulate another solution to the dilemma of poor mothers compelled to work outside the home: mothers' or widows' pensions. In the view of prominent Progressives such as Jane Addams, day nurseries only added to such women's difficulties by encouraging them to take arduous, low-paid jobs while their children suffered from inadequate attention and care. Thus she and her Hull House colleagues, including Julia Lathrop, who would go on to become the first chief of the U.S. Children's Bureau when it was founded in 1912, called for a policy to support mothers so they could stay at home with their children. Unlike child care, the idea of mothers' pensions quickly gained popular support because it did nothing to challenge conventional gender roles. Indeed, some reformers argued that mothers, like soldiers, were performing a "service to the nation" and therefore deserved public support when they lacked a male breadwinner. Pensions "spread like wildfire" (Skocpol 1992, 424) as several large national organizations, including the General Federation of Women's Clubs and the National Congress of Mothers, mounted a highly successful state-by-state legislative campaign for state-funded mothers' pensions. By 1930, nearly every state in the union had passed some form of mothers' or widows' pension law, making this the policy of choice for addressing the needs of low-income mothers and pushing child care further into the shadows of private charity.

Despite the rhetoric, however, mothers' pensions could not fully address the problems of poor and low-income mothers, and many women had no alternative but to go out to work. In most states, funding for pensions was inadequate, and many mothers found themselves ineligible because of highly restrictive criteria or stringent, biased administrative practices. African American women in particular were frequently denied benefits, in the North as well as the South, on the grounds that they, unlike white women, were accustomed to working for wages and thus should not be encouraged to stay at home to rear their children. Because pension coverage was sporadic and scattered, maternal employment not only persisted but increased, adding to the demand for child care. Philanthropists were hard put to meet this growing need using private funding alone. With mothers' pensions monopolizing the social policy agenda, however, they had no prospect of winning public funding for day nurseries.

This pattern continued into the 1920s, as the U.S. Children's Bureau (CB) conducted a series of studies of maternal and child labor in agriculture and industry across the country. Although investigators found many instances of injuries, illnesses, and even fatalities resulting from situations in which infants and toddlers were either left alone or brought into hazardous workplaces, the CB refused to advocate for federal support for child care; instead, it worked to strengthen mothers' pensions so that more mothers could stay at home. CB officials were influenced, in part, by the thinking of experts such as the physician Douglas Thom, an advocate of child guidance who argued that "worn and wearied" wage-earning mothers who had no time for their children's welfare stifled their development (quoted in Michel 1999, 110). At the same time, the reputation of day nurseries continued to slide as efforts to upgrade their educational component flagged due to lack of funds, and nursery schools, the darlings of Progressive-Era early childhood educators, began to capture the middle-class imagination.

The Depression and then World War II had a mixed impact on the fortunes of child care. On the eve of the Great Depression, fewer than 300 nursery schools were in operation, compared to 800 day nurseries, but as unemployment rose, day nursery enrollments fell sharply and charitable donations also declined, forcing 200 day nurseries to close down between 1931 and 1940. Meanwhile, at the urging of prominent early childhood educators, the Works Progress Administration (WPA), a key New Deal agency, established a program of Emergency Nursery Schools (ENS). Primarily intended to offer employment opportunities to unemployed teachers, these schools were also seen as a means of compensating for the "physical and mental handicaps" (quoted in Michel 1999, 120) caused by the economic downturn. Nearly 3,000 schools, enrolling more than 64,000 children, were started between 1933 and 1934; over the next year, these were consolidated into 1,900 schools with a capacity for approximately 75,000 students (cited in Michel 1999, 119). The program covered forty-three states and the District of Columbia, Puerto Rico, and the Virgin Islands. Unlike the earlier nursery schools, which were largely private, charged fees, and served a middle-class clientele, these free, government-sponsored schools were open to children of all classes.

Designed as schools rather than as child care facilities, the ENS were only open for part of the day, and their enrollments were supposedly restricted to the children of the unemployed. They did, however, become a form of de facto child care for parents employed on various WPA work-relief projects. Unlike that of the day nurseries, the educational component of the ENS was well developed because of early childhood educators' strong interest in the program. Organizations such as the National Association for Nursery Education, which was eager to promulgate the ideas of progressive pedagogy, even sent in their own staff members to supervise teacher training and to oversee curricula. The educators were frustrated, however, by inadequate facilities and equipment and by difficulties in convincing teachers with conventional classroom experience to adopt a less-structured approach to working with young children. By the late 1930s, the ENS also began to suffer from high staff turnover as teachers left to take up better-paying jobs in defense plants. Between 1936 and 1942, nearly 1,000 schools were forced to close down.

Although the approach of World War II reduced the unemployment crisis in the United States, it created a social crisis as millions of women, including many mothers, sought employment in war-related industries. Despite a critical labor shortage, the federal government was at first reluctant to recruit mothers of small children, claiming that "mothers who remain at home are performing an essential patriotic service" (quoted in Michel 1999, 131). Gaining support from social workers, who opposed maternal employment on psychological grounds, government officials dallied in responding to the unprecedented need for child care. In 1941 Congress passed the Lanham Act, which was intended to create community facilities in "war-impact areas," but it was not until 1943 that this was interpreted as authorizing support for child care. In the meantime, Congress allocated $6 million to convert the remaining ENS into child care facilities. The organization of new services bogged down in interagency competition at the federal level and in the considerable red tape involved when local communities applied for federal funding. According to the government's own guidelines, one child care slot was required for every ten female defense workers; however, when the female labor force peaked at 19 million in 1944, only 3,000 child care centers were operating, with a capacity for 130,000 children—far short of the 2 million places that were theoretically needed.

Public opinion was slow to accept the dual ideas of maternal employment and child care. The popular media frequently reported on the spread of "latchkey children" and on instances of sleeping children found locked in cars in company parking lots while their mothers worked the night shift. Such stories served to castigate "selfish" wage-earning mothers rather than to point up the need for child care. At the same time, children's experts warned parents that children in group care might suffer the effects of "maternal deprivation" and urged them to maintain tranquil home environments to protect their children from the war's upheaval. What child care there was did little to dispel public concerns. Hastily organized and often poorly staffed, most centers fell far short of the high standards early childhood educators had sought to establish for the ENS. One exception was the Child Service Centers set up by the Kaiser Company at its shipyards in Portland, Oregon. Architect-designed and scaled to children's needs, they offered care twenty-four hours a day (to accommodate night-shift workers), a highly trained staff, a curriculum planned by leading early childhood experts, and even a cooked-food service for weary parents picking up their children after an arduous shift.

Despite its inadequacies, federally sponsored New Deal and wartime child care marked an important step in American social provision. Congress, however, was wary of creating permanent services and repeatedly emphasized that public support would be provided "for the duration only." Soon after V-J Day, funding for the Lanham Act was cut off, forcing most of the child care centers to shut down within a year or two. But the need for child care persisted, as maternal employment, after an initial dip due to postwar layoffs, actually began to rise. Across the country, national organizations like the Child Welfare League of America, along with numerous local groups, demonstrated and lobbied for continuing public support. These groups failed to persuade Congress to pass the 1946 Maternal and Child Welfare Act, which would have continued federal funding for child care, but they did win public child care provisions in New York City, Philadelphia, and Washington, D.C., and in California. During the Korean War, Congress approved a public child care program but then refused to appropriate funds for it. Finally, in 1954, Congress found an approach to child care it could live with: the child care tax deduction. This permitted low- to moderate-income families (couples could earn up to $4,500 per year) to deduct up to $600 for child care from their income taxes, provided the services were needed "to permit the taxpayer to hold gainful employment."

The tax deduction offered some financial relief to certain groups of parents, but reformers were not satisfied, for such a measure failed to address basic issues such as the supply, distribution, affordability, and quality of child care. In 1958, building on the experience they had gained in lobbying for postwar provisions, activists formed a national organization devoted exclusively to child care, the Inter-City Committee for Day Care of Children (ICC, later to become the National Committee on the Day Care of Children). The organization was led by Elinor Guggenheimer, a longtime New York City child care activist; Sadie Ginsberg, a leader of the Child Study Association of America; Cornelia Goldsmith, a New York City official who had helped establish a licensing system for child care in that city; and Winifred Moore, a child care specialist who had worked in both government and the private sector. Unlike its predecessor, the National Federation of Day Nurseries (which had been absorbed by the Child Welfare League of America in 1942), the ICC believed that private charity could not provide adequate child care on its own; instead, the new organization sought to work closely with government agencies like the U.S. Children's Bureau and the U.S. Women's Bureau (WB) to gain federal support.

The ICC experimented with a number of different rationales for child care, generally preferring to avoid references to maternal employment in favor of stressing the need to "safeguard children's welfare." In 1958 and 1959, the ICC helped mobilize grassroots support for several child care bills introduced into Congress by Senator Jacob Javits (R-New York), but to no avail. The ICC did succeed in convincing the CB and WB to cosponsor a National Conference on the Day Care of Children in Washington, D.C., in November 1960. At that conference, several government officials pointed to the growing demand for labor and to what now appeared to be an irreversible trend toward maternal employment, but many attendees continued to express ambivalence about placing young children in group care. Guggenheimer, however, noted that mothers would work "whether good care is available or not. It is the child," she emphasized, "that suffers when the care is poor" (quoted in Michel 1999, 232). Guggenheimer did not call directly for government support for child care, but she made it clear that private and voluntary agencies could no longer shoulder the burden. The CB and WB, under the direction of chiefs appointed by President Dwight D. Eisenhower, were reluctant to take the lead on this issue, but the president-elect, John F. Kennedy, in a message to the conference, expressed his awareness of the problem, stating, "I believe we must take further steps to encourage day care programs that will protect our children and provide them with a basis for a full life in later years" (quoted in Michel 1999, 235).

Kennedy's message, along with subsequent statements, implied that his administration sought a broad-based approach to child care. In a widely circulated report, the President's Commission on the Status of Women acknowledged that maternal employment was becoming the norm and pointed out that child care could not only help women who decided to work outside the home but also serve as a developmental boon to children and advance social and racial integration. But the Kennedy administration could not muster sufficient political support to push through a universal child care policy. Instead, in two welfare reform bills, passed in 1962 and 1965, Congress linked federal support for child care to policies designed to encourage poor and low-income women to enter training programs or take employment outside the home. The goal was to reduce the number of Americans receiving "welfare" (Aid to Families with Dependent Children, or AFDC) and prevent women from becoming recipients in the first place.

From 1969 to 1971, a coalition of feminists, labor leaders, civil rights leaders, and early childhood advocates worked with Congress to legislate universal child care policy, but their efforts failed when President Richard M. Nixon vetoed the Comprehensive Child Development Act of 1971. As a result, for the next three decades, direct federal support for child care was limited to policies targeting low-income families. At the same time, however, the federal government offered several types of indirect support to middle- and upper-class families in the form of tax incentives for employer-sponsored child care and several ways of using child care costs to reduce personal income taxes. In the 1980s, under the Reagan administration, the distribution of federal child care funding shifted, as expenditures for low-income families were dramatically reduced while those benefiting middle- and high-income families nearly doubled. Such measures stimulated the growth of voluntary and for-profit child care, much of which was beyond the reach of low-income families. These families received some help from the Child Care and Development Block Grant (CCDBG), passed in 1990, which allocated $825 million to individual states.

The Personal Responsibility and Work Opportunity Reconciliation Act of 1996 replaced AFDC with time-limited public assistance coupled with stringent employment mandates. Acknowledging the need for expanded child care to support this welfare-to-work plan, Congress combined CCDBG, along with several smaller programs, into a single block grant—the Child Care and Development Fund. Although more public funds for child care were available than ever before, problems of supply and quality continue to limit access to child care for welfare recipients who are now compelled to take employment, and moderate-income families must cope with ever-rising costs for child care. For all families, the quality of child care is compromised by the high rate of turnover among employees in the field, in itself the result of low pay and poor benefits.

Because of its long history and current structure, the American child care system is divided along class lines, making it difficult for parents to unite and lobby for improved services and increased public funding for child care for all children. When it comes to public provisions for children and families, the United States compares poorly with other advanced industrial nations such as France, Sweden, and Denmark, which not only offer free or subsidized care to children over three but also provide paid maternity or parental leaves. Unlike the United States, these countries use child care not as a lever in a harsh mandatory employment policy toward low-income mothers but as a means of helping parents of all classes reconcile the demands of work and family life.

Sonya Michel

See also: Child-Saving; Foster Care; Maternalism; Maternalist Policy; Orphanages; Welfare Policy/Welfare Reform

References and Further Reading

Berry, Mary Frances. 1993. *The Politics of Parenthood: Child Care, Women's Rights, and the Myth of the Good Mother*. New York: Viking.

Goodwin, Joanne L. 1997. *Gender and the Politics of Welfare Reform: Mothers' Pensions in Chicago, 1911–1929*. Chicago: University of Chicago Press.

Levy, Denise Urias, and Sonya Michel. 2002. "More Can Be Less: Child Care and Welfare Reform in the United States." In *Child Care at the Crossroads: Gender and Welfare State Restructuring*, ed. Rianne Mahon and Sonya Michel. New York: Routledge.

Michel, Sonya. 1999. *Children's Interests/Mothers' Rights: The Shaping of America's Child Care Policy*. New Haven: Yale University Press.

Rose, Elizabeth. 1998. *A Mother's Job: The History of Day Care, 1890–1960*. New York: Oxford University Press.

Skocpol, Theda. 1992. *Protecting Soldiers and Mothers: The Political Origins of Social Policy in the United States*. Cambridge, MA: Harvard University Press.

Child Labor

Child labor generally means wage work done by children and adolescents, which is viewed as harmful to their growth and overall development. Children had always worked in the United States, but in the mid-nineteenth century, the term "child labor" took on a negative connotation. Prior to the Civil War, most American children labored on family farms or as slaves. A smaller group, like Benjamin Franklin, worked

"Child-Labor in Southern Cotton Mills," Irene M. Ashby, 1901

Come with me to an Alabama town, where there is a large cheerful-looking factory. Walking up the long, orderly building, deafened by the racket, yet fascinated by the ingenious machinery, you become suddenly aware of a little gray shadow flitting restlessly up and down the aisles—a small girl, and with bare feet and pale face. She has a worn and anxious aspect, as if a weight of care and responsibility rested already on her baby shoulders. She either does not look at you at all or she turns her eyes but for a moment, unchildlike in their lack of interest, looking back immediately to the spinning frame. A thread breaks first at one end of the long frame, then at the other. The tiny fingers repair the damage at the first place and she walks listlessly to the other. Something goes wrong above, and the child pushes forward a box to stand on that she may reach it. With a great shock it dawns on you that this child is working. . . .

I was prepared to find child-labor [in Alabama], for wherever easily manipulated machinery takes the place of human muscles the child is inevitably drawn into the labor market, unless there are laws to protect it. But one could hardly be prepared to find in America today white children, six and seven years of age, working for twelve hours a day—aroused before daybreak and toiling till long after sundown in winter, with only half an hour for rest and refreshment. . . . Some [mills] run the machinery at night, and little children are called on to endure the strain of all-night work—and are sometimes kept awake by the vigilant superintendent with cold water dashed into their faces.

Source: Irene M. Ashby, "Child-Labor in Southern Cotton Mills," *World's Work* 2 (October 1901): 1290–1295. Reprinted in *The Rebuilding of Old Commonwealths and Other Documents of Social Reform in the Progressive Era South,* ed. William A. Link (New York and Boston: Bedford Books, 1996), 87–88.

as unpaid apprentices in artisan shops. Such work was often difficult and brutal, as Franklin attested in his autobiography, but the intimacy of working for family and friends tempered criticism of the practice.

The Industrial Revolution marked a shift away from children's traditional work roles. In 1790, Samuel Slater of Rhode Island hired nine children, aged seven through twelve, to work in a large room filled with spinning wheels. George Washington's treasury secretary, Alexander Hamilton, welcomed such efforts as a means of easing what seemed to be a growing problem of poverty among widows and fatherless children. The standard practice of paying children less than half the wage given to adult men, along with a perception that young workers were more docile, made child labor popular with employers. In addition, 50 percent of the U.S. population in the decade prior to the Civil War was age seventeen or younger. Consequently, wage-earning children became a growing part of the nation's workforce as the country moved to a more industrial and urban-based economy.

The growth in wage labor among children contrasted sharply with the development of a new middle-class ideal depicting childhood as a distinct period of life separate from adult responsibilities. Urban, middle-class couples had fewer children and sent them to school longer. The shift from farm to factory lessened families' dependence on household and agricultural production. Children spent more time in school as education beyond the elementary grades became an important step to white-collar employment.

Despite the growing acceptance of the middle-class definition of childhood, a rising proportion of children in working-class families

Little spinner in Mollahan Cotton Mills, Newberry, South Carolina, December 3, 1908. These and other photographs were used to draw public attention to the exploitation of child laborers, as indicated in the original caption: "Many others as small." (Photo by Lewis W. Hine, Library of Congress)

were taking jobs in the nation's factories, mines, and streets. In 1842, Massachusetts and Connecticut passed the nation's first restrictions on child labor, limiting the workday for children under twelve to ten hours a day, six days a week. In 1884, New York outlawed contract labor of young people living in reform schools. Illinois passed a law in 1893 prohibiting the employment of children under fourteen for more than eight hours a day or at night. By 1889, New York and Colorado had prohibited industrial employment for anyone under fourteen. But all such laws were poorly enforced and failed to cover many working children. Those doing piecework at home, laboring in sharecropping fields, or working as migrant agricultural workers were not counted as child laborers and were not covered by legal protections.

Even with the limitations in existing data, it is clear that the employment of children for wages increased as the nation industrialized. According to the 1870 census, about one in every eight children in America worked for wages. The 1900 count showed that the ratio was one in every six, and the proportion continued to grow through 1910. Reformers pointed to the trends as a threat to the nation's future. They argued that children who were spending so much time on the job were neglecting school, which contributed to high rates of morbidity, mortality, and serious injury and made the youngsters more likely to become dependent adults unable to care for themselves or their families.

In 1907, reformers organized the National Child Labor Committee (NCLC) in order to lobby for restrictions on child labor. From 1908 to 1921, the NCLC paid Lewis Hine to take photographs of child laborers that would pull at the nation's heartstrings and create public sympathy for reform legislation. President William Howard Taft signed an act establishing the U.S. Children's Bureau on April 9, 1912. Over the next three decades, the NCLC worked closely with the U.S. Children's Bureau to promote child labor reforms at both the state and federal levels.

The effort faced strong opposition from manufacturers and newspaper editors. In addition, many working-class parents saw little advantage to keeping their children in school instead of sending them to work. Despite such resistance, in 1916 Congress passed the Keating-Owen Act. Just before the law was to go into effect, the U.S. Supreme Court praised the law's intent but declared its method unconstitutional (*Hammer v. Dagenhart*, 1918). In 1924, Congress passed a constitutional amendment outlawing child labor, but by 1932 only six states had voted for ratification of the measure and twenty-four had rejected it.

From 1910 to 1930, state laws making school attendance compulsory contributed to a decline in the percentage of wage-earning children despite the failed effort to win a constitutional amendment. New technologies also made the use of child labor less economical. Although the onset of the Great Depression temporarily reversed this trend, child welfare advocates and labor unions pressured Franklin D. Roosevelt's administration to devise child labor regulations in the 1933 National Industrial Recovery Act (NIRA). The NIRA ended, however, when the U.S. Supreme Court declared it unconstitutional on May 27, 1935. Sensing a new attitude in the Supreme Court by the late 1930s, advocates included child labor regulations in the 1938 Fair Labor Standards Act (FLSA). The new law was very similar to the 1916 Keating-Owen Act, prohibiting the employment of those under fourteen and placing restrictions on workers fourteen through seventeen. In its 1941 decision in *United States v. Darby*, the Supreme Court reversed its earlier *Hammer v. Dagenhart* ruling against child labor regulation as well as its holdings against state and federal regulation of labor standards generally. Reformers understood, however, that even the 1938 FLSA did not protect all children, especially those working in agriculture. Nevertheless, child labor has declined in the United States since its passage. The legal employment of those under fourteen has been eliminated, but older adolescents continue to work for wages, although most do so while attending school. Despite the decline in child labor, more U.S. teens work for wages than in other industrialized nations.

There is no single explanation for the decline in most types of exploitative child labor. A growing emphasis on education, developing attitudes about the inappropriateness of wage labor among children, and smaller families interacted with the growth of technology and social changes to lessen child labor. Poverty is a continuing cause of children's employment throughout the world. As in the past, children from poor minority or immigrant families or those living in agricultural areas remain the most likely to work for wages.

Kriste Lindenmeyer

See also: Fair Labor Standards Act (FLSA); Progressive Era and 1920s

References and Further Reading

Bremner, Robert H., et al. 1974. *Children and Youth in America: A Documentary History*. Vols. 2, 3. Cambridge, MA: Harvard University Press.

Lindenmeyer, Kriste. 1997. *"A Right to Childhood": The U.S. Children's Bureau and Child Welfare, 1912–1946*. Urbana: University of Illinois Press.

Nasaw, David. 1991. *Children of the City: At Work and at Play*. New York: Oxford University Press.

Trattner, Walter I. 1970. *Crusade for Children: A History of the National Child Labor Committee and Child Labor Reform in America*. Chicago: Quadrangle Books.

Child Support

Child support is the financial contribution a noncustodial parent is required by law to make for a child's upkeep, once a child support order has been secured by the custodial parent. Federal policy is most interested in child support as an income source for poor, single-mother families.

The United States is unique among industrialized democracies in its emphasis on private solutions for children's poverty. Child support collection, which ties children's economic welfare to income from noncustodial parents, is a major component of the U.S. social welfare system. But child support is generally an inadequate solution to child poverty because when single-parent families are poor, the other parent usually is also poor, and child support is difficult to collect and distribute fairly. In addition, the reliance on child support as a solution to poverty poses significant problems for families. For example, in those instances where the noncustodial parent is abusive or where the noncustodial parent is generous with time and affection but cannot afford to give money, child support policy robs custodial parents of the right to make appropriate decisions for their families.

History of Child Support and Poverty Programs

American child support laws came into existence largely to protect against indigence for children whose fathers divorced or abandoned their mothers. Divorce was relatively rare in colonial America, but the divorce rate increased steadily during the nineteenth century. As both divorce and abandonment increased, courts were willing to impose civil child support obligations on the absent father. The concern about the rising divorce rate coincided with several social developments, including the development of an ideal of childhood in which young children were specially cared for and educated. At the same time, the traditional English rule of favoring fathers in child custody contests gave way to a preference for maternal custody for the child. Divorced or abandoned mothers therefore needed support in order to care for their children, who would take longer to become economically independent.

In the first part of the twentieth century, both state support and child support were governed by state and local law. Family law in each state established a child support claim for custodial parents after divorce. Many states provided "mothers' pensions" for poor single mothers, but the target recipients of these programs were widows. Private charities also provided assistance to mothers considered worthy of such assistance, again usually widows. The possibility that there might be a father who could provide support was not an issue for such charities.

The Great Depression changed the way income assistance was provided for poor single mothers with children. Private charities and local relief programs could not meet the overwhelming needs caused by the Depression. The New Deal's Aid to Dependent Children program (ADC) made federal money available to states that maintained cash-assistance programs for single mothers and their children. Although states imposed many conditions on mothers in exchange for this assistance, state programs did not require mothers to secure paternal child support as a condition of aid. By and large, child support remained something middle-class or wealthy families might receive as a consequence of divorce.

The first link between ADC and child support came in 1950 with the enactment of a provision requiring state welfare agencies to notify local law enforcement agencies whenever aid was provided to a child who had been abandoned by a parent (Section 402[a][11] of the Social Security Act as enacted by Section 321 of Public Law 81–734 [1950]). Referred to as NOLEO (an acronym for "Notify law enforcement officials"), the requirement left it up to the states to follow through on attempts to locate an absent parent or to collect assistance from him. In 1965, Congress allowed states attempting to locate a parent who owed child support to an AFDC child to have access to information from the federal government on that parent's location and employment status. And in 1967, Congress allowed states to obtain from the Internal Revenue Service (IRS) the address of an absent parent who owed child support. In addition, states were required to designate an organizational unit to oversee the establishment of paternity and the collection of child support and to cooperate with law enforcement officials in other states (Public Law 90–248).

Despite these requirements, states were erratic in their attempts to collect child support, with some states doing nothing and few making serious efforts. Some states required mothers receiving aid to institute support actions or otherwise cooperate in finding the absent parent. However, under the legal doctrines established in other cases, the fact that there was no federal requirement of cooperation with child support enforcement permitted several courts to rule that state-level cooperation requirements amounted to additional conditions of eligibility not provided for in federal law (*Lascaris v. Shirley*, 420 U.S. 730, 95 S. Ct. 1190, 43 L. Ed. 2d 583 [1975] [per curiam], *aff'g Shirley v. Lavine*, 365 F. Supp. 818 [S.D.N.Y.1973] [three-judge court]).

Linking Child Support and Income Support: Child Support Enforcement Act of 1975 and Beyond

In 1975, Congress passed a massive statutory scheme designed to require mothers who needed public assistance to cooperate in efforts to enforce child support and to require states to enforce child support obligations from absent parents. The Child Support Enforcement Act added to Title IV-D of the Social Security Act an entire section designed to improve collection of child support from absent fathers (Public Law 93–647 [1975], the Social Security Amendments of 1974 creating Part D of Title IV of the Social Security Act, Sections 402[a][25], [26]; Sections 451 *et. seq.*).

The impetus for this congressional action was a fear that federal welfare expenditures were growing too rapidly and that one of the causes of that growth was parents' failure to take primary responsibility for the financial needs of their children. Dissatisfied with state child support enforcement efforts, Congress believed both that children and custodial parents needed help in securing child support and that noncustodial parents should reimburse the government for welfare expenses incurred for children they did not adequately support. Although welfare families were the focus of federal child support enforcement legislation, government assistance in collecting child support proved widely popular, leading Congress to include families not receiving welfare within the scope of the newly enacted Child Support Enforcement Act.

The new Title IV-D imposed a variety of requirements on both the states and recipients. Added were new eligibility requirements mandating that applicants or recipients assign their rights to support to the state and cooperate with the state in establishing paternity and securing support. The act also authorized the federal government to oversee the child support program in the states, to monitor and require reports, and to refer cases for wage garnishment to the IRS. States were required to establish paternity for AFDC recipients and for others who applied for services, to collect child support payments directly and distribute them as specifically directed by statute, to establish a parent locator service, and to cooperate with other states in locating absent parents and securing support. Federal employees who owed child support were subject to wage garnishment.

Title IV-D was a revolutionary effort by the federal government to oversee child support collection. Support for the effort was widespread in Congress, and the law was subsequently expanded and toughened. In 1977, Title IV-D was amended to expand wage garnishment provisions and to include medical support. In 1980, Congress authorized increased federal financial participation in the program in the form of a 90 percent match for child support enforcement–related expenses for welfare families and an authorized match for expenditures on non-welfare families. In addition, services were expanded for non-AFDC families. In 1984, spousal support was brought within the domain of Title IV-D, and Congress significantly toughened requirements for the states, now requiring such improved enforcement mechanisms as mandatory income withholding, expedited processes, state income tax interceptions, and the bringing of paternity actions up to a child's eighteenth birthday. In addition, improved interstate procedures were required, and the statute made it clear that all services must be available to both non-AFDC and AFDC families. In 1988, the Family Support Act was passed, emphasizing parents' responsibility for their children. Child support enforcement was again expanded, requiring compliance with child support guidelines, setting numerical goals for the establishment of paternity, requiring genetic testing in contested cases, and requiring immediate wage withholding in almost all cases. Notification requirements were also added for families for whom the IV-D system was collecting support.

In 1996, the Personal Responsibility and Work Opportunity Reconciliation Act repealed AFDC and in its place established the Temporary Assistance for Needy Families (TANF) program. TANF replaced the AFDC entitlement program with a block grant to the states. In addition to repealing the federal entitlement to assistance and giving the states broader discretion over program design, TANF placed a time limit on receipt of assistance and imposed strict work requirements on all recipients. Although Congress granted states greater flexibility in administering many aspects of welfare, it also imposed strong federal requirements with respect to child support enforcement. The 1996 welfare law increased federal oversight over child support enforcement and toughened punishments for parents who default. In addition, the 1996 law required states to impose a minimum 25 percent reduction of benefits on TANF families whose mothers failed to cooperate with establishing paternity or collecting child support.

The increase in the federal government's role in child support enforcement was accompanied by increased blaming of absent parents for the problems of poverty and increased calls to punish parents who failed to pay child support. In 1998, Congress enacted the Deadbeat Parents Punishment Act, which made it a federal felony, subject to two years in prison, to cross state lines with the intent of evading a child support obligation. In addition, the statute made it a crime to willfully fail to support a child residing in a different state.

Child Support Enforcement: Help for Some Families

Child support enforcement can provide additional income for some families. The attempt to obtain support from absent parents can be effective for families whose absent parent has significant earnings or resources. In that case, children will be far better off with financial help from their father than they would be relying on the state to supply inadequate welfare benefits. Mothers who need public assistance and know that the father could contribute to the support of his children are very interested in securing that support, and their major complaint about the child support enforcement system is that it is not effective enough. The importance of child support to many families is indicated by the lawsuits brought to enforce Title IV-D requirements when custodial parents feel their state is not doing enough to collect support (see *Blessing v. Freestone*, 520 U.S. 329 [1997]). Although there are questions as to whether these suits can be maintained in federal court, the fact that they continue to be brought is an indication of how desperate many families are to receive help in obtaining child support from the absent parent.

It should be noted that child support collections help only those families that do not receive welfare. A welfare recipient for whom child support is collected does not receive any part of it if the child support obligation is less than the welfare grant—unless the state chooses to pass through the child support collections or some part of them to the recipient. Thirty-one states keep all child support collected on behalf of welfare recipients as a kind of reimbursement for welfare. Of the remaining states, all but two pass through no more than fifty dollars to the welfare family.

Although welfare and child support are inextricably linked, the vast majority of collections made by the Title IV-D program are actually on behalf of non-AFDC families. In 1998, of $14,347,000 in child support collected, $11,697,800, or 81.5 percent, was for non-AFDC families (U.S. House of Representatives, Committee on Ways and Means 2000, 538–539). This raises the question of how effective child support enforcement has been in helping the poorest families. On the other hand, for those families that do receive it, child support can be an important income supplement, even serving to keep those families above poverty. For children in all divorced families, child support is between 26 and 29 percent of the family income. For children in poor families not receiving public assistance, child support constitutes 36 percent of income (Roberts 2002, 2). For some families, therefore, child support can make an important difference.

Child Support Enforcement: Harm for Some Families

On the other hand, for some families, the child support enforcement system can cause serious harm. First, the requirement that custodial parents cooperate with child support enforcement is difficult for a woman who may desperately need public aid but who may not be able to identify the father of her child, may not be able to locate him, may not have enough information to satisfy welfare workers in charge of pursuing child support, or may know he cannot pay and not want to risk sending him to jail. Some states have imposed very specific requests for information on applicants for aid, and if applicants cannot provide the information, their applications are denied or the family is otherwise penalized or denied benefits. These policies punish families where the absent parent has disappeared or otherwise abandoned the family. They also punish children born as the result of casual liaisons. In Massachusetts, for example, mothers and children were denied aid if they could not provide the Department of Transitional Aid with the name of the absent father and at least two specified pieces of information about him. In cases where the father had left town without giving the mother any information, these pieces of information were not available, and aid was denied. A lawsuit filed in 1996 required Massachusetts to allow mothers to swear under oath that they had no further information, but until then, many families with no contact with an absent father were denied needed aid. Cases such as this continue to occur in other states, resulting in denials of aid to needy families where custodial parents are doing all they can to cooperate.

For women in violent relationships, cooperation with child support enforcement requirements can create serious danger for themselves and their children. As many as 60 percent of women receiving welfare have been victims of domestic violence as adults (compared to 22 percent of women in the general population), and as many as 30 percent reported abuse within the previous year (Tolman and Raphael 2000, 660). Although the child support law requires states to include a "good cause" exception that excuses cooperation with child support if it is likely to result in harm to the mother or child, the exception is rarely used. In fact, studies of abused and battered women indicate that they are ashamed of having been battered and that they fear disclosing any details of the abuse—fearing both that the abuser will find out and that sharing information with authorities will result in loss of their children to child protective services. In addition, custodial parents asked to cooperate with child support enforcement are sometimes not told they have a right not to cooperate if they can show good cause, and those who do claim good cause sometimes cannot prove it. Several studies have indicated that in relationships where there is domestic violence, child support enforcement activities can trigger further violence. The prevalence of violence in the lives of poor families who need income support and the inadequacy of current protections should lead policymakers to further modify child support cooperation requirements. Applicants' statements that they are afraid to pursue child support should be accepted without the need for further verification, and penalties should never be imposed when fear is a factor in failure to cooperate.

In addition to the problems that cooperation requirements bring for some custodial parents, for many poor families the entire premise of child support collection is flawed. Although most noncustodial fathers are better off than their children, a significant minority are just as poor themselves. The Urban Institute National Survey of America's Families reports that 37 percent of nonresident fathers of poor children are also poor. If the goal of social welfare policy is to give some baseline measure of economic security to poor families with children, it is clear that there are many families for whom this cannot happen through child support. Child support cannot be a substitute for a more comprehensive program of ensuring basic income support for poor families with children.

Sherry Leiwant

See also: Aid to Families with Dependent Children (ADC/AFDC); Domestic Violence; Welfare Policy/Welfare Reform

References and Further Reading

Abramovitz, Mimi. 1996. *Regulating the Lives of Women*. Boston: South End Press.

Broeck, Jacobus ten. 1964–1965. "California's Dual System of Family Law: Its Origin, Development, and Present Status." *Stanford Law Review* 16: 900; 17: 614.

Fineman, Martha L. A. 1995. "Masking Dependency: The Political Role of Family Rhetoric." *Virginia Law Review* 81: 2181, 2203.

Hansen, Drew D. 1999. "The American Invention of Child Support: Dependency and Punishment in Early American Child Support Law," *Yale Legal Journal* 108: 1123–1127.

Jones, Mary Somerville. 1987. *An Historical Geography of the Changing Divorce Law in the United States*. New York: Garland.

Roberts, Paula. 2002. "The Importance of Child Support Enforcement." Center on Law and Social Policy Report. Spring. Washington, DC: Center for Law and Social Policy.

Tolman, Richard M., and Jody Raphael. 2000. "A Review of Research on Welfare and Domestic Violence." *Journal of Social Issues* 56: 655–682.

Trattner, Walter I. 1984. *From Poor Law to Welfare State: A History of Social Welfare in America*. 3d ed. New York: Free Press.

U.S. House of Representatives, Committee on Ways and Means. 2000. *2000 Green Book*. October 6. Washington, DC: GPO.

Child Welfare

The term "child welfare" refers to the arrangements a society makes for children whose parents cannot or will not take proper care of them. The public child welfare system in the United States has historically dealt with the needs of poor children. The class structure of child welfare can be traced to the Elizabethan Poor Law of 1601, which encouraged state intervention in indigent families for social ends while protecting the authority of wealthy parents over their children. Public assistance to indigent families and child welfare services for neglected children are related programs addressing family poverty. Public aid was historically disparaged, and destitute children were indentured and committed to almshouses during the eighteenth century and placed in orphanages by child-savers during the nineteenth century. Progressive reformers, who saw child poverty as a social problem, successfully campaigned for aid for indigent mothers to prevent the need to place their children in orphanages and asylums. Aid to Dependent Children, established in 1935 as part of the New Deal, was also designed to avoid separating poor children from their mothers. The function of child welfare was transformed in subsequent decades to child protection and focused on investigating charges of child maltreatment, rehabilitating guilty parents, and placing their children in foster care.

There is a high and well-established correlation between poverty and cases of child abuse and neglect. Researchers have posited a number of explanations for this association, including the extreme stress caused by economic hardship, the heightened exposure of poor families to government surveillance, and a definition of neglect that includes inadequate provision of food, clothing, shelter, and medical care to children. The number of families in the child welfare system is a function of the U.S. child poverty rate, which, despite its recent decline, is still exceptionally high by international standards. Before World War II, Black children were largely excluded from public and private child welfare services. Destitute or troubled Black children were likely to be labeled "delinquent" and sent to prison. The proportion of nonwhite children in the public child welfare caseloads steadily increased after 1945, however. In 2000, almost half of all children in foster care nationwide were Black.

The federal government abandoned the progressive understanding of child maltreatment as a social problem in the 1970s. In an attempt to secure bipartisan support for government spending on poor children, liberals dissociated

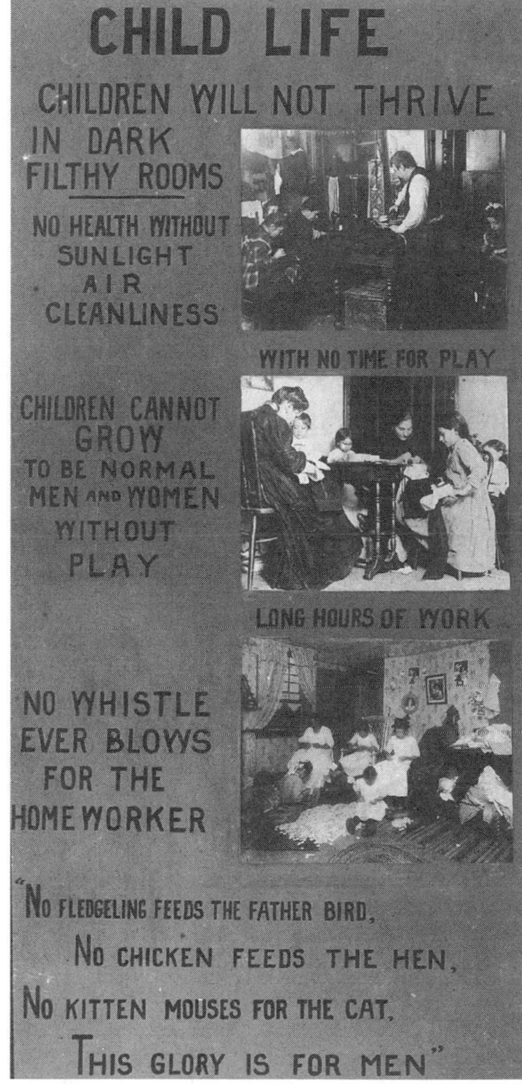

Lewis Hines Exhibit panel. (Library of Congress)

efforts to combat child abuse from unpopular poverty programs. Congress passed the Child Abuse Prevention and Treatment Act of 1974, which considered child maltreatment to be a symptom of parents' mental depravity instead of a symptom of poverty and other societal inequities. The focus of state child welfare agencies shifted from child well-being to child protection. Since then, the number of children receiving child welfare services has declined dramatically because state and federal governments have spent more money on removing children from their families than on providing services to children living at home.

The chief service provided by the public child welfare system is foster care. The foster care population—as well as the proportion of the federal budget devoted to out-of-home care—skyrocketed between 1980 and 2000. The number of children in foster care had climbed to 568,000 by 1999 (U.S. Department of Health and Human Services 2000, 1). One explanation for the shift in services is that contemporary families have more-serious problems, such as HIV/AIDS, substance abuse, and homelessness, forcing agencies to direct a larger portion of their resources to foster care. The shift may also be linked to the philosophy of child protection that addresses family problems only after children have already experienced harm.

Federal and state child welfare policies have reflected both family preservationist and child-saving philosophies. In the late 1970s, hearings revealed that federal reimbursement policy created incentives for state child welfare agencies to place children in foster care instead of providing services to intact families. Congress attempted to correct this bias by passing the Adoption Assistance and Child Welfare Act of 1980, which requires state agencies to make "reasonable efforts" to prevent the need for out-of-home placement and to safely return children in foster care to their parents. Because of the child protection philosophy, the passage of laws that mandate reporting of child abuse, and insufficient funding of family preservation programs, however, the foster care population increased after passage of the 1980 law. The federal child welfare law was amended in 1997 by the Adoption and Safe Families Act in response to criticism that caseworkers were interpreting the "reasonable efforts" mandate to keep maltreated children in dangerous homes and that too few children in foster care were being adopted. The new law directs state authorities to make the health and safety of children in foster care their "paramount concern," establishes swifter timetables for terminating biological parents' rights, and provides financial incentives to states to increase the number of foster children placed in adoptive homes. Although some commentators applaud the emphasis on safety and adoption, others fear that the 1997 law represents an abandonment of efforts to preserve poor families. The passage of the Adoption and Safe Families Act on the heels of the 1996 Personal Responsibility and Work Opportunity Reconciliation Act marks the first time in U.S. history that the federal government requires states to protect children's safety but not to provide economic assistance to poor families.

Dorothy E. Roberts

See also: Aid to Families with Dependent Children (ADC/AFDC); Child-Saving; Foster Care; Orphanages; Poorhouse/Almshouse; Social Work; Welfare Policy/Welfare Reform

References and Further Reading

Lindsey, Duncan. 1994. *The Welfare of Children*. New York: Oxford University Press.

Nelson, Barbara J. 1984. *Making an Issue of Child Abuse: Political Agenda Setting for Social Problems*. Chicago: University of Chicago Press.

Pelton, Leroy H. 1989. *For Reasons of Poverty: A Critical Analysis of the Public Child Welfare System in the United States*. New York: Praeger.

Roberts, Dorothy. 2002. *Shattered Bonds: The Color of Child Welfare*. New York: Basic Books.

U.S. Department of Health and Human Services. 2000. Administration for Children and Families. "The AFCARS Report: Current Estimates as of October 2000." www.acf.dhhs.gov/programs/cb.

The Children of Sanchez, *Oscar Lewis*

The Children of Sanchez is best known among historians of poverty as the book in which anthropologist Oscar Lewis first fully articulated his influential theory of the "culture of poverty." Based on ethnographic and life-history research in a *vecinidad*, or "slum tenement," of Mexico

City, the book offers an often-sensationalistic portrait of the day-to-day lives of the Sanchez family, told in the first-person voices of individual family members based on tape-recorded interviews. Although Lewis had begun to develop the "culture of poverty" concept in his 1959 book *Five Families*, it was in the later publication that he elaborated on his earlier observations to present it as a model for understanding poverty in the developing countries of Latin America, Asia, and Africa during the post–World War II era. What these developing countries had in common, Lewis argued—and what distinguished his culture of poverty from more-traditional peasant communities—was that they were in the throes of a massive and rapid transition to modern industrial capitalism, leaving a residue of impoverished people at the very margins of economic and social life. Assuming the mantle of their "student and spokesman," Lewis presented theirs as a distinctive way of life, "a design for living which is passed down from generation to generation," characterized not only by the material conditions of poverty and unemployment but, more fatefully, by a deep-seated psychological orientation that—left unaddressed—would render them incapable of adjusting to the demands of modern economic and social life (Lewis 1961, xxiv).

Generated in the context of U.S. efforts to prevent the spread of communism by encouraging capitalism and political democracy in developing nations, Lewis's theory gained greater notoriety in its application to the ghettos and rural "pockets" of concentrated poverty in the United States. Presented in less-scholarly terms in popular books such as Michael Harrington's *Other America* (1962) and Harry Caudill's *Night Comes to the Cumberlands* (1963), the "culture of poverty" resonated with the notion of poverty as a separate social reality, affecting an isolated minority in a society otherwise characterized by mass prosperity. In reality, as Harrington himself was soon to point out, the experience of poverty was very much part of "mainstream" experience and included substantial numbers of the employed. But what made Lewis's theory controversial among scholars—while adding to its popular appeal—was its designation of what he called psychological "traits" that closely corresponded to widely held stereotypes of social "deviance" among the poor. Based on a combination of observation and deeply flawed psychological tests, Lewis's inventory of psychological traits eventually swelled to a virtual laundry list of behaviors that verged on self-parody, even though Lewis himself was basically sympathetic to the people he wrote about. By the late 1960s, the culture of poverty had been roundly criticized and largely dismissed among scholars and antipoverty activists and was increasingly associated with conservative arguments that whole classes of poor people and poor places were simply beyond social intervention. Nevertheless, and despite the paucity of scholarly evidence supporting it, the basic concept of a socially deviant, psychologically pathological culture continues to exert widespread influence as an explanation for the persistence of poverty and as a "scientific" label for the undeserving poor.

Alice O'Connor

See also: Deserving/Undeserving Poor; *Night Comes to the Cumberlands; The Other America;* Poverty Research; "Underclass"

The economic traits which are most characteristic of the culture of poverty include the constant struggle for survival, unemployment and underemployment, low wages, a miscellany of unskilled occupations, child labor, the absence of savings, a chronic shortage of cash. . . .

Some of the social and psychological characteristics include living in crowded quarters, a lack of privacy, gregariousness, a high incidence of alcoholism, frequent resort to violence in the settlement of quarrels, frequent use of physical violence in the training of children, wife beating, early initiation into sex, free unions of consensual marriages, a relatively high incidence of the abandonment of mothers and children, a trend toward mother-centered families . . ., a strong predisposition to authoritarianism, and a great emphasis upon family solidarity—an ideal only rarely achieved. Other traits include a strong present time orientation with relatively little ability to defer gratification and plan for the future, a sense of resignation and fatalism based upon the realities of their difficult life situation, . . . and finally, a high tolerance for psychological pathology of all sorts. . . .

A critical attitude toward some of the values and institutions of the dominant classes, hatred of the police, mistrust of government and those in high position, . . . gives the culture of poverty a counter quality and a potential for being used in political movements aimed against the existing social order. . . .

[T]he material in this book. . . highlights the social, economic, and psychological complexities which have to be faced in any effort to transform and eliminate the culture of poverty from the world. It suggests that basic changes in the attitudes and value systems of the poor must go hand in hand with improvements in the material conditions of living.

Source: Oscar Lewis, *The Children of Sanchez: Autobiography of a Mexican Family* (New York: Random House, 1961), xxvi–xxvii.

Child-Saving

Child-saving—the impulse to mount a variety of reforms in the name of protecting children—has long been recognized as a recurring theme in U.S. social welfare history. However, "child-saving" also has a more specific historical meaning, as the basis of a movement, with roots in the early nineteenth century, to control juvenile crime by establishing special institutions targeting youth considered wayward, delinquent, or criminal.

Rise of the Child-Saving Movement

By the early 1900s, social workers and other reformers had created a new and separate system of justice for youth. Throughout the nineteenth century, special, prisonlike institutions were developed to control the activities of delinquent youth. But it was not until the close of the century that an initiative was taken to rationalize these efforts into a coherent system of juvenile justice, composed of juvenile courts, probation, child guidance clinics, social services, and reformatories. The conventional view of the new juvenile justice system suggests that it was an enlightened effort to alleviate the miseries of urban life and to respond to the needs of poor children. A more critical view suggests that the child-saving movement, as it was called, used benevolent language to disguise a class-based system of punishment.

The child-saving movement was led by wealthy philanthropists who were alarmed by the changes in public life generated by urbanization, industrialization, and the influx of immigrant cultures. Although the child-saving movement, like most reforms of the Progressive Era (1900–1920), drew its most active and visible supporters from middle-class women's groups and from professionals, including social workers, it relied on the political and financial support of ruling elites to implement its visionary plans.

The child-savers created new categories of youthful misbehavior (later known as "status offenses") and sought to extend governmental control, without the safeguards of due process, over a wide range of youthful behavior, including incorrigibility, loitering, disobedience, and disorderly conduct. The child-saving movement minimized the significance of individual rights in the sense that it believed in the maximum use and benign character of governmental intervention. With close links to the prohibitionist movement, the child-savers argued that social progress depended on broad police powers and close supervision of working-class children's daily lives.

Between 1825, when the New York House of Refuge was founded to house juvenile delinquents, and 1899, when the first juvenile court was established in Chicago, the child-saving movement created a separate set of institutions that transformed both the definition and regulation of youth crime. The reformers themselves were convinced that their interventions were "in the best interests of the child," and many immigrant families turned to the child-savers for help in controlling their wayward children. But the new custodial institutions created for youth imposed harsh regimes on their wards: military exercises, severe discipline, and long hours of hard labor.

Moreover, issues of class, race, and gender marked policies of the juvenile justice system. African American youth were placed in segregated reformatories with inferior resources; American Indian youth were forced into boarding schools and stripped of their cultural heritage; campaigns by women's organizations to rescue "wayward girls" meant that young women were disproportionately arrested for running away from home, sexual behavior, and other status offenses; and middle-class delinquents were largely exempt from court referrals and imprisonment. This double standard in the application of juvenile justice policies has permeated public policies regarding the control of delinquency for over 100 years.

Reform of Child-Saving

Between the 1940s and the early 1970s, a new generation of reformers introduced programs in community-based corrections that attempted to correct injustices generated by the child-saving movement. In the 1940s, several states developed separate correctional institutions to deal with young offenders. The model for this development was the California Youth Authority (CYA), which was responsible for supervising the imprisonment of young men and women between the ages of sixteen and twenty-one. The focus in the CYA was on the "rehabilitative ideal," which emphasized psychologically oriented programs, such as group therapy and counseling.

In the wake of the civil rights movement and other movements for social change, far-reaching reforms were initiated in education, community development, welfare, public health, and job training. Beginning in the 1960s, the federal government took the initiative in developing a national perspective on juvenile justice, emphasizing prevention and alternatives to incarceration in large institutions. President Lyndon B. Johnson's Commission on Law Enforcement and Administration of Justice (known as the Crime Commission), created in 1965, established the guidelines for this shift in policy and issued a comprehensive assessment of American juvenile justice in 1967. In the mid-1960s, the first federal legislation on juvenile delinquency created such innovative programs as the Neighborhood Youth Corps, the Legal Services Corporation, and Head Start. These programs were later incorporated into President Johnson's War on Poverty.

In 1966, the U.S. Supreme Court required due process rights for juveniles. It found, in the words of Justice Abe Fortas, "that the child receives the worst of both worlds: that he gets neither the protections accorded to adults nor the solicitous care and regenerative treatment postulated for children" (*Kent v. United States*, 383 U.S. 541, 556). In 1967, the U.S. Supreme Court, in its landmark ruling *In re Gault* (387 U.S. 1), expanded due process rights for juveniles, including the right to counsel and the privilege against self-incrimination.

Demise of Child-Saving

In 1968, a shift to a more punitive, anticrime philosophy was signaled in President Richard M. Nixon's "war on crime" and the passage of the Omnibus Crime Control and Safe Streets Act. A nationwide study reported in the early 1970s that, after a long decline in the rate of juvenile incarceration, almost 500,000 juveniles were being processed annually through local jails. Moreover, efforts to reduce the disproportionate imprisonment of youth of color had clearly failed. In 1976, the National Assessment of Juvenile Corrections found that African American youths accounted for 33 percent of the reformatory population in sixteen sample states (Vintner 1976).

In the 1990s, the emphasis on prevention and rehabilitation as public policies for addressing juvenile crime disappeared from public discourse. Since 1992, forty-five states have passed laws making it easier to prosecute juveniles as adults. In addition, more than thirty states have created juvenile boot camps, which emphasize military-style discipline and physical labor, a return to the regime of the nineteenth-century reformatory. Moreover, of twenty-three states that permit the execution of youthful offenders, seven (Georgia, Louisiana, Missouri, Oklahoma, South Carolina, Texas, and Virginia) have carried out executions since 1976. There have been fourteen such executions in the last twelve years, more than in all other countries combined that permit executions of people who commit capital crimes while under the age of eighteen (Rimer and Bonner 2000, 16).

The impact of punitive policies has fallen hardest on children of color. By 1996, African American males accounted for 44 percent of all cases referred from juvenile to criminal courts (Office of Juvenile Justice and Delinquency Prevention 1999, 130–132). A federal study found that although minority youth constituted about 32 percent of the youth population in the country in 1995, they represented 68 percent of the incarcerated juvenile population (Hsia and Hamparian 1998). By 1997, two-thirds of all incarcerated juveniles were African Americans, Latinos, or American Indians (Office of Juvenile Justice and Delinquency Prevention 1999, 150, 155, 195). A study by the National Council on Crime and Delinquency found that African American girls had an overall 1 in 188 chance of being incarcerated before their eighteenth birthday, compared to a 1 in 454 chance for Latinas and a 1 in 1,000 chance for white girls (Chesney-Lind and Shelden 1998, 138–139, 158–159).

By the mid-1990s, juvenile court systems in large cities were overwhelmed by huge caseloads and insufficient resources and were under political pressure to emphasize punishment rather than rehabilitation. Chicago now has one of the largest juvenile court systems in the country, with a staff of more than 600 and an annual budget that exceeds $20 million. On any given day, there are between 1,500 and

Anti–child labor poster, "A Child's Creed . . ." Created by Lewis W. Hine. (Library of Congress)

2,000 cases pending on each judge's docket, which adds up to about 75,000 delinquency, abuse, and neglect cases awaiting disposition. Caseloads in Cook County are twice the national standard, and an average case is dispensed with every twelve minutes. Of the close to 13,000 kids who come through Chicago's detention center each year, the overwhelming majority are poor, African American (80 percent) or Latino (15 percent), and male (90 percent). In the city where the child-saving movement originated, law and order now prevails (Ayers 1997).

Anthony M. Platt

See also: Juvenile Delinquency; Progressive Era and 1920s

References and Further Reading

Ayers, William. 1997. *A Kind and Just Parent: The Children of Juvenile Court*. Boston: Beacon Press.

Brown, Claude. 1965. *Manchild in the Promised Land*. New York: Macmillan.

Chesney-Lind, Meda, and Randall G. Shelden. 1998. *Girls, Delinquency, and Juvenile Justice*. Belmont, CA: Wadsworth.

Hsia, Heidi M., and Donna Hamparian. 1998. *Disproportionate Minority Confinement: 1997 Update*. Washington, DC: U.S. Department of Justice.

Krisberg, Barry, and James F. Austin. 1993. *Reinventing Juvenile Justice*. Newbury Park, CA: Sage.

Markowitz, Gerald, and David Rosner. 1996. *Children, Race, and Power: Kenneth and Mamie Clark's Northside Center*. Charlottesville: University Press of Virginia.

Office of Juvenile Justice and Delinquency Prevention. 1999. *Juvenile Offenders and Victims: 1999 National Report*. Washington, DC: U.S. Department of Justice.

Platt, Anthony M. 1977. *The Child Savers: The Invention of Delinquency*. Chicago: University of Chicago Press.

President's Commission on Law Enforcement and Administration of Justice. 1967. *Juvenile Delinquency and Youth Crime*. Washington, DC: GPO.

Rimer, Sara, and Raymond Bonner. 2000. "Whether to Kill Those Who Killed as Youths." *New York Times*, August 22.

Vinter, Robert D., ed. 1976. *Time Out: A National Study of Juvenile Correctional Programs*. Ann Arbor, MI: National Assessment of Juvenile Corrections.

Christian Fundamentalism

A broad category encompassing three different social formations within Protestantism, Christian fundamentalism arose between the late 1800s and the early 1990s. Each of the formations—antimodern fundamentalism, separatist fundamentalism, and the New Christian Right—invoked the claim that the Bible is free of errors in order to authorize particular statements about how society ought to be structured and how one ought to live. Despite that common tactic, the statements advanced by each formation and the corresponding impacts on social welfare policies have differed radically.

Antimodern fundamentalism emerged as a theological position in the second and third decades of the twentieth century. Its leading figures argued for governmental programs to protect citizens from the unjust effects of Social Darwinism and laissez-faire economics. In the 1930s, antimodern fundamentalism retreated from secular public affairs and took on a separatist character. In addition, these fundamentalist leaders launched critiques of communism and the welfare state. In 1942, the National Association of Evangelicals was formed to distinguish evangelical Christians from separatist fundamentalists. The dispute over separatism marks an important distinction between the self-identified fundamentalists and the New Christian Right, which liberal Protestants, academics, and journalists generically characterize as "fundamentalist." New Christian Right fundamentalism criticizes the welfare state, yet its contemporary proponents advocate a "compassionate conservatism" that involves governmental action and "charitable choice," which engages churches and other faith-based groups in government programs.

The first fundamentalist social formation coagulated around theological antimodernist projects among different Protestant denominations in the United States during the late nineteenth and early twentieth centuries. "Modernists" suggested that Christian theology must address methods of biblical criticism and Darwinian theories of evolution. The Niagara Bible Conference of 1883, which marked the beginning of the antimodern fundamentalist formation, rejected any appeal to or incorporation of biblical criticism methodologies. Organized by a variety of Baptist and Presbyterian denominations, the conference affirmed five doctrinal points: the inerrancy of scripture, the divinity of Jesus, the virgin birth, substitutionary atonement, and the bodily resurrection and physical return of Jesus.

The loose coalition of institutions, people, and media that made up this first formation included the Moody Bible Institute, established in Chicago in 1899, and the American Bible League, founded in 1902; the scholars representing the dominant perspective at Princeton's Theological Seminary; and the periodicals *Watchword, Truth,* and *Our Hope*. Between 1910 and 1915, a California businessman, Lyman Stewart, financed the publication of twelve pamphlets called *The Fundamentals*. The pamphlets reasserted the doctrinal points from the Niagara Bible Conference; attacked biblical criticism, modernism, and the teachings advanced by Catholics, Christian Scientists, and Mormons; and rejected Darwin's theory of evolution. In 1920, Rev. Curtis Lee Laws, editor of the Baptist publication *Watchman-Examiner,* used the term "fundamentalist" to describe organizations and people who affirmed the basic principles outlined in *The Fundamentals*. He made distinctions not only between fundamentalists and liberal Protestants but also between fundamentalists and other Bible-believing Protestants (such as conservatives, premillennialists, landmarkers).

Unlike the New Christian Right fundamentalism of the late twentieth century, antimodern fundamentalists supported governmental programs designed to protect citizens from economic risks. William Jennings Bryan, one of the more famous antimodern fundamentalists, defeated the incumbent president Grover Cleveland to become the party's presidential nominee at the 1896 Democratic National Convention. Although Bryan lost the presidential race, he led the Democrats to push for antitrust prosecutions, farming subsidies, union protections, a federal income tax, and legislation to limit working hours and provide minimum wages. Bryan grounded his political stance on biblical authority and argued against a laissez-faire economy that encouraged Social Darwinism. Unlike modernist advocates of the Social Gospel movement, Bryan challenged strict separation between church and state by stating that Bible classes should be a mandatory part of public education. In 1925, the World's Christian Fundamentals Organization solicited Bryan to prosecute John T. Scopes for teaching evolution in public schools. Although the prosecution won the legal battle, the fundamentalist position encountered much ridicule from mainstream media.

The 1930s mark the beginning of Christian fundamentalism's second formation, which is characterized primarily by separatism from or lack of participation in allegedly secular public affairs. The networking infrastructure of this formation included a variety of Baptist associations, the Dallas Theological Seminary, Bob Jones University, the Westminster Theological Seminary, the Orthodox Presbyterian Church, a number of independent Bible churches and schools, the World Council of Bible Believing Churches, and the Christian Missionary Alliance. In 1941, the separatist fundamentalist Carl McIntire helped establish the American Council of Christian Churches (ACCC), which opposed ecumenical bodies like the National Council of Churches. During his radio show, *The Twentieth Century Reformation Hour,* he preached against the alleged dangers of communism and critiqued the welfare state.

In 1942, dissenting fundamentalists formed the National Association of Evangelicals to distinguish themselves from separatist fundamentalists. Evangelical bodies such as the Fuller Seminary, Youth for Christ, and the Billy Graham Evangelistic Association focused their attention on preaching "the good news" to the larger public. Despite the large and growing numbers of people who invoked the authority and inerrancy of the Bible, only those who maintained a separatist position (for example, J. Frank Norris, Carl McIntire, Billy Hargus, John Rice, Bob Jones Sr., Bob Jones Jr., and Jerry Falwell) continued to call themselves "fundamentalists." The dispute over separatism signals the beginning of a taxonomic shift in which fundamentalism began to lose its appeal as a term of self-characterization. Academic and popular discourses frequently collapsed the distinctions between fundamentalists and evangelicals.

Before World War II, fundamentalist statements about the role of the family revolved primarily around the importance of child rearing and family prayer. After World War II, both fundamentalists and evangelicals focused more attention on "the family" through critiques of divorce, birth control, abortion, and homosexuality. In 1977, Dr. James Dobson founded the organization Focus on the Family as a response to increasing concern for the American family. Despite the growing emphasis on patriarchal authority and hierarchy, evangelicals maintained ambivalent and varied relationships to feminism as well as to lesbian and gay issues. For example, the Evangelical and Ecumenical Women's Caucus (EEWC), formed in the early 1970s, endorsed the proposed Equal Rights Amendment, supported inclusive language in Bible translation and Christian publications, affirmed the ordination of women, criticized discriminatory hiring policies in Christian institutions, and supported different sexual orientations and gender expressions. Dissent over the EEWC's position on homosexuality led to the 1986 formation of Christians for Biblical Equality (CBE), whose statement of faith excludes homosexual families from "the patterns God designed for us." One can witness the heterogeneous positions of evangelicals on other family-related issues (such as abortion and child rearing) and social welfare, issues of war and peace, racism, poverty, and violence in quarterly publications of the *Daughters of Sarah*, the "magazine for Christian Feminists."

During the 1960s and 1970s, fundamentalists and evangelicals developed a large television media infrastructure. Self-identified fundamentalist Jerry Falwell televised his weekly Sunday service, the *Old-Time Gospel Hour*, and evangelicals created the Christian Broadcasting Network, Trinity Broadcasting Network, LeSea Broadcasting, and the Praise the Lord Ministry. In 1979, Falwell abandoned his separatist stance and founded an organization for all Bible-believing Protestants, who, he argued, made up a "Moral Majority" of Americans. Liberal Protestants, academics, and journalists referred to the Moral Majority as the New Christian Right or the Religious Right.

The New Christian Right fundamentalist formation campaigned against legalized abortion, homosexuality, and the proposed Equal Rights Amendment while advocating prayer in public schools, increased defense spending, and anticommunist foreign policy. In the 1960s, Falwell had defended segregation and criticized religious leaders who participated in the civil rights movement, but in 1982, he approvingly compared the Moral Majority's influence and strategy to that of the civil rights movement. The Moral Majority strongly supported and influenced Ronald Reagan's presidency. During the late 1980s, mainstream media reported several financial and sexual scandals that indicted leaders of the New Christian Right, and in 1989, Falwell disbanded the Moral Majority, claiming that it was no longer necessary because the Religious Right was solidly in place.

After the 1980s, only the separatist Bible-believing Protestants continued to refer to themselves as fundamentalists. Although the term "fundamentalist" was and is frequently used to characterize Christian and non-Christian groups who reject some tenets of secularism, deployments of the term function primarily at a rhetorical rather than an analytic level. Contemporary descendants of New Christian Right fundamentalists and evangelicals include Pat Robertson's Christian Coalition (1989) and Bill McCartney's Promise Keepers (1990). Both preach the importance of what they call "family values." Unlike Falwell's Moral Majority, the Christian Coalition is not opposed to ecumenical relations with other denominations and religions. The Promise Keepers profess an interest in and attention to racial reconciliation.

Unlike separatist fundamentalism, the New Christian Right formation and its descendants support interactions between church and state. Indeed, they call upon government to codify and enforce their moral values in such policies and initiatives as the Hyde Amendment, which prohibits Medicaid funding for abortions; federally subsidized abstinence-only education; and federally mandated marriage promotion. To advance the role of religious groups in public policy, born-again Christian President George W. Bush's Faith-Based Initiative would permit New Christian Right religious entities, as well as mainline churches, to directly participate in government programs. An expansion of the "charitable choice" provision in welfare law, the Faith-Based Initiative enables religious groups to compete for government grants to deliver social services ranging from job training to fatherhood promotion.

Karen deVries

See also: Charitable Choice; Family Structure; New Right; Philanthropy; Salvation Army; Sexism; Social Gospel; Voluntarism; Welfare Policy/Welfare Reform; Welfare State

References and Further Reading

Bendroth, Margaret Lamberts. 1999. "Fundamentalism and the Family: Gender, Culture, and the American Pro-Family Movement." *Journal of Women's History* 10, no. 4 (Winter).

Harding, Susan. 2000. *The Book of Jerry Falwell*. New Jersey: Princeton University Press.

Kazin, Michael. 1999. "The Forgotten Forerunner (William Jennings Bryan)." *Wilson Quarterly* 23, no. 4 (Autumn).

Marsden, George M. 1991. *Understanding Fundamentalism and Evangelicalism*. Grand Rapids, MI: William B. Eerdmans.

Churches

See Black Churches; Catholic Church; Charitable Choice; Missionaries; Protestant Denominations

Citizens' Crusade against Poverty (CCAP)

The Citizens' Crusade against Poverty (CCAP), a national coalition of labor unions, businesses, churches and synagogues, charitable foundations, advocacy groups, and grassroots organizations, advocated for poor people's rights between 1965 and 1968.

The president of the United Auto Workers, Walter Reuther, became the CCAP chairman at its founding in 1965. Leading members of the organization included former Office of Economic Opportunity (OEO) staff members Richard Boone and Edgar Cahn, as well as philanthropist Robert L. Choate. The board of directors represented a veritable who's who of civil rights advocates, labor leaders, American Indians, and religious figures.

In 1966, after playing a significant role in developing the War on Poverty's controversial Community Action Program, Richard Boone became the CCAP's executive director and oversaw the expansion of its activities. In addition to publishing the *Citizens' Crusade against Poverty Bulletin*, the organization sponsored conferences on issues related to impoverishment and distributed special pamphlets, such as "New Schools for the Cities: Designs for Equality and Excellence" (1967).

Following the motto "Reform is more frequently a problem of power than of knowledge," Boone directed the Citizens' Crusade toward a series of action programs (Boone 1967, 374). With additional support from churches, the Ford Foundation, the Stern Family Fund, labor unions, and individuals, the CCAP cosponsored the Southern Rural Action Project in Alabama, Georgia, and Mississippi; a community worker-training program; a grassroots information system to link local self-help groups; and a fund to provide emergency help for local organizations. The Citizens' Crusade advocated on behalf of the Child Development Group of Mississippi (CDGM)—a civil rights affiliated Head Start program that generated tremendous controversy for challenging the South's segregated status quo—when the OEO threatened to cut off further funding for that organization. By 1966, the Citizens' Crusade had become increasingly critical of the War on Poverty's shortcomings and bureaucratization. Other grassroots CCAP activities included developing strategies for training nonprofessionals to work with other members of their own communities.

One of the CCAP's most significant undertakings, a survey conducted between July 1967 and April 1968 by the Citizens' Board of Inquiry into Hunger and Malnutrition, led to the publication of *Hunger USA*, the report of the survey's findings. This study revealed the dramatic problem of starvation and hunger in the United States. The Citizens' Crusade investigated hunger and starvation as statistical categories but probed their political and power dynamics as well. For instance, the study revealed that large amounts of federal subsidies were being distributed to agricultural producers in the very areas where poverty remained most endemic. Indeed, in 1970, one observer credited the CCAP with serving "a unique role in spurring America's most recent rediscovery of hunger" (Brown 1970, 116).

The Citizens' Crusade served an important role in the politics of social policy from 1965 to 1968 by agitating for reform, organizing and training poor people, and conducting investigations into the areas of education, hunger, and economic development. In 1968, the Center for Community Change (CCC), a coalition of nonprofit organizations, absorbed the Citizens' Crusade against Poverty.

Daniel M. Cobb

See also: Antihunger Coalitions; Center for Community Change; Community Development; Community-Based Organizations; War on Poverty

References and Further Reading

Boone, Richard. 1967. Prepared statement in the hearings before the Subcommittee on Employment, Manpower, and Poverty of the Committee on Labor and Public Welfare. *Examination of the War on Poverty*. 90th Cong., part 1, 374–388.

Brown, Larry. 1970. "Hunger USA: The Public Pushes Congress." *Journal of Health and Social Behavior* 11, no. 2: 115–126.

Citizenship

Citizenship is the status of full membership within a political community. Democratic citizenship confers rights on individuals as well as obligations to promote the well-being of the polity. In the United States, citizenship is understood primarily in political terms—that is, as having the right to vote and the duty to serve on juries. But meaningful membership in a political community also includes civil and, especially, social rights. Civil rights include basic legal guarantees, such as governmental protection of life, liberty, and property, and also each individual's right to equitable and equal treatment by the government. Social rights are the individual's entitlement to basic economic provision as a basis for the exercise of civil and political rights. Social rights include minimal economic security, educational opportunity, health care, housing, and the like. Social rights are weak and undeveloped in the United States, which constrains the governmental response to poverty. As explained by the British social theorist T. H. Marshall (1950), political, civil, and social rights are so intertwined that without public policies promoting greater social and economic equality, citizenship as a whole is severely compromised.

Since at least the mid-nineteenth century, reformers (often predominantly women) have struggled to extend the meaning of citizenship to include access to minimal basic social provision. The idea that economic security is a component of citizenship did not win favor until the New Deal, and even then only for certain favored constituencies and only because they could claim to have "earned" their benefits. The "mothers' pensions" of the Progressive Era were a breakthrough for social provision, but they did not include a concept of rights, either for applicants or for recipients. Likewise, under New Deal social policies, public assistance recipients were not considered to have a "right" to benefits.

Struggles around citizenship in the United States have focused on the progressive incorporation of members of different groups into full voting membership in the polity. One group that did not have to struggle as a group for participatory rights was the white, male working class. This was due to the early-nineteenth-century extension of the franchise to adult white men regardless of their wealth or status as property owners. Some have argued that as a result of "early suffrage" for adult, white, male workers, U.S. worker movements did not develop robust claims linking political equality to economic security. Thus, the constituency most closely associated with the development of social rights in the western European polities becoming industrialized at the same time was not, in the United States, an agent of social democracy.

Despite the democratic principles enshrined in the Constitution and the Declaration of Independence, even rights to political participation were not automatically enjoyed by all individuals. In the early decades of the U.S. republic, the status of citizen (in the political sense) was reserved for free, white, propertied men—men deemed by their property ownership to be both "independent" and capable of engaging in public service. Although propertyless white men did not have to struggle to win formal political citizenship, deliberate changes in electoral laws needed to be made to incorporate them. Further political democratization did not occur until after the Civil War, when, at least in theory, the Fifteenth Amendment formally extended voting rights to Black males. However, a combination of violence, poll taxes, economic threats, and other exclusionary policies prevented most African Americans (whether male or female) from effectively exercising those rights until the passage of the Voting Rights Act of 1965. Although some states accorded women the right to vote as early as the final decade of the nineteenth century, women were not guaranteed a right to vote at the national level until the passage of the Nineteenth Amendment in 1920. Native American Indians born in the United States were formally admitted to full political citizenship in 1924; Asian immigrants were denied access to citizenship until 1952.

As this brief history suggests, although the ideal of citizenship in the United States is one of inclusion, in reality, formal laws and informal practices have promoted exclusion. A number of dichotomies animated exclusion, beginning with early distinctions between propertyless workers and propertied citizens and including distinctions between workers slave and free, between workers and women, and between women and citizens. These oppositions, in turn, have been overlaid with others, most significantly the oppositions between private and public, deserving and undeserving, and independence and dependence. During virtually the entire course of U.S. history, the inclusion of some has been defined with respect to the exclusion of others.

At least until the early nineteenth century, citizenship was accorded only to those who were defined as "independent," who had the means to participate "unencumbered" in the public realm. Such a definition excluded slaves, wage workers, and white women, who were expected to be dependent on others for their support. Citizenship was also assigned to the public domain, so the private or domestic work of caring for families was not viewed as being in the realm of "citizens." Although this ideology excluded virtually all women from full citizenship rights on the grounds of their dependence, early U.S. political ideology did offer some women an alternative basis for incorporation into the polity. "Republican mothers"—a status reserved for the white wives of citizens and white mothers of future citizens—were valued for their domestic activities, especially for their contribution to the care and education of democracy's next generation. This gendering of citizenship was also deeply racialized. No republican virtue was attributed to the dependency of enslaved women, and even after emancipation, free Black women, Latinas, and many immigrant women were restricted from participating fully in the ideal of female domestic dependence. Most women of color and many southern and eastern European women were expected to work for wages, but at rates that did not allow for self-sufficiency.

Throughout much of the nineteenth century, women social reformers actively promoted roles for women in political life—as spokespeople for moral concerns and as advocates for the poor. Concerned to protect those for whom the dislocations of industrial capitalism were especially severe, these reformers were quite successful in winning attention to the needs of women and children both as wage workers and as domestic dependents. Progressive women reformers of the early twentieth century inserted claims for social provision into the larger political agenda and gave currency to the idea that a democratic government sometimes has responsibilities to its citizens. They based their claims on the arguments that women were uniquely vulnerable because they were dependent and that they were uniquely deserving as the domestic mothers of future citizens. When political citizenship finally was granted to (white) women, it was won in part by women reformers, who promised that because women differed from men they would contribute uniquely to the polity.

But both the more prudentialist arguments for women's suffrage and the arguments for state-supported welfare benefits for women and children reinforced the sense that only women could be dependent adults and still merit the status of citizen. Female social reform activists had deliberately used those understandings of women's domesticity and dependence to argue for social welfare measures that women (and later men) would not otherwise have had. Thus, although women attained formal political citizenship rights when they secured the right to vote in 1920, women's citizenship was conceived as being different from men's. Although (primarily white) women had equal voting rights with men, women remained unequal to men in other aspects of citizenship, such as jury duty and obligations for military service. The gendered nature of democratic citizenship in the United States implanted confusing paradoxes at the core of U.S. understandings of citizenship. For certain women, dependence was considered compatible with citizenship. But for legitimately dependent women citizens, social provision was treated as a special need rather than as a component right of citizenship. Because legitimate dependency was understood in racialized gender terms, Black, Latino, and Asian women were effectively excluded from more-generous social welfare provisions aimed at "deserving" women. Meanwhile, programs to address the problems of dependent *men* became virtually impossible to conceive, let alone to enact. As contemporary welfare "reform" policies such as the Personal Responsibility and Work Opportunity Reconciliation Act (1996) make clear, universal social citizenship rights are far from guaranteed by—

or even recognized as a goal of—U.S. social policies; if anything, the language of "dependence" and "independence" has only come more strongly to the fore, further marginalizing those who cannot support themselves by their own wages or who are not supported by the wages of others with whom they live.

Feminist advocates and scholars have called attention to the fact that no one in existing (or even imaginable) political or social communities is truly independent. They have argued that meaningful political communities must attend to the necessary *interdependencies* of their members. They have noted, furthermore, that relationships of dependence (which certainly characterize families, among other social institutions) are often unequal and that such inequality should not necessarily stand in the way of fully equal citizenship rights. What follows from such an awareness is an argument for a system of social provision that is adequate, generous, and nondemeaning—one that honors the rights of citizenship.

Those who are dependent in society need and deserve to be cared for, but the structures of social provision in the United States operate on the assumption that most of the work of care will be undertaken in families (largely by women) and not for pay; that is, they assume a privatized system of care and social reproduction. If families cannot provide that care themselves, they are expected to hire others who will do so—again, usually women (often recent immigrants), who are also expected to perform this work at very low wages. But those who enable society to function by caring for its dependents (in the form of child care, education, health care, and the like) must be recognized as performing crucial work for the common good. Because this work is socially necessary and important both to the individuals who receive care and to the polity, it ought to be adequately compensated.

In the United States, even when social programs take caregivers' contributions into account, such as in the survivors' insurance program, access to benefits depends on one's familial status and relationships. Women are assumed to be supported by their husbands—by husbands' wages, by husbands' workplace-based pensions, or by husbands' Social Security. Meanwhile, husbands, children, and the elderly are supposed to be able to count on the women in their families to care for them. People who do not fit into the married heterosexual family model are, then, marginalized and left with far inferior benefits (if any at all). Thus, for example, widowed mothers who receive income support through survivors' insurance not only never have to endure intimate surveillance from welfare agencies but also receive far more generous benefits than do single mothers who need welfare. Especially with the new emphasis on marriage promotion, welfare targets poor, unmarried mothers for sexual regulation, to the detriment of their basic civil rights of citizenship. This harms not only unmarried heterosexual mothers but also gays and lesbians who cannot marry, because their "intimacy constellations" are not recognized by state or federal law.

In the twenty-first century, citizenship is highly stratified: Certain groups enjoy firmer political and civil rights in addition to a modicum of social entitlements while other groups are asked to relinquish rights in exchange for economic survival. Poverty, gender, race, culture, and sexuality each affect the experienced reality of citizenship—in its civil and political, as well as its social dimensions. Outright exclusions, such as prohibitions on lesbian and gay marriage and military service throughout the nation or felony disenfranchisement in many states, belie the universal guarantee of political citizenship. The impairment of basic reproductive, parental, and associational rights for poor women who receive social provisions belies the democratization of civil rights in the twentieth century. The persistent distinction between poor people who need social provision and better-off people who are deemed to have "paid" for it through social insurance makes clear that we are far from having achieved a recognition of social rights as an aspect of citizenship in the United States.

Martha Ackelsberg

See also: Civil Rights Acts, 1964 and 1991; Liberalism; Republicanism

References and Further Reading

Marshall, T. H. 1950. "Citizenship and Social Class." In *Citizenship and Social Class and Other Essays*. Cambridge: Cambridge University Press.

McDonagh, Eileen. 2002. "Political Citizenship and Democratization: The Gender Paradox." *American Political Science Review* 96, no. 3 (September): 535–552.

Nelson, Barbara. 1984. "Women's Poverty and Women's Citizenship." *Signs* 10, no. 2 (Winter): 209–231.

Orloff, Ann Shola. 1993. "Gender and the Social Rights of Citizenship: The Comparative Analysis of Gender Relations and Welfare States." *American Sociological Review* 58, no. 3 (June): 303–328.

Civil Rights Acts, 1964 and 1991

The Civil Rights Act of 1964 (Public Law 88–352) was a landmark law in its prohibition of discrimination on the basis of race, color, sex, national origin, or religion in employment, government programs, and public accommodations. The historic legislation occurred in the same political context as the Johnson administration's War on Poverty and was driven primarily by the goal of achieving racial and economic equality.

The 1964 Civil Rights Act was the second major civil rights law in U.S. history, following by 100 years the seminal 1866 Civil Rights Act. Despite the 1866 act's guarantee of "the full and equal benefit of all laws" to all persons, subsequent laws and court decisions made racial discrimination and unequal rights the norm. Of major significance was the *Plessy v. Ferguson* (163 U.S. 537 [1896]) decision, in which the U.S. Supreme Court established a "separate but equal" doctrine. *Plessy* was not overturned until *Brown v. Board of Education of Topeka, Kansas* (347 U.S. 483 [1954]), when the Court held that segregated schools were inherently unequal and thus unconstitutional.

The milestone 1964 act was a result of the protracted struggle for political and economic redress sought by the civil rights movement, ignited by Rosa Parks's refusal in 1955 to give up her seat to a white person on a Montgomery, Alabama, bus. Civil rights acts were enacted in 1957 and 1960, but they were weak and limited because of southern opposition to the use of federal power to check the states' control of race relations and racial hierarchy. To varying degrees, states in both the North and the South supported or permitted social, political, and economic discrimination, effectively segregating neighborhoods, schools, and employment opportunities. However, discrimination and segregation by law were especially prevalent in the South, where poll taxes, literacy tests, "grandfather" clauses, and Jim Crow laws were common. After a six-month legislative process in which a number of compromises were made in order to gain the support of some southern Democrats, the 1964 Civil Rights Act was enacted by a bipartisan coalition on July 2, 1964.

The goals of the Civil Rights Act of 1964 were expansive. Its eleven titles incorporated numerous provisions, such as prohibitions on job and housing discrimination, which had not been addressed in previous civil rights legislation. Title I (and Title VIII) stipulated voting rights protections. Title II prohibited discrimination on the basis of race, color, religion, or national origin in public facilities such as restaurants, theaters, and motels. Title III forbade segregation of public facilities "owned, operated, or managed by or on behalf of any State or subdivision thereof" (Section 301[a]). Title IV required desegregation of public education and gave enforcement authority to the U.S. Department of Justice. Title V established a Civil Rights

President Lyndon B. Johnson signs the Civil Rights Act of 1964, legislation intended to eliminate racial discrimination in places of public accommodation and in employment. (Phillips Scott/Lyndon B. Johonson Library)

Commission to investigate and hear cases of denial of equal protection in voting, education, housing, public facilities, and employment, among other areas.

Titles VI and VII are especially relevant to antipoverty goals. Title VI barred discrimination because of race, color, or national origin in any program receiving federal funds or contracts, including education, training, and welfare. This ban extended to cases where the "primary objective of the Federal financial assistance is to provide employment" (Section 604). The Office of Federal Contract Compliance was established in 1965 in the U.S. Department of Labor to monitor this provision.

Title VII forbade discrimination in employment because of race, color, religion, sex, or national origin and required equal employment opportunity by employers, employment agencies, and unions with more than twenty-five employees. A 1972 amendment reduced this number to fifteen employees and expanded Title VII coverage to federal, state, and local government employees.

Proponents of Title VII recognized that discrimination was a source of unemployment, underemployment, and low wages for people of color and for women. The provisions of Title VII accordingly prohibited discrimination in all manner of employment decisions, from union apprenticeship programs to hiring, promotion, and firing. By the 1970s, Title VII was understood to also prohibit discrimination in the employment environment, giving rise to proscriptions against racial harassment on the job and, by the 1980s, to sexual harassment, as well.

Title VII set up an administrative agency, the Equal Employment Opportunity Commission (EEOC), to enforce its provisions. Initially, the EEOC was empowered only to investigate and negotiate the settlement of unlawful employment practices through conciliation and voluntary compliance. Because the EEOC was perceived to lack force, the Civil Rights Act was amended in 1972 to give the EEOC power to take employers who discriminated to court. In addition, Title VII permitted individuals who filed timely grievances to sue employers directly if the EEOC process did not remedy their discrimination.

Title VII litigation during the 1970s opened up jobs to people of color and women. Not only were most explicit forms of discrimination, such as race- or sex-based job classifications, struck down, but apparently neutral policies that produced discriminatory effects on the basis of race came under judicial purview beginning with *Griggs v. Duke Power Co.* (401 U.S. 424 [1971]). This "disparate impact" framework for gauging discrimination was extended to sex-based discrimination in *Dothard v. Rawlinson* (433 U.S. 321 [1977]). By the late 1970s, attorneys for unions, most notably labor and civil rights lawyer Winn Newman, also began to deploy Title VII to try to close the wage gap.

The 1980s, however, was a period of lax civil rights enforcement and efforts to curtail the scope of Title VII and to overturn some of its legal precedents. Efforts to remedy discrimination, such as affirmative action, were derided and condemned as "reverse discrimination." Conservatives charged that white men were being discriminated against and excluded from jobs and promotions simply because they were not minorities or women. Reagan-era litigation produced judgments that advanced these views by making it more difficult to win disparate impact cases and by questioning the government's authority to create race-conscious remedies absent a showing of intentional discrimination or of verifiable harm to the group(s) that would benefit from the remedy.

The Civil Rights Act of 1991 (Public Law 102–166), enacted November 21, 1991, was Congress's response to the Supreme Court's decisions of the 1980s weakening Title VII. It sought to confirm the principles of the 1964 act by codifying the disparate impact framework and by allowing victims of discrimination to seek monetary damages from employers. Like the 1964 act, the 1991 act was passed by a Democratic-majority Congress.

Taken as a whole, the 1991 act not only tightened and buttressed the 1964 act's civil rights protections but also provided explicit procedures and mechanisms by which to remedy and compensate victims of employment discrimination. Title I of the 1991 act spelled out remedies for civil rights violations and changed the burden of proof to make it easier for minorities and women to win damages in litigation. Also, disparate impact, not disparate intent, became the legal standard in assessing discrimination complaints involving ostensibly neutral employer policies. The 1991 act also provided for jury trials in conjunction with awarding monetary damages as a remedy for victims of discrimination. Since the 1970s, the 1866 Civil Rights Act (section 1981) had been interpreted to provide monetary damages in race discrimination cases, so the 1991 act was especially helpful to women in sex-based discrimination cases. Until 1991, sex-based discrimination claims, including sexual harassment, were eligible only for equitable relief, such as job reinstatement or back pay. However, the administration of George H. W. Bush insisted on calibrating and capping damages available to plaintiffs in sex-based discrimination cases: a maximum of $50,000 for businesses with 100 or fewer employees (95 percent of all businesses) and a ceiling of $300,000 for those employing over 500 people. As a legal weapon to fight inequality in employment, Title VII plays an important role against the racial and sex/gender distribution of poverty. However, just how strong a weapon Title VII can be depends on individuals' access to the EEOC, lawyers, and the courts and on the willingness of courts to deploy Title VII against discrimination's many iterations and forms.

Cheryl M. Miller

See also: Affirmative Action; Civil Rights Movement; Gender Discrimination in the Labor Market; Racial Segregation; Racism; Slavery; Unemployment; Voting Rights Act, 1965; War on Poverty

References and Further Reading

Burstein, Paul. 1985. *Discrimination, Jobs, and Politics: The Struggle for Equal Employment Opportunity in the United States since the New Deal*. Chicago: University of Chicago Press.

Dale, Charles V. 1991. *The Civil Rights Act of 1991: A Legal Analysis of Various Proposals to Reform the Federal Equal Employment Opportunity Laws*. Washington, DC: Congressional Research Service.

Employment Policy Foundation. 2002. "The Consequences of Providing Compensatory and Punitive Damages under Title VII." *Backgrounder*. Washington, DC. At http://www.epf.org. Accessed April 1, 2002.

Le Loup, Lance T., and Steven Shull. 1993. *Congress and the President: The Policy Connection*. Belmont, CA: Wadsworth.

McCrone, Daniel, and Richard Hardy. 1978. "Civil Rights Policies and the Achievement of Racial Economic Equality, 1948–1975." *American Journal of Political Science* 22 (February): 1–17.

Miller, Cheryl M., and Hanes Walton Jr. 1994. "Congressional Support of Civil Rights Public Policy: From Bipartisan to Partisan Convergence." *Congress and the Presidency* 21 (Spring): 11–27.

Civil Rights Movement

Between 1955 and 1965, a growing African American mass movement for civil and voting rights focused national attention on racial segregation and poverty, especially in the South. Across the nation, Blacks initiated lawsuits, legislative lobbying campaigns, and militant protest movements for school desegregation, voter registration, and equal access to public accommodations and jobs. Mass activism led to the Civil Rights Act of 1964 and the Voting Rights Act of 1965 and shaped the political conditions under which President Lyndon B. Johnson declared the War on Poverty and Congress passed the Economic Opportunity Act in 1964 (although historians still disagree on the degree to which the declaration of War on Poverty was a response to civil rights activism). Two periods saw the twentieth century's greatest declines in Black poverty (measured both in terms of family incomes and in terms of the ratio of Black to white family incomes): the early to middle 1940s and the middle to late 1960s. These periods shared three intertwined elements whose conjunction produced dramatic and lasting changes: mass activism at the grassroots level, a responsive national government committed to antidiscrimination policies, and quickening economic growth that lifted the incomes of nearly all workers (Cross 1987, 431, 501).

In reality, the mid-twentieth-century civil rights movement was only a phase in the ongoing national Black freedom struggle, many of whose activists had long dreamed of economic justice as well as civil and political rights. Critics have alleged that middle-class civil rights leaders failed to identify and attack the structural roots of Black poverty, especially in the ghettos that exploded in violence between 1964 and

1968. The view has validity for the period between 1950 and 1962. But it neglects the cross-class dynamism of the civil rights unionism of the 1940s, and it overlooks the degree to which even "middle-class" leaders of the middle to late 1960s linked civil rights, political empowerment, economic justice, and the quality of life in Black communities. As civil rights struggles broadened to include working-class and poor Blacks, activists fought for decent jobs and housing, adequate welfare, union representation, political power (beyond just voting rights), and an end to institutional racism (in police departments, housing authorities, schools, and even in welfare and antipoverty agencies themselves).

During the New Deal, the National Association for the Advancement of Colored People (NAACP) and the National Urban League (NUL) lobbied to extend Social Security benefits, unemployment compensation, minimum wages, and collective bargaining protections to agricultural and domestic workers (Blacks disproportionately occupied these poorly paid occupational niches) (Hamilton and Hamilton 1997, ch. 2). By 1941, with the World War II economy rapidly reducing unemployment and poverty among whites, Black trade unionist A. Phillip Randolph organized the March on Washington movement. The threat of mass protest was enough to persuade President Franklin D. Roosevelt to establish a Fair Employment Practices Commission in 1941 to fight discrimination in defense industries. At the same time, leftist interracial unions in the Congress of Industrial Organizations (CIO) pushed to integrate shop floors, union halls, and seniority ladders. These unions also pressed for expanded social insurance, minimum wages, full employment, and antidiscrimination legislation. Civil rights unionists swelled the ranks of the NAACP, whose members boosted Black voting dramatically outside the Deep South. Economic growth, mass mobilization, and antidiscrimination policy all combined to lift Black incomes. The ratio of Black to white median incomes rose from 37 percent to 55 percent in the 1940s (Cross 1987, 431).

By the early 1950s, anticommunist efforts had suppressed many of these organizations, stalling the drive to "organize the unorganized," especially in southern industries. Mainstream civil rights organizations narrowed their focus to the extension of voting rights and the integration of schools, transportation, and restaurants. The U.S. Supreme Court's 1954 ruling in *Brown v. Board of Education of Topeka, Kansas* (347 U.S. 483 [1954]) inaugurated a twelve-year civil rights era, when dramatic Black protests and violent white resistance filled the nation's newspapers and television screens with dramatic images from the South. Even then, when constitutional protections and issues of "dignity" remained central, activists agitated for jobs and welfare for the poor. At the outset of the famous bus boycott in Montgomery, Alabama, in 1955–1956, the Montgomery Improvement Association (MIA) demanded that the bus company hire Black drivers *before* full desegregation of bus seating. The Welfare Department gave relief to untold numbers of protesters suddenly impoverished by white economic reprisals. The MIA's president, Martin Luther King Jr., went on to found the Southern Christian Leadership Conference (SCLC), coordinating protests in Albany, Georgia (1962), and Birmingham, Alabama (1963). In each case, local leaders demanded employment in the downtown stores along with desegregated service. SCLC also launched Operation Breadbasket in 1962, which staged consumer boycotts to open jobs in specific firms (Jackson 1994, chs. 2–4).

Local organizers formed the core of the mass movement, however. Black students who formed the Student Nonviolent Coordinating Committee (SNCC) after the sit-in movement in 1960 became an activist vanguard, raising consciousness about the intersections of racism and poverty. Women such as Ella Baker, Gloria Richardson, and Fannie Lou Hamer inspired the students to embrace a radical idea: Even

Civil rights advocates lead hundreds of thousands of Americans in a march on Washington, D.C., in a multiracial demonstration for equal rights and opportunity in August 1963. (Flip Schulke/Corbis)

the poorest African Americans could lead their own fight for citizenship rights. Moving into the poorest southern rural communities to register voters in 1961, the students saw how closely poverty was related to tools of white oppression: disenfranchisement, violence, and economic reprisals. Locals like Hamer endured beatings, job losses, and evictions from their plantations for simply attempting to register. (Hamer became a full-time organizer for the Mississippi Freedom Democratic Party in 1963.) By 1965, the SNCC in Mississippi had fostered the Poor People's Corporation (providing credit for local economic projects) and the Mississippi Freedom Labor Union (organizing over 1,000 farm workers to fight for minimum wages, medical coverage, and better working conditions). Hamer founded Freedom Farm, where displaced sharecroppers cooperatively raised their own food. It is no wonder that at the 1963 March on Washington, of all the speakers, SNCC's John Lewis spoke most concretely about violence, powerlessness, and poverty in Mississippi, where Blacks received "starvation wages . . . or no wages at all" (Jackson 1994, chs. 3, 5; Carson 1981, 83, 94, 172).

"What good are integrated restaurants or theaters if Black people cannot afford the meal or the ticket?" was a question being asked across the political spectrum by 1963. A. Philip Randolph—distressed with Black job losses in manufacturing due to "automation"—proposed a March on Washington for Jobs and Freedom. The march drew 250,000 protesters to the Lincoln Memorial on August 28, 1963. Reporters covered King's "I Have a Dream" speech and the nearly unanimous support for President John F. Kennedy's civil rights bill. They scarcely noticed demands for public works employment, for a two-dollar-an-hour minimum wage (extended to domestic workers), and for prohibitions on job discrimination not contained in Kennedy's bill. NAACP lobbying and direct-action protests by SCLC strengthened President Johnson's Civil Rights Act, signed in August 1964. That act outlawed discrimination in public accommodations and incorporated a new Title VII barring employment discrimination, to be enforced by a new Equal Employment Opportunity Commission. President Johnson and President Richard M. Nixon later issued executive orders strengthening enforcement and mandating affirmative action in government agencies and contractors. Finally, in 1965, voting rights protests in Selma, Alabama, again placed pressure on Johnson to sponsor the Voting Rights Act of 1965.

Hundreds of civil rights activists became antipoverty warriors after Congress passed the Economic Opportunity Act in August 1964. St. Louis Congress of Racial Equality (CORE) activist Ivory Perry used his position in the federally funded Human Development Corporation to organize job protests, rent strikes, welfare rights groups, and a campaign to monitor and prevent poisoning from lead paint in poor children. Independently, Syracuse CORE leader George Wiley went on to form the Poverty Rights Action Center in Washington, D.C., supporting the organization of the National Welfare Rights Organization in 1967. On a larger scale, the NUL, under Whitney M. Young's leadership, won funding for programs such as the National Skills Bank (a referral service) and On-the-Job-Training (an apprenticeship program in private industry). The NUL drew generous federal and foundation support for its programs (from 1965 to 1970, its budget grew eightfold to $14.5 million) (Lipsitz 1988; Jackson 1993). Meanwhile the NAACP lobbied for civil rights enforcement and school desegregation. Herbert Hill's Labor Department filed complaints charging violations of Title VII by government contractors and labor unions. Local chapters protested discrimination at federally sponsored construction sites. The Legal Defense Fund, however, did not shift major resources into the fight against job discrimination until after 1970 (Jaynes and Williams 1989, 185).

Leaders and activists grew increasingly critical of cutbacks in the poverty program, of the Vietnam War and its negative impact on funding, and of congressional restrictions on citizens' participation in poverty programs. Leaders proposed a policy reorientation outstripping what Johnson ever conceived for his War on Poverty. Whitney Young's 1963 Marshall Plan for the Negro and King's 1964 Bill of Rights for the Disadvantaged both anticipated in scope A. Philip Randolph's 1966 Freedom Budget for All Americans, which was endorsed by all major civil rights groups. The Freedom Budget called for a tenfold increase in antipoverty outlays: $185 billion over ten years for public works, income support, and new housing construction designed "to wipe out the slum ghetto" (Jackson 1994, ch. 6; Hamilton and Hamilton 1997, 147–153).

By 1966, a third summer of urban violence underscored to many critics that rights groups had not effectively organized working-class and poor Blacks around issues important to *them*. In response, King and the SCLC mobilized several thousand Chicago Blacks to end "slum colonialism" in the summer, staging a series of "open-housing" marches in white suburbs. Yet lacking the "nonviolent army" they had expected and without support from Chicago's Mayor Richard J. Daley or President Johnson, King failed to realize his dream of an enforceable local agreement and a national civil rights act with open-housing provisions. Congress only passed the Fair Housing Act of 1968 after dozens of riots followed King's assassination in April 1968.

Conservatives blamed criminals and socially outcast poor people for the riots, but surveys found that young Black men arrested for "rioting" were no less educated than nonrioters. And they were protesting against grievances broadly

"Where Do We Go from Here?" Martin Luther King Jr., presidential address to the Southern Christian Leadership Conference, Atlanta, August 16, 1967

We must develop a program that will drive the nation to a guaranteed annual income. Now, early in this century this proposal would have been greeted with ridicule and denunciation, as destructive of initiative and responsibility. At that time economic status was considered the measure of the individual's ability and talents. And, in the thinking of that day, the absence of worldly goods indicated a want of industrious habits and moral fiber. We've come a long way in our understanding of human motivation and of the blind operation of our economic system. Now we realize that dislocation in the market operations of our economy and the prevalence of discrimination thrust people into idleness and bind them in constant or frequent unemployment against their will. Today the poor are less often dismissed, I hope, from our consciences by being branded as inferior or incompetent. We also know that no matter how dynamically the economy develops and expands, it does not eliminate all poverty.

. . . the movement must address itself to the question of restructuring the whole of American society. . . . We are called upon to help the discouraged beggars in life's marketplace. But one day we must come to see that an edifice which produces beggars needs restructuring. . . . You begin to ask the question, "Who owns the oil?" You begin to ask the question, "Who owns the iron ore?" You begin to ask the question, "Why is it that people have to pay water bills in a world that is two-thirds water?"

Source: From *I Have a Dream: Writings and Speeches That Changed the World*, ed. James M. Washington (San Francisco: HarperSanFrancisco, a division of HarperCollins, 1992), 170, 173, 177.

shared in their communities: against police brutality; against inadequate jobs, housing, education, and welfare; and in general, against unresponsive "power structures." The Black Panther Party, begun in an Oakland, California, antipoverty office in 1966, combined revolutionary rhetoric, confrontations with police, advocacy of national "full employment" policies, and local services like programs to provide free breakfasts for children and screening for sickle-cell anemia. Economic nationalists such as Floyd McKissick of CORE increasingly turned to strategies of "Black capitalism" supported by foundations and the Nixon administration. Community development corporations involved activists in housing rehabilitation or social service programming around issues as diverse as lead paint removal and adult literacy. Campaigns for "fair lending" and national legislation garnered funds for some neighborhood revitalization (Fisher 1994, 182).

The 1968 Poor People's March on Washington embodied King's final dream of using mass multiracial demonstrations to compel the government to provide "jobs or income now." King reached out to organize rural and urban poor, welfare recipients, the working poor, and the unemployed. Leadership conflicts and episodes of violence in Resurrection City, a tent city built by 3,000 poor people on the Mall in Washington, D.C., after King's assassination, garnered most press attention. Yet an interracial coalition of activists did advance proposals for jobs programs, expanded income support, an end to hunger, and the empowerment of the poor in the War on Poverty. Unfortunately, the Poor People's March faced a lame-duck president and a Congress more determined to pass repressive legislation than to extend the welfare state. Activists went back to their communities with little more than a modest expansion in the food stamp program. The welfare rights movement fought on through the early 1970s, but Black activism waned along with white-majority support for civil rights (Jackson 1994, ch. 8).

The civil rights acts and the war on poverty were unable to eradicate racism and poverty, yet they did help raise Black incomes and improve the quality of life in Black communities. Between 1964 and 1969, tax cuts and military spending pushed unemployment to historic lows, and tight labor markets, job training programs, and antidiscrimination policy spelled economic gains for Blacks. The Black middle class grew substantially; yet especially as incomes polarized and the economy slowed in the 1970s and 1980s, continued discrimination in employment and housing, persistent school segregation, and the "feminization of poverty" worsened the fortunes of the bottom third of Black America. Still, between 1959 and 1969, Black poverty rates had declined from 55 percent to 34 percent; unemployment dipped from 10 percent to 6.2 percent; and the ratio of Black to white median income rose from 52 percent to 61 percent. None of this eradicated racism: Black unemployment rates were consistently double those of whites, and census undercounts masked a much larger "subemployment" rate (including the unemployed, part-time workers, and workers no longer looking for work) that especially affected Black youth, whose official unemployment rates actually rose during the decade. The rising economic tide, it seemed, lifted boats that already occupied privileged positions higher than others. White poverty declined by 40 percent in the 1960s, whereas Black poverty declined 25 percent. The percent of the poverty population that was Black therefore increased from 25.1 percent in 1959 to 32.1 percent in 1973 (the year the nation's poverty rate hit its historic low at 11.1 percent) (Brimmer 1974, 148–150; Levy 1998, 27, 34, 96, 176).

Exacerbating these problems was the growing gap between family incomes in poorer cities and wealthier suburbs, up from 12 percent in 1959 to 21 percent in 1985. A similar tale can be told of diverging Black fortunes in housing. Working and middle-class Blacks took up new housing opportunities under the Fair Housing Act of 1968, leaving older central cities poorer. By 1990, indices of segregation nationwide had declined only slightly (Levy 1998, 143; Farley 1996, 51, 55–58; Jaynes and Williams 1989, 90).

Black communities and incomes benefited from political empowerment, but in limited ways. In 1965, 280 Blacks held elected office nationwide (31 percent of them in the South). After the Voting Rights Act, the number more than quintupled, to 1,469 in 1970 (48 percent in the South) and more than quadrupled again by 1985 to 6,016 (63 percent in the South). James Button has shown that in six southern cities, Black political power translated into improved police and fire protection, paved streets, and Black employment in public works and recreation. Though far from achieving equality (especially as professionals and managers), Blacks made dramatic progress in private employment as a result of the civil rights movement. Button's survey of employers in the six southern cities revealed that before 1960, only 12 percent had hired any Blacks, but that by the late 1970s, the proportion of employers who had hired Blacks had jumped to 81 percent. Still, only 31 percent of Black-majority cities in the entire South had Black mayors by 1985. Even in the North, where 70 percent of the Black-majority cities had Black mayors in 1985, the resources those mayors could devote to services and employment were shrinking, as federal aid dried up and tax bases shrank because of business relocation and middle-class flight. Grassroots activists also complained of a "new patronage system . . . a spoils system for the [Black] middle and upper classes" that limited public benefits to the poor (Jaynes and Williams 1989, 238–239, 251; Button 1989, 143, 148–151, 186–187).

Yet the combination of popular and government activism had indeed spelled dramatic gains in the 1960s. As a recent review of the economic literature concludes, the combined effects of desegregation in jobs and schooling, the rise in voter participation, federal enforcement efforts, antipoverty programs, and a relatively robust economy were substantial, though they cannot be disentangled by standard econometric tests. "With the greatest relative black improvement coming in the South, which was the target of a comprehensive Federal effort to dismantle segregation in schooling, voting, accommodations and employment, the inference is buttressed that Federal civil rights policy was the major contributor to the sustained improvement in black economic status that began in 1965," the study concluded (Donohue and Heckman 1991, 1641). Mass activism and civil rights advocacy had made this revolution possible (Donohue and Heckman 1991, 1641, 1629).

Thomas F. Jackson

See also: Affirmative Action; African American Migration; African Americans; Black Panther Party; Civil Rights Acts, 1964 and 1991; Community Development; Community Organizing; Highlander; Kerner Commission Report; National Association for the Advancement of Colored People (NAACP); National Urban League; Operation Breadbasket; Poor People's Campaign; Racial Segregation; Racism; Service and Domestic Workers, Labor Organizing; Tenant Organizing; Voting Rights Act, 1965; War on Poverty; Welfare Rights Movement

References and Further Reading

Brimmer, Andrew F. 1974. "Economic Developments in the Black Community." In *The Great Society: Lessons for the Future*, ed. Eli Ginzberg and Robert M. Solow, 146–163. New York: Basic Books.

Button, James W. 1989. *Blacks and Social Change: Impact of the Civil Rights Movement in Southern Communities*. Princeton: Princeton University Press.

Carson, Clayborne. 1981. *In Struggle: SNCC and the Black Awakening of the 1960s*. Cambridge, MA: Harvard University Press.

Cross, Theodore. 1987. *The Black Power Imperative*. New York: Faulkner.

Donohue, John J., III, and James Heckman. 1991. "Continuous versus Episodic Change: The Impact of Civil Rights Policy on the Economic Status of Blacks." *Journal of Economic Literature* 29, no. 4 (December): 1603–1643.

Farley, Reynolds. 1996. "Black-White Residential Segregation." In *An American Dilemma Revisited*, ed. Obie Clayton Jr., 45–75. New York: Russell Sage Foundation.

Fisher, Robert. 1994. *Let the People Decide: Neighborhood Organizing in America*. New York: Twayne.

Hamilton, Dona Cooper, and Charles V. Hamilton. 1997. *The Dual Agenda: Race and Social Welfare Policies of Civil Rights Organizations*. New York: Columbia University Press.

Jackson, Thomas F. 1993. "The State, the Movement, and the Urban Poor: The War on Poverty and Political Mobilization in the 1960s." In *The "Underclass" Debate: Views from History*, ed. Michael B. Katz, 403–439. Princeton: Princeton University Press.

———. 1994. "Recasting the Dream: Martin Luther King, Jr., African-American Political Thought, and the Third Reconstruction, 1955–1968." Ph.D. diss., Stanford University. Revision forthcoming as *Dilemmas and Dreams: Martin Luther King, Jr. and Black America's Search for Economic Justice*. Chapel Hill: University of North Carolina Press.

Jaynes, Gerald, and Robin M. Williams Jr., eds. 1989. *A Common Destiny: Blacks and American Society*. Washington, DC: National Academy Press.

Levy, Frank. 1998. *The New Dollars and Dreams*. New York: Russell Sage Foundation.

Lipsitz, George. 1988. *A Life in the Struggle: Ivory Perry and the Culture of Opposition*. Philadelphia: Temple University Press.

Payne, Charles M. 1995. *I've Got the Light of Freedom: The Organizing Tradition and the Mississippi Freedom Struggle*. Berkeley and Los Angeles: University of California Press,

Civilian Conservation Corps (CCC)

In November 1932, Franklin Delano Roosevelt was elected president of the United States, in large part because he promised active government solutions to the widespread unemployment and poverty ravaging the nation during the

Great Depression. During what would later be called "the Hundred Days," Roosevelt introduced several measures to help alleviate the immediate suffering Americans were experiencing. One of them was the Civilian Conservation Corps (CCC). Calling the Seventy-third Congress into emergency session on March 9, 1933, FDR proposed to recruit and train thousands of unemployed young men to combat the destruction and erosion of the nation's natural resources. With this program, he hoped not only to pump money into the moribund economy but also to save two of the nation's precious resources—its young men and its land—from going to waste. Congress approved of the program immediately, sending the Emergency Conservation Work (ECW) Act to the president's desk for his signature on March 31. Until the demise of the CCC in 1942, over 3 million men worked on its various conservation projects, including reforestation, forest protection, soil-erosion prevention, flood control, wildlife restoration, and public range and park development.

FDR wasted no time getting the program under way and appointed Robert Fechner as the CCC's director. The logistics of mobilizing 250,000 young men who hailed mainly from the East to work in camps located mostly in the West were difficult, requiring the involvement of the armed forces. The influence of the armed forces could be seen in the program's regimented management style. Men wore uniforms and were expected to address their superiors with deference, as in, "Yes, sir!" But other government departments were involved in the administration of the CCC as well: The Departments of Agriculture and Interior were responsible for planning and coordinating the work the CCC would perform, and the Department of Labor handled the processing and selection of applicants.

Applicants were required to be unmarried men aged eighteen to twenty-five who came from families on government relief. Exceptions were made for men with special skills or experience and for veterans of the Spanish American War and World War I. The men worked forty hours a week and earned thirty dollars a month in addition to free room, board, and clothing. They were only allowed to keep five dollars for themselves, and the rest was sent directly to their families. The initial enrollment period was six months, but men were eligible to reenlist for up to two years. Many men learned trades and skills that renewed their confidence during the hard times and gave them a competitive advantage when they returned to the labor market.

The CCC was perhaps the most popular of the New Deal programs approved during the Roosevelt administration. It created much-needed jobs for young men and produced tangible results. CCC workers planted over 3 billion trees from 1933 to 1942, erected nearly 3,500 fire towers, laid down 97,000 miles of fire roads, and devoted millions of man-days to fighting fires, floods, and soil erosion. At its peak in 1935–1936, over 500,000 men were enrolled in the CCC at one time, operating in 2,650 camps in every state across the country. Hoping to balance the budget during an election year, FDR introduced a budget to Congress that drastically reduced the amount of funds allocated to the popular program. Members of Congress were deluged with letters of protest, and under the weight of public opinion, they were forced to reject the president's proposal.

The program's popularity would continue until the late 1930s, when unemployment began to decline and the country began focusing its attention on the looming threat of Nazism across the ocean. In 1942, Congress defunded the program after a review committee concluded that the CCC, designed as a temporary relief program, was no longer necessary, especially as the country had to marshal its limited resources for the war effort.

Robert J. Lacey

See also: Great Depression and New Deal; Public Works Administration; Relief; Works Progress Administration (WPA)

References and Further Reading

Civilian Conservation Corps Alumni. "Roosevelt's Tree Army: A Brief History of the Civilian Conservation Corps." http://www.cccalumni.org/history1.html.

Hill, Edwin G. 1990. *In the Shadow of the Mountain: The Spirit of the CCC*. Pullman: Washington State University Press.

Nolte, C. 1997. *Civilian Conservation Corps (the Way We Remember It)*. Paducah, KY: Turner Publishing.

Classism

The term "classism" refers to the network of attitudes, assumptions, beliefs, behaviors, and institutional practices that maintain and legitimatize class-based power differences that privilege middle- and higher-income groups at the expense of the poor and working classes. It is made up of three independent but related dimensions: prejudice (that is, negative attitudes toward the poor and working classes), stereotypes (that is, widely shared, socially sanctioned beliefs about the poor and working classes), and discriminatory behaviors that distance, avoid, or exclude poor or working-class persons.

Rooted in socially constructed assumptions about deservingness and deviance, classist stereotypes characterize the poor as lazy, unable to defer gratification, lacking respect for or interest in education, and unwilling to work. These beliefs make middle-class experiences normative and confer on poor and working-class persons the status of devalued "other." Classist stereotypes intersect with sexist and racist beliefs, further stigmatizing low-income women and poor people of color. Such intersections are evident in stereotypes of poor women, particularly welfare recipients, as sexually available, amoral, permissive mothers and of poor men of color as irresponsible fathers, criminals, and members of a menacing "underclass." Classist stereotypes also underlie individualistic attributions for poverty, which emphasize personal causes of poverty (such as lack of motivation, poor work ethic) rather than structural explanations (for example, discrimination, low wages).

Like other forms of discrimination (such as sexism or racism), classist discrimination occurs on both the interpersonal and institutional levels, ranging from subtle or covert to blatant or overt. Both interpersonal and institutional classism create and maintain a climate of hostility for poor and working-class persons. Interpersonal classism includes face-to-face behaviors that distance or derogate low-income individuals, such as avoiding cross-class interactions, labeling (with such terms as "white trash," "welfare queens"), and treating the poor as inferior. Institutional classism refers to the marginalization of poor and working-class individuals within social institutions. Examples include limited access to high-quality health care, affordable safe housing, legal representation, well-equipped schools, and employment in the primary labor market. Classist assumptions and discriminatory practices are also embedded in policies that seek to regulate the behaviors of public assistance recipients by making the receipt of funds contingent on compliance with program rules and that focus on changing poor people rather than poverty conditions. Penalties that reduce or eliminate benefits to recipients who do not fulfill work requirements and "family cap" regulations that deny additional benefits to women who have another child while receiving welfare are examples of two such penalties.

Heather E. Bullock

See also: Deserving/Undeserving Poor; Poor Whites; Racism; Sexism; "Underclass"

References and Further Reading

Bullock, Heather E. 1995. "Class Acts: Middle Class Responses to the Poor." In *The Social Psychology of Interpersonal Discrimination*, ed. Bernice Lott and Diane M. Maluso, 118–159. New York: Guilford Press.

Feagin, Joseph R. 1975. *Subordinating the Poor: Welfare and American Beliefs*. Englewood Cliffs, NJ: Prentice-Hall.

Gans, Herbert J. 1995. *The War against the Poor: The*

Underclass and Antipoverty Policy. New York: Basic Books.
Jarret, Robin L. 1996. "Welfare Stigma among Low-Income African American Single Mothers. *Family Relations* 45: 368–374.

Cloward, Richard

See Regulating the Poor; War on Poverty; Welfare Rights Movement

Committee on Economic Security

See Aid to Families with Dependent Children (ADC/AFDC); Great Depression and New Deal; Social Security Act of 1935; Unemployment Insurance

Communist Party

From the early 1930s until the early 1950s, the Communist Party of the United States of America (CPUSA) was an importance influence in American society, in labor and various protest movements, in cultural and artistic life, in many state governments, and even for a short time in national politics. Particularly during the 1930s, the CPUSA was the major organizer of poor people, the unemployed, and African Americans. Yet the CPUSA is hardly uncontroversial. On the one hand, from the early 1920s until the late 1950s, it was the dominant left-wing group in the United States, highly interracial and ethnically diverse, the most militant and successful of trade union organizers, and the foremost fighter for equality for African Americans, women, and other minorities, as well as the leading proponent in the struggle of the unemployed, poor people, students, and others. On the other hand, it was an unabashed, uncritical apologist for the brutal crimes of the Stalin regime in the Soviet Union, and it was an unrelenting, sometimes repressive, critic of others on the left.

History of the CP

The U.S. Communist Party was born in 1919 out of the left wing of the U.S. Socialist Party (SP) when the entrenched SP leadership refused to allow the left-wing majority to take control democratically of the organization. Losing most of its more dynamic members, refusing to support the 1917 Russian Revolution led by V. I. Lenin and Leon Trotsky, and revealing a lack of commitment to democracy among its own members, the SP virtually died at this time. In September 1919, two communist parties were formed. The larger, the Communist Party of America (CPA), had approximately 24,000 members. The other group, the Communist Labor Party (CLP), with approximately 10,000 members, was led by John Reed (the hero of Warren Beattie's film *Reds*), a journalist who wrote *Ten Days That Shook the World*, a popular, heroic account of the Russian Revolution of 1917. In 1921, the Communist International (CI) forced the two parties to merge. In 1929, the party changed its name to the Communist Party of the United States of America.

The 1920s were a difficult time for all radical groups, and the Communist Party was no exception. Membership stabilized at around 10,000, reaching a low point of around 7,500 in 1930. Nevertheless, in the 1920s, the CP engaged in numerous activities, its members gained valuable experience, and the party itself achieved the prestige and roots that would allow it to make dramatic gains during the 1930s. CP members led a large textile strike in Passaic, New Jersey, in 1926, and another in Gastonia, North Carolina, in 1929. The Communists were also involved in the key defense cases of the day, including that of Nicola Sacco and Bartolomeo Vanzetti, two Italian American anarchists who were executed in 1927 for supposedly committing a bank robbery and double murder.

The CP's activities allowed it to recruit leading radicals from virtually every left-wing milieu. Many Industrial Workers of the World (IWW) members joined the party, including "Big Bill" Haywood, the most prominent IWW leader of the day. The CP recruited Black socialists, and important activists from Marcus Garvey's United Negro Improvement Association, some of whom were taken aback at the commitment to Black rights by many of the CP's white members. In the 1930s, prominent intellectuals flocked to the CP. Few gravitated toward the SP, for as John Dos Passos explained in 1932, "[b]ecoming a Socialist right now would have just about the same effect on anybody as drinking a bottle of near-beer." None of the attraction of the CP at this time was based on its support for liberal Democratic Party politicians or for any watered-down version of radical politics. The result of the activities of the CP during the 1920s is described by James Cannon, one of the party's leaders until his 1928 expulsion for Trotskyism:

> This Communist Party held the line of class struggle and revolutionary doctrine in that long, ten-year period of boom, prosperity and conservatism before the crash of 1929. It was in that period—fighting for revolutionary ideas against a conservative environment . . . , refusing to compromise the principle of class independence—that the Communist Party gathered and prepared its cadres for the great upsurge of the thirties. (Cannon 1971, 92)
>
> Despite its reduced membership, the Communist Party entered the thirties—the period of the greatest radical revival—as the dominating center of American radicalism. It had no serious contenders. (Cannon 1971, 93–94)

The 1930s

In the fall of 1929, the stock market crashed, and the U.S. economy ground to a halt, with many industries, including the automobile, mining, and textile industries, virtually collapsing. Official jobless estimates went from 492,000 in October 1929 to over 4 million in January 1930. CP mass activity and membership growth both skyrocketed.

The earliest mass activity took place among the unemployed. The largest unemployed organization of the early 1930s was the CP-led Unemployed Councils, concentrated in large cities throughout the country. Protests by the unemployed, often massive and militant, began immediately with the onset of the Depression. On March 6, 1930, over 1 million people demonstrated across the country under CP leadership. Concerted activity by the unemployed seems to have touched virtually every part of the land. The South, the West, the Northeast, the Midwest—all were affected. In large cities, including Atlanta, Baltimore, Milwaukee, Minneapolis, Pittsburgh, San Francisco, Seattle, Toledo, and many more, large-scale activity by and organization of the unemployed took place. Records show activity in small and medium towns, including Indianapolis and Terra Haute, Indiana; Lewiston, Maine; Camden, New Jersey; Ashtabula and Warren, Ohio; Charlestown and Fairmont, West Virginia; Racine, Wisconsin; and even in small towns in Mississippi.

Some of the activities of the unemployed organizations were on a large scale. In New York City, for example, in late January 1930, 50,000 people attended the funeral of a Communist Party activist killed by the police. A similar funeral in Detroit in 1932 for four party activists killed by the police at a protest march on Ford's River Rouge plant was attended by 20 thousand–40 thousand people: "Above the coffin was a large red banner with Lenin's picture" (Klehr 1984, 33, 59). Perhaps the high point of such activity was in Chicago. In one incident in 1931, 500 people in a Chicago southside African American neighborhood brought back furniture to the home of a recently evicted widow.

The police returned and opened fire; three people lay dead. The coffins were viewed, again under an enormous portrait of Lenin. The funeral procession, with 60 thousand participants and 50 thousand cheering onlookers, was led by workers carrying Communist banners: "Within days, 2,500 applications for the Unemployed Councils and 500 for the Party were filled out" (Klehr 1984, 322–323). Even in cities in the Deep South, including Atlanta, Birmingham, and New Orleans, racially integrated mobilizations of the unemployed took place.

What most distinguished the CP during the 1930s from other radical groups was its position and commitment to the fight against Black oppression. No previous largely white U.S. radical group had focused attention on the plight of Blacks. The CP's efforts in the battle for Black liberation even penetrated into its extensive immigrant membership. As Mark Naison notes: "Not only Jews felt moved by the Party's position: Finnish, Polish, Hungarian, Irish, Italian, and Slavic Communists became passionate exponents of the Party's position on the Negro Question" (1983, 43). One result of the CP position was to place special emphasis on organizing African Americans in the South, leading the CP to publicize and fight against the lynching of Blacks there. In 1931, the CP took the initiative in a case that was to gain it major political leadership among Blacks throughout the whole country: the case of the Scottsboro boys, nine Black youths seized on a freight train in rural Alabama and accused of raping two white girls who had been riding with them.

The CP's most massive successes, however, were undoubtedly within the labor movement, especially the Congress of Industrial Organizations (CIO). Had it not been for its conciliatory tactics toward more-conservative CIO leaders, the CP would have had the early leadership of the auto union and would have had greater influence in the steel, oil, and rubber industries, in which it played a leading role in organizing.

The Decline of the CP

After World War II ended in 1945, the influence of the CP began to decline. There are two primary reasons why the CP declined and disappeared so ignominiously. First, after 1935, the CP never regained an anticapitalist, radical, social transformatory perspective. Despite certain periods of renewed militance, largely dictated by the exigencies of Soviet foreign policy, its perspective remained largely reformist. This approach robbed it of its ability to attract the most militant and radical youth and workers. During the 1950s, for example, it trailed in the wake of the National Association for the Advancement of Colored People. In the 1960s, it was unprepared to support, much less lead, either the radicals in the civil rights movement or the student and antiwar movements. Yet the mild social democratic domestic politics to which the CP aspired, epitomized by its antimonopoly perspective (an alliance of all "progressive" forces, including the more democratically inclined capitalists) required a greater allegiance to the U.S. ruling class than its Soviet ties would permit. Thus, it was not spared increased repression when Soviet and U.S. aims came into conflict. The nature of its Soviet ties also led it to squander its moral capital as either a domestic radical or reformist organization.

The Impact of the CP

The CP was not by and large an electoral party and should not be evaluated as such. Nevertheless, it did, at its height, have an important electoral impact. In Connecticut, Oregon, Massachusetts, Michigan, and Ohio, it was a significant force in the influential labor party politics there, as well as in later left politics within these states' Democratic Parties. It also had substantial influence within the Democratic Parties of California and Wisconsin. In Minnesota, for a time, the CP and its popular-front allies controlled the Minnesota Farmer-Labor Party, the dominant political party in the state. In New

York State, it had significant control of the American Labor Party, which controlled the swing vote between the Democrats and Republicans in the state. New York City had two Communist city councilmen, Benjamin Davis Jr. and Pete Cacchione, along with other political supporters on the city council. Its support in New York City was significant enough that it had an alliance with Governor Herbert Lehman, who returned the favor by vetoing a legislative bill that would have banned the CP. It had two firm congressional supporters, Vito Marcantonio from New York and John Bernard from Minnesota, along with a close alliance with Harlem congressman Adam Clayton Powell Jr.

Support for the CP was widespread among artists, entertainers, and intellectuals, from Hollywood personalities to Nelson Algren, Leonard Bernstein, Harold Cruse, John Dos Passos, Theodore Dreiser, W. E. B. Du Bois, Ralph Ellison, Josephine Herbst, Granville Hicks, Langston Hughes, Doris Lessing, Paul Robeson, Pete Seeger, Upton Sinclair, Richard Wright, José Yglesias, and many more. Among sports figures, not only did the CP have the support of boxers Joe Louis and Henry Gibson, Brooklyn Dodger second baseman Jackie Robinson, and Negro League star Josh Gibson, but New York Yankees third baseman Red Rolfe and Chicago Cubs star Rip Collins wrote regular sports columns in the *Daily Worker*. Many prominent African American entertainers and musicians attended or performed at CP functions at one time or another. Among them were Count Basie, Cab Calloway, Miles Davis, Roy Eldridge, Duke Ellington, Ella Fitzgerald, Dizzy Gillespie, Lionel Hampton, W. C. Handy, Coleman Hawkins, Billy Holiday, Lena Horne, Leadbelly, Charlie Parker, Art Tatum, Chick Webb, Josh White, Mary Lou Williams, and Teddy Wilson.

This support was based on the work that the CP had accomplished. The party organized African Americans, exposed and fought against the many manifestations of white supremacy at a time when it was not popular to do so, and won large numbers of whites to support these struggles. The CP had a large number of talented Black leaders and was, by all accounts, racially egalitarian in its own organization. According to enthusiastic reports in the Black press, the CP was the main organization to force these issues into the public consciousness. It and the African American workers whom it often organized were the impetus for making issues of race central to the perspective of the CIO. Finally, it was CP organizers who provided the main shock troops in the organizing of industrial unions. All these good deeds coincided with the party's subordination to the foreign policy dictates of Moscow, its slavish submission on central issues, including its apologies for the crimes of Stalin, and its failure to maintain its original anticapitalist perspective after the mid-1930s. Thus, the Communist Party of the United States of America provides key lessons for future radical movements of what to do as well as what not to do.

Michael Goldfield

See also: Great Depression and New Deal; Progressive Era and 1920s; Socialist Party; Trade/Industrial Unions

References and Further Reading

Cannon, James P. 1971. *Speeches for Socialism*. New York: Pathfinder Press.

———. 1973. *Speeches to the Party: The Revolutionary Perspective and the Revolutionary Party*. New York: Pathfinder Press.

Cochran, Bert. 1977. *Labor and Communism: The Conflict That Shaped American Unions*. Princeton: Princeton University Press.

Draper, Theodore. 1957. *The Roots of American Communism*. New York: Viking.

———. 1960. *American Communism and Soviet Russia*. New York: Viking.

Goldfield, Michael. 1980. "The Decline of the Communist Party and the Black Question in the U.S.: Harry Haywood's *Black Bolshevik*." *Review of Radical Political Economics* 12, no. 1 (Spring).

———. 1985. "Recent Historiography of the Communist Party U.S.A." In *The Year Left*, ed. Mike Davis, Fred Pfeil, and Michael Sprinker, vol. 1. London: Verso.

Horne, Gerald. 1994. *Black Liberation/Red Scare: Ben*

Davis and the Communist Party. Newark: University of Delaware Press.

Klehr, Harvey. 1984. *The Heyday of American Communism: The Depression Decade*. New York: Basic.

Klehr, Harvey, John Earl Haynes, and Kyrill M. Anderson. 1998. *The Soviet World of American Communism*. New Haven: Yale University Press.

Naison, Mark. 1983. *Communists in Harlem during the Depression*. Chicago: University of Illinois Press.

Community Action Program

See Community Development; Community Organizing; Community-Based Organizations; War on Poverty

Community Chests

Community Chests served as fund-raising organizations for voluntary health, recreation, and welfare agencies for hundreds of communities in the United States from the 1920s through the 1960s. By the 1960s and 1970s, most had been renamed as local United Way organizations. Founded initially to reduce the dizzying array of appeals from charitable groups to local businessmen, Community Chests sought agreements by local charities to forgo individual fund-raising efforts and instead to receive a portion of a single community-wide fund-raising effort conducted by the Community Chest. Control over disbursing funds often gave Community Chests a deeply influential role in the activities of the organizations they funded. Community Chest agencies at midcentury generally represented the most popular and least controversial elements of the voluntary sector.

Although a number of cities in the late nineteenth and early twentieth centuries experimented with the idea of "federated financing," it was World War I that spurred the Community Chest movement. After the war, local organizations to coordinate multiple appeals for foreign relief were converted by local elites into Community Chests for local agencies; the number of Community Chests swelled from 17 in 1917 to 80 in 1922 to 335 in 1929 (Borst 1930, 95). Local charities gained generally higher revenues in exchange for Community Chest supervision of agency budgets, giving Community Chests deep influence over agency program and staffing. In most places, the conservative orientation of Community Chests guaranteed that only groups that focused on well-accepted service provision, rather than on advocacy or even service to stigmatized groups, would be funded.

The primary beneficiaries of Community Chests prior to the New Deal were organizations providing financial assistance to the poor, but those organizations were strained by the Great Depression. Though Community Chests raised a record $101 million in 1932, they could not meet the needs of the unemployed and were overshadowed by federal intervention in welfare in the New Deal. Though diminished in scope, Community Chests capitalized on public welfare to shift their dollars to such nonwelfare programs as the Boy Scouts, YMCAs, and family counseling programs. World War II again stimulated efforts to organize and consolidate charity campaigns, and the Community Chest movement emerged from the war with 797 chests raising $197 million in 1947 (United Way of America 1977, 108). The stability of the Community Chests was augmented by the increasingly routinized contributions from major corporations and their employees, particularly with the help of labor unions in the postwar period.

In the postwar period, despite gradually expanding coffers, Community Chests encountered several major challenges. First, by the 1950s, they were facing competing appeals from a number of major national health associations that lobbied for funds for research for heart disease, tuberculosis, and other causes. Donor dissatisfaction with multiple appeals spurred a second wave of federation between Community Chests and health agencies, resulting in "United

Funds" and, by the 1970s, the United Way. United Fund practices were protested in the late 1960s by groups and organizations that had been generally excluded from membership, particularly minority groups and women's organizations. Such protests liberalized United Way policies somewhat, but they also spurred the organization of "alternative" federations of voluntary organizations made up of underrepresented groups. In 2000–2001, over 1,400 United Way organizations raised $3.91 billion (United Way of America 2001).

Andrew Morris

See also: Philanthropy; Voluntarism

References and Further Reading

Borst, Homer. 1930. "Community Chests and Councils." In *Social Work Yearbook of 1929*, ed. Fred S. Hall, 95–100. New York: Russell Sage Foundation.

Murphy, Michael. 1977. "Financing Social Welfare: Voluntary Organizations." In *Encyclopedia of Social Work*, 478–484. Silver Spring, MD: National Association of Social Workers Press.

Seely, John R., et al. 1957. *Community Chest: A Case Study in Philanthropy*. Toronto: University of Toronto Press.

United Way of America. 1977. *People and Events: A History of the United Way*. Alexandria, VA: United Way of America.

———. 2001. "Basic Facts about the United Way."

Community Development

"Community development" is a term that came into common use in the 1960s to describe multifaceted economic and social improvement initiatives, located in neighborhoods and areas of disproportionate poverty, both urban and rural, and based on the idea that community or "place-based" investments were vital components of an overarching strategy to combat poverty. These initiatives had their roots in the settlement house movement of the Progressive Era, in some New Deal programs, in neighborhood-based juvenile delinquency prevention programs, and in numerous other neighborhood institutions. However, in their urban application in the 1960s, they were more deeply grounded as a response to racial segregation and in ideas of resident self-determination. In their rural and small-city applications, community development activities emanated from a realization that broader economic changes had injured or left behind geographical areas of significant size. Federal policies in the 1960s encouraged multidimensional and comprehensive approaches to reviving these areas. These approaches often took the form of "community development corporations" (CDCs), especially in urban settings. There are some 2,000 CDCs in existence now, although most are small and limit their work to the construction or rehabilitation of low-income housing. Federal support for place-based efforts has proceeded by fits and starts since the 1960s, with most innovation occurring as a result of support from private foundations. During the 1980s, particular emphasis was placed on combining social services with economic development and with an overarching aim of "community building"; as of 2001, roughly fifty schemes around the country could be described as "comprehensive community initiatives" (CCIs). Currently, leaders in the field are focusing on ways to connect inner-city initiatives to the regional economy, to "smart growth" projects, and to outside political and economic actors, and they are also focusing on approaches to comprehensiveness that build out from entities like youth programs and community health centers rather than on such traditional core activities as housing and commercial development.

The place- or community-based approach to fighting poverty has historically evolved against a backdrop of economic restructuring, migration, and public policy and the attendant political struggles that have shaped and reshaped the fortunes of affected communities. Of particular importance in the emergence of community development in the 1960s were the Great Migrations between 1890 and the 1960s, which brought millions of African Americans from the rural South to the nation's cities, as well as large numbers of whites from declining mining and agricultural areas and places from which industry had relocated. Pervasive forces of segregation, both official and customary (including widespread violence), confined African Americans of all economic strata to inner-city neighborhoods. Previous generations of immigrants who had initially settled in similar situations had moved out as their economic circumstances improved. In contrast, even with the impetus of the civil rights movement in the late 1950s and early 1960s, the demographics of the disproportionately Black inner city did not change. At the same time, the chronic problems of left-behind rural areas, most prominently Appalachia, began to attract increasing public notice.

Public policy had a strong effect in setting the stage and creating the need for community development, reinforcing and supporting private discrimination. The federal Home Owners' Loan Corporation worked in tandem with bankers and real estate brokers to prevent African Americans from purchasing homes not only in white neighborhoods but in their own neighborhoods as well. The Federal Housing Administration, the Veterans Administration, and private lending institutions were explicitly discriminatory in their lending policies. Decisions regarding locations for public housing under the Housing Act of 1937 reinforced segregation. In the 1950s, urban renewal and siting decisions for interstate highways destroyed stable Black neighborhoods and consequently weakened community ties.

As the 1960s began, seeds of change had been planted. The civil rights movement was under way. Its focus was primarily on state-mandated segregation in the South, but in the African American community in general a broader impatience was developing that would erupt into urban violence before long. Poverty was inching its way into public focus. The Ford Foundation began a multisite initiative known as the Gray Areas program, which was premised on providing education and work skills to young people in poor communities and on developing the capacity of local bureaucracies that were supposed to serve low-income people. This program attracted the attention of the administration of newly elected President John F. Kennedy, which at the time was developing its own initiative against juvenile delinquency, with Attorney General Robert Kennedy as point person. This in turn led to a federal-Ford partnership to sponsor Mobilization for Youth (MFY) on the Lower East Side in New York City. MFY developed the idea that comprehensive community-based services, legal aid, and education would help prevent juvenile delinquency and in addition emphasized organizing local residents to demand more-responsive public policies. The Gray Areas program and MFY became the models for what emerged under President Lyndon B. Johnson as the Community Action Program (CAP), which became a signature program of his officially declared War on Poverty and was administered by the Office of Economic Opportunity. The CAP provided a framework of employment and legitimacy within which inner-city neighborhood leaders could press for change in and concerning their communities. Each of these items was a building block toward the set of activities in urban settings that came to be known as community development.

Seeds of change had been planted on the rural side as well. In 1956, Senator Paul Douglas of Illinois began pressing for legislation to address depressed areas left in the lurch by industrial relocation and changes in mining and agricultural economics. These efforts eventuated in the Area Redevelopment Act of 1961 and the Appalachian Regional Development Act of 1965.

The racial unrest of the mid-1960s was a catalyst in the emergence of the first initiatives and policies that reflected the contemporary idea of urban community development. The violence in the Watts neighborhood of Los

Angeles, which occurred less than a month after President Johnson signed the Voting Rights Act of 1965 into law, was pivotal. Policymakers in the newly created federal U.S. Department of Housing and Urban Development began conceptualizing a design for multifaceted initiatives directed at improving the conditions of life on a neighborhood-wide basis, the outcome of which was the Model Cities program enacted in 1966. Originally proposed as a small number of demonstrations, each generously funded, the program as it emerged from Congress was highly diluted and spread the funding in small doses among dozens of places. It never came close to achieving its promise.

Senator Robert Kennedy, seeking his own way to make a difference, took the lead in initiating the Bedford-Stuyvesant Restoration Corporation in a low-income part of Brooklyn in New York City. The ambitious "Bed-Stuy" effort aimed to harness public and private funding to attract new plants from outside and otherwise stimulate new economic activity, rehabilitate housing, make the neighborhood safer, and in general create a more cohesive community. Analogous models already existed, such as the Watts Labor Community Action Committee in Los Angeles and the Woodlawn Organization in Chicago, but Kennedy's highly visible foray attracted greater attention. Kennedy and his New York senatorial colleague, Republican Jacob Javits, succeeded in attaching to the Economic Opportunity Act of 1966 a new Special Impact Program (SIP) to provide federal funds for neighborhood-based community development schemes. A key difference between Model Cities and the Special Impact Program was that the funding for the former went through the city government whereas the funds for SIP went directly from Washington to the community development corporation in the neighborhood.

As these urban efforts were taking shape, rural community development was also receiving attention, most prominently through the 1965 legislation that was specially directed at the Appalachian region. The theory was that extra federal investment in roads and other infrastructure would help attract and retain business, which would in turn contribute to jobs and economic stability. At the same time, states and localities around the country offered and have continued to offer tax abatements and other incentives to attract manufacturing and other economic activity, and some communities have in fact been winners in this beggar-thy-neighbor sweepstakes. By the 1990s, favored strategies to promote rural economic development included attracting a prison and, in Indian communities, establishing a casino.

Inner-city community revitalization has always confronted the dilemma that focusing on separate development could be taken to mean acceptance of exclusion from the larger society—"gilding" the ghetto, according to critics, rather than "dispersing" it through integration. In reality, however, investing in segregated communities more often represented a response to rather than an acceptance of segregated conditions. Thus, some Black leaders, espousing the idea of "Black power," advocated an active strategy of separatism and self-sufficiency as a counterforce to the prevailing economic power of the white establishment. Others turned to the task of attracting outside investment and nurturing local enterprise as a way of making a virtue of necessity, in effect seeking to combat the walls of segregation by making urban areas more desirable places to live.

Despite expressions of enthusiasm in the outside world, funding for community development—especially federal funding—did not keep pace with its initial promise and before long began to drop off. Federal funding was greatly reduced during the Richard M. Nixon's presidency, with SIP nearly disappearing and Model Cities being changed into the Community Development Block Grant (CDBG), under which mayors had the discretion to decide where to spend the funds with little oversight from Washington. Modest federal support for low-income housing remained available, and CDCs that focused on the construction and rehabilitation of affordable housing grew in number (although, on balance, the nation's supply of affordable housing has diminished steadily for more than two decades).

Even more fundamentally, social conditions in inner-city neighborhoods grew worse. Notwithstanding the racial backlash, the Fair Housing Act of 1968 and related changes in federal policies on housing financing opened up places outside the inner city to African Americans who could afford to leave. Equally important, jobs and industry as well as housing opportunities had been steadily shifting to the suburbs. Thus, while the large growth in the Black middle class in the 1960s gave more African Americans the wherewithal to move, rising joblessness and the widespread destruction in inner-city neighborhoods in the riots made it less attractive to stay. Many who could afford to move did so. Many of the business-, professional-, and working-class residents who had sustained economic stability in neighborhoods left. Discrimination in the housing and housing finance markets was far from eliminated, but enough change occurred to enable substantial out-migration (although not necessarily to integrated neighborhoods).

Through the 1970s and 1980s, deterioration in the living conditions in inner cities far outpaced the achievements of CDCs and other community development activities. Although not all of the nonpoor departed, the ensuing concentration of poverty was enough to tip the neighborhoods in dangerously synergistic ways. Crime and violence went up, births to unmarried teens shot up, high school completion dropped, and drug and alcohol use increased (especially in the 1980s). Communities that had been reasonably healthy lost cohesion, and their political capacity to demand adequate services, let alone investment, grew weaker. The economic deterioration in the inner city was made worse by the structural changes occurring in the economy generally, with higher-paying jobs disappearing to deindustrialization and ground being lost by everyone at the lower end of the labor market. Minorities living in areas of concentrated poverty were hit worst of all.

Political responses targeted at the inner city during the 1970s were mostly pallid. President Jimmy Carter offered the Urban Development Action Grant (UDAG) program, but its approach was primarily a downtown-development strategy, and its main promise to low-income residents was the possibility of work (generally low-wage work) in the hotels and other facilities created with UDAG funds. On the other hand, the Home Mortgage Disclosure Act, signed by President Gerald Ford in 1975, and the Community Reinvestment Act, signed by President Carter in 1977, were important spurs to more-responsive action by financial institutions. By the 1980s, federal urban policy had turned to what some characterized as active disinvestment; substantial budget cuts were accompanied by policies that both encouraged increased industrial relocation and globalization and favored suburban development. Presidents Ronald Reagan and George H. W. Bush and some in Congress talked about enterprise zones that would offer tax incentives for job creation in distressed neighborhoods, but federal legislation to create such incentives was not enacted during those presidencies. Income maintenance in various forms remained available, but little was offered in the way of school improvement, assistance with transition to the job market, economic development, or job creation.

Despite the increasing hardship, some CDCs persevered and grew throughout the period. In the Central Ward of Newark, New Jersey, the New Community Corporation, which was founded in the 1960s, grew to have an annual budget of more than $100 million and more than 1,400 employees. Bethel New Life in Chicago, the Dudley Street Neighborhood Initiative in Boston, and the more recently created

Community Building in Partnership in Baltimore have received national attention.

National foundations, seeking to fill the void in federal policy during the 1980s, undertook a new wave of activities. The Ford, Rockefeller, and Annie E. Casey Foundations all put substantial funding into multicity initiatives, with varying degrees of success. One of the most interesting foundation thrusts occurred in the South Bronx in New York City. To help in that very blighted area, the Surdna Foundation created the Comprehensive Community Revitalization Program (CCRP), which served as a highly effective go-between to help a number of CDCs get resources and connections in the outside world. Much of the South Bronx has been transformed as a result of the work of those CDCs and the CCRP.

New entrants joined the scene. Long-standing community organizers like the Industrial Areas Foundation and the Association of Community Organizations for Reform Now (ACORN) turned some of their energy to bricks and mortar. A highly publicized example is Project Nehemiah, which began as an endeavor by two dozen churches in the East New York section of Brooklyn. Project Nehemiah produced about 2,200 affordable single family homes in a very distressed part of the city. It stimulated federal legislation, which in turn helped others build thousands of units of Nehemiah homes around the country.

During the 1990s, organizations with a base in activities besides housing and economic development began to branch out to generate a new wave of comprehensive community-building efforts. Rheedlen Centers for Children, located in Harlem in New York City, began as a program for truants, grew into a set of after-school programs, and is now a community institution (renamed the Harlem Children's Zone) with activities radiating out from school buildings to make streets safer and to establish violence-free zones. Many community health and mental health centers, drug treatment programs, and human service providers have found themselves becoming more comprehensive and more rooted in and connected to the community as they have seen the need to respond to as many of the needs as possible of those who come in the door to partake of the primary activity of the organization.

President Bill Clinton brought federal policy back into the community development world in the 1990s, although with nowhere near the success that adherents had hoped for. The Empowerment Zone/Enterprise Communities (EZ/EC) program was enacted in 1993 with a guaranteed ten-year appropriation of $1 billion. This sum was to fund six urban empowerment zones with $100 million each and three rural empowerment zones with $40 million each; the remaining $280 million was to be divided among ninety-five enterprise communities (two-thirds urban and one-third rural), which would therefore receive slightly under $3 million each. Firms newly locating in or expanding in EZ and EC areas would also receive tax advantages, with the incentives for EZ zones being more generous than those for the EC zones. Applicants were to engage in a widely collaborative planning process, and awards were to be based on the quality of the planning process as well as the quality of the plan. Plans were to be broadly conceived; permissible activities included almost anything that would improve the quality of life for residents or assist them in improving their economic and social status.

As with Model Cities, the funds were spread too thin. The six urban zones could have as many as 250,000 people each, subdivided into three separate portions of the city. Each subzone could thus be larger than a typical neighborhood, and the ten-year life of the program meant that each subzone would receive an average of $3.33 million annually in grant funds, in addition to the value of the tax incentives. Further, because the target areas did not have to coincide with the home bases of existing organizations, there was no natural role for any particular group or groups.

This, coupled with the large role assigned to the mayors and governors, caused the planning and implementation process to become highly politicized. By the end of the decade, it was clear that the accomplishments of the overall program, although tangible, did not add up to a consistently positive pattern among all of the participating localities.

The challenges to the community development field were quite different in 2000 from what they had been in 1990. The economics of central cities had improved markedly over the decade, in significant part because the economy of the nation as a whole improved so much. Business and professional people tired of long commutes, and young couples wanting to avoid commuting in the first place, began buying and renovating homes in central cities, often in low-income neighborhoods. Neighborhoods such as Harlem in New York City, 47th Street in Chicago, and U Street in Washington, D.C., took on a very different look. Mayors began making decisions about amenities and infrastructure designed to support the burgeoning process of gentrification. Magnet schools began to appear in gentrifying neighborhoods.

These trends were good for urban tax bases but were not especially good for low-income people, who were often forced out of neighborhoods in which they had resided for a long time. At the same time, many units of high-rise public housing were demolished in a number of cities, and little organized effort was made to help people relocate. The combined effects produced more dislocation than at any time since the days of urban renewal in the 1950s. And all of this occurred at a time when the supply of affordable housing was becoming more constricted than ever, with rents in most urban areas skyrocketing to a point where even families with full-time workers found it impossible to both pay the rent and eat.

Many of those dislocated from the inner cities reappeared in now-deteriorating inner-ring suburbs. Here they joined many representatives of another key phenomenon of recent years: the large-scale immigration that has created an unprecedented diversity in a nation that already prided itself on being a haven for people seeking a better life. Our nation is more multiracial, multiethnic, and multicultural than ever. This is both an opportunity and a challenge.

A final set of developments that affects the agenda for community development inheres in the welfare changes of 1996 and their effect on low-income communities. As of 2003, it was at least true that many people formerly on welfare had jobs of some kind, but it was also true that many people had lost their cash assistance or had been refused help when they applied for it and had no work either. The result was that those at the bottom of the income scale were actually worse off than they had been before the welfare law was enacted, and these people disproportionately resided in the distressed neighborhoods that had been the focus of community development activities.

These developments and trends all affect the agenda for community development as the new century gets under way.

Those working on community development in distressed inner-city neighborhoods must contend with the process of gentrification. The challenges are to attract people of higher incomes and to hold on to residents with rising incomes who are tempted to move away, while not displacing longtime low-income residents. Reestablishing a mixture of incomes in a currently distressed neighborhood is an important goal but one that is not easy to accomplish. If there is to be a new stability, the conditions that reflect the neighborhood's distress must be improved. The neighborhood must be safe, schools must be improved, trash must be collected, and streets must be maintained. Even then, the easier course for those with power to make and impose decisions, whether collectively or through the market, will be to force low-income people out.

Gentrification is just one of the forces from outside the neighborhood that have to be confronted. These forces include what might be called "structural racism": all of the factors that bring about a disproportionate racial impact with regard to employment, education, housing, health care, law enforcement, administration of public benefits, and more. Urban distressed neighborhoods cannot be fixed in a vacuum. Outside forces played a critical role in creating and perpetuating these neighborhoods' distress, and a greater focus on the continuing operation of those forces is essential. People should have a genuine choice about where they live and work. Those who work on reviving distressed neighborhoods should consider their responsibility to help promote that genuineness of choice at the same time as they continue to create a greater sense of community in their own space.

In many cities, though not all, major improvements in employment levels cannot be achieved without attending to the fact that so many of the existing jobs are situated in suburban areas. With the greater emphasis on work that has emanated from the 1996 welfare legislation, community development actors who wish to be comprehensive need to consider undertaking activities that help people get and keep jobs in the regional economy. Helping establish or actually operating child care and transportation services and taking action to combat race discrimination in the job market are increasingly recognized as part of the community development mission, as is a more regional perspective.

Meanwhile, the venue for community development work may well be changing. Inner-ring suburbs are changing rapidly, and unless care is taken, many will shortly replicate the current problems of inner-city neighborhoods.

Even more fundamentally, the changing "face" of America due to the growing numbers of immigrants from the countries of Latin America, Asia, Africa, and the Caribbean includes a changing face of poverty and near-poverty. Hispanics constituted a disproportionate part of the population of distressed neighborhoods even in 1990, and the 2000 census revealed further diversification of the minority populations in poor neighborhoods. All who are living in circumstances that call for a comprehensive community development agenda need to find ways to cooperate and collaborate rather than compete.

Finally, renewed attention to funding streams, both public and private, is essential if progress is to be made. The more comprehensive an organization's approach to the task of community development, the more sources of funding it will need to tap to do its work. A continued effort to create a simplified and responsive federal funding stream remains in order, as is intensified action to create new private funding institutions dedicated to the work, and to attract more attention from existing financial institutions.

Peter Edelman

See also: African American Migration; Community-Based Organizations; Housing Policy; Racial Segregation; Rural Poverty; Urban Poverty; Urban Renewal; War on Poverty

References and Further Reading

Downs, Anthony. 1981. *Neighborhoods and Economic Development*. Washington, DC: Brookings Institution.

Edelman, Peter. 2001. *Searching for America's Heart: RFK and the Renewal of Hope*. Boston: Houghton Mifflin.

Ferguson, Ronald F., and William T. Dickens, eds. 1999. *Urban Problems and Community Development*. Washington, DC: Brookings Institution.

Grogan, Paul S., and Tony Proscio. 2000. *Comeback Cities: A Blueprint for Urban Neighborhood Revival*. Boulder, CO: Westview Press.

Halpern, Robert. 1995. *Rebuilding the Inner City*. New York: Columbia University Press.

Massey, Douglas S., and Nancy A. Denton. 1993. *American Apartheid: Segregation and the Making of the Underclass*. Cambridge, MA: Harvard University Press.

Orfield, Myron. 1997. *Metropolitics: A Regional Agenda for Community and Stability*. Washington, DC: Brookings Institution.

Pierce, Neal R., and Carol F. Steinbach. 1990. *Enterprising Communities: Community Based Development in America*. Washington, DC: Council for Community Based Development.

Rusk, David. 1999. *Inside Game/Outside Game: Win-*

ning Strategies for Saving Urban America. Washington, DC: Brookings Institution.

Schorr, Lisbeth B. 1997. *Common Purpose: Strengthening Family and Neighborhoods to Rebuild America*. New York: Doubleday.

Community Organizing

Community organizing is the strategic and tactical processes through which residents of a geographically and socially delimited area are brought together to exert pressure in the pursuit of what they perceive to be their immediate or long-term collective interests. Community organizing against poverty requires strategies aimed at eradicating political impoverishment as well as economic deprivation.

Community organizing strategies vary in their assumptions about both the need for a permanent organizational structure and, when such entities are deemed necessary, the degree to which they should be organized or structured. They could involve, for example, simple ad hoc mobilization of area residents for a brief protest against police brutality or against specific actions by a slum landlord or an unresponsive local school principal. Or the primary goal might be the establishment of a powerful and permanent community organization that will represent a wide range of both immediate and long-term community interests. Community interests could range from such basic goods as needed traffic stop signs or adequate playgrounds and recreational facilities, to responsive city services like police protection, trash pickup, and public assistance, to ambitious economic development projects and initiatives to build affordable housing.

Community organizing was a popular strategy for addressing various needs of the poor (especially the urban poor) throughout the twentieth century, but the number of community organizations proliferated beginning in the 1960s. Yet if there is one name that is emblematic of community organizing in the United States, it is that of Saul Alinsky, whose ideas had been implanted decades earlier, during the Depression-ravaged 1930s. During the 1940s, Alinsky helped earn his reputation as a grassroots community organizer through effective challenges to what he saw as the elitism and paternalism of settlement house workers. Alinsky's community organization approach was heavily influenced by his work with the Chicago Area Project anti–juvenile delinquency program that was established by Clifford Shaw under the auspices of the Illinois Institute for Juvenile Research in the 1930s. Its model of community action stressed the involvement of area residents and the cultivation of indigenous leadership but focused primarily on changing individuals rather than the social structures that contribute to poverty in urban America.

While working with the Chicago Area Project, Alinsky began organizing the families, churches, and other neighborhood organizations of stockyard workers into the Back of the Yards Neighborhood Council (BYNC), the prototype for his brand of militant community organizing. One of the early reform targets of the BYNC was the community organization strategy of area settlement house workers and social workers. Their approach was limited, largely to the coordination of the activities of area social agency heads. In contrast, Alinsky's strategy emphasized the development of indigenous leadership and the use of conflict tactics to force community change.

In 1940, Alinsky founded the Industrial Areas Foundation as a nonprofit group to organize residents to address the many social problems plaguing their older, working-class neighborhoods in highly industrialized regions of the United States. Alinsky's local BYNC and his national Industrial Areas Foundation initiated an important movement for participatory democracy and self-determination among inner-city residents. In Alinsky's highly replicable model of community organizing, professional organizers should organize communities so as to maximize indigenous leadership and to build an independent and self-sustaining base of community power for area residents. The irony of Alinsky's approach and contribution to community organizing is that despite his emphasis on the building of people's organizations based on indigenous leadership, it was Alinsky more than anyone else who was responsible for the growth of community organization as a profession, run, of course, by professionals.

In the 1960s, the Woodlawn Organization (TWO), a community organizing group advised by Alinsky, quickly became one of the largest, most effective, and best-known community organizations serving an African American community. Its growth was accelerated in 1960 by a major urban renewal battle between the University of Chicago and the adjoining Woodlawn community when, without bothering to consult Woodlawn's largely low-income, African American residents, the university announced plans to clear a mile-long, block-wide strip of the Woodlawn community for its South Campus.

Like the BYNC, TWO was not a single organization. Instead, it was organized as an umbrella for many already-existing community organizations. TWO offered a replicable model of community organization for low-income African American urban communities throughout the United States that was far more independent than programs developed under the financial sponsorship of private foundations or the federal government. With the assistance of professional community organization consultants, organizations like TWO were organized by indigenous leaders for area residents, to establish a permanent, locally run organizational base through which to pursue what the residents determined to be their community interests.

A major reason for the proliferation of community organizations in the 1960s was the support received from the federally funded community action programs during the War on Poverty. The earliest of the project precursors to those community action programs, and the one generally regarded as the most influential, was the Mobilization for Youth (MFY) project on Manhattan's increasingly Puerto Rican and African American Lower East Side. Organizers in MFY and other projects, like the Harlem Youth Opportunity Unlimited project—also initiated in New York City before the War on Poverty—tested the potential and the limits of community action as a strategy for changing the power structures of low-income urban communities.

The dominant theoretical guideposts for MFY, and later for the War on Poverty, were provided by Richard Cloward's and Lloyd Ohlin's (1960) "opportunity theory." Opportunity theory legitimized the establishment of a wide range of community-based social programs through its assumption that juvenile delinquency could be reduced if the opportunities available to inner-city youth were expanded. MFY's community organization strategy challenged settlement houses in at least two major ways that paralleled previous conflicts between Alinsky organizations and settlement houses. First, MFY's community organization strategy called for the sponsorship of grassroots organizations that were homogeneous in both class and ethnicity. Second, it assumed that conflict (for example, through social protest) was a legitimate and viable mechanism of institutional reform. Furthermore, those who held to the tenets of opportunity theory believed that if projects like MFY were to be viable, they must include community organization mechanisms that were effective in ensuring that local institutions were responsive to the needs of area residents.

MFY supported numerous protests and other community actions, especially those associated with the civil rights movement. Its staff participated in the 1963 March on Washington and in Martin Luther King Jr.'s Poor People's Campaign, supported local African American and Puerto Rican leaders in efforts to develop a police department civilian-review board, and sponsored voter registration campaigns for low-income residents. They also organized community residents on behalf of welfare rights and affordable housing.

During the 1960s, welfare rights campaigns, tenant associations, and neighborhood safety groups emerged in cities throughout the United States in response to the immediate survival needs of residents in poor urban neighborhoods. For example, Johnnie Tillmon, who became a leader in the National Welfare Rights Organization, helped found the Aid to Needy Children (ANC) Mothers Anonymous of Watts, one of the first welfare rights groups in the country. The ANC program provided welfare assistance to poor mothers and their children. ANC Mothers Anonymous and other grassroots community groups were organized by local residents and focused on advocating for their rights at the local level. Welfare rights organizing developed on a national scale when former university professor George Wiley and other welfare rights workers established the National Welfare Rights Organization (NWRO) in 1966. In doing so, Wiley was influenced by Frances Fox Piven's and Richard Cloward's (1977) call for "A Strategy to End Poverty" that originally appeared in the *Nation* in 1966. Unfortunately, the gender, race, and class politics within the NWRO contributed to the shift away from grassroots organizing on the part of the national leadership. For example, Guida West reports that "conflicts over male dominance . . . gradually surfaced and led to fragmentation" of the NWRO (1981, 367).

A contemporary group that carries on the work of community organizing in working-class neighborhoods is the Association of Community Organizations for Reform Now (ACORN). According to ACORN (2002), there are 500 ACORN chapters in forty U.S. cities. It was established in 1970 as the Arkansas Community Organization for Reform Now to determine if the NWRO could expand its membership base beyond poor, mostly African American women receiving public assistance. Although ACORN has been described as a neo-Alinsky organization, it differs from Alinsky-style organizations in important ways. For example, ACORN's organizational strategy and tactics were modeled after the work of Alinsky's coworker, Fred Ross. Where Alinsky aimed to organize existing institutions in urban areas (for example, churches and recreational facilities) into a super organization of organizations, Ross learned from organizing low-income Mexican Americans in the more rural Southwest that issues important to area residents could best be identified and addressed through meetings held in their homes. Consequently, those methods became known as the "house meeting, issue organizing approach" (Boyte 1980, 94).

ACORN's goal is not to build a powerful community organization but, instead, to place the power directly in the hands of "the people." The organization views inequality in the distribution of power to be its ultimate issue, and it assumes that power inequality cannot be addressed merely at the local community level. With its commitment to addressing issues of concern to a wide range of citizens, ACORN's multi-issue approach grew into a multistate and later a national organization that employed not only pressure politics but also electoral politics.

By drawing most of its financial resources from its family membership dues and from door-to-door solicitations, ACORN has been able to maintain a great deal of autonomy. However, there are also limitations to its model of community organization. For example, ACORN's extreme pragmatism and need to appease a broad-based constituency reduces its effectiveness in addressing socially divisive issues like racism, sexism, and class exploitation. Although ACORN has been credited with providing organizational opportunities and empowerment for working-class women, there is also a tendency for its day-to-day decision making and operations to be dominated by its more middle-class staff rather than by its members.

Community organizing can build effective power bases for increasing the access of poor people to social welfare and other economic resources at the local level and in some cases beyond. Although community organizing alone cannot produce fundamental changes in the class, gender, and racial structures that are ultimately responsible for the high rates of poverty and economic inequality in the United States, it can provide some relief and reform for those who need it most.

Noel A. Cazenave and Nancy A. Naples

See also: Association of Community Organizations for Reform Now (ACORN); Living-Wage Campaigns; Poor People's Campaign; Tenant Organizing; War on Poverty; Welfare Rights Movement

References and Further Reading

Association of Community Organizations for Reform Now (ACORN). 2002. Web site. http://www.acorn.org.

Boyte, Harry C. 1980. *The Backyard Revolution: Understanding the New Citizen Movement*. Philadelphia: Temple University Press.

Cazenave, Noel A. 1993. "Chicago Influences on the War on Poverty." *Journal of Policy History* 5: 25–50.

Cloward, Richard, and Lloyd Ohlin. 1960. *Delinquency and Opportunity*. Glencoe, IL: Free Press.

Delgado, Gary. 1986. *Organizing the Movement: The Roots and Growth of ACORN*. Philadelphia: Temple University Press.

Fisher, Robert. 1984. *Let the People Decide: Neighborhood Organizing in America*. Boston: Twayne.

Naples, Nancy A. 1998. *Community Activism and Feminist Politics: Organizing across Race, Class, and Gender*. New York: Routledge.

Piven, Frances Fox, and Richard A. Cloward. 1977. *Poor People's Movements: Why They Succeed, How They Fail*. New York: Vintage Books.

West, Guida. 1981. *The National Welfare Rights Movement: The Social Protest of Poor Women*. New York: Praeger.

Community-Based Organizations

Community-based organizations are instruments through which residents of particular geographic areas work together to preserve or improve local conditions. For much of the history of the United States, American citizens and immigrants have organized themselves privately on the local level to serve their own interests, often in response to gaps in public services. Among the most common forms of community-based organizations are improvement associations, settlement houses, neighborhood councils, block clubs, community development corporations, and coalitions of organizations patterned according to the teachings of organizer and theorist Saul Alinsky. These groups have pursued such goals as material provision for residents, infrastructure improvements, government services, and political influence. Community-based organizations have varied enormously in their scale, structure, relationship with other established institutions, and activities. Some have counted only a city block their area of concern; others have been coalitions encompassing entire metropolitan regions. Participants have organized some groups spontaneously, and large civic organizations and the federal government have sponsored the creation of others. Some organizations purposefully sought publicity for their activities; other groups, ephemeral and inwardly focused, have escaped public attention.

Urban political structures in the nineteenth century encouraged neighboring property owners to cooperate with one another. Home owners who wanted such communal amenities as sidewalks and sewers extended into their neighborhoods had to petition their city council to provide them; they also promised to pay for the improvements through a special assessment. In order to guarantee sufficient funds for expensive local infrastructure projects, property owners were required to secure commitments from a majority of their neighbors. Collecting such petitions was usually the single goal of the individuals who arranged them, but insofar as the requests brought neighbors together for the purpose of improving the area, these efforts set the stage for the emergence later in the century of more-permanent groups. Poor and working-class people also pooled their resources to provide for each other's needs in emergencies. Fraternal organizations and lodges created life insurance and medical service funds to provide members with services they could not afford individually. Some of these organizations were primarily oriented to such social services, but others provided members with social activities, entertainment, and camaraderie.

In the era before the creation of the federal safety net, private charities provided for some of the material needs of poor people. Reformers mistrustful of the condescension of elite charities toward their clients established settlement houses, where they lived as "residents" among the people they hoped to serve. Settlement houses offered a broad array of direct services and legislative programs to buffer poor urbanites from the ravages of the industrial economy. They also provided gathering spaces where local residents could pursue cultural activities. The most famous American settlement, Chicago's Hull House, provided facilities for immigrant artisans to pursue their native arts and crafts, forums in which residents could perform and view theatrical and musical entertainments, and opportunities for political education. In the early twentieth century, some settlements founded community centers that focused more directly on channeling the energies of local residents toward neighborhood betterment. Settlement houses did not disappear with the rise of new styles of community-based organizing, but they did sometimes change their focus and structure. The Hull House complex, for example, was destroyed in the early 1960s to make way for the campus of the University of Illinois, but it continued to exist in the form of several distinct "Jane Addams Centers" scattered throughout the city.

Although settlement houses and other philanthropic organizations provided services directly to needy residents, another strand of urban activism sought to stimulate organizations that would provide solutions to a broad array of problems that residents perceived in their neighborhoods. Nineteenth-century organizations of property owners who paid for infrastructure evolved into local "improvement associations" of residents who hoped to keep their neighborhoods clean and orderly in order to enhance their living conditions and property values. Such organizations sponsored local sanitation and beautification campaigns and petitioned elected officials for physical improvements such as street lighting and parks, as well as for better service from police and fire departments. Improvement associations in white neighborhoods often included the preservation of racial homogeneity in their mandates, actively seeking to prevent nonwhites from taking up residence in the area. Related community groups, with more narrowly conceived interests, sponsored the adoption of racially restrictive covenants, so that members of minority groups, such as African Americans, Asians, and Jews, could be legally prevented from living in the area, except as resident domestic servants.

Civic groups with an interest in the working class and the poor realized that the middle and upper classes were not alone in their interest in promoting desirable neighborhoods. Local branches of the National Urban League, an African American organization dedicated to helping southern migrants adjust to city life, urged the formation of block clubs to build community in the urban setting. As early as 1920, the Pittsburgh Urban League sponsored a block club in the predominantly working-class, African American Hill District. In the 1920s and again after World War II, the Chicago Urban League staff pounded the pavement to encourage African Americans to create block clubs and to knit those organizations into regional federations. In Cincinnati between 1917 and 1920, Wilbur C. Phillips experimented with a "social unit plan" to help service providers and recipients coordinate children's health care and identify other community needs. Similarly, citywide civic organizations around the nation fostered the development of local community councils to plan for their areas' general improvement or to address specific problems such as juvenile delinquency.

Alinsky, usually regarded as the father of community organizing, transformed such ad hoc practices by establishing a philosophy, a method, and a profession. He gained his initial organizing experience in Chicago, where in the late 1930s he helped Joseph Meegan found the Back of the Yards Neighborhood Council. In his 1946 call to arms, *Reveille for Radicals,* Alinsky described how ordinary people could challenge establishment institutions by forming "people's organizations" that concentrated individuals' disparate energies into a single group. The key to Alinsky's approach was that the people must organize and act on their own behalf rather than allowing others to represent their interests. Alinsky argued against conciliation, urging activists not to shrink from using conflict tactics to exercise political power and demand change.

Alinsky translated his philosophy into action through the Industrial Areas Foundation (IAF), established in 1940 to hone and disseminate the techniques of community organizing, in part by maintaining a core staff of organizers for hire by nascent community groups. The IAF trained a cadre of professional community organizers for whom creating new organizations was more important than individually addressing the interests of particular neighborhoods. The organizer's job was to cultivate local leadership skills, so that neighborhoods could sustain their activities indefinitely on their own. IAF staff successfully organized new, highly effective, publicity-oriented groups in Chicago, Rochester, and other cities. IAF-trained groups often found themselves battling community groups that fronted for other institutions and powerful political interests, as when the Woodlawn Organization (TWO) in Chicago challenged urban renewal plans—supported by the University of Chicago and the business/middle-class-oriented Hyde Park–Kenwood Community Conference—that threatened to displace Black residents and institutions in the neighborhood. Large, Alinsky-style groups often encouraged the creation of new, smaller groups as a means of fostering locally driven improvement and also of bolstering their own base of support. Some potential groups found IAF's terms too restrictive and expensive and sought alternative routes to community organization. Adopting the pieces of Alinsky's dicta that suited their needs, new community organizations flourished around the country in the 1960s and 1970s, without Alinsky's imprimatur but inspired by his principles.

The movement to help otherwise politically disempowered groups of people to help themselves through community organizing gained momentum in the 1960s, drawing additional inspiration from Michael Harrington's *Other America* (1962) and the southern civil rights movement, which emphasized that the absence of political organization and power were significant dimensions of poverty. An array of new programs sought to promote the engagement of poor people in civic and political affairs, on the theory that participation itself could solve local problems. In 1963, members of Students for a Democratic Society formed the Economic Research and Action Project (ERAP) to build community organizations in urban areas. About 300 participants, principally college students or recent graduates, fanned out in cities like Cleveland and Newark over the next several years, hoping to build an interracial social movement among the poor. President Lyndon B. Johnson's War on Poverty required the "maximum feasible participation" of poor people in its local administrative bodies. Federally funded community action agencies also hired residents as paraprofessional staff members. These approaches were by no means limited to urban areas; U.S. Senator Paul Wellstone (D-Minnesota) documented the labors of residents of a Minnesota county in his book *How the Rural Poor Got Power* (1978). Many community organizations used their newfound power to lobby local government officials. Community organizations called for the installation of stop signs, traffic lights, and playgrounds and for better service from sanitation, welfare, and education authorities. Other groups challenged elected officials, calling for an end to police brutality and to urban renewal projects that threatened their neighborhoods with highway building or downtown business and high-end, luxury development plans. Perhaps most famously, residents of the area around Love Canal, New York, challenged the state's handling of a local toxic site. Although occasionally successful in winning particular remedies, these efforts were insufficient to undo poverty in neighborhoods that were becoming increasingly vulnerable as traditional sources of working-class jobs left for suburban areas and overseas.

Many local activists realized that greater community-mindedness, by itself, could do little to address the effects of deindustrialization and economic restructuring on neighborhoods that relied on the proximity of stable, high-paying, working-class jobs. New federal programs in the 1970s, most notably the Community Development Block Grant, provided monies with which city mayors could target particular neighborhoods for improvement and better services. Community organizations created community development corporations (CDCs) to coordinate efforts to attract grants from the government and private sources. CDCs aimed to fix the housing stock, attract commercial and manufacturing jobs, and create medical and child care services within the neighborhood. In contrast to Alinsky-inspired efforts, which encouraged residents to challenge political structures, CDCs tended to focus their energies on enterprises to revitalize local economies. Existing community organizations, such as Bethel New Life in Chicago, also reorganized their missions to take advantage of the new opportunities for bricks and mortar and for economic improvement in their areas. Complementing the efforts of formal CDCs and community organizations were the ongoing and often informal and invisible operations conducted by networks of poor people (primarily women) to meet their own needs collectively by providing child care, food, cash, and other forms of mutual assistance.

The late twentieth century witnessed new trends in the practice of community-based organizing in the United States. First, local community organizations linked themselves into regional and even national networks of groups. The Association of Community Organizations for Reform Now (ACORN) has branches around the country. The IAF, on the principle that the influence of allied groups can aid in providing pressure for the interests of particular constituents, has been developing regional networks of organizations. For example, in 1997, IAF launched United Power for Action and Justice, a group that covers the whole of the metropolitan Chicago area. Second, community organizations have distanced themselves from Alinsky's philosophy of conflict. Rather than deploying abrasive and spectacular protests against centers of power, "relational organizing" emphasizes building up networks of personal connections. The shift to more-cordial relationships also allowed for the easier integration of religious groups, whose ethical mandates included behaving in a neighborly fashion, into organizing efforts. Finally, the "community building" approach to revitalizing poor neighborhoods has sought to draw on the existing skills of residents and local institutions instead of conceptualizing such areas as a list of problems to be solved.

Amanda I. Seligman

See also: Association of Community Organizations for Reform Now (ACORN); Civil Rights Movement; Community Development; Community Organizing; Hull House; Industrial Areas Foundation (IAF); Mutual Aid; National Urban League; New Left; *The Other America;* Settlement Houses; Tenant Organizing; Urban Renewal; War on Poverty

References and Further Reading

Alinsky, Saul D. 1969. *Reveille for Radicals.* New York: Vintage Books. Originally published 1946.

Beito, David T. 2000. *From Mutual Aid to the Welfare State: Fraternal Societies and Social Services, 1890–1967*. Chapel Hill: University of North Carolina Press.

Betten, Neil, and Michael J. Austin. 1990. *Roots of Community Organizing, 1917–1939*. Philadelphia: Temple University Press.

Halpern, Robert. 1995. *Rebuilding the Inner City: A History of Neighborhood Initiatives to Address Poverty in the United States*. New York: Columbia University Press.

Mooney-Melvin, Patricia. 1986. *American Community Organizations: A Historical Dictionary*. New York: Greenwood Press.

Warren, Mark R. 2001. *Dry Bones Rattling: Community Building to Revitalize American Democracy*. Princeton: Princeton University Press.

Contingent Work

Contingent work is an employment arrangement where the employee/employer relationship is understood from the outset to be of limited duration. The terms "contingent work" and "nonstandard work" are often used interchangeably. Contingent work relationships are understood to be of limited duration, while nonstandard work includes part-time work and all employment relationships that are not regular, full-time employment.

Contingent and nonstandard employment arrangements have become increasingly important as a result of a series of economic pressures. Profit pressures on companies, driven largely by increased competition and improved technology, have given rise to contract work and temporary employment as strategies for reducing labor costs. The growth in these forms of contingent employment have provided further evidence of dual labor markets: one labor market with a core of stable jobs that are well insulated from economic volatility and peripheral jobs that are more exposed to economic volatility. Contingent work has also resulted from the reduced importance of firm-specific skills, that is, skills acquired on the job. Firm-specific skills raise employee productivity and provide some measure of security for workers since an employer cannot hire a similarly skilled worker from outside the firm. Some researchers have argued that the reduction in firm-specific skills has allowed firms to convert more jobs into contingent jobs. At the same time, the number of women in the labor force, particularly mothers, has increased demand for flexible work schedules. Although many of the contingent arrangements do not offer real flexibility, part-time work provides reduced schedules that allow both women and men to care for family responsibilities. Overall, however, there is only limited evidence that increases in contingent employment have been driven by workers' needs for flexibility, as opposed to employer practices.

Demographics of the Contingent Labor Force

In 2001, 31.0 percent of women worked in nonstandard employment, compared to 22.8 percent of men. These shares are virtually unchanged since 1995 (the first data available) (Kalleberg et al. 1997). The least remunerative types of nonstandard work—part-time, temporary, and on-call jobs—continue to be dominated by women. Overall, women are considerably overrepresented in nonstandard work arrangements: In 2001, 54.5 percent of nonstandard workers were women, compared with 46.9 percent of all workers (author's calculations from the February 2001 Current Population Survey). Economy-wide, more than one in seven U.S. workers is employed in a contingent job; including part-time work in the calculation raises the share of the nonstandard employment to more than one in four workers. Contingent work, however, encompasses heterogeneous groups of workers. Contingent and nonstandard employment can be split, broadly, into two classifications: employment arrangements that are entrepreneurial and employment arrangements that are obligated to an employer. Entrepreneurial arrangements typically include self-employment, independent contracting, and contract company workers and comprise approximately one-fourth of the contingent workforce. Workers in these arrangements tend to be more skilled and better educated and to receive higher compensation. In contrast, the majority of contingent workers (73 percent) are in obligated arrangements, in which an employee works for a single employer for a limited time or under a reduced schedule. These arrangements include part-time or temporary help and on-call/day laborers. Workers in these arrangements tend to be less skilled and lower paid.

Compensation in Contingent Work

Compensation for the obligated arrangements is considerably less than compensation for the entrepreneurial arrangements. For example, in 1999, average hourly wages ranged between $10.84 (temporary help) and $13.19 (on-call/day laborers) for the obligated arrangements. By contrast, average hourly wages for the self-employed were $17.68 and for contract company workers were $19.09. Full-time workers received $15.83 per hour in 1999. (All figures are the author's analysis of the February 1999 Current Population Survey.) Contingent workers also experienced considerable differences in non-wage compensation such as health insurance and pension coverage. As of 2001, workers in temporary help, on-call/day laborers, and part-time employment had very low levels of health insurance coverage; their overall coverage rates were 46.9 percent, 69.1 percent, and 76.6 percent respectively, as compared to 88.2 percent for workers in regular full-time employment (these figures include coverage of any sort). Pension coverage shows a similar pattern. For low-wage workers, the bottom of the earnings distribution is overrepresented with workers in contingent arrangements. More than 22 percent of part-time workers and 17 percent of on-call/day laborers earn less than $5.50 per hour. By contrast, only 4.5 percent of regular, full-time workers earned below that amount (author's analysis of February 1999 Current Population Survey data).

Preferences for Work Arrangements

Among analysts and researchers of nonstandard employment, there is a long-standing debate about the extent to which these work arrangements reflect workers' demands for work/life balance versus employers' efforts to reduce costs. Two nonwork factors play an important role in this debate: being simultaneously enrolled in school and employed, and having young children.

Many workers use nonstandard employment to enable them to enroll in school. However, the majority of eighteen-to-twenty-four-year-old nonstandard workers are not enrolled in school. Part-time workers, especially males, are the most likely among nonstandard workers to be enrolled in school, and the self-employed (including self-employed independent contractors) are the least likely. But overall, only 13.2 percent of women and 13.7 percent of men are *both* employed in nonstandard arrangements and enrolled in school.

Proponents of nonstandard arrangements also point to the benefits of nonstandard work in balancing work with family responsibilities. For the most part, these family responsibilities fall on women, yet women between the ages of eighteen and forty-five with children under six years old do not show a strong preference for nonstandard employment. Overall, they are about 8 percentage points more likely to choose nonstandard employment than are women without children under six. Most of that share comprises women who work in part-time jobs. This preference should perhaps not be surprising, since the needs of parents with young children typically involve dependable schedules, like those provided by regular part-time work, rather than schedules that vary from week to week with only limited control by the worker, such as those often offered in temporary jobs or self-employment.

The percentage of women workers in nonstandard arrangements who prefer standard employment remained relatively constant between 1999 and 2001. Women working part-time hours showed a small decrease (from 18.0 percent to 17.4 percent) in their preference for a full-time job; the drop was larger among men (from 27.1 percent to 23.4 percent). For the first time since the Contingent Work Survey has been conducted, more than half (50.4 percent) of all women in temporary jobs say they prefer their current work arrangement. Men working at temporary help agencies were the least satisfied with their work arrangement. Overall, temporary help and on-call work were the arrangements that workers liked least, but less than half of all women in these arrangements wanted a regular full-time job.

Workers at the bottom of the skills distribution are likely to enter the labor force through temporary help, part-time, and on-call/day labor employment. These forms of work provide access to the labor market but very little job security and only limited opportunity for advancement. Still, there are instances where workers use these job experiences to secure higher-paying jobs in the future. Nevertheless, the current emphasis on placing workers in jobs rather than in education or training programs may mean placing them in low-paying contingent work that does not lead to economic self-sufficiency.

Jeffrey B. Wenger

See also: Day Labor; Domestic Work; Labor Markets; Unemployment

References and Further Reading

Barker, Kathleen, and Kathleen Christensen. 1998. *Contingent Work: American Employment Relations in Transition*. Ithaca, NY: Cornell University Press.

Houseman, Susan. 2001. "Why Employers Use Flexible Staffing Arrangements: Evidence from an Establishment Survey." *Industrial and Labor Relations Review* 55, no. 1 (October): 149.

Kalleberg, Arne L., Edith Rasell, Naomi Cassirer, Barbara F. Reskin, Ken Hudson, David Webster, Eileen Appelbaum, and Roberta M. Spalter-Roth. 1997. *Nonstandard Work, Substandard Jobs: Flexible Work Arrangements in the U.S.* Washington, DC: Economic Policy Institute and Women's Research and Education Institute.

Wenger, Jeffrey. 2003. "Share of Workers in Nonstandard Jobs Declines." Briefing paper. Washington, DC: Economic Policy Institute.

Contract with America

See New Right

Convict Labor

Convict labor is the institutional employment of prisoners in public or private enterprise.

In contrast to other forms of forced labor, convict labor has been persistently defended as a reform measure that rehabilitates the prisoner's work discipline or "ethic," making him or her eligible for the freedom and citizenship of a liberal democracy and useful to a capitalist economy. In reality, convict labor has historically meant the exploitation of the un- or semiskilled poor and the racially stigmatized. Although convict labor has often succeeded as a disciplinary tool against prisoners and against organized labor, it has generally failed to reintegrate prisoners into the market economy and civil society.

Convict labor has been at the core of the U.S. prison system since its inception. In the late eighteenth and early nineteenth centuries, incarceration in a penitentiary increasingly replaced the tradition of corporal punishment for the poor that had come to be the norm in the young republic. In Philadelphia's Eastern State Penitentiary (1790), prisoners ate, slept, and worked isolated in single cells. Under New York's "congregate" system at Auburn Prison (1823), convicts inhabited separate cells but ate and worked together under a strict rule of silence. Whereas Pennsylvania's system proved costly to the state

Chain gang of convicts engaged in road work. Pitt County, North Carolina, 1910. The inmates were quartered in the wagons shown in the picture. Wagons were equipped with bunks and moved from place to place as convict labor was utilized. The central figure in the picture is J. Z. McLawhon, who was at that time county superintendent of chain gangs. The dogs are bloodhounds used for running down any convict attempting escape. (Library of Congress)

and harmful to the prisoners' sanity, New York's penitentiaries developed more productive prison workshops modeled after innovations in the emerging factory system. Hats, tools, shoes, and other products of convict labor were either reserved for state use—particularly in time of war—or were sold to private merchants on a piece-price basis. Auburn became the model for America's penal institutions because it united the intention of turning convicts into "useful" participants in a market society with a businesslike pursuit of profit.

Mechanics and craftsmen protested the use of convict labor from the very beginning. They hailed labor as the foundation of social mobility and citizenship, to be reserved for the free and "virtuous poor." But the growing opposition of "free labor" against the state monopoly on convict labor only resulted in the growing involvement of private contractors who used convicts as a cheap and easily disciplined labor pool that could replace organized workers.

With the breakdown of chattel slavery in the South following the Civil War, convict labor became the new institution of social discipline and economic exploitation, since the Thirteenth Amendment to the U.S. Constitution (1863) still permitted slavery as "a punishment for crime." At first, the introduction of "Black Codes," officially instituting separate systems and standards of criminal justice for Blacks and whites in the South, led to a sharp rise in the number of African American prisoners. Subsequently, the Jim Crow legal system continued to provide a racially defined prison labor force. Wardens sold their convicts' labor per day, offering discounts on the old and infirm. This "lease system" allowed private firms to exploit the "slaves of the state" and encouraged them to feed and dress them as poorly as they pleased. Often the lease system was worse than slavery, since the lessee had no interest in the prisoners' welfare or survival. African American convicts worked and died on the plantations of Louisiana and Mississippi but also in railroad construction and in iron and coal mines in Alabama, Georgia, and Tennessee, where they were also used as strikebreakers. Less deadly but no less exploitative was the work in the growing manufacturing industry in the Jim Crow South.

Beginning in the 1890s, progressive reformers initiated a gradual shift from the exploitation of convict labor for private profit to the use of prisoners in public works. Southern states abolished the lease system between 1894 (Mississippi) and 1927 (Alabama) and instead worked prisoners on farms and in chain gangs in road construction and in other public projects. Similarly, the piece-price contracts between state prisons and private companies in industrial production gradually declined from the early 1880s until World War II, pushed by the growing labor movement's complaints about unfair competition as well as by manufacturers who could increasingly rely on a sufficient labor pool outside the prison walls.

Federal restrictions on convict labor culminated in the Sumners-Ashurst Act of 1940, which prohibited the interstate commerce in convict-made goods for private use, regardless of state law. Five years earlier, the New Deal administration had created the Prison Industries Reorganization Administration (PIRA) to restructure the state and federal prison systems for the employment of convicts in production for government agencies. Although the demands of World War II created a temporary flurry of activity, institutional limitations, the defensive stand of labor unions, and lackluster inmate participation in often-monotonous and poorly paid work projects made it difficult for convict labor to compete with ever more efficient free enterprise even for government contracts.

In the 1970s, prison administrators worked on a renewed expansion of convict labor in order to defuse the riot-inducing tensions that arose with the confinement and forced immobility of thousands of convicts in the nation's "big houses." The Free Venture Model of the Law Enforcement Assistance Administration (LEAA) and the 1979 Prison Industry Enhancement Act (PIEA) reintroduced convict labor for private enterprise at minimum wages, from which the institution deducts room and board, victim's compensation, and family support. At the same time, the prison population has rapidly increased, mainly because of longer sentences for nonviolent or low-level offenses like drug use or graffiti spraying. Thus, convict labor in the 1980s and 1990s has been just one element in a prison-industrial complex that has expanded parallel to the disinvestment in poor communities and public infrastructure. Incarceration in contemporary America thus underwrites not just the employment of prisoners as an immobile, cheap, low-skill labor force but also their profitable warehousing, which maintains rather than alleviates poverty and racial discrepancies.

Volker Janssen

See also: Crime Policy; Indentured Servitude; Poorhouse/Almshouse; Slavery

References and Further Reading

Burton-Rose, Daniel, Dan Pens, and Paul Wright, eds. 1998. *The Celling of America: An Inside Look at the U.S. Prison Industry*. Monroe, ME: Common Courage Press.

Gildemeister, Glen A. 1987. *Prison Labor and Convict Competition with Free Workers in Industrializing America, 1840–1890*. New York: Garland Publishing.

Lichtenstein, Alex. 1996. *Twice the Work of Free Labor: The Political Economy of Convict Labor in the New South*. London and New York: Verso.

Coxey's Army

In 1894, in the midst of a severe economic depression, at least 1,000 people tried to take part in the first in a long tradition of popularly organized marches on Washington, D.C., on behalf of social and economic justice. Jacob Coxey, a businessman and social reformer from Ohio, and Carl Browne, a labor activist from California, led a group of almost 500 men who arrived in the capital in late April. On May 1, the entire group marched to the Capitol building, where Browne's and Coxey's actions resulted in their arrest and imprisonment for trespassing on the grounds of the Capitol. Related police action had already taken place at the state and local level in partially successful attempts to prevent more marchers from reaching Washington to join the protest army. The goal of the march was to attack the rampant unemployment that directly affected many of the marchers. The marchers put forth a comprehensive plan that asked the federal government to issue no-interest bonds worth $500 million to towns, cities, and counties. The money was to be used for public works projects such as road building and other improvements, and the projects would also serve to employ thousands of unemployed workers. Under the plan, workers would be guaranteed a minimum wage of $1.50 a day, almost 80 percent above the norm (Hoffman 1970, 219, 257). In short, the proposal was for a massive program of federal deficit spending that would end the economic depression by employing thousands of workers and expanding the money supply. It was a proposal that received no serious congressional or presidential attention, but Coxey's and Browne's unique method of marching directly to Washington to demand change captured the imagination of many supporters of reform. At the same time, their methods caused great alarm among those within the traditional political system.

The debate that surrounded Coxey's Army and its demands mirrored many other debates about how to respond to poverty and unemployment in the United States. Like more-moderate reformers, Coxey and Browne clearly believed that direct relief payments to workers were inappropriate; they wanted help in the form of jobs. But unlike many reformers, they also wanted these jobs to establish a minimum wage for workers—an idea that was unacceptable to the majority of legislators in the United States. And like some economic reformers with a national dimension to their thinking, they understood that federal policy—especially deficit spending and a looser money supply—could have a fundamental effect on the broader economy of the nation. Again, however, most politicians of the time believed that the appropriate response to economic crisis was for governments to spend less, since their revenues were less.

In mobilizing the poor to demand changes, Coxey and Browne had many counterparts in the vibrant labor and social reform culture of the late 1880s and 1890s. Yet their method of demanding change by going directly to the nation's capital was unique and untested. Thus, the arrest of the leaders in Washington, the use of police measures by state and local officials to prevent other groups from joining them, and the dismissal of their demands by national leaders were not surprising. In the wake of Coxey's Army, gradual changes in both national policy and political culture would make their demands seem less exceptional. Perhaps most significant, their method of protest—the march on Washington—would be memorably and effectively embraced in subsequent decades by veterans, by civil rights activists, and by a broad coalition of poor people's advocates, all demanding significant changes in federal government social policy.

Lucy G. Barber

See also: Bonus Army; Civil Rights Movement; Economic Depression; Federalism; Minimum Wage; Poor People's Campaign; Relief; Unemployment

References and Further Reading

Barber, Lucy G. 2002. *Marching on Washington: The Forging of American Political Tradition*. Berkeley and Los Angeles: University of California Press.

Hoffman, Charles. 1970. *The Depression of the Nineties: An Economic History*. Westport, CT: Greenwood Press.

Schwantes, Carlos A. 1985. *Coxey's Army: An American Odyssey*. Lincoln: University of Nebraska Press.

Crime Policy

Crime disproportionately harms the poor and hampers antipoverty strategies. But efforts to combat crime often perpetuate rather than alleviate poverty. In 2001, the rate of violent crime suffered by those with an income under $15,000 was more than twice that of those with an income over $50,000 (Rennison 2002, 5). Yet proactive policing, mass incarceration, and legal restrictions on ex-offender activity also exacerbate the poverty of offenders, their families, and even their neighborhoods.

Traditionally, men, the young, members of racial and ethnic minorities, and the poor have most often been victims of crime. Although victimization rates declined in the 1990s for all income groups, the poor benefited least from these reductions (Thacher 2003, 29). Women also benefited less. Nearly one-third of all crimes affecting women are committed by intimate partners or family members, compared to less than 10 percent for men (Rennison 2002, 1). Thus, reductions in crime, unless targeted at family violence, do less to protect women.

Crime is concentrated in neighborhoods that suffer from other economic and social problems. Early scholars posited a direct link between poverty, social disorganization, and crime. More-recent research has focused on the institutional and individual factors that accompany social disinvestment and in turn help foster crime. Neighborhoods with high crime rates are then caught in a vicious cycle: Crime makes it hard to attract the home owners, business investments, schools, or public amenities that could help residents move out of poverty (DiIulio 1989).

Many crime policies, therefore, target poor neighborhoods. In one approach, police respond aggressively to small crimes in the expectation that maintaining order will deter more-serious crimes. In another, police use data to help them focus their efforts on "hot spots" where multiple crimes occur. These approaches can also be combined in community policing, in which police collaborate with local residents to identify priorities and build relationships in the neighborhood. But aggressive police activity can also lead to mistakes that fall most heavily on the poor as innocent people in crime-prone areas are subject to additional scrutiny and sometimes mistaken accusations. Thus, residents in areas of concentrated disadvantage, who are usually people of color, are highly cynical about legal fairness and police behavior even though they condemn deviance and violence at higher rates than do whites (Sampson and Bartusch 1998).

Imprisonment, the most widely used crime policy, also has a dual quality. Prison keeps criminals off the streets, and incarceration rates, largely stable through most of the early twentieth century, have risen rapidly since the 1970s. But these prisoners are overwhelmingly poor. In 1991, a survey of state prisoners showed that 53 percent had had an income of under $10,000 a year before they entered prison. Yet 67 percent had been working, 55 percent of them full-time, in the month before their arrest (Beck et al. 1993, 3). Most prisoners are also people of color. In 2001, 44.5 percent of all inmates were Black, and 17.4 percent were Latino (Harrison and Beck 2002, 12). Men made up 93.4 percent of the prison population, but the number of female prisoners increased by 36 percent between 1995 and 2001 (Harrison and Beck 2002, 1).

It has been predicted that over a quarter (28.5 percent) of all Black men in the United States will serve a prison sentence in their lifetime, compared to 16 percent of Hispanic men but only 4.4 percent of white men (Bonczar and Beck 1997, 1). These disparate life chances are linked to three major policy changes: the increased use of incarceration, reductions in the sentencing discretion of judges, and the abolition of parole. Drug laws, which now routinely carry a prison sentence, have been applied disproportionately to drugs that minority groups use and sell. Racial disparities in the charges brought for similar offenses, combined with long minimum sentences, cause the burden of sentencing changes to fall upon Blacks. The abolition of parole prevents many offenders from reducing their sentences for good behavior and for participation in rehabilitation programs (Leadership Conference on Civil Rights and Leadership Conference Education Fund 2000).

Poor communities also suffer from incarceration and from the legal restrictions imposed upon ex-offenders. Within neighborhoods, incarceration can remove criminals from their likely victims, but it can also disrupt informal networks that enforce social control. Communities that experience high rates of incarceration are also communities to which ex-prisoners return and pose a heavy financial and social burden. Ex-offenders have difficulty finding employment, they are often prohibited by law from living in public housing or receiving assistance from benefit programs, they can destabilize family arrangements that were established in their absence, and they add to the stigma that poor neighborhoods already experience (Clear, Rose, and Ryder 2001).

Ann Chih Lin

See also: Classism; Convict Labor; Domestic Violence; Juvenile Delinquency; Picturing Poverty (II); Racism

References and Further Reading

Beck, Allen J., Darrell Gilliard, Lawrence Greenfeld, Caroline Harlow, Thomas Hester, Louis Janowski, Tracy Snell, James Stephan, and Danielle Morton. 1993. *Survey of State Prison Inmates, 1991*. NCJ-136949. Washington, DC: U.S. Department of Justice, Bureau of Justice Statistics.

Bonczar, Thomas P., and Allen J. Beck. 1997. *Lifetime Likelihood of Going to State or Federal Prison*. NCJ-160092. Washington, DC: U.S. Department of Justice, Bureau of Justice Statistics.

Clear, Todd R., Diane R. Rose, and Judith A. Ryder. 2001. "Incarceration and the Community: The Problem of Removing and Returning Offenders." *Crime and Delinquency* 47, no. 3: 335–351.

DiIulio, John J. 1989. "The Impact of Inner-City Crime." *The Public Interest* 96: 28–46.

Harrison, Paige M., and Allen J. Beck. 2002. *Prisoners in 2001*. NCJ-195189. Washington, DC: U.S. Department of Justice, Bureau of Justice Statistics.

Leadership Conference on Civil Rights and Leadership Conference Education Fund. 2000. "Justice on Trial: Racial Disparities in the American Criminal Justice System." http://www.civilrights.org/publications/reports/cj/index.html.

Rennison, Callie. 2002. *Criminal Victimization 2001*. NCJ-194610. Washington: U.S. Department of Justice, Bureau of Justice Statistics.

Sampson, Robert J., and Dawn Jeglum Bartusch. 1998. "Legal Cynicism and (Subcultural?) Tolerance of Deviance: The Neighborhood Context of Racial Differences." *Law and Society Review* 32, no. 4: 777–804.

Thacher, David. 2003. "The Rich Get Richer and the Poor Get Robbed: Inequality in U.S. Criminal Victimization, 1974–2000." Working paper. Ann Arbor: University of Michigan, Ford School of Public Policy.

"Culture of Poverty"

See The Children of Sanchez; Dependency; Deserving/Undeserving Poor; Poverty Research; "Underclass"

The Dangerous Classes of New York, *Charles Loring Brace*

In 1853, Charles Loring Brace helped found the Children's Aid Society in New York, a group dedicated to child welfare in the city. Nineteen years later, he published *The Dangerous Classes of New York*, a study of the lives of poor children and an assessment of the work of the society. As the title suggests, Brace believed that "the class of a large city most dangerous to its property, its morals and its political life, are the ignorant, destitute, untrained, and abandoned youth" (Brace 1872, ii).

The book detailed the problems of crime, prostitution, alcoholism, overcrowding, and homelessness and argued that difficult living conditions and neglectful parenting were the primary causes of youthful indolence and violence. Yet Brace firmly believed that wayward children could rise above their circumstances with proper education and the good example of middle-class reformers. In this vein, he insisted that charitable giving must be coupled with instruction in industriousness and self-reliance. He supported industrial education and almshouses for the homeless, but he especially favored placing orphans, or children from families deemed irresponsible (sometimes because of religious or cultural differences; immigrant and Catholic parents were those most likely to be found "unworthy"), with "respectable," especially rural, families. Brace and other society members advocated sending children to farm families in the West, and over 20,000 children left New York for the western states on "orphan trains" between 1853 and the 1930s. Some found loving families; others were separated from their own families and lived more like servants than adopted children.

The passage below demonstrates Brace's distrust of relief, his faith that children could be "saved" from pauperism through the discipline of work, and his belief that in order to be truly successful, charity must improve the character of its recipients—while keeping a sharp eye on the bottom line.

Sarah Case

See also: Child Labor; Child Welfare; Child-Saving; Deserving/Undeserving Poor; Homelessness; Immigrants and Immigration; Urban Poverty

[The Children's Aid Society] has always sought to encourage the principle of Self-help in its beneficiaries, and has aimed much more at promoting this than merely relieving suffering. All its branches, its Industrial Schools, Lodging-houses, and Emigration [removal to the West], aim to make the children of the poor better able to take care of themselves; to give them such a training that they shall be ashamed of begging, and of idle, dependent habits, and to place them where their associates are self-respecting and

industrious. . . . [W]e have taken advantage of the immense demand for labor through our rural districts. . . . Through this demand we have been enabled to accomplish our best results, with remarkable economy. We have been saved the vast expense of Asylums, and have put our destitute children in the child's natural place—with a family. Our Lodging-houses also have avoided the danger attending such places of shelter, of becoming homes for vagrant boys and girls. They have continually passed their little subjects along to the country, or to places of work, often forcing them to leave the house. In requiring the small payments for lodging and meals, they put the beneficiaries in an independent position, and check the habits and spirit of pauperism. . . . The Industrial Schools, in like manner, are seminaries of industry and teachers of order and self-help.

Source: Charles Loring Brace, *The Dangerous Classes of New York, and Twenty Years' Work among Them* (New York: Wynkoop and Hallenbeck, 1872), 441–442.

Day Labor

Day labor is a type of temporary employment that is distinguished by impermanence of employment, hazards in or undesirability of the work, the absence of fringe and other typical workplace benefits (such as breaks or safety equipment), and the daily search for employment.

Two types of day labor industries exist: informal and formal. Informal day labor is characterized by workers who congregate in open-air, curbside, or otherwise visible markets, such as empty lots, street corners, parking lots, designated public spaces, or the storefronts of home-improvement establishments, to solicit temporary daily work. Soliciting work in this manner is an increasingly visible part of the urban landscape, and the practice is growing in the United States and worldwide in countries and regions such as Mexico, Japan, and South America. Several important characteristics identify the informal day labor industry and its participants: The market is highly visible, with large hiring sites spread throughout metropolitan Chicago, Los Angeles, New York, and other cities in the Southwest, the South, and the Northwest. Most day laborers are male, foreign-born, recently arrived, and unauthorized, and most have low levels of education and a poor command of English. As a result, the workers in this industry are highly vulnerable and exploited. The informal day labor market primarily provides temporary job opportunities that last from one to three days in the broadly defined construction industry, which includes home refurbishment, landscaping, roofing, and painting. In some regions, it also provides limited light industrial and factory work.

The formal day labor industry is tied to for-profit temporary staffing agencies or "hiring halls" and primarily places workers in manual work assignments at or around minimum wage. These temp agencies or hiring halls are less ubiquitous than informal sites, and they are located in enclosed hiring halls with boarded windows or other neighborhood-based establishments. As in the informal day labor market, many of the participants are undocumented recent immigrants and have low levels of education. However, the workers in formal day labor are more diverse than those in the informal market and also include nonimmigrants, women, and a substantial homeless population. Participants in this market are similarly vulnerable and exploited, as is evidenced by low wages, infrequent employment, workplace injuries, and such ancillary employment charges such as check cashing fees for payroll and costly transportation charges to get to the work site. The formal day labor markets, in addition to construction work, also offer temporary employment in light industrial work, factory work, loading and unloading, and warehouse work.

Both informal day labor and formal day labor are unstable, neither provides benefits or workplace protections, and both pay poorly and are

Day laborers pick broccoli in Salinas, California. Day laborers earn low wages near, and often below, the minimum wage rate and are generally paid in cash at the end of the workday. (Morton Beebe/Corbis)

characterized by such workplace abuses as instances of nonpayment, lack of regular breaks, and hazardous work.

The practice of men and women gathering in public settings in search of work dates back to at least medieval times, when the feudal city was originally a place of trade. In England during the 1100s, workers assembled at daily or weekly markets to be hired. Statutes regulated the opening of public markets in merchant towns and required agricultural workers (foremen, plowmen, carters, shepherds, swineherds, dairymen, and mowers) to appear with tools to be hired in a "common place and not privately" (Mund 1948, 106). In the United States, during the early to middle 1800s, day laborers recruited from construction crews worked for the track repairmen of railroad companies. Casual laborers (often off from construction jobs) worked in a variety of unskilled positions (brakemen, track repairmen, stevedores at depots, emergency firemen, snow clearers, mechanic's assistants). Some of these workers were recent immigrants, Chinese and Mexicans in the West and Germans and Irish in the East. Between 1788 and 1830, hundreds of day laborers ("stand-ups," as they were known then) worked along the waterfront, and more than half of New York City's male Irish workers were day laborers. In 1834, a "place was set aside on city streets in New York where those seeking work could meet with those who wanted workers" (Mund 1948, 96). This exchange worked for both men and women, with employment for women (primarily African American) concentrated in the domestic labor market sector.

The growth and development of day labor in the United States and elsewhere has very real implications for thousands of workers and their employers. In its simplest form, day labor provides a distinct service to employers who wish to forgo traditional forms of hiring workers and who prefer not to undertake the time-consuming and costly activities associated with providing "regular" employment. The gains to employers from hiring day laborers are clear: Day laborers are easy to find, plentiful, and relatively inexpensive to hire. Employers are spared the liability costs and paperwork associated with providing benefits and observing fair labor standards. A subcontractor needing help to finish a project can easily hire a day laborer for several hours or several days to tidy up, remove debris, clean the site for inspection, or do other types of unskilled and skilled tasks. Similarly, a home owner wishing to move from one home to another or to uproot a tree in his or her backyard need not hire an expensive contractor for such seemingly simple but labor-intensive jobs. The existence of the day labor market also makes it easy for employers to circumvent paying the higher rates that a non–day laborer on a job or project would normally get, and, more generally, to avoid creating more permanent jobs in favor of the cheaper alternative.

Day labor also has some potential benefits for workers, who would not otherwise be employed. In addition, day laborers get paid in cash (usually untaxed), can walk away from a dangerous or particularly dirty job, and can negotiate a wage for a fair day of work. For some day laborers, this occupation provides a flexible alternative to a regularly scheduled job, autonomy from a difficult employer, and the opportunity to learn different skills. However, such potential benefits should not outweigh the reality that day labor plays on the vulnerabilities of unorganized and otherwise marginalized workers and can be effectively used to undermine labor protections for workers more generally.

Abel Valenzuela Jr.

See also: Agricultural and Farm Labor Organizing; Bracero Program; Contingent Work; Domestic Work; Fair Labor Standards Act (FLSA); Immigrants and Immigration; Informal Economy; Migrant Labor/Farm Labor; Service and Domestic Workers, Labor Organizing

References and Further Reading

Mund, Vernon. 1948. *Open Markets: An Essential to Free Enterprise*. New York: Harper and Brothers.

Peck, Jamie, and Nik Theodore. 2001. "Contingent Chicago: Restructuring the Spaces of Temporary Labor." *International Journal of Urban and Regional Research* 25, no. 3: 471–496.

———. 2002. "The Temporary Staffing Industry: Growth Imperatives and Limits to Contingency." *Economic Geography* 78, no. 4: 463–493.

Valenzuela, Abel, Jr. 2001. "Day Laborers as Entrepreneurs?" *Journal of Ethnic and Migration Studies* 27, no. 2: 335–352.

———. 2002. "Working on the Margins in Metropolitan Los Angeles: Immigrants in Day Labor Work." *Migraciones Internacionales* 1, no. 2: 5–28.

———. 2003. "Day-Labor Work." *Annual Review of Sociology* 29: 307–333.

Valenzuela, Abel, Jr., Janette A. Kawachi, and Matthew D. Marr. 2002. "Seeking Work Daily: Supply, Demand, and Spatial Dimensions of Day Labor in Two Global Cities." *International Journal of Comparative Sociology* 43, no. 2: 192–219.

Debt

Debt is incurred when a person receives money or goods in exchange for a promise to repay the amount borrowed plus interest. People borrow for many reasons. They borrow to pay for an education, to start a business, or to move to a place where there are greater opportunities. They borrow to improve their current well-being by obtaining consumer goods. Sometimes people are forced to borrow to meet immediate needs, such as medical services, rent, or food. Borrowing is an exchange that can benefit both borrowers and lenders, but the possibility that the borrower might not repay the debt can make it difficult to achieve this mutual benefit. Individuals who find it difficult to convince lenders that they will repay the debt find it difficult to borrow. People with low incomes and few assets have a particularly difficult time convincing lenders they will repay debts. Historically, this has made it difficult for poor people to borrow, a significant problem in an economy in which access to credit has become increasingly important for achieving upward mobility and higher standards of living. It has also made them more vulnerable to shady creditors charging exorbitantly high interest rates. For these and other reasons, policies affecting the repayment of debts have been at the center of many public policy debates throughout American history.

The Poor Pay More

The interest on a debt is the sum of two parts. The first part represents the value of the money to the lender and would be the interest rate charged to someone who, in the lender's view, is completely certain to repay the debt. The second part is a risk premium that covers the costs of trying to ensure repayment and the losses when a borrower does not pay. The more likely it seems to the lender that the borrower will not be willing or able to repay the debt, the greater the risk premium.

Because they find it difficult to convince lenders that they will be willing and able to repay their debts, poor borrowers pay higher risk premiums. Borrowers sometimes try to reduce the risk for lenders by offering collateral. If the debt is not paid, the lender can claim the collateral. Poor households typically do not have the kinds of assets, such as real estate, that banks accept as collateral. Lenders attempt to lower risk by screening debt applicants and by spending time and money collecting delinquent debts. The costs of screening, such as charges for obtaining a credit report, tend not to vary a great deal with the size of the debt. Because the loans that the poor seek are often small, the costs of screening are large relative to the size of the debt. When a borrower does not pay, the lender can turn to such legal remedies as garnishment of wages to collect the debt, but poor households often find that their wages do not provide much security to a lender.

Poor people often find that it is not possible to obtain a debt through formal credit markets at any price. Banks and other lenders in the formal credit market are not willing to increase the interest rate too much because the consequent increase in the size of the debt payments makes it more likely the debtor will default. The inability to obtain credit through the formal credit market leads the poor to turn to "fringe banks," such as pawnshops, check cashing outlets, or loan sharks. Over the course of American history, the access of the poor to formal credit markets has increased, but many of the poor still have to turn to fringe banking.

Fringe Banking

The use of fringe banking to obtain credit has been prevalent throughout American history. During the colonial period, a large number of people who came to the American colonies came as indentured laborers. A laborer who signed an indenture contract was required to work for the owner of the contract for a specified number of years. The indenture was only for a specific period of time, for instance seven years, but the owner of the contract did have extensive rights to control the behavior of the servant. People were willing to accept such an arrangement because of their lack of access to formal credit. Moving to America was regarded as an opportunity for improvement, but the cost of transportation was greater than the average person could afford. There were no banks that would lend a large sum of money to a poor person to migrate across an ocean. A legally binding indenture contract enabled the borrower to use his or her future labor as collateral.

Debt peonage in the South after the Civil War illustrates another side of alternative credit markets, a side in which debt became a burden rather than an opportunity. African Americans were emancipated, but having few assets, they had to turn to country stores for credit to purchase necessities. The interest rate on a loan at a southern country store could be as much as 70 percent. Borrowers who could not pay their debts after harvest were often required to commit the next year's crop (that is, a crop lien) as collateral. The combination of high interest rates and crop liens were often enough to create long-term indebtedness to the store owner, a situation that came to be referred to as "debt peonage."

During the twentieth century, access to formal credit markets expanded. Part of the increase is attributable to credit market innovations that enabled low-income households to obtain loans at reasonable rates more easily. Finance companies were created to facilitate the purchase of durable consumer goods (such as cars, large appliances, or furniture) on installment plans. Because the durable goods acted as collateral for the debt, African Americans appear to have experienced less discrimination in finding installment loans than in finding other types of consumer credit. In addition, a coalition of small lenders and the Russell Sage Foundation drafted a Uniform Small Loan Law that many states enacted. The law provided for licensing of small lenders and allowed them to charge higher interest rates than most usury laws had allowed.

It may seem that a usury law that sets maximum interest rates should benefit the poor, but usury laws can have just the opposite effect. Because the costs of lending to the poor are high relative to the amounts borrowed, conventional lenders typically do not find small debts profitable. In the absence of a legal small-debt market, poor borrowers have to turn to unregulated lenders. The Uniform Small Loan Law raised legal interest rates on small debts, but it made it possible to obtain these debts from legitimate businesses.

The second half of the twentieth century witnessed a continued opening of credit markets. Part of this expansion was the result of continued innovation, such as the introduction of credit cards. Another part of the opening of credit markets was due to changes in public policy. The Fair Housing Act of 1968 and the Equal Credit Opportunity Act of 1974 were enacted to reduce discrimination in credit markets. Although there is evidence that discrimination against women has declined, considerable evidence suggests that racial discrimination still exists in credit markets, especially mortgage markets.

Although lenders in formal credit markets have continued to expand their services, many poor borrowers still have to resort to fringe banks. Despite charging interest rates that are often higher than 200 percent, pawnshops thrived during the 1980s and 1990s, as did check cashing outlets and rent-to-own stores. The increased dependence of poor households on fringe banking was caused by reduced access to the formal banking system due to increased fees for small accounts, the closing of branches in low-income communities, and decreases in the real incomes of poor households.

Debt and Public Policy

Conflicts over policies affecting debt have been a staple of American politics. Public policy influences the relationship between lenders and borrowers in several ways. The law determines when borrowers can have their debts discharged. The law also determines the means that lenders can use to try to enforce repayment.

Public policy toward borrowers was a controversial topic in the years immediately following the American Revolution. Conflicts between Federalists and Anti-Federalists over the adoption of the Constitution were, in part, conflicts over debt. States were prohibited from impairing the obligation of contracts, which was interpreted as barring them from passing any legislation that would discharge a debt incurred before the legislation was passed.

In general, law in early America supported strict enforcement of debt contracts. Imprisonment for debt was not uncommon, though within debtors' prisons, the rich and the poor were often treated differently. Some wealthy borrowers went to prison rather than turn over their assets to lenders. In debtors' prison, the wealthy sometimes lived in private quarters with their own furnishings.

Class differences also appeared in the first federal debt relief law, the Bankruptcy Act of 1800. The law enabled insolvent debtors to obtain a discharge of their debts, but proceedings had to be initiated by a creditor who was owed at least $1,000. The law provided no relief to poor borrowers who owed small sums.

As the economy developed, attitudes toward debt and insolvency evolved. Many people came to believe that macroeconomic forces such as financial crises and deflation were often more responsible for economic failure than was individual behavior. Changes in attitudes toward borrowers led to changes in public policy. Most states ended imprisonment for debt. During the series of financial crises that struck the United States at roughly ten-year intervals during the nineteenth century, states passed moratoriums on debt repayments and stay laws to protect destitute debtors from legal action by creditors. States also enacted homestead laws declaring that all or part of a person's home or farm could not be taken to pay his or her debts and exemption laws specifying other assets that could not be taken.

The 1898 Bankruptcy Act marked an important turning point for many borrowers. Although the law was primarily the result of lobbying by associations of manufacturers and wholesalers, it enabled any insolvent borrower to file for bankruptcy and receive a discharge of his or her debts. The Bankruptcy Act was extensively amended by the Chandler Act in 1938. With the expansion of consumer credit in the 1920s, there was a rapid expansion in the number of bankruptcy cases filed by wage earners. Studies suggested that many people would have preferred to pay off all or part of their debts if they could have done so over a longer period of time. After the Chandler Act, bankruptcy offered two alternatives for insolvent borrowers. In Chapter 7 cases, debtors turn their nonexempt assets over to the court and receive a discharge of most of their debts. In Chapter 13 cases, borrowers propose a plan to pay all or part of their debts over time. Although the introduction of Chapter 13 was intended as a benefit to bankrupt wage earners, the vast majority of consumers have chosen to use Chapter 7 and receive an immediate discharge.

The number of bankruptcy cases rose from 226,476 in 1979 to over 1 million in 1996. The rapid increase in bankruptcy cases gave rise to intense lobbying by the credit industry to amend the bankruptcy law. The National Consumer Bankruptcy Coalition, composed of VISA, Mastercard, the American Bankers Association, and other creditor associations, began lobbying for bankruptcy legislation in 1997. Ironically, their efforts have focused on making borrowers pay off more of their debts by forcing them into Chapter 13, which was originally intended as an option to benefit bankrupt wage earners. Proponents of the revision argue that the increases in bankruptcy are due to an overly generous bankruptcy law and the declining social stigma of bankruptcy. Opponents of the revision cite overly aggressive marketing of consumer credit and unstable incomes as the causes of increased bankruptcy. They suggest that the revision would actually turn the federal government into a collection agency for creditors. The future of public policy toward poor borrowers will probably depend on the outcome of this ongoing debate over bankruptcy law.

Bradley A. Hansen

See also: Capitalism; Community-Based Organizations; Housing Policy; Indentured Servitude

References and Further Reading

Calder, Lendol. 1999. *Financing the American Dream:*

A Cultural History of Consumer Credit. Princeton: Princeton University Press.

Caplowitz, David. 1963. *The Poor Pay More: Consumer Practices of Low Income Families*. New York: Free Press.

Caskey, John. 1994. *Fringe Banking: Check Cashing Outlets, Pawnshops, and the Poor*. New York: Russell Sage Foundation.

Coleman, Peter. 1974. *Debtors and Creditors in America: Insolvency, Imprisonment for Debt, and Bankruptcy, 1607–1900*. Madison: State Historical Society of Wisconsin.

Mann, Bruce. 2002. *Republic of Debtors: Bankruptcy in the Age of American Independence*. Cambridge, MA: Harvard University Press.

Olney, Martha. 1998. "When Your Word Is Not Enough: Race, Collateral, and Household Credit." *Journal of Economic History* 58: 408–431.

Ross, Stephen, and John Yinger. 2002. *The Color of Credit: Mortgage Discrimination, Research Methodology, and Fair Lending Enforcement*. Cambridge: MIT Press.

Skeel, David. 2001. *Debt's Dominion: A History of Bankruptcy Law in America*. Princeton: Princeton University Press.

Dependency

There are many forms of dependency, but "welfare dependency" in particular has received much attention in Western societies, especially in recent years in the United States. Agitation for reform of the Elizabethan Poor Law of 1601 in England beginning in the late eighteenth century was grounded in good part on arguments by Thomas Malthus and others regarding the deleterious moral and economic effects of relief to the poor. Malthus helped develop what Albert Hirschman and others in the twentieth century have called the "perversity thesis"—that is, the idea that aid to the poor was actually bad because it led them to give up trying to adhere to social standards regarding work and family. This sort of thinking quickly made its way across the Atlantic, and it has been an enduring presence in debates about public assistance in the United States for over 200 years.

More than any other idea, the perversity thesis has influenced welfare policy discourse in the United States. The welfare reforms of the 1990s are a dramatic example of the enduring legacy of the perversity thesis. By the 1990s, welfare dependency had come to be seen in significant policy circles as replacing poverty as the key social welfare issue. Influential arguments such as those by Charles Murray in his 1984 book *Losing Ground* had laid the basis for suggesting that only with the abolition of welfare would it be possible to even contemplate the eradication of poverty. Bill Clinton successfully campaigned for the presidency in 1992 promising to "end welfare as we know it." He then in 1996 felt obligated to sign the Personal Responsibility and Work Opportunity Reconciliation Act so that he could campaign for reelection claiming he had kept his promise. The law's preamble stressed the need to attack welfare dependency as a root cause of many of the most serious social ills afflicting the nation. The law abolished the sixty-one-year-old cash assistance program Aid to Families with Dependent Children (AFDC) and replaced it with a block grant program, Temporary Assistance for Needy Families (TANF), giving states the option to run their welfare programs largely as they saw fit as long as they reduced welfare dependency and put recipients to work according to specified quotas. The 1996 law placed time limits on the receipt of federally funded benefits, capping such benefits after five years. It allowed states to set even stricter time limits, which a number of states in fact did. The welfare rolls were slashed at an unprecedented rate. All this took place in the name of ridding society of the scourge of welfare dependency.

The analysis used to identify welfare dependency as a root cause for social ills has been consistently questioned by scholars, activists, concerned citizens, and numerous other observers. Yet welfare dependency has proven to have a powerful rhetorical appeal, suggesting personal irresponsibility, freeloading, and failure to adhere to basic work and family values. Focusing on welfare receipt as a form of dependency facilitates likening it to other questionable forms of dependency, and in particular to drug dependencies. Welfare dependency has historically been denigrated in various ways; it has sometimes been criminalized, sometimes medicalized, and often both at the same time. Other dependencies, such as being dependent on a male breadwinner in a traditional two-parent family, are not denigrated. Single mothers who rely on welfare are seen as needing to be weaned from a bad form of dependency whereas women who are dependent upon a male in a traditional marriage are not. The underlying assumption that distinguishes these two forms of dependency has to do with who is practicing personal responsibility according to ascendant work and family norms in a market-centered society. Rarely is this assumption challenged, and as a result, welfare dependency continues to be articulated in welfare policy discourse as a fundamental problem rather than as a necessary aid to families adversely affected by prevailing social and economic relations.

Sanford F. Schram

See also: Aid to Families with Dependent Children (ADC/AFDC); Deserving/Undeserving Poor; Malthusianism; Poor Laws; Welfare Policy/Welfare Reform; "Working Poor"

References and Further Reading

Hirschman, Albert O. 1991. *The Rhetoric of Reaction: Perversity, Futility, Jeopardy*. Cambridge, MA: Harvard University Press.

Katz, Michael B. 2001. *The Price of Citizenship: Redefining the American Welfare State*. New York: Metropolitan Books.

Murray, Charles. 1984. *Losing Ground: American Social Policy, 1950–1980*. New York: Basic Books.

Schram, Sanford F. 2000. *After Welfare: The Culture of Postindustrial Social Policy*. New York: New York University Press.

Somers, Margaret, and Fred Block. 2001. "From Poverty to Perversity: Markets, States, and Institutions over Two Centuries of Welfare Debate." Unpublished manuscript. Ann Arbor: University of Michigan.

Deserving/ Undeserving Poor

Since the early nineteenth century, the mainstream public discourse on poverty has distinguished between the "deserving" poor, who are poor through no fault of their own, and the "undeserving" poor, whose poverty seems to derive chiefly from low work motivations, moral failings, or "dependency" on charity. Such distinctions rest on the assumption that poverty is a matter of personal responsibility (rather than the product of power relationships and political economic structures) and can be overcome by some sort of personal transformation (Katz 1989, 7). Laden with racial and gendered meanings, the distinction between the deserving and undeserving poor has been integrally linked to the moral valuation of wage labor, military service, and nuclear family life. In both rhetoric and public policy, women and racial minorities have been substantially excluded from the ranks of the deserving poor.

The racial and gendered meanings of the deserving and undeserving poor have been inextricably linked to the evolution of U.S. social welfare policy. The public discourse has portrayed programs serving large numbers of white males—such as Old Age Insurance (OAI) (commonly known as Social Security), veterans' pensions, work relief, and job training—as helping deserving recipients by rewarding and encouraging wage labor and military service. Programs such as OAI are generally understood to be contributory and universal, providing entitlements, not handouts. By contrast, the recipients of means-tested relief programs (who are disproportionately female and nonwhite) are considered undeserving and are required to provide proof, sometimes extensive, of their ongoing need, worthiness, and willingness to obey certain behavioral rules in order to receive assistance. Relief programs such as general assistance and Aid to Families with Dependent Children (AFDC) are portrayed as antithetical to the

American work and family ethic, easily taken advantage of by those who seek to avoid full-time employment or nuclear family life.

Public perceptions of the deserving and undeserving poor have changed considerably over the course of American history. In the seventeenth century, when there was widespread scarcity, the public generally viewed poverty as inescapable and divinely sanctioned. Poor people received pity and assistance; their poverty was not interpreted as a sign of weakness or moral failure. Indeed, poverty was thought to provide an opportunity for those who were divinely ordained to be affluent to fulfill their charitable obligations. Poor-relief policies in the early colonies were based on British poor laws from the Elizabethan era. Local governments had an obligation to provide resources (either through the provision of "outdoor" [in-home, or noninstitutional] relief or "indoor" [institutional, in poorhouses or similar institutions] relief) to poor members of their communities but not to visitors, who were sent back to their place of origin.

The idea that one could distinguish between the deserving and undeserving poor took shape in the nineteenth century and was closely linked to rising rates of immigration and urbanization and to the growth of a capitalist-industrial economy. As the costs of poor relief increased and poverty became more visible, communities began to distinguish between those considered genuinely needy because they were incapable of work due to old age, sickness, or disability, and the able-bodied, who were considered capable of work and thus undeserving of assistance. Women who were sexually active outside of marriage were also placed under the rubric of the undeserving.

In the early nineteenth century, the public discourse on poverty also began to judge and classify the poor according to their reliance on government assistance. Critics of poor relief charged that government assistance produced the undeserving poor by undermining recipients' work ethic, encouraging them to idleness, and destroying their character. In the second half of the nineteenth century, public criticism of relief increased and contributed to a wholesale scaling back of relief provisions. In many cities, public officials either drastically reduced the value of their relief grants or abolished them altogether. White middle-class proponents of scientific charity, organized in charity organization societies (COSs), began to play an increased role in the administration of poverty assistance. COS leaders, such as Josephine Shaw Lowell, argued that private agencies could best address the behavioral roots of poverty and advocated screening and investigating the poor to separate the worthy from the unworthy.

The late nineteenth century also marked the emergence of Civil War pensions, the first federal government social provision for recipients considered deserving. The provision of pensions to Union veterans received considerable public support, and public authorities did not screen recipients for need or morality. By contrast, the relief provided to freed slaves by the Freedmen's Bureau was criticized for encouraging idleness and inspired considerable debate about just which Blacks were "deserving" of assistance.

In the 1890s, poverty intensified, and it became increasingly clear to public authorities that private charity could not solve the problem. In response to campaigns by white middle-class women, states began to institute programs to grant pensions to single mothers. Known as mothers' aid or mothers' pensions, these programs tried to free their recipients from the stigma of relief by instituting strict screening practices and eligibility requirements intended to ensure that only deserving women received assistance. Program administrators primarily provided assistance to desperately poor white widows. They classified deserted, separated, and unmarried mothers as ineligible for assistance, refused to help those who had assets of nearly any kind, and discriminated against immigrants and African Americans.

During the Great Depression, the extent of poverty throughout the nation made the idea that poverty resulted from moral failings increasingly untenable. The federal government provided citizens with relief, but "the dole" continued to elicit criticism for encouraging idleness. In 1934, President Franklin D. Roosevelt described relief as "a narcotic, a subtle destroyer of the human spirit" (Katz 1986, 226). To decrease the number of people dependent on relief, New Deal policymakers created new groups of deserving recipients of government assistance by establishing new social welfare programs linked to wage work. The public job programs created by the Works Progress Administration and the Civilian Conservation Corps provided large numbers of able-bodied white men with jobs and thus received considerable public support for helping the deserving poor in the spirit of the American work ethic.

The Social Security Act (SSA) of 1935 created the Aid to the Blind program and in 1954 added Aid to the Disabled. Recipients of these programs were regarded as deserving because blindness and disabilities were considered faultless, well-defined, and unalterable causes of poverty. The SSA also created OAI, unemployment insurance (UI), and Aid to Dependent Children (ADC). To ensure that the primarily white urban male recipients of OAI and UI did not get branded as undeserving, the designers of these programs made them universal (not means or morals tested), funded them through designated payroll taxes, and emphasized that the programs were contributory and offered earned benefits rather than relief.

Architects of the ADC program (renamed AFDC in 1962) also tried to ensure that the single mothers and children who benefited from the program did not get identified as undeserving. Yet they did this in ways that ultimately contributed to the stigmatization of ADC recipients: States were permitted to police and regulate recipients through strict moral and financial requirements, to refuse assistance to certain recipients who would then have to accept very low-waged work without it, to provide only meager amounts of financial assistance, and to subject women to home visits from caseworkers who disqualified lone mothers who were found to be involved with men. The 1939 Social Security Act Amendments further facilitated the stigmatization of ADC recipients as undeserving when they created a separate policy for widowed mothers whose husbands had been covered under the Social Security system. The Survivors' Insurance program offered more generous benefits, without intimate surveillance and regulation, to these widows and children, deeming them deserving in comparison to ADC mothers who were divorced, never-married, or married to men whose jobs were not covered by Social Security.

Over the course of the 1940s and 1950s, the public discourse on poverty began to single out ADC as a grant for the undeserving poor. In the 1930s and early 1940s, politicians and journalists in northern cities described the program as "child aid"—a grant for innocent poor children—and the ADC program commanded a fair amount of public support. However, in the late 1940s and 1950s, with the civil rights movement becoming a significant political force and facing escalating postwar migration of African Americans to northern cities, conservative politicians and journalists began to claim that welfare grants in these cities encouraged Blacks to migrate. By the 1960s, the mainstream public discourse on ADC focused almost exclusively on African American recipients and on mothers rather than children, describing these women as profoundly undeserving of government financial support. Many media reports portrayed ADC recipients as promiscuous, lazy, unmarried Black women who abused alcohol and neglected their children.

In the late 1950s and 1960s, some left-wing academics and liberal social critics inadvertently fueled the public discourse on the undeserving poor through studies that focused on the behavioral roots of poverty. In 1959, anthropologist Oscar Lewis distinguished what he called a "culture of poverty" from economic deprivation, crystallizing an image that had a profound impact on poverty discourse and policies. Lewis argued that the culture of poverty was a way of life, passed down from generation to generation, characterized by powerlessness, apathy, promiscuity, and marital dissolution. The notion of a culture of poverty (popularized by the publication of antipoverty activist Michael Harrington's *Other America*) influenced the liberal architects of the Great Society programs of the 1960s. Rather than address larger political economic issues, they tried to equip the poor with skills, empowerment, and physical well-being through programs providing health care, education, job training, and services. Such programs did not create jobs, redistribute wealth, cure racism, or address sexism. In addition, because many programs were based on the idea that poverty was cultural, they reinforced the notion that poverty was the product of behaviors and attitudes and hence the fault of the poor.

The lack of integrated political or macroeconomic analyses in mainstream liberal approaches to fighting poverty made them vulnerable to appropriation by conservatives, who used the idea of a culture of poverty to provide a description of the undeserving poor. In the 1980s, conservatives, most notably Charles Murray in his book *Losing Ground*, furthered their attack on the poor by arguing that the welfare system itself (particularly AFDC) rewarded and produced the behaviors of the undeserving poor. Substituting the image of a "culture of welfare" for the "culture of poverty," conservatives argued that welfare was a way of life passed down from generation to generation. In this view, AFDC discouraged poor people from seeking employment and forming nuclear families while rewarding them for so-called promiscuous behavior. With the increased acceptance and incidence of white middle-class women's employment, critics of AFDC also began to condemn female welfare recipients for not holding jobs.

In the 1980s, the public discourse on poverty began to focus on the urban "underclass," a term often used as a euphemism for the undeserving poor. The "underclass" is a moral category covering the poor who fail to conform to the behavioral and attitudinal norms of mainstream middle-class society. Rhetorically separating the undeserving poor from the deserving "working poor," the "underclass" usually refers to African Americans living in inner cities. Much important liberal scholarship on the "underclass," most notably the work of sociologist William Julius Wilson, has located its roots in the spatial isolation and chronic unemployment of African American men. However, the public discourse tends to obscure such analyses: Women of the "underclass" are often described as promiscuous welfare recipients or prostitutes; the men are usually described as willfully flouting the American work ethic by hanging out on street corners and engaging in drug selling and other criminal activities instead of seeking employment.

Throughout U.S. history, the notion of the undeserving poor has been challenged. For instance, the social survey movement of the early-twentieth-century Progressive Era emphasized the ways that unemployment, low wages, and labor exploitation contributed to poverty. Similarly, in more recent years, left-wing academics and social critics have focused on power relationships and political and economic structures. Poor people have also been strident critics of both the discourses and the public policies that promote ideas about the undeserving poor. They have formed welfare rights organizations and campaigns for living wages, and they have engaged in protests against police brutality and racial profiling. However, because discourses about the undeserving poor have been so integrally linked to powerful and highly charged ideas about race and gender, the work ethic, the marital family, and Anglo-Saxon morality, they have held remarkable cultural power. Indeed, the notion of the undeserving "underclass" drove the movement to end welfare during the 1990s, culminating in the elimination of AFDC in 1996.

Lisa Levenstein

See also: Aid to Families with Dependent Children (ADC/AFDC); *The Children of Sanchez;* Dependency; Gender Discrimination in the Labor Market; *Losing Ground;* Means Testing and Universalism; Public Opinion; *Public Relief and Private Charity;* Racism; Relief; Self-Reliance; Sexism; Social Security Act of 1935; "Underclass"; Welfare Policy/Welfare Reform; Welfare Rights Movement; Work Ethic

References and Further Reading

Gilens, Martin. 1999. *Why Americans Hate Welfare: Race, Media, and the Politics of Antipoverty Policy.* Chicago: University of Chicago Press.

Gordon, Linda. 1994. *Pitied but Not Entitled: Single Mothers and the History of Welfare, 1890–1935.* New York: Free Press.

Katz, Michael B. 1986. *In the Shadow of the Poorhouse: A Social History of Welfare in America.* New York: Basic Books.

———. 1989. *The Undeserving Poor: From the War on Poverty to the War on Welfare.* New York: Pantheon Books.

Levenstein, Lisa. 2000. "From Innocent Children to Unwanted Migrants and Unwed Moms: Two Chapters in the Public Discourse on Welfare in the United States, 1960–1961." *Journal of Women's History* 11, no. 4: 10–33.

Lieberman, Robert C. 1998. *Shifting the Color Line: Race and the American Welfare State.* Cambridge, MA: Harvard University Press.

Mink, Gwendolyn. 2002. *Welfare's End.* Ithaca, NY: Cornell University Press.

Murray, Charles. 1984. *Losing Ground: American Social Policy, 1950–1980.* New York: Basic Books.

O'Connor, Alice. 2001. *Poverty Knowledge: Social Science, Social Policy, and the Poor in Twentieth-Century U.S. History.* Princeton: Princeton University Press.

Patterson, James T. 1981. *America's Struggle against Poverty, 1900–1980.* Cambridge, MA: Harvard University Press.

Devolution

See Federalism

Dillingham Commission

In 1907, the Dillingham Commission was organized and given the task of conducting the most extensive study of immigration patterns in U.S. history. Named after its chairman, Republican Senator William Paul Dillingham of Vermont, the committee was the result of Progressives' demands that the social sciences be applied to determine the best manner of addressing what was increasingly being seen as an immigration crisis. The great waves of immigrants pouring into the United States by the early 1900s alarmed many Americans who blamed immigrant communities for bringing poverty, illiteracy, prostitution, crime, poor morals, and low wages to cities like Boston, Chicago, and New York. The Dillingham Commission's findings supported the restrictionist posture that such biases had presaged; major immigration policy recommendations included literacy tests for prospective immigrants, higher immigration taxes, and quotas to regulate how many individuals could come to the United States from each country.

Such recommendations were based largely on the committee's conclusion that the national origins and character of the immigrant population had shifted. They identified three main waves of immigration to the country. The first, from 1815 to 1860, was composed of roughly 5 million immigrants, mostly of English, Irish, German, and other northwestern European nationalities. The second wave, from 1865 to 1890, grew to 10 million, still largely of northwestern European origin. However, the third wave, from 1890 to 1914, was distinctly different. It included 15 million immigrants, many of them Italian, Jewish, Turkish, Austro-Hungarian, Russian, Greek, and Lithuanian. The Dillingham Commission considered such southeastern European immigrants far less desirable than their northwestern European predecessors and closely associated this demographic shift with the rise in strikes, unemployment, crime, and other evidence of social unrest that accompanied late-nineteenth-century industrialization and urbanization. Couched in the language of unbiased social science, the committee's 1911 final report provided official sanction for a host of discriminatory, anti-immigrant policies that followed, such as those aimed against Japanese immigration (also "undesirable") to the West Coast of the United States. It introduced the concept of restrictive quotas based on national origins, although these would not be implemented until the 1920s. The report also reinforced prevailing stereotypes of the "new" immigrants based on its findings during an extended tour of Europe. For example, the Dillingham Commission compiled a directory of immigrant groups that is riddled with culturally biased descriptions and highly racialized imagery. Slavs were characterized as possessing fanaticism "in religion," as being "[careless] as to the business virtues of punctuality and often honesty," and as indulging in "periods of besotted drunkenness . . . [and] unexpected cruelty," while southern Italians were described as "excitable, impulsive, impracticable . . . [and having] little adaptability to highly organized society" (U.S. Immigration Commission 1911, 82–83, 129).

Some of the Dillingham Commission's early proposals were defeated. Dillingham's first campaign at the conclusion of the committee's study demanded implementation of literacy tests for potential immigrants, a measure passed by Congress but then vetoed by President William Howard Taft in 1912. However, the growing nativism of the early twentieth century allowed Dillingham to gain congressional support for a similar bill in 1917. When President Woodrow Wilson vetoed the bill, Congress overrode his veto. This victory for Dillingham was followed by another: In 1921, the first national-origin quota system for immigration was enacted. This crucial turning point was the culmination of the work of the Dillingham Commission and its report, and it would leave the ugly scar of restrictionism motivated by racial stereotyping on U.S. immigration policy for decades to come.

Rebecca K. Root

See also: Immigrants and Immigration; Immigration Policy

References and Further Reading

Lund, John M. 1994. "Boundaries of Restriction: The Dillingham Commission." *History Review* (University of Vermont), 6 (December). http://chipmunk.uvm.edu:6336/dynaweb/histrev/hrvol6/@Generic__BookTextView/1197;cs=default;ts=default.

U.S. Immigration Commission [Dillingham Commission]. 1911. *Abstracts of Report of the Immigration Commission*. Vol. 5, *Dictionary of Race and Peoples*. Washington, DC: GPO.

Disability

Disability and poverty have been linked in complex ways throughout American history. Disability rights activists argue that this linkage has more to do with societal attitudes and government policies toward people with disabilities than with the physical, mental, or emotional conditions that constitute any individual's particular disability. One-quarter of children with disabilities currently live in poverty, as do approximately one-third of working-age adults with disabilities (Kaye 1997, 73). Direct and indirect discrimination in education, job training, and employment contribute to the fact that of the 10 percent of American adults with a work disability—"a limitation in the amount or kind of work they are able to perform, due to a chronic condition or impairment" (LaPlante et al. 1996, 1)—two-thirds do not participate in the labor force. Despite some improvement, physical, communication, and architectural barriers continue to limit access to workplaces more than a decade after the 1990 passage of the Americans with Disabilities Act (ADA). Inadequate, restrictive, and contradictory government policies further contribute to disabled people's poverty rates. Gender and age discrimination compound the cascading effect of widespread prejudice against people with disabilities. The cumulative effects of poverty, conversely, contribute to high rates of disability among poor people in the United States; substandard living and work conditions, along with poor-quality health care, often lead to the impairments that make up a disability.

To the extent that income correlates with education, disabled people are at a disadvantage. Far fewer disabled than nondisabled people complete either high school or college. Despite legislation mandating the fullest possible inclusion of disabled children in mainstream public school classrooms, disabled children continue to receive substandard instruction, often in segregated classrooms. Physical, communication, and attitudinal barriers still impede their full participation. People with disabilities thus frequently enter the job market lacking competitive skills and training (Kaye 1997, 74).

Employed disabled adults work disproportionately at part-time and low-wage jobs. It is less common now than it was historically for disabled adults to work in "sheltered workshops," or segregated workplaces where people with disabilities perform unskilled labor, often on a piecework basis (Shapiro 1994, 143). In the competitive job market, disabled workers face prejudice from employers and other barriers to full workplace participation. Although the ADA and other legislation are attempts to eradicate such discrimination, it persists in all sectors of the labor market. From hirings to promotions to firings, employers' and coworkers' attitudes and behavior hinder disabled people's work experience. Moreover, basic compliance with the transportation and physical access mandates of the ADA lags, leaving workplaces largely inaccessible to many.

Those without paid employment must rely upon the federal Supplemental Security Income (SSI) and Social Security Disability Insurance (SSDI) income-maintenance programs, whose benefits fail to raise many families out of poverty. Of working-age disabled adults who do not work, nearly 40 percent live in poverty. A poverty rate of 11.4 percent among elderly disabled people contrasts with a 6.5 percent rate for those without disabilities (Kaye 1997, 18). Women with disabilities, who face combined prejudices based on gender and disability in both the labor and marriage markets, are especially likely to live in poverty. Of women receiving SSI, 52.7 percent fall below the poverty line (Kaye 1997, 18). For single disabled mothers of young children, the rate is 72.9 percent (LaPlante 1996, 3). Yet many people with disabilities cannot afford to abandon the welfare system for the job market, because even a meager earned income will cause them to lose valuable health care and personal assistance benefits. Disability activists have argued for decades that the economic betterment of people with disabilities requires ridding the social welfare system of such "work disincentives" while increasing income subsidies dramatically.

Much disability activism has focused on economic justice. In 1934, the League for the Physically Handicapped, a New York group with 300 disabled members, staged a sit-in at the Washington, D.C., offices of the Works Progress Administration (WPA), demanding jobs and antidiscrimination protection from the WPA (Shapiro 1994, 64). Just as league members demanded "Jobs, Not Tin Cups," disabled people today profess a sincere desire to work; a 1994 Harris poll found that 79 percent of disabled adults without jobs wanted to be working (Kaye 1997, 24). Since the 1970s, disability rights activists have fought against direct discrimination in employment while also demanding full access to venues of education, training, and employment. They have opposed public policy that keeps people with disabilities both poor and dependent. Thus, the disability rights agenda has included battles for accessible transportation and buildings, basic prerequisites to participation in the labor force. Activists push for workplace accommodations such as Braille signs and text telephones, the absence of which make workplaces inaccessible to thousands of blind and deaf workers. They want rational government policies that support efforts to live in the community rather than in nursing homes or other institutions, where lifelong dependency supplants independent living and wage earning. Recognizing the importance of passing and enforcing such legislation as the ADA, they also see that the fight to end prejudice and discrimination against people with disabilities must be fought at every level of society, including the ideological and the cultural.

Lauri Umansky

See also: Disability Policy; Supplemental Security Income

References and Further Reading

Asch, Adrienne, and Michelle Fine, eds. 1988. *Women with Disabilities: Essays in Psychology, Culture, and Politics*. Philadelphia: Temple University Press.

Kaye, H. Stephen. 1997. *Disability Watch: The Status of People with Disabilities in the United States*. Introduction by Paul K. Longmore. Oakland, CA: Disability Rights Advocates.

LaPlante, Mitchell P., Jae Kennedy, H. Stephen Kaye, and Barbara L. Wenger. 1996. *Disability and Employment*. San Francisco: Disability Statistics Rehabilitation Research and Training Center.

Longmore, Paul K., and Lauri Umansky, eds. 2001. *The New Disability History: American Perspectives*. New York: New York University Press.

Scotch, Richard K., and Edward D. Berkowitz. 1990. "One Comprehensive System? A Historical Perspective on Federal Disability Policy." *Journal of Disability Policy Studies* 1, no. 3 (Fall): 1–19.

Shapiro, Joseph P. 1994. *No Pity: People with Disabilities Forging a New Civil Rights Movement*. New York: Times Books.

Disability Policy

The United States, in the words of the historian Edward Berkowitz, "has no disability policy" (1987, 1). Instead, it has knit together three types of disability policy—income-maintenance programs, rehabilitation programs, and antidiscrimination programs—that sprang from three different and sometimes conflicting sources: retirement policy, welfare policy, and civil rights policy. The extent of governmental powers and funding, moreover, are equally complex, consisting of various combinations of state and federal funds, national grants, tax policy, and private agreements with employers and insurance carriers.

The three income-maintenance programs are workers' compensation, Social Security Disability Insurance (SSDI), and Supplemental Security Income (SSI). Workers' compensation constituted the first national program for workers in the United States, and it was one of the country's earliest social policies. Beginning in 1911 in Wisconsin and New Jersey, workers' compensation programs were aimed at workers who had been injured on the job. By 1949, all the states and the District of Columbia had created their own programs. Workers' compensation removed money, medical care, and other services to injured workers from the hands of employers, the courts, and the community. Before this program, an employee's only recourse for receiving financial compensation for his or her medical costs was to sue an employer.

Workers' compensation is a state-federal program that is funded by employers' taking out workers' compensation insurance with private companies. After an individual reports an injury, a company doctor determines whether the injury is work related. If it is, the workers' compensation insurance pays for recovery. Once the individual reaches what is known as "maximum medical improvement," a payment schedule indicates the amount of compensation he or she will receive for a permanent disability or a permanent partial disability. Schedules essentially list a price for the loss of every body part or a life. Initially only amputations of extremities (fingers, hands, toes, and feet) and limbs (arms and legs) were listed, but by 1915, loss of vision and hearing were included on most schedules. In the 1920s, moreover, schedules included permanent partial disabilities. Industrial diseases, such as those that result from exposure to asbestos, are largely absent from the schedules. The one notable exception is black lung disease, which had its own compensation program established in 1969.

In light of its complicated state-federal structure and its private funding from insurance companies, workers' compensation has been resistant to most reform. Nonetheless, one wave of national reform occurred in the 1970s because benefits had not kept up with inflation throughout the 1950s and 1960s. Another wave of reform happened on a state-by-state basis in the mid-1980s after costs (primarily medical) escalated at a rate far beyond that of inflation. By the mid-1990s, employer costs had dropped, and costs stayed constant for the rest of the decade, since thirty-four states had enacted legislation between 1991 and 1994 that was designed to diminish the cost of job injuries by, among other things, reducing the number of workplace injuries.

The second income-maintenance program is SSDI. Unlike workers' compensation, this federally funded disability insurance program does not require any causal connection between a particular job or workplace and the disability. A person's benefits depend on how long he or she has worked. Coverage is almost universal, with 95 percent of all jobs covered. Instituted by an amendment to the Social Security Act in 1956, SSDI serves approximately 4.5 million people. Social Security was one of the cornerstones of the New Deal, and funding for all Social Security programs is based on the principle of social insurance. What is more, SSDI is financed by a payroll tax on employers and employees rather than by private insurance.

Over time, SSDI has become more inclusive. Originally created for workers over fifty, in 1960 the Social Security Act was amended to make anyone with a work history eligible. It also gives benefits to widows and widowers over age forty-nine. In 1980, President Ronald Reagan instituted reforms to remove people from the SSDI rolls. All those with nonpermanent disabilities were required to be reevaluated every three years. But Reagan's reforms generated opposition. By 1984, amendments that included a "medical improvement standard" partially undid the Reagan reforms. This standard stipulates that benefits will continue for beneficiaries who have medical conditions that have not improved and who remain out of work or who have a small income or wages.

The Ticket to Work and Work Incentives Improvement Act of 1999 constitutes the most recent reform. This legislation allowed former SSDI recipients to keep receiving Medicare health benefits for eight and one-half years after starting a job. Except for legally blind people (who could earn up to $1,100), a former SSDI recipient could not earn more than $700 per month (these allowances were subsequently raised to $1,350 per month for legally blind and $810 per month for disabled people) from "substantial gainful employment" and continue to qualify for transitional Medicare (U.S. Social Security Administration 2004).

Although under SSDI, applicants can have no dispute with employers, who themselves have no monetary incentive to contest their claims, legal contests do occur with the disability determination services. SSDI is run by the states but regulated by the U.S. Department of Health and Human Services, and officials in these services determine eligibility. Numerous opportunities for appeal are available if someone is denied benefits. The first appeal is brought before a federal administrative law judge; such judges have more discretion than a state disability examiner, who is not bound to follow the strict procedures contained in the Program Operating Manuel System. Most people now hire lawyers to help them through the eligibility process, particularly during an appeal. In fact, eligibility varies greatly from state to state and from year to year. For instance, in a one-year period, Alaska denied SSDI benefits to 63 percent of all applicants, whereas Iowa denied them to only 36 percent.

Unlike SSDI, which is a right if someone has made the requisite amount of contributions, SSI, the third income-maintenance program, is considered a welfare policy. Created in 1972, SSI became operational in 1974 to provide aid to the aged, the blind, and the disabled. Like other welfare programs, eligibility for SSI is based on a means test. Applicants must prove that they are indigent. If a person is ineligible for SSDI due to an insufficient work history, Social Security officials will advise him or her to file for SSI. Approximately 5.2 million people receive SSI on grounds of disability. When the program became operational in 1974, approximately 40 percent of recipients were blind or disabled; by 1997, this figure had almost doubled, with 79 percent of recipients being blind or disabled. From 1965 until the early 1980s, SSI also paid for the institutional care of severely disabled people. In 1981, under the Omnibus Budget Reconciliation Act, the federal government established the Home and Community Based Care Waiver Program. This program allows states to pay for home- and community-based care if the program is "cost neutral," that is, if the average costs under the waiver are equal to or less than the cost of services without the waiver.

Vocational rehabilitation constitutes another part of disability policy. Vocational rehabilitation, however, is by far the smallest program in terms of expenditures. Although private programs were created as early as the mid-nineteenth century for the poor and the disabled, the federal government started rehabilitating veterans only during World War I. In 1920, the Vocational Rehabilitation Act was passed, creating a program for all citizens, although it was not until 1954 that the program was fully funded and formed. Operated by the states with federal funding, vocational rehabilitation gives people with disabilities the chance to meet counselors who help them find educational opportunities and provide equipment and medical services that might make them employable.

In the 1970s, vocational rehabilitation became the statutory basis for the rights orientation in current disability policy. In 1973, the program was amended by the Rehabilitation Act, which included Section 504 prohibiting discrimination against people with disabilities by any agency or organization that receives public funds, such as a university. Section 504 became a blueprint for disability rights advocates, and in 1990, the Americans with Disabilities Act (ADA) was passed, extending rights to people with disabilities in the private sector. Approximately 55 million people with physical and mental impairments are covered by this legislation.

The ADA contains four substantive titles protecting people from discrimination in the workplace, in programs that provide governmental services or benefits, and in private places of public accommodation such as stores, offices, and restaurants. It also mandates that interstate or intrastate telephone services make provisions to enable hearing- and speech-impaired individuals to communicate with hearing people. The ADA stipulates that disabled people must be given reasonable accommodations in the workplace and that such state and local government services as mass transit, public education, or public accommodations must be accessible to disabled people. The public accommodations provisions, however, do not mandate that the modifications must place disabled people in the same situation as people without disabilities. For instance, a restaurant need not provide a menu written in Braille as long as a waiter will read the menu aloud to a person with vision problems.

Recourse against discriminatory action by employers or in such facilities as transportation systems or service establishments, whether public or privately owned, is found in the federal courts. Disabled people may sue a prospective or an existing employer either for discriminatory treatment during the hiring process or for not furnishing reasonable accommodations. People may also sue a state government or a private establishment if a public accommodation, such as a tax office or dentist, is not accessible. Moreover, the public accommodations provisions allow courts to enjoin practices that do not accommodate disabilities—for example, if a builder fails to include a ramp to a building.

A decade after its enactment in 1992, people with disabilities who thought the new law would protect them from discrimination have become disenchanted with the federal courts' interpretation of certain aspects of this civil rights law. In the employment context, the most heavily litigated section of disability law, federal courts have decided in employers' favor in 80 to 90 percent of all suits (O'Brien 2001, 14). In a series of cases about employment, moreover, the Supreme Court has rendered such a narrow interpretation of the provisions that few people qualify for coverage under the ADA. The disability rights extended under the governmental services and public accommodations provisions in Titles II and III have been more successful in protecting people with disabilities, with 70 percent (O'Brien 2004, 22) and 46 percent (O'Brien 2001, 18–19) of the cases favoring defendants, respectively.

Ruth O'Brien

See also: Disability; Social Security Act of 1935

References and Further Reading

Anderson, Linda, Paul A. Sundet, and Irma Harrington. 2000. *The Social Welfare System in the United States: A Social Workers' Guide to Public Health Programs*. Boston: Allyn and Bacon.

Berkowitz, Edward D. 1987. *Disabled Policy: America's Programs for the Handicapped*. New York: Cambridge University Press.

Fishback, Price V., and Shawn Everett Kantor. 2000. *A Prelude to the Welfare State: The Origins of Workers' Compensation*. Chicago: University of Chicago Press.

O'Brien, Ruth. 2001. *Crippled Justice: The History of Modern Disability Policy in the Workplace*. Chicago: University of Chicago Press.

———. 2004. "Introduction." In *Voices from the Edge: Narratives about the Americans with Disabilities Act*, ed. Ruth O'Brien, 3–28. New York: Oxford University Press.

Thomason, Terry, John F. Burton Jr., and Douglas Hyatt. 1998. *New Approaches to Disability in the Workplace*. Madison, WI: Industrial Relations Research Association.

Disasters

Disaster relief programs established key cultural and political precedents for the American welfare state, including the distinction between the deserving and undeserving poor. As Michele Landis has shown (1998, 1999), several of the first federal assistance efforts—such as a congressional subsidy of $20,000 to residents of Alexandria, Virginia, who had lost property in a fire in 1827, and sixteen payments to traders whose merchandise had been damaged or destroyed before delivery between 1799 and 1801—compensated Americans who could not be held accountable for their plight. Often presidents acted independently to provide emergency aid for citizens or groups they believed to be deprived for reasons beyond their control. Yet Congress and the Executive Office consistently denied funds to parties who appeared to be responsible for their own condition, including merchants who lost goods while traveling in waters known to contain pirates.

Early disaster relief also favored property owners and businesses. In the late eighteenth century, individuals and private parties made the first requests for state assistance. But between 1800 and 1825, businesses and property holders organized into class-based interest groups for the purpose of securing political support. The federal government established a new bureaucratic apparatus to manage and adjudicate emerging requests for public relief from catastrophic events. It made few accommodations to address the everyday deprivation of the unemployed, who—in the minds of most political officials—had authored their own misfortunes. By the early nineteenth century, then, the government had established an institutional structure that legitimated assistance to the advantaged while marginalizing the destitute.

The rhetoric of disaster has played an enduring and significant role in American welfare politics, and it was particularly crucial during the contentious debates over the legitimacy and constitutionality of the New Deal. In their battles with laissez-faire conservatives, advocates for expanded public unemployment insurance and social security programs represented the Depression as a national catastrophe that deserved traditional forms of disaster relief. When Franklin D. Roosevelt, congressional leaders, and government attorneys defended their call for public assistance, they told "the history of disaster relief . . . in order to show how the New Deal was consistent with this precedent for federal assistance and thus legitimate" (Landis 1999, 273). As Senator Robert La Follette argued in Congress, "Will the Senator from Delaware explain, if he can, what difference it makes to a citizen of the United States if he is homeless, without food or clothing in the dead of winter, whether it is the result of flood, or whether it is due to an economic catastrophe over which he had no control? I see no distinction" (quoted in Landis 1999, 257). This reasoning helped convince Congress, the courts, and the public, paving the way for the introduction of new social protection programs for Americans whose misery was "undeserved."

If the New Deal broadened the meaning of disaster, the Disaster Relief Act of 1950 established new parameters for federal policy responses to extreme environmental events. The original Disaster Relief Act (Public Law 81–875) legislation granted limited benefits to state and local governments for "alleviating suffering and damage resulting from a major peacetime disaster." The program's initial budget of $5 million was too small to provide much help, but the act established legal and political mechanisms that states and Congress would quickly use to expand the scope and increase the costs of disaster relief. Between 1950 and 1980, Congress passed fourteen additional acts, including the sweeping disaster relief acts of 1970 and 1974. During the 1970s, spending on direct assistance for disaster victims approached $4 billion, but the criteria for eligibility remained vague, and the Executive Office used its own discretion in determining what constituted a national disaster.

In 1979, the government created the Federal Emergency Management Agency (FEMA) to oversee the emerging assistance programs. FEMA expanded the scope of disaster relief even further, extending its reach into risk management by creating subsidized insurance programs and construction projects to support private development in regions with known vulnerability to hazardous weather, such as coastal Florida and California (see Steinberg 2000). Since the early 1980s, states have increased the number of requests for federal assistance, and presidents have largely complied. The average number of disasters declared by the White House rose from twenty-five in 1984–1988, to thirty-three in 1988–1992, and to forty-five in 1993–1997. Yet Congress has not provided sufficient funds for disaster relief, and in addition to the regular FEMA budget, financing comes from supplemental appropriations that take dollars away from other programs. Between 1992 and 1998, special disaster appropriations ranged between $2 billion and $8.2 billion annually. But the federal government compiles no systematic data on disaster spending, and the twenty-six departments and agencies administered by FEMA operate with little accountability (see Platt 1999, ch. 1).

There are means tests for most individual-level disaster relief programs and rigid caps on others. (Individual and family grants, for example, are capped at roughly $14,000.) But public assistance from FEMA has no such restrictions, and "affluent communities covered by declarations may receive 75 percent and 100 percent of their recovery costs from the federal government, even if they carry or could afford to carry disaster insurance" (Platt 1999, 17). The poor are doubly disadvantaged because the funds used to compensate the disaster victims who lost expensive property are often taken directly out of social protection programs targeting "the truly disadvantaged." In 1995, for example, Congress cut funds for low-income housing, job training, and home energy assistance to pay for a $6 billion bill that largely funded the state and property owners who suffered damage in the Northridge (California) earthquake (Steinberg 2000, 193). The initial compensation plans for victims of the September 11, 2001, disaster also allocated far greater benefits to the affluent. Using actuarial standards that determined economic losses based on expected future earnings, the administrators of the Victims Compensation Fund offered benefits ranging from $400,000 to more than $4 million, depending on the salaries of the victims.

None of these programs provide assistance for the most deadly of the so-called natural disasters in the United States: heat waves. Although political officials and the media are most interested in the property damage inflicted by earthquakes, tornadoes, hurricanes, and floods, during a typical year heat waves kill more Americans than all these disasters *combined* (see Klinenberg 2002). A disaster policy designed to save lives and provide social protection would focus on reducing human vulnerability to extreme events and addressing the everyday crises that make exogenous forces so dangerous. It would also limit private development in areas with known disaster risks. But in the United States, insuring private property has always been a greater political priority, and—as in other areas of social policy—disaster policies that protect the vulnerable remain in short supply.

Eric Klinenberg and Elif Kale-Lostuvali

See also: Epidemic Disease

References and Further Reading

Klinenberg, Eric. 2002. *Heat Wave: A Social Autopsy of Disaster in Chicago*. Chicago and London: University of Chicago Press.

Landis, Michele. 1998. "'Let Me Next Time Be "Tried by Fire"': Disaster Relief and the Origins of the American Welfare State, 1789–1874." *Northwestern University Law Review* 92, no. 3: 967–1034.

———. 1999. "Fate, Responsibility, and 'Natural' Disaster Relief: Narrating the American Welfare State." *Law and Society Review* 33, no. 2: 257–318.

Platt, Rutherford, ed. 1999. *Disasters and Democracy: The Politics of Extreme Natural Events*. Washington, DC: Island Press.

Steinberg, Ted. 2000. *Acts of God: The Unnatural History of Natural Disaster in America*. Oxford and New York: Oxford University Press.

Discrimination

See Ageism; Classism; Gender Discrimination in the Labor Market; Heteronormativity; Homophobia; Racial Segregation; Racism; Sexism

Domestic Violence

Domestic violence and women's poverty are undeniably linked. Each year, approximately 1.5 million women in the United States are physically or sexually assaulted by an intimate partner (Tjaden and Thoennes 2000, 9). Domestic violence survivors face a pattern of psychological assault and physical and sexual coercion by their intimate partners. Although survivors face a number of barriers to escaping abuse, poverty is among the most formidable. This is true for survivors for whom leaving the abuser means giving up economic security and for those already trapped in poverty. As many as 60 percent of women on welfare report having been a victim of intimate violence at some point in their adult lives, and as many as 30 percent report having been the victim of abuse within the preceding year (Tolman and Raphael 2000, "Prevalence" section).

Abusers retain control over survivors by

ensuring the survivors' economic dependency or instability. Although most domestic violence survivors report that they engage in wage work or that they want to work, some are prohibited from working by their abuser. Others are denied access to economic resources, including checking accounts or credit cards. Many abusers interfere with work, education, or training through phone calls, harassment, or threats of violence at the workplace. Twenty-five to fifty percent of survivors report having lost a job due to abuse (Tolman and Raphael 2000, table 3). This economic insecurity is compounded for survivors who, because of race, ethnicity, disability, and the like, face discriminatory barriers to reemployment.

Despite the economic risks involved, most domestic violence survivors attempt to flee the abuse. Means of escape differ among women. Some go to family. Others go to domestic violence shelters, which provide only temporary accommodation. In addition, domestic violence is a primary cause of homelessness (U.S. Conference of Mayors 2000), a plight that poses significant barriers to survivors' workforce participation.

Assistance for survivors is often crafted to accommodate the model of a white woman survivor and fails to incorporate the experience or meet the needs of many immigrant women, women of color, lesbians, gay men, or disabled or drug- or alcohol-addicted survivors. Because these survivors fail to fit the model, they are more vulnerable to discriminatory state action, such as being perceived as violent and thus subject to mandatory arrest laws or not having an interpreter's assistance in response to 911 calls. These survivors are frequently unable to access formal channels of assistance.

Many domestic violence survivors depend on welfare to provide the economic support necessary to escape the violence. Certain requirements of the welfare law present potential problems for domestic violence survivors. These include (1) the requirement that welfare recipients engage in a work activity within two years, (2) the requirement that they establish paternity and cooperate with child support enforcement, and (3) the five-year lifetime limit on welfare receipt (42 U.S.C. 601[a]). Access to benefits is available to battered immigrant women only on a limited basis (8 U.S.C. 1641[c]), and eligibility requirements make it difficult for most immigrant survivors to qualify.

The work requirements of the welfare program established in 1996 (Temporary Assistance for Needy Families [TANF]) can expose survivors to more violence and can make it difficult to maintain eligibility for welfare. Recipients who are currently experiencing abuse report that their abuser sabotages work efforts by increasing the violence before a big event such as an exam or interview, refusing to provide transportation or child care at the last minute, or inflicting guilt on the survivor for leaving the children (Lyon 2000, 5). States need to adapt to the needs of survivors by waiving work requirements where necessary and by making work requirements more flexible to assist survivors in overcoming barriers to sustained employment and economic security.

Paternity establishment and child support enforcement requirements may also be dangerous. Recent studies of welfare recipients indicate that many survivors want child support regulations to be enforced against the abuser (Tolman and Raphael 2000, "Child Support" section). Doing so can be dangerous either for the survivor or for the child. Court proceedings increase batterers' access to the mother and child and can be used by the abuser as a vehicle for continued harassment. Moreover, child support enforcement opens up the issue of visitation and custody, threatening the safety and security of the child. Although some survivors may need waivers from the entire process, others may need the state to institute policies and procedures (such as excusing her from court visits, protecting contact information, and ensuring that abusers are not granted unsafe visitation or custody) so that survivors can safely take advantage of pending child support reforms, which will aid welfare recipients in achieving economic security.

Domestic violence survivors are remarkably resilient. Nevertheless, survival can be a long, hard process. Survivors may take longer than five years to free themselves from the abuse and its effects. They may cycle between wage work and welfare, may need to overcome post-traumatic stress, and may need to deal with other violence-related problems. Moreover, domestic violence is linked to increased incidence of drug and alcohol abuse, which can create barriers to work, education, and training and can even threaten welfare eligibility. Hence, the five-year lifetime limit on welfare eligibility threatens survivors' physical, psychic, and economic security.

A Family Violence Option was put into the 1996 welfare law to provide states with the opportunity to waive welfare requirements that make escaping domestic violence more difficult or that unfairly penalize current or former survivors (42 U.S.C. 607[a][7][A][iii]). Thirty-four states and the District of Columbia have adopted the Family Violence Option, and ten states have similar domestic violence policies. The Family Violence Option is, however, just a state option, administered at a state's discretion. But even if the Family Violence Option was mandatory for states, survivors who are reluctant to expose intimate partners to the criminal justice system would not benefit. The challenge for survivors under the TANF welfare regime is to win implementation policies that provide full disclosure of available waivers and services while respecting survivors who do not wish to reveal their abuse to the government. Once informed, survivors must be free to choose what they decide will work best for them, and that choice must be honored and carried out in such a manner as to protect their safety and confidentiality. Only then will survivors be empowered to attain economic self-sufficiency and a life free from violence.

Jacqueline K. Payne

See also: Feminisms; Gender Discrimination in the Labor Market; Welfare Policy/Welfare Reform

References and Further Reading

Davis, Angela. 2000. "The Color of Violence against Women." *Color Lines* 3, no. 3 (Fall). http://www.arc.org/C_Lines/CLArchive/story3_3_02.html.

Lyon, Eleanor. 2000. "Welfare, Poverty, and Abused Women: New Research and Its Implications." Harrisburg, PA: National Resource Center on Domestic Violence. http://www.vawnet.org/NRCDVPublications/BCSDV/Papers/BCS10_POV.pdf.

Tjaden, Patricia, and Nancy Thoennes. 2000. *Full Report of the Prevalence, Incidence, and Consequences of Violence against Women: Findings from the National Violence against Women Survey*. Washington, DC: United States Department of Justice, National Institute of Justice.

Tolman, Richard M., and Jody Raphael. 2000. "A Review of Research on Welfare and Domestic Violence." *Journal of Social Issues* 56, no. 4: 655–682.

U.S. Conference of Mayors. 2000. *A Status Report on Hunger and Homelessness in America's Cities: 2000*. Washington, DC: U.S. Conference of Mayors.

Domestic Work

Domestic work encompasses the wide range of labor required to meet the day-to-day needs of households, tasks that generally include cleaning, cooking, laundry, and child or other dependent care. Although sometimes romanticized in ideologies aimed at reaffirming the virtues of female "domesticity" in the "traditional" male-breadwinner family, in reality this work has historically been socially undervalued as "women's work," generally uncompensated when performed by household members and, when not, largely relegated to low-paid women of color and immigrant women in the United States.

The predominance of poor women of color and immigrant women in domestic work in the United States must be understood within two contexts: (1) the historical use of U.S. welfare policy to channel women of color into paid domestic work, and (2) the contemporary use of international finance policies to compel third world women to migrate in search of work in these and other service jobs.

Welfare scholar Mimi Abramovitz proposes that the welfare state has historically mediated capitalism's conflicting demands that women provide two functions: to remain in the home to reproduce and maintain the labor force, and to undertake traditionally "female" low-wage work in the paid labor force. Government policy resolves this conflict, Abramovitz says, by encouraging and subsidizing some women to remain home and nurture the workforce while forcing others into low-wage work (Abramovitz 1996, 313–318). Historically, U.S. welfare policy has been designed to channel women of color into paid domestic work on the rationale that women of color were more suitable for employment outside of the home and should be coerced to do agricultural or domestic work to meet market demands. This assumption was often translated into practice by, for example, denying Black families public assistance through explicit administrative measures such as the so-called suitable home and employable mother (that is, employable outside her own home) rules of the 1940s through the 1960s. The practice was also instituted more covertly by caseworkers' making eligibility determinations that barred or expelled women of color from welfare rolls, thus pushing them from their homes into the local labor market for domestic or agricultural work (Bell 1965, 34, 64). At the same time, U.S. social welfare and labor market policies have historically operated to keep the domestic workforce marginalized and low paid. In policy debates that acknowledged the preponderance of women and people of color in these jobs, domestic (as well as agricultural) workers were deliberately excluded from Social Security, unemployment insurance, collective bargaining, minimum wage, and other bedrock protections of the New Deal welfare state. Not until the 1970s, following several decades of struggle that won such benefits as Social Security coverage, were domestic workers brought under the minimum wage, overtime, and other provisions of the original 1938 Fair Labor Standards Act. Even so, employer compliance is far from universal and is not rigorously enforced.

Today, we see a parallel channeling of Latina and Asian Pacific Islander immigrant women into domestic work, again through the denial of aid to these women in U.S. welfare and immigration policy. In addition, this coercion of third world women into service work in the United States begins even before they arrive in this country. Immigrant women workers are recruited, or, in effect, imported, from the third world for labor in the United States and other first world nations both through illicit trafficking and through formal international agreements benefiting both sending and receiving countries' governments and employers, particularly structural adjustment policies (SAPs). Through SAPs, first world creditor nations attach preconditions to their loans to third world indebted nations, requiring debtor nations to cut social spending and wages, open their markets to foreign investment, and privatize state enterprises. SAPs wreak havoc on the lives of women in third world nations, devastating subsistence economies and social service systems in such a way that women's nutrition, health, education, employment possibilities, and work conditions are vastly diminished. These ravages make it so difficult for women to survive and sustain their families that they must leave their home countries, and often leave their families behind, in search of work in the first world as domestic servants or other service workers.

The subsequent denial of all forms of aid to immigrants in "host" countries, such as the United States, seals the fate of these women, making them more willing to take the most scorned, low-paid service jobs once they arrive. The demise of social supports in the first world has created both an expanded demand for care workers and a lack of alternatives to this low-wage service work. Thus, the demolition of social supports in the third world through SAPs not only parallels the dismantling of the welfare state in the United States and elsewhere but also serves to reinforce the channeling of immigrant women workers into service work as the only viable choice. These women's vulnerability is further exacerbated in the current global market and political structure, which enables both sending and "host" countries' governments and private employers to avoid any accountability for overseas workers.

Ironically, many of these women are employed by the very International Monetary Fund and World Bank officials or foreign diplomats in the United States who are responsible for the design and implementation of the policies destroying their home countries' economies and social support systems. A Human Rights Watch report of June 2001 documents the extreme abuses migrant domestic workers suffer at the hands of these elite, powerful employers. The exploitation of immigrant women and women-of-color domestic workers by middle-class employers in the United States is also widespread and is increasingly being exposed, documented, and challenged.

In the face of these abuses, immigrant women domestic workers across the country and internationally are organizing to fight back, developing new messages and alternative strategies to address these challenges against great odds (Chang 2000, 136–146, 202–205). Immigrant women are playing central and leading roles in both mainstream and nontraditional labor organizing, fighting for domestic worker rights in the United States, challenging the trafficking of migrant women, and fighting the destructive SAPs that force them to leave their home countries and families.

Grace Chang

See also: Fair Labor Standards Act (FLSA); Service and Domestic Workers, Labor Organizing; Social Security Act of 1935

References and Further Reading

Abramovitz, Mimi. 1996. *Regulating the Lives of Women: Social Welfare Policy from Colonial Times to the Present*. Boston: South End Press.

Bell, Winifred. 1965. *Aid to Dependent Children*. New York: Columbia University Press.

Chang, Grace. 2000. *Disposable Domestics: Immigrant Women Workers in the Global Economy*. Boston: South End Press.

Human Rights Watch. 2001. "Hidden in the Home: Abuse of Domestic Workers with Special Visas in the United States." Report, New York, June 14.

Dual Labor Market

See Labor Markets

Du Bois, W. E. B.

See The Philadelphia Negro; Poverty Research; Social Surveys

Dust Bowl Migration

The Dust Bowl migration of the 1930s plays an important and complicated role in the way Americans talk about the history of poverty and public policy in the United States. For almost seventy years, the story of white families from Oklahoma and neighboring states making their way to California in the midst of the Great Depression has been kept alive by journalists and filmmakers, college teachers and museum curators, songwriters and novelists, and of course historians. Although it was but one episode out of many struggles with poverty during the 1930s, the Dust Bowl migration became something of synecdoche, the single most common image that later generations would use to memorialize the hardships of that decade. The continuing fascination with the Dust Bowl saga also has something to do with the way race and poverty have interacted over the generations since the 1930s. Here is one of the last great stories depicting white Americans as victims of severe poverty and social prejudice. It is a story that many

The automobile was often the only hope for the future to many families fleeing from the Dust Bowl in the Southwest during the depression years of the 1930s. Pictured here is a migrant cotton field worker and family on their way to the West. Photograph taken in the early 1930s. (Bettmann/Corbis)

Americans have needed to tell, for many different reasons.

The story begins in the summer of 1935. That is when the economist Paul Taylor realized that something new was happening in California's agricultural areas, particularly the wondrously productive San Joaquin Valley, which supplied two dozen different kinds of fruits and vegetables to the nation's grocery stores and the highest-quality cotton fiber to its textile mills. The workers who picked those crops had been mostly Mexicans, Filipinos, and single white males before the Depression. Now, Taylor, an expert on farm labor issues, noticed more and more whites looking for jobs as harvest laborers, many of them traveling as families, a lot of them with license plates from Oklahoma, Texas, and Arkansas.

Those states had suffered greatly in the early 1930s, both from escalating joblessness and from a severe drought that for several years denied much of the Great Plains sufficient rain to produce its usual complement of wheat and cotton. The drought had also produced a spectacular ecological disaster. Wind-driven dust storms had arisen in a broad swath of counties in western Kansas and the Oklahoma and Texas panhandles on several occasions between 1933 and 1935, each time filling the air with millions of tons of finely plowed topsoil and blackening skies for a thousand miles as the clouds moved east. The dust storms brought press attention and later government intervention to the affected area, soon known as the "Dust Bowl."

Taylor was thinking about drought and dust as he pounded out an article for *Survey Graphic* magazine. The article profiled the families from Oklahoma, Texas, and Arkansas showing up in large numbers in the fields of California. They came with great hope, like the westward-moving pioneers of old, he wrote, but they were heading into disappointment. What awaited them was a shortage of work and low wages for what was available. Housing would be a tent camp or a shack thrown together of scraps. Taylor worried about their future even as he attached to them a label that he knew would bring sympathy. He called them "refugees," refugees from "dust, drought, and protracted depression" (Taylor 1935, 348). The journalists who read his article and rushed into the San Joaquin Valley to see and write more about the newcomers substituted the more evocative label "Dust Bowl refugees," assuming that the terms and locations were equivalent. In fact they were not. The actual Dust Bowl counties were sparsely populated and contributed few refugees to the migration stream that was pouring into California. Most of those who did migrate came from eastern sections of Oklahoma and from Texas, Arkansas, and Missouri, which knew drought and depression but little dust.

Historians have since clarified some of the dimensions of the misnamed migration. Numbers are elusive, but it is safe to say that 300,000–400,000 Oklahomans, Texans, Arkansans, and Missourians moved to California and settled there during the 1930s (Gregory 1989). This would have been a significant population transfer in any era, but it was particularly momentous in the context of the Depression, when internal migration rates for other parts of the country were low and when high unemployment made any kind of relocation risky.

Distinctive too were certain demographic features of the migrant population. Whites made up roughly 95 percent of those moving (Gregory 1989). African Americans were well represented in the populations of Oklahoma, Arkansas, and Texas, and some left during the 1930s, but African Americans usually moved to the cities of the North. It was not until World War II that large numbers of African Americans would move to the West Coast. Among the migrating whites, gender was pretty evenly balanced, and the number of families was quite large. A small family headed by young adults was the most common profile.

Many of the people moving westward were not farm folk. At least half had been living in a town or city and doing some kind of blue-collar or, less frequently, white-collar work before unemployment or stories of California opportunities encouraged them to pack the car and hit the road. Most of these migrants headed for the cities of California, where they usually found jobs and a decent standard of living in fairly short order. They were the overlooked half of the ill-named Dust Bowl migration; their urban stories were lost in the concern and fascination that centered on the relocating farm families who had chosen to look for work in the agricultural valleys of California.

John Steinbeck and Dorothea Lange created the most memorable portraits of what some families faced in those areas. Lange toured farm labor camps in the spring of 1936, snapping photographs of ragged children and worried parents living in tents and waiting for work. Some families were completely out of funds and food. Lange's most famous picture, "Migrant Mother," showed a gaunt young widow holding her three daughters, her careworn face suggesting that hope was running out. John Steinbeck wrote a set of newspaper articles that year depicting in similar terms the desperate plight of thousands. Then he sat down to write the book that became, three years later, *The Grapes of Wrath*. His 1939 fictional account of the Joad family, who lose their Oklahoma farm to dust and avaricious bankers and then set out for the California promised land, only to find there even greater challenges and hardships, became an instant best seller and a classic of American fiction, the publishing phenomenon of the decade. When Hollywood followed up with an equally

Destitute pea pickers in California. Mother of seven children, age thirty-two, Nipomo, California. This photograph, taken by Dorothea Lange and titled "Migrant Mother," is among the most famous images of want in the Great Depression. (Library of Congress)

brilliant movie directed by John Ford, the image of the Dust Bowl migration was secure. These works of art—by Steinbeck, Ford, Lange, and others—gave the Joads and their kind a place in American history that has lasted to this day.

Fortunately, the poverty that drew the artists was much less permanent. Even as *The Grapes of Wrath* was flying off bookshelves in 1939, conditions were beginning to improve in rural California, thanks first to federal aid programs and then to the World War II defense boom that pulled many of the migrants out of the fields and raised wages for those remaining. Still, incomes for many former Oklahomans, Arkansans, and Texans would remain low for some time. As late as the 1970s, poverty experts in the San Joaquin Valley talked about "Okies" as a disadvantaged population and could point to poverty and welfare-use rates that exceeded norms for other whites. But the bigger story was the climb up from poverty that most families experienced in the decades after the Depression. Taking advantage of the wide-open job markets for white male workers that characterized the wartime and postwar eras, the Dust Bowl migrants and their children made steady, if unspectacular, progress up the economic ladder.

If the poverty associated with the Dust Bowl migration was transitory, the impact on public policy and on popular understandings of poverty was more lasting. This high-profile episode, with its sympathetic white victims and its powerful storytellers, helped reshape the terrain of poverty-related policymaking in various ways, especially around the issues of interstate migration and farm labor. Poor people crossing state lines would have a clear set of rights in the aftermath of the Dust Bowl migration, and the plight of farmworkers would be more visible even as the Joads left the fields to families with darker skins and different accents.

Until 1941, states felt free to restrict interstate mobility, focusing that power, when they used it, on the poor. To discourage indigents from crossing state lines, many states maintained tough vagrancy laws and required those applying for public assistance to prove many years of residence in the state. California had been especially hostile to poor newcomers. In 1936, the Los Angeles Police Department established a border patrol, dubbed the "Bum Blockade," at major road and rail crossings for the purpose of turning back would-be visitors who lacked obvious means of support. Withdrawn in the face of threatened lawsuits, this border-control effort was followed by a less dramatic but more serious assault on the right of interstate mobility. California's Indigent Act, passed in 1933, made it a crime to bring indigent persons into the state. In 1939, the district attorneys of several of the counties most affected by the Dust Bowl influx began using the law in a very public manner. More than two dozen people were indicted, tried, and convicted. Their crime: helping their relatives move to California from Oklahoma and nearby states. The prosecutions were challenged by the American Civil Liberties Union, which pushed the issue all the way to the U.S. Supreme Court. In 1941, the court issued a landmark decision (*Edwards v. California,* 314 U.S. 160) ruling that states had no right to restrict interstate migration by poor people or any other Americans.

Farm labor systems were not as easily changed, but there too the Dust Bowl migration left a lasting legacy, helping bring to public attention and into the policy arena the unique vulnerabilities of a sector of the labor force that most Americans had previously ignored. Publicity was the major contribution. The plight of white families in the fields and labor camps of California in the late 1930s aroused media attention on an unprecedented scale and forced public officials and urban consumers to contemplate, often for the first time, the systems of labor operating in rural areas. Farm employers had long enjoyed exemption from many of the customs, laws, and labor unions that protected most urban workers. As a result, farm laborers suffered forms of exploitation and at times degrees of poverty that exceeded urban experience.

The attention did facilitate some policy development. The federal government created some modest services for farmworkers during the 1930s: a camp program in California and Arizona run by the Farm Security Administration, a health service, and an emergency relief program. These were dismantled in the 1940s at the insistence of growers, but some of these services did not entirely disappear. County authorities took over the camps and began to provide certain health and education services to the farm labor families. These were insufficient but not completely insignificant. Moreover, states not affected by the Dust Bowl migration also paid more attention to farmworkers in the decades following *The Grapes of Wrath*. However modest the programs, the plight of rural workers could no longer be completely ignored.

In part, that was because the news media had been retrained by the dramatic stories that came out of California in the 1930s. In the decades to come, print journalists and television journalists would return again and again to the subject of farmworker poverty, finding in it a repeated source of compassion and outrage that pretty much followed the media formulas of the Dust Bowl era. That was certainly true of the CBS documentary *Harvest of Shame*, which shocked television viewers in 1960. Narrated by Edward R. Murrow and focusing on migratory farmworkers, who were by then mostly Mexican Americans in the West and African Americans in the East, the program worked with images and sympathies that Dorothea Lange and John Steinbeck had helped to create.

Race has always been central to the story of the Dust Bowl migration. Paul Taylor knew in 1935 when he wrote his first article about the "drought refugees" that their white skins and Anglo-Saxon names could win attention and sympathy that would not so readily attach to the Mexican and Asian farmworkers who normally struggled in the valleys of California. Steinbeck, too, used the paradox, emphasizing in a dozen ways that Americans of their pedigree were not supposed to experience what the Joads experienced.

As the Dust Bowl saga has worked its way into history, race has become still more important. The continuing fascination with this subject over the decades has had as much to do with racial politics as with the events themselves. As poverty became more and more racialized and as struggles over social welfare programs became increasingly contentious, the Dust Bowl migration took on new meanings and new functions. By the 1970s, an aging generation of former migrants and their upwardly mobile offspring were ready to memorialize the experiences of the 1930s, and another set of storytellers were ready to help. A new round of journalism, novels, history books, TV documentaries, and country music songs has been the result, much of it fed by a late-twentieth-century need for stories of poverty, hardship, and eventual triumph in which the victim-heroes are white. These latter-day Dust Bowl accounts have sometimes promoted conservative agendas, as in the collection of songs that Merle Haggard produced in the late 1960s and 1970s celebrating the struggles of his parents and implying that the poverty of their generation was more noble than the poverty of contemporary America. Unwilling to acknowledge kinship with the Mexican Americans who replaced them in the fields or to admit the importance of government assistance in Dust Bowl survival strategies, some former migrants constructed self-histories that added to racial distances. But others among the new storytellers see the meanings differently. In keeping alive the Dust Bowl migration saga, they remind America that poverty has had many faces, that disparaging the victims is senseless and cruel, and that the poor and helpless of one era will hopefully escape that fate in the next.

James N. Gregory

See also: Agricultural and Farm Labor Organizing; *The Grapes of Wrath; Harvest of Shame;* Migrant Labor/Farm Labor; New Deal Farm Policy; Picturing Poverty (I); Rural Poverty; *Survey* and *Survey Graphic;*

Vagrancy Laws/Settlement Laws/Residency Requirements

References and Further Reading

Gregory, James N. 1989. *American Exodus: The Dust Bowl Migration and Okie Culture in California*. New York: Oxford University Press.

LeSeur, Geta J. 2000. *Not All Okies Are White: The Lives of Black Cotton Pickers in Arizona*. Columbia: University of Missouri Press.

Morgan, Dan. 1992. *Rising in the West: The True Story of an "Okie" Family from the Great Depression through the Reagan Years*. New York: Knopf.

Shindo, Charles J. 1997. *Dust Bowl Migrants in the American Imagination*. Lawrence: University Press of Kansas.

Stein, Walter. 1973. *California and the Dust Bowl Migration*. Westport, CT: Greenwood Press.

Steinbeck, John. 1939. *The Grapes of Wrath*. New York: Viking.

Taylor, Paul. 1935. "Again the Covered Wagon." *Survey Graphic* 24, no. 7 (July).

Weber, Devra. 1994. *Dark Sweat, White Gold: California Farm Workers, Cotton, and the New Deal*. Berkeley and Los Angeles: University of California Press.

Earned Income Tax Credit (EITC)

The Earned Income Tax Credit (EITC) is a refundable tax credit for the working poor, enacted by Congress in 1975. Recipients receive a credit against income tax liability and a cash payment if the credit exceeds taxes owed. At the time of its initial passage, legislators viewed the EITC as a work-friendly alternative to conventional public assistance programs—a way to supplement low wages rather than provide more-generous welfare payments. Although Congress attacked welfare "as we know it" in the 1980s and 1990s, the EITC grew in size and scope. But popularity had its price. Although the benefit generally retains bipartisan political support, by the 1990s, some conservatives were turning against it, claiming that it had become a welfare subsidy rather than a tax offset, that it discouraged people from working more, and that it suffered from poor targeting and high costs.

As early as 1970, Congress considered the idea of tax credits for the "working poor," who were generally ineligible for cash welfare or benefits under Aid to Families with Dependent Children (AFDC). In part, this was a response to the declining wage levels and higher tax burdens that workers were beginning to experience, but the subsidy idea was also an alternative to then-popular proposals to expand welfare significantly by providing income guarantees to all low-income people, whether employed or not. Senator Russell Long (D-Louisiana) introduced a "work bonus" to offset regressive Social Security taxes, encourage work effort, and reduce welfare dependency. Congress rejected Long's plan in 1970 and again in 1972, 1973, and 1974. With the economy slipping into recession in late 1974, however, Congress endorsed the tax-credit approach to stimulate work effort among low-income workers. The Tax Reduction Act of 1975 included an "earned income credit" equal to 10 percent of the first $4,000 of earned income. The credit phased out at 10 percent and vanished completely when income levels reached $8,000, making it a relatively modest supplement.

For the next three years, the EITC underwent slight modification. In 1977, however, domestic policy planners in President Jimmy Carter's administration transformed the credit. President Carter's welfare reform initiative proposed tripling the size of the EITC to encourage claimants to choose work over welfare. Members of Congress praised the liberalized EITC as a pro-work, pro-growth, low-cost antipoverty program. Although the president abandoned his welfare reform proposal in 1978, Congress independently enlarged the EITC. By the end of the 1970s, the EITC had become "everybody's favorite program" (Lynn and Whitman 1981, 247).

The EITC survived welfare retrenchment in the early 1980s. The Economic Recovery Tax Act of 1981 removed 400,000 families from the welfare rolls and increased the nation's poverty rate by 2 percentage points (Patterson 1994, 213). But the EITC escaped the budgetary knife. A bipartisan group of liberals and conservatives preserved and enlarged the credit. An expanded EITC appealed to liberals concerned with the working poor and with deteriorating wages and rising income inequality. A larger EITC appealed to conservatives because it reduced their responsibility for the growing disparity between rich and poor, a long-term trend accelerated by President Ronald Reagan's tax and social policy cuts. A liberalized EITC also benefited low- and middle-income families, reinforcing the pervasive "family values" rhetoric. Especially important, it was promoted by both liberals and conservatives as a "nonwelfare" approach to providing income support to the poor—indicating the degree to which liberals as well as conservatives had come to distance themselves from welfare.

In 1986, 1990, and 1993, bipartisan efforts in Congress expanded the EITC by raising the maximum benefit level and phase-out rate (the rate at which benefits fall as income rises), by extending the break-even point (the point at which benefits zero out), and by guaranteeing the credit's integrity by indexing it for inflation. The cumulative effect of the changes between 1986 and 1996 raised EITC expenditures by 1,191 percent (U.S. House of Representatives 1998, 872).

At the same time, these expansions began to draw political attention and controversy to a program once seen as part of the "hidden" (because administered through the tax system rather than as an outright grant) welfare state (Howard 1999). The EITC had grown too big and too fast, critics argued. The benefit levels were profligate, the phase-out rate created implicit work disincentives, and the break-even point amounted to welfare for the middle class. Dissatisfaction with the EITC crested in the mid-1990s when the IRS reported that the program suffered from unusually high error rates: Of EITC benefits, 40 percent went to ineligible taxpayers. Although later studies showed these error rates to be exaggerated, and due in part to honest mistakes, critics charged that the EITC subsidized defrauders and cheats.

Supporters of the EITC leapt to its defense. Congress had expanded the credit to offset increased payroll taxes, real decreases in the minimum wage, and higher excise taxes. Moreover, the EITC had grown in response to bipartisan efforts. Presidents Ronald Reagan and George H. W. Bush initiated early expansions, while President Bill Clinton considered a larger EITC the cornerstone of his pledge to "make work pay." By 1996, the EITC was all that kept millions of individuals out of poverty. The 1996 welfare reform act pushed welfare claimants toward work, and the EITC eased the transition.

In response to these controversies, supporters and administrators of the EITC addressed its high error rates. The Treasury Department simplified the procedures for EITC claimants and made it easier for the IRS to verify eligibility for EITC. Congress authorized the IRS to levy penalties for EITC abuse and provided special appropriations for EITC compliance. By 1997, the IRS reported that error rates had fallen dramatically.

In addition, researchers revealed that the EITC's work disincentives were less severe than critics charged. Empirical studies relying on tax-return microdata found that the EITC produced unambiguous incentives for single workers to participate in the labor force and statistically significant increases in aggregate labor force participation.

Indeed, the prevailing evidence suggests that the EITC represents one of the U.S. welfare state's most effective weapons against poverty. Although not designed to get at the underlying roots of such problems as deteriorating wages for low-income workers, higher taxes for the working poor, and a widening divide between rich and poor, it counteracts the economic effects of these problems. In 1997, the Council of Economic Advisors reported that the EITC had lifted 4.3 million persons out of poverty, including 2.2 million children under eighteen, more than any other government program (Council of Economic Advisors 1999, 114). The EITC has proven so effective at the federal level that more than a dozen states have enacted low-income tax credits.

Dennis J. Ventry Jr.

See also: Tax Policy; Welfare Policy/Welfare Reform; "Working Poor"

References and Further Reading

Council of Economic Advisors. 1999. *Economic Report of the President*. Washington, DC: GPO.

Howard, Christopher. 1999. *The Hidden Welfare State*. Princeton: Princeton University Press.

Lynn, Laurence E., Jr., and David deF. Whitman. 1981. *The President as Policymaker: Jimmy Carter and Welfare Reform*. Philadelphia: Temple University Press.

Meyer, Bruce, and Douglas Holtz-Eakin, eds. 2002. *Making Work Pay*. New York: Russell Sage Foundation.

Patterson, James. 1994. *America's Struggle against Poverty: 1900–1994*. Cambridge, MA: Harvard University Press.

U.S. House of Representatives. Committee on Ways and Means. 1998. *1998 Green Book*. Washington, DC: GPO.

Ventry, Dennis J., Jr. 2000. "The Collision of Tax and Welfare Politics: The Political History of the Earned Income Tax Credit." *National Tax Journal* 53, no. 4, part 2 (December): 983–1026.

Economic Depression

Economic depressions are severe downturns in economic activity characterized by extensive unemployment and business failures. They have punctuated the overall trend of economic growth in the United States and are generally caused by weaknesses in the financial sector, adverse international events, economic restructuring, and governmental policy mistakes. The Great Depression (1929–1940) dwarfs all other American depressions, including important depressions in the 1850s, 1870s, and 1890s, the post–World War I depression, and the deep recession of the early 1980s. Depressions have triggered important political realignments and policy responses, especially the New Deal of the 1930s. Economic depressions exacerbate poverty, but the overall trend of economic growth throughout U.S. history means that the level of absolute poverty during later depressions was generally substantially *lower* than the level of poverty during good economic times from earlier periods.

In a recession, real (that is, inflation-adjusted) gross domestic product (GDP) falls in consecutive quarters. A depression is a *severe* recession, but there is no precise line separating the two. The depth of a depression is usually measured by the decline in real GDP or by the level to which the unemployment rate rises. Unfortunately, both statistics become harder to estimate the further one goes back in American history.

In the colonial and early national periods, the economy was dominated by agriculture. In 1800, about 89 percent of the labor force was either self-employed farmers or slaves. Therefore, the impact of economic downturns was not to generate massive unemployment but to cause defaults on loans, business failures, and falling incomes and prices. By 1850, the proportion of self-employed farmers and slaves had declined to 70 percent and the rising share of wage workers made for higher unemployment rates during recessions and depressions. By 1900, only 20 percent of the population were self-employed farmers, and the share of workers in the manufacturing, mining, and construction sectors—where demand can be very cyclical—had risen to 30 percent. The percentage of workers in these sectors peaked at 36 percent in 1950 and fell to 22 percent by 1990. Thus, some would argue that the potential for depressions in the U.S. economy rose throughout the nineteenth century and peaked in the first half of the twentieth century, before diminishing with the shift toward service-sector employment.

Economic downturns during the colonial era were often tied to conditions in Britain and occurred consistently at the ends of wars. The downturn in Britain at the end of the French and Indian War pushed it to tighten its control of the colonial American economy, which helped trigger the Revolutionary War. The British naval blockade and occupation of ports, especially from 1778 to 1780, caused considerable economic distress during the Revolution. The end of the Revolution brought a flood of imports, restrictions on exports and shipping, and an overall restructuring of ties with Britain, which triggered widespread bankruptcies among merchants and manufacturers and a decline of prices by about 25 percent. The economic crisis was deepened by tax increases to pay off state war debts and by a weak central government with little capacity to restore economic stability and probably helped precipitate the adoption of the Constitution. Unfortunately, quantitative measures of overall economic pain during these downturns are virtually nonexistent.

The rapid expansion of the U.S. economy in the first half of the 1800s was punctuated by a series of economic depressions. The first occurred in 1808 and was due to President Thomas Jefferson's trade embargo; national income declined by about 9 percent, and the northern ports suffered considerable unemployment. Agricultural workers' standards of living fell as the price of exported products (mainly staple crops) dropped by about one-quarter, while the price of imports (mostly manufactured goods) rose by roughly one-third. Trade disruption before and during the War of 1812 also brought localized depressed conditions.

Depression struck again from 1819 to 1821, fueled by a 50 percent drop in the price of cotton and a sharp contraction of the money supply and credit. Large-scale urban unemployment emerged for the first time in U.S. history, and the price of land collapsed, especially in the South. Although manufacturing employment may have fallen by two-thirds, national unemployment probably did not exceed 4 percent. Many states reacted by enacting laws relieving debtors, and the crisis led to demands for democratization of state constitutions and hostility toward banks and "privileged" corporations.

The financial Panic of 1837 was probably set in motion by a contraction of the money supply and credit due to Bank of England policies, although some argue that the land and fiscal policies of President Andrew Jackson's administration helped drain gold from eastern banks, prompting bank suspensions. The panic brought a rapid decline in prices and a widespread drop in real wages—which fell by 15 to 20 percent for artisans in the Midwest and South between the two crisis periods of 1831–1835 and 1836–1840—but it does not seem to have caused widespread unemployment. A brief recovery was followed by another crisis beginning in the summer of 1839 and lasting until 1843. This depression is usually linked to a borrowing binge by frontier states to fund transportation improvements, in anticipation of future taxes and revenues. When these states and their bankers overextended themselves, they were forced to cease work on their transportation projects; property values collapsed, there were runs on banks in the frontier states, and ultimately nine states, mostly southern and western, defaulted on their debts. Overall, prices fell over 35 percent, but there was not massive unemployment.

Robert Fogel (1989) argues that the 1850s brought a "hidden" depression that transformed American politics and the economy. The depression was not characterized by extraordinarily high unemployment rates—which probably peaked at 6 to 8 percent during the recession of 1857. Instead, the depression's impact was concentrated on native-born craftsmen, tradesmen, and petty merchants in the North, who made up nearly one-sixth of the labor force. The root cause of this "hidden" depression was the period's exceptionally high immigration rate, with 14 immigrants reaching the United States for every

1,000 persons in the U.S. population each year from 1847 to 1854. This 10 percent increase in the population flooded especially into northeastern cities, glutting labor markets, pushing down wages, displacing workers, increasing rents, and triggering epidemics. Fogel estimates that real wages declined by 25 to 50 percent, although other sources conclude that the declines were smaller—perhaps 20 percent among common laborers, for example. The political response included nativism and demands for land reform (for example, free homesteads), free primary education, and tariff protection, a policy package that was combined with abolition to fuel the rise of the Republican Party and hence may have been a catalyst for the Civil War.

Economic conditions were very weak during the Civil War, with the economy contracting for three consecutive years from 1861 to 1863 and real wages of laborers falling over 20 percent, but there were no widespread business failures or unemployment.

Average incomes doubled in the second half of the 1800s, but recurrent economic depression plagued the economy. The economic crisis that began in 1873 was probably the second-worst of the nineteenth century (after the depression of the 1890s). One of Wall Street's largest firms, Jay Cooke and Company, overextended itself attempting to finance a second transcontinental railroad, the Northern Pacific. With the railroad only partly completed, the European market for American railroad bonds dried up after the Vienna stock market crashed. Cooke's subsequent failure set off an economic crisis in the United States, as investors' optimism turned to pessimism. Railroad construction, which had reached 7,000 miles per year, fell below 2,000 miles in 1875, and about one-fifth of the track mileage in the country was owned by companies in bankruptcy. Wage cutting by railroads triggered an unprecedented round of strikes and violence in 1877 in the Middle Atlantic states and the Midwest. Strong economic growth did not return until 1879; public relief rolls surged, and the unemployment rate probably topped 10 percent for the first time in the country's history. Another steep recession beginning in 1884 brought a two-year economic dip, with industrial output falling 16 percent and the unemployment rate climbing to roughly 6 to 7.5 percent.

The depression of the 1890s is considered the second-worst in the nation's history. The economy shrank by about 7 percent in 1893, shrank again in 1894, rebounded in 1895, and contracted again in 1896. Christina Romer (1986) estimates that unemployment rose to 8 percent in 1893, hit 12 percent in 1894, and remained at 11 or 12 percent for five long years, until 1898. (Romer's figures are generally preferred to earlier estimates suggesting an unemployment peak of 18 percent in 1894.)

This depression's origin follows the pattern of many other economic downturns. It began with a drop-off in the British economy, a major source of investment capital in the United States. The American economy began to shrink early in 1893, and then in May a "panic" swept financial centers after European creditors redeemed American securities for gold; critics of powerful financial interests said these investors were wary about ongoing congressional debates about monetary policy and feared that the U.S. commitment to the gold standard was in jeopardy. The gold drain forced eastern banks to call loans, and short-term interest rates soared, causing many businesses to fail and others to suspend investments. The debate about silver versus gold continued at least until William McKinley defeated William Jennings Bryan in the 1896 presidential election. Farmers were especially hard-hit by the depression, as wholesale farm prices fell by over 20 percent from 1893 to 1896. Part of their response to the depression was populism, which advocated an inflationary expansion of the money supply through the increased coinage of silver and increased governmental regulation of railroads and other big businesses. Local governments expanded welfare relief and established public works projects. However, when Jacob Coxey and his "army" of unemployed men marched from Ohio to Washington, D.C., in 1894, agitating for federal work relief, they (and other similar groups) were turned away empty-handed. A wave of strikes, especially the American Railway Union's strike against the Pullman Company, precipitated considerable violence in 1894, leading to aggressive federal intervention against labor organizing and, in the case of the Pullman strike, to suppression by federal troops. A final reaction was the enactment of a federal income tax law in 1894, but the U.S. Supreme Court declared it unconstitutional.

During the first three decades of the twentieth century, rapid technological advances, an unprecedented rise in education levels, and an *eightfold* increase in average income levels ended absolute poverty for almost all Americans. But the economy faced its worst-ever depression, before largely escaping this menace after 1940. The century's first sharp recession came in 1907–1908, when unemployment reached 6 to 8 percent. Several months *after* the recession began, a short panic gripped Wall Street amid a run on New York's trust banks. A syndicate led by J. P. Morgan squelched the run, but the primary impact of this episode was the development of a political consensus that the banking system was unstable and in need of a central bank, which was established in 1913 as the Federal Reserve System ("the Fed"). The onset of World War I brought on a recession, with unemployment rates reaching 7 or 8 percent in 1915, and the war's end was followed by a sharp recession that is sometimes labeled a depression. The demobilization from the war effort, a substantial drop in government spending, requisite economic restructuring, and the Fed's tight money policy brought a rapid deflation. Wholesale prices fell a startling 46 percent, and unemployment reached 9 to 12 percent in 1921. The swift recovery from this intense contraction may have led policymakers initially to underestimate the seriousness of the Great Depression eight years later (Romer 1986; Fearon 1987).

The Great Depression began in 1929, hit bottom in 1933, and lasted throughout much of the 1930s. Its worldwide scope, its magnitude, and its duration set it apart from economic crises before and since. The value of economic output (real GDP) in the United States fell by 27 percent from 1929 to 1933. Simultaneously, prices fell by about one-quarter. The unemployment rate, which had averaged 5 percent in the 1920s, soared from 3 percent in 1929 to 25 percent (36 percent of nonfarm workers) in 1933 and averaged 14 percent for the decade of the 1930s. Industrial output fell substantially in many of the world's economically developed nations, with the United States taking the hardest hit (a drop of 45 percent), followed by Germany (41 percent) and Canada (32 percent) (Fearon 1987).

The Great Depression's causes are very complex and have been the subject of intense debate among economic historians. Most explanations point to weaknesses in credit markets—both internationally and within the United States—that sapped consumer spending and killed investment.

Stock prices surged upward from 1926 to September 1929, then lost 36 percent of their value in the next year and 84 percent of their value before hitting bottom in June 1932. Many link the run-up in stock prices to a speculative frenzy encouraged by financial manipulation and overextended financing and argue that this played a key role in the market's subsequent fall. The collapse destroyed much wealth, and this helped cut consumer spending somewhat, but most historians argue that the stock market mostly reflected investors' outlooks rather than driving the economy.

What caused the unusually severe contraction of consumer spending in 1930 that marked the beginning of the Great Depression? One plausible answer is that the proportion of household income going to pay off household debt had doubled during the 1920s, much of that debt being installment debt tied to the booming automobile market, with large down payments and short contracts. Missed installment payments could result in repossession and the forfeiture of the down payment and the payments already made. Rather than defaulting on these loans when the recession brought declining incomes and uncertainty, buyers responded by cutting back other spending, with overall real consumption expenditures falling by over 6 percent from 1929 to 1930. Unfortunately, this had a multiplier effect, forcing firms to reduce output and to lay off additional workers. The drop in demand also caused a fall in prices, and this deflation further handcuffed the economy by making it harder for businesses to earn a profit and by increasing the real value of business and household debts.

The collapse in spending was compounded by weaknesses in the banking system, which converted a nasty recession into the Great Depression. Most banks in the United States had only a single branch, and their loans were tied almost completely to the local economy. When low prices meant that many farmers could not repay their loans, this caused a wave of bank failures in the South in late 1930. Along with the failure of a large New York City bank, these failures began to make depositors leery of keeping their funds in banks. Bank failures climbed during 1931, cresting after Britain left the gold standard in September. The Federal Reserve Bank responded to Britain's move by trying to assure international investors that the United States would not abandon gold. It *increased* interest rates, increasing the dollar's attractiveness for international investors but undercutting troubled banks seeking to borrow funds rather than sell their assets in response to their depositors' withdrawals. Finally, the entire banking system froze up in early 1933. A bank run prompted Michigan's governor to declare a statewide bank "holiday" in February 1933. Depositors rushed to banks in nearby states to withdraw needed funds, precipitating mandatory shutdowns in neighboring states. After all the dominoes fell, most of the banks in the nation were closed. The loss of confidence in the banking system was crucial because it caused depositors to withdraw their funds, leaving banks with few resources to lend. Reduced lending resulted in reduced spending. Finally, the withdrawals caused the overall money supply to shrink, which generated more deflation and its negative consequences.

President Herbert Hoover tried vigorously to restore the economy to health. He signed the Smoot-Hawley Tariff in June 1930, which raised taxes on imports. It is not clear whether this helped the economy much, and in response, America's largest trading partner, Canada, retaliated by increasing its tariffs on U.S. exports. Another response was the establishment of the Reconstruction Finance Corporation to lend money to banks and other businesses, but a congressional requirement that the names of these borrowers be published derailed the program's effectiveness, since it advertised to depositors that their banks were in weak shape. The larger response to the Great Depression came with the election of 1932. President Franklin D. Roosevelt and the Democratic Party adopted a raft of new programs, most of which substantially increased the role of the federal government in the economy. Among these responses were government building projects, income supports to farmers, bank deposit insurance, laws promoting unions and collective bargaining, the creation of an agency overseeing the stock market, and the establishment of the Social Security system, unemployment insurance, and a minimum wage.

Unfortunately, because the damage from the Depression (especially in the banking system) was so acute and because some of the new policies were severely flawed (especially the National Recovery Act, which encouraged industries to form cartels and *reduce* output) and may have discouraged wary investors, the recovery from the Depression was slow and painful, with a second recession hitting in 1937 and the unemployment rate remaining at or above 10 percent until the end of the decade.

World War II effectively ended the Great Depression by putting the nation back to work. Widespread fears that the nation would return to depression after the war prompted the federal government to adopt the Employment Act of 1946 (originally named the Full Employment Act, but retitled when conservative lawmakers grew wary of the implied commitment), which committed the government to do something to prevent depression, recessions, and other macroeconomic malfunctions. Fortunately, perhaps because of increased stability within the economy itself or perhaps due to government policies (including such automatic stabilizers as unemployment insurance and proactive economic management by the Fed), the United States has avoided depression since the 1930s.

The closest the nation came was a series of recessions beginning in October 1973, when Arab exporters imposed an oil embargo on the United States, the price of oil rose by 150 percent, and the unemployment rate climbed to 8.5 percent in 1975. This was followed by a second "energy crisis" due to the Iranian revolution and the Iran-Iraq War, which caused another doubling of oil prices between 1979 and 1980. These oil shocks caused a significant restructuring of the economy, since many industrial practices relied on cheap energy. Simultaneously, industry was battered by increased foreign competition, especially from Japan. The crisis reached its worst point after the Fed purposely reduced money supply growth in 1981 in an ultimately successful attempt to squeeze inflation, which had reached 13.5 percent per year, out of the economy. The result was an unemployment rate that averaged a bit below 10 percent in 1982 and 1983 (U.S. Bureau of Labor Statistics). Depression-like conditions gripped certain portions of the country, especially the industrial "Rust Belt," from Pennsylvania to Wisconsin, which was the home of much heavy industry, including auto and steel manufacturing. Policy responses to these downturns included some protectionist trade measures (as for autos), increased efforts to stabilize the world's oil supply, and a move toward deregulating the economy, a move motivated by evidence that overregulation had encouraged economic weaknesses and decreased the flexibility of the economy.

Robert Whaples

See also: Coxey's Army; Great Depression and New Deal; Unemployment

References and Further Reading

Fearon, Peter. 1987. *War, Prosperity, and Depression: The U.S. Economy, 1917–1945*. Lawrence: University Press of Kansas.

Fogel, Robert. 1989. *Without Consent of Contract: The Rise and Fall of American Slavery*. New York: Norton.

Glasner, David, ed. 1997. *Business Cycles and Depressions: An Encyclopedia*. New York: Garland Publishing.

Hall, Thomas E., and J. David Ferguson. 1998. *The Great Depression: An International Disaster of Perverse Economic Policies*. Ann Arbor: University of Michigan Press.

Higgs, Robert. 1987. *Crisis and Leviathan: Critical Episodes in the Growth of American Government*. New York: Oxford University Press.

Huston, James L. 1987. *The Panic of 1857 and the Coming of the Civil War*. Baton Rouge: Louisiana State University Press.

Lebergott, Stanley. 1964. *Manpower in Economic Growth: The American Record since 1800*. New York: McGraw-Hill.

Romer, Christina. 1986. "Spurious Volatility in Historical Unemployment Data." *Journal of Political Economy* 94, no. 1: 1–37.

Steeples, David, and David Whitten. 1998. *Democracy in Desperation: The Depression of 1893*. Westport, CT: Greenwood Press.

U.S. Bureau of Labor Statistics. Web site. http://www.bls.gov/.

Economic Justice for All (EJA), *U.S. Catholic Bishops*

Economic Justice for All (EJA), published by the U.S. Catholic Bishops in 1986, is a significant, broadly consultative, American contribution to a long tradition of Catholic concern for the poor and vulnerable, focused on those marginalized or mistreated by modern economic systems. Addressed simultaneously to U.S. Catholics and all justice-seeking citizens, the five-chapter "letter" draws on and updates economic-ethical teaching initiated by Pope Leo XIII's groundbreaking 1891 *On the Condition of Labor (Rerum Novarum)*. Centering on communally situated political *and* economic rights and responsibilities issuing from the God-given dignity of every human being, *EJA* argues that a properly functioning, just economy offers all members access to material well-being through dignified participation and proposes socio-moral principles and practical policy directions toward that end.

EJA's drafters organized extensive hearings, feedback, and listening sessions that gathered input from experts, working persons, and poor people themselves. The resulting document employs personalist criteria for evaluating any economic arrangement or practice: What does it do *for* and *to* people, and *how are people empowered to participate in it?* (U.S. Catholic Bishops 1996, ch. 1, para. 1). Its analysis is permeated by an "option for the poor," which makes the litmus test for a just economy the degree to which its most vulnerable members are enabled to attain a decent livelihood (ch. 2, paras. 51–52, 86–87, 123). Amid unprecedented abundance, poverty is a "scandal" (Introduction, para. 16) demanding alleviation.

Chapter 2's religiously grounded economic-ethical framework articulates a tri-dimensional goal of "basic" economic justice. *Commutative justice* requires "fairness in agreements and exchanges between individuals and private groups" such as wage labor contracts and employer-employee relations; *distributive justice* evaluates society's allocation of income, wealth, and power "in light of its effects on persons whose basic material needs are unmet"; *social justice* affirms persons' duty to be active, contributing participants in society, and institutions' duty to make such participation possible (paras. 69–72). Basic justice entails "a floor of material well-being on which all can stand" pursuant to "minimal levels of communal participation for all," for to be treated or abandoned as if one is a nonmember of the human race is "the ultimate injustice" (para. 77). Since work is crucial to economic participation and livelihood, high unemployment and job discrimination are morally intolerable. Materially advantaged citizens have special obligations to undertake individual initiative, but even more, they are obligated to carry out collective action to examine and revise "institutional relations and patterns that distribute power and wealth inequitably."

Chapter 3 treats selected economic policy issues: unemployment, poverty, food and agriculture, the U.S. economy, and developing nations. Here, *EJA* proposes reforms that drew criticism for their "liberal, New Deal" slant. With their primary expertise being spiritual and moral, the bishops conceded that their policy proposals are open to debate, but they challenged disputants to offer equally concrete alternatives consonant with the *nonnegotiable* economic justice principles previously outlined. The final two chapters consider intrachurch economic practices and spiritual resources for Christian justice seekers and call for a "bold new American experiment" wherein varied social actors collaborate in a "partnership for the common good" dedicated to extending substantive economic rights to every member of the human community.

Christine Firer Hinze

See also: Catholic Church; Catholic Worker Movement; Living-Wage Campaigns

References and Further Reading

O'Brien, David, and Thomas A. Shannon, eds. 1996. *Catholic Social Thought: The Documentary Heritage*. Maryknoll, NY: Orbis Books.

U.S. Catholic Bishops. 1996. *Economic Justice for All*. 10th anniversary ed. Washington, DC: NCCB/USCC Publications.

Economic Report of 1964, *Council of Economic Advisors*

The Council of Economic Advisors (CEA) *Economic Report of 1964* is a key document in the history of poverty in the United States, and indeed, in the history of twentieth-century liberalism. For the first time in the history of the world's most prosperous society, the administration's chief economists were proclaiming that eliminating poverty was not only within reach but was to be a goal of the nation's economic policy. The approach outlined in the report marked the culmination of a sequence of broader political, intellectual, and institutional developments that had led to President Lyndon B. Johnson's declaration in January 1964 of a War on Poverty and that put his economic advisers in the forefront of planning.

The more immediate context was the CEA-led effort, starting early in the administration of John F. Kennedy and continuing through Lyndon Johnson's succession to the presidency after Kennedy's assassination in late November 1963, to mobilize the administration behind a high-growth, full-employment economic policy through a combination of growth-stimulating tax cuts and expanded social welfare spending. As part of this agenda, the CEA in 1963 began to lobby within the administration for a major attack on poverty as a top policy priority—and a theme for the upcoming presidential campaign. The longer-range context was the emergence of what was popularly known as the "new economics" in the decades following World War II, based on the theories of British economist John Maynard Keynes—who proposed a more activist role for government fiscal policy (a tax-and-spend policy) in order to manage the economy and promote full employment—as well as on more recent developments that emphasized the importance of "human capital" investments to enable individuals to take advantage of the opportunities provided by economic growth. The Kennedy and Johnson administration economists fully embraced these ideas and made the CEA the vehicle for their growing influence on federal policymaking.

Their 1964 report, written in the immediate aftermath of President Kennedy's assassination and in response to President Johnson's decision to escalate their proposed "attack" on poverty into a full-scale "war," reflects the core ideas of the new economics, proposing economic growth and full employment as the chief weapons against poverty, coupled with expanded investments in education and training, antidiscrimination measures to ensure access to labor markets and related opportunities, and improvements in New Deal–era social welfare programs to protect those outside the labor force from the risk of poverty. It also reflects the then-current thinking that poor people in America—by most measures a large and varied group representing at least one-quarter of the population—were an "other" America, living in a "world apart," rather than an integral part of the economy of prosperity. Above all, it reflects the tremendous optimism that characterized liberal economics and liberalism more generally in the mid-1960s, and nowhere more clearly than in the report's underlying convictions that the rational science of economics had uncovered the keys to ongoing economic growth and that ending poverty could be achieved without substantial, politically controversial redistributions of resources and power.

The following excerpt is taken from chapter 2, "The Problem of Poverty in America."

Alice O'Connor

See also: Economic Theories; Economic/Fiscal Policy; Labor Markets; Liberalism; War on Poverty

In his message on the State of the Union, President Johnson declared all-out War on Poverty in America. This chapter is designed to provide some understanding of the enemy and to outline the main features of a strategy of attack.

Eliminating Poverty—a National Goal

There will always be some Americans who are better off than others. But it need not follow that "the poor are always with us." In the United States today we can see on the horizon a society of abundance, free of much of the misery and degradation that have been the age-old fate of man. Steadily rising productivity, together with an improving network of private and social insurance and assistance, has been eroding mass poverty in America. But the process is far too slow. It is high time to redouble and to concentrate our efforts to eliminate poverty.

Poverty is costly not only to the poor but to the whole society. Its ugly by-products include ignorance, disease, delinquency, crime, irresponsibility, immorality, indifference. None of these social evils and hazards will, of course, wholly disappear with the elimination of poverty. But their severity will be markedly reduced. Poverty is no purely private or local concern. It is a social and national problem. . . .

The poor inhabit a world scarcely recognizable, and rarely recognized, by the majority of their fellow Americans. It is a world apart, whose inhabitants are isolated from the mainstream of American life and alienated from its values. It is a world where Americans are literally concerned with day-to-day survival—a roof over their heads, where the next meal is coming from. It is a world where minor illness is a major tragedy, where pride and privacy must be sacrificed to get help, where honesty can become a luxury and ambition a myth. Worst of all, the poverty of the fathers is visited upon the children. . . .

Although poverty remains a bitter reality for too many Americans, its incidence has been steadily shrinking. The fruits of general economic growth have been widely shared; individuals and families have responded to incentives and opportunities for improvement; government and private programs have raised the educational attainments, housing standards, health, and productivity of the population; private and social insurance has increasingly protected families against loss of earnings due to death, disability, illness, old age, and unemployment. Future headway against poverty will likewise require attacks on many fronts: the active promotion of a full-employment, rapid-growth economy; a continuing assault on discrimination; and a wide range of other measures to strike at specific roots of low income. As in the past, progress will require the combined efforts of all levels of government and of private individuals and groups.

All Americans will benefit from this progress. Our Nation's most precious resource is its people. We pay twice for poverty: once in the production lost in wasted human potential, again in the resources diverted to coping with poverty's social by-products. Humanity compels our action, but it is sound economics as well.

Source: Council of Economic Advisors, *Economic Report of 1964* (Washington, DC: GPO, 1964), 55–56.

Economic Theories

Introduction

Poverty and social policy have always been topics of concern in economics. Beginning with Adam Smith's classic work *The Wealth of Nations*, economists have worked to define, measure, explain, and prescribe cures for poverty. There are a wide range of economic theories of poverty and corresponding social policies. They share the notion that poverty is an economic condition in which one cannot meet basic needs. However, what constitutes "need" varies widely across economic theories, as do ideas about the way the economy works.

Generally, economic theories argue that the main cause of poverty is lack of income-sustaining employment, of adequate wages, and/or of compensation for work, such as caregiving and child rearing, that is socially vital but not formally recognized as "work" worthy of compensation. As such, almost all economic theories of poverty and social policy focus on three related but separate areas of economic analysis. The first analyzes labor markets and with them wage and employment levels. The second area examines economic growth and development to determine macroeconomic levels of employment and income-generating potential. The third area looks at income distribution and inequality to help assess relative poverty and to better focus on certain groups that are especially vulnerable to poverty.

How economists understand poverty dictates their prescriptions to cure it. Since economists seem to carry disproportionate weight in policy discussions, the economic theories that policymakers adhere to often carry disproportionate weight in how poverty is understood and addressed.

We delineate our discussion of economic theories of poverty historically. We focus first on the "grand" theories developed before World War II. We then turn to more modern theories, spawned initially by the expansion in the number of independent nation-states in the 1950s and the accompanying development concerns, and subsequently, in the 1960s, by the War on Poverty in the United States.

Economic Theories before the 1940s

Prior to the 1940s, economic theories of poverty initially focused on production, or "supply," as the engine of growth and economic well-being and gradually came to incorporate the role of "demand," or consumption, in affecting the status of workers and the general level of macroeconomic market activity. If the manufacturing class did not produce enough to hire workers or if workers were paid wages below subsistence levels, then poverty would result. Early writings (1776–1870s) tended to be most concerned with the development of a laboring class and the difficulties posed by newly developing capitalist production. Later writings (1880s–1930s) focused more on how workers were integrated into already-established labor markets in rapidly industrializing economies.

Classical Political Economy

Classical political economists writing in the late eighteenth and early nineteenth centuries (Adam Smith, David Ricardo, and Thomas Malthus) argued that, provided there was ample production, workers as a group would receive a wage share that was sufficient to cover a basic standard of living. In the absence of enough production, poverty would result. Smith in particular is well known for his theory that individuals pursuing their own self-interest and the "invisible hand" of the market would coordinate production and generate adequate wages. Still, he and other classical political economists recognized that economic growth and income distribution involved exchanges among large groups (or classes)—such as workers, landlords, and manufacturers—and that wage levels were grounded in custom as well as in economic "laws" and were largely based on subsistence levels.

For classical political economists, poverty in the form of insufficient wages for the laboring classes would result if nation-states impeded trade or if population growth pushed agricultural production to use increasingly marginal land. The resulting insufficient food production would benefit landowners by pushing the rents they receive up while putting a squeeze on workers' wages and manufacturers' profits. Although Ricardo promoted free trade and restrictions on landlords as way to stave off poverty, Malthus argued strongly for population control through moral restraint, convinced that agricultural production would never increase as fast as the population and that widespread deprivation would result. Reflecting the influence of this gloomy Malthusian outlook, economics would henceforth be known as the "dismal science."

Marxist Theory

Karl Marx also saw society as being drawn into distinct and opposing classes. Writing in the middle to late 1800s, Marx argued that capitalism is driven by "exploitation" of the working class by the profit-seeking property-owning class (capitalists). Exploitation occurs because workers produce the entire product in society yet are only paid for a portion of it. The rest—surplus—goes to capitalists by virtue of their ownership of the equipment and materials used in production as well as by virtue of their control over the production process itself. Although workers as a class are typically paid their "value" (a historically determined subsistence standard of living), poverty is still endemic in Marx's capitalism. Indeed, unemployment (and with it, poverty for some) is an important self-regulating function in capitalist production. At full employment, workers' strength allows them to increase wages at the expense of profits. Capitalists respond by firing workers, creating a "reserve army of labor." These "armies" consist of the workers available for employment but not currently employed, who will be willing to take lower wages and worse working conditions than the currently employed, driving down wages and boosting profits. Over time, Marx predicted an immiseration of the working class by two distinct means. First, capitalists, in their drive to produce more profits, would draw previously untapped workers into the labor force (immigrants, women, workers in overseas production) and pay them less than the currently employed labor force, driving wages down further and further. Second, Marx argued that profit rates would fall over time as capitalists substitute capital for labor. This substitution leaves more and more workers unemployed. For Marx, nothing short of changing the mode of production (capitalism) and the rules of ownership (private property) to achieve a more egalitarian system would alleviate poverty.

Neoclassical/Marginal Productivity Theory

In the late 1880s, Leon Walras in France, Carl Menger in Austria, and W. S. Jevons in England simultaneously generated the so-called marginalist school in economics, the precursor to contemporary neoclassical economics. Unlike previous economic analyses, this school of thought focused on the behavior of individual firms, consumers, and workers. Based on a utility theory of value (which holds that the price of a good or service will be determined by how useful people find it), this new school of thought used abstract reasoning and calculus to develop equilibrium models of the economy. Equilibrium is achieved when the amount producers can supply at a given price exactly equals the amount consumers want to buy. Importantly, the signals that markets send to consumers and producers when not in equilibrium push the prices in each market and the entire economy to equilibrium conditions. Thus, the market, according to this theory, is self-regulating and requires no outside intervention. This includes the labor market, which implies that as long as wages can fluctuate freely, there should be no unemployment. If workers are unwilling to accept prevailing market wages, they will not be employed and will receive no wages, making poverty, in effect, a condition of their own choosing.

The marginal productivity theory of wages was first articulated by American economist John Bates Clark in his 1898 book *The Distribution of Wealth: A Theory of Wages, Interest, and Profits*. Rather than seeing profit as surplus (what is left over after paying rent, wages, and materials) in an inherently class-conflicted production process, Clark argued that profits, wages, and interest are fair payments based on each economic factor's contribution to production. Workers, like all "inputs" to production, are paid an amount equal to their marginal productivity—in this case, how much the last worker employed adds to the value of goods produced. Workers get what they are "worth," and as long as the labor market works in an unimpeded fashion, there should be no unemployment. Poverty is unlikely if workers are willing to work as many hours as necessary to achieve self-sufficiency.

Historical/Institutionalist Theories

Noting the inadequacy of neoclassical laissez-faire economics to explain the vast disparities of income and the concentrations of wealth in late-nineteenth-century capitalism, institutionalist, or "social," economists developed a different understanding of the economy, based on the idea that markets are fundamentally social and political institutions and need to be studied as such. Associated with the historical school in Germany, this group of political economists became well established in U.S. academic circles and government bureaus during the Progressive Era. Thorstein Veblen and John R. Commons were among the best-known proponents of this approach. Unlike previous schools of economic thought, this group included women, most notably Edith Abbott, the University of Chicago–trained economist who conducted pioneering statistical studies of female industrial workers and played a prominent role in "maternalist" and child welfare movements. Further, the leading African American social scientist W. E. B. Du Bois was also trained in German historical methods, an approach he used to understand race relations in the United States.

The rise of large-scale industrial capitalism brought the realities of industrial production—the concentration of the population into urban areas, wage work, the sweatshop—into everyday life and helped spur the movement for a more activist, regulatory state. This was the context within which institutionalist scholars launched major investigations of workplace and labor conditions. Armed by such investigations, they argued that economic outcomes are not determined by scientific models but, rather, are shaped by custom, law, institutions, and powerful coordinated actors. Government policy could be used to reduce poverty and other harmful impacts of the rapid economic changes wrought by industrial capitalism, but the development of such policy required proper knowledge of the problem and empirical documentation. Institutionalists also distinguished among different groups, arguing that they often faced different economic conditions and opportunities for employment opportunities. Of particular concern were immigrant, Black, and women workers. In the institutionalist school, poverty was not seen as a function only of the conditions of the labor market; rather, it was seen as also being shaped by the ways tradition and prejudice (including prevailing ideas about people of color, immigrants, and women) prevented workers from participating in certain industries and occupations.

Keynesian Economic Theory

Writing in the mid-1930s, during the most extensive worldwide economic downturn since the inception of capitalism, John Maynard Keynes rejected his own training and practice in marginalist equilibrium analysis. In its place, he argued that capitalist economies were not self-equilibrating. Insufficient demand for goods and services that had already been produced would result in unemployment. Unemployment would further reduce aggregate demand, making matters worse. With unemployment comes poverty and social unrest. Keynes argued that uncertainty about the future and the proclivity toward speculation among investors meant that they could not be relied upon to correct macroeconomic instability and unemployment. Consumers, lacking income due to high levels of unemployment, were not equipped to provide relief either. Rather, Keynes argued that government action—purchasing goods and services or reducing taxes so consumers could purchase more—would ultimately bring the economy back to acceptable levels of unemployment. Economic growth and sufficient demand would reduce unemployment and poverty, but it was up to government and monetary authorities to manage growth, employment, and income levels through policy interventions. Initially controversial, Keynes's "demand-side" explanation, and especially its

John Maynard Keynes. Keynes argued that government action during economic downturns—purchasing goods and services or reducing taxes so consumers could purchase more—would ultimately bring the economy back to acceptable levels of growth and employment. (Library of Congress)

emphasis on the need for government spending and intervention, came to be a centerpiece of economic thinking about poverty and economic well-being until the late 1970s and early 1980s, when "supply-side" theories reemerged.

Post–World War II Theories of Poverty

Post–World War II prosperity among industrialized nations as well as growth in the number of new nation-states brought a new direction for poverty theory and research in economics. A major focus of this work concerns why certain groups, certain regions, or certain countries are poor despite the achievement of prosperity among other groups or countries. Most use the theories discussed above as their base or springboard. We briefly discuss eight threads of poverty theory in contemporary economics.

Development Theories

The aftermath of World War II and the gradual independence of formerly colonized countries contributed to a growing concern about what became known as "underdevelopment," in reference to the lack of industrial, manufacturing, or other large-scale productive capacities. Underdevelopment and the lack of economic growth and production were seen to be the main cause of poverty in third world countries, at least in absolute terms. Typically, economic development and modernization of productive capacities have been posed as the solutions.

Broadly speaking, economic development theories tend to range from neoclassical to Marxist approaches. Neoclassically based development theories emphasize market-based solutions. This school focuses on market growth rather than on income distribution, arguing that economic growth raises living standards. Marxist and some institutionalist-based development theories argue that the historical colonial relationship is the cause of underdevelopment and poverty. Only after the postcolonial dependency relationship is broken can countries proceed with equitable development, emphasizing egalitarian distribution of resources even at the expense of rapid growth.

Development theories have historically focused on industrialization. However, development theorists differ on how best to industrialize and on what role the state should play in the process. Some countries emphasize the "big-bang" approach, an attempt to simultaneously address macroeconomic and development policy problems through massive state initiatives. Others focus on structural adjustments to the existing economy, introducing market friendly economic liberalization policies. Some promote export promotion strategies based on the notion that nations should specialize in the kind of production in which they have a comparative advantage in world markets. Still others espouse import substitution, a strategy in which countries start producing the products that would otherwise have to be imported. Most development theories emphasize economic growth, with the conviction that it reduces poverty by improving everyone's living standard. It is not clear, however, that growth and redistribution policies can always or easily go hand in hand.

Discrimination

Beginning in the late 1950s with Gary Becker's book *The Economics of Discrimination* (1957), economists have engaged in a debate about the role discrimination plays in markets and in the disparities they produce. As long as discrimination exists, certain groups will be denied full and equal access to markets, possibly contributing to poverty in the form of less or no income, inferior health status, inadequate housing, or unequal educational opportunities. Discrimination theories focus on explaining the uneven distribution of economic resources and poverty of specific groups of people delineated by where people live or by differences in race, ethnicity, religious affiliation, sexual preference, immigration status, or gender. Neoclassical discrimination theories focus on individuals as the agents of discrimination, while Marxist and institutional theorists focus on structural and institutionalized forms of discrimination.

Becker, a neoclassical economist, originally argued that labor market discrimination could exist in the form of an individual's tastes and preferences; a racist employer, for example, who prefers to hire whites will pay them higher wages regardless of their skill levels. When this does occur, it could help explain lower wages or occupational segregation of workers facing discrimination even though they have qualifications equal to those of other workers. However, Becker soon rescinded this argument, instead claiming that market competition bids away discrimination. Firms without a "taste" for discrimination would readily hire equally productive workers at their going wages, while discriminating firms would pay a price—higher wages for preferred workers—for refusing to hire qualified workers regardless of race, sex, or other characteristics. When this happens, in Becker's theory, the nondiscriminating firms boost profits, driving firms that discriminate out of business. Thus, the competitive market should then "bid away" discrimination, since it is unprofitable. In a similar vein, in the 1970s, neoclassical economists argued that it was possible for "statistical discrimination" to exist. In this case, employers screen workers not on a case-by-case basis but based on average characteristics of a group. This results in hiring or wage discrimination against individuals who belong to groups whose average productivity (along with wages) are lower than others. But soon afterward, neoclassical economists rebuked this argument. Firms under competitive conditions will develop ways to ferret out equally productive workers, eliminating statistical discrimination. Today, few neoclassical economists argue that discrimination exists when markets are allowed to operate unhampered.

Marxist and institutional economists argue that discrimination exists even with competitive markets. Racial, ethnic, and gender discrimination has been ingrained in economic institutions and customs over centuries and still exists even in the face of antidiscrimination laws and vast changes in individual views. These theorists argue that wage levels, occupational opportunities, educational systems, and housing patterns have been shaped by centuries of discrimination, resulting in persistent inequality. Entire groups of people are much more likely to be poor due to current and previous institutional and individual discrimination.

Human Capital

In lieu of discrimination as a way to explain inequality, neoclassical economists, again led by Gary Becker (1964), turned to human capital theory to explain why some people had high levels of unemployment or low wages and, by extension, high poverty rates. Human capital theory, extending Clark's marginal productivity arguments to a matter of individual choice, argues that workers' investments in themselves determine wage levels. Workers who do not pursue education and training opportunities or on-the-job experience will have lower marginal productivity and hence lower wages and a higher likelihood of being poor. Alleviating poverty requires policies, such as tax credits for education, that boost individual incentives to invest in human capital.

Labor Market Segmentation

Developed in the 1970s by institutionalist economists (see Doeringer and Piore 1971) and further expanded in the 1980s by Marxist economists (see Gordon, Edwards, and Reich 1982), labor market segmentation theory argues that there are distinct labor markets with distinct wage structures, advancement opportunities, job-related benefits, and portals of entry. There are basically two segments to the labor market—primary and secondary—and three labor groupings: independent primary, subordinate primary, and secondary workers. These groups roughly correspond to white-collar professional jobs, blue-collar skilled and semiskilled manufacturing and service work, and unskilled, high-turnover jobs, respectively. Primary-sector jobs have select ports of entry based on education levels, personal networks, and discriminatory hiring practices. Secondary workers, most often women, teens, and people of color, receive low wages and few benefits and have little or no opportunity for job advancement. Where people fall in the job structure helps explain poverty. Poverty levels are further exacerbated by the growth in secondary jobs led by the free flow of manufacturing jobs to other parts of the world. For labor market segmentation theorists, improving the wage and work conditions in these secondary jobs is key to reducing poverty, as are policies that improve educational attainment, combat discrimination, and prevent nepotism.

Theories of Regional Poverty

Researchers sometimes separate the issues of rural poverty from those of urban poverty. Rural poverty, for example, is seen as a function of lack of wage employment or other forms of income-generating opportunities. Development strategies, population shifts, and economic growth patterns often make subsistence farming untenable, resulting in increased rural poverty as well as migration to urban areas. Urban poverty is also a result of insufficient income-generating activities, but it often exists amid expanding economic opportunities and vibrant market activity. In absolute terms, urban poverty standards tend to be higher, simply because urban lifestyles tend to be more expensive than rural lifestyles. The costs of housing, transportation, and food items are relatively higher in urban areas.

There is a dynamic relationship between rural and urban poverty. Migration from rural areas contributes to the problems of urban poverty, since most of the rural migrants tend to be poor. Because urban poverty is more visible to politicians and policymakers, it has tended to draw more attention than rural poverty. In the 1970s, however, policymakers began to pay more attention to the interconnectedness between rural and urban poverty dynamics and the notion of "urban bias" (Lipton 1976). This new awareness has led to "meso" policy solutions directed toward infrastructure and other rural development activities.

Underclass and Social Exclusion

The notion of an "underclass," characterized by poverty-producing behavior, occupies one of the central positions in poverty debates in contemporary writings across all ideological spectrums. Typically, those who write about the underclass in the United States describe it as a subset of the urban poor—usually African American—whose members' behaviors or lifestyles largely deviate from those of the rest of society. Arguments diverge as to the source of these behaviors. Not all of the urban poor exhibit poverty-producing behaviors, nor are all of those who show so-called deviant behavior poor.

A lack of desire or motivation to be employed, the lure of criminal activities, and out-of-wedlock childbirth are the behaviors most frequently cited in this literature as reasons for persistent poverty and the cause of sustained or intermittent nonemployment (see Jencks and Peterson 1991). Lack of employment limits people from getting the resources needed to escape poverty and precludes their developing the social and cultural networks that would help them break away from poverty-producing behaviors. Employment is required to eradicate underclass poverty.

William Julius Wilson (1987), a prominent underclass researcher in the United States, argues that urban deindustrialization accounts for the concentrated urban poor. The loss of manufacturing work accelerated middle-class suburbanization, which in turn destroyed interclass networks in ghetto neighborhoods, made illegal activity more attractive, and generated negative attitudes toward low-wage employment. The underclass poor, he argues, will disappear when economic conditions improve and when decent-paying jobs and job training become available. Another, more conservative perspective, presented by Charles Murray (1984) and others, argues that cash and in-kind assistance, such as welfare benefits and food stamps, encourage poor people not to seek employment, to have more children, and to engage in "off-the-books" economic activity. The solution, conservatives argue, is to eliminate or drastically reduce public assistance and instead to provide incentives (usually negative) to discourage what is seen as deviant behavior and to encourage employment.

Outside the United States, researchers focus on the notion of social exclusion (International Institute for Labour Studies [IILS] 1996). They seek to understand the processes by which particular segments of the population end up being systematically excluded from mainstream economic, political, and civic and cultural activities. Although social exclusion does not equate to poverty in a literal sense, its proponents argue that it is a process that leads to poverty.

The social exclusion debate focuses on broad institutional and structural forces. Unemployment, lack of income, lack of education and good health, and other inadequacies that largely characterize conditions of people in poverty are the outcomes of the process of social exclusion. Broadly speaking, social exclusion takes three major forms: First, people are denied access to the labor market and other income-generating activities, thereby rendering them unable to acquire economic resources to have adequate consumption. The long-term result is that the excluded poor will deviate socially from the mainstream lifestyle. Second, social exclusion occurs when people lack access to participation in a wide range of political activities, including actions that directly result in improving one's own life. The third form of exclusion includes the denial of access to civic, social, and cultural organizations, networks, and functioning. This can occur at the local or community level as well as the broader regional, national, and global level.

Like U.S. underclass theorists, social exclusion theorists see employment as a major policy solution. Among the more widely advocated policy solutions are universal social rights and social insurance to promote opportunities for inclusion in labor markets and other social, cultural, and political activities.

Capacity and Poverty

Most economists construe poverty to mean a lack of income. However, economist Amartya Sen

(1999) and others argue that poverty results from a lack of "capacity" to earn income, to make informed decisions, or to fight discrimination or injustice. This lack of capacity inhibits income-generating potential, constituting the root cause of poverty. Capacity may be constricted by poor health; unsafe living conditions; gender, caste, or class restrictions; or inability to access education opportunities. Taking these issues into consideration, the U.N. Development Program (2000) includes a capability poverty measure (CPM) for every nation in its annual publication *Human Development Reports* (UNDP 2000).

Capability researchers focus on physical and social well-being as a way to measure poverty. They argue that it is important to use capability measurements in terms of education, health, nutrition, gender disparity, and ethnic disparity as proxies for measurements of well-being, since these are highly correlated with the achievements (or functioning) needed to avoid poverty. Similarly, the notions of basic social rights and freedoms are also incorporated in the capability concept of well-being. Social rights and freedoms, proponents argue, are necessary to allow people to develop the capacity to participate fully in society.

Debates continue as to what determines individual capacity. For some, it is a function of individual choices and efforts. For others, individual capacity is largely determined by broader institutional and structural forces, which provide incentives for or pose threats to the way people develop capacities. Capability researchers argue that improvement in individual capacities can lead to poverty reduction through educational, health, and nutritional measures as well as other measures to eliminate gender and ethnic discrimination.

Feminist Economic Theories

Adult women make up the majority of the adult poor everywhere. Further, lone-mother families face higher poverty rates than do other families. Clearly, gender plays a distinct role in understanding the causes and cures of poverty. Although economists have often recognized that women, especially mothers, are disproportionately poor, it has taken the development of explicitly feminist economic theories to explain why.

Feminist economists point to the role that caregiving—as distinct from employment, economic growth, and inequality—plays in understanding poverty. Women's role in providing care for family members as well as for others restricts their labor market participation and remuneration. All systems of economic production are vitally dependent on care work. However, care work has been undervalued economically, socially, and politically. In capitalist economies, care work has precluded the participation of many women—especially white women—in the labor force and has often shunted women of color into care work jobs. In addition, undervaluing care work results in low wages for women who perform care work for pay. Nancy Folbre (2001) calls this the care penalty. Women, then, are particularly vulnerable and much more likely to be poor than men.

Low pay and primary responsibility for care work makes many women dependent on men for income. Hence, without male income, these women are poor. As women's labor force participation has increased and in some countries as women's demands for equal treatment in the labor market have been met, many more women without children have been able to live independently and not in poverty. Still, even in advanced industrialized countries, lone mothers have the highest poverty rates of all families.

Feminist economists promote policies that reduce the care penalty, such as equal-pay legislation, generous family allowances, child care stipends or provision, and paid parental leave policies.

Randy Albelda and Udaya Wagle

See also: Capitalism; Classism; Economic/Fiscal Policy; Employment Policy; Globalization and Deindustrialization; Income and Wage Inequality; Labor Markets; Malthusianism; Rural Poverty; "Underclass"; Unemployment; Urban Poverty

References and Further Reading

Becker, Gary S. 1957. *The Economics of Discrimination*. Chicago: University of Chicago Press.

Becker, Gary S. 1964. *Human Capital: A Theoretical Analysis with Special Reference to Education*. New York: Columbia University Press for National Bureau of Economic Research.

Doeringer, Peter B., and Michael J. Piore. 1971. *Internal Labor Markets and Manpower Analysis*. Lexington, MA: Heath.

Folbre, Nancy. 2001. *The Invisible Heart: Economics and Family Values*. New York: New Press.

Gordon, David M., Richard Edwards, and Michael Reich. 1982. *Segmented Work, Divided Workers. The Historical Transformations of Labor in the United States*. New York: Cambridge University Press.

International Institute for Labour Studies (IILS). 1996. *Social Exclusion and Anti-Poverty Strategies*. Geneva, Switzerland: Author.

Jenks, Christopher, and P. E. Peterson, eds. 1991. *The Urban Underclass*. Washington, DC: Brookings Institution.

Lipton, Michel. 1976. *Why Poor People Stay Poor: A Study of Urban Bias in World Development*. Cambridge, MA: Harvard University Press.

Murray, Charles. 1984. *Losing Ground: American Social Policy, 1950–1980*. New York: Basic Books.

Sen, Amartya K. 1999. *Development as Freedom*. New York: Knopf.

U.N. Development Program (UNDP). 2000. *Human Development Report, 2000*. New York: Oxford University Press.

Wilson, William J. 1987. *The Truly Disadvantaged: The Inner City, the Underclass, and Public Policy*. Chicago: University of Chicago Press.

Economic/Fiscal Policy

Introduction

Although economic deprivation has always been part of the American experience, the issues and policies that frame current understandings of poverty in America took shape in the 1930s. There are two reasons for this, and they serve as the basis for much of this entry. First, the Great Depression made it abundantly clear that poverty was not necessarily a function of personal failure, such as lack of motivation or skills, but was linked to economic conditions. Second, a role for the federal government in poverty reduction was firmly established. Through macroeconomic policy—taxing and spending decisions and regulation of financial markets—the government can improve economic conditions, decreasing poverty.

The Great Depression was a massive failure of the free market, and while no poverty statistics comparable to today's measures are available from that period, it was surely the case that at least one-third and perhaps one-half of the nation suffered severe income restrictions at some point in those years. Although the causes of the Depression are not the subject of this entry, the important point is that no one could realistically blame the poor or the unemployed for their predicament. For many policymakers, not least of all President Franklin D. Roosevelt, it was clear that steps had to be taken both to get the economy moving again and to protect those who were being battered by its failure.

The theoretical foundation for this dramatically new mind-set toward the economy originated with the great British economist John Maynard Keynes. Before Keynes, it was widely held that an "invisible hand" guided market economies to the best outcomes. Once markets were created and the rules of the game, such as property rights, were established and defended, rational economic agents would engage with each other in ways that would automatically lead to the best results for all parties. Any interventions, including well-intentioned efforts to help the downtrodden, would only lead to counterproductive distortions of market outcomes.

Keynes, however, looked out at the ravaged landscape of the 1930s and realized that sometimes the invisible hand is all thumbs. His key insight was the realization that market economies, unless properly managed from above, regularly fail to utilize all their available resources. The result is higher unemployment, lower incomes, and higher poverty rates. By invoking policies to put the fallow resources (including the unemployed) to work, the government can give the invisible hand a firm nudge, speed up growth, and lower, perhaps even eradicate, poverty. To no small degree, the ongoing American (and to a lesser extent, European) debate about poverty policy is an argument over whether Keynes was right.

Knowingly or not, Roosevelt implemented a Keynesian program. The 1930s saw the creation of a broad and lasting set of federal policies designed both to protect the disadvantaged from market failures and to strengthen their ability to bargain with the owners of capital for a larger share of the fruits of growth. At the same time, New Deal economic policy aimed to jump-start capital toward productive ends again. With the establishment of Unemployment Insurance, the minimum wage, Aid to Dependent Children (the first federal safety net program for the families of poor single mothers, who were generally not expected to work in the paid labor market), the Wagner Act encouraging collective bargaining, and Social Security (which provides benefits to both workers and nonworkers), the Roosevelt administration created a large regulatory structure that strove to use government intervention to promote growth, provided a social safety net for those unable or unexpected to work, and began to empower workers as well.

Through these interventionist policies, along with large temporary public-sector job programs such as the Works Progress Administration and the Civilian Conservation Corps, the Roosevelt administration staved off severe privation for many poor families. Equally important, these policies represented an explicit acknowledgment that the market economy could not be counted upon to generate enough growth to reduce poverty. But the key theme, in terms of poverty policy, is that such policies viewed poverty as flowing from a lack of economic opportunity, not from a lack of personal initiative. Thus, by the early 1940s, the themes that still dominate the poverty debate in industrialized economies were established. To what extent is poverty a market failure or a personal failure? How far can macroeconomic management go toward reducing poverty, or will such management simply thwart the invisible hand? What is the role of the safety net? Is it reasonable to believe that the poor can be protected from harsh aspects of the market economy, or will such efforts simply generate perverse incentives, encourage exploitative behaviors, and engender an impoverished culture of dependency?

With these questions in mind, this essay broadly reviews five decades, from 1950 to 2000, of the American poverty experience and the specific role of macroeconomic policy. We find, unsurprisingly, that the pendulum swings back and forth between the polarities explicit in these questions. But, in our view, that should not be taken to imply that both sides are equally right. We think the evidence shows that a full employment economy with publicly provided "work supports" (subsidies designed to meet the gap between earnings and needs), along with a safety net for families that cannot work, is needed to reduce poverty to the lowest possible level. In the absence of this policy set—and it is a set that has never been fully employed in the United States—the lack of progress against poverty here should not be surprising.

1950s and 1960s: Strong Economic Growth and Activist Government Lead to Large Declines in Poverty

In the immediate post–World War II period, macroeconomic policy as a tool of government also took on its modern shape. The U.S. Congress passed the Employment Act of 1946, which called upon the federal government to use all means available to promote "maximum employment, output, and purchasing power." The Council of Economic Advisors was established to advise the president on economic policy, and the president was charged with providing an annual economic report to Congress. Congress established the Joint Economic Committee to help both houses of Congress keep tabs on such federal agencies as the Department of the Treasury and the Federal Reserve Board.

The 1950s were characterized by a huge postwar boom, fueled by individual consumers (with both newly available veterans' benefits and pent-up savings that had accumulated during the war when there was little to buy) and by the Cold War arms race with the Soviet Union. The relatively stable, high-paying jobs that resulted from this combination of consumer demand and massive government investment in the military-industrial complex helped spread prosperity widely. The labor movement, empowered by New Deal–era legislation, also played a central role, as did federal programs that subsidized suburbanization and helped put home ownership within reach of a broader segment of the white working class. The highest-ever proportion of U.S. workers enjoyed union membership, and they bargained and won pensions and health insurance. The middle class grew, and the birthrate soared. President Dwight D. Eisenhower golfed, while mommies stayed home to raise the kids in new suburban developments and daddies went to work.

Despite this idyllic picture of the 1950s, not everyone benefited equally. Recessions in 1948–1949, 1954, and 1958 saw unemployment rates of 5.9, 5.4, and 6.8 percent, respectively. The unemployment rates of Blacks and other minority races were 9.0, 9.9, and 12.6, respectively, in the same recessions. The federal government's response to the recessions was minimal; the Eisenhower administration was more worried about the dangers of inflation than about the dangers of unemployment. Moreover, despite the Employment Act, the 1950s saw little use of macroeconomic policy to fight poverty. Rather, poverty was addressed by the expansion of the Social Security system to cover domestic, agricultural, and professional workers as well as employees of many state and local governments, so that coverage was nearly universal by 1956. Benefits for disabled workers and family members were also added in 1956. Aid to Dependent Children was also expanded to include assistance to the mother and other adults in low-income families in addition to children; the name of the program was changed to Aid to Families with Dependent Children (AFDC) in 1962. The Department of Health, Education, and Welfare, which administered these programs, issued the first official poverty rate in 1959, when 22.5 percent of the population were estimated to be poor.

President John F. Kennedy, elected in 1960, experienced another recession early in his administration, but his Council of Economic Advisors was far more activist in striving to achieve full employment. They set 4 percent as the target unemployment rate, and when the economic recovery proceeded slowly, with unemployment remaining over 5 percent through 1964, they engineered a tax cut, which worked to stimulate the economy. The expansion was supported by the Federal Reserve Board, now far less concerned about inflation and willing to expand the money supply so that high interest rates would not choke off the recovery. Their coordinated actions maintained the longest sustained period of economic expansion known until that time (105 months).

Kennedy also asked his advisers to report on poverty, for he had observed deep "pockets"—or concentrated areas—of unemployment and poverty when he campaigned in economically depressed parts of the country, such as Appalachia. Structural unemployment was recognized as a phenomenon that might not be reduced much by a strong economy if people remained in geographic areas that were underdeveloped. Kennedy's advisers developed plans for several antipoverty programs. In the 1960s, urban poverty in the northern cities also drew increased attention from policymakers. More than 1 million American Blacks had abandoned impoverished farms in the South decades earlier and had flocked to northern cities where they could find work. Now increasingly excluded from the growth they witnessed around them, their dissatisfaction, coupled with the need for greater legal rights in the South, where racial segregation still reigned, fueled the civil rights movement.

Michael Harrington's *Other America,* published in 1962, increased public awareness and helped build public support for government intervention. After President Kennedy's assassination, President Lyndon B. Johnson succeeded in enacting several antipoverty programs, known as the War on Poverty, in 1964, including Head Start, the Community Action Program, the Model Cities program, and Volunteers in Service to America (VISTA). Medicare and Medicaid, longer-lasting programs, were enacted in 1965.

The War on Poverty complemented macroeconomic policy with targeted economic development and job-training programs to address pockets of poverty. More resources were also poured into education. Head Start sought to give poor children an equal place at the starting gate. Graduating from high school became a nearly universal experience, and the development of the community college system in the 1960s brought higher education to many. Although conservatives subsequently criticized the War on Poverty as a failure, in reality, macroeconomic policy was especially effective in the 1960s in reducing poverty, as Richard Freeman (2001, 108) has shown. Programs like Head Start have been shown to make a lasting difference in achievement levels of poor youth, and the Community Action Program and Model Cities contributed to the redistribution of political power to the poor. Medicaid and Medicare now deliver health care to 70 million Americans.

Meanwhile, in addition to the extraordinary spate of federal government antipoverty activism spurred by the combination of prosperity and social movements, other changes were occurring to move American society away from the stereotyped 1950s image. Nowhere were these changes more evident than in the family. As the decade of the "second wave of feminism" was getting under way, women's increased education, the invention of the birth control pill, and the Vietnam War all pulled women into the workforce, and the traditional one-earner, two-parent family began its long decline.

The 1970s: Transitioning away from Activism

After falling from 22.4 percent to 12.1 percent between 1959 and 1969, poverty barely budged over the 1970s, ending the decade at 11.7 percent (U.S. Census Bureau 2001b). Given the ambitious and successful antipoverty agenda of the 1960s, this was a discouraging result, and it set up the major retrenchment of antipoverty policy that was to follow in the next decade. In this sense, the 1970s represent a transitional period in the history of how poverty is viewed in the United States. The nation moved from the belief that strong macroeconomic growth in tandem with greatly expanded investments in the poor would reach even those entrenched corners of poverty identified by Harrington, to the view that poverty was more a personal problem or, from the perspective of some social scientists, a cultural problem. In this context, the dominant view was heading toward the position that government interventions are likely to do more harm than good.

The dynamic of the transition is revealing in and of itself. Over the first half of the decade, momentum from the 1960s led to continued expansion of certain War on Poverty programs. Spending on antipoverty programs such as means-tested transfers actually accelerated in the first half of the decade. The Comprehensive Employment and Training Act (CETA) was passed in 1973, and the Earned Income Tax Credit—a wage-subsidy for workers in low-income families with children—followed in 1975.

The second half of the decade introduced a decidedly new trend. Overall spending on means-tested programs as a share of gross domestic product was unchanged, but spending on direct cash assistance through AFDC, which grew 49 percent in real terms in the period 1970–1975, fell 7 percent in the period 1975–1980 (the decline was attributable to both falling real benefit levels and lower welfare caseloads). Spending on in-kind benefits (such as food stamps) continued and even increased, but the stage was set for a broad attack on these programs as well. As Sheldon Danziger and Robert Haveman have noted, "By the late 1970s, the optimistic belief that government could solve most social problems had turned to the pessimistic attitude that 'nothing works'" (2001, 4).

At the same time, the economy stumbled through two recessions, and the ability of Keynesian style macromanagement to achieve full employment became highly suspect. In fact, the dominant ideology in economics shifted toward the belief that government intervention in the economy was most likely to generate not low unemployment but high inflation. As if to prove the point, the latter years of the decade were characterized by what came to be called "stagflation": high unemployment and high inflation. The fact that the latter resulted more from the sharp increase in the cost of imported oil than from harmful macroeconomic policy was lost in the shifting ideology of the moment.

At this point, conservative poverty analysts saw an opening to gain public support by attacking the War on Poverty, particularly those programs that provided cash transfers to the poor. Ronald Reagan ran on a platform that attacked "welfare queens" who were bilking the system, and conservative social scientists began to argue that not only were U.S. antipoverty efforts ineffective, they were harmful. For example, these critics argued that welfare was responsible for the increase in mother-only families, particularly among minorities, a group whose poverty rates were much higher than average. In fact, virtually every aspect of the policies and institutions that grew out of the Depression and New Deal came under conservative fire for either stifling economic growth or creating perverse incentives. By the 1980 presidential election, the pendulum had swung far from the optimistic activism of prior decades.

The 1980s

Although the Reagan campaign made the political case against the poverty policies of the 1960s, social scientist Charles Murray made the analytic case. His book *Losing Ground,* published in 1984, argued that poverty programs, particularly AFDC, reduced work incentives and encouraged women to become single mothers. According to Murray's research, far from solving the problem, these programs had the unintended consequence of deepening poverty.

Though his evidence was not particularly convincing, Murray's work was taken very seriously. Common sense, backed up by quantitative research, did suggest that some welfare recipients worked and married less than would have been the case in the absence of welfare. But Murray and those around him vastly exaggerated the magnitude of these findings, ultimately claiming that dramatic reduction of the welfare state would reduce poverty much further than would continuing to finance what he considered to be counterproductive behaviors. These ideas resonated with the Reagan revolution against government.

With the first Reagan budget, growth in some means-tested benefits slowed, particularly AFDC, due to both a decline in real benefit levels and a tightening of eligibility criteria. Other spending, however, quietly expanded, particularly for Medicaid and EITC, the latter of which was included in the Tax Reform Act of 1986. As Reagan himself said about the act, it is "the best antipoverty bill, the best profamily measure, and the best job-creation program ever to come out of the Congress of the United States" (Reagan 1986). Here one sees the seeds of a subtle shift: a distinction between the worthy and the unworthy poor that would become very important in the next decade.

In addition to all this focus on the impact of incentives, major economic changes that were to have a profound impact on poverty were also occurring. First of all, the so-called supply-side revolution—the notion that deregulation and deep tax cuts would stimulate faster overall growth—was not having its intended effect. Growth was moderate over the decade and unemployment remained high. Second, there was a sharp increase in economic inequality. Both of these trends, particularly the latter, led to higher poverty.

The problem of higher-than-expected poverty was first noted in the latter part of the decade, when it became clear that poverty rates were falling less than expected. Even though growth was slower in the 1980s than in previous decades, the economy did expand, and given historical relationships between growth and poverty reduction, poverty should have fallen more than it did. Though few analysts recognized it at the time, the main reason for this disconnect between economic growth and poverty—the "rising tide" was *not* lifting all boats—was the sharp increase in inequality.

The 1980s saw the continuation and acceleration of this late–1970s trend toward higher levels of economic inequality, and this meant that what growth did occur over the 1980s went largely to those at the top of the income scale. Inequality created a wedge between economic growth and poverty reduction. Despite the fact that real per capita income grew 23 percent over the decade, the real family income of those in the bottom 20 percent fell by 4 percent (U.S. Census Bureau 2001a) and poverty increased by 1 percentage point (these values are taken from 1979–1989, since both these years are business-cycle peaks).

This increase in poverty over the 1980s is very instructive. As noted in the introduction, for poverty to decline, both market and nonmarket forces must work in tandem. Growth must be fast enough to generate low unemployment, which in turn raises the employment and earnings opportunities of low-income working families. In addition, the safety net must be in place both to help close the earnings/needs gap faced by many low-wage workers even in good times and to catch those who are unable to work. Although the 1980s saw some expansion of work supports, particularly the EITC, neither economic conditions nor social provisions were working very hard to reduce poverty, and the result was higher poverty amid growth.

The 1990s

Perhaps more than is often realized, the 1990s were a fairly clear continuation of the 1980s, though with a few salient differences. For example, the dominant 1980s view that the welfare system, primarily AFDC, created perverse incentives to reduce labor supply and bear children out of wedlock persisted in the 1990s and ultimately led to the end of welfare as an entitlement (that is, a program where all eligible families can receive benefits). Another similarity was the continuation and even refinement of the distinction between the "worthy" and "unworthy" poor, with work in the paid labor market being the major determinant of worthiness. Stressing this distinction, President Bill Clinton greatly expanded the EITC and raised the minimum wage as well (although Reagan had done the former, he had avoided the latter).

On the other hand, the second half of the decade featured a very different economy from that of the 1980s. For the first time since the 1960s, the economy grew quickly enough to drive the unemployment rate down to a thirty-year low of 4 percent in 2000. The movement toward full employment led to the first persistent real wage gains among low-wage workers in decades and slowed the seemingly inexorable growth in inequality. After peaking at 15.1 percent in 1993, poverty fell to 11.3 percent in 2000. Although this was certainly an impressive decline, it is worth noting that in 1973, the rate was 11.1 percent (U.S. Census Bureau 2001b). After twenty-seven years, the nation was about back where it started.

The replacement of AFDC with the Temporary Assistance for Needy Families (TANF) program is an excellent microcosm for viewing the shift in poverty policy over the decades, both positively and negatively. The framers of welfare reform were most concerned about reducing dependency on government and building self-sufficiency. Contrast this view with that of the New Deal depression fighters of the 1930s or the Keynesian economists and antipoverty warriors of the 1960s, who clearly saw a positive role for the federal government in improving the life circumstances of the poor—and indeed, of all Americans—and did not see themselves as fostering dependency. Many who supported TANF wanted to get the federal government out of the poverty business for good, and provision of welfare was thus highly devolved down to the state level, while welfare beneficiaries were subject to a lifetime limit of five years (states were free to reduce this limit, and many did so).

On the other hand, TANF, at least as implemented in the second half of the 1990s, was not a dramatic retreat from antipoverty initiatives. Because of the block grant structure of the program and the sharp decline in welfare caseloads, spending per recipient climbed steeply over the latter 1990s. Numerous states used these resources to finance a system of work supports—child care, health care, transportation, training—designed to smooth the path from welfare to work. With these work supports in place, including the expanded EITC, and the strong economy at their backs, some of those who left welfare found jobs and lifted their incomes well above what they would have had on welfare.

Of course, they also had more expenses (child care in particular), fewer cash welfare benefits, and, too often, the loss of food stamps and Medicaid. They also faced many of the hurdles and stressors that less-skilled workers face in the low-wage labor market, including inflexible and erratic schedules and difficulty making ends meet on their meager earnings, even with the more generous EITC. In addition, a smaller group of poor single mothers were excluded from the program due to tougher rules and, in many localities, because of TANF administrators who viewed their mandate as cutting the welfare rolls or who simply discouraged applying. Research shows that this group is far poorer than they were under AFDC and that they have far less access to health insurance and food stamps (Lyter, Sills, and Oh 2002).

The United States ended the decade with a highly decentralized, devolved system tilted very heavily toward the elderly and the working poor and providing little help for able-bodied people outside the paid labor force. Although poverty expenditures as a share of the economy have changed little since the mid-1970s, that spending is far more tied to work than it was in the past. In this regard, the current system depends more on economic growth than did previous incarnations; that is, antipoverty policy, at least for the nonelderly, does much less to counter the effects of economic slowdown than it did in the past. Earnings and related credits (the EITC), as opposed to public assistance, now make up a much larger share of the income of low-income families, particularly for single mothers. This worked to reduce poverty in the latter 1990s, when the economy moved toward full employment, but it is a source of concern moving forward.

Conclusion

The history of poverty and poverty policy since the 1930s is a rich one, reflecting many shifts in ideology that kept the pendulum in fairly constant motion. The themes were set up right from the beginning, when the Great Depression revealed seismic cracks in the market system and dragged a huge proportion of the citizenry into privation. The notion that the federal government had a role and in fact a responsibility to implement an antipoverty strategy was fully established.

In response to this great market failure, the Roosevelt administration built a set of regulations and institutions that served to empower workers, regulate the excesses of the market, and provide a safety net for the most disadvantaged. At the same time, Keynesian economists realized that left to its own devices, the market would too often underperform, and the invisible hand needed guidance as often as not. Without being too reductionist, it is fair to say that the rest of what followed over the next sixty years was largely a debate over whether this was the right way to fight poverty.

We think the record shows that it was and is. This is not wholly to deny conservative critics who argue that some poverty programs created perverse incentives that led to unintended consequences. But we judge these effects to be economically small, in that they have had much less influence on behaviors and outcomes than is claimed by their critics. The record shows that fighting poverty calls for a strong macroeconomy running at full capacity in tandem with a set of supports to help lift the incomes of the working poor to a level that enables them to meet their needs. Finally, despite the contemporary desire to get government out of the business of providing for the poor, a safety net is still needed to catch those who fall out of the labor market when the economy stumbles and to provide for the needs of those unable to work.

Jared Bernstein and Heidi Hartmann

See also: Aid to Families with Dependent Children (ADC/AFDC); Area Redevelopment Act; Earned Income Tax Credit (EITC); Economic Theories; Employment Policy; Great Depression and New Deal; Labor Markets; 1940s to Present; Tax Policy; War on Poverty; Welfare Policy/Welfare Reform

References and Further Reading

Amott, Teresa, and Julie Matthei. 1996. *Race, Gender, and Work: A Multi-Cultural Economic History of Women in the United States*. Boston: South End Press.

Blank, Rebecca. 1998. *It Takes a Nation: A New Agenda for Fighting Poverty*. Princeton: Princeton University Press.

Council of Economic Advisors. Various years. *Economic Report of the President*. Washington, DC: GPO.

Danziger, Sheldon, and Peter Gottschalk, eds. 1993. *Uneven Tides: Rising Inequality in America*. New York: Russell Sage Foundation.

Danziger, Sheldon H., and Robert H. Haveman, eds. 2001. *Understanding Poverty*. Cambridge, MA: Harvard University Press; New York: Russell Sage Foundation.

Freeman, Richard. 2001. "The Rising Tide Lifts . . . ?" In *Understanding Poverty*, ed. Sheldon H. Danziger and Robert H. Haveman. Cambridge, MA: Harvard University Press; New York: Russell Sage Foundation.

Harrington, Michael. 1962. *The Other America: Poverty in the United Sates*. Baltimore: Penguin.

Keynes, John Maynard. 1936. *The General Theory of Employment, Interest, and Money*. New York: Harcourt, Brace.

Lyter, Deanna, Melissa Sills, and Gi-Taik Oh. 2002. "Children in Single-Parent Families Living in Poverty Have Fewer Supports after Welfare Reform." Briefing paper. Washington, DC: Institute for Women's Policy Research.

Mishel, Lawrence, Jared Bernstein, and Heather Boushey. 2002. *The State of Working America, 2002–03*. Ithaca, NY: Cornell University Press.

Murray, Charles. 1984. *Losing Ground: American Social Policy, 1950–1980*. New York: Basic Books.

O'Connor, Alice. 2001. *Poverty Knowledge: Social Science, Social Policy, and the Poor in Twentieth-Century U.S. History*. Princeton: Princeton University Press.

Peterson, Janice, Xue Song, and Avis Jones-DeWeever. 2003. *Before and after Welfare Reform: The Work and Well-Being of Low Income Single Parent Families*. Washington, DC: Institute for Women's Policy Research.

Reagan, Ronald. 1986. "Remarks on Signing the Tax Reform Act of 1986." October 22, South Lawn, White House. Ronald Reagan Presidential Library Archives.

U.S. Census Bureau. 2001a. Table F-3, "Mean Income Received by Each Fifth and Top 5 Percent of

Families (All Races): 1966 to 2001." http://www.census.gov/hhes/income/histinc/f03.html.
———. 2001b. Table 2, "Poverty Status of People by Family Relationship, Race, and Hispanic Origin: 1959 to 2001." http://www.census.gov/income/histpov/hstpov2.lst.

Education Policies

Education in the United States serves multiple, often contradictory, purposes. Education promotes a healthy economy by producing a trained workforce. It advances democratic ideals, at least in theory encouraging individuals to reach their fullest potential and providing common training for future citizens. It stabilizes the polity by socializing and assimilating marginalized groups. In the process of fulfilling these mandates, education both reinforces and mitigates the racism, classism, sexism, homophobia, and ableism that perpetuate poverty in the United States.

During the colonial period, education typically was a family matter; children were trained at home and formal education was for the most part reserved for select, wealthy, white males. Still, as early as 1647, the Massachusetts Bay Colony court decreed that communities should have elementary and Latin schools so that children could be tutored in Calvinism and could learn to read their Bibles (Mondale et al. 2001, 6). The expansion of commerce and the development of an industrial economy in the early nineteenth century generated calls to "prepare the children for the labors of the mills" (Bowles and Gintis 1986, 162) through a system of free public education. By the 1850s, seven states had provisions for public education (Mondale et al. 2001, 12).

At midcentury, Horace Mann became the head of the newly formed Massachusetts State Board of Education, serving from 1837 to 1848. One of the foremost leaders in educational innovation and reform, Mann claimed that public education created a ready and compliant work force, a united society, and "good" citizens who were less likely to engage in crime. Also referring to education as "the great equalizer," Mann lobbied for a school system that would be tax supported and nonsectarian (Mann [1853] 1990, 3). Mann's initiatives dramatically increased the number of children enrolled in Massachusetts public schools and the resources devoted to these schools.

Education innovations abounded in other contexts as well during second half of the nineteenth century. The 1862 Morrill Act provided for the establishment of state universities and land-grant colleges. "Reform schools" combining education and juvenile rehabilitation were launched. The first compulsory education laws were enacted. Legislation made it illegal for Native American children to be taught in their own language. Professional education theorists and administrators became a dominant force in deliberations about schooling. Meanwhile, with the end of Reconstruction, racial segregation and deprivation became an organizing principle for education in the South.

Late-nineteenth-century industrialization, economic instability, and social movements precipitated reform efforts in every aspect of U.S. society, including education. During the Progressive Era, new educational philosophies stressed unity of the school with the community and what has come to be called "child-centered learning" (Mondale et al. 2001, 11). John Dewey was at the forefront of this reform. In *Democracy and Education* (1916), he outlined the social role of education, both formal and informal, positioning education as a dynamic process of growth that allows all children—including the poor—to realize their greatest potential in partnership with the community. In focusing on the integration of knowledge and experience, Dewey envisioned liberal education as necessary for social equalization, full human and community development, and thus the success and vibrancy of the democratic community.

Progressives argued that education should be "tailored to the child." This impetus, perhaps rooted in devotion to social justice, led to some reforms that produced stratification rather than equality. The movement spawned special curricula for poor and working-class children; tracking for "appropriate" education on the basis of students' ethnicity, race, gender, and economic backgrounds; special gender-based vocational education programs for those tracked into "practical" fields; and the development and popularization of "intelligence" testing and academic aptitude testing (Gordon 1992). The first substantive federal education initiative, the Smith-Hughes Vocational Education Act of 1917, supported these developments by funding industrial (boys), agricultural, and domestic arts (girls) education in secondary schools and extension programs.

Although the Smith-Hughes Act was an important step in U.S. education policy, the federal government left virtually all education policy to the states until the middle of the twentieth century. In turn, states deferred to local communities and did little to correct disparities of educational provision across jurisdictions within their own borders. States did take on a bigger role in the regulation and funding of education in the post–World War II period, although most states did not interfere with the local bases of education financing and provision. Although a preference for neighborhood schools and community control remained strong throughout the twentieth century, the U.S. Supreme Court's decision in *Brown v. Board of Education of Topeka, Kansas* (347 U.S. 483 [1954]) and the civil rights movement precipitated major changes in the federal government's role in education policy.

In its 1954 *Brown* decision, the Court unanimously declared racially segregated schools to be inherently unequal schools. In a 1955 follow-up decision, *Brown v. Board of Education II* (349 U.S. 294 [1955]), the Court required that segregated schools be desegregated with "all deliberate speed." These two decisions made education a constitutional, and therefore a national, matter. Although *Brown* did not overturn the state and local basis of education (indeed, it affirmed it), the declaration of a fundamental national guarantee of equality in education triggered federal action to enforce it.

Congress responded in part with Title IV of the Civil Rights Act of 1964, providing a statutory prohibition on racial segregation in public schools. Congress's primary response to the new national principle of equal educational opportunity was to deal with the effects of segregation, both racial and economic, in the 1965 Elementary and Secondary Education Act (ESEA). Title I of this landmark law addressed the educational opportunities of economically disadvantaged students; amendments over the years have added provisions for disabled students, for bilingual education, for schooling for migrant children, and for education in correctional facilities.

These measures have expanded educational access, but they have not necessarily equalized the quality of education. The federal share of total educational expenditures hovers at only around 6 percent—hardly enough to overcome discriminatory distribution of educational services by states and localities. The local property tax remains the basis of school financing in most jurisdictions, providing ampler resources and facilities to schools in wealthier districts. In 1973, in *San Antonio Independent School District et al. v. Rodriguez et al.* (411 U.S. 1), the U.S. Supreme Court upheld Texas's school financing scheme based on property taxes. The Court argued in part that it could not discern discrimination against poor people in the Texas policy, that wealth classifications do not trigger special, heightened constitutional review, and that education is not a fundamental right, though it is "an important function of state and local governments."

Without a constitutional "right to education" that individuals can deploy, the best avail-

San Antonio Independent School District et al. v. Rodriguez et al. *(1973) 411 U.S. 1*

This suit attacking the Texas system of financing public education was initiated by Mexican-American parents whose children attend the elementary and secondary schools in the Edgewood Independent School District, an urban school district in San Antonio, Texas. They brought a class action on behalf of school children throughout the State who are members of minority groups or who are poor and reside in school districts having a low property tax base. . . .

We must decide, first, whether the Texas system of financing public education operates to the disadvantage of some suspect class or impinges upon a fundamental right explicitly or implicitly protected by the Constitution, thereby requiring strict judicial scrutiny. . . .

The individuals, or groups of individuals, who constituted the class discriminated against in our prior cases shared two distinguishing characteristics: because of their impecunity they were completely unable to pay for some desired benefit, and as a consequence, they sustained an absolute deprivation of a meaningful opportunity to enjoy that benefit. . . . Neither of the two distinguishing characteristics of wealth classifications can be found here. . . .

First, in support of their charge that the system discriminates against the "poor," appellees have made no effort to demonstrate that it operates to the peculiar disadvantage of any class fairly definable as indigent, or as composed of persons whose incomes are beneath any designated poverty level. . . .

Second, neither appellees nor the District Court addressed the fact that, unlike each of the foregoing cases, lack of personal resources has not occasioned an absolute deprivation of the desired benefit. The argument here is not that the children in districts having relatively low assessable property values are receiving no public education; rather, it is that they are receiving a poorer quality education than that available to children in districts having more assessable wealth. . . . A sufficient answer to appellees' argument is that, at least where wealth is involved, the Equal Protection Clause does not require absolute equality or precisely equal advantages. . . . For these two reasons—the absence of any evidence that the financing system discriminates against any

able federal remedy for the unequal distribution of state and local educational resources is federal spending, which includes whatever conditions Congress attaches to federal spending. The challenge during the late twentieth century was to increase federal contributions to elementary and secondary education. However, partisans of local control, opponents of Title I programs for poor schools and students, and proponents of less government effectively blocked significant increases to federal ESEA expenditures. In 2002, President George W. Bush won passage of his "No child left behind" legislation, which expands the federal role in schooling without substantially expanding the federal financial commitment. Most significantly, the new law targets "failing schools" for loss of federal support and, in fact, for closing. Failing schools are identified by their students' performance on standardized tests.

The federal government has carved out a more extensive, though no less controversial, role in postsecondary education, including in private colleges and universities. The federal role in higher education has produced some profound changes.

Three centuries ago, the impetus for establishing colleges was the desire for an educated clergy. The first educational and public policies were unspoken but absolute: Higher education definable category of "poor" people or that it results in the absolute deprivation of education—the disadvantaged class is not susceptible of identification in traditional terms. . . .

We thus conclude that the Texas system does not operate to the peculiar disadvantage of any suspect class. But in recognition of the fact that this Court has never heretofore held that wealth discrimination alone provides an adequate basis for invoking strict scrutiny, appellees have not relied solely on this contention. They also assert that the State's system impermissibly interferes with the exercise of a "fundamental" right and that accordingly the prior decisions of this Court require the application of the strict standard of judicial review. . . . It is this question—whether education is a fundamental right, in the sense that it is among the rights and liberties protected by the Constitution—which has so consumed the attention of courts and commentators in recent years. . . .

[T]he importance of a service performed by the State does not determine whether it must be regarded as fundamental for purposes of examination under the Equal Protection Clause. . . . Education, of course, is not among the rights afforded explicit protection under our Federal Constitution. Nor do we find any basis for saying it is implicitly so protected. . . . Even if it were conceded that some identifiable quantum of education is a constitutionally protected prerequisite to the meaningful exercise of either right, we have no indication that the present levels of educational expenditure in Texas provide an education that falls short. . . . This is not a case in which the challenged state action must be subjected to the searching judicial scrutiny reserved for laws that create suspect classifications or impinge upon constitutionally protected rights. . . .

While it is no doubt true that reliance on local property taxation for school revenues provides less freedom of choice with respect to expenditures for some districts than for others, the existence of "some inequality" in the manner in which the State's rationale is achieved is not alone a sufficient basis for striking down the entire system. . . . [A]ny scheme of local taxation—indeed the very existence of identifiable local governmental units—requires the establishment of jurisdictional boundaries that are inevitably arbitrary. It is equally inevitable that some localities are going to be blessed with more taxable assets than others. . . . It has simply never been within the constitutional prerogative of this Court to nullify statewide measures for financing public services merely because the burdens or benefits thereof fall unevenly depending upon the relative wealth of the political subdivisions in which citizens live.

was intended only for white, propertied men "of good character." Not until 1837 were women admitted to any college (Oberlin) along with men of all races, and not until the Morrill Act of 1862, more than 200 years after Harvard opened its doors in 1636, did federal policy provide for the postsecondary education of some women in the new network of public colleges and universities. Even so, colleges accepted the entry of young women, students of color, the poor, immigrants, and the disabled into academia on a very limited basis (Kates 2001). Those men of color and women who did pursue higher education were typically tracked into fields deemed appropriate to their social station, and they were barred in some cases from fields considered the province of white men.

Perhaps the most significant federal policy affecting higher education was the G.I. Bill, signed into law on June 22, 1944. Most notably, the G.I. Bill invested billions of dollars in education for millions of veterans, opening up educational opportunities to lower- as well as middle-class men. However, G.I. Bill educational benefits were initially of more limited value to Blacks and other veterans of color, who faced racial exclusions in admissions policies and other discriminatory barriers. At the same time, women lost educational opportunities. Because priority was given to veterans, poor undergraduate and graduate women found it more difficult to be admitted and were denied financial assistance (Gordon 1992, 113). Although the G.I. Bill did not call for discrimination against women, women were but a tiny fraction of the armed forces until late in the twentieth century.

In the 1960s and 1970s, a spate of legal and legislative actions fostered policy changes designed to open access to education to women, nonwhites, and the poor. Title VI of the Civil Rights Act of 1964, banning race discrimination in institutions that receive federal funds, and the federal student loan program began to change patterns of admissions and financial support. In 1971, the U.S. Congress approved an Omnibus Higher Education Bill. This legislation included Title IX, which prohibits sex discrimination, including discrimination in the treatment of pregnant students, in all federally assisted educational programs, including admissions, academic programs, and athletics. Title VII of the Civil Rights Act, which prohibits discrimination in employment, was also extended to cover employees in all educational institutions. In addition, in 1972, guidelines were issued to implement executive orders requiring federal contractors, including schools, to institute affirmative action programs to ensure equal treatment. Affirmative action has been a critical tool for securing access to higher education for women and people of color.

Today, women outnumber men in college, in part due to the access guaranteed by Title IX and facilitated by affirmative action. But for the most part, women in higher education are predominantly white, middle-class, and able-bodied. Poor women, students of color, and disabled students remain vastly underrepresented in colleges and universities (Rothman 1999, 18; U.S. Census Bureau 2000a). In addition, disproportionate numbers of women earn degrees in fields with lower status and lower pay than the fields white men enter; and in the job market, the degrees that women, workers of color, and the disabled hold are worth less than are their counterparts' credentials (Chronicle of Higher Education Almanac 1998a, 1998b).

Bias is also evident in policy determining the offer of financial aid in colleges and universities across the nation. Even though women far surpass men as adult, part-time, independent, low-income, and thus "financially needy" students, women receive only 68 percent of what male students receive in financial aid earnings, 73 percent of what men are awarded in grants, and 84 percent of what men receive in loans for low-income undergraduates (Dahlberg forthcoming, 368; Malveaux 2002, 3). Students from low-income families made up only 6 percent of the student population in 1996, as opposed to 18.7 percent from middle-income families and 41.1 percent from high-income families (Chronicle of Higher Education Almanac 1998a, 18). Profoundly poor women, especially those on public aid, are dissuaded from entering educational programs because of welfare legislation that supports "work first" rather than educational advancement. As a result of 1996 welfare policy legislation, the number of poor families participating in programs leading to postsecondary degrees was cut from 648,763 in 1995 to 340,000 in 1998–1999 (Adair 2001, 226; Greenberg 1999, 3). Similarly, despite the passage of the Americans with Disabilities Act in 1990, disabled students, and particularly low-income disabled students, have yet to become full participants in the American educational system (Jordan 2001).

In 2000, there was a clear correlation between educational credentials and financial security. The more higher education an individual accrues, the less likely she or he is to become or remain poor. Yet primary, secondary, and postsecondary education continues to impede participation by the poor and to track white women and people of color into fields that do not offer the best incomes. Many educators argue that contemporary educational practices of tracking and uniform testing exacerbate these gaps in education.

Contemporary issues of vocational education, multilingual education, and school vouchers threaten to deepen class and race gaps in education, and accordingly they generate intense debate. A "back to basics" testing movement has been supported by those who favor standardized tests and curricula that prioritize basic skills over critical thinking and intellectual freedom. As in the past, these standardized tests are often used to track students into specific courses, schools, curricula, and occupational sectors. Opponents of tracking claim that the practice contradicts the tenets of an equal education because inferior educational resources are allocated to students in nonacademic tracks. Poor children and children of color are overrepresented in these tracks.

Monolingual education also reinforces the access and opportunity gap in education at all levels. Supporters of bilingual education encourage schools to build on children's native language and culture and to draw students into substantive learning by teaching them in their first languages until they have grade-level command of English. Increasingly vocal critics argue, meanwhile, that in order to succeed in the nation, (primarily poor) immigrant children must acquire English quickly and exclusively.

Perhaps the starkest challenge to poor people's educational opportunity is the school voucher movement, which is also a challenge to public schools. Supporters of vouchers believe that free-market competition will improve both students' and schools' performance, especially for the poor and for students of color. Armed with vouchers, students could abandon "failing schools" by using their vouchers to pay for alternative private education, or they could simply vote with their feet by switching to a successful public school. Opponents fear that both vouchers and public school choice will drain funds away from the poorest schools and will disadvantage the poorest students who will not be able to afford to travel long distances to the school of their "choice," let alone afford private education with meager vouchers. To many, the voucher/school choice debate is a Rubicon, as the disappearance of underfunded schools in poor districts will reinstitute educational apartheid.

Vivyan C. Adair

See also: Affirmative Action; Civil Rights Acts, 1964 and 1991; Disability; Gender Discrimination in the Labor Market; G.I.. Bill; Immigrants and Immigration; Industrialization; Progressive Era and 1920s; Racial Segregation; Vocational Education; Welfare Policy/Welfare Reform

References and Further Reading

Adair, Vivyan. 2001. "Poverty and the (Broken) Promise of Higher Education in America." *Harvard Educational Review* (Harvard University Press), 71, no. 2 (Summer): 217–239.

Bowles, Samuel, and Herbert Gintis. 1986. *Schooling in Capitalist America: Educational Reform and the Contradictions of Economic Life*. New York: Basic Books.

Chronicle of Higher Education Almanac. 1998a. "Highest Level of Educational Attainment of 1998." *Chronicle of Higher Education* (Ohio State University Press) 16, no 1.

———. 1998b. "College Enrollment by Race and Ethnic Group." *Chronicle of Higher Education* (Ohio State University Press) 16, no 1.

Dahlberg, Sandra. Forthcoming. "Families First: But Not in Higher Education." In *Reclaiming Class: Women, Poverty, and the Promise of Education in America*, ed. Vivyan Adair and Sandra Dahlberg. Philadelphia: Temple University Press.

Dewey, John. [1916] 1997. *Democracy and Education*. New York: Simon and Schuster.

Gordon, Lynn D. 1992. *Gender and Higher Education in the Progressive Era*. New Haven: Yale University Press.

Greenberg, Michelle. 1999. *How State Welfare Laws Treat Postsecondary Education*. Washington, DC: Center for Law and Social Policy.

Jordan, I. King. 2001. "Colleges Can Do Even More for People with Disabilities." *Chronicle of Higher Education* 47, no. 40.

Kates, Susan. 2001. *Activist Rhetorics and American Higher Education 1885–1937*. Carbondale and Edwardsville: Southern Illinois University Press.

Malveaux, Julianne. 2002. "Speaking of Education: Hard Times for Poor Students." *Issues in Black Education*, May 23: 41–43.

Mann, Horace, and Mary Mann. [1853] 1990. *On the Art of Teaching*. New York: Applewood Books.

Mondale, Sarah, Sarah B. Patton, Carl Kaestle, James Anderson, Diane Ravitch, and Larry Cuban, eds. 2001. *School: The Story of American Public Education*. Boston: Beacon Press.

Rothman, Robert. 1999. *Inequality and Stratification: Race, Class, and Gender*. New Brunswick, NJ: Prentice Hall.

U.S. Census Bureau. 2000a. "Money Matters: Money, Income, and Education, 1999." *Population Profile of the United States: 1999*. Washington, DC: Author.

———. 2000b. "Disability and Income." *Population Profile of the United States: 1999*. Washington, DC: Author.

———. 2000c. "Annual Demographic Survey." *Current Population Series*. Washington, DC: Author.

Employment and Training

Employment and training programs provide public or publicly subsidized instruction in job skills to individuals who are unemployed, in poverty, or at risk of falling into either category. Job skills may include finding and retaining jobs, skill education in the classroom (vocational education) or worksite skill training (on-the-job training). The large-scale employment and training programs initiated in the United States in the early 1960s aimed at first to assist unemployed breadwinners who had been displaced by trade policies, by automation, or by industrial decline. Over time, employment and training became more closely tied to the welfare system, with programs increasingly motivated by the desire to reduce welfare dependency and welfare expenditures. Employment and training programs have increasingly emphasized job-search skills rather than extensive training.

Americans who seek to improve their employment skills have always depended heavily on their own initiative, their employers' efforts, and private labor market institutions. Despite the tradition of free public schooling and of postsecondary education for higher-status occupations, the United States provided little direct job training to help the poor and jobless improve their position in the labor market. The federal government's Smith-Hughes Act of 1917 supported vocational education for high school students. This program quickly came to be dominated by agricultural training for white southern farmers; vocational education for women consisted primarily of home economics and secretarial training.

The New Deal provided numerous work-relief programs for millions of jobless Americans in the 1930s. These programs aimed to provide temporary income rather than long-term skills or jobs. A few New Deal initiatives established enduring models for job training that informed policy in the 1960s and 1970s: part-time jobs for students (the National Youth Administration), employment and training in conservation (the Civilian Conservation Corps [CCC]), adult basic education, literacy training, and defense vocational training.

After World War II, interest in employment and training policy increased as economic planning became more widely accepted. The G.I. Bill extended education and training benefits for veterans, a population expected to swell the ranks of the unemployed after the war. Federal support for vocational education expanded substantially. Liberal senators briefly floated a proposal to spend $100 million annually for retraining and relocating the jobless in high-unemployment areas in 1949. A decade later, a Senate committee recommended federal grants for a "nationwide vocational training program" to deal with the problem of jobless Americans who lacked the skills to adjust to the changing economy.

By the early 1960s, national policymakers considered job training an important remedy for the problem of long-term unemployment among older male breadwinners. Automation, free trade, and industrial change had eliminated the jobs of many heads of households. Growing concern about this problem resulted in the Area

Redevelopment Act (ARA) in 1961 and the Manpower Development and Training Act (MDTA) in 1962. The ARA authorized job training as part of a package of aid to "depressed" areas with unusually high jobless rates. The MDTA provided grants to every state for retraining workers through the vocational education system and on-the-job training. As many as 300,000 individuals were enrolled in MDTA-sponsored programs in the mid-1960s; about 40 percent were female, and a third were African American. MDTA trained people to serve as typists, machine tool operators, nurse's aides, auto mechanics, secretaries, and cooks. MDTA avoided the institutionalized racial discrimination in vocational education and the U.S. Employment Service in the South. The U.S. Labor Department increasingly tried to bypass these systems entirely by contracting directly with employers for on-the-job training.

As unemployment declined in the early 1960s, policymakers grew more interested in using employment and training to address poverty. The Public Welfare Amendments of 1962 extended benefits for families with an unemployed parent who were receiving Aid to Families with Dependent Children (AFDC) and encouraged the states to expand social services, including job training, to welfare recipients by providing federal funding for three-quarters of the cost of "rehabilitation" services. The Economic Opportunity Act of 1964 (the War on Poverty) expanded the population eligible for help and expanded the employment and training help available, most notably by providing "work experience" (temporary paid employment to bring welfare recipients into the labor market). The Office of Economic Opportunity (OEO) provided direct funding to community-based organizations, especially in minority communities, that could provide employment and training services directly to target populations. Philadelphia's Opportunities Industrialization Center (OIC) program, founded by the Reverend Leon Sullivan, was the most influential community-based employment and training program. Organizations such as OIC, the National Urban League, and Service Employment and Redevelopment (SER)–Jobs for Progress today remain important institutions in the delivery of employment and training services across the United States. Inspired by the New Deal's CCC, the War on Poverty's Job Corps (established in 1964) has provided residential education and job training for youth aged sixteen through twenty-four. In 1968, in the aftermath of riots in major American cities, President Lyndon B. Johnson's administration implemented the Job Opportunities in the Business Sector program, the first substantial program to subsidize private-sector jobs for the poor.

Baffling complexity plagued the job-training system by the end of the 1960s. The Labor Department alone was trying to control over 10,000 separate contracts with community-based organizations, private employers, unions, and state and local agencies. President Richard M. Nixon's "New Federalism" initiative proposed to combine these grants and delegate administration to state and local governments. A lengthy battle between the president and Congress resulted in the Comprehensive Employment and Training Act (CETA) of 1973. CETA delegated substantial authority to over 400 state and local governments, which would receive block grants for job training. Congress insisted that CETA include a program for public employment to counter recessions and for areas with high joblessness. By the late 1970s, CETA employed over 700,000 individuals. Programs such as the Job Corps continued as separate, federally administered programs.

During the 1970s, CETA came to be seen as a policy failure. The program's rapid growth, its decentralization, and its emphasis on public job creation made CETA vulnerable to abuse in many places. Public funds were used for patronage jobs in some areas; other areas used CETA to ease their budget crises by cutting regular payrolls and rehiring workers with CETA funds.

Media attention to training programs for professional card dealers and other questionable occupations further undermined the program. Though CETA was amended in 1978 to correct some of these problems and to target disadvantaged youth, the acronym was irretrievably tainted.

As CETA lost credibility, a backlash against welfare and perceived welfare dependency was encouraging sentiment for using employment and training to discipline welfare recipients. The Work Incentive (WIN) Program of 1967 marked an early sign of this sentiment. WIN took a step toward requiring job training as a prerequisite for receiving welfare. Welfare recipients could lose their eligibility if they refused to take suitable jobs or to enroll in job-training programs. By the end of the 1970s, support was strong for replacing welfare with "workfare," that is, providing temporary income support for needy people on the condition that they work or participate in job training.

President Ronald Reagan's administration eliminated spending for CETA's public employment programs in 1981. As joblessness increased in 1982, the Reagan administration reluctantly agreed to reauthorize federal job-training programs. The Job Training Partnership Act of 1982 (JTPA), which replaced CETA, explicitly targeted the poor and economically disadvantaged, cementing the connection between U.S. employment and training policy and the welfare system. No JTPA funds were to be used for income support for trainees. Federal job-training grants were channeled through state governments to local Private Industry Councils (the majority of whose members had to come from the business community), which would manage local employment and training policy. Despite efforts to consolidate employment and training programs, the federal government still funded 163 separate job-training programs in 1995.

Subsequent changes in national welfare policy have inspired further changes in employment and training policy. The Family Support Act of 1988 created the Job Opportunities and Basic Skills (JOBS) training program, which required states to place 20 percent of welfare recipients in workfare programs by 1995 and emphasized job training and education for those considered at risk of long-term dependency. Because the program permitted the states considerable discretion in achieving the program's goals and because a severe economic recession soon followed its enactment, the cash-strapped states invented new, cheaper approaches to expediting the removal of welfare recipients from the rolls. Programs in San Diego, California, and in Arkansas emphasized helping welfare recipients find new jobs as quickly as possible without any additional job training. This approach, which often places people in low-paying, insecure jobs, has been ensconced in policy as the "work-first" principle followed in many localities.

In 1992, presidential candidate Bill Clinton sought to combine education and job-training services for welfare recipients with a time limit on benefits. Conservative Republicans, who won congressional majorities in 1994, insisted on mandatory work requirements. The Personal Responsibility and Work Opportunity Reconciliation Act of 1996, which replaced AFDC with Temporary Assistance for Needy Families (TANF), limited the number of months an individual could receive income support over his or her lifetime and required recipients to enroll in work or job training. TANF permitted states to experiment with these workfare requirements. The Wisconsin Works program, implemented in 1997, ended cash assistance to the poor and substituted a system of job-placement services and supports for poor people, depending on their employment readiness. The lessons of the Wisconsin, San Diego, Arkansas, and other experiments made it attractive for states to emphasize job-search assistance before job training for many welfare recipients. Two other considerations have been important in this "work-first" emphasis. One is that effective job training requires a bigger up-front investment of time and money. The other is that the new federal welfare law—and the incentives it offers the states—is focused solely on reducing the welfare rolls as quickly as possible rather than on moving people out of poverty.

These changes in welfare policy affected national employment and training policy in 1998, when the Workforce Investment Act (WIA) replaced JTPA. Unlike previous programs, which had emphasized the education and the development of skills before job search, WIA emphasized immediate job-search, job-placement, and job-retention skills (such as interviewing, punctuality, and workplace literacy). WIA also attempted to create "one-stop" service delivery, with the intent to create single locations that would blend the job-training programs of JTPA with unemployment insurance, the employment service, vocational education, veterans programs, trade adjustment assistance, and, it was hoped, TANF and school-to-work programs.

Despite the bold rhetoric of the MDTA, CETA, and other programs of the 1960s and 1970s, U.S. expenditures on employment and training never approached the levels of such expenditures in many European nations, and they have declined considerably since the late 1970s. When JTPA ended in the 1990s, it had provided training for about the same number of people as MDTA had thirty years earlier, despite substantial growth in the eligible population. Initially conceived as programs to help male breadwinners adjust to economic change, American employment and training programs steadily became an adjunct of the welfare system, serving a clientele that was disproportionately young, minority, and female. The entry-level jobs encouraged by employment and training policy are aimed at reducing dependency at the lowest cost rather than at increasing the quality of the labor supply.

The evidence that job training has helped youth or men is inconclusive. Job training and job services evidently provide modest benefits for women. Even the best job-training programs do not raise earnings enough to make a substantial difference in the poverty status of poor mothers. The most successful programs seem to be those conducted by employers themselves. "Creaming" (that is, selecting the most job-ready candidates for training services) and "substitution" (that is, substituting publicly subsidized trainees or employees for one's own employees in order to reduce payroll costs) persistently plague these programs. Meanwhile, American employment and training policy in the near future will continue to be driven by American welfare policy.

David Brian Robertson

See also: Area Redevelopment Act; Employment Policy; Unemployment; U.S. Department of Labor; War on Poverty; Welfare Policy/Welfare Reform; Workfare

References and Further Reading

Baumer, Donald C. 1985. *The Politics of Unemployment*. Washington, DC: Congressional Quarterly Press.

Nightingale, Demetra Smith, and Robert H. Haveman, eds. 1995. *The Work Alternative: Welfare Reform and the Realities of the Job Market*. Washington: Urban Institute Press.

Peck, Jamie. 2001. *Workfare States*. New York: Guilford Press.

Riemer, Frances Julia. 2001. *Working at the Margins: Moving off Welfare in America*. Albany: SUNY Press.

Weir, Margaret. 1992. *Politics and Jobs: The Boundaries of Employment Policy in the United States*. Princeton: Princeton University Press.

Employment Policy

At the end of World War II, employment policy developed out of the liberal-labor vision of a right to a job for all able to work or seeking work, which the federal government would guarantee. Responding to widespread fears of mass unemployment, Montana's Democratic Senator James E. Murray drew upon the legacy of wartime planning and economic coordination to propose the Full Employment Act of 1945. The resulting Employment Act of 1946 contained not new obligations or entitlements but, rather, an economic planning mechanism and commitment to promoting "maximum employment, production, and purchasing power" (Joint Economic Committee 1966, 9). The act instructed the president to transmit an economic report at the beginning of each legislative session, and it formed two new agencies, the Council of Economic Advisors (CEA) in the executive branch and the congressional Joint Economic Committee, to gather data and analyze economic trends, with the first acting in an advisory capacity and the second directing congressional attention to the economy. Over the years, the CEA attempted to shore up aggregate demand through fiscal devices, seen in the 1964 tax cut, rather than to address structural barriers to employment, which became the purview of targeted regional development and manpower training programs under the War on Poverty. Policymakers disconnected overall economic health from social welfare.

By the 1940s, policy intellectuals inside and outside the government had turned to the writings of British economist John Maynard Keynes. His ideas permeated the National Planning Association, an elite Washington group composed of agriculture, business, and labor interests, and the National Farmers Union, the most liberal group in the farm lobby, which joined the fiscal division of the Bureau of the Budget to push for economic planning for full employment. Keynesians argued for state investment and expenditure to raise purchasing power and to stimulate job creation in the private sector, with jobs programs being a last resort. In 1943, the National Resources Planning Board, located in the Executive Office of the President, issued *Security, Work, and Relief Politics*, a report that announced a "New Bill of Rights" that began with the right to work. President Franklin D. Roosevelt reinforced this idea with his Economic Bill of Rights of January 1944 and subsequent speeches during the presidential campaign of that year. Congressional planning committees were already grappling with the consequences for employment of terminating war contracts and converting production for postwar uses. Upon assuming the presidency, Harry S. Truman embraced the concept of full employment.

Murray's Senate Committee on Military Affairs strongly claimed in its 1944 report, "Legislation for Reconversion and Full Employment," that only government could ensure full employment. The bill Murray introduced a few months later, cosponsored by liberal Democrats such as New York's Robert Wagner and Republican mavericks like Oregon's Wayne Morse and North Dakota's William Langer, placed the responsibility for employment and prosperity squarely with the government. It mandated a National Production and Employment Budget, greater coordination of economic policy, and public spending to compensate for lost private investment. Significantly, the original wording restricted the government's guarantee of employment to "all Americans who have finished their schooling and who do not have full-time housekeeping responsibilities" (Bailey 1950, 243). Such a proposal assumed that married women who had entered wartime factories were temporary workers. The government, declared cosponsor Senator Joseph C. O'Mahoney (D-Wyoming), should not encourage employment among "people . . . who ought to be at home helping to raise families" or engage in policies to "break up the family" (quoted in Kessler-Harris 2001, 20). Although the bill sent to the House dropped this language, full employment never meant that all would be fully employed; rather, only those recognized as workers were covered.

Organized labor and liberal groups, such as the National Association for the Advancement of Colored People and the National Catholic Welfare Conference under the auspices of the Union for Democratic Action (which became Americans for Democratic Action), lined up behind the 1945 bill. The Congress of Industrial Organizations felt that the bill would buffer economic shocks but that only its own more robust program of higher wages, price controls, extended Social Security and unemployment compensation, fair taxation, aid to housing and education, and improved race relations would guarantee full employment. In contrast, major business lobbyists, including the American Farm Bureau Federation, charged that the bill would lead to inflation and would replace private enterprise with statism. In the midst of the largest strike wave in history, with fears of rising prices replacing concerns over unemployment, the more conservative House of Representatives adopted a weakened bill. Truman accepted the resulting act as a first step.

The CEA would come to serve as an advocacy group for the president as much as a compiler of economic information, improving the executive's ability to evaluate the economy. Whether it would promote Keynesian ideas depended on presidential appointments and the influence of the council on both the president and more-established agencies. Liberal Democrats would come to dominate the Joint Economic Committee, which was limited to holding hearings and thus had little substantive impact on enacting the employment demands of trade union allies.

Though the Employment Act of 1946 made no mention of inflation, balance of payments, or redistribution of income, these issues would face the CEA over the next two decades. Central to postwar policy was a presumed trade-off between employment and inflation. Rather than stressing employment, the first *Economic Report of the President,* in 1947, asked trade unions to moderate wage demands lest prices rise, anticipating the idea of wage-price guidelines. Although price controls ended before the 1948 election, the Korean War brought deficit spending and limited price, wage, and credit controls. Leon Keyserling, then the council's chair, pushed economic growth to obtain high employment without fluctuations in prices, but cold war spending made "little direct contribution to increased standards of living" (Norton 1977, 123).

Federal spending tied to foreign policy, rather than macroeconomics, ignited postwar growth, so neither employment policy nor Keynesian pump priming actually drove economic policy. Congress nearly cut off funding for the CEA in 1953, and President Dwight D. Eisenhower's appointments, led by Arthur Burns, were not inclined to push government intervention. Moderation of economic fluctuations became the goal. By 1956, economists believed that a conflict existed between high employment, rapid growth, and stable prices. Despite more-frequent recessions (1949, 1954, 1958, and 1961–1962), each with greater unemployment, policymakers praised the general level of economic prosperity. They sought a technical outcome—a balanced budget at full employment—without much interference in the workings of the private labor market.

Though Walter Heller and the other economists appointed by President John F. Kennedy to the CEA were liberal Keynesians, they separated social from economic policies. By increasing growth, they argued, unemployment would diminish and so would poverty. Though the CEA's 1962 *Economic Report* admitted that families "headed by women, the elderly, nonwhites, migratory workers, and the physically or mentally handicapped" were left out of prosperity, they still insisted that growth and full employment would end poverty (O'Connor 2001, 152). Through new statistical measures, administration economists like Robert Solow and Arthur Okun associated decreased poverty with numerical goals, such as 4 percent rates for both unemployment and growth. Against this aggregate growth position were trade unionists, as well as conservatives, who saw unemployment as structural. The conservatives argued that any rate of unemployment over 5 or 6 percent would generate inflation, while labor saw automation displacing industrial, especially minority, workers (who were mostly male). Thus, labor and its left-liberal supporters promoted active job creation, retraining, minimum-income guarantees, and other market interventions by government.

To combat the recession of 1962, when automatic stabilizers appeared to be ineffective, Heller and the CEA recommended tax cuts. Deficit spending would generate a "full employment budget," that is, "the excess of revenues over expenditures that would prevail at 4 percent employment" (Norton 1977, 181). Although the CEA believed tax cuts to be more "efficient" in producing the necessary deficits to stimulate the economy, it did not dismiss increased spending. Rather, congressional diffidence over spending bills blocked other options; here a spillover effect from southern Democratic opposition to social welfare spending reinforced the tax-cut approach. Kennedy lacked the political clout to initiate any bold move against rising unemployment, especially since poverty and joblessness increasingly appeared connected to distressed regions and hidden people, as Michael Harrington noted in *The Other America* (1962).

Kennedy-Johnson initiatives targeted structural unemployment but never with adequate resources. The 1961 Area Redevelopment Act (ARA) provided loan guarantees and training and technical grants to high-unemployment areas. The 1962 Manpower Development and Training Act (MDTA) would make employable skilled men who had been dislocated by technology. To end youth unemployment, the War on Poverty initiated the Jobs Corps and Neighborhood Youth Corps, programs geared to changing the characteristics of individuals rather than to transforming labor markets or redistributing income.

African Americans, who undoubtedly had the highest unemployment rates in the nation, became identified with the War on Poverty, bringing racial politics to the forefront of employment policy. Some policymakers began to believe, as one House task force put it, that "a successful employment program would in itself help to solve many of the problems of social disorganization" (quoted in Weir 1992, 92). The 1968 Kerner Commission Report on urban riots recommended public employment; jobs were a top priority of the 1968 Poor People's Campaign, as they had been for the 1963 March on Washington. The fiscal drain of the Vietnam War and a general political reluctance to provide the poor with government jobs led to an emphasis on creating incentives for private-sector employers to open up jobs and job training. But neither business nor unions felt subsidized job training was in their interest. The most effective jobs program for African Americans turned out to be the growth of public-sector employment.

The Humphrey-Hawkins Full Employment and Balanced Growth Act (1978) responded to the growing unemployment of the mid-1970s by combining a renewed interest in economic planning with full-employment guarantees. It joined together a bill proposed by former vice president Senator Hubert Humphrey (D-Minnesota) to create an Economic Planning Board, based on the ideas of Nobel laureate Wassily Leontief, with one initiated by Representative Augustus Hawkins (D-California) to provide a job for all who would work, based on the demands of the Congressional Black Caucus. As an amendment to the 1946 Employment Act, it would "put full employment back in the Employment Act," Humphrey declared in 1976, by setting a goal of reaching 3 percent unemployment in four years (quoted in Weir 1992, 135). Liberals found the bill useful during the election to tarnish opponents, but actual political support was lukewarm. Moreover, intellectual advocates were outside the mainstream of an increasingly neoclassical economics profession, and only the liberal industrial unions, like the United Auto Workers, were fully behind the bill. It was judged inflationary by President Lyndon B. Johnson's former budget director Charles Schultze during congressional hearings, and support dropped off. President Jimmy Carter signed a bill in 1978 that targeted a 4 percent unemployment rate within five years without committing the government to providing either jobs or any mechanism to reach that goal.

Full employment lost support of elite policymakers during the stagflation of the 1970s. Associated with African Americans, its political feasibility diminished with the election of Ronald Reagan. Job training programs were cut back, and punitive welfare-to-work schemes, developed over the previous twenty years, replaced the right to a job as government's main employment policy. Attention thus shifted from the unemployed white male breadwinner to the unmarried minority mother as the subject of poverty and the object of reform.

Eileen Boris

See also: Civil Rights Movement; Economic/Fiscal Policy; Employment and Training; Unemployment

References and Further Reading

Bailey, Stephen Kemp. 1950. *Congress Makes a Law: The Story behind the Employment Act of 1946*. New York: Columbia University Press.

Hamilton, Dona Cooper, and Charles V. Hamilton. 1997. *The Dual Agenda: The African-American Struggle for Civil and Economic Equality*. New York: Columbia University Press.

Joint Economic Committee. 1966. *Twentieth Anniversary of the Economic Act of 1946: An Economic Symposium*. Washington, DC: GPO.

Kessler-Harris, Alice. 2001. *In Pursuit of Equity: Women, Men, and the Quest for Economic Citizenship in 20th-Century America*. New York: Oxford University Press.

Mucciaroni, Gary. 1990. *The Political Failure of Employment Policy, 1945–1982*. Pittsburgh, PA: University of Pittsburgh Press.

Norton, Hugh S. 1977. *The Employment Act and the Council of Economic Advisors, 1946–1976*. Columbia: University of South Carolina Press.

O'Connor, Alice. 2001. *Poverty Knowledge: Social Science, Social Policy, and the Poor in Twentieth-Century U.S. History*. Princeton: Princeton University Press.

Weir, Margaret. 1992. *Politics and Jobs: The Boundaries of Employment Policy in the United States*. Princeton: Princeton University Press.

End Poverty in California (EPIC)

End Poverty in California (EPIC) was the campaign platform turned social movement that transformed California's politics during the Great Depression by making socialist reform a distinct possibility in one of the nation's largest and most politically significant states. Muckraking novelist, critic, and socialist Upton Sinclair promised to "end poverty in California" if elected governor in 1934. Sparking one of the most exciting and controversial gubernatorial elections in American history, both Sinclair's grassroots popularity and his ultimate defeat attest to the possibilities and the limitations of reform during the Great Depression.

In 1933, Sinclair, who was well known for such widely read reform novels as *The Jungle* (1906), switched his party affiliation from Socialist to Democratic as he contemplated a campaign for the California governorship. He hoped that associating with the Democratic Party and with President Franklin D. Roosevelt's New Deal would make his views more palatable to the public and would increase his chances of electoral victory. He also published a small book entitled *I, Governor of California and How I Ended Poverty—A True Story of the Future*, which served as the basis for his 1934 End Poverty in California (EPIC) gubernatorial campaign. The EPIC plan consisted of twelve points, each of which was intended to quell the economic depression facing the region. Sinclair wanted the state to appropriate unused lands and factories to build "production-for-use" (rather than for profit) communities. He also wanted to shift the burden of taxation to the wealthy, proposing heavy, graduated income and inheritance taxes as well as large taxes on corporations and utilities. Capitalizing on an issue popular in California due to the state's many aging residents, he advocated pensions for the elderly and the disabled. Invigorated by Sinclair's proposals, EPIC clubs formed all over the state and brought

Upton Sinclair, The Epic Plan, *1934*

1. A legislative enactment for the establishment of State land colonies, whereby the unemployed may become self-sustaining and cease to be a burden upon the taxpayers. A public body . . . will take the idle land . . . and erect dormitories, kitchens, cafeterias, and social rooms, and cultivate the land. . . .
2. A public body . . . will be authorized to acquire factories and production plants whereby the unemployed may produce the basic necessities required for themselves and for the land colonies, and to operate these factories and house and feed and care for the workers. . . .
3. A public body . . . will . . . issue scrip to be paid to the workers and used in the exchanging of products within the system. . . .
4. An act . . . repealing the present sales tax, and substituting a tax on stock transfers . . .
5. An act . . . providing for a State income tax . . .
6. An increase in the State inheritance tax . . .
7. A law increasing the taxes on privately owned public utility corporations and banks.
8. A constitutional amendment revising the tax code of the State . . . exempt[ing] from taxation . . . homes and ranches [assessed at] less than $3000. Upon properties assessed at more than $5000 there will be a tax increase. . . .
9. A constitutional amendment providing for a State land tax upon unimproved building land and agricultural land which is not under cultivation . . .
10. A law providing for the payment of a pension of $50 per month to every needy person over sixty years of age . . .
11. A law providing for the payment of $50 per month to all persons who are blind, or who by medical examination are proved to be physically unable to earn a living . . .
12. A pension of $50 per month to all widowed women who have dependent children . . . increased by $25 per month for each additional child . . .

Source: Upton Sinclair, *Immediate Epic: The Final Statement of the Plan* (Los Angeles: End Poverty League, 1934). Reprinted in *The Era of Franklin D. Roosevelt, 1933–1945: A Brief History with Documents*, ed. Richard D. Polenberg (Boston and New York: Bedford Books, 2000), 120–122.

many previously apolitical men and women into the American democratic process.

Sinclair convincingly won the Democratic Party's gubernatorial nomination, but he simultaneously became a lightning rod for controversy. He never gained the support of the state Democratic Party bosses, who believed that the writer was too radical. For much the same reason, President Roosevelt refused to endorse him and took pains to distance himself from Sinclair's left-leaning ideas. This lack of support from the party establishment struck a significant blow against Sinclair's chances. Sinclair also galvanized a relentless conservative opposition intent on his defeat. Industrial leaders loathed him, and newspapers, almost unanimous in their opposition, printed propaganda against him. One common practice was to attribute the words of a fictional Sinclair character to the candidate himself, making him look absurd. For the first time, Hollywood leaders became explicitly politically active as well. Short propaganda films dressed up as prefeature "newsreels" were aired throughout the state and showed "hoboes"—who were actually actors—pouring into California for government "handouts" in anticipation of a Sinclair victory. Louis B. Mayer, the head of Metro-Goldwyn-Mayer studios, threatened to leave the state if Sinclair won. The most important campaign issue, however, was religion. As a result of his novel *The Profits of Religion* (1918), the press painted Sinclair as a subversive hostile to Christianity. Although many clerics supported him anyway, popular leaders like Aimee Semple McPherson attacked the candidate as an atheist and a communist.

In the end, Sinclair's grassroots supporters could not overcome the power and the money of the many forces aligned against him. But the campaign was not a total defeat. EPIC candidates won many seats in the State Assembly, and EPIC clubs helped revive Californian progressivism. Thousands of new Democrats were registered, and in order to beat Sinclair, Republican victor Frank Merriam pledged to bring the programs and ideas of the New Deal to California, which he subsequently did. In the era of Roosevelt, Huey Long, and Francis E. Townsend, the Sinclair campaign provided another example of the opportunities and the limitations of poverty relief and wealth redistribution available to reformers during the Depression. EPIC also stands out for its bold objective: ending poverty through political and policy action, a goal that would not again be embraced until the affluent 1960s, with President Lyndon B. Johnson's declaration of "unconditional war on poverty" in 1964.

Matthew A. Sutton

See also: Great Depression and New Deal; Social Security Act of 1935; Socialist Party; Townsend Movement; War on Poverty

References and Further Reading

Harris, Leon. 1975. *Upton Sinclair, American Rebel*. New York: Thomas Y. Crowell.

Mitchell, Greg. 1992. *The Campaign of the Century: Upton Sinclair's Race for Governor of California and the Birth of Media Politics*. New York: Random House.

Rice, Richard, William Bullough, and Richard Orsi. 1996. *The Elusive Eden: A New History of California*. 2d ed. Boston: McGraw-Hill.

Rising, George G. 1997. "An Epic Endeavor: Upton Sinclair's 1934 California Gubernatorial Campaign." *Southern California Quarterly* 79: 101–124.

Entitlements

See Aid to Families with Dependent Children (ADC/AFDC); Citizenship; Social Security Act of 1935; Welfare Policy/Welfare Reform

Environmentalism

Environmentalism is a social movement that began in the late nineteenth century whose purpose was the preservation of natural forests and wildlife refuges. Since that time, it has evolved to include efforts to eliminate environmental inequities that result in the location of poor and minority communities on or near toxic lands. The concern with environmental inequities is called the "environmental justice movement." It consists of over 400 grassroots organizations in the United States, Canada, and Mexico. Although organizations originally established for preservation may also engage in activities around environmental justice, there is an ideological distinction between environmentalism and environmental justice.

Environmentalism was born in the writings of Ralph Waldo Emerson and Henry David Thoreau, who believed in a spiritual link between man and nature. In the late 1800s, several organizations dedicated to the conservation of lands and wildlife emerged—the Audubon Society and the National Parks and Conservation Association, among others. The most prominent such organization was the Sierra Club. The beauty of the Yosemite Valley in California transformed John Muir, a naturalist, during what was to be a brief visit. He made California, and the exploration of the valley and the Sierra Nevada mountains, his life's work. Muir led the campaign to establish Yosemite National Park, and in 1892, he helped establish the Sierra Club. Muir was its first president.

Since it began, the Sierra Club has been a powerful lobbying organization for the preservation of the wilderness. In the early twentieth century, the organization encouraged the establishment of the National Park Service. In the mid-1970s, the Sierra Club began to advocate for energy conservation policies and clean air. By the end of the twentieth century, the Sierra Club had turned to the effects of globalization on the environment.

In the middle to late 1960s, a period of significant social and political change in the United States, a worldwide movement grew to create more respect for the planet through the elimination of pollution and the reduction of waste. This led to the first international Earth Day on April 22, 1970. The activities of the Greenpeace environmental group heightened global awareness of environmentalism. Greenpeace is an international organization established in 1971 to protect endangered species. In their efforts to prevent the extinction of whales and seals, Greenpeace members employed the nonviolent resistance tactics of the civil rights movement by manning small boats that hovered between the hunters and their prey.

In the late 1970s, the Love Canal incident, which demonstrated the threat that toxic waste posed to humans, became a national political issue. Love Canal was a working-class neighborhood in Niagara Falls, New York. The homes and apartments in the neighborhood had been built on top of a landfill that had been used by several chemical plants located along the Niagara River. The nearly 42 million pounds of toxic chemicals dumped by these plants seeped into the yards and playgrounds in Love Canal. In 1978 and 1980, President Jimmy Carter declared Love Canal an environmental emergency area, and 950 families were evacuated. This was the beginning of a national awareness of the possibility of exposure to toxins in residential areas and of the consequent threat to human health.

In 1978, drivers for Ward Transformer Company, one of the largest transformer-repair companies in the United States, sprayed more than 200 miles of North Carolina roadsides with oil containing polychlorinated biphenyls (PCBs). This toxic chemical is a carcinogen and may cause birth defects and liver and skin disorders. In an attempt to decontaminate the roadsides, the state decided to collect the tainted soil and bury it in a landfill in Warren County, North Carolina. Warren County, which is 60 percent African American, fought this decision on the grounds that because the county is composed of a group that has been historically discriminated against, exposing those residents to the PCBs contained in the soil was a civil rights violation. A series of demonstrations resulted in the arrests of over 350 people. Although residents did not succeed in blocking the location of the landfill in their community, the struggle attracted the attention of national civil rights leaders and Black elected officials. The Warren County struggle, for many, marks the beginning of the environmental justice movement.

Since the Warren County incident, the environmental justice movement has been slowly gaining momentum. Citizens in the mostly Black community of Chester, Pennsylvania, combat toxins from various waste disposal, waste treatment, and incinerator sites in their community. Residents of New Orleans, Louisiana, fight efforts to rebuild a housing project near a toxic landfill linked to higher rates of breast cancer for residents who live near it.

In 1987, the Commission for Racial Justice, under the auspices of the United Church of Christ, published *Toxic Wastes and Race in the United States: A National Report on the Racial and Socio-Economic Characteristics of Communities with Hazardous Waste Sites*. Using an analysis of demographic patterns, the report found that race was significantly associated with the location of commercial hazardous waste facilities.

This report and the activities of environmental justice activists have led to the recognition of environmental justice as an issue of national importance.

In 1994, President Bill Clinton signed Executive Order 12898, which required the U.S. Environmental Protection Agency to address environmental justice issues as part of its mission. It also established the Interagency Federal Working Group on Environmental Justice, which was composed of sixteen other agencies. These agencies are responsible for collecting data on the impact of environmental hazards on minority and poor communities, for promoting public participation in the policymaking process related to the health of humans and the environment, and for ensuring the enforcement of health and environmental statutes. Since the passage of this order, the Environmental Protection Agency has established a national environmental justice program as well as individualized programs for each of its ten regions.

Andrea Y. Simpson

See also: Community Organizing; Community-Based Organizations

References and Further Reading

Bullard, Robert. 1990. *Dumping in Dixie: Race, Class, and Environmental Quality*. Boulder, CO: Westview Press.

———, ed. 1993. *Confronting Environmental Racism: Voices from the Grassroots*. Boston: South End Press.

Cole, Luke W., and Sheila R. Foster. 2001. *From the Ground Up*. New York: New York University Press.

Epidemic Disease

The American health experience has been shaped by the shifting nature of the country's economic, social, and political life. In particular, experience with epidemic disease among women and men, the aged and the young, African American and white, and the rich and poor have all been affected by such factors as the isolation of rural communities, the development of an economy based on commerce and industry, the growth of large urban and industrial centers, race and racism, changing housing and working conditions, and the development of extremes in poverty and wealth.

From early in American history there has been an intimate connection between health status and social developments. Although recent research (e.g., Ulrich 1990) appears to contradict some of the rosier conclusions of earlier studies, many studies of colonial New England written in the 1970s reveal an extraordinarily successful experience with disease as measured by available statistics on average length of life. According to Philip Greven (1972) and other colonial historians, men living in the first Andover, Massachusetts, settlement and elsewhere lived into their sixties, seventies, and eighties while their English counterparts were dying in their midthirties.

In contrast, although yellow fever and malaria, both mosquito-borne diseases, were both widely reported in seventeenth-century New England, their impact on the colonists of Jamestown, Virginia, was inordinately greater. The first Virginia colonies were plagued by starvation, which led to susceptibility to malaria, yellow fever, and a variety of other epidemics. Constant infirmity, infertility, and early death marked their experiences.

The differing experiences with disease in New England and Virginia were probably related to the distinct social and economic bases for these colonies. The New England colonies were settled by families seeking to establish stable, self-sufficient communities based on sustainable agriculture. The Virginia colonies, on the other hand, were settled largely as exploitative settlements of men who sought to plunder the land and the peoples of the area to extract wealth in the form of the cash crop, tobacco. The lack of commitment to establishing permanent, ongoing settlements helps explain the relative dearth of women among the first generations of colonists, their inability to establish successful economic and social institutions, and their inability to ward off starvation and susceptibility to epidemic diseases.

Early Epidemics: Smallpox

Smallpox, an acute viral disease whose symptoms are high fever and dark red spots that soon fill with pus and disfigure its victims, was perhaps the most fearsome disease of the colonial period. Introduced to the Americas by European colonists, the disease had an especially devastating effect on the Native American populations, who, because of their lack of contact with the disease, had virtually no immunity to it. While various English and Spanish settlements were periodically swept by an epidemic that caused varying degrees of distress, Native American populations throughout the colonies were devastated. In the nineteenth century, some U.S. Army units gave blankets previously used by smallpox and measles victims to Indian tribes, thereby destroying their communities and destroying resistance to westward expansion.

In some early smallpox epidemics, it was observed that a technique called "variolation" practiced by African American slaves seemed to be effective in protecting the Black population from the disease's worst ravages. The focus of intense public and religious debate in the early eighteenth century, the technique consisted of transplanting scabs and pus of smallpox victims into open wounds of healthy individuals. These people then developed a mild set of symptoms and, thereafter, immunity. This technique was adopted by European Americans and helped in the development of inoculation and vaccination as effective preventives.

By the end of the eighteenth and early nineteenth centuries, an extensive commercial economy combined with a growing, increasingly urbanized and poor population to make epidemic diseases a much greater threat to Americans. Epidemic disease, once a local phenomenon circumscribed by the relative lack of mobility among self-sufficient and isolated rural communities, began to sweep through the nation along the well-established trade routes. By the middle of the nineteenth century, the highly crowded and increasingly poor urban centers experienced death rates that were as high as those of European cities. Cholera, dysentery, tuberculosis, and a host of other water- and air-borne infectious conditions were endemic in the country's teeming urban centers, such as Boston, New Orleans, New York, Philadelphia, and elsewhere.

In the decades following the Revolution and continuing through the nineteenth century, a number of new water-borne and air-borne conditions began to sweep through urban poor communities. Cholera, a disease that caused severe dehydration through acute diarrhea, made dramatic and fearsome sweeps through the growing ports and cities of the nation in 1832, 1848, and 1865. In the absence of sewerage systems, pure water, systematic street cleaning, pure or fresh food or milk, and decent methods for preserving or freezing meats, diphtheria, whooping cough, and any number of fevers and flus became constant threats to babies and young children in the filthy urban trading centers of the nation. By the second half of the century, death and disease rates in American cities had increased substantially, and Americans' average length of life was by then no better than that of Europeans.

Tuberculosis, perhaps the most pervasive and deadly disease historically, emerged as the focus of intense concern as its primary symptoms—hacking coughs, fever, loss of weight, and night sweats—took on a seemingly dangerous aspect in the crowded and poverty-stricken urban environment of the late nineteenth century. Despite the fact that the disease probably peaked in significance in the middle years of the century and began to decline as a major cause of mortality after the 1880s, public health professionals and charity workers began to focus on this condition in the early years of the twentieth century.

The Use of Disease to Stigmatize the Poor

The changing experience of disease was often used as part of a broader political agenda that sought to stigmatize the poor and identify immigrants as a cause, rather than as victims, of disruptions in the life of the community. This use was particularly important in the nineteenth century amid the urbanization, industrialization, and large-scale immigration that transformed the nation's economy and environment. Especially in eastern port cities and most pointedly in New York, the demographic and physical transformation of the country was hard to miss: An English-speaking, largely Protestant community became, by the 1880s, home to thousands of Catholic and Jewish immigrants, who made up a poor and largely impoverished industrial working class. While some embraced these socioeconomic and demographic changes as signs of future growth and possibility, others expressed alarm at the increasingly visible poverty, illness, crowding, and "foreignness" of the city. To more-established residents, most of them Protestants, the connection between "plagues and people" seemed clear. Epidemic diseases, such as smallpox, cholera, typhoid, yellow fever, and a host of intestinal diseases, became powerful symbols of uncontainable social decline and were largely blamed on the immigrant poor.

In New York City, the elite class bemoaned the passing of a "golden age" in the city's history, but those memories were in large measure nostalgic and highly selective. High death rates and pestilence had long affected rich and poor communities alike. Yet patterns of disease in recent decades appeared to contemporaries to confirm the community's decay. "By mid-century, New York had among the worst health statistics in the nation. Vital statistics gathered by the City showed that while one out of every 44 people died in 1863 in Boston and one of 44 in Philadelphia, New York's rate was one in 36 . . . Despite the fact that endemic conditions such as tuberculosis and diarrheal diseases among children were more important contributors to mortality . . . than epidemic diseases, the appearance of scourges such as cholera had a very real significance as symbols of the apparent rapidity" with which American life was being transformed (The Living City/NYC).

The Sanitary Condition of the City

Amid this atmosphere of alarm over the "conditions of the poor," civic leaders launched major investigations into the social and environmental as well as the individual causes and consequences of disease, and with those investigations they began to pave the way for the public health movement, and its advocacy of improved sanitation, in the United States. In 1865, just as the Civil War was ending and shortly following the infamous draft riots of 1863, the Council of Hygiene and Public Health of the Citizens' Association of New York issued a report entitled *Sanitary Condition of the City*. Dedicated to the benefit of "all classes in the city," the report provided over 300 pages of detailed description of the city's physical, social, and moral character. Coming at the end of a bloody war that had split apart not only the nation but the communities of New York City as well, the report reflected both the hopes and the fears of the merchant leaders who had commissioned it.

Beginning with the observation that "pestilential diseases" laid bare "the impotence of the existing sanitary system," the report noted that outbreaks of disease paralyzed the commercial and political life of the community: "The people are panic-stricken [and] the interests of commerce suffer by the insensible and certain *loss of millions*." In a city of less than 1 million people, fully 7,000 to 10,000 lives could be saved, it was estimated, if proper sanitary practices could be developed (*Sanitary Condition of the City* 1865, xii). Disease was a hindrance to the new economy, and health was a commodity that could be measured in dollars and cents. An organized response to the high disease rates was a political and social necessity. Equally important, the report depicted disease as a matter of public morals and safety as well. "The mobs that held fearful sway in our city during the memorable out-break of violence in the month of July, 1863, were gathered in the overcrowded and neglected quarters of the city," the report reminded the reader. "The high brick blocks and closely-packed houses where the mobs originated seemed to be literally *hives of sickness and vice*" (xvi).

The observation that housing, politics, morals, and health were all intertwined underscored the council's perception of what needed to be done for the city in the coming years. Of first importance was the need to document and quantify the degree of suffering, the inadequacy of health and social services, and the horrors of urban and especially tenement life. Hence, with a voyeur's acuity, an elite's sense of authority, and the moral righteousness of missionaries, the council set out to expose the physical and social conditions that led to the spread of disease in mid-nineteenth-century New York. Their emphasis in these investigations was on the links between the physical environment—especially sanitary and tenement conditions—and individual behavior and morality as mutually reinforcing causes of illness. Similarly, their advocacy of improved sanitation was accompanied by calls for behavioral change. In this sense, the early public health literature did little to dispel the idea that poor people, "foreigners," and people of color were at least partly to blame for their own vulnerability to disease and for the threat that disease posed to other parts of the city.

Death and Disease in the New Environment

Underlying the social geography of disease documented by sanitary investigations were patterns of economic development and land use in urban centers that had created some of the world's worst crowding and most-depressing health statistics. By the middle years of the century, epidemics of typhus, yellow fever, cholera, and other diseases swept through the tenements and urban slums with fearsome impact. Despite the fact that epidemics were relatively minor contributors to overall death rates, the highly visible and often dramatic experience of seeing people literally dying in the streets had an enormous impact, affecting where and how cities developed. In the late eighteenth century, yellow fever had caused elites to flee from cities to relatively distant suburbs, beginning a spatial segregation of the rich and poor that would develop over the next century.

The commercial city of the late nineteenth century had created a skewed market for land and housing, which provided landlords and absentee owners with enormous profits and denied to workers and their families wholesome living quarters. Older, early-eighteenth-century housing patterns, in which artisans and working people lived and worked in the same dwelling, were replaced by land use patterns that separated work from home, wealthy from poor, immigrant from native, and owner from occupant. The market for housing created "unnatural" social relationships and market-driven scarcities of housing and land, which, in turn, created the preconditions for the disastrous health experience as market values replaced human values in the legal and social environment (Blackmar 1989).

The "sanitarians" who led reform efforts generally saw themselves as more than technical experts or professionals trained in a specific skill. Some had come from elite merchant families, and others had been trained in the ministry. They defined their mission as much in moral as in secular terms, and they believed that illness, filth, class, and disorder were intrinsically related. Individual transgression and social decay were equally at fault for poor health. In this period, before the widespread acceptance of the notion that specific pathogens caused particular diseases, public health workers, medical practitioners, and laypeople alike understood disease in highly personal and idiosyncratic terms. Much of public health practice as well as medical therapeutics rested on the belief that disease was a reflection of individuals' special social, personal, hereditary, and economic circumstances. An individual's maladies were based, in part, on his or her peculiarities and life. It was the special relationship between an individual and a complex, highly particularized environment that was at the root of illness.

With the revolution in bacteriology that followed the discoveries of Louis Pasteur, Joseph Lister, and Robert Koch in the middle decades of the nineteenth century, a new faith in laboratory science emerged not only among physicians but also among public health workers. "Bacteriology thus became an ideological marker, sharply differentiating the 'old' public health, the province of untrained amateurs, from the 'new' public health, which belonged to scientifically trained professionals," pointed out Elizabeth Fee (1987, 19). Despite the different professional mandates of public health workers and physicians, members of both professions who identified themselves with the science of medicine and public health began to share a common faith in the significance of the disease-specific germ entity in causing tuberculosis. A new model was gaining greater acceptance: A bacillus made people sick. The slums of large cities came to be seen as "breeding grounds" that were "seeded" with tuberculosis bacilli waiting to infect the susceptible victim. Tuberculosis came to be viewed as a disease that could be transmitted to susceptible individuals by means of air impregnated with bacteria from dried sputum, breathing, and so on. The dusting of furniture could throw into the air the "dried sputum" of tuberculars. Crowded public spaces or unclean home conditions with moist, warm, and stagnant air were seen as the most likely conduits for the disease.

New Public Health and Old Health Conditions

Despite decades of agitation and a rapidly evolving view of disease causation, the nation still faced daunting environmental hazards. In 1912, New York's Public Health Department issued its annual report, which, in language as dispassionate as any, detailed the continuing environmental problems that New Yorkers faced. The Public Health Department picked up over 20,000 dead horses, mules, donkeys, and cattle from the city's streets during the year and recorded 343,000 complaints from citizens, inspectors, and officials about problems ranging from inadequate ventilation and leaking cesspools and water closets to unlicensed manure dumps and animals kept without permits. It also removed nearly half a million smaller animals, such as pigs, hogs, calves, and sheep. While such environmental hazards had by then become familiar, somewhat startling was the emergence of changing patterns of death in the city. Officials wondered whether the nature of disease in the city was undergoing a perceptible shift. The infectious diseases of the nineteenth century, such as smallpox, typhoid fever, diphtheria, and pulmonary tuberculosis, appeared to be claiming fewer and fewer of the city's children and young adults. But cancer, heart disease, and pneumonia were claiming larger and larger numbers of elderly. To public health officials, these findings were significant in two ways. On the one hand, they showed measurable progress in the battle against infectious diseases. On the other hand, the report suggested a need to broaden the focus of public health policy to reduce mortality from diseases increasingly associated with middle and old age.

As the approach among public officials became more medicalized and scientific, their conceptualization of the public health challenge became less individual and personalized. Unlike in the early nineteenth century, when writers' works had a moral undertone, in the twentieth century a distinctly commercial tone overtook public health activities. History had taught health officials that "the full benefits of the methods and practice of sanitary science are available to any intelligent and well-organized community which will make the necessary expenditures, [and that] it may be truly said that within certain limits *public health is purchasable*" (*Annual Report* 1912, 12).

The health problems the nation faces today are largely of our own making as a society and are also potentially under our own control. AIDS, tuberculosis, SARS, and diseases associated with poverty and homelessness are in a very real way social creations and, therefore, can be addressed through social decisions. In a 1992 essay on what he calls "framing" disease, Charles Rosenberg noted that "disease is at once a biological event, a generation-specific repertoire of verbal constructs reflecting medicine's intellectual and institutional history," and "a sanction for cultural values." Pointing out that disease is a "social phenomenon," he illustrates that in large measure, "disease does not exist until we have agreed that it does, by perceiving, naming, and responding to it" (Rosenberg 1992, xiii).

Yet disease takes specific forms at different moments in history. Not only do we define different symptoms as pathological events, but we also create the physical environments and social relationships that allow for the emergence of very real new problems. In a very real way, we create our environment, and hence we create the conditions within which diseases thrive. Whether infectious disease in the nineteenth century, AIDS, cancer, heart disease, or tuberculosis today, or cholera, silicosis, or yellow fever in earlier times, the manner in which we address disease becomes emblematic of a specific society at a particular moment in history. Just as physicians, the elites, and the politicians in the mid-nineteenth century presented cholera as a moral as well as medical stigma, so too do we use disease as metaphor. We need only recall that as recently as the 1980s, newspapers, politicians, and public health professionals presented AIDS as a disease peculiar to Haitians and gay men, to realize how deeply social values and specific historical circumstance shape our understanding of disease and how quickly our assumptions about the causes and victims of disease can change.

Ironically, the success of the postwar decades in developing a wider and wider range of technological innovations left the nation almost unprepared for the new scourge of the 1980s, AIDS. Public health departments were underfunded and understaffed, and a generation of public health and medical practitioners had been reared in the belief that medical science and technology could protect us from widespread epidemics. In addition, the fact that the 1970s were marked by a giant fiasco—in which millions of dollars were spent on the development and distribution of a vaccine for a swine flu epidemic that never occurred—undermined our ability to mobilize against a disease that primarily affected gay men, intravenous drug users, and their partners. Some have also accused government and research scientists of deliberate inaction because of the association of AIDS with immorality among groups already disliked by large cross-sections of the population.

The nation's reaction to epidemic infectious disease has varied greatly over time. Once perceived to be a local problem of divine origin, epidemics became national in scope and became understood in highly medicalized terms. Yet the reaction and public response to illness is largely shaped by our perceptions of its victims and the social circumstances in which we live.

David Rosner

See also: Health Policy; Housing Policy; Urban Poverty

References and Further Reading

Annual Report of the Department of Health of the City of New York for the Years 1910–1911. New York, 1912.

Blackmar, Elizabeth. 1989. *Manhattan for Rent, 1785–1850*. Ithaca, NY: Cornell University Press.

Crosby, Alfred. 2003. *America's Forgotten Pandemic:*

The Influenza of 1918. 2d ed. New York: Cambridge University Press.

Duffy, John. 1990. *The Sanitarians: A History of American Public Health*. Urbana: University of Illinois Press.

Fee, Elizabeth. 1987. *Disease and Discovery: A History of the Johns Hopkins School of Hygiene and Public Health, 1916–1939*. Baltimore: Johns Hopkins University Press.

Greven, Philip. 1972. *Four Generations: Population, Land, and Family in Colonial Andover, Massachusetts*. Ithaca, NY: Cornell University Press.

The Living City/NYC. Web site. http://156.145.78.54/htm/decades/1860.htm.

Rosenberg, Charles E. 1987. *The Cholera Years*. Chicago: University of Chicago Press.

———. 1992. "Introduction: Framing Disease: Illness, Society, and History." In *Framing Disease: Studies in Cultural History*, ed. Charles E. Rosenberg and Janet Golden. New Brunswick, NJ: Rutgers University Press.

Rosenkrantz, Barbara. 1972. *Public Health and the State: Changing Views in Massachusetts, 1842–1936*. Cambridge, MA: Harvard University Press.

Sanitary Condition of the City: Report of the Council of Hygiene and Public Health of the Citizens' Association of New York. 1865. New York.

Ulrich, Laurel Thatcher. 1990. *A Midwife's Tale: The Life of Martha Ballard, Based on Her Diary, 1785–1812*. New York: Vintage Books.

Eugenics

Eugenics is the scientific theory and social movement that sought to ensure human betterment by applying the principles of evolutionary biology to human populations. Sir Francis Galton, a British amateur scientist, began arguing in 1883 that human improvement could be best secured through efficient management of human heredity. Just as humans had bred faster horses and fatter cattle, scientists could eliminate physical and mental disabilities and solve a host of social problems through rational control of human reproduction and immigration. The idea of human betterment appealed to many middle-class and white social reformers, who used it to justify a variety of social reforms in the early twentieth century. But the formal eugenics movement focused on several reforms: marriage restrictions, institutionalization and compulsory sterilization of mentally and physically disabled persons, and restrictions on immigration. Supporters of eugenics believed that heredity determined everyone's potential and that science could identify those persons whose hereditary endowment made them likely to be diseased or unsuccessful in life. In turn, legal restrictions—or negative eugenics—could be instituted to weed out the unfit, while state-funded incentives—or positive eugenics—could be used to encourage fit persons to have more children. Despite developments in biology that discredited most of their hereditarian assumptions, eugenicists continued to believe that all the characteristics important to success in life were biologically determined. Following the notion that social class reflected one's inherent worth, eugenicists often confused wealth with biological fitness. Likewise, eugenicists confused white political supremacy with biological superiority. Thus, eugenic definitions of fitness lent scientific credence to traditional U.S. elitist and racial prejudices. As a consequence, for decades to come, the impact of the policy successes achieved by eugenicists in the 1910s and 1920s fell most heavily on the poor, especially women and ethnic minorities.

Eugenics came to public attention through the publication in the first and second decades of the twentieth century of a number of scientific studies of human heredity. In a 1912 study called *The Kallikaks*, Henry Goddard traced the family tree of a mentally retarded girl, describing a family history in which miscreants, paupers, and prostitutes propagated at high rates. He concluded that the unregulated reproduction of people of limited intelligence constituted a menace. His recommended solution to this menace of the feebleminded was to institutionalize such individuals in sex-segregated facilities where they could receive vocational training and be prevented from procreating. In 1915, *The Jukes*, a study claiming to have traced the more than 700 descendants of a single Dutch immigrant through five generations, provided another portrait linking feeblemindedness to poverty, crime, prostitution, and excessive fertility. *The Jukes* and numerous other less well known family pedigrees were produced by workers at the Eugenics Record Office. Opened in 1907 with funding from the Carnegie Foundation, the Eugenic Records Office served as the headquarters of the American Eugenics Society. The office, run by Charles Davenport and Harry Laughlin, was the primary source of eugenic research until it was closed in 1939. The definition of feeblemindedness that Goddard used in writing *The Kallikaks* was based on results of the newly developed IQ tests. Although eugenicists believed IQ tests provided an accurate measure of inborn intelligence, eugenic family pedigrees were grounded in social prejudice more than in objective testing. The feeblemindedness identified in these studies was often based only on visual observations of white, middle-class fieldworkers. Following the American myth that any capable person, through hard work and thrift, could improve his or her social standing, eugenicists believed poverty resulted from low intelligence or other hereditary inadequacy. Thus, eugenic investigators usually skipped testing and just interpreted poor living conditions or periodic unemployment as evidence of underlying biological inadequacy.

Eugenicists feared that those with weak heredity were also, in addition to being social failures, naturally inclined to have very large families. Following Charles Darwin's observations that more-evolved species have fewer offspring than do less-evolved species, Herbert Spencer, a nineteenth-century British sociologist, concluded that as the capacity for rational thought increased, reproductive capacity decreased. Darwin's sea turtles laid hundreds of eggs, but only a few hatchlings survived. On the other hand, mammals, particularly humans, had very few offspring, and most lived to adulthood. Eugenicists quickly applied this logic to the differential fertility rates reported after the 1910 census. Eugenicists understood this differential rate to be the result of the difference in biological quality between native-born middle-class persons and working-class ethnic immigrants. Eugenicists also feared that the increasingly popular social welfare programs would actually undercut evolution by allowing unfit individuals to survive and reproduce. The differential fertility rate suggested to eugenicists that the proportion of unfit persons might actually be increasing. These fears spurred their efforts to secure sterilization of the unfit and to impose legal restrictions on marriage. By the mid-1930s, forty-one states prohibited the marriage of the feebleminded and twenty-seven states required their compulsory sterilization. Harry Laughlin was an expert witness in the 1927 U.S. Supreme Court case *Buck v. Bell*, which upheld sterilization laws. Following eugenic logic, the Court held that "in order to prevent our being swamped with incompetence," compulsory sterilization was justified. The Court held that it was in the interests of public welfare for society to "prevent those who are manifestly unfit from reproducing their kind" (quoted in Reilly 1991, 87).

The last reform that eugenicists pursued was the restriction of immigration. Eugenicists believed that the capacity for self-government, like every other important human characteristic, was grounded in biology and was most highly developed in those races that evolved in the German forests and the English countryside. Therefore, heavy immigration from other regions, they feared, might dilute the instinct for democracy within the U.S. population and thereby threaten to undermine the U.S. government. Arguing before Congress in 1921 that the IQ tests and physical exams given to World War I recruits demonstrated that recent immigrants were of an inferior stock, Harry Laughlin helped persuade Congress to limit immigration to the United States from all of Asia, Africa, and the southern and eastern regions of Europe.

Carole R. McCann

Buck v. Bell 274 *U.S.* 200 (1927)

This is a writ of error to review a judgment of the Supreme Court of Appeals of the State of Virginia, affirming a judgment of the Circuit Court of Amherst County, by which the defendant in error, the superintendent of the State Colony for Epileptics and Feeble Minded, was ordered to perform the operation of salpingectomy upon Carrie Buck, the plaintiff in error, for the purpose of making her sterile. The case comes here upon the contention that the statute authorizing the judgment is void under the Fourteenth Amendment as denying to the plaintiff in error due process of law and the equal protection of the laws.

Carrie Buck is a feeble minded white woman who was committed to the State Colony above mentioned in due form. She is the daughter of a feeble minded mother in the same institution, and the mother of an illegitimate feeble minded child. She was eighteen years old at the time of the trial of her case in the Circuit Court, in the latter part of 1924. An Act of Virginia, approved March 20, 1924, recites that the health of the patient and the welfare of society may be promoted in certain cases by the sterilization of mental defectives, under careful safeguard, &c.; that the sterilization may be effected in males by vasectomy and in females by salpingectomy, without serious pain or substantial danger to life; that the Commonwealth is supporting in various institutions many defective persons who if now discharged would become a menace but if incapable of procreating might be discharged with safety and become self-supporting with benefit to themselves and to society; and that experience has shown that heredity plays an important part in the transmission of insanity, imbecility, &c. . . .

The judgment finds the facts that have been recited and that Carrie Buck "is the probable potential parent of socially inadequate offspring, likewise afflicted, that she may be sexually sterilized without detriment to her general health and that her welfare and that of society will be promoted by her sterilization," and thereupon makes the order. . . .

It is better for all the world, if instead of waiting to execute degenerate offspring for crime, or to let them starve for their imbecility, society can prevent those who are manifestly unfit from continuing their kind. The principle that sustains compulsory vaccination is broad enough to cover cutting the Fallopian tubes. Jacobson v. Massachusetts, 197 U.S. 11. Three generations of imbeciles are enough.

Judgment affirmed.

See also: Birth Control; Feminisms; Reproductive Rights; Welfare Policy/Welfare Reform

References and Further Reading

Kevles, Daniel. 1985. *In the Name of Eugenics*. Berkeley and Los Angeles: University of California Press.

McCann, Carole. 1994. *Birth Control Politics in the United States, 1916–1945*. Ithaca, NY: Cornell University Press.

Reilly, Philip. 1991. *The Surgical Solution: A History of Involuntary Sterilization in the United States*. Baltimore: Johns Hopkins University Press.

Roberts, Dorothy. 1997. *Killing the Black Body: Race, Reproduction, and the Meaning of Liberty*. New York: Pantheon Books.

Trent, James. 1994. *Inventing the Feeble Mind: A History of Mental Retardation in the United States*. Berkeley and Los Angeles: University of California Press.

Evans, Walker

See Let Us Now Praise Famous Men; Picturing Poverty (I); *Survey* and *Survey Graphic*

Factories in the Field, *Carey McWilliams*

In 1939, writer and lawyer Carey McWilliams published *Factories in the Field: The Story of Migratory Labor in California*, a scathing indictment of the state's exploitative agricultural system during the Great Depression. Published just two months after *The Grapes of Wrath*, McWilliams's work was considered a praiseworthy nonfiction companion to John Steinbeck's legendary novel. After traveling extensively throughout California's fields, working as a labor organizer, and spending countless hours perusing old newspaper accounts and government records, McWilliams produced what he called "a hidden history" of the misery endured by migrant farmworkers in the state of California. *Factories in the Field* was the first comprehensive exposé of the harmful effects of corporate agriculture on farmworkers and the environment and is now considered a classic work of social history and investigative journalism.

McWilliams was particularly interested in showing his reader how the growth of corporate agriculture turned independent and hardworking farmers into a throng of low-paid farmworkers toiling on gigantic factory farms. He argued that the corporate agricultural system was largely the product of government policies—including water subsidies, marketing orders, and price supports—that favored agribusiness over the family farm. More accurately portraying modern farmworkers as members of the proletariat, just like their counterparts in urban factories, McWilliams called for their right to collective bargaining. There may have been no turning back from the rise of agribusiness, but this, according to McWilliams, made eliminating the artificial distinction between farmworkers and factory workers even more pressing.

During the Depression, over 1 million people moved to California, at least 150,000 of whom became farmworkers, expanding the farm workforce from 200,000 to 350,000 people. Many of these migrants, hailing mainly from the Midwest, drove up to farmhouses and asked for work, expecting that they would work as farmhands until they had saved enough money to buy their own farm. But the new system of industrialized agriculture precluded such a possibility for the vast majority of farm laborers. The urban factory model of product specialization and division of labor had effectively insinuated itself into California's agricultural system, making the family farm a thing of the past.

During his brief tenure as head of California's Division of Immigration and Housing from 1939 to 1942, McWilliams tried to help migrant farmers as much as he could. He stepped up inspections of grower-owned labor camps, which he found particularly troublesome because on-farm housing made farm laborers too dependent on their employers. He also abolished rules that denied relief to migrants who refused to accept farm jobs paying low wages, a policy that effectively forced growers to raise wages.

As a result of his book and his policies, the Associated Farmers, a coalition of agribusiness interests, called McWilliams "Agricultural Pest No. 1, worse than pear blight or boll weevil" (quoted in Julian 2002). Republican gubernatorial candidate Earl Warren promised to fire McWilliams during his campaign and followed through on that promise after his election in 1942.

Robert J. Lacey

See also: Agricultural and Farm Labor Organizing; Dust Bowl Migration; Migrant Labor/Farm Labor

References and Further Reading

Julian, Kate. 2002. "Carey Quite Contrary." *In These Times*, February 1. http://www.inthesetimes.com/issue/26/07/culture1.shtml.

McWilliams, Carey. 1939. *Factories in the Field: The Story of Migratory Labor in California*. Boston: Little, Brown.

———. 1979. *The Education of Carey McWilliams*. New York: Simon and Schuster.

Two News Girls. Edward F. Brown, Investigator. Location: Wilmington, Delaware. Photo by Lewis W. Hine. (Photograph from the records of the National Child Labor Committee, U.S. Senate) (Library of Congress)

Fair Labor Standards Act (FLSA)

Part of the New Deal program to alleviate poverty and stimulate the economy by increasing Americans' purchasing power, the Fair Labor Standards Act (FLSA) of 1938 established a national minimum-wage rate and maximum-hours standard for workers in covered occupations, and it restricted employment of children younger than sixteen. The act's initial impact was limited by its low minimum-wage rate and its exemption of many low-paying, long-hour occupations. Over the decades, a succession of amendments broadened FLSA coverage and raised the minimum wage, although the wage rate has not kept abreast of cost-of-living increases or brought the earnings of a full-time worker with dependents above the poverty line.

The FLSA originated in a movement begun in the 1890s by female reformers to improve the working conditions of women. Reformers focused on women because discrimination by employers and unions kept women's labor standards especially low and because the courts and labor unions resisted government regulation of men's labor standards. After ruling in 1905 that restricting men's hours was an unconstitutional violation of men's "freedom of contract," the U.S. Supreme Court in 1908 sustained an Oregon ten-hour-day law for women on the ground that women's role as "mothers of the race" justified state intervention. From 1909 to 1937, many states enacted maximum-hours and minimum-wage laws for women, often after campaigns by the National Consumers League and Women's

Trade Union League. Male trade unionists' lukewarm support reflected their concern that legislated standards would undercut unionization and collective-bargaining agreements.

The Great Depression demonstrated that state labor laws could not check the downward pressure on standards exerted by interstate competition. State legislators were reluctant to enact or enforce standards higher than those of states that were their economic rivals. The resulting variations encouraged industries to relocate to lower-wage, lower-standard states. In turn, the threat of industry migration undermined unionization efforts as well as wage and hour standards. This competition, especially apparent in the textile and garment industries and more generally between northern manufacturers and lower-paying southern manufacturers, produced new enthusiasm for wage-hour regulation among labor leaders and some employers. A national standard would limit the threat that employers would relocate to a state with lower wages or longer hours, they argued, and would bolster unionization and labor protection efforts.

National labor standards were adopted on an industry-by-industry basis under the National Recovery Administration (1933–1935) until that program was found unconstitutional. In 1937, the U.S. Supreme Court reopened the door to national wage-hour policy by upholding both a Washington State minimum-wage law for women and the National Labor Relations Act of 1935. Thereafter, support from organized labor, especially the new Congress of Industrial Organizations, was indispensable to enacting the FLSA over intense opposition from low-wage employers and a congressional coalition of southern Democrats and conservative Republicans.

The FLSA's initial impact was more symbolic than material. It applied only to employees deemed to be in "interstate commerce" and therefore within Congress's legal jurisdiction—initially about 11 million workers, or one-fifth of the labor force. For them, the act set an hourly minimum wage of twenty-five cents, to increase to forty cents over seven years. Twenty-five cents per hour represented a raise for only about 300,000 of the covered workers; overtime provisions entitled another 1.4 million workers to raises. Women, Black men, and southerners were overrepresented among these beneficiaries because they were concentrated in low-wage occupations (for example, in the garment, textile, fertilizer, and lumber industries). But the vast majority of workers who earned below-subsistence wages for backbreaking hours were excluded from the original FLSA. The act held domestic servants and retail workers to be outside interstate commerce, and agricultural workers were exempted because of the political power of their employers. These exclusions denied protection to most minority workers and many white women. However, these groups stood to gain the most from the FLSA if coverage could be expanded.

Despite its limitations, the FLSA was a significant intervention in the labor market. By setting a national floor for standards and limiting the attractiveness of relocating a factory across state borders, it improved the bargaining position of organized workers and offset some obstacles to organizing others. Unionization rates did not surge in the wake of the FLSA's passage, but this outcome reflected a rightward shift in national politics rather than the FLSA's impact. The act's effects were subsequently limited further by the underfunding of the Wage and Hour Division of the U.S. Department of Labor, which was responsible for enforcing the legislation.

After the U.S. Supreme Court upheld the FLSA in 1941, liberal and labor groups waged an ongoing struggle to raise the minimum wage and expand coverage. Amendments in 1949, 1955, 1961, 1966, 1974, 1977, 1989, and 1996 brought the minimum wage to $5.15 per hour by 1997. The 1949 amendments reduced the act's total coverage, despite new formal restrictions on industrial homework in the garment industries.

Muller v. Oregon, *208 U.S. 412 (1908)*

On February 19, 1903, the legislature of the State of Oregon passed an act . . . , the first section of which is in these words: "SEC. 1. That no female (shall) be employed in any mechanical establishment, or factory, or laundry in this State more than ten hours during any one day. The hours of work may be so arranged as to permit the employment of females at any time so that they shall not work more than ten hours during the twenty-four hours of any one day." The single question is the constitutionality of the statute under which the defendant was convicted so far as it affects the work of a female in a laundry. . . .

We held in *Lochner v. New York*, 198 U.S. 45, that a law providing that no laborer shall be required or permitted to work in a bakery more than sixty hours in a week or ten hours in a day was not as to men a legitimate exercise of the police power of the State, but an unreasonable, unnecessary and arbitrary interference with the right and liberty of the individual to contract in relation to his labor. . . . That decision is invoked by plaintiff in error as decisive of the question before us. But this assumes that the difference between the sexes does not justify a different rule respecting a restriction of the hours of labor. . . .

It is undoubtedly true, as more than once declared by this court, that the general right to contract in relation to one's business is part of the liberty of the individual, protected by the Fourteenth Amendment to the Federal Constitution; yet it is equally well settled that this liberty is not absolute and extending to all contracts, and that a State may, without conflicting with the provisions of the Fourteenth Amendment, restrict in many respects the individual's power of contract. . . . That woman's physical structure and the performance of maternal functions place her at a disadvantage in the struggle for subsistence is obvious. This is especially true when the burdens of motherhood are upon her. Even when they are not, by abundant testimony of the medical fraternity continuance for a long time on her feet at work, repeating this from day to day, tends to injurious effects upon the body, and as healthy mothers are essential to vigorous offspring, the physical well-being of woman becomes an object of public interest and care in order to preserve the strength and vigor of the race. . . .

Still again, history discloses the fact that woman has always been dependent on man. . . . Though limitations upon personal and contractual rights may be removed by legislation, there is that in her disposition and habits of life which will operate against a full assertion of those rights. She will still be where some legislation to protect her seems necessary to secure a real equality of right. . . . Differentiated by these matters from the other sex, she is properly placed in a class by herself, and legislation designed for her protection may be sustained, even when like legislation is not necessary for men and could not be sustained. . . . Even though all restrictions on political, personal and contractual rights were taken away . . . it would still be true that she is so constituted that she will rest upon and look to him for protection; that her physical structure and a proper discharge of her maternal functions—having in view not merely her own health, but the well-being of the race—justify legislation to protect her from the greed as well as the passion of man. The limitations which this statute places upon her contractual powers, upon her right to agree with her employer as to the time she shall labor, are not imposed solely for her benefit, but also largely for the benefit of all. . . .

In 1961, the FLSA was extended to new groups, including retail employees. An Equal Pay Act for women was incorporated into the FLSA in 1963. In 1966, civil rights and labor groups finally won coverage for agricultural workers. The 1974 amendments extended protection to domestic workers, after the women's movement forced a revaluation of household labor. Many remaining specific exemptions were removed in 1977. The 1974 and 1977 amendments increased penalties for violations.

The FLSA came under heavier fire after 1977 as conservatives regained political power. Targeting the minimum wage in particular, conservatives have argued that it actually lowers employment by raising the cost of labor—an argument that is widely disputed in the economics literature. Such opposition, along with broader efforts to undermine the political power of labor, contributed to a steady erosion in the value of the minimum wage. In the 1980s, President Ronald Reagan's administration also rescinded some FLSA restrictions on industrial homework. Enforcement suffered as the staffing levels of the Wage and Hour Division declined and as staff substituted telephone conciliations for on-site investigations. The 1996 increase in the minimum wage was concurrent with the Personal Responsibility and Work Opportunity Reconciliation Act, intended to force welfare mothers into employment. In 2000, a Senate committee heard arguments for raising the minimum wage to reduce the gender-based pay gap, a proposal that faced diminished prospects under the administration of President George W. Bush.

Landon R. Y. Storrs

See also: Agricultural and Farm Labor Organizing; Earned Income Tax Credit (EITC); Family Wage; Great Depression and New Deal; Living-Wage Campaigns; Minimum Wage; Service and Domestic Workers, Labor Organizing; Trade/Industrial Unions; Wagner Act; Welfare Policy/Welfare Reform; "Working Poor"

References and Further Reading

Boris, Eileen. 1994. *Home to Work: Motherhood and the Politics of Industrial Homework in the United States*. New York: Cambridge University Press.

Hart, Vivien. 1994. *Bound by Our Constitution: Women, Workers, and the Minimum Wage*. Princeton: Princeton University Press.

Nordlund, Willis J. 1997. *The Quest for a Living Wage: The History of the Federal Minimum Wage Program*. Westport, CT: Greenwood Press.

Palmer, Phyllis. 1995. "Outside the Law: Agricultural and Domestic Workers under the Fair Labor Standards Act." *Journal of Policy History* 7, no. 4: 416–440.

Storrs, Landon R. Y. 2000. *Civilizing Capitalism: The National Consumers' League, Women's Activism, and Labor Standards in the New Deal Era*. Chapel Hill: University of North Carolina Press.

Family Assistance Plan (FAP)

See Aid to Families with Dependent Children (ADC/AFDC); Welfare Policy/Welfare Reform

Family Structure

Poverty and family structure are deeply connected in any consideration of poverty and social welfare policy in the United States. The idea that something is wrong with families that do not look like the imagined norm—married mother, breadwinner father, and children—has been central to debates about the causes of poverty and the requisites of social policy since the nineteenth century. Especially since the release in 1965 of the Moynihan Report, *The Negro Family: The Case for National Action*, these "deviant" or "problem" families have been typified in the social policy and popular imagination as young, female headed, and Black. Meanwhile, even as family structure has become more diversified in the United States, on the whole welfare policy has become increasingly preoccupied with the nuclear family ideal and with pushing poor women into marriage.

The assumption that single-mother family structures cause poverty has been the linchpin of neoliberal and conservative arguments that social policy should be used to reconstitute single-mother families as heterosexual marital units. In *Losing Ground: American Social Policy, 1950–1980*, Charles Murray set the tone for policy discussions during the 1980s and 1990s regarding race, welfare, and the composition of families.

The view that the family ought to include an adult male married to a female partner continues to dominate discussions of poverty and families. This view guided the policy decision that poverty should be alleviated by biological fathers rather than by government. Hence, the 1996 welfare reform imposed harsh requirements and time limits on poor unmarried women with children, instructing them either to secure financial support from a man or to support themselves by working full-time in the labor market.

The assumption that nonmarital mother-headed families are deviant is the product of race, class, and gender dynamics and generates race, class, and gender consequences. The African American family is a powerful case in point.

From the beginnings of enslavement in America, the security and permanency of Black family bonds were at the mercy of slave owners. Although evidence suggests that African Americans were quite creative in maintaining family ties under the system of slavery (Gutman 1976, 10), enslavement still undermined Black families in quite powerful ways. For example, in slaveholding states, marriages between enslaved women and men were not legally recognized. In addition, enslaved mothers and fathers had no parental rights to their children. African Americans responded to these and other legal disabilities and structural vulnerabilities by defining family broadly, a practice probably rooted in western African ways and traditions and re-created in the American context (Gutman 1976, 212). Despite the resiliency of Black families even under slavery, racism has marked as inferior those Black families that do not conform to father-headed marital norms.

African American men and women collectively experience racism, but in somewhat different ways. The massive marginalization of African American men from the economy and the racial and gender segregation in the labor market are two dynamics that direct the fates of African American families. Since nuclear family formation is predicated on the model of the male breadwinner, such family forms have become more and more difficult to form and maintain in the absence of viable work for too many Black men.

African American women also suffer. Black women may be more likely to find work or are forced into work through the welfare system's workfare demands, but too often the work is low paid, keeping these women and their families mired in poverty. And in too many instances the families are without decent child care, housing, or health care.

The public policy debate has been intensely focused on the family structure of women on welfare, especially African American mothers who are not married and who head their families. Yet all families have been brought under scrutiny by the drumbeat of marital family values. The idea that something is wrong with the American family is the general tenor of much of this analysis. Conservative analysts such as Murray and Daniel P. Moynihan and more liberal analysts such as William J. Wilson (1987) and William A. Darity and Samuel L. Myers (1995) argue that reconstituting the heterosexual father-led family is key to reducing poverty. The idea that fathers should be present or that fathers should pay and be visible in families has dominated discussion since the 1980s. Whether the analyst takes the tack that there are too few "marriageable men" (Wilson 1987; Darity and Myers 1995) or that there is something fundamentally pathological about the culture and value choices of Black families (Moynihan 1965; Murray 1984), the endpoint is the same. There is only one family structure that matters: a married nuclear family headed by a male.

These positions have been countered by the argument that actual American families are varied in their forms, ranging from nuclear to blended to single parent. Some feminist welfare scholars challenge the patriarchal assumptions running through much of the current policy recommendations for poor women, which press for marriage and, if not marriage, work (Albelda and Withorn 2002). Women-of-color feminists such as Bonnie Thornton Dill and Maxine Baca Zinn (Dill, Zinn, and Patton 1999) and progressive white feminists such as Stephanie Coontz (1992) point to the sexual division of labor, the structure of the economy, and gender discrimination as the mainsprings of women's poverty and family decisions. Many feminists also argue that patriarchal violence, not a shortage of patriarchs, also leads to family decisions such as the decision to parent alone. Although the decision to leave an abusive partner can expose a mother and her children to poverty, single-mother families are not the only families that can be poor. Sixteen percent of families are still in poverty, as compared to one in two of single-female-headed households (National Committee on Pay Equity 2001, 310). Further, 20 percent of married African American families with children aged six and under are poor (Aulette 1994, 142). A number of feminists argue that these statistics say more about gender, class, and racial inequality than they do about any particular household form per se.

We do know that gender, poverty, and family structure are connected. Many women are poor, but single women who are family heads are the poorest of the poor (Burnham 2002, 49). We know that race and ethnicity matter. Women of color, especially, are profoundly economically disadvantaged, and their children are among the poorest of all children (Burnham 2002, 49). Many of these women are working, but they simply do not earn enough money to get their families out of poverty. Nonetheless, one of the most prominent antiwelfare demands is that women on welfare work.

In a service-driven economy where many jobs pay minimum wage without benefits, it is not surprising that families, whatever their structure, remain poor. The minimalist welfare state has contributed to this state of affairs. Job training, general assistance, and affordable housing have been all but eliminated for poor families. Moreover, low-wage workfare and the elimination of health and child care supports can make having a job too costly to lead out of poverty.

Rose M. Brewer

See also: Aid to Families with Dependent Children (ADC/AFDC); Gender Discrimination in the Labor Market; Heteronormativity; Racism; Sexism; Welfare Policy/Welfare Reform

References and Further Reading

Albelda, Randy, and Ann Withorn, eds. 2002. *Lost Ground*. Boston: South End Press.

Aulette, Judy Root. 1994. *Changing Families*. Belmont, CA: Wadsworth.

Burnham, Linda. 2002. "Welfare Reform, Family Hardship, and Women of Color." In *Lost Ground*, ed. Randy Albelda and Ann Withorn, 43–56. Boston: South End Press.

Carby, Hazel. 1987. *Reconstructing Black Womanhood*. New York: Oxford University Press.

Coontz, Stephanie. 1992. *The Way We Never Were: American Families and the Nostalgia Trap*. New York: HarperCollins.

Darity, William A., and Samuel L. Myers Jr. 1995. "Family Structure and the Marginalization of Black Men: Policy Implications." In *The Decline in Marriage among African Americans*, ed. M. B. Tucker and C. Mitchell-Kernan, 263–308. New York: Russell Sage Foundation.

Dill, Bonnie Thornton, Maxine Baca Zinn, and Sandra Patton. 1999. "Race, Family Values, and Welfare Reform." In *A New Introduction to Poverty: The Role of Race, Power, and Politics*, ed. Louis Kushnick and James Jennings, 263–286. New York: New York University Press.

Gutman, Herbert G. 1976. *The Black Family in Slavery and Freedom: 1750–1925*. New York: Vintage Books.

Moynihan, Daniel Patrick. 1965. *The Negro Family: The Case for National Action*. Washington, DC: U.S. Department of Labor.

Murray, Charles, 1984. *Losing Ground: American Social Policy, 1950–1980*. New York: Basic Books.

National Committee on Pay Equity. 2001. "The Wage Gap: Myths and Facts." In *Race, Class, and Gender in the United States*, ed. Paula Rothenberg, 5th ed., 292–304. New York: Worth Publishers.

Rothenberg, Paula, ed. 2001. *Race, Class, and Gen-*

der in the United States. 5th ed. New York: Worth Publishers.
Wilson, William J. 1987. *The Truly Disadvantaged: The Inner City, the Underclass, and Public Policy.* Chicago: University of Chicago Press.

Family Wage

The family wage—that is, a wage sufficient to support a family—was a main demand among male unionists and social reformers in the nineteenth and early twentieth centuries. This wage reduced poverty among working-class families and enabled many wives and children to avoid employment (Carlson 1996). However, it justified overt discrimination against women and child workers and legal barriers to female employment. It also perpetuated poverty among nondependent women, especially single mothers, and remained out of reach for most unskilled and minority workers (Hartmann 1979).

Heidi I. Hartmann (1979) claimed that the family-wage system was a patriarchal bargain between capitalists and socially privileged adult male workers. Although capitalists wanted to ensure working-class reproduction, these workers wanted to reduce labor market competition, ensure their social dominance, and benefit from women's unpaid domestic labor. Indeed, many adult, white, native-born, male workers, especially those in craft unions, raised their wages by excluding women and other kinds of workers from union membership and better-paying jobs. However, most employers provided the family wage reluctantly in response to pressure from workers and their allies. A notable exception was Henry Ford, who adopted family wages to avoid unionism (Carlson 1996). Male workers' and employers' interests in job segregation and exclusionary wage and employment policies were also more variable, and contingent, than Hartmann suggested (Milkman 1979).

Social reformers, including maternalist reformers, designed U.S. welfare programs to replace the family wage when the male breadwinner was absent or lost his job. Welfare policies in the late nineteenth and early twentieth centuries thus reinforced traditional expectations that women (especially white, native-born widows) should stay at home with their children and be dependent on their husbands. Unequal benefits also reinforced the income inequalities associated with the family wage (Gordon 1994).

The family-wage economy was still evident in the 1950s, when the income ratio among married couples with and without an employed wife approached one. This ratio rose after 1970 as the male-female wage gap narrowed. This was partly due to greater union support for the principle of "equal wages for equal work" in response to feminist demands and partly due to women's rising labor force participation. Enforcement of the Civil Rights Act of 1964 and affirmative action also reduced gender discrimination at work (Carlson 1996). As the economy restructured and the labor movement declined, male wages also shrank, while the ideal of supporting a family on the wages on one earner—male or female—became increasingly difficult to attain. Today, most unions pursue "living wages" rather than "family wages." Even so, the family-wage ideology and the male-female wage gap still persist.

Ellen Reese and Acela Minerva Ojeda

See also: Civil Rights Acts, 1964 and 1991; Feminization of Poverty; Gender Discrimination in the Labor Market; Income and Wage Inequality; Labor Markets; Living-Wage Campaigns; Maternalist Policy; Social Security Act of 1935; Trade/Industrial Unions; "Working Poor"

References and Further Reading

Carlson, Allan C. 1996. "Gender, Children, and Social Labor: Transcending the 'Family Wage' Dilemma." *The Sociological Review* 44: 204–224.
Gordon, Linda. 1994. *Pitied but Not Entitled: Single Mothers and the History of Welfare, 1890–1935.* New York: Free Press.
Hartmann, Heidi I. 1979. "The Unhappy Marriage of Marxism and Feminism: Toward a More Progressive Union." *Capital and Class* 8: 1–33.
Milkman, Ruth. 1979. "Organizing the Sexual Division of Labor: Historical Perspectives on 'Women's

Work' and the American Labor Movement." *Socialist Review* 49: 95–150.

Farm Security Act

See New Deal Farm Policy

Farm Security Administration Photographs

See Dust Bowl Migration; Great Depression and New Deal; Picturing Poverty (I); Rural Poverty

Federalism

Federalism is a constitutional principle providing for two layers of government: a central government and a lower level of governments, known as provinces, cantons, republics, commonwealths, or states, with some kind of representation of the lower units in the central government and usually some provision for guaranteeing the integrity of the lower units in the national polity.

To understand how federalism works, one needs to look beyond the formal principle to the actual division and allocation of precise functions and powers between the two levels in each system.

For the first 150 years of history under the Constitution, the United States clearly lodged more-substantive functions and powers in the states (the "constituent governments") than has been true of any other federal system. This was the "intent of the framers," as expressed in Article I, Section 8 of the original 1789 Constitution, which specifically delegated a few powers to the national government and reserved all other powers to the states. That principle of division was reaffirmed by the Tenth Amendment in 1791, providing that "the powers not delegated to the United States by the Constitution, nor prohibited by it to the States, are reserved to the States respectively, or to the people."

For all of the nineteenth century and the first thirty-three years of the twentieth, these principles allocating powers between the two levels of government were observed and applied in the real world of government in the United States. The policies of the national government were largely those of internal improvements (infrastructure), operations of the postal service, disposal of large portions of the vast public lands acquired by conquest, the recording of patents and copyrights, the establishment of uniform standards for currency and for weights and measures, and the surveying of the land and the counting of the population. Except for the grants and other services mentioned here, the national government did not reach individuals directly, especially in efforts to regulate the conduct of individuals. Although the Constitution granted power to the national government to regulate commerce "among the several states," during its first seventy years it only made one major effort to regulate commerce, and that was the Fugitive Slave Act of 1850, which actually contributed to the Civil War. The nation did not even have a standing army of any consequence until after World War II. It had something of a Navy, but national armies were demobilized after wars; the nation depended on its distance from other nations to buy time while mobilizing against an attack.

Two late-nineteenth-century efforts by the national government can be considered antecedents of the revolutions in government that were to come during the New Deal and after: regulating monopolies and regulating the railroads. However, these were meek exceptions proving the rule that for the first century and a third of its history, the national government left most of the governing to the states. For example, there were no national property laws;

no national morality, marriage, divorce, child support, or child custody laws; no laws providing for the rendering of contracts, the structuring of firms into partnerships and corporations, or the enforcement of contracts; no national labor laws; no national laws providing for universal compulsory primary and secondary education; no national laws regulating the professions and vocations; no laws concerning vagrancy, dependency, disability, or public obligations to the poor (until the 1930s); and, perhaps most significant, no national criminal laws except for a few strictly limited to interstate crimes. And the list does not end there. *For over two-thirds of American history, the states did almost all the fundamental governing in the United States*.

The American federal system did change after 1933, in what has been popularly designated "the Roosevelt Revolution." But, especially with regard to federalism, it must be considered a mild revolution spread across more than thirty years, within a traditional system that had persisted through two-thirds of the nation's history under the Constitution up until 1933. That traditional system lasted long enough to shape U.S. governmental institutions and political culture. Moreover, despite the growth of the national government since 1933 and the constitutional validation of this growth in 1937 and in the 1960s, the result was addition rather than redistribution of powers: The national government grew, *but not at the expense of the states*.

Two constitutional revolutions in the 1930s established genuine national supremacy in economic affairs. One led to the national regulatory state; the other led to a national redistributive state. The first culminated with *National Labor Relations Board v. Jones and Laughlin Steel Corporation* (301 U.S. 1 [1937]), giving the national government power to confront capitalism and to impose a number of restrictions on corporate power in areas once considered "intrastate" and beyond the reach of Congress. In the second constitutional revolution, also in 1937, the Supreme Court, in *Steward Machine v. Davis* and *Helvering v. Davis*, validated national redistributive powers by refusing to question the goals or purposes for which tax revenues were spent. That is, the national government could spend as it willed, even when taking from the rich to give to the poor, as long as the tax providing the revenues was constitutional (and the income tax had been declared constitutional not by the Court but by the ultimate means, a constitutional amendment, the Sixteenth Amendment, 1913).

The third revolution was delayed until the 1960s (nearly ten years after the 1954 decision in *Brown v. Board of Education of Topeka, Kansas* [347 U.S. 483] set the stage), when a series of Supreme Court decisions recognized the supremacy of the national government on all questions revolving around the rights of individual citizens. This third constitutional revolution in federalism occurred almost exactly 100 years after what was to have been the revolution in federalism for which the Civil War was fought and for which the Fourteenth Amendment was the instrument of ultimate victory. The *Brown* Court's interpretation of the Fourteenth Amendment incorporated virtually all the clauses of the Bill of Rights to apply as protections against state and local governments, whereas up until the 1960s (with the exception of parts of the First and Fifth Amendments), the Bill of Rights only applied to rights against the national government. (Until then, liberty was a matter of geography.) The incorporation of the Bill of Rights became powers enabling the national government to intervene not only against the states and local governments but also against corporations, churches and other private associations, and schools and other public corporations in matters involving exclusiveness, favoritism, harassment, and other forms of discrimination on the basis of race, religion, sex/gender, and national origin. In other words, a large number of important economic and human rights standards were nationalized and thus made uniform throughout the country.

Not only were state governments now subjected to the same uniform rights standards as applied to all private and semipublic associations, but states were now also subjected to enforceable national standards prescribing *how* they could exercise their powers to control their citizens. For example, powers over persons accused of crimes remained full and plenary, but right to counsel and immunity against forced confession were rules governing *how* to use state power that can (and does) prevent successful state prosecutions. But it is important to add immediately that even with all of that apparently revolutionary change in federalism, almost nothing of *what* states can do was taken away from them. Thus, even as America's third century began, only a small proportion, a tiny proportion, of the *substance* of federalism, the substance of state government power, has changed. With the exception of federal territories like the District of Columbia, there are *still* no national property laws, still no national corporate laws, still no national professions and occupations laws, still no national family laws governing divorce, custody, or morality, and so on and so forth. The states remain supreme in all these areas, and more. In fact, there are still no uniform standards even on crimes or their punishment—which is why thirty-seven states provide capital punishment for various crimes and thirteen states do not, and why possession of an ounce or two of cocaine or heroin can produce very severe sentences in some states and very light sentences or mere probation in other states. This is also why even the sacred practices of electoral democracy are so varied from state to state.

It should be clear on the basis of all this that the *substance* of power distribution between national and lower levels—not the mere division itself—is the significant factor defining federalism and the influence of federalism on political institutions and practices. This also makes federalism the major factor in the answer to why there has been no socialism in America. The variations among state laws on property, exchange, corporations, and accumulation would have presented even the most ardent, imaginative, and ingenious Marxist a forbidding task of mounting a successful and sustained national critique against a nation and an elite of capitalism.

But variations among state laws do not alone explain how federalism in the United States inhibited sustained political critique of and opposition to capitalism. Just as important is the inherent conservatism of state and local governments. This conservatism follows from the responsibility of the states to maintain social order. Thus, just as there is significant variability among states in our federal system, there is an equal measure of continuity, which is imposed on the states by the powers reserved to the states by the Constitution. The powers reserved by the U.S. Constitution to the states are broad and significant. This is precisely what makes the United States far more of a confederated system than most other federal states. In other federal states, principally Canada and Australia, the powers of the states are the enumerated powers, while all other powers are reserved to the national government. In the United States, it is the national government's powers that are enumerated, while all other powers are left to the states. This was the primary method for limiting the national government, on the logical principle that if some powers are enumerated, other powers are not to be included and are therefore reserved for no other government or for some other specified layer of government.

Even more to the point, constitutional law in the United States treats the "reserved powers" of the states as the "police power," whose traditional definition is the power of the sovereign to regulate the health, safety, and morals of the community. It is worth noting that the terms "police" and "policy" are descendants of a common ancestor, *polis*, the Greek term designating the primal source of power and authority in any constituted community. The conservatism of the states and localities arises out of the fundamental responsibility of states and localities to maintain public order, and the maintenance of public order requires keeping people in their places. This is what "states' rights" has always meant. Because this designation originated in the American South and was associated with racial segregation, states' rights was associated with racism, but in recent years it has been sanitized and goes well beyond race. But the conservatism of states' rights remains.

That natural or innate conservatism of the states and their local principalities has been played down by conservatives and overlooked by liberals who embrace the virtues of community and the need for social capital. That conservatism is also overlooked by those who, liberal or conservative, sincerely accept the argument that government is best that is closest to the people. The test of these tendencies can only be observed and assessed in real policy situations, and the best cluster of cases for the test will be found in the liberal urban policies of the 1960s. Devolution of the federal powers to the states and local governments was quite popular in the 1960s and was advertised as a virtue of the popular urban redevelopment programs. What was not appreciated by the most vociferous Democratic supporters of national urban policy was that devolution of federal power and federal money to local governments was the price Democratic policymakers had to pay to get enough conservative support in Congress to pass the programs and to finance them. All during the 1950s and on into the 1960s, as urban policy expanded, the chair of the housing subcommittee of the House Banking and Currency Committee—which had the key influence over the framing, financing, and implementation of all urban redevelopment programs—was Albert Rains, conservative Democrat from a northern Alabama congressional district known at the time for explicit, policy-directed use of federal money to create a Black ghetto in a city that was more than 30 percent Black and that had never had a ghetto before. More subtly, but appreciated by virtually all urbanites, was the fact that every American city was more segregated—along class as well as racial lines—after urban redevelopment than before. Federal money—devolved without clear national standards, based on the virtuous principle of maximum local participation—had simply provided the resources to segregate and resegregate cities (along racial but also class and other lines) to an extent that they would not otherwise have had the resources to accomplish.

Devolution reemerged in the 1980s, but in the hands of conservatives it was much more logically carried out than it had been in earlier efforts. Liberals went along, like lambs to the slaughter, dazzled by the reputed virtues of local autonomy and states' rights, oblivious (despite 1960s experience) to the ideological bias against their own interests. The 1996 welfare reform was the ultimate post-1960s case study of conservative victory with the support of the "false consciousness" of the now-organized and self-conscious Democratic centrists, who had moved rightward to devolution music and globalization cadences, with President Bill Clinton as drum major. The effect can best be seen in the Personal Responsibility and Work Opportunity Reconciliation Act (PRWORA) of 1996. Its most explicitly conservative feature was the abrupt and complete termination of Aid to Families with Dependent Children (AFDC) and its replacement by Temporary Assistance for Needy Families (TANF). Termination of AFDC meant the end of uniform national standards for entitlement to income support for single parents who meet means tests. Replacement by TANF meant turning over most federal welfare appropriations to the states to dispense and implement at their discretion. National guidelines set conditions states should observe, but these left wide discretion for states to be more restrictive and regulative if they wish. For example, the broadest new federal standard in the 1996 law is a new lifetime limit of five years of eligibility for welfare; and in the process, the recipient must be looking for work and show evidence he or she is working thirty hours per week or trying to find work. The states are disciplined by a national participation quota specifying that 50 percent of a state's recipients must be working thirty hours a week (a participation rate that President George W. Bush's administration wants to raise to 70 percent, notwithstanding its paeans to states' rights). States can meet these requirements by cutting recipients off welfare altogether or by assigning them to some kind of nonsalaried "workfare" calculated at the rate of the minimum wage.

States are given discretion under the federal law to increase the restrictiveness of the welfare requirements, with tighter time limits and more elaborate and discouraging administrative procedures. Federal law also provides financial incentives to states to regulate poor women. The 1996 law's "illegitimacy" bonus, for example, offers additional funds to states that most successfully reduce nonmarital births by encouraging contraception, marriage, or the relinquishment of nonmarital babies at birth. Just as the work requirement forces single mothers to choose between work and child care, so do the federal and state marriage policies force single mothers to choose between the right to privacy even in poverty versus possible escape from poverty through marriage or through compulsory "residential coparentage" with the biological father (who may well have imposed himself on her to produce the child). This returns us to the conservative principle of keeping people in their places: "TANF's pronouncements and punishments regarding childbearing and childrearing by single mothers proceed from assumptions about racial failure and disproportionately affect mothers of color. . . . TANF proponents attribute the need for welfare to the moral or cultural deficits of racialized individuals rather than to racialized opportunities and economic conditions" (Mink 2002, 5).

The 1996 welfare reform has given so much discretion to state and local administration that welfare has been transformed from a welfare assistance state to a welfare police state. This is a throwback to nineteenth-century policies. There was always considerable charity in the United States, private charity through churches and other private philanthropies as well as local governments. But charity was always linked to morality, and morality toward poverty and dependency took the form of a clear and rigid distinction between the "deserving" poor and the "undeserving" poor. From its American beginnings in Buffalo in the 1870s, a charity organization movement spread throughout the cities of the United States. And it was truly a national movement, with local societies linked together through their awareness of each other and through a uniform ideology and operational code. The code had two principles, one scientific and one moral. Scientific charity worked from a causal model that held that the poverty of the deserving poor was caused by misfortune—such as the loss of the breadwinner—and the poverty of the undeserving poor was caused by "idleness, filth and vice." This led directly to the moral dimension, a genuine moral imperative, caught well in an early speech of Reverend S. Humphreys Gurteen, founder of the first American charity organization: "We shall have ourselves alone to blame if the poor, craving for human sympathy, yet feeling their moral deformity, should some fine day wreak their vengeance upon society at large." As the charity organization movement grew through local charity organization societies, it formed a national group in the 1890s, and its name conveys almost everything about its philosophy, its ideology, and its operational code: The National Conference of Charities and Corrections (NCCC). And its chief mechanism for penetrating the slums was "INVESTIGATE," a word published in caps by founder Gurteen. Research for information on the poor was necessary "to apply scientific methods to human relationships." The purpose was "to bring about transformations of character" (Boyer 1978, 115–116, 119, 121) through rewards to the deserving poor and punishments to the undeserving poor.

The purpose of all this is to unmask federalism, in order not to denounce it but to bring objective understanding to it. Constitutional or policy decisions that distribute powers between the national level and the state level are never neutral. The policy direction driven by that choice should be made clear, if not by the policymakers then at least by the policy observers.

After September 11, 2001, there was an interruption of the trend toward devolution because the attack was deemed to be an act of war requiring national mobilization for defense against terrorism and eventually for an all-out world war against it. There was an immediate reassertion of national supremacy, and it mainly took the form of national policies restricting civil liberties and expanding national defense and certain other industries and areas considered strategic. Whether these new national powers are short-lived or permanent, they are specialized. In all other areas, devolution of national government continues. Thus it remains as important now as it was before 9/11 that we understand that *devolution does not mean less government*. On the contrary, devolution means rearrangement of and realignment of powers and functions between the levels of government, which often ends in more government but always ends in government better designed for the needs of an expanding, globalizing capitalism.

The attack on the national level of government, which began in earnest with Ronald Reagan after 1980, was genuinely antigovernment in its effort to eliminate as many as possible of the regulatory rules that were seen as adverse to economic expansion. But a free market, defined as one free of all government, was neither Adam Smith's idea nor American practice. Beyond the many national economic regulations the Republicans left in place, there were many programs they actually embraced: for example, protecting intellectual property, maintaining and extending national standards, protecting trade from cartels and other forms of piracy, keeping currencies stable, and defending, supporting, and often bailing out capital markets.

Still more government was needed and sought at the state level. Globalization involves not only the expansion of the capitalist economies but also their penetration of societies through profit, contract, technology, bureaucracy, science, and other such modernizations that threaten to undermine traditional values and established bases of authority. A proper regard for that social environment requires state provision for statewide laws and local governments strong enough for maintenance of the social order. It is either falsehood or the highest form of false consciousness to embrace the extreme antigovernment laissez-faire cause while also embracing states' rights and strong local government.

Rational citizens need both levels of governing, national and local, and it is normal and probably healthy that the two major parties in the United States are divided along national versus state lines, central versus local lines. But no one should be asked to accept federalism as a virtue in itself. Federalism is not a neutral principle. Federalism is a mask for a substantive, ideological, particular policy-oriented direction. Federalism in real, twenty-first-century time is a particular remedy for a particular problem. Federalism comprehends a variety of arrangements that are useful when properly understood. In other words, federalism is a constitutional medicine that has to be properly labeled with all its ingredients, followed by the warning, NOTE WELL: FEDERALISM CAN BE HARMFUL TO YOUR HEALTH.

Theodore J. Lowi

See also: Charitable Choice; Privatization; Social Security Act of 1935; Welfare Administration; Welfare Policy/Welfare Reform; Welfare State

References and Further Reading

Boyer, Paul. 1978. *Urban Masses and Moral Order in America, 1820–1920*. Cambridge, MA: Harvard University Press.

Ferejohn, John, and Barry Weingast, eds. 1997. *The*

New Federalism: Can the States Be Trusted? Stanford, CA: Hoover Institution Press.
McRoberts, Kenneth. 1997. *Misconceiving Canada—The Struggle for National Unity*. New York: Oxford University Press.
Mink, Gwendolyn. 1998. *Welfare's End*. Ithaca, NY: Cornell University Press.
———. 2002. "From Welfare to Wedlock." Unpublished paper.
Peterson, Paul E. 1995. *The Price of Federalism*. Washington, DC: Brookings Institution.
Pusey, Michael. 1991. *Economic Rationalism in Canberra—A Nation Building State Changes Its Mind*. Cambridge: Cambridge University Press.
Whittington, Keith E. 1998. "Dismantling the Modern State? The Changing Structural Foundations of Federalism." *Hastings Constitutional Law Quarterly* 25, no. 4 (Summer): 483–527.

Feminisms

The term "feminism" now refers to a family of ideas and movements that challenged male dominance and fostered women's status, flourishing since the late eighteenth century. The term became common only in the twentieth century and was used widely only in relation to the so-called second-wave women's movement arising in the late 1960s.

At the end of the twentieth century, second-wave feminism was typically understood in the United States as a movement of elite, white, and largely professional-class young women, for whom issues of poverty and welfare were not a high priority. There is a great deal of truth in this characterization, but significant exceptions have been overlooked. Moreover, that judgment rests on a selective and narrow definition of what constitutes a women's movement, disregarding a great deal of grassroots activism among poor women. This activism has remained less visible because its participants were poor, did not always keep records, and were not able to command media or scholarly attention.

The movement usually referred to as second-wave feminism developed in two separate streams: One, a formally structured national set of organizations, coalesced around the National Organization for Women (NOW), organized in 1966. This stream, including primarily adult women and a few men, sought equality for women within such mainstream institutions as government, employment, and labor unions in civic and public life particularly. Another stream, beginning at the end of that decade, never coalesced into a dominant national organization. Informally named "women's liberation," it attracted primarily young women college graduates, many of whom had been active in the antiwar and civil rights movements. Ironically, this larger and more radical stream concentrated on changing personal, social, and cultural life. It focused on issues that had not been previously considered political, such as housework, beauty, reproductive rights, violence, and sexuality. By contrast, the NOW stream, with its greater emphasis on reforming institutionalized sexism, at first focused more on issues relevant to poor women, such as wage and job discrimination. It pursued these reforms primarily through lobbying for legislation and litigating for judicial decisions.

By the 1970s, the radical women's liberation stream, influenced as it was by Marxist theory and civil rights and New Left practice—particularly community organizing—began to challenge the bases of poverty, for example, inequality, exploitation, and racism. In discussions in consciousness-raising groups and in numerous pamphlets and underground press articles, these feminists began to analyze the gendered aspects of poverty. They examined wage and education gaps between men and women, the impact of raising children and doing housework on the market value of women's labor, and the costs of sexual harassment. They showed how the sexual division of labor in the home made women poorer than men, especially when they became lone mothers, because women were almost always the primary parents, because men were irresponsible in providing for children, but also because there were class and race inequalities among men. They showed that violence against women and lack of reproductive control also contributed to imprisoning women in poverty. "We define our best interest as that of the poorest, most brutally exploited woman. We repudiate all economic, racial, educational or status privileges that divide us from other women," wrote the influential radical-feminist group Redstockings in 1969.

Despite this rhetoric, the movement was not adequately committed or prepared to build a cross-class or cross-race movement. Good intentions were not enough. Women of color and poor white women rarely joined feminist organizations, in some cases because they had not been invited and in some cases because they were offended by the whiteness and middle-classness of the agenda as well as the membership. The majority of white, middle-class women simply did not see the race and class nature of their outlook and agenda. Most consciousness raising tended to produce generalizations and even theories about women's oppression that were actually particular to privileged, white, college-educated women. These included antagonism toward the family and the idealization of paid work as liberatory, ignoring the fact that poverty and discrimination drove so many women into low-paying, boring, even dangerous jobs. Women's liberation was primarily a movement of healthy young adults, and its concerns were the concerns of its constituency. It neglected the problems of older women, the disabled, or the ill, many of whom are poor.

The myth that poor women only care about directly economic issues was contradicted by the strongly positive response among poor women to a wide range of feminist ideas. Battered women's shelters have disproportionately served poor women of all races, who have the fewest means of escape from abusive relationships. The women's movement conducted massive consciousness raising about violence against women, through publicizing individual cases, through defending women who had killed their assailants, and through holding speak-outs in which women testified about their experiences. The movement had significant success in forcing police, judges, doctors, and social workers not to trivialize domestic violence or blame the victims. Sexual harassment disproportionately victimizes poor women, as does rape, and many poor women have responded enthusiastically to initiatives against these forms of violence.

The women's movement was particularly influential in the field of health, where neglect of women's particular problems, such as breast cancer, affects poor women more than prosperous women. The women's movement won increased funding for research on women's health and changed medical attitudes toward women as patients, although women who attend public clinics continue to receive inferior care. Feminist pressure forced drug companies to quit testing unsafe drugs on poor and minority women and required them to publicize information about negative side effects. Feminist rhetoric called for community-controlled free health care and child care, but feminist organizations lacked the clout to create such institutions.

The feminist record on reproductive rights is representative of its generally mixed scorecard with respect to poor women. The legalization of abortion brought down the price of abortions and made them safer and more easily accessible to poorer women. But then the Hyde Amendments, attached to annual appropriations bills for the Departments of Labor and Health and Human Services yearly since 1977, prevented the use of Medicaid funds for abortion except in cases of extreme danger to a woman's life. The women's movement did not adequately mobilize against these class-based restrictions, and the pro-choice orientation of the abortion-rights movement became increasingly individualist and blind to inequality among women. But the radical and socialist feminist streams of the movement initiated two other crusades that changed both consciousness and practice, arguing that women needed not just birth control or abortion but overall reproductive rights, including the right to bear and raise healthy children as well as the right not to procreate. A feminist-led campaign against sterilization abuse—the coerced sterilization of poor women, largely women of color and welfare recipients—was a considerable success. Feminist reproductive rights groups such as Committee for Abortion Rights and against Sterilization Abuse forced state and federal governments to insist on informed consent. Feminists also raised consciousness about women's need for better child care provisions, asserting a demand for free universal high-quality child care, although what was achieved is still far from meeting the need.

Two particular areas—jobs and welfare—need to be examined in evaluating the feminist approach to women's poverty. The feminist movement, along with civil rights, had a significant effect in reviving the union movement. When the feminist movement began in the late 1960s, working women were largely unorganized and confined to the secondary, predominately nonunion, sector. Since then, women have not only formed the constituency of the most successful union drives—as health and hospital workers, clerical workers, and service workers—but have also provided the leadership and energy for organizing. The grassroots advocacy organization 9to5, National Association of Working Women grew out of an organizing project of Boston's Bread and Roses that involved the predominantly female clerical workforce. In 1974, 3,200 women from fifty-eight different unions met in Chicago with great optimism to found the Coalition of Labor Union Women (CLUW). CLUW had chapters in many cities, trained women for union leadership, and pressured unions to include women in apprenticeship programs, to make child care a priority, to fight sexual harassment, and to get unions to support abortion rights and the Equal Rights Amendment (ERA). Despite feminism's dominant image as exclusively middle class, it was developing strongly within labor unions. Although CLUW did not long remain a significant force, labor union feminism remains very much alive. Wherever unionization is growing today, it is largely through the recruitment of women, especially women of color, not only as members but also as organizers. Within the unions, feminist consciousness led to numerous challenges to male domination of leadership, some of them successful, and to the injection of new issues, such as child care and parental leave, into bargaining. The women's movement gave rise not only to women's caucuses but also to far more risky gay and lesbian caucuses within unions. The labor movement had opposed the ERA from 1923 to 1976, when feminist pressure changed the position of the American Federation of Labor–Congress of Industrial Organizations (AFL-CIO). Although the amendment did not pass, the multiyear battle for an ERA educated many Americans about sex inequality in the workforce. Similarly, feminists perceived the limitations of "equal pay for equal work" regulations, since women could rarely get equal work but, instead, were confined to female job ghettoes, and hence they initiated campaigns for pay equity and "comparable worth."

Feminists' contribution to creating a decent welfare system fell short because these largely middle-class activists did not feel the same personal urgency toward improving the antediluvian U.S. welfare system that they felt toward combating employment discrimination. But in the case of welfare, too, a lot depends on the definition of a women's movement. In the 1960s and early 1970s, a strong welfare rights movement arose from a Los Angeles initiative in the African American Watts neighborhood. The movement quickly spread among both Black and white women, in the South, in Appalachia, in the Northeast, and in the West. The group they formed, the National Welfare Rights Organization (NWRO), always powered by Black women's organizing energy, claimed 20,000 members at its peak in 1968, with many additional welfare recipients participating in local events. NWRO conceived of welfare as fundamentally a women's issue, and its first chairwoman, Johnnie Tillmon, wrote a much-circulated article arguing this point in 1972. Poverty, and particularly the poverty of mothers and children, she argued, is constructed by the gendered division of labor that assigns child rearing to women and then devalues this labor. "Welfare is a women's issue," Tillmon wrote.

> For a lot of middle-class women in this country, Women's Liberation is a matter of concern. For women on welfare it's a matter of survival. . . . If I were president, I would solve this so-called welfare crisis in a minute and go a long way toward liberating every woman. I'd just issue a proclamation that "women's" work is real work. . . . For me, Women's Liberation is simple. No woman in this country can feel dignified, no woman can be liberated, until all women get off their knees. That's what N.W.R.O. is all about—women standing together, on their feet. (Tillmon 1972)

Although the mainstream women's movement remained distant, left feminists took up the fight for welfare rights. Although most NWRO members did not call themselves feminists, in fact they were fighting for women's rights, and some women's liberation groups, notably socialist-feminist organizations, participated in welfare organizing. For example, Bread and Roses contributed to building Boston's Mothers for Adequate Welfare (MAW).

NWRO did not last long, however. In the 1960s and early 1970s, welfare rights activists won some decisive victories in the courts, aided by feminist and civil rights lawyers. The Supreme Court outlawed several standard practices of welfare administration that interfered with recipients' rights and privacy. But as a well-funded conservative revival in the 1980s escalated antiwelfare sentiment and as the women's movement declined, the stigma on welfare grew so much that it became virtually impossible to organize large-scale support to defend welfare from cutbacks. Meanwhile, NWRO experienced internal conflict: Its overwhelmingly female rank and file began to clash with its original head, the veteran civil rights leader George Wiley, on many points.

When the main welfare program, Aid to Families with Dependent Children, was repealed in 1996, the women's movement put up little resistance. This absence reflects both the largely middle-class and professional base of feminism at the time and the fact that the continuing struggle to defend abortion rights was claiming such a large proportion of feminist energy.

Rosalyn Baxandall and Linda Gordon

See also: Civil Rights Movement; Domestic Violence; Gender Discrimination in the Labor market; NOW Legal Defense and Education Fund; Reproductive Rights; Welfare Rights Movement

References and Further Reading

Baxandall, Rosalyn, and Linda Gordon, eds. 1995. *America's Working Women*. 2d ed. New York: Norton.

———, eds. 2000. *Dear Sisters: Dispatches from the Women's Liberation Movement*. New York: Basic Books.

Cobble, Dorothy Sue, ed. 1993. *Women and Unions: Forging a Partnership*. Ithaca, NY: ILR Press.

Evans, Sara. 2003. *Tidal Wave: How Women Changed America at Century's End*. New York: Free Press.

Naples, Nancy A. 1998. *Grassroots Warriors: Activist Mothering, Community Work, and the War on Poverty*. New York: Routledge.

Tillmon, Johnnie. 1972. "Welfare Is a Women's Issue." Reprinted at http://www.msmagazine.com/spring2002/tillmon.asp.

Feminization of Poverty

The feminization of poverty is the concentration of poverty among female-headed families in the United States. Although 28 percent of all poor families with children were female headed in 1959, 61 percent of them were female headed in 1978. Since then, that percentage has tended to

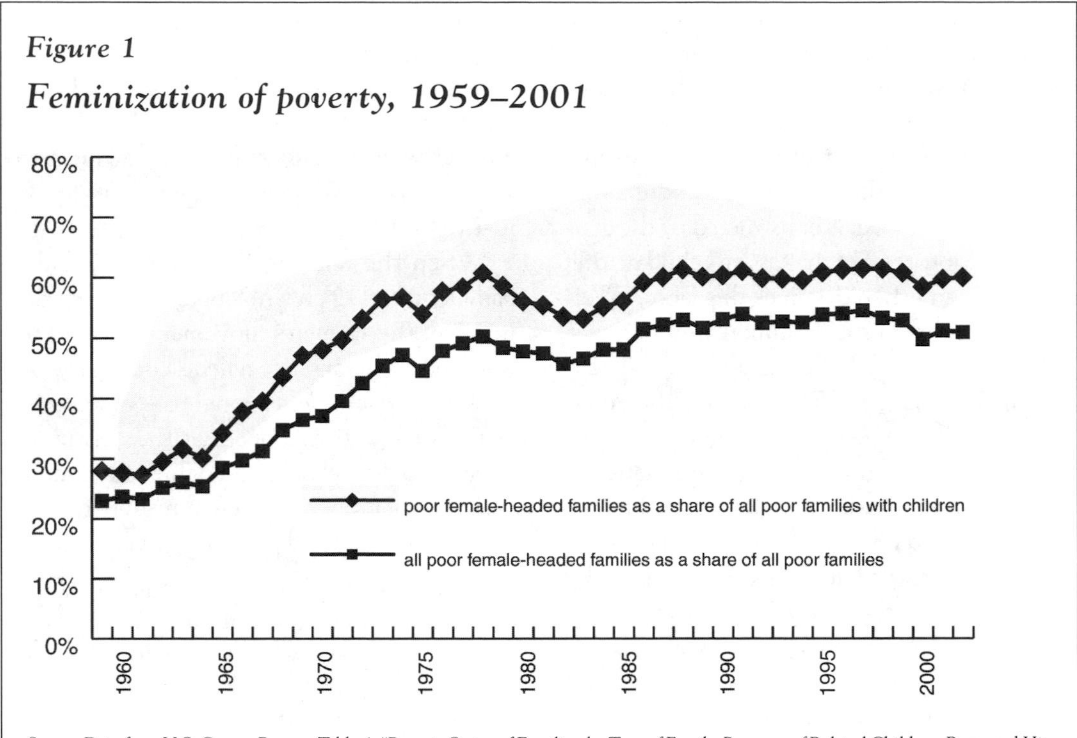

Figure 1
Feminization of poverty, 1959–2001

Source: Data from U.S. Census Bureau, Table 4, "Poverty Status of Families, by Type of Family, Presence of Related Children, Race, and Hispanic Origin: 1959 to 2002." Historical Poverty Tables. http://www.census.gov/hhes/poverty/histpov/hstpov4.html (October 6, 2003).

fall during recessions (when more married-couple families become poor) and to rise during economic expansions, but otherwise it has been stable (U.S. Census Bureau 2003).

Sociologist Diana Pearce coined the phrase "feminization of poverty" in 1978. At that time, the United States had experienced nearly two decades of rapid demographic change, especially divorce and extramarital childbearing, which left ever-larger numbers of women and children in households without adult men sharing formal responsibility for the family's economic welfare. Departing from prevailing views about the causes of poverty, Pearce argued that greater economic growth, education, and training would not be sufficient to address the poverty of families headed by women alone. Rather, the crux of the problem was that these women bore a disproportionate share of the responsibility for raising children. More children than ever before depended almost exclusively on their mothers for monetary support. Yet women's earnings typically have been insufficient to support families due to labor market discrimination and to the many conflicts between work and family care. The lack of adequate child support payments from the fathers of their children and the low levels and restrictive criteria for public income support have greatly exacerbated mothers' vulnerability to poverty.

Poverty among female-headed families is not new. However, as Linda Gordon (1994) observed, the problem of single motherhood as we know it today emerged in the late nineteenth and twentieth centuries, as wage labor removed men from household production and as geographic mobility and large cities made it more difficult for traditional patriarchal communities to enforce a degree of paternal responsibility.

The "feminization of poverty" concept has been criticized for its insensitivity to racial and class differences in the causes of poverty. As Linda Burnham (1985) pointed out, a one-dimensional focus on gender overstates the vulnerability of professional women to poverty. It also exaggerates the ability of Black men to reduce Black family poverty through marriage, by disregarding their higher rates of unemployment and incarceration. Mary Jo Bane (1986) found that 55 percent of the difference between Black and white poverty rates resulted from higher Black poverty rates for the *same* household type, and only 44 percent from the greater tendency of Black families to be female headed. Burnham also argued that the "feminization of poverty" obscured the roots of poverty in working-class exploitation.

Elaine McCrate

See also: Aid to Families with Dependent Children (ADC/AFDC); Child Support; Child Welfare; Family Structure; Feminisms; Gender Discrimination in the Labor Market; Sexism

References and Further Reading

Bane, Mary Jo. 1986. "Household Composition and Poverty." In *Fighting Poverty: What Works and What Doesn't,* ed. Sheldon H. Danziger and Daniel H. Weinberg, 209–231. Cambridge, MA: Harvard University Press.

Burnham, Linda. 1985. "Has Poverty Been Feminized in Black America?" *Black Scholar* 16, no. 2: 14–24.

Folbre, Nancy. 1984. "The Pauperization of Motherhood: Patriarchy and Public Policy in the United States." *Review of Radical Political Economics* 16, no. 4: 72–88.

Gordon, Linda. 1994. *Pitied but Not Entitled: Single Mothers and the History of Welfare, 1890–1935.* New York: Free Press.

Pearce, Diana. 1978. "The Feminization of Poverty: Women, Work, and Welfare." *Urban and Social Change Review* 11, nos. 1–2: 28–36.

U.S. Census Bureau. 2003. Table 4, "Poverty Status of Families, by Type of Family, Presence of Related Children, Race, and Hispanic Origin: 1959 to 2002." Historical Poverty Tables. October 6. http://www.census.gov/hhes/poverty/histpov/hstpov4.html.

Food Banks

Food pantries, food banks, and soup kitchens deliver emergency food assistance to the poor. Although government policy supports and shapes emergency food assistance, food pantries, food banks, and soup kitchens are often represented as providing nongovernmental food assistance to the poor. Technically, food pantries offer groceries directly to the poor, whereas food banks collect and warehouse food for distribution to food pantries. Many programs offering food directly to the poor, however, call themselves food banks. Soup kitchens, in contrast to food banks and food pantries, offer prepared meals for the needy to be eaten on-site in a dining room. The increasingly complex infrastructure of food provision in the United States has been built with government and religious assistance, as well as with huge charitable contributions of time, money, and food.

Soup kitchens appear to have been established first in Ireland with the passage of the Soup Kitchen Act of 1847 to provide soup for the starving during the Great Potato Famine (Glasser 1988). In the early years of the United States, poor relief drew heavily on English models that emphasized local municipal responsibility for the poor. In 1893, soup kitchens sprang up in the United States in response to a financial market collapse. In 1932, in the midst of the Great Depression, desperation for food manifested itself in food store riots and public horror at the destruction of unmarketable produce. At this time, the public concern about food distribution centered on the paradox of scarcity amid abundance, or "breadlines knee-deep in wheat" (Poppendieck 1986). Janet Poppendieck has argued that the administrations of Presidents Herbert Hoover and Franklin D. Roosevelt formulated programs to address not hunger per se but this visual paradox. The Federal Emergency Relief Administration, created by Congress under President Roosevelt in 1933, authorized federal relief that sometimes took the form of groceries or even orders for goods. Food deemed surplus because of its low market value was purchased by the government for redistribution to the impoverished via food banks (Poppendieck 1986). To this day, government-subsidized surplus food stocks the shelves of food banks and food pantries nationwide.

Religious organizations have also played a prominent role in food provision, at times operating from a combination of charitable, evangelical, or political purposes, and are increasingly reliant on government subsidy for their services. The Salvation Army and the Catholic Worker movement represent two very different Christian charitable endeavors to feed the poor, and their historical trajectories illuminate the complicated politics of entitlement and paternalism wrapped up in soup kitchens.

Appearing in the United States in 1880 from England, the Salvation Army brought its project of moral and spiritual reform in order to recover what were then widely referred to as "the sinking classes." This form of so-called muscular Christianity aimed to wage a spiritual war on moral deprivation, and most particularly drunkenness, by first extending shelter and food and then saving souls. Recruits to the Salvation Army, mostly men in these early years, were expected to commit themselves to self-discipline and a demanding work ethic. Foreshadowing later patterns in social service delivery, needy recruits might themselves eventually become Salvation Army employees, most commonly not as Salvationists but as civilian employees. During the twentieth century, as the government became more involved in food assistance, the Salvation Army social services programs came to rely increasingly on government subsidies, becoming a "nonprofit for hire" as welfare policy shifted toward privatization and contracting out in the 1980s (Smith and Lipsky 1993). In the fiscal year ending in September 2000, the U.S. Salvation Army reported that 15 percent of its operating budget came from government funding, in line with a report of 17 percent in 1980 (Salamon 1995, 94). Thus, despite its evangelical religious mission, the Salvation Army kitchens reside in what has been aptly called the "shadow state," the voluntary sector responsible for significant social services, existing outside of conventional democratic oversight and yet subject to state oversight (Wolch 1990). The Salvation Army, in keeping with its place within the shadow state, provides not only food assistance but also alcohol and drug treatment and job training as part of its evangelical dispensation. A recent study of volunteers in a Salvation Army social services shelter kitchen found that many of the men volunteering there, often men of color and of working-class or lower-middle-class origins, welcomed the self-discipline of the Salvation Army and its attendant concern for their ability to become good providers for their families (Allahyari 2000).

In 1933, Dorothy Day, a newly converted Roman Catholic and newspaper reporter inspired by the political agitation of Peter Maurin in France, began publication of the *Catholic Worker* newspaper. Day and Maurin advocated "personalist" hospitality, challenging others to work in intimate contact with the poor by living in voluntary poverty, to treat the poor as "the Ambassadors of God" (Maurin 1977), to extend not moral judgment but love, and to feed the poor while agitating for radical social transformation. Day and Maurin shunned involvement with the state, and Day explained to their followers that she intended the Catholic Worker to function as a social movement, not a charity. By the mid 1990s, over 100 Houses of Hospitality had been established to feed and sometimes house the poor. These houses sought to carry on Day's vision of social transformation, but they were not always able to transcend prevailing social norms. Thus, in some cases "hospitality" would be provided in settings graced by flowers and other middle-class touches, where groups of volunteers, often white and middle class, gave of their time and resources to prepare the meal for the guests. Many of these volunteers remained far removed from direct, personalist interaction with the poor and with social change politics, however. A recent study of a Catholic Worker kitchen found that religious and civic groups took responsibility for feeding the poor as a way of giving back to their communities and of putting into practice their moral and spiritual beliefs. Many struggled, however, with the mandate to treat all the poor as the ambassadors of God. The broader cultural imperative to bifurcate the poor into the worthy and unworthy made difficult their loving acceptance of the seemingly able-bodied guests, many of them male. As the examples of the Catholic Worker and the Salvation Army show, the politics beneath food distribution entail welfare ideologies about the "deserving" and "undeserving" poor (Allahyari 2000).

The provision of emergency food accelerated dramatically during the 1980s. The deepest recession since the Great Depression, intensified by decreased federal spending on welfare benefits, resulted in a growing impoverished population. The homeless emerged as a new national concern in the early 1980s. During this decade, food pantries, food banks, and soup kitchens grew explosively as the networks in which they were embedded became increasingly complicated. For example, food banks numbered approximately two dozen at the beginning of the decade but had proliferated to over 100 by the middle of the decade. In New York City, City Harvest established innovative "food rescue" programs to make nearly expired and perishable food available to food distribution programs; by the end of the decade, Foodchain provided such programs with a national organization (Poppendieck 1998). By 2004, America's Second Harvest, the largest self-described national domestic hunger relief organization, estimated it was annually distributing over 1 billion pounds of food to over 23 million hungry Americans (America's Second Harvest 2004). The charitable choice provision of the 1996 welfare reform act may encourage even more faith-based programs to augment and expand their feeding programs with government funds.

Progressive critics of the burgeoning charitable sector have argued that the sanctified nonprofit sector glorifies the Christian commitment to charity at the expense of redistribution of wealth (Wagner 2000) and that when the politics of emergency food distribution displace the politics of entitlement, the moral urgency to social change wanes (Poppendieck 1998). Comparing emergency food distribution programs to the food stamp program reveals that food pantries, food banks, and soup kitchens, even despite attempts to ease class divisions by treating the recipients with dignity in their kitchens or permitting recipients the right to choose and bag their groceries, nonetheless still remove the recipients from mainstream food markets. In other words, the inequalities implicit in the charitable relationship replace the entitlement implicit in the use of food stamps within conventional market settings (Poppendieck 1998).

Rebecca A. Allahyari

See also: Antihunger Coalitions; Catholic Worker Movement; Charitable Choice; Food Stamps; Hunger; Salvation Army; Voluntarism; Welfare State

References and Further Reading

Allahyari, Rebecca Anne. 2000. *Visions of Charity: Volunteer Workers and Moral Community*. Berkeley and Los Angeles: University of California Press.

America's Second Harvest. 2004. "Fact Sheet." http://www.secondharvest.org/site_content.asp?s=316.

Glasser, Irene. 1988. *More Than Bread: Ethnography of a Soup Kitchen*. Tuscaloosa: University of Alabama Press.

Maurin, Peter. 1977. "The Duty of Hospitality." In *Easy Essays*. Quincy, IL: Franciscan Press. Reprinted at http://www.catholicworker.com/maurin.htm#Hospitality.

Poppendieck, Janet. 1986. *Breadlines Knee-Deep in Wheat: Food Assistance in the Great Depression*. New Brunswick, NJ: Rutgers University Press.

———. 1998. *Sweet Charity? Emergency Food and the End of Entitlement*. New York: Viking.

Salamon, Lester M. 1995. *Partners in Public Service: Government-Nonprofit Relations in the Modern Welfare State*. Baltimore: Johns Hopkins University Press.

Smith, Steven Rathgeb, and Michael Lipsky. 1993. *Nonprofits for Hire: The Welfare State in the Age of Contracting*. Cambridge, MA: Harvard University Press.

Wagner, David. 2000. *What's Love Got to Do with It? A Critical Look at American Charity*. New York: New Press.

Wolch, Jennifer R. 1990. *The Shadow State: Government and Voluntary Sector in Transition*. New York: Foundation Center.

Food Stamps

Administered by the U.S. Department of Agriculture (USDA), the food stamp program has subsidized food consumption for qualified poor families for almost half a century. Although the program has experienced many changes in administrative rules, eligibility requirements, benefit levels, and budgeting patterns, the basic structure has remained relatively the same since its first run from 1939 to 1943 and through its modern manifestation from 1961 to the present. Through the USDA, the federal government has issued food coupons (these "stamps" came in paper form until the 1990s, when debit cards and other electronic formats became more widely used) to low-income U.S. residents, who have used those coupons to increase their ability to buy approved food items and food-producing seeds and plants. Until 1977, largely to encourage recipients to stay in the active workforce, food stamp rules mandated that participants purchase their coupons (which were redeemable at a variable rate higher than the original cash purchase). With the Food Stamp Act of 1977, the federal government eliminated the purchase requirement and began distributing benefits according to a formula based on the difference between a family's income and a federal minimum food budget. Despite troubling allegations of fraud and serious criticism of the program's administration, the food stamp program has been a relatively successful and quietly accepted social welfare program that has served as an important tool for economic management. Over the years, the program has helped enhance the food budgets of millions of participants, while also helping consumer and agricultural markets by expanding consumption of agricultural products, increasing sales at grocery stores, and generating sales tax revenue.

The program has enjoyed substantial support from a broad coalition of interests, including farmers, grocers, food processors, federal administrators, social welfare professionals, antihunger activists, and professional lobbyists. Their support has helped to turn the food stamp program into a pillar of the American welfare state. According to the USDA's Food and Nutrition Service (which administers the food stamp program), participation in the food stamp program reached a high of 27 million individuals in 1994, while in 2000 almost 17 million individuals received food stamp benefits. This falloff is due in part to the severe restrictions on eligibility

Massachusetts Application for Food Stamps

Things you need to provide . . . :

1. Proof of Identity. . . .
2. Proof of Residence. . . .
3. Utility Bills. . . .
4. Non-citizen Status. . . .
5. Bank Accounts. . . .
6. Earned Income. . . .
7. Self-Employment. . . .
8. Child Care or Adult Dependent Care Expenses. . . .
9. Unearned Income. . . .
10. Rental Income. . . .
11. Medical Expenses. . . .
12. Child Support Payments. . . .

This food stamp transaction at a supermarket produces a couple of bags' worth of food for the young consumer at left. The day marks the beginning of the federal food stamp program, with the city's 1.1 million persons on welfare and 800,000 other persons eligible to participate. August 31, 1970, New York, New York. (Bettmann/ Corbis)

imposed by the Personal Responsibility and Work Opportunity Reconciliation Act of 1996, which cut off food stamps for most legal immigrants as a way of paying for its provisions. The approximately 17 million people who receive benefits represented almost 60 percent of the residents eligible for the program. The appropriation for the food stamp program has grown to approximately one-fifth of the total USDA budget. In 2000, the program received an appropriation of over $21 billion, which was down from a high in 1996 of almost $29 billion. Although appropriations have generally increased, benefits remain relatively small. In 2000, the average individual benefit was a mere seventy-three dollars per month.

The growth of the food stamp program involved several phases. The outline of the modern version began with a New Deal effort designed to reduce agricultural surplus and, to a lesser extent, to alleviate hunger. Beginning in 1939, participants could buy coupons to buy certain surplus items. The program enjoyed relatively extensive participation as approximately 4 million Americans took part, but in 1943, the program was discontinued as a result of increased war production and other factors. Several congressional attempts to revive the program in the late 1940s and the 1950s failed. In 1961, however, President John F. Kennedy used executive authority to initiate eight pilot programs loosely modeled after the New Deal program. Over the next three years, the number of projects expanded, and on August 31, 1964, President Lyndon B. Johnson signed the Food Stamp Act, making the Kennedy-inspired program a permanent fixture of American social policy. Institutional and budget constraints kept expansion incremental and slow. In 1967, however, a "rediscovery" of hunger and the highlighting of hunger problems in the Deep South created enormous pressure for the liberalization of eligibility requirements and benefit levels. The pressures of the civil rights movement and the War on Poverty shifted the emphasis of the program away from its agricultural roots toward its future in service to more-urbanized areas. Between 1970 and 1975, policymakers liberalized eligibility, increased benefits, expanded the program to every county in the United States, and replaced state-level eligibility standards with uniform national ones. In conjunction with a rise in unemployment due to an economic downturn, those policy reforms greatly accelerated participation in the food stamp program, especially from 1973 to 1975 and from 1978 to 1980. Expenditures almost doubled between 1974 and 1977. The rise in participation and spending caused concern among fiscal and social conservatives and fueled political attacks against food stamps and other means-tested social welfare programs. Those attacks contributed to major cuts during President Ronald Reagan's first administration. Despite those attacks, the program persisted as an indispensable part of American social policy.

The piecemeal development of the food stamp program reflects many classic features of American social welfare policy. The program has never been universal or comprehensive, many of its formulators have tried to use it as a way to regulate work, and it has depended on local implementation and administration. Like other means-tested programs, it has perpetuated a distinction in the welfare state between social assistance programs and social insurance programs. Moreover, the food stamp program's growth has been motivated most effectively by pity and fear, and it has often reflected serious American racial dilemmas. Throughout its existence, the program has straddled the interests of its various constituencies. From the experimental agricultural relief program of the late New Deal to the pilot program of John F. Kennedy's New Frontier to the

Food Stamp Penalty Warning

- . . . Individuals who make a fraudulent statement or representation about their identity or place of residence to receive multiple food stamp benefits simultaneously, will be barred from the Food Stamp Program for ten years.
- Individuals who trade (buy or sell) food stamp benefits for a controlled substance/illegal drug(s), will be barred from the Food Stamp Program for a period of two years for the first finding, and permanently for the second finding.
- Individuals who trade (buy or sell) food stamp benefits for firearms, ammunition or explosives, will be barred from the Food Stamp Program permanently.
- Individuals who trade (buy or sell) food stamp benefits having a value of $500 or more, will be barred from the Food Stamp Program permanently.
- Individuals who are fleeing to avoid prosecution, custody or confinement after conviction for a felony or are violating a condition of probation or parole, are ineligible to participate in the Food Stamp Program.
- Individuals who fail to comply without good cause with Food Stamp Work Requirements, will be disqualified from the Food Stamp Program for a period of three months for the first finding, six months for the second finding and twelve months for the third finding. If the individual found to have failed to comply for a third time is the head of the food stamp household, the entire household shall be ineligible to participate in the Food Stamp Program for a period of six months.

enormous entitlement program of the middle 1970s, program formulators had to purchase support from various interests, concede to the wishes of powerful local and state politicians—especially congressional leaders from the South—and contend with severe budget constraints. What began as an experimental program to alleviate the burdens of agricultural surplus traveled a peculiar path to become America's chief program to alleviate hunger.

Kent B. Germany

See also: Antihunger Coalitions; Citizens' Crusade against Poverty (CCAP); Food Banks; Hunger; Means Testing and Universalism; Nutrition and Food Assistance; War on Poverty; Welfare Policy/ Welfare Reform

References and Further Reading

Berry, Jeffrey M. 1986. *Feeding Hungry People: Rulemaking in the Food Stamp Program*. New Brunswick, NJ: Rutgers University Press.

Eisinger, Peter K. 1998. *Toward an End to Hunger in America*. Washington, DC: Brookings Institution.

King, Ronald F. 2000. *Budgeting Entitlements: The Politics of Food Stamps*. Washington, DC: Georgetown University Press.

Kotz, Nick. 1971. *Let Them Eat Promises: The Politics of Hunger in America*. Garden City, NY: Anchor.

Foster Care

Foster care is the chief service that the public child welfare system provides to poor children in America. Although foster care typically refers to care by nonrelative families, it also encompasses other types of substitute care for children, including group homes and kinship foster care. Foster care is grounded in a long history of addressing the needs of poor children by rescuing them from their families. Its origins in the United States have been traced to the colonial child indenture system that provided for the apprenticeship of orphaned or indigent children in exchange for their necessities until they reached the age of twenty-one. In the late nineteenth century, charitable organizations began a child-saving movement to remove indigent children from their parents and place them in orphanages and asylums. Beginning in 1853, Charles Loring Brace, secretary of the Children's Aid Society in New York, sent destitute children on trains to work on farms in the Midwest. The first White House Conference on the Care of Dependent Children in 1909 recommended that dependent children be placed in local and carefully selected foster homes instead of in institutions. By the second half of the twentieth century, foster care was an established part of child welfare, conceived of as a temporary service for children while their biological parents were rehabilitated. Most experts agree, however, that the foster care system is overburdened and often damaging to children and their families. Foster care also demonstrates the state's willingness to more generously support poor children in the care of strangers than in the care of their parents.

The number of children in foster care remained stable in the two decades following World War II. The foster care population increased steeply after the discovery of battered child syndrome in 1962 and the subsequent passage of state laws that mandate the reporting of child abuse. Child maltreatment began to be understood as a national epidemic caused by parental depravity rather than as a social problem associated with poverty. Foster care was transformed from a largely voluntary refuge for orphans and children whose parents could not care for them to an involuntary system for children coercively taken from parents charged with abuse and neglect. However, family poverty, not the severity of child maltreatment, is the best predictor of placement in foster care.

The foster care system came under criticism during the 1970s for keeping children in substitute care for too many years and for moving children too frequently from home to home. Congressional hearings also revealed that federal reimbursement policy created incentives for state child welfare agencies to place children in foster care instead of providing services to intact families. Congress passed the Adoption Assistance and Child Welfare Act of 1980, which sought to end foster care "drift" (the problem of children languishing in foster care for extended periods without permanent placements or reunification with their families), prevent unnecessary removals of children, and encourage permanency planning for children in foster care. The foster care population as well as the proportion of the federal child welfare budget devoted to foster care nevertheless skyrocketed in the period between 1980 and 2000. The number of children in foster care climbed to 568,000 by 1999 (U.S. Department of Health and Human Services 2002b). At the same time, the number of children who received services in their families fell dramatically.

As the foster care population grew, so did the proportion of nonwhite children, especially Black children, in the system. The child welfare system virtually excluded Black children until World War II, when services shifted from institutions to foster care and from private to public agencies. In 2000, 40 percent of all children in foster care nationwide were Black, even though Black children constituted only 17 percent of the nation's youth (U.S. Department of Health and Human Services 2002a). Most Black children who are referred to child protective services are removed from their parents and placed in foster care. Black children also remain in foster care longer, are moved to new placements more often, and are less likely either to be reunited with their parents or adopted than are white children. During the 1990s, Black foster children were increasingly placed in the care of relatives, a practice known as "kinship foster care." Kinship foster care is now the main type of out-of-home placement for Black children in some cities. The exploding foster care population and a shortage of licensed nonrelative foster homes made relatives an attractive placement option for child welfare agencies.

Although federal policy now encourages kinship foster care, it gives states wide latitude in creating the system of financial support for kin caregivers. Relative caregivers can receive benefits under Temporary Assistance for Needy Families (TANF), or they can receive foster care stipends if they are licensed. Foster care payments are much larger than TANF benefits and are multiplied by each child in the relative's care. Some experts believe that this disparity works as an incentive for needy families to seek formal placement of children in kinship foster care instead of relying informally on relatives to help with caregiving. These families must make the children state wards and submit to regulation by child welfare authorities to receive the more generous foster care stipends needed to meet their children's needs.

Dorothy E. Roberts

See also: Aid to Families with Dependent Children (ADC/AFDC); Child Welfare; Child-Saving; *The Dangerous Classes of New York;* Orphanages; Poorhouse/Almshouse; Social Work

References and Further Reading

Bernstein, Nina. 2001. *The Lost Children of Wilder: The Epic Struggle to Change Foster Care.* New York: Pantheon Books.

Lindsey, Duncan. 1994. *The Welfare of Children.* New York: Oxford University Press.

Pelton, Leroy H. 1989. *For Reasons of Poverty: A Critical Analysis of the Public Child Welfare System in the United States.* New York: Praeger.

Roberts, Dorothy. 2002. *Shattered Bonds: The Color of Child Welfare.* New York: Basic Books.

U.S. Department of Health and Human Services. Administration for Children and Families. 2002a. "AFCARS Report." http://www.acf.hhs.gov/programs/cb/publications/afcars/report7.htm.

———. 2002b. "National Adoption and Foster Care Statistics." http://www.acf.hhs.gov/programs/cb/dis/afcars/publications/afcars.htm.

Frazier, E. Franklin

See Moynihan Report; *The Negro Family in the United States;* Poverty Research

Freedmen's Aid

Freedmen's aid was educational, material, medical, employment, and related social welfare assistance provided to former slaves, first by private groups and eventually by the federal government, during and after the American Civil War of 1861–1865. In addition to caring for newly emancipated slaves, the freedmen's aid movement became an important venue for female reform and social welfare activism in the post–Civil War period, setting the stage for the creation of the Freedmen's Bureau. An unprecedented extension of federal government authority on behalf of African American former slaves, the bureau and the movement it grew out of were bold experiments in social policy. At the same time, freedmen's aid efforts were limited by the combination of racial paternalism and prejudice that kept even the most committed white reformers from treating Blacks as social and economic equals.

Freedmen's aid efforts began even as the Civil War was raging, initiated by northern teachers, ministers, abolitionists, businessmen, and military personnel. Freed from bondage by the social upheaval of the war, thousands of slaves sought safety and freedom behind Union lines. Though initially reluctant to serve as emancipators, the Union army soon adopted Gen. Benjamin Butler's policy, articulated in May 1861, that considered slaves to be enemy "contraband." Former slaves proved an invaluable source of labor to the Union military, and the army began to enlist Black soldiers in 1862. But the army also faced a humanitarian crisis as it tried to feed and house slave families crowded into army camps. In order to aid the military, northern reformers established freedmen's aid societies, which raised money and sent boxes of clothing and books to the South. In addition, teachers and reformers traveled to the South. Following Union victories in Confederate states, these reformers took over the management of abandoned plantations, established special camps for former slaves, and set up schools, stores, soup kitchens, and employment agencies. Though in many ways an extension of the antislavery movement, freedmen's aid organizations included Republican businessmen, members of Methodist, Baptist, and other denominational missionary societies, and female members of soldier's aid societies as well as abolitionists. The two largest organizations aiding former slaves were the American Missionary Association and the secular American Freedmen's Union Commission.

Northern reformers and the military continued to cooperate during Reconstruction. Their efforts contributed to the transformation of charity in the post–Civil War period, when private associations began working closely with state and local governments, adopting social science methods to evaluate the causes of poverty and to formulate policy. Following the recommendations of the American Freedmen's Inquiry Commission, whose members had observed freedmen's aid efforts throughout the South, Congress established the Bureau of Refugees, Freedmen, and Abandoned Lands (Freedmen's Bureau) in March 1865 as a temporary guardian for former slaves. The bureau was a division of the Department of War, and the military staff of the bureau negotiated employment contracts, oversaw the establishment of freedmen's schools, and distributed relief. The bureau also protected the basic rights of former slaves, fighting such remnants of slavery as the practice of apprenticing freedchildren against the will of their parents. Though the government and the military distributed rations, fuel, and clothing, they focused principally on developing a wage labor system in the South. Gen. Oliver Otis Howard, the commissioner of the Freedmen's Bureau, promoted the partnership between his government agency and private aid societies in the North, arguing that these societies should provide direct relief while the bureau prepared former slaves for participation in a capitalist economy. But freedmen's aid societies also viewed charity with suspicion. Northerners worried that slavery had

Recently freed sick and old slaves line up at the Freedmen's Bureau to receive rations, ca. September 22, 1866. (Corbis)

made freedpeople dependent on whites and the government, and they wanted to promote the self-reliance of African Americans. The military staff of the Freedmen's Bureau and the leadership of the freedmen's aid movement formulated their policies to encourage freedpeople's self-support and independence from public and private charity.

The staff of the Freedmen's Bureau pushed education as the most effective means of preparing former slaves for wage labor and citizenship, and education proved the most successful aspect of its cooperation with northern aid societies. Freedmen's aid societies recruited and paid teachers, while the bureau built schoolhouses and paid for transportation. Hundreds of women served as teachers in schools throughout the South. Most "Yankee schoolmarms" stayed in the South for only a few years, or as long as their parent society could cover their salaries, but others, including Laura Towne, Caroline Putnam, and Sallie Holley, remained in the South for the rest of their lives. Teachers served as intermediaries between the North and former slaves; they also distributed clothing and offered other aid to African Americans in their districts.

Though men such as Edward L. Pierce, Lyman Abbott, J. Miller McKim, and General Howard often served as the public face of the freedmen's aid movement, northern women provided the organizational base as members of aid societies, distributors of relief, and teachers. Applying skills learned in antislavery and soldier's aid societies, women raised funds, hired teachers, and oversaw the daily operations of their associations. Northern societies also employed women as "freedmen's agents" to distribute material aid to former slaves and to work as visitors in cities like Alexandria, Virginia, and Washington, D.C., where refugees had congregated. Soon the Freedmen's Bureau, too, began to employ women as visitors and employment agents, contributing to the growing number of women in the civil service following the war. Nevertheless, women's participation in freedmen's aid proved controversial. As the freedmen's aid movement turned its focus to wage labor, education, and political rights, bureau agents and other reformers viewed women's charitable activities as harmful to the self-sufficiency of former slaves.

Former slaves saw the Freedmen's Bureau as an ally, but the bureau's policies could be detrimental to freedpeople's interests. Former slaves turned to the Freedmen's Bureau for protection again unscrupulous employers and former owners. For as long as the bureau existed, freedpeople hoped in vain to buy or rent confiscated and abandoned Confederate land, viewing landownership as the best means to economic and personal independence. The bureau itself, however, focused on wage labor above other aspects of freedom and often coerced former slaves into signing labor contracts. Bureau agents and former slaveholders expected freedwomen, including married women and women with children, to continue working on southern plantations, impinging upon their desire to care for their families. Despite the poverty of many freedpeople and the evidence of their industry and self-reliance, the Freedmen's Bureau cut back on material aid, fearing its effects on the character of former slaves. Thus, even as reformers advocated for former slaves, their racial assumptions about the indolence of African Americans ultimately shaped their policies.

Frederick Douglass criticized the freedmen's aid movement for its paternalism. Other free Blacks in both the North and the South responded to whites' concern over alleged African American dependency by founding aid societies that emphasized self-help. Northern Blacks realized that their status in American society also depended on the outcome of the emancipation experiment, and they sought to prove their qualification for citizenship through freedmen's relief. Organizations like the African Civilization Society sent teachers to the South, found jobs in the North for southern migrants, raised money, and established orphanages. In the South, mutual aid societies helped the elderly, poor, and sick. By forming these organizations, African Americans stressed their independence from whites and from the government, responding to those who denied their capacity for self-reliance. In both the North and the South, African American women taught school and administered material aid.

After Congress passed the Fourteenth (1868) and Fifteenth (1870) Amendments, granting African American men civil and political rights, public and political support for the freedmen's aid movement diminished due to complacency, the decline of Reconstruction, and massive resistance in the South. Most Americans believed that with the vote, former slaves could protect themselves. Initially established as a temporary agency, the Freedmen's Bureau fought for political support and adequate funding throughout its existence. Opponents rejected both the implied expansion of federal power and the wisdom of a national welfare program for former slaves. The Freedmen's Bureau ceased most of its operations in 1868, finally closing in 1872. Freedmen's aid societies also struggled to raise funds. Since the Freedmen's Bureau had funded a significant part of their educational work, the bureau's demise forced many aid societies to close by 1870. And yet, although the freedmen's aid movement officially ended when the federal government withdrew its support for Reconstruction in 1877, many individuals and denominational aid societies continued to sponsor African American schools in the South through the end of the century.

Carol Faulkner

See also: African Americans; Racial Segregation; Racism; Sharecropping; Slavery

References and Further Reading

Berlin, Ira, Barbara J. Fields, Steven F. Miller, Joseph P. Reidy, and Leslie S. Rowland. 1992. *Slaves No More: Three Essays on Emancipation and the Civil War.* New York: Cambridge University Press.

Bremner, Robert H. 1980. *The Public Good: Philanthropy and Welfare in the Civil War Era*. New York: Knopf.

Cimbala, Paul A., and Randall M. Miller. 1999. *The Freedmen's Bureau and Reconstruction: Reconsiderations*. New York: Fordham University Press.

Jones, Jacqueline. 1980. *Soldiers of Light and Love: Northern Teachers and Georgia Blacks, 1865–1873*. Athens: University of Georgia Press.

McPherson, James M. 1964. *The Struggle for Equality: Abolitionists and the Negro in the Civil War and Reconstruction*. Princeton: Princeton University Press.

Friendly Visitors

See Charity; Charity Organization Societies; Society for the Prevention of Pauperism

Galbraith, John Kenneth

See The Affluent Society

Gender Discrimination in the Labor Market

Gender is a key factor in understanding poverty, employment, and social welfare. Gender discrimination has affected women differently depending on their class, race, ethnicity, immigrant status, first language, and sexual orientation. Gender discrimination has taken many forms: in laws that govern families, in assumptions that shape opportunities, in social policies that ease economic insecurity, and in the labor market. This entry will discuss gender discrimination in the labor market.

Gender discrimination does not occur in isolation from other statuses and identities. Especially in the labor market, where social forces and statuses interact, gender cannot provide the sole explanation for discrimination because gender itself is shaped by other important social categories, such as race, ethnicity, class, and other dimensions of social difference. Therefore, our discussion of women's wages, occupations, and poverty is placed within the framework of an intersectional analysis—one that works to reveal how the intersections of gender, race, ethnicity, and social class come together to influence these aspects of social and economic organization.

The Feminization of Poverty

The term "feminization of poverty" was first coined by Diana Pearce (1978) in an article in which she drew attention to the increasing numbers of female-headed households that were currently living in poverty. This term created a kind of "research moment" whereby a great deal of attention was drawn to the growing numbers of households with only a single (almost always female) parent in the home, as these households became a greater proportion of the poor. Pearce pointed out that there were nearly twice as many poor female-headed families in 1976 as there had been in 1950, and she indicated that this trend showed no signs of abating. Her explanation for the high concentration of single-mother families in poverty stressed women's low wages and marital status as well as the role of welfare in perpetuating the placement of women in low-paying, low-skill jobs.

Critics of the term "feminization of poverty" charge that it obscures some of the continuing differences in who is likely to become and remain poor. Linda Burnham brought an intersectional approach to this topic when she wrote, "These distortions [within the feminization of poverty analysis] are the inevitable result of a theory that abstracts women as a group out of the overall socioeconomic trends in U.S. capitalist development" (1986, 70). Burnham argued that by conceiving of poverty as solely a gendered issue, the causes of Black women's poverty are overlooked, white women's vulnerability to poverty is overestimated, and the perpetuation of a poor working class by capitalist systems is ignored. Pearce herself updated her own work with a subsequent article in 1988 that detailed how "the proportion of persons in poverty who are in families maintained by women has risen for all groups, with the most dramatic shifts occurring in Black families" (1988, 502).

Sara McLanahan, Annemette Sorensen, and Dorothy Watson (1989) investigated the ratio of poor women to poor men, the poverty rates of women and of men (each as a proportion of the total of their respective sex), and finally the ratio of the women's poverty rate to the men's poverty rate. In addition, they also compared data for Blacks and whites in all of these categories. The authors found that Black people are more likely to be poor and that the ratio between Black men and Black women is very similar to the respective ratio between white men and white women. In addition, for women in their early childbearing years (eighteen to twenty-four), living arrangements were found to be significant in increasing poverty ratios between women and men. This article was important in identifying some of the structural connections between gender and poverty. Both race and gender are implicated in the experience of poverty. Nevertheless, more information is needed to explore how women of color might experience this intersection in ways that mutually reinforce the consequences of racism, classism, and sexism. Increasingly, research on gender and poverty examine how race *and* gender *and* class (as well as other dimensions of difference) together explain the causes and consequences of poverty. These kinds of analyses could reveal some of the social processes that reinforce the greater likelihood for women of color to become and remain poor and white women's greater likelihood to avoid poverty or have shorter spells of poverty.

The literature surrounding the feminization of poverty is multifaceted and reflects much of the policy-related debate on the subject. Often, there is an implied blaming of single mothers, either because they did not stay married or, even worse, because they "chose" to have children outside of marriage. Bonnie Thornton Dill, Maxine Baca Zinn, and Sandra Patton have analyzed "racialized political narratives that blame poor single and [Latina] immigrant mothers for social ills like drug addiction, poverty, crime and gang violence" (1998, 6), connecting these media-produced tropes to the maintenance of misperceptions about the causes and the perpetuation of poverty. Dill, Zinn, and Patton's analysis revealed the underlying connections among systems of power (based on race, class, and gender) that privilege a particular family form (that is, white, two-parent, and middle class) through ideological and political manipulation of social institutions.

Zinn (1992) elaborated on some of the consequences of these processes. She showed that even in situations where there are two parents in the home, if those parents happen to be Black or Latino, they are more likely to be living in poverty than they would be if they happened to be white. Mary Jo Bane's (1986) work related this fact to a phenomenon she calls "reshuffled poverty." Families with a lone female head due to marital breakup are often living in poverty, but when this head is a woman of color, it is more likely that the family was already living in poverty prior to the marital breakup. Thus, the family's structure has very little to do with the state of poverty when race is taken into account.

Single mothers of all races are subject to lower pay rates, thus further increasing the likelihood that their families live in poverty. But when the family head is a white woman, it is more likely that the family fell into poverty at the time of a marital breakup. Bane emphasized the import of this finding, writing, "if this argument is correct, child and spousal support may help alleviate the poverty of many white households, but it can only make the smallest dent in the problem of Black poverty" (1986, 231). This illustrates how an intersectional approach can lead to the formulation of policies and interventions. This approach demonstrates that for Black and Latina women, getting or staying married does not offer the same kinds of economic protections that it might for white women. And yet marital status is commonly (mis)understood as a key factor in the feminization of poverty.

The Wage Gap

The gender wage gap is the difference in pay received by male and female workers. Although this difference shrank throughout the second half of the twentieth century, it remains significant. Currently, the gap in median annual earnings between full-time, year-round female and male workers, after narrowing during the 1980s, has closed to approximately 73 percent (see the accompanying table for breakdown by race). This difference is exacerbated for women of color; studies have shown that marital status and children do not change the facts that white women earn more than Black and Latina women and that white men tend to earn more than all other groups of workers.

Table 1

2000 median annual earnings for year-round, full-time workers as a percentage of white male earnings

	Men	*Women*
Black	78%	64%
Hispanic	63%	52%
White	100%	72%

(*Data source:* U.S. Census Bureau, CPS Survey, March 2001, as compiled by the National Committee on Pay Equity)

Education does not ameliorate the gap; for example, according to Randy Albelda and Chris Tilly (1997), men with only a bachelor's degree still earn more than women with a master's degree. This remains true at every level of education: Men earn more for each year of education than do women. These differences in wages persist even when such factors as industry and experience have been controlled.

The causes of income inequality are manifold. Some of the difference between men's and women's wages has to do with human capital issues. Women, on average, have less work experience and job tenure than do men (although this is less true among younger cohorts of women). Yet Paula England, Karen Christopher, and Lori I. Reid (1999) have offered evidence that measures of seniority and experience are most effective in explaining differences in wages among whites but do not readily explain differences in wages among people of color. What they call the "generic" account of gender-based income disparities does not explain the disparities between the incomes of Black women and men, although it can offer insight into Latino/a differences. An alternative explanation that focuses on the organization of work, rather than on the human resources of women workers, is occupational segregation, which is discussed below. Closely related to occupational segregation are discussions of comparable worth that argue that "women's work is regarded as less skilled or unskilled *because women do it*" (Kemp, 1994). Long-term data has shown that once a formerly male-dominated profession opens to women, it quickly becomes a female-dominated one, and overall wages decline. More work is needed in this area to determine how race intersects with gender and class to reinforce segregationist trends. Other factors contributing to the existence of income inequality include the division of labor in the household and lifelong social pressures to conform to standard gender roles.

Reductions in the wage gap have been brought about by various factors; for instance, more white women now remain in the workforce after childbirth, resulting in an increase in overall job experience and tenure (Stevenson and Donovan 1996). A second partial explanation for the reduction in the wage gap is the overall decrease in men's wages. As the manufacturing sector declined in the late 1970s, abolishing many well-paid jobs, the relative difference between men's and women's wages declined as well. Although the income gap has shrunk, it remains likely that it will continue to persist as long as structural factors, such as occupational segregation, play a role in its perpetuation.

"Occupational segregation" is the phenomenon of women and men tending to be concentrated in different types of jobs. For example, Francine Blau and Maryanne Ferber found that women tend to be concentrated in administrative support and service occupations whereas men dominate the operator/laborer jobs and precision craft and repair occupations (1992, 120). In general, the jobs that women hold have less status and are lower paid, even when the jobs require similar skill levels and educational background. Barbara Reskin, in her study of racial occupational segregation among women workers, found considerable evidence that many "women's jobs" are almost as segregated racially as they are by gender. She wrote, "segregation by race and ethnicity . . . preserves racial and ethnic inequality both by maintaining the social distance between groups and by generating earnings disparities" (1999, 200). She argued that both race and ethnicity must be taken into account to understand occupational segregation among women. Albelda and Tilly (1997), using the terms "glass ceiling" and "sticky floor," discussed the kinds of segregation that women and women of color encounter. The term "glass ceiling" refers to the blocking of upward advancement that women often face, and "sticky floor" refers to segregation into low-paying jobs.

In addition, scholars of comparable worth have pointed out that women working in "women's jobs" tend to be paid less than men working in "men's jobs," even when the jobs require similar skills, responsibilities, and efforts, and that this is exacerbated when women of color are the majority of workers in that job: "Occupations with high concentrations of women of color are among the lowest paid in the labor force (e.g., cleaners, child care workers, and sewing machine operators)" (Dill, Cannon, and Vanneman 1987, 63), and yet "male jobs" that have equivalent skill requirements are paid more. Programs aimed at ameliorating these pay inequities, like comparable worth, come under considerable political debate. Dill, Cannon, and Vanneman (1987) have argued that Black women, in spite of being in different kinds of jobs, would benefit from the institution of "equal pay for equal work" laws in multiple ways. First, those Black women who work in occupations similar to those of white women would benefit directly, and those Black women who work in segregated occupations, if rewarded on the basis of the education and experience of the jobholders, would benefit on average even more than would white women. In addition, such a program would benefit men of color, who are more likely to work in "women's jobs" than are white men, both by increasing their own earnings and by increasing household income through increases in the earnings of women of color.

Consequences of the combined effects of occupational segregation by race and gender include stagnation in low-paying, low-skill jobs with limited benefits for Blacks, Latinas, and many immigrant women of color. Women, especially single mothers, often need jobs that can meet their child care needs, but these are exactly the kinds of jobs that are difficult to find and keep. The service industry is where many find jobs that can fit their needs for flexibility, yet those are often dead-end jobs. As a consequence, these kinds of jobs have a high turnover, thus lessening the likelihood that their holders will acquire long-term work experience. In addition to the wage gap and occupational segregation, women also tend to work additional hours at home, doing the majority of household work (Hochschild and Machung 1989).

These terms—"feminization of poverty," "wage gap," and "occupational segregation"—describe some of the unique challenges that women and particularly women of color face in the labor market. As Valerie Polakow wrote, "Many women are poor for the same reason men are poor—because they lack education, skills, live in a poor job area, or are minorities. But women are also poor because they are both nurturers of and providers for their children; and because they are disadvantaged in the labor market" (1993, 61). The challenges women face are even greater when the experiences of women of color are moved to the center of analysis. When this is done, the institutional context, both past and present, must be acknowledged as a major contributing factor. Gender inequality in the workplace remains intrinsically bound to racial and ethnic inequality. Larger national and international trends that document increasing global inequality warn that if the systems of oppression are not ameliorated, current trends that divide the world into the "haves" and the "have-nots" will continue to worsen and exacerbate racial, gender, and class differences.

Amy E. McLaughlin and Bonnie Thornton Dill

See also: African Americans; Deserving/Undeserving Poor; Domestic Work; Family Structure; Feminization of Poverty; Heteronormativity; Income and Wage Inequality; Latino/as; Racism; Sexism; "Working Poor"

References and Further Reading

Albelda, Randy, and Chris Tilly. 1997. *Glass Ceilings and Bottomless Pits: Women's Work, Women's Poverty*. Boston: South End Press.

Bane, Mary Jo. 1986. "Household Composition and Poverty." In *Fighting Poverty: What Works and What Doesn't*, ed. Sheldon H. Danziger and Daniel H. Weinberg, 209–231. Cambridge, MA: Harvard University Press.

Blau, Francine, and Maryanne Ferber. 1992. *The Economics of Women, Men, and Work*. Englewood Cliffs, NJ: Prentice-Hall.

Burnham, Linda. 1986. "Has Poverty Been Feminized in Black America?" In *For Crying Out Loud: Women and Poverty in the United States*, ed. Rochelle Lefkowitz and Ann Withorn. New York: Pilgrim Press.

Dill, Bonnie Thornton, Lynn Weber Cannon, and Reeve Vanneman. 1987. *Pay Equity: An Issue of Race, Ethnicity, and Sex*. Washington, DC: National Committee on Pay Equity.

Dill, Bonnie Thornton, Maxine Baca Zinn, and Sandra Patton. 1998. "Valuing Families Differently: Race, Poverty, and Welfare Reform." *Sage Race Relations Abstracts* 23, no. 3 (August): 4–30.

England, Paula, Karen Christopher, and Lori I. Reid. 1999. "Gender, Race, Ethnicity, and Wages." In *Latinas and African American Women at Work: Race, Gender, and Economic Inequality*, ed. Irene Browne, 139–182. New York: Russell Sage Foundation.

Hochschild, Arlie, with Anne Machung. 1989. *The Second Shift: Working Parents and the Revolution at Home*. New York: Viking.

Kemp, Alice. 1994. *Women's Work: Degraded and Devalued*. Englewood Cliffs, NJ: Prentice-Hall.

McLanahan, Sara, Annemette Sorensen, and Dorothy Watson. 1989. "Sex Differences in Poverty: 1950–1980." *Signs: Journal of Women in Culture and Society* 15, no. 1: 102–122.

Pearce, Diana. 1978. "The Feminization of Poverty: Women, Work, and Welfare." *Urban and Social Change Review* 11: 28–36.

———. 1988. "Farewell to Alms: Women's Fare under Welfare." In *Women: A Feminist Perspective*, ed. Jo Freeman, 493–506. Mountain View, CA: Mayfield.

Polakow, Valerie. 1993. *Lives on the Edge: Single Mothers and Their Children in the Other America*. Chicago: University of Chicago Press.

Reskin, Barbara F. 1999. "Occupational Segregation by Race and Ethnicity among Women Workers." In *Latinas and African American Women at Work: Race, Gender, and Economic Inequality*, ed. Irene Browne, 183–204. New York: Russell Sage Foundation.

Stevenson, Mary Huff, and Elaine Donovan. 1996. "How the U.S. Economy Creates Poverty and Inequality." In *For Crying Out Loud: Women's Poverty in the United States*, ed. Diane Dujon and Ann Withorn, 67–78. New York: Pilgrim Press.

Zinn, Maxine Baca. 1992. "Family, Race, and Poverty in the Eighties." In *Rethinking the Family: Some Feminist Questions*, ed. Barrie Thorne and Marilyn Yalom, 71–90. Boston: Northeastern University Press.

General Assistance

General Assistance (GA) is typically defined as programs funded by state or local governments that provide cash assistance or in-kind benefits to very low-income individuals who are not eligible for such federal public assistance programs as Temporary Assistance for Needy Families (TANF) or Supplemental Security Income (SSI). The history of GA is fundamentally about societal judgments about who should work and about American persistence in denying generous and dignified public aid to those who are not working but are deemed able to do so.

Like all U.S. social welfare programs for the poor, GA's roots are found in the traditions of the English poor laws. In the late nineteenth century, public "outdoor relief" (aid to people in their homes, as opposed to "indoor," or institutional, aid) was considered so morally harmful that reformers sought to abolish it. As Josephine Shaw Lowell wrote in 1884, "human nature is so constituted that no man can receive as a gift what he should earn by his own labor without a moral deterioration" (cited in Coll 1969, 45). To ensure that only the most "deserving" among the poor—that is, individuals incapable of or morally excused from work, and their financial dependents—received public aid, officials thoroughly investigated the lives of applicants and monitored recipients. Humiliating treatment and dismally meager benefits discouraged all but the most desperate from seeking assistance.

During the Progressive Era, many states began to adopt public assistance programs for two categories of individuals—widowed mothers and the elderly—deemed worthy of aid because they had socially acceptable reasons for not working. Although "mothers' aid" and especially "old-age assistance" benefits were more generous than traditional "relief," in practice, they often differed little from the harsh programs they were meant to replace. Mothers' aid programs investigated applicants, judged the "suitableness" of their homes, and subjected them to ongoing supervision. Benefits were insufficient to support a family; the majority of recipients engaged in some form of wage labor.

Although the widespread unemployment of the Great Depression highlighted the need for a public safety net, Depression-era rhetoric and policies nonetheless emphasized work as the arbiter of deservingness. The Social Security Act of 1935 institutionalized the provision of public aid based on a distinction between "employables" and "unemployables." Unemployment insurance paid benefits to "employables" experiencing temporary spells of unemployment. Old Age Assistance and Old Age Insurance (that is, Social Security) supported "unemployable" retired workers, and Aid to Dependent Children (later Aid to Families with Dependent Children [AFDC]) targeted "unemployable" widowed and deserted mothers who lacked a male breadwinner to provide for their children.

With the passage of the Social Security Act, the federal government "quit this business of relief" (Franklin D. Roosevelt in 1935, quoted in Coll 1995, 33). Working-age adults without dependents who could not support themselves because of chronic unemployment, barriers to employment, or underemployment—the residual "unemployables"—were left to depend on wildly divergent and unevenly implemented state and local GA programs. But just as important, in the somewhat arbitrary world of public assistance, GA became the program of last resort for individuals who fell through the cracks of other programs, whether working-age adults, children, or the elderly.

In 1950, Congress passed a means-tested public assistance program for individuals who could not work because of permanent disability, picking up about a quarter of the nation's general assistance rolls. Then, in 1972, legislation folded means-tested assistance for the elderly (that is, for those who did not qualify for Social Security), the blind, and the disabled into a single federal program, Supplemental Security Income (SSI).

Unlike AFDC, SSI was completely federally financed, and its benefits were more generous than those of AFDC.

By the 1970s, the residual place of state and local GA programs in the U.S. welfare state was set. Unemployment insurance and Social Security provided for individuals with strong labor force attachment who found themselves in need because of temporary unemployment or old age. These socially acceptable reasons for being in need were rewarded by social insurance programs with strong federal oversight and relatively predictable and generous benefits. Individuals without strong labor force attachment were forced to rely on less generous, means-tested public assistance. The most "deserving" among this group—impoverished elderly, blind, or disabled individuals—could turn to the federally controlled SSI program. Single mothers—whose children were considered deserving even though their own deservingness was in doubt—could apply for federal-state AFDC benefits, which, though meager, provided a legal entitlement until 1996. The most "undeserving" of all—working-age adults, men and women alike, without dependents—were left to the vagaries of chronically underfunded state and local GA programs. GA continued to serve its traditional role as the safety net of last resort for other groups.

States began to crack down on GA in the 1980s, restricting eligibility, strengthening work requirements, and establishing time limits for those deemed employable. The trend accelerated with federal efforts to replace AFDC with Temporary Assistance for Needy Families, to make work requirements the centerpiece of reform, and to establish time limits for receipt of federally subsidized public assistance. In the late 1990s, GA caseloads reached their lowest levels in twenty-five years. As unemployment rises and more families are denied access to TANF because of time limits and penalties, it remains to be seen whether states and localities will expand GA programs to meet the growing need or whether increasing numbers of very low-income people will be left without a safety net of any sort.

Nancy K. Cauthen

See also: Deserving/Undeserving Poor; Federalism; Great Depression and New Deal; Poor Laws; *Public Relief and Private Charity;* Relief; Social Security Act of 1935; Welfare Policy/Welfare Reform; Work Ethic

References and Further Reading

Amenta, Edwin. 1998. *Bold Relief: Institutional Politics and the Origins of Modern American Social Policy*. Princeton: Princeton University Press.

Cauthen, Nancy K. 1998. "From Quiet Concern to Controversy: The Transformation of Aid to Dependent Children, 1935–1967." Ph.D. diss., New York University.

Coll, Blanche D. 1969. *Perspectives in Public Welfare: A History*. Washington, DC: U.S. Department of Health, Education, and Welfare.

———. 1995. *Safety Net: Welfare and Social Security, 1929–1979*. New Brunswick, NJ: Rutgers University Press.

Gallagher, Jerome L., Cori E. Uccello, Alicia B. Pierce, and Erin B. Reidy. 1999. *State General Assistance Programs, 1998*. Washington, DC: Urban Institute Press.

George, Henry

See Progress and Poverty; Property; Wealth

G.I. Bill

The G.I. Bill is the informal name used to refer to a set of social programs initially established for returning veterans of World War II and later extended to those who served during the undeclared wars in Korea and Vietnam and in the all-volunteer military since 1984. These programs continued the American tradition of extending generous social benefits to those who had fulfilled what was considered the highest obligation of citizenship: military service. In contrast to the direct, retrospective cash payments ("bonuses") that were granted to veterans of the wars from the American Revolution through World War I, which were paid only years after the military service, the G.I. Bill offered immediate assistance to veterans as a way to improve their long-term economic prospects. The most popular features included educational and training benefits that enabled veterans to attend college or vocational schools or to receive on-the-job training at government expense, and a loan-guarantee program to assist in the purchase of homes, farms, or businesses.

The formal title of the original G.I. Bill was the Servicemen's Readjustment Act of 1944 (Public Law 78–346). Public officials sought measures to ease the readjustment of veterans to civilian life, but they worried that the end of the war would bring a return to Depression-era unemployment levels as veterans reentered the job market. Fearful of instigating more veterans' protests like that of the Bonus Army in the early 1930s—during which thousands of World War I veterans camped in the U.S. capital for months until forcibly evicted—planners in President Franklin D. Roosevelt's administration suggested that veterans who had served for at least six months should be eligible for one year of education and training, with a limited number selected on a competitive basis to continue for more years. After the administration's bill was introduced in Congress, the American Legion crafted a far more sweeping alternative that promised up to four years of education for all veterans. The organization mobilized an enormous grassroots and public relations campaign in support of the legislation. Other veterans' groups disputed the legislation, advancing more-traditional programs targeting disabled veterans alone. Some university officials testified before Congress that the educational provisions would degrade their institutions by allowing unqualified individuals to pursue further education. Southern representatives opposed extending extensive benefits to African American veterans. Nonetheless, a blend of the most generous features of the administration and American Legion bills was enacted and was signed into law by Roosevelt on June 22, 1944.

The original G.I. Bill offered a wide array of benefits to World War II veterans. All veterans were entitled to a "mustering-out" payment of $100 to $300 per person. In addition, they could draw twenty dollars per week in "readjustment allowances," for as many as fifty-two weeks, until they found a job; these benefits were far more accessible than those available through unemployment insurance, which varied from state to state and was characterized by restrictive eligibility criteria. Although policymakers had worried that veterans would use what became known as the "52–20 Club" benefits to their full extent, in fact only 14 percent did so; the average veteran drew the benefits for 19.7 weeks. The loan guaranty provisions were utilized by 29 percent of veterans. The construction industry received an enormous boost as 4.3 million veterans purchased homes at low-interest rates through the program, and 200,000 purchased farms or started businesses. By 1955, nearly one-third of the new housing starts nationwide owed their backing to the Veterans Administration (President's Commission on Veterans' Pensions 1956, 275, 300–304).

The educational and training benefits were used by 51 percent of veterans—7.8 million individuals. Among beneficiaries, 28 percent attended colleges and universities, 45 percent went to schools below the college level, especially trade and vocational training programs, and the remainder utilized on-the-job or on-the-farm training (President's Commission on Veterans' Pensions 1956, 287). Any veteran with an honorable discharge who had served for at least ninety days of active duty was eligible. Beneficiaries could attend the educational institution of their choice, as long as they gained admission through the standard procedures. The G.I. Bill covered all tuition and fees up to a total of $500 per year, and veteran students also received monthly subsistence payments of $75 if single, $105 with one dependent, and $120

A new crop of ex-soldier students acquires school supplies on January 28, 1945. Books and notebooks, as well as tuition and other fees, up to a total of $500 for an ordinary school year, were furnished to World War II veterans under the G.I. Bill. (UPI/Bettmann/Corbis)

with two or more dependents. Veterans who had served for ninety days qualified for one year of education at government expense, with an additional month of education for each additional month of service up to a maximum of forty-eight months.

Colleges, after having struggled to survive the lean years of the Depression and the war, were inundated with new students: Veterans made up half of the undergraduate population nationwide by 1949. Many institutions adjusted to space shortages and to the different needs of veteran students, who were older and more likely to be married and to have children, by building new temporary housing for veterans and their families. Veterans were most likely to use the higher education provisions if they were younger, had higher levels of education prior to the war, and had been encouraged to pursue an education while growing up. Prior to the war, higher education had been limited primarily to white, native-born, higher-status Protestants; the G.I. Bill helped include more Jews, Catholics, immigrants and children of immigrants, and individuals from working-class and lower-middle-class families. Although the G.I. Bill made college affordable to many who could not have attended otherwise, it also permitted individuals who could have attended regardless to go to more-expensive and often higher-status institutions than they could have otherwise and to attend full-time, completing their degrees more quickly than they would have otherwise. Veterans could use the benefits to study in whatever field they wished. The G.I. Bill produced professionals in a broad array of fields, including 450,000 engineers, 238,000 teachers, 91,000 scientists, 67,000 doctors, 22,000 dentists, and 17,000 writers and editors. The program boosted educational attainment among beneficiaries by three years. The government financial assistance served to ameliorate the effects of socioeconomic factors that had long determined who went to college and how much education they ultimately received.

Although the higher education provisions were administered easily through existing colleges and universities, the demand for vocational training spurred the widespread development of new programs. The number of trade schools tripled within six years of the G.I. Bill's enactment. Administrators experienced challenges in ascertaining the quality of such programs, and they uncovered many cases of programs overcharging the government for the service provided. Nonetheless, such programs enabled veterans to acquire training in a wide array of vocations, including accounting, auto mechanics, plumbing, masonry, refrigeration, pipe fitting, small engine repair, electrical work, and television or telephone repair. In addition, thousands of veterans attended flight school or business school or completed their primary or secondary education. Veterans who had less education prior to military service and whose parents had less education were especially likely to use the vocational training benefits.

African American veterans' experiences of the G.I. Bill differed from those of white veterans and varied by specific program and by region of residence in the postwar era. Many found that the Veterans Administration was less likely to approve their claims for readjustment allowances. Those who sought low-interest mortgages often found that banks turned them away. African Americans' use of the educational provisions was impeded by the fact that the vast majority lived in the South, where they faced a segregated educational system. The historically Black colleges were overwhelmed by the influx, nearly doubling their 1940 enrollment levels by 1950. These institutions enjoyed neither the resources nor the accreditation bestowed on the white universities, and nowhere did they provide students the opportunity for graduate study at the doctoral level or for an accredited degree in engineering. Nonetheless, in all regions of the country, including the South, African American veterans used the education and training benefits at higher rates than did white veterans (Mettler 2005). Thousands of others migrated to the North and West and utilized the provisions in integrated institutions. Regardless of region, Black beneficiaries of the education and training program were especially likely to regard it as life-altering, inasmuch as it provided them with opportunities to which they would not otherwise have had access.

The G.I. Bill elevated the status of American men relative to women largely because of the composition of the military and because tuition benefits were limited to those who had served. Although more women served in the military during World War II than in any earlier period, they made up less than 2 percent of the armed forces (Mettler 2005). Women who had served in the Army Air Force were not granted full military status and thus were ineligible for the benefits. And yet, despite the prevalent cultural messages about domesticity that confronted women in the postwar era, 40 percent of female veterans used the educational provisions (U.S. Senate, Committee on Veterans' Affairs 1973, 163). Sixty thousand attended college on the G.I. Bill, and others used the vocational provisions to learn bookkeeping, cosmetology, and secretarial skills. Married women veterans using the benefits were denied subsistence payments for their husbands. Unlike prior forms of veterans' benefits, the G.I. Bill was not provided to wives or widows of veterans. Due to the increased access to higher education for men and the perpetuation of obstacles to women's enrollment in some schools and programs, women's presence among undergraduate students declined from 40 percent in 1940 to 31 percent in 1950 (Mettler 2005).

Besides extending generous rights of social citizenship to beneficiaries through expanded access to education, the G.I. Bill also prompted higher levels of involvement in civic and political activity during the postwar era. Veterans who used the educational benefits joined greater numbers of civic organizations and became more active in politics than did veterans with the same level of education and socioeconomic background who did not use the G.I. Bill benefits. The policy design of the program, featuring universalism and treating beneficiaries as rights-bearing individuals, appeared to have positive effects beyond elevating socioeconomic status. These effects were most pronounced for those from low to moderate socioeconomic backgrounds, since they experienced full incorporation into the polity as first-class citizens. In addition, some developed a sense of owing back to society in exchange for the generous program from which they had benefited. The extended educational levels facilitated by the G.I. Bill helped cultivate the skills, networks, and resources that allow individuals to engage in public life. All of these dynamics enhanced individuals' predisposition to participate in civic activities (Mettler 2002).

The original G.I. Bill quickly gained popularity among citizens and policymakers, and it served as a template for subsequent policymaking. Congress extended comparable benefits through the Korean G.I. Bill (Public Law 82–550) in 1952, the Cold War GI Bill (Public Law 89–358) in 1966, and another version (Public Law 90–77) for veterans of the undeclared war in Vietnam in 1967. Each version's educational and training benefits were extended on somewhat less-generous terms than those of its predecessor. The Korean and post-Korean versions limited training to a maximum of thirty-six months and permitted veterans to be trained for one and a half times as long as they had been on active duty. Veterans of Vietnam had to have served a minimum of eighteen months to qualify for the benefits. In 1984, Congress established a system of educational benefits comparable to the G.I. Bill for veterans of the all-volunteer military. This program was regarded as a recruitment tool, but it required contributions from those who served.

The G.I. Bill continued to foster greater social inclusion of those who had engaged in military service. The percentage of veterans using the educational and training programs hovered around 40 percent in the 1950s and 1960s, and growing proportions of beneficiaries attended college, including 51 percent among those who had served during the Korean War and 57 percent among those who had served in Vietnam (U.S. Senate, Committee on Veterans' Affairs 1973, 161–174). The end of legalized segregation in the United States enabled African Americans to become more likely to use the G.I. Bill benefits than other veterans and to experience the greatest increase in their subsequent earnings after program usage.

Suzanne Mettler

See also: Bonus Army; Education Policies; Veterans' Assistance

References and Further Reading

Mettler, Suzanne. 2002. "Bringing the State Back into Civic Engagement: Policy Feedback Effects of the G.I. Bill for World War II Veterans." *American Political Science Review* 96, no. 2 (June): 351–365.

———. 2005. *Civic Generation: The G.I. Bill in the Lives of World War II Veterans*. New York: Oxford University Press.

Olson, Keith W. 1974. *The G.I. Bill, the Veterans, and the Colleges*. Lexington: University Press of Kentucky.

Onkst, David H. 1998. "First a Negro . . . Incidentally a Veteran": Black World War Two Veterans and the G.I. Bill of Rights in the Deep South, 1944–1948." *Journal of Social History*, Spring: 517–543.

President's Commission on Veterans' Pensions. 1956.

Veterans' Benefits in the United States. Washington, DC: GPO.

Ross, David R. B. 1969. *Preparing for Ulysses: Politics and Veterans during World War II*. New York: Columbia University Press.

U.S. Senate, Committee on Veterans' Affairs. 1973. *Final Report on Educational Assistance to Veterans: A Comparative Study of Three G.I. Bills*. Washington, DC: GPO.

Globalization and Deindustrialization

In the 1970s, profound transformations began to occur in the shape of the world economy, with enormous consequences for world poverty, inequality, and social policy. The two most widely used concepts to describe this restructuring are *globalization*, the increasing interdependence of the world's national and local economies, and *deindustrialization*, the diminishing importance of manufacturing to the world's most advanced economies.

Both of these developments have roots that predate the 1970s—world historians have traced the ebbs and flows of truly world-spanning economic connections back to the voyages of Columbus, if not earlier, and industrial employment declined in certain regions of Europe and North America in the 1920s. However, since about 1970, two factors have accelerated both processes and given them some unprecedented characteristics. Advances in transportation and communication technologies—including long-distance jets, giant container ships, satellite networks, and the Internet—have made connections across the globe much faster and easier, increasing the sheer volume and density of flows of money, goods, people, ideas, and political influence. More important, a dramatic shift in world politics has transformed the ways the world economy is governed. Supporters of government regulation of markets and redistribution of wealth through welfare states lost influence to supporters of neoliberal economic philosophies, so-called because they were inspired by the classical, liberal free-market ideas of the eighteenth and nineteenth centuries. Neoliberals have called for an end to government interference in the world's markets in the interest of global growth and prosperity. In practice, they have reconfigured the role of governments—and of other institutions that set the rules for the world economy—to prioritize the interests of multinational corporations and financiers. As a result, contemporary neoliberal forms of globalization and deindustrialization have increased economic inequality worldwide.

Deindustrialization was the first concept to enter the public debate about global economic restructuring, as news of dramatic plant closings increased in North America and Europe during the 1970s and intensified during the worldwide recession of the 1980s. Commentators coined the term "Rust Belt" to denote the empty hulls of factories strewn across the urban landscapes of the U.S. Northeast and Midwest, the British Midlands, the German Ruhrgebiet, and other historic heartlands of the Industrial Revolution. In the United States, factory closings were quickly linked to worldwide transformations, first to America's increasing competition with Europe and Japan over the products of heavy industry like steel and automobiles. Later, textiles, electronics, and other consumer items imported from Southeast Asia and Latin America gained visibility, and the loss of factory jobs in the United States was linked to corporations' practice of moving or outsourcing their production overseas and to free-trade treaties. In the 1990s, the word "globalization" gained currency as a way to highlight these broader contexts of deindustrialization, and globalization played an important role in the fierce debate over such free-trade institutions as the North American Free Trade Agreement (NAFTA), the World Trade Organization (WTO), and the Free Trade Agreement of the Americas (FTAA).

Economic statistics give some indication of

the increasing magnitude of contemporary deindustrialization and its link to the globalization of trade and investment. In the United States in 1947, manufacturing was the largest sector of the economy, employing 26.5 percent of the workforce. By 1996, that figure had diminished to 15 percent, half the size of the rapidly growing service sector, smaller than that of the retail sector, and about equal to government employment. The decline began slowly, and it accelerated in the late 1960s, when Europe and Japan rebuilt industrial plants destroyed in World War II and began to compete effectively with U.S. industry. It is important to remember, though, that in 1995, this "triad" of advanced economies together still accounted for nearly three-quarters of the world's exports of vehicles and other machinery and two-thirds of its steel and other metals (Levy 1999; Smith 1999).

The flip side of deindustrialization in the wealthiest countries has been the dramatic increase in industrial activity in the world's developing and transitional economies. Between 1980 and 1995, their share of vehicle and machinery exports rose from about 5 percent to 22 percent, and their share of textile exports surpassed half of the world's total. This increased export activity was part of a general growth in global trade. The world's total exports, measured as a percentage of gross domestic product (GDP), grew by a fifth from 1973 to 1992. During that time, Asia's GDP nearly doubled and Latin America's grew by a half (Baker, Epstein, and Pollin 1998). Much of this trade was between different foreign subsidiaries of multinational corporations based in the West, often involving unfinished goods and auto parts heading toward the next appointed location on the "global assembly line." Foreign direct investment in such things as factory buildings and equipment, another critical measure of the interconnectedness of the world economy, also increased during the same period, from 4.5 percent of world output in 1975 to 10.1 percent in 1995 (Baker, Epstein, and Pollin 1998). It must be noted, however, that both the volume of trade and foreign direct investment were about as high or higher in the free-market world economy of the nineteenth century, suggesting that today's globalization represents a new expansionary phase in a much longer historical pattern of global integration, which has been interrupted by periods of relatively decreasing or slower-growing numbers of connections.

The character of deindustrialization in advanced economies like the United States also reflects movements of goods and investment capital within the country, particularly from central cities to suburbs and from the Rust Belt toward the Sun Belt of the South and Southwest. As a result, American deindustrialization was very uneven, and in some places manufacturing actually expanded. Cities whose economies were highly focused on heavy industry suffered the most. In 1947, 340,000 people worked in Detroit's factories, heavily concentrated in auto making. Thirty years later, the number had dropped by almost two-thirds, to 138,000. Buffalo, another bastion of heavy industry, lost 41,000 factory jobs, a third of the city's total, in the recession years 1979–1983 alone (Sugrue 1996; Perry and McLean 1991, 361). By contrast, New York City, which has a more diversified economy and little heavy industry, more closely followed the national average. Many suburban areas, even in the Rust Belt, actually saw gains in industrial employment. Though the city of Philadelphia, for example, lost almost two-thirds of its industrial jobs between 1958 and 1986, manufacturing in its suburban ring actually continued to rise throughout the period and by the 1990s had more than two and a half times as many factory jobs as the historic city (Stull and Madden 1990, 28).

Cities in the South and Southwest also followed different trends from those of the country as a whole. Houston's industrial employment expanded dramatically during the oil boom of the 1970s, when the rest of the country stagnated, but then plummeted during the 1980s as oil prices declined. The Los Angeles region lost many heavy industry jobs related to aerospace and defense during the late 1980s and early 1990s, but its overall manufacturing employment has climbed continuously, and in 1990 its 1.3 million factory jobs made it one of the largest centers of industrial employment in the world (Waldinger and Bozorgmehr 1996, 219). Finally, it is important to remember that the overall flight of manufacturing from the United States masks the resurgence of particularly low-paid work in "sweatshops," especially in apparel, electronics assembly, and food processing, which are predominantly staffed by women and immigrants. Such sweatshops in the United States reflect uneven racial and gender patterns within the transformation of manufacturing worldwide. Once a high-wage white male preserve, the factory has increasingly become a low-wage ghetto for women and people of color.

In the United States, debates over the social impact of globalization and deindustrialization have focused on the relatively specific question of free-trade treaties, as enshrined in NAFTA and the WTO and as proposed in the FTAA. There is a consensus that such treaties do cause many older plants to close and that deindustrialization results in immediate pain to the individuals, families, and communities involved. Neoliberal supporters of free trade argue, however, that this pain represents a cost American society must bear if it is to benefit from unfettered capitalism's promise of greater economic efficiency and a long-term upward cycle of global growth. They argue that blue-collar workers and the American economy as a whole will reap much richer rewards from specializing in higher-skilled "knowledge-based" work such as that offered in the dynamic service sector and in export-oriented jobs. According to neoliberals, benefits will also come from the greater variety of ever less expensive consumer goods available in the globalized marketplace. The poor of the developing world, meanwhile, will be able to give up subsistence agriculture for factory work, ultimately narrowing the gap between the first and third worlds. In their most triumphal moments, especially after the fall of the Soviet bloc and again during the late 1990s, neoliberals proclaimed the "end" of history's endless ideological conflicts and heralded a "new economy" made possible by new technologies and global connections, blessed by upward-spiraling stock market indexes, a reconciliation of low unemployment and low inflation, and a victory over the boom and bust of the business cycle.

Critics of this story argue just the opposite. They argue that free trade treaties, rather than creating a rising tide that lifts all boats, result in a "race to the bottom" by forcing first world workers to compete directly with workers receiving vastly lower wages in developing countries. Even the *threat* of a plant closing—ever more credible in the age of globalization—has forced workers and their unions to make wage concessions, while corporate practices of outsourcing production to foreign suppliers cause other wage and job declines. As a result, critics argue, a quarter century of expanding global trade and investment has fulfilled few of the free-marketeers' long-term promises. The economic booms of the 1950s and 1960s, the period of regulated world markets, produced a large increase in wages in the United States, a dramatic decline in poverty, and a decline in inequality of income and wealth. By contrast, during the free-trade 1980s and 1990s, economic booms have been accompanied by stagnating wages and poverty rates and by soaring inequality, only minimally redressed during such fragile episodes of hypergrowth as the high-tech bubble during the late 1990s. Even the celebrated low unemployment rates of the 1980s and 1990s were higher, on average, than those from 1950 to 1970. Meanwhile, the world's average annual economic growth rate has slowed down, not accelerated, since the expansion of trade and investment in the 1970s and 1980s. Inequality between the advanced economies and developing economies has also widened. In 1960, according to the

World Bank, the richest 20 percent of the world's population earned about thirty times more than the poorest 20 percent. By 1993, that gap had grown to a factor of seventy (U.N. Development Program 1999). In almost all of the wealthiest countries and in the majority of developing countries, disparities of income and wealth have also grown.

However, confining the debate about global economic restructuring to trade treaties and migrating factories understates the breadth of the *political* roots of contemporary economic inequality, not only in declining barriers to trade but throughout all the institutions that govern the world economy. Neoliberals often maintain that globalization is an impersonal and unstoppable process; as British Prime Minister Margaret Thatcher put it, "There Is No Alternative." But "TINA," as this rhetorical strategy is called, obscures the extensive and deliberate, if often internally divided, campaigns of political mobilization that neoliberals have organized from 1970 to the present to promote their vision for the world economy. The first of these political efforts were ideological and occurred within universities, think tanks, and the mass media. A second strand of mobilization occurred within the structures of international finance. From these bases, neoliberals had numerous successes in transforming government policy and corporate practice worldwide, culminating in attacks on workers' rights, antidiscrimination law, and welfare states and contributing to the wage declines and growing inequality that is often attributed to economic restructuring.

Before 1970, the custodians of nineteenth-century classic liberal laissez-faire were largely confined to academia in the United States, most notably the University of Chicago. Their first political successes came in that world of ideas, as neoliberals such as Friedrich von Hayek and Milton Friedman gradually pushed the economics profession to the right and then extended their influence into law schools and business schools. In the 1970s, highly active and well-connected conservative think tanks emerged in the United States and Britain, gaining ever more influence within the mass media. Ultimately, these efforts contributed to the victories of President Ronald Reagan in the United States and Prime Minister Margaret Thatcher in the United Kingdom, at which point neoliberal influence reached into two of the world's most powerful governments.

Meanwhile, neoliberals gained another set of political victories within the often-overlooked but vastly powerful realm of global finance. In 1973, the future Federal Reserve chairman, Paul Volcker, helped President Richard M. Nixon dismantle the system of regulated international currency markets, which were themselves a legacy of free-market critic John Maynard Keynes and the international Bretton Woods Agreement he helped broker in 1944. As the value of the world's monetary denominations began to "float" freely in relation to each other, huge new opportunities opened up for short-term speculation in what has been called the "global casino." Currency markets began to grow as traders bet huge sums on minute fluctuations in currency values. The amount of money that switched hands in these frenetic "hot money" markets exploded from $15 billion a day in 1973 to $1.3 trillion a day in 1993—a staggering sum equal to the value of an entire year's worth of global trade in goods and services (Baker, Epstein, and Pollin 1998). In the process, the interests of financial markets achieved considerable power over governments, as traders kept an eye out for local trends and policies the financial press deemed "unsound" or "inflationary," including wage growth and increases in social welfare spending. When conditions were not to their collective liking, they could sell off currencies with frightening speed. Such a "run" on the U.S. dollar in 1979 forced President Jimmy Carter to appoint Volcker as Federal Reserve chairman. Volcker's "monetarist" solution to inflation, inspired by Friedman, created the deepest recession since the 1930s, probably closing more U.S. factories in a few years than any single free-trade treaty, and dramatically undercutting the power of organized labor.

That recession also had enormous consequences for poverty the world over. The Fed's high interest rates precipitated the Latin American debt crisis and the inauguration of the structural adjustment programs (SAP) of the International Monetary Fund (IMF) and World Bank. Under these agreements, debtor nations across the world received rescheduled loans in exchange for giving up sovereignty to IMF or World Bank advisers and their neoliberal "bitter medicine." Countries undergoing structural adjustment would invariably cut wages, public payrolls, and social welfare, education, and health budgets. They would also focus on expanding exports; by the 1990s, the cumulative effect of SAPs across the world was to glut markets in raw commodities and some industrial goods, often undercutting the fragile national economies they were designed to save and increasing the debt burden on the developing world. Meanwhile, currency traders in the "hot" deregulated global money markets helped precipitate terrible financial crises in Mexico, Southeast Asia, Russia, Brazil, and Argentina during the late 1990s, wiping out in a few days many of the gains achieved by the expansion of manufacturing in those economies.

Events like these have bolstered arguments that globalization has rendered the nation-state obsolete. But it is clear that national governments have not retreated at all from the management of the world economy, as free-market doctrine itself would suggest. Instead, when neoliberal political leaders gained power, governments—and the U.S. federal government above all—played a giant role in *promoting* free-market global policies, most often in the interests of multinational corporations and financiers. Very often these policies required building broad electoral coalitions, and many of the world's most important political parties have made it an important part of their business to sell neoliberal orthodoxy. These developments are not confined to traditional parties of the right: The U.S. Democratic Party under Bill Clinton and the British Labour Party under Tony Blair both enthusiastically supported many neoliberal economic policies as part of their ostensibly centrist "third way" political efforts.

As neoliberal ideas increasingly dominated all sides of the official political debate in the United States since the mid-1970s, the U.S. federal government has made many contributions to free-market global restructuring—so many that the phrase "Washington consensus" was coined as a synonym for orthodox neoliberalism. The United States led the way in deregulating international financial markets in the 1970s and was among the first to abrogate so-called capital controls on foreign investment. The U.S. Treasury Department is a major force behind the policies of the IMF and the World Bank, and the United States is the single most important member of the WTO. Its support of lower trade barriers has been stalwart, from the General Agreement on Trades and Tariffs (GATT) to NAFTA to the FTAA to the new "Doha round" (named for the WTO's fourth ministerial conference, held in Doha, Qatar) of multilateral trade talks on investment, agricultural goods, and services. But more important than tariff reductions have been the skewed ways such trade treaties seek to govern world trade. Minimal protections for labor and the environment coexist with heavy emphasis on protecting corporations' intellectual property rights and—as in NAFTA's Chapter 11—an insistence on corporations' right to sue governments over social and environmental regulations deemed injurious to their investments. Meanwhile, the U.S. government has also been among the world's most avid proponents of "privatization," the selling of government assets to corporations, often at bargain prices. It has spent untold billions of taxpayer dollars on such "corporate welfare" expenditures as subsidies, tax breaks, military contracts, investment protection insurance, export promotion, and bailouts. And its hands-off approach to urban and industrial policy allowed corporations to play local and state governments against each other as they scrambled to attract investment through ever more lavish inducements, thus depleting already-strapped public coffers and further straining municipal welfare and education budgets.

But the U.S. government's neoliberal global policymaking has not been confined to trade agreements and corporate welfare. It has also been instrumental in undercutting labor regulations, civil rights protections, and welfare programs worldwide, with measures that have probably contributed the most to overall stagnation in wage rates in advanced economies and to the growth in economic inequality. Indeed, although globalization and deindustrialization have become catchall explanations for wage declines in the manufacturing sector, they do not explain similar stagnation in all sectors of the economy, including the knowledge-based and export-related sectors and the less globally transportable service sector—the very kinds of jobs neoliberals believed would provide prosperity for the great majority of Americans.

The rollback of workers' rights across all sectors of the U.S. economy was probably the most significant political victory of corporate neoliberalism and the most important contributor to wage stagnation. It was the result of intense electoral organizing by such business groups as the National Chamber of Commerce, the National Association of Manufacturers, and their various very active political action committees (PACs). Ronald Reagan's firing of striking air traffic controllers in 1981 set the tone for federal policy that was heavily sympathetic to employers in their battles with labor unions. Under Reagan, the National Labor Relations Board (NLRB) became a willing vehicle for decertifying unions, and so-called right-to-work laws that undercut labor organizing spread throughout the states. Employers meanwhile pressed forward with their project of creating an ever more "flexible" workforce, not only using the threat or the practice of moving abroad but also investing much more heavily in nonunion factories than in union ones, establishing parallel production plants in different locations so that production could be sustained during strikes, celebrating CEOs who specialized in "downsizing" firms, and hiring increased numbers of temporary workers. Between 1970 and 1994, union membership rates in the United States fell by half, from 27 percent of all workers to 14 percent. The downward pressure on wages caused by deunionization was compounded by successful corporate opposition to hikes in the minimum wage, which fell by a third of its real value during Reagan's presidency and in the early 1990s bottomed out at a hair above what it could buy in 1948 (Levy 1999).

Corporate neoliberals have also targeted civil rights law and affirmative action, a crusade that allows them to combine their distaste for government intervention in society with the politically popular argument that African Americans and other people of color have received too much help from the federal government. During the 1980s and 1990s, Presidents Reagan and George H. W. Bush weakened the scope of the Equal Employment Opportunity Commission (EEOC) by forcing plaintiffs in racial discrimination suits to prove biased intent on the part of employers. Such policies allowed racial discrimination in job markets to persist, sustaining the racial inequalities in the job market that overlap broader patterns of economic inequality. In addition, efforts were made to undercut the Community Reinvestment Act, the only federal effort to reverse a long history of racial discrimination by banks in housing credit.

The project to weaken the U.S. welfare state, finally, reflects one of the basic tenets of neoliberal philosophy. Volcker's high interest rates during the 1980s and early 1990s, along with Reagan's expensive corporate tax cut, his trillion-dollar military expansion, and the ballooning federal deficits that resulted, created a general sense that government was at the limit of its resources. This, in turn, provided an exploitable backdrop for attacks on welfare. In addition, the vocabulary of racial and gender conservatism—the basis for Reagan's "welfare queen" stereotype—was also indispensable in creating the impression that such relatively modest programs as Aid to Families with Dependent Children (AFDC) were a threat to national well-being. As the actual value of welfare payments declined—by 40 percent during the 1980s alone—antiwelfare rhetoric grew, and in 1996, under President Bill Clinton's policy to "end welfare as we know it," poor people's entitlement to federal assistance was repealed. The saga of welfare reform overshadowed a whole array of cuts to the broader fabric of the welfare state, including unemployment insurance, workers' compensation, public housing, and health care.

These same trends of decreasing worker protection, declines in civil rights, and declines in welfare states have parallels in societies around the world—whether under the auspices of the IMF in the developing world, in the face of financial crises such as those in Latin America in 1995, 1998, and 2001, in Southeast Asia in 1997, and in eastern Europe in 1998, or under the stewardship of American-inspired neoliberal or "third-way" governments in wealthier societies such as Britain, Canada, Italy, Spain, Australia, and New Zealand. Deliberate, globalized political efforts to suppress wages and welfare programs have caused the principal pipelines that distribute the world's economic resources throughout society to silt up considerably, and the enormous pools of wealth and privilege at the very top of society have grown.

The realization that this kind of global restructuring is not only the result of technological change and the "invisible hand" of the market but also the product of political choices has inspired a growing movement opposed to neoliberal globalization in recent years. Margaret Thatcher's claim that "there is no alternative" to today's forms of economic restructuring implies that anyone who opposes such changes is either parochial (antiglobalization, and hence against all international connections) or foolhardy, resisting what amounts to a force of nature. However, the tenuous alliances of resistance that have developed across countries, among labor unions, nongovernmental organizations, environmentalists, civil rights activists, the women's movement, and advocates of the poor, actually represent an alternative form of globalization. In protests against structural adjustment throughout the developing world during the 1980s and 1990s; in the "battle in Seattle" in 1999 against the WTO; in the "summit-hopping" demonstrations in Cancun, Genoa, New York, Prague, Quebec City, and Washington, D.C., and at the World Social Forum in Pôrto Alegre, Brazil, coalitions of labor, environmental, and human rights activists have advocated a more equitable, more sustainable, and more democratic global restructuring. Political struggles, which cross oceans and boundaries, have always crucially determined the nature of global economic restructuring, and struggles between neoliberals and their emboldened opposition will no doubt do much to shape the next stage in world history.

Carl H. Nightingale

See also: Capitalism; Industrialization; Liberalism; New Right; Trade/Industrial Unions; World Bank

References and Further Reading

Baker, Dean, Gerald Epstein, and Robert Pollin. 1998. *Globalization and Progressive Economic Policy*. Cambridge: Cambridge University Press, published in association with the Political Economy Research Institute and the University of Massachusetts.

Bluestone, Barry, and Bennett Harrison. 1982. *The Deindustrialization of the United States: Plant Closings, Community Abandonment, and the Dismantling of Basic Industry*. New York: Basic Books.

Cowie, Jefferson. 1999. *Capital Moves: RCA's 70-Year Quest for Cheap Labor*. Ithaca, NY: Cornell University Press.

Fukuyama, Francis. 1992. *The End of History and the Last Man*. New York: Free Press.

Levy, Frank. 1999. *The New Dollars and Dreams*. New York: Russell Sage Foundation.

Milkman, Ruth. 1997. *Farewell to the Factory: Auto Workers in the Late Twentieth Century*. Berkeley and Los Angeles: University of California Press.

Nightingale, Carl. 1998. "The Global Inner City: Towards an Historical Analysis." In *W. E. B. DuBois, Race, and the City*, ed. Michael B. Katz and Thomas J. Sugrue. Philadelphia: University of Pennsylvania Press.

Perry, David, and Beverly McLean. 1991. "The Aftermath of Deindustrialization: The Meaning of 'Economic Restructuring' in Buffalo, New York." *Buffalo Law Review* 39: 345–384.

Rodgers, Daniel T. Forthcoming. "The Revival of Market Ideology." In *Thinking through the Seventies*, ed. Casey Blake and Kenneth Cmiel. Chicago: University of Chicago Press.

Smith, Dan. 1999. *State of the World Atlas*. London: Penguin.

Stull, William J., and Janice Fanning Madden. 1990. *Post-Industrial Philadelphia: Structural Changes in the Metropolitan Economy*. Philadelphia: University of Pennsylvania Press.

Sugrue, Thomas J. 1996. *The Origins of the Urban Crisis: Race and Inequality in Postwar Detroit*. Princeton: Princeton University Press.

Tabb, William K. 2002. *Unequal Partners: A Primer on Globalization*. New York: New Press.

U.N. Development Program. 1999. *Human Development Report, 1999: Globalization with a Human Face*. New York: Oxford University Press.

Wachtel, Howard. 1990. *The Money Mandarins: The Making of a Supranational Economic Order*. 2d ed. Armonk, NY: Sharpe; London: Pluto Press.

Waldinger, Roger, and Mehdi Bozorgmehr. 1996. *Ethnic Los Angeles*. New York: Russell Sage Foundation.

"Gospel of Wealth," Andrew Carnegie

Described by historian Robert Bremner as "the most famous document in the history of American Philanthropy," Andrew Carnegie's article "Wealth" detailing his philosophy on philanthropy appeared in *North American Review* in 1889 (Bremner 1988, 100). Retitled by critics and more popularly known as "The Gospel of Wealth," this article contained musings and advice to peers on the "proper administration of wealth" (Carnegie 1889, 653).

During his lifetime (1835–1919), self-made industrialist Carnegie, like many of his Gilded Age contemporaries, accumulated many millions of dollars. In his later years, Carnegie contemplated how to dispose of his wealth before death. "Wealth" celebrated accumulated wealth, defending the growing distance between the rich and poor in American society and tying it to the benefits shared by all in a growing consumer society. A strong supporter of individualism, private property, laissez-faire economics, and American democracy, Carnegie did not seek to challenge the social order or government of his times; rather, he outlined the best way for the rich to support the maintenance of American society through the careful distribution of their wealth.

Carnegie believed there were three options for wealthy persons: Wealth could be passed on to family, handed out as bequests, or distributed through the active donation of money during one's lifetime. The first two options, he believed, would lead to great evils. Inheritance created a class of idle, spoiled children; bequests often led only to the establishment of memorials. The third, however, would allow for great men of business to apply their skills and knowledge to the disbursement of wealth for the betterment of society.

Carnegie encouraged the wealthy to live frugally, to provide only as necessary for their heirs, and to administer the remainder of their wealth as would the trustees of a charitable fund. Extolling the suitability of wealthy men for this job, Carnegie described "the man of wealth [as] thus becoming the mere agent and trustee for his poorer brethren, bringing to their service his superior wisdom, experience, and ability to administer, doing for them better than they would or could do for themselves" (Carnegie 1889, 662). Carnegie encouraged careful charitable choices, helping those who were worthy.

His emphasis was on "help[ing] those who will help themselves" (Carnegie 1889, 663). He advocated funding projects that facilitated self-improvement, including the creation of parks, the support of art, and the building of public institutions—especially, by his own example, libraries.

Although Carnegie's contemporaries did not follow his suggestions, living lavishly and passing on a great deal of wealth to their heirs, "Wealth" has become an anthem for the Gilded Age. For his part, Carnegie did follow his own instructions, establishing major philanthropic institutions, including the Carnegie Foundation for the Advancement of Teaching, the Carnegie Endowment for International Peace, and the Carnegie Corporation in the early 1900s and giving away some $350 million during his lifetime.

Laura Tuennerman-Kaplan

See also: Philanthropy; Social Darwinism; Wealth; Wealth, Distribution/Concentration

References and Further Reading

Bremner, Robert. 1988. *American Philanthropy*. 2d ed. Chicago: University of Chicago Press.

Carnegie, Andrew. 1889. "Wealth." *North American Review* 148 (June): 653–664.

The Grapes of Wrath, *John Steinbeck*

John Steinbeck's novel *The Grapes of Wrath*, published in 1939, chronicled the massive Dust Bowl migration to the West Coast during the Great Depression by telling the story of the Joads, an extended family of Oklahoma tenant farmers pushed off the land by a combination of drought and agricultural consolidation, who park all their belongings on a makeshift truck and head out to California in search of work and a new start. On one level, it is a powerful story of one family's personal struggle for survival amid devastating loss, hardship, and relentless disappointment as they meet with hostility and watch the promise of gainful employment disappear. On another, it tells the story of a generation forced to suffer the outcome of the horrific economic collapse that left one-fourth of America's labor force unemployed by 1933. In the novel, we see this generation questioning the justice of the capitalist system and the morality of the nation. Through characters like the ex-preacher Jim Casey and Rose of Sharon Joad, we see how the human spirit endures even in the face of hopelessness and the loss of faith in God and all that has held their lives together before.

Even as he personalized the migrant experience, Steinbeck used it to offer a structural critique and to warn of where mass desperation might lead. Those who, like the Joads, sought work in the promised land of California found themselves surrounded by thousands of others as desperate and hungry as they. These masses lived together in poverty and fear—and later in anger—in makeshift communities formed at the edges of cities and dubbed "Hoovervilles" in recognition of President Herbert Hoover's policies of neglect. The Joads make the abstraction of surplus labor come alive, as they join the abundant supply of people desperate to work and as they watch their wages continue to fall until a family could not earn enough to survive. They absorb mounting hatred and hostility, and they are sneeringly dubbed "Okies" by resentful and nervous Californians. And they witness the worst injustices of the capitalist system, which Steinbeck starkly portrays through the eyes of his characters: "A homeless, hungry man, driving the road with his wife beside him and his thin children in the back seat, could look at the fallow fields which might produce food but not profit, and that man would know how a fallow field is a sin and the unused land a crime against the thin children" (Steinbeck [1939] 2002, 319).

Such stark realism is tempered only by the glimpses of strength in the men and women who cling to one another and to hope in order

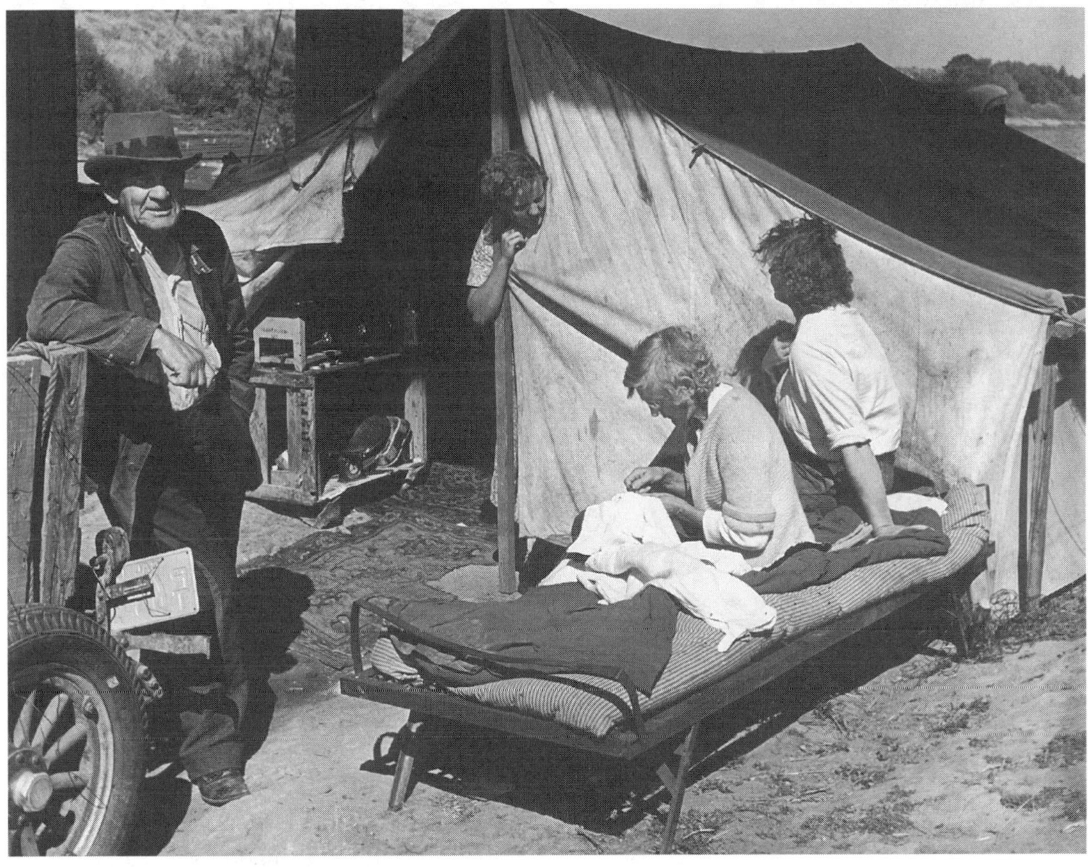

A family, one of many left homeless by the Great Depression, goes about their daily business outside the tent where they live. Photographer Horace Bristol was with John Steinbeck when he interviewed this family, among others, during research for his book The Grapes of Wrath. *(Horace Bristol/Corbis)*

to go on. Ma Joad and her daughter, Rose of Sharon, are two of the most memorable women characters in American literature. Ma Joad is willing to make any sacrifices to keep her family together, and Rose of Sharon's great act of generosity at the close of the novel indicates Steinbeck's continued belief that such people could never be defeated so long as they had their compassion and anger to keep them alive.

The heartbreaking truth of the novel, winner of the 1940 Pulitzer Prize and a major element in Steinbeck's receiving the 1962 Nobel Prize for Literature, shook the nation and led many to accuse Steinbeck of communist sympathies. Since publication, *The Grapes of Wrath* has sold over 14 million copies and has left an indelible, even if controversial, impression on the American consciousness.

Rebecca K. Root

See also: Agricultural and Farm Labor Organizing; Dust Bowl Migration; Economic Depression; Great Depression and New Deal; Poor Whites; Rural Poverty

References and Further Reading

Steinbeck, John. [1939] 2002. *The Grapes of Wrath*. New York: Penguin USA.

Wyatt, David, ed. 1990. *New Essays on* The Grapes of Wrath. New York: Cambridge University Press.

———. 1999. *Readings on* The Grapes of Wrath. San Diego, CA: Greenhaven.

Hagood, Margaret

See Mothers of the South

Harrington, Michael

See Catholic Worker Movement; *The Other America;* Socialist Party; War on Poverty

Harvest of Shame, *Edward R. Murrow*

Noted journalist Edward R. Murrow created *Harvest of Shame*, a documentary chronicling the plight of migrant farmworkers, for CBS television in 1960. Originally broadcast on Thanksgiving Day, the hour-long film succeeded in shocking middle-class Americans about the living and working conditions of those who actually produced the nation's food supply. The film follows families on their annual treks between Florida and New York and up the West Coast and presents interviews with migrant workers and representatives of advocacy groups, government agencies, and grower organizations. It also captures the hardships faced by migrant workers as they deal with miserable shelter, lack of schooling for their children, the disruptions of constant travel, and pitifully low wages. Using documentary techniques to underscore the shame of such conditions amid great bounty, the film advocates for better regulation of living and working conditions. *Harvest of Shame* is credited with using an appeal to common sense, decency, and the American conscience to create pressure for such reforms as the congressional repeal of the Bracero Program—the U.S.-Mexican agreement that brought Mexican workers to fill the demand for cheap labor on American farms—in 1964. Nevertheless, migrant labor conditions remain unevenly regulated at best. Considered pathbreaking as a documentary, *Harvest of Shame* was named number eleven in New York University's School of Journalism list of the 100 most influential pieces of journalism of the twentieth century.

Sarah Case

See also: Agricultural and Farm Labor Organizing; Bracero Program; Dust Bowl Migration; Migrant Labor/Farm Labor; Picturing Poverty (I); Picturing Poverty (II); Rural Poverty

References and Further Reading

Garcia, Matt. 2002. *A World of Its Own: Race, Labor, and Citrus in the Making of Greater Los Angeles, 1900–1970*. Chapel Hill: University of North Carolina Press.

Hahamovitch, Cindy. 1997. *The Fruits of Their Labor: Atlantic Coast Farmworkers and the Making of Migrant Poverty, 1870–1945*. Chapel Hill: University of North Carolina Press.

Head Start

See Child-Saving; Maternalism; Maternalist Policy; War on Poverty

Health Policy

Poverty is a powerful predictor of poor health, early mortality, and disability. In the United States, the poor are disproportionately women and children and from communities of color. Researchers have documented the relationship between poverty and many health problems, including infant mortality, cardiovascular and heart disease, cancer, diabetes, arthritis, and AIDS. In 1990, the probability of Black inner-city male adolescents surviving to age forty-five was lower than the probability that white adolescents nationwide would survive to age sixty-five (Geronimus 2000, 1). In 1990, the infant mortality rates for African Americans (17.9 per 1,000), Native Americans (10.7 per 1,000), and Puerto Ricans (10.2 per 1,000) far exceeded those for whites (7.4 per 1,000) (Wingard 1997, 41). Although researchers disagree about why poverty and poor health are correlated, the correlation is probably a combined result of material hardship, inequality, and inadequate health care. Public policies affecting health care access and delivery can attenuate the relationship between poverty and poor health.

Health policy includes government measures affecting individual and public health as well as the organization, financing, and regulation of health care services. The United States, the only major Western industrialized country without national health insurance, has a mixed private-public health system dominated by private services and financing. Government programs to increase access to health care developed primarily in the twentieth century. In a system governed by the principle that health care is a commodity rather than a citizenship right, economically disadvantaged groups face limited access to preventive health care and medical services *and* to resources that promote health (such as good jobs, safe housing, and healthful nutrition). In the late twentieth century, health care was the largest U.S. industry, accounting for one-seventh of the gross domestic product. This industry included about 6,000 hospitals, 1,200 insurance companies, and over 600,000 physicians (Byrd and Clayton 2000,16). These powerful interests wield vast power to shape health policy, although activists from labor, civil rights, women's, welfare rights, homeless, disability rights, and AIDS movements have effected major health care reforms benefiting the poor.

Explicit federal health policy was limited before the Civil War, but de facto policies resulted from the economic, social, and military activities of all levels of government. Beginning at the time of early European settlement, the health of indigenous peoples, slaves, women, children, workers, and racial-ethnic and sexual minorities was sharply affected by economic exploitation, political disenfranchisement, and relative exclusion from the mainstream health system. Most people, except the wealthy, relied on families, healers, and midwives for health care before the nineteenth century. Until the late nineteenth century, hospitals served more as social welfare institutions than as medical ones, and they were widely regarded as places of last resort. The first public hospital was established in 1798, when the Merchant Marine Health Services Act mandated care for sick and disabled seamen.

An era of intensified government participation in health policy began in the mid-nineteenth century. State governments established requirements for medical licenses and for licensing medical schools; the federal government regulated patent medicines. The medical infrastructure grew during the Civil War to handle civilian and military casualties. After the war, health care devolved back to states and localities, with two exceptions: the network of Freedmen's Bureau clinics and hospitals that provided care to ex-slaves until they were closed in 1872 and a medical division in the Bureau of Indian Affairs (BIA) that, for eighteen years, provided minimal health care for Native Americans. Previous Native American experiences with nonindigenous health care had been through missionaries and the army.

As the health care system expanded in both size and complexity, physicians were firmly at the helm. Following the founding of the American Medical Association (AMA) in 1847, the medical profession was transformed to the high-status, powerful, affluent group it is today (Starr 1982). Modern private facilities and medical advances transformed public attitudes about hospitals, ushering in an era in which hospitals became more numerous and powerful. The Flexner Report (1910) led to an upgrading of medical education by reducing the number of medical schools and graduates, both outcomes endorsed by the AMA. Health care was largely a fee-for-service enterprise, and many low-income people had limited access to medicine's improved services except through public health facilities. Health care was highly segregated by race. In 1910, African American physicians represented 2 percent of the profession (Byrd and Clayton 2000, 384), but Black health professionals and patients, like other people of color, faced segregation and discrimination in the health care system.

The federal government's more active involvement in health policy was in part a response to the mobilization of social reformers, especially progressive women. They organized for improvements in public health, regulation of factory and other working conditions, improved sanitation in urban slums, and protections for consumers. In 1899, congressional legislation led to the hiring of physicians and personnel for the growing public health system. In 1912, the U.S. Public Health Service was formed, replacing the Marine Hospital Service. New scientific knowledge about the sources of infectious disease led to a new emphasis in public health on personal hygiene and medicine rather than social and environmental reform. Congress passed exclusionary immigration laws with "medical excludability" provisions. Although the development of public health services increased access to medical care for low-income people, support for public health was generated by fears of contagious disease, anti-immigrant sentiment, and racism.

Early-twentieth-century labor and other progressive activists constituted a powerful political force that organized to change the appalling working and living conditions of the poor. Organized labor won important victories, but few men of color or women benefited because unions neglected them and the jobs they held. Maternalist activists secured an important victory in the aftermath of women winning the vote when Congress passed the Maternity and Infancy Act of 1921 (the Sheppard-Towner Act). This bill established a grant-in-aid program to subsidize health services for mothers and their children. The program was terminated less than a decade later, mainly due to AMA opposition. Activists such as Margaret Sanger fought for legalization of family-planning services, especially for poor women, a campaign that would take decades to be successful.

In 1921, Congress passed the Snyder Act reauthorizing the BIA to provide medical services. The BIA retained this role until 1954, when the Indian Health Service (IHS) was created as a division of the Public Health Service. Many Native organizations criticized BIA health services for their inadequacy, insensitivity, and eugenic policies.

The role of the federal government in funding and providing medical care developed further in the context of World War I, when Congress provided compensation to disabled military veterans. In 1921, the U.S. Veterans Bureau was created, an agency that today, as the Veterans Administration (VA), operates a vast network of hospitals, clinics, long-term care facilities, and special programs to serve eligible veterans.

The AMA became a staunch opponent of government involvement in medical provision and joined the American Hospital Association (AHA) in the 1920s to oppose such measures as national health insurance. Fearing that inclusion of national health insurance would mean defeat of the Social Security Act of 1935, President Franklin D. Roosevelt declined to include it in the legislation. The Social Security Act had two health-related titles: Title V established grants to states for maternal and child health care, and Title VI allocated funds to state and local public health programs. The federal government supported the growth of the health care infrastructure with resources for public hospitals and clinics and for the training of health care personnel and with growing support for biomedical research. The National Institutes of Health was created in 1930.

Private, voluntary health insurance developed as an alternative to national health insurance. During the Depression, the "Blues" were established when revenues for health were scarce. Hospitals slowly began to offer prepayment plans (Blue Cross) beginning in 1929. State medical societies followed suit with insurance plans (Blue Shield) to pay for physician services in the late 1930s. Most poor families could not afford these plans and were reliant on Depression-era relief programs that began to provide more assistance for medical care.

Health insurance became more widely available after World War II when unions used collective bargaining to win employer-provided health insurance as a benefit for members and their dependents. By late 1954, 12 million workers and 17 million family members had health insurance as a result of collective bargaining (Starr 1982, 313). However, before the victories of the civil rights and women's movements, women of all races and men of color generally had limited access to jobs that offered health insurance benefits. Tying health insurance to employment also disadvantaged the elderly who were not employed.

In 1960, many poor people lacked access to primary and preventive health care services, especially the poor of color, the rural poor, and poor women, children, and elderly persons. Low-cost services were available mainly from public hospitals, located primarily in cities; from local health departments; from some private practitioners, especially rural or minority practitioners, who provided free or low-cost care to the indigent; and from federal programs, such as the Indian Health Service, that served specific populations. Because the IHS served only those enrolled in federally recognized tribes, many Native Americans were ineligible for these services. In 1960, Congress passed the Kerr-Mills Act, a voluntary program of medical assistance for the medically indigent elderly. Only about half the states participated in the program.

Certain veterans also received medical services. Veterans with extensive service-related disabilities are automatically eligible for VA health services. Other veterans can receive VA services if they are enrolled with the VA. Eligibility for enrollment is based on criteria determined by Congress (extent of disability, recipient of a Purple Heart, former prisoner of war, medical indigence, and the like) and the level of service allowed by congressional appropriations. Some veterans, especially veterans of the wars in Vietnam and the Persian Gulf, struggled for coverage for medical conditions that the VA has refused to recognize as service-related, especially those related to exposure to toxic substances. Spouses and dependents of former military personnel who died or who became 100 percent disabled due to service-related injuries have, since the early 1970s, received reimbursement for many medical expenses through health coverage provided by the VA.

In the 1960s, a new generation of health activists from the civil rights, women's, and antipoverty movements demanded more from the government. Their activism paid off with President Lyndon B. Johnson's declaration of a War on Poverty, inaugurating the Great Society programs that greatly expanded access to health care. Most significant were two Great Society programs passed in 1965: Medicare and Medicaid.

Medicare is a social insurance program for those sixty-five or older who are eligible for Social Security or Railroad Retirement benefits or who are permanently disabled. Eligibility is based on having forty required quarters of covered employment, a prerequisite that was phased in yearly increments beginning in 1965. Coverage is also extended to those who have been totally disabled for a period of two years and who have become eligible for Social Security Disability Insurance. Medicare is financed by payroll taxes paid by both employers and employees.

Medicare has uniform national standards for eligibility and benefits and is financed and administered by the federal government. The program has two parts: Part A reimburses hospital costs and selected other costs and is financed through payroll taxes. Part B reimburses fees paid to physicians and is financed by premiums and general tax revenues. Medicare pays for hospital bills, physician services, outpatient hospital care, and some home and ambulatory care and skilled nursing facility costs. It does not pay for prescription drugs, long-term care, or vision or dental services. Beneficiaries pay a deductible for services and coinsurance for physician services. Medicare is not a means-tested program. Program goals include increasing the access of the elderly to medical care and protecting the elderly from extensive medical debt. It has been very successful in achieving these ends. A 1963 study showed that half the elderly had no health insurance (Rowland 1993, 15). Almost all the elderly now have Medicare coverage, and Medicaid supplements the program for those elderly whose incomes are below the poverty line. However, those elderly who have not worked enough paid quarters in the Social Security system or who have not been married to such workers remain ineligible for Medicare. This group is disproportionately made up of women and people of color who have either not been employed in covered occupations, not worked enough quarters, or lost eligibility because of divorce or who are married to someone over sixty-five but are not yet themselves age sixty-five. If they are not eligible for Medicaid, they will fall through the cracks of the unraveling medical safety net.

Medicaid is a means-tested program financed by both federal and state governments on a matching basis. Medicaid is administered by the states, which set eligibility and coverage criteria. Because states determine eligibility and other rules and benefits, there is wide variation in benefits and rules across states. Medicaid is the major source of public assistance for health care services for low-income families and for long-term care services for the elderly and the disabled. It was intended to create expanded health care access for recipients of Aid to Families with Dependent Children (AFDC) and other persons who met eligibility criteria. However, many physicians do not participate in the program because reimbursement rates are often low, lower than for Medicare. This creates hardships for recipients, particularly in rural areas where there are few physicians. But the program has greatly increased access to health care for the poor. In 1964, the poor averaged 3.8 physician visits per year, compared to 4.7 for other families; similarly, the poor averaged 179 hospitalizations per 1,000, compared to the nonpoor who averaged 202 hospitalizations (Rowland 1993, 110). By 1978, the differences between the poor and nonpoor in utilization of health services had narrowed considerably (Rowland 1993, 110). Despite its success, the program is far less popular with the public and politicians than is Medicare.

Congress passed at least seventy-five other health-related bills during the 1960s and 1970s, many designed to improve both access to and the quality of health care for the poor and for the nation as a whole. Some legislation targeted the health needs of "medically underserved" groups (for example, migrant workers, schoolchildren, the mentally ill, and the rural poor). Others sought to improve health through federal regulation of the environment, pollution, drinking water, tobacco products, and occupational health and safety. One of the earliest and most successful federal health initiatives of this period was the national immunization system, created in the early 1960s, that has dramatically decreased vulnerability of children and adults to nine vaccine-preventable diseases. Yet a persistent gap in immunization levels exists: Children and adults who live in areas of concentrated poverty or who are homeless, immigrants, or families of migrant workers are significantly less likely to be fully immunized.

Congressional support for family planning in 1970 and legalization of abortion in 1973 followed feminist activism for reproductive choice, and both have led to improved maternal health outcomes. Funds for health manpower training and affirmative action policies helped diversify the health professions by race, ethnicity, and gender. Never before or since has health policy done so much to expand access to health care and address social and environmental health risks.

Credit for this era of health reform belongs to activists from the civil rights, welfare rights, women's, consumer health, and environmental movements and the responsiveness of the Democratic Party. Health activism went beyond access issues to advocate and model change in health service delivery. Grassroots health programs—free clinics, community clinics, and women's clinics—were founded by and secured some of their revenues from federal social programs. Health care advocacy also led to changes in or the defense of hard-won policies. Feminists defended women's right to abortion. Communities of color and some women's health advocates sought protection of poor women of color from sterilization abuse and from medical experimentation without informed consent. Groups demanded and won community-controlled health clinics in poor communities. Feminists made visible the issue of violence against women and secured changes in the legal and health care systems for survivors of rape, domestic violence, and sexual assault. An important policy setback in 1976 was passage of the Hyde Amendment, prohibiting the use of federal Medicaid funds for abortion. Although some states use the state portion of Medicaid to pay for abortion, poor women's reproductive rights were severely curtailed by this and other legislation sought by the powerful antichoice movement.

In the 1980s, rising health costs and the fiscal and social conservatism of the administrations of Presidents Ronald Reagan and George H. W. Bush brought a halt to the era of progressive health policy. Since 1980, health policy has been preoccupied with containing costs and with reducing the federal commitment to social programs. Public-sector health programs have had their budgets slashed. State revenues for health care diminished as the combined effects of conservative-driven "taxpayer revolts," devolution policies, and escalating costs for Medicaid and Medicare strained state budgets. Policies of the 1980s and 1990s have led to "corporatization" of medicine and health policy (Starr 1982; Navarro 1994). The Reagan administration's 1981 and 1982 budgets reduced expenditures for social programs (including Medicaid and Medicare) dramatically; these expenditures fell from 11.2 percent to 10.4 percent of the gross national product (GNP) between 1981 and 1985. Total grants to state and local governments (which included funding for health care) declined from 1.6 to 1.2 percent of the GNP (Navarro 1994, 29). These reductions were part of a larger trend in policy that shifted federal expenditure away from social programs to increased military spending and led to an unprecedented redistribution of wealth upward, economic polarization, and reduced economic security for low- and moderate-income people.

Despite these cutbacks, expenditures for health care, including Medicaid and Medicare, have soared since the 1980s. Intensified competition, "managed care," and reductions and changes in federal financing of Medicaid and Medicare emerged as the policy solutions to a health care "crisis" that was defined in terms of runaway costs and excessive government involvement. In addition to outright cuts in Medicaid and Medicare, other policy changes included switching from an actual cost-based reimbursement policy to a prospective payment system (PPS), which specifies predetermined rates for diagnosis categories for Medicare hospital reimbursements. Many categorical health and social programs were consolidated into state block grants, with a 25 percent reduction in funds. Medicare deductibles were increased, and a host of administrative and financing rule changes in both Medicare and Medicaid strained the ability of health care providers, states, and localities to sustain the health care safety net for the growing populations of the poor, the uninsured, and the elderly.

Nevertheless, the costs of both private and public insurance programs continued to skyrocket. The reasons are complex. Growing rates of poverty and unemployment, a reduction in the number of families covered by private health insurance, the overall aging of the population, and general population growth have multiplied the numbers who are eligible for publicly subsidized coverage. Expensive medical technologies, medical litigation, the consequences of heightened health care competition, and costly diseases, such as AIDS, were among the additional factors. Health insurance companies offset rising costs with higher health care premiums. Some employers shifted to lower-cost (and lower-benefit) health plans, stopped offering insurance, and hired more part-time or contingent workers, who rarely receive health benefits. Between 1980 and 1992, there was a 22 percent increase in the number of uninsured and a 42 percent increase in the amount Americans paid for out-of-pocket medical costs (Navarro 1994, 198). Low-income families were the hardest hit by these changes, but higher health premiums and loss of coverage have affected many other families.

In the mid-1980s, "managed care" began to replace fee-for-service health delivery, a trend encouraged by government policies. Managed care encompasses preferred provider organizations (PPOs), health maintenance organizations (HMOs), and other arrangements. PPOs accept discounted payment from insurers in return for guaranteed revenues, and consumers retain some choice in providers. HMOs require members to receive care from a select group of providers and hospitals in their network. Managed care has transformed many health providers into employees or contractors, constraining professional autonomy and imposing caps on their earnings. By 1998, 85 percent of employees with employer-provided health coverage and more than half of Medicaid beneficiaries were enrolled in managed care plans (Lewin and Altman 2000, 16, 29).

Health care advocacy took on new urgency as health care inequities intensified and access shrank for many. A 1985 report by the federal Task Force on Black and Minority Health exposed glaring health inequities between people of color and whites. The Pepper Commission Report (1988) documented the problem of long-term care for the elderly and disabled. A 1990 General Accounting Office report revealed systematic gender inequities in medical research and health care. AIDS activists were vocal about the inadequacy of health services and health coverage for people with AIDS, disproportionately the poor and members of racial or ethnic minorities. In public opinion polls and in commissioned studies, many health providers and consumers expressed dissatisfaction with managed care.

Upon election to the presidency in 1992, Democrat Bill Clinton promised that health care reform would be a top priority. Advocates for national health insurance and a single-payer health plan hoped the time had come for universal health coverage. But the powerful health insurance, business, AMA, and AHA lobbies opposed both of these ideas, advocating instead managed care solutions. After heated debate, Congress failed to pass health care reform. There were limited policy reforms. The 1993 Family and Medical Leave Act provides job protection for unpaid leave to care for family members, and the 1996 Health Insurance Portability and Accountability Act helps employees keep group health insurance coverage when they change jobs, become self-employed, or are temporarily unemployed. Neither of these bills was much help for the poor, who can rarely afford to take unpaid leave and who seldom have employer-provided insurance.

Congressional passage of the Personal Responsibility and Work Opportunity Reconciliation Act in 1996 profoundly affected both health care access and health in poor families. Legal immigrants to the United States after 1996 are now ineligible for most forms of public assistance except for emergency medical services. Medicaid, formerly available to welfare recipients, was decoupled from the new Temporary Assistance for Needy Families (TANF) program, a change supposed to promote coverage for poor families with employed breadwinners. However, the proportion of low-income families insured by Medicaid fell almost 25 percent between 1995 and 2000 (Broaddus et al. 2002). Slight increases in the household incomes of many working families left them ineligible for Medicaid even when they had no employer-provided health coverage. In addition, new federal waivers to the Medicaid program (1115 and 1915b) contributed to falling Medicaid enrollment, since states were permitted to put aside certain Medicaid requirements if doing so generated cost savings and were budget neutral or made it easier to implement mandatory managed care for certain categories of individuals. Because states set their own standards for Medicaid eligibility, coverage can vary significantly from state to state. In addition, whether or not states reach out aggressively to eligible populations and whether or not they inform eligible former welfare recipients that they may continue to receive Medicaid both affect the degree to which poor people receive medical benefits in each state. As a result, the number of poor covered by Medicaid in the mid-1990s ranged widely, from a high of 60 percent in Washington, D.C., to a low of 29 percent in Nevada.

Welfare-to-work policies have created hardships for welfare-eligible families in which a breadwinner or child suffers from a disability. A recent study found that of the single-mother population receiving TANF in 1997, 46 percent included either a mother or child with a disability (Lee, Sills, and Oh 2002, 5). In addition to the problems these families face from restrictive welfare-to-work policies, many also lost Supplemental Security Income (SSI) when stricter definitions of disability were introduced. The income from SSI had been part of the safety net for the poor since the mid-1970s, but the new regulations cut millions of disabled children, adults with substance abuse problems, and legal immigrants from the program. This combination of policies has left many families without the resources they need to care for children with disabilities and has forced many disabled adults to try to find and keep jobs despite their disabilities.

In 1997, Congress passed the State Child Health Insurance Plan (SCHIP), a program that increases health coverage for low-income children in households with incomes just above the poverty line. Since the inception of the program, the percentage of poor children with health coverage has risen modestly. On the other hand, poor adults are now less likely to receive health coverage, a problem that has only worsened with the economic woes of 2001–2002. In 2000, only 20 percent of low-income families received Medicaid (Broaddus et al. 2002). Since the mid-1990s, the growing number of uninsured and underinsured Americans must rely on a weaker health safety net. A recent study issued by the Institute of Medicine concludes that the nation's health safety net has been deeply compromised by growth in the numbers of uninsured individuals, the impact of mandated Medicaid managed care, and the decline in federal and other funds available to support public health and subsidized health programs (Lewin and Altman 2000, 8).

Sandra Morgen

See also: Birth Control; Disability Policy; Epidemic Disease; Maternalist Policy; Mental Health Policy; Reproductive Rights; Social Security; Supplemental Security Income; Welfare Capitalism; Welfare Policy/Welfare Reform

References and Further Reading

Broaddus, Matthew, Shannon Blaney, Annie Dude, Jocelyn Guyer, Leighton Ku, and Jaia Peterson. 2002. "Expanding Family Coverage: States' Medicaid Eligibility Policies for Working Families in the Year 2000." Washington, DC: Center on Budget and Policy Priorities.

Byrd, W. Michael, and Linda Clayton. 2000. *An American Health Care Dilemma: A Medical History of African Americans and the Problem of Race*. New York: Routledge.

———. 2002. *An American Health Care Dilemma: Race, Medicine, and Health Care in the United States, 1900–2000*. New York: Routledge.

Dixon, Mim, and Yvette Roubideaux. 2001. *Promises to Keep: Public Health Policy for American Indians and Alaska Natives in the 21st Century*. Washington, DC: American Public Health Association.

Geronimus, Arline T. 2000. "To Mitigate, Resist, or Undo: Addressing Structural Influences on the Health of Urban Populations." *American Journal of Public Health* 90, no. 6: 867–873.

Lee, Sunhwa, Melissa Sills, and Gi-Taik Oh. 2002. "Disabilities among Children and Mothers in Low-Income Families." Washington, DC: Institute for Women's Policy Research.

Lewin, Marion Ein, and Stuart Altman, eds. 2000. *America's Health Care Safety Net: Intact but Endangered*. Washington, DC: National Academy Press.

Navarro, Vincente. 1994. *The Politics of Health Policy: The US Reforms, 1980–1994*. Cambridge, MA: Blackwell.

Romero, Diane, Wendy Chavkin, Paul Wise, Lauren Smith, and Pamela Wood. 2002. "Welfare to Work? Impact of Maternal Health on Employment." *American Journal of Public Health* 92, no. 9: 1462–1468.

Rowland, Diane. 1993. "Health Care of the Poor: The Contribution of Social Insurance." In *Medical Care and the Health of the Poor*, ed. David Rogers and Eli Ginzberg, 107–121. Boulder, CO: Westview Press.

Starr, Paul. 1982. *The Social Transformation of American Medicine*. New York: Basic Books.

Wingard, Deborah. 1997. "Patterns and Puzzles: The Distribution of Health and Illness among Women in the United States." In *Women's Health: Complexities and Differences*, ed. Sheryl Ruzek, Virginia Olesen, and Adele Clark, 29–45. Columbus, OH: Ohio University Press.

Heteronormativity

Heteronormativity refers to the ideological system that confers legitimacy exclusively upon kinship networks that conform to the marital heterosexual nuclear family model.

In contemporary American public policy, the citizen is often treated by the government as a lone individual. The right to vote, for example, is conferred upon the individual adult, while professional licenses are granted to individuals who possess the appropriate credentials. But in welfare policy, the government usually considers the recipient as a member of a "household" or a "caregiver/dependent" relationship. Under Temporary Assistance for Needy Families (TANF) law, the adult applicant must show not only that she or he is needy but that she or he is the custodial parent of a dependent child and that the sum total of the household's income and assets do not exceed subsistence levels. Welfare policy, however, does not just situate the needy individual in a household; it also attempts to transform that household into the ideal marital heterosexual family. Single mothers in the TANF program cannot receive benefits unless they assist the government in identifying the biological fathers of their dependent children and in obtaining support payments from them. The men in question often lack the economic resources needed to lift their children's households above the poverty line. The women themselves do not have any choice in the matter, and the government's demand for their cooperation can be especially problematic when the TANF recipient is fleeing domestic abuse. Welfare policy experts from across the political spectrum nevertheless champion the child support system on ideological grounds, since it makes the single mother's kinship network conform more closely to the traditional heterosexual model.

In 2002, in an even more blatant example of heteronormativity, President George W. Bush's administration proposed a new initiative in the TANF program, namely, the promotion of marriage as a solution to poverty. Indeed, several states were already using TANF funds and state welfare monies to award cash bonuses to welfare recipients when they get married, to support marriage preparation classes for the poor, and to provide resources to religious leaders coordinating statewide promotion of marriage campaigns. Again, the economic rationale fails to account for this policy development. Many married heterosexual couples fall below the poverty line, while many single-father-headed households are relatively well-off. Furthermore, the academic literature suggests that a child's well-being does not depend on the marital status or sexual orientation of his or her parent. In the end, the support for the marriage promotion welfare initiative is grounded in the ideological belief that children should be born and reared only in the context of a family headed by a heterosexual married couple.

The term "heteronormativity" was coined by "queer theorist" Michael Warner. Drawing inspiration from radical lesbian, gay, bisexual, and transgender activism, Warner argued that genuine social change requires much more than the mere tolerance of sexual minorities and the passage of antidiscrimination legislation. It necessitates, more fundamentally, a radical transformation of the dominant culture that celebrates reproductive marital heterosexual relationships. For Warner, heterosexuality—like all sexualities—is socially constructed, but where heteronormativity is hegemonic, heterosexual culture misrecognizes marital heterosexuality not only as "natural" but as essential to the perpetuation of any possible social order. The queer critique of heteronormativity, then, is profoundly anti-assimilatory. In its view, lesbians and gays should not seek to become "just like" heterosexuals, since heterosexual culture is deeply problematic. Queer critique goes beyond the struggle for equality for lesbians and gays by challenging the infinite number of ways in which biological reproduction, the family, gender roles, child rearing, social relationships, and public policies are conceptualized as if there were no alternative to the marital heterosexual nuclear family (Warner 1993).

Heteronormative critique takes in a much broader range of subjects than the analysis of sexism and homophobia. The latter terms refer exclusively to the discriminatory treatment of discrete classes of individuals: women and lesbians and gays. The concept of heteronormativity refers to the entire social, cultural, and political system that privileges marital heterosexuality above all other forms of intimate relationships. The term "heteronormativity" can be used, for example, to address the sociocultural and political tactics used to discipline heterosexuals themselves: It can identify the symbolic and material rewards that are given to heterosexual men and women who marry and restrict their sexual expression and reproduction to the marital context. The ambitious scope of the term is reminiscent of Monique Wittig's notion of the "straight mind" (Wittig 1992) and Adrienne Rich's "compulsory heterosexuality" (Rich 1993). Social policy literature tends to focus exclusively on political and legal analyses. Heteronormativity theory usefully directs our attention to the fact that social change must entail broad-ranging and deep-seated cultural transformation.

There are, nevertheless, several limitations to this critical discourse. First, heteronormativity theory, as it was originally developed in the lesbian, gay, and bisexual studies literature, constructs society according to one all-encompassing division: heterosexuals versus homosexuals. It assumes that heterosexuals are a basically homogeneous group that enjoys substantial material and status advantages over homosexuals. In its original form, then, the theory was not well positioned to understand the ways in which single mothers on welfare have been demonized not in spite of their heterosexuality but precisely because of their reproductive heterosexuality. Although heteronormative critique implicitly sheds light on the celebration of marital heterosexuality over all other kinship networks, including single parenting, the extension of the theory to the discriminatory treatment of nonconforming heterosexuals was stalled at first by many queer theorists' insistence on the overwhelming power of heterosexual privilege (Cohen 1997). Queer theorists appear to have learned from their critics on this point, and they are now taking into account the exclusion of nonconforming heterosexuals—namely, the nonmarried—from heterosexual privilege (Warner 1999).

On a more abstract level, heteronormativity theory suggests that the sphere of dominant ideas about the primacy of marital heterosexuality and the sphere of values—"normativity"—are one and the same. This construction situates all deviants and rebels "outside of society," as it were. Since all rebellion takes place outside *the* corrupt value system, all rebellious acts are equally valid. A more complex approach to ideology and power, such as Gramscian hegemony theory, is a useful antidote here insofar as it directs our attention to the fact that every subject—even the most excluded—is always working within some sort of value system and is always negotiating within various networks of power.

Finally, heteronormativity theory conflates the concepts of legitimization and normalization. Michel Foucault uses the latter term to refer specifically to the way modern institutions, such as schools, the medical profession, government agencies, and so on, use statistical methods to measure trends in the population and to compare each individual to the population average, or "norm." Because the application of demography and causal social theory models—such as the widely rejected notion that marriage causes an increase in household income, so that we ought to promote marriage to solve poverty—remain quite influential in welfare policy debates, it is important that we retain this Foucauldian insight.

Anna Marie Smith

See also: Gender Discrimination in the Labor Market; Homophobia; Sexism; Welfare Policy/Welfare Reform

References and Further Reading

Cohen, Cathy. 1997. "Punks, Bull Daggers, and Welfare Queens: The Real Radical Potential of 'Queer' Politics." *glq*, no. 3: 437–485.

Mason, Mary Ann, Arlene Skolnick, and Stephen Sugarman, eds. 2002. *All Our Families: New Policies for a New Century*. New York: Oxford University Press.

Rich, Adrienne. 1993. "Compulsory Heterosexuality and Lesbian Existence." In *The Lesbian and Gay Studies Reader*, ed. Henry Abelove, Michèle Aina Barale, and David Halperin, 227–254. New York: Routledge.

Stacey, Judith. 1997. *In the Name of the Family: Rethinking Family Values in the Postmodern Age*. Boston: Beacon Press.

———. 1998. *Brave New Families: Stories of Domestic Upheaval in Late-Twentieth-Century America*. Berkeley and Los Angeles: University of California Press.

Warner, Michael. 1993. "Introduction." In *Fear of a Queer Planet: Queer Politics and Social Theory*, ed. Michael Warner, vii–xxxi. Minneapolis: University of Minnesota Press.

———. 1999. *The Trouble with Normal: Sex, Politics, and the Ethics of Queer Life*. New York: Free Press.

Wittig, Monique. 1992. *The Straight Mind*. Boston: Beacon Press.

Highlander

Established in eastern Tennessee in 1932, Highlander has been the site and source of adult education programs that have trained thousands of rural and industrial grassroots leaders seeking to create a new social, economic, and political order that simultaneously enriches the indigenous culture of Appalachia and the South. Through residential workshops, extension projects, and community-based initiatives, the Highlander staff has acted on the belief that poor and working-class adults can draw upon their collective experiences to define their concerns and determine for themselves the most effective course of action to address them. Using this approach, the school helped unionize southern workers during the 1930s and 1940s. It anticipated and reacted to the dynamics of the civil rights movement during the 1950s and 1960s. It cultivated an Appalachian citizens' network connected to similar groups in the Deep South and other parts of the world in the 1970s and 1980s. Its most recent programs have grappled with intersecting economic and environmental crises while promoting points of unity among culturally diverse groups. Highlander's sustained record of activism testifies to its ability to employ its core pedagogy to help others resist exploitation and to empower communities so that they might achieve economic justice.

During its first thirty years, what was originally known as the Highlander Folk School, located near Monteagle, Tennessee, worked through the organized labor and civil rights movements to address the systemic roots of poverty and inequality in the South. The school allied itself with the burgeoning labor movement, aiding striking coal miners, woodcutters, textile mill hands, and government relief workers. In the late 1930s, Highlander joined the southern organizing drive of what would become the Congress of Industrial Organizations (CIO). It also directed large-scale labor education programs in eleven southern states and developed a residential program that sought to support a broad-based, racially integrated, and politically active southern labor movement. Frustrated by the declining militancy of the CIO after World War II and by the labor movement's inability to forge a sustained farmer-labor coalition, staff members broadened their focus by launching a series of interracial workshops on desegregation almost a year before the U.S. Supreme Court's historic ruling in *Brown v. Board of Education of Topeka, Kansas* (347 U.S. 483 [1954]). The school thereafter became an important educational center of the civil rights movement, and its Citizenship School program, initiated on the South Carolina Sea Islands, helped thousands of Black southerners gain not only the literacy skills needed to register to vote but also the capacity to mobilize new voters in support of political and economic reform. These programs made Highlander the target of a barrage of attacks by antiunionists and segregationists that eventually resulted in the revocation of the folk school's charter by the state of Tennessee in 1961.

Despite the demise of the folk school, Highlander was able to secure a charter for the Highlander Research and Education Center in 1961 and had already begun operations in Knoxville, Tennessee, advocating the development of a multiracial poor people's coalition and giving greater attention to the complex troubles facing the poor and powerless in Appalachia. Moving the center to its present location near New Market, Tennessee, in 1972, the staff pursued the goal of democratizing economic and political power in Appalachia, though without the frames of reference that had been offered by the more defined labor and civil rights movements. Increasingly, the center's workshops, participatory research projects, and long-term leadership development efforts led to the realization that such issues as land ownership, taxes, toxic substances, health care, and economic dislocation crossed regional as well as national lines. In response, Highlander sought to establish links to local struggles around the world. Though timely, informative, and often effective, such work confronted new dilemmas as grassroots organizations received diminishing support, dissent became more diffused, and the economies of both Appalachia and the South declined.

Highlander has persisted nonetheless, building its current programs upon its seventy-year history and more consciously providing a space for extending connections across race and nation, class and gender, languages, and sexual orientations. Its staff continues to work with groups from African American, Latino, and white communities experiencing economic displacement, demonstrating how the knowledge and skills gained during workshop experiences can be translated into action back home. By not attaching itself to a single issue, organization, or movement and by recognizing and learning from the shortcomings of earlier reform efforts that left the basic problems facing the poor largely untouched, Highlander has been able to remain true to its mission of using education for fundamental change.

John M. Glen

See also: African Americans; Appalachia; Civil Rights Movement; Community Organizing; Poor Whites; Racial Segregation; Rural Poverty; Trade/Industrial Unions

References and Further Reading

Glen, John M. 1996. *Highlander: No Ordinary School.* 2d ed. Knoxville: University of Tennessee Press.

Horton, Aimee I. 1989. *The Highlander Folk School: A History of Its Major Programs, 1932–1961.* Brooklyn, NY: Carlson.

Horton, Myles, with Judith Kohl and Herbert Kohl. 1990. *The Long Haul: An Autobiography.* New York: Doubleday.

Home Health Care Work

Home health care is the often low- or unpaid labor involved in attending to the needs of sick, disabled, and elderly people. Historically provided by women as part of family or community responsibilities, throughout the post–World War II decades, the work of caregiving has increasingly been contracted out to a low-paid, disproportionately female health care workforce. Considered a "labor of love" when provided by a family member, this kind of work is demanding, requires a variety of skills, and can be emotionally draining. Socially and economically undervalued though it is, caregiving work remains essential to the well-being of individuals, families, and society writ large.

Caring for sick and disabled kin dominated women's lives throughout the nineteenth century. Beginning as early as girlhood and extending into middle and old age, caregiving simultaneously exacted a terrible toll and conferred significant benefits. A constellation of forces has transformed the content and cultural meaning of care.

Although many men participated in caregiving during the nineteenth century, the primary responsibility for family and community nursing rested with women. Few formal services relieved their obligations. Most families were reluctant to entrust ill relatives to the few hospitals that existed. Without telephones and automobiles, summoning physicians involved considerable time and effort, even if the family could afford the fees physicians charged. Skepticism about physicians further deterred many people from relying on them.

Nineteenth-century caregiving work had three recognized and socially valued components: instrumental, spiritual, and emotional. Only later would their importance be diminished, as health care came to be increasingly medicalized and professionalized. Instrumental caregiving services in the nineteenth century included not just cooking, cleaning, and assisting sick people with feeding and mobility but also delivering skilled medical care. Women dispensed herbal remedies, dressed wounds, bound broken bones, sewed severed fingers, cleaned bedsores, and removed bullets. At the time, knowledge acquired through practical education was considered to be as important as that gleaned in the laboratory and taught in schools. Consequently, some women could translate caregiving skills into paid employment as nurses and midwives.

Struggling to establish themselves as professionals, nineteenth-century doctors denigrated women's healing knowledge and tried to restrict the information available to the public. But many doctors were well aware of their own educational deficiencies. A few later acknowledged how much they had learned from older women caregivers.

Because sickness and death were religious as well as medical events, caregiving had an important spiritual dimension. Enslaved healers in the antebellum South sought to address both the metaphysical and the natural causes of disease. The healers also sought to connect patients to their ancestors. Although fewer whites associated healing with spirituality, white women routinely reported reading the Bible to care recipients, praying with them, and urging them to accept death openly and peacefully.

Nineteenth-century medicine also dignified the emotional component of care. Most doctors agreed that attention, sympathy, and reassurance facilitated healing. In addition, prevailing medical beliefs encouraged doctors to value personal relationships as a source of knowledge.

The forces that altered caregiving between 1890 and 1940 included the mass production of goods and services for the home, the increase in the rate of women's participation in the labor force, the rise of the formal health care system, and the growth of physicians' authority. Such changes affected different groups of caregivers in different ways. Caregiving remained grueling for women who could not afford the new domestic technologies. The job of mediating between family members and health care services also was especially difficult for low-income women. Because few hospitals and clinics were located in poor neighborhoods, women had to travel long distances to take patients to the doctor or to visit them in the hospital. Some caregivers had no access to relevant services. And some had to fend off the medical assistance that charity workers, public health nurses, and government officials sought to impose.

The new scientific optimism undermined the cultural value of these three major components of caregiving. Caregivers' knowledge was increasingly denigrated as superstition, acceptance of God's will was disparaged as resignation, and solicitude was condemned as indulgence. This shift in cultural values had the most serious consequences for the least privileged women. Although the increased confidence in medical science created a pretext for physicians to lavish attention on the education of all mothers, poor women, immigrant women, and women of color were especially likely to be perceived as needing instruction. Such women also were considered especially likely to be discouraged and resigned and to be swayed by excessive emotion and thus to indulge sick and disabled family members. White middle-class women, as charity workers, public health nurses, and occasionally government officials, helped construct the portrait of poor women, immigrant women, and women of color as superstitious, fatalistic, and irrational. Such a depiction not only skewed the services provided to those groups but also contributed to the denigration of an activity with which all women were associated.

Caregiving has continued to undergo profound transformation since 1940. As the rate of women's participation in the labor force has soared, women have increasingly faced the conflict between jobs in the paid labor force and care. The aging of the population has meant that growing numbers of women must provide elder care.

The growth of health care financing programs after World War II led to a dramatic upsurge in the use of institutions. But the movement between home and medical facilities has not been unidirectional. The population of the nation's mental hospitals plunged between 1955 and 1975. Since the mid-1970s, states have attempted to curb Medicaid expenditures by keeping people out of nursing homes. And the growth of managed care since the early 1990s has led to a drop in the length of stay in hospitals, again shifting care back to the home.

The high-tech equipment that often follows patients out of the hospital and into the home setting has transformed caregiving work. Some technologies must be constantly monitored, and many require family caregivers to perform extremely complex tasks. Nineteenth-century women struggled to retain jurisdiction over skilled medical care, but caregivers today complain about being entrusted with responsibilities that far exceed their capabilities.

Caregiving remains especially onerous for poor women today. The low-status jobs they can obtain tend to have little or no flexibility in hours or days worked. Despite the growth of health care financing programs, many continue to confront barriers to such assistance. Very few can purchase medical equipment or supplies, retrofit their homes to accommodate a sickroom or wheelchair, or "buy out" of their obligations by hiring other women. Meanwhile, home health care workers are disproportionately women of color and are among the lowest paid of all workers in the United States.

Emily K. Abel

See also: Disability; Domestic Work; Epidemic Disease; Gender Discrimination in the Labor Market; Health Policy; Service and Domestic Workers, Labor Organizing

References and Further Reading

Abel, Emily K. 2000. *Hearts of Wisdom: American Women Caring for Kin, 1850–1940*. Cambridge, MA: Harvard University Press.

Leavitt, Judith Walzer. 1986. *Brought to Bed: Child-Bearing in America, 1750–1950*. New York: Oxford University Press.

Ulrich, Laurel Thatcher. 1990. *A Midwife's Tale: The Life of Martha Ballard, Based on Her Diary, 1785–1812*. New York: Knopf.

Homelessness

Destitute people living without permanent shelter have been a part of the American experience since the early colonial period, but the size and demographics of the homeless population, as well as the causes of homelessness, have varied over time. Throughout the nineteenth and early twentieth centuries, the number of homeless moved jaggedly upward in a cyclical pattern inversely related to general economic conditions, reaching a high point in the 1930s. After World War II, the homeless population sharply declined and became confined to deteriorating skid row sections of cities. Homelessness remained at a fairly low level until the late 1970s, when the sudden appearance of large numbers of destitute "street people" in urban areas marked the beginning of a surge in the homeless population that would continue into the early twenty-first century. Although homelessness today is not nearly as significant as it was during the 1870–1940 period, it is much nearer the historical norm than was true of the immediate post–World War II era.

Prior to the 1730s, "sturdy beggars" or "the wandering poor" (as the homeless were called before 1800) were relatively rare. Much of the homelessness at this time was sporadic, the result of dislocations caused by disasters, plagues, or, especially, warfare, such as the Indian-white conflict of 1675–1676 in Massachusetts known as King Phillip's War. The second half of the eighteenth century, however, saw the emergence of a more conspicuous homeless population, especially in New York, Philadelphia, and other cities along the eastern seaboard. Although the French and Indian War (1756–1763) and the American Revolution were responsible for some of this increase, fundamental economic and social changes were more-important causes. As the American economy became more tied to the world market, inequalities of wealth grew, and the number of poor people at risk of falling into homelessness increased. Prior to 1820, former indentured servants, apprentices, and unskilled laborers made up the majority of the homeless population. Although white males made up a majority of this group, there were also significant numbers of homeless women. Relative to their share of the population in the cities, African Americans were overrepresented among the homeless because of the number of runaway slaves and desperately poor former slaves in the North who became homeless after being freed between 1790 and 1815.

In the decades preceding the Civil War, nascent industrialization and urbanization created new conditions that fostered homelessness. Mechanization of some industries increased productivity but drove down wages and led to a decline in artisanal independence. Fluctuations in the economy also became more frequent. The unemployment and general economic insecurity resulting from the depressions of 1817–1823, 1837–1843, and the late 1850s increased the levels of homelessness significantly, especially in northern cities. During the 1830–1860 period, women, many of them widows, continued to make up as much as a third of the urban homeless, but the number of homeless Blacks declined sharply as Black communities in the North matured and Black churches began to provide rudimentary assistance to the poor. Instead, by the 1850s, destitute Irish immigrants, male and female, made up as much as half the homeless population in many locales. The homeless of the antebellum period were not distributed equally across all regions of the country. In the South, the institution of slavery impeded the growth of homelessness by placing the poorest segment of the population under the control of individual slaveholders. In the North, vagrancy was much more prevalent in the East Coast metropolitan corridor and surrounding areas than in the thriving small towns and rural areas of the Midwest.

Throughout the colonial and early national period, charitable groups and local governments responded to the homeless in both positive and negative ways. Harsh vagrancy laws existed but were only sporadically enforced. Vagrants were sometimes imprisoned, but more often they received a public whipping followed by expulsion from the community. Citizens sympathetic to the homeless responded in equally irregular fashion, setting up ad hoc committees to provide food for the destitute, then disbanding when the immediate crisis had passed. Such intermittent, largely unplanned activities were typical of premodern approaches to homelessness. After 1820, the growth of large private charities in New York and other cities led to the first significant organized response to the homeless. Organizations like the Association for the Improvement of the Condition of the Poor (founded in 1843) dominated public debate over the increasing number of vagrants and beggars on city streets. Charity theorists, espousing a harsh, moralistic view of poverty, criticized traditional, haphazard ways of responding to the homeless as "sentimental" and "unscientific." Ignoring the economic causes of much homelessness, they largely blamed the homeless for their own condition. In an effort that was only occasionally successful, the large philanthropies campaigned to eliminate outdoor poor relief (that is, relief not provided in institutions such as poorhouses) and replace it with workhouses in which all able-bodied paupers, homeless or not, would be incarcerated.

Homelessness remained predominantly local until the severe depression of the 1870s, when for the first time large numbers of men began riding illegally on trains. The use of railroads by tramps brought the specter of homelessness to every area of the country and inaugurated an intense debate over how to deal with a group now perceived as a national problem. The homeless of the industrial era (1870–1940) were greater in number than at any other time in American history and were distinctive in a number of ways. Some went "on the road" in search of work, while others became long-term residents of a particular city. There was considerable overlap between the two groups, but the mobile homeless tended on the average to be much younger than those who remained in one locale. This duality would continue to define homelessness until the 1940s, when riding the freights fell off sharply.

The post–Civil War decades witnessed a steady decline in the number of female homeless, primarily because of the growth of urban charities aiding women and, after 1910, the institution of mothers' pensions for single women with children. By the early twentieth century, women made up no more than about 10 or 15 percent of the urban homeless, and until the 1930s, it was rare for women to ride the freights. African Americans, who until about 1915 had remained mostly in the South and had worked primarily as sharecroppers or servants, also were underrepresented among the homeless. After World War I, however, the incorporation of a sizable number of Black migrants into the industrial economy of the urban North brought with it a substantial rise in Black homelessness.

Regardless of their gender or race, the homeless at this time were overwhelmingly drawn from the ranks of blue-collar workers. Skilled laborers were almost as likely as the unskilled to experience homelessness, but until the 1930s even lower-level white-collar workers were usually able to avoid this fate.

It is not surprising that there were so many tramps and beggars during the industrial era, a time when there was no unemployment insurance, no workmen's compensation (prior to 1910), and no government-sponsored old-age pensions. The unemployment accompanying periodic economic depressions, a natural result of an unregulated economic system, was a major underlying cause of much homelessness. Unemployment also arose from automation, seasonal work, strikes, or simple overproduction. Industrial accidents, which rendered tens of thousands of workers unemployable each year in the early twentieth century, also played a significant role in creating homelessness. An unemployed or disabled worker was most likely to become homeless, however, if he lacked sufficient family or community support. It was for this reason that immigrants from China or southern and eastern Europe, despite wretched poverty, seldom experienced homelessness. Relatively large families and high levels of community cohesion among these groups acted as support systems that prevented many at-risk individuals from falling into complete destitution. Partly because of the much smaller size of their families, native-born whites were more likely than other groups to become homeless during the 1870–1940 period.

During the Victorian era, the attitude of government and large urban charities toward the homeless was often distrustful or punitive. Beginning in the 1840s and 1850s, city governments began to set aside rooms in police stations where the destitute could sleep overnight. These decrepit, filthy accommodations represented a minimalist policy of dealing with the homeless population, a group that many believed deserved nothing better. In the 1880s and 1890s, local branches of the Charity Organization Society (COS) set up privately run lodging houses for tramps. The primary purpose of these "wayfarers' lodges" was to separate the "worthy" unemployed workman from the disreputable tramp by requiring a "work test" of those who stayed overnight. Before receiving breakfast, the male lodgers were required to chop wood or break stone for one or two hours. In COS lodges that provided accommodations for both sexes, women were also required to work, usually by doing laundry or scrubbing floors. Although the accommodations in the wayfarers' lodges were more humane than the police station tramp rooms, the homeless who used them complained of the poor food, humiliating treatment, and rules that limited a lodger's stay to only a few days.

In the 1870s and 1880s, hostility to tramps also led to the passage of harsh vagrancy laws and a concerted effort by police to round up and arrest street beggars. It soon became evident, however, that it was not possible to legislate the homeless out of existence. The size and mobility of the homeless population made enforcement of such laws difficult, but equally important was the fact that the average citizen did not always share the antagonistic views of public officials and the middle-class press toward this impoverished class. For the most part, the homeless of the industrial era survived not through assistance from government or the COS but because there were many local neighborhood charities, religious groups outside the mainstream, and individuals who sympathized with the down-and-out. Despite their own poverty, immigrants and racial minorities were reputed to be generous in feeding tramps, and the Salvation Army (established in the United States in 1891) and evangelical Protestant groups who established "gospel missions" for the homeless in inner-city areas usually made no distinction between the "worthy" and "unworthy" poor. Attempts by police and the COS to eliminate street begging were largely unsuccessful because too many Americans, especially from the working class, sympathized with panhandlers.

Progressive-Era reformers broadened the middle class's understanding of the causes of poverty and promoted a more humane approach by city governments to the homeless. Robert Hunter's *Poverty* (1904), Alice Willard Solenberger's 1914 Chicago study, *One Thousand Homeless Men*, and Nels Anderson's *Hobo: The Sociology of the Homeless Man* (1923) all stressed the diverse causes of homelessness and argued that the homeless, like other poor people, deserved to be treated as individuals. The professionalization of social work at this time also promoted a less-punitive approach to the homeless and a greater recognition of the effects of unemployment, work accidents, and poverty in creating homelessness. Between 1900 and 1920, most large cities outside the South established municipal lodging houses. While retaining some of the negative features of the wayfarers' lodges, these facilities for the homeless usually eliminated the work test and the three- or four-day limit on use of the shelters. The South's approach to homelessness remained distinctive. Most southern cities did not have municipal shelters. Where they did exist, they were racially segregated, and smaller southern communities continued to use draconian vagrancy laws against the homeless (especially African Americans) much more frequently than did police in the North.

After a decade of relatively moderate homelessness during and after World War I, the Great Depression brought this issue back to the forefront of public consciousness. Homelessness touched people from all walks of life in the 1930s. Although white males still made up a majority of the down-and-out, there was a substantial increase in the numbers of homeless women, families, and, especially, Blacks. For the first time, a significant number of white-collar workers showed up in soup lines. Illegal train riding became more commonplace than at any time since the 1890s, shantytowns constructed by the homeless sprang up in cities across the nation, and officials struggled to deal with unprecedented demands on private and public shelters. Out of this crisis came a New Deal agency, the Federal Transient Service (FTS), the first federal program in American history designed specifically to aid the homeless. Established in 1933 as a part of the Federal Emergency Relief Administration (FERA), the FTS organized 300 urban centers and over 300 rural camps for "federal transients" (defined as anyone who had lived less than one year in a particular state). The general treatment of and facilities for the transients, especially food and sleeping quarters, was far superior to that of most private or municipal shelters, and the FTS made a significant break with past neglect by making free medical and dental care available to the homeless. In addition, FTS urban centers developed a wide range of educational programs for residents, and the rural camps provided much on-the-job training. In a little over two years, about 1 million people took part in FTS programs.

In the fall of 1935, the FTS was abruptly phased out, as the New Deal shifted its attention to public works projects, Social Security, and workers' rights. The result, across the country, was a sharp rise in the number of street beggars, people sleeping in parks, and men riding the rails. Within two years, they would be joined by destitute farm families attempting to make their way from the Dust Bowl states to California. This resurgence of visible homelessness, however, was short-lived. By 1941, war preparedness allowed some of the destitute to regain employment, and American participation in World War II further drew many formerly homeless persons into the regular workforce. Postwar economic expansion, coupled with benefits from Social Security, Aid to Dependent Children, and the G.I. Bill, reinforced this trend, helping many who had temporarily become homeless during the Depression to avoid becoming so again. A core group of the homeless, however, consisting mostly of older men, were unable to adjust to the new economic circumstances. These individuals' irregular work histories prevented them from receiving pensions and limited their Social Security benefits. Increasingly in the 1950s and 1960s, this aging homeless population, no longer mobile and now limited to short-term employment as casual laborers, became confined to the deteriorating skid row sections of the nation's cities.

In the 1960s and 1970s, urban renewal programs led to the demolition of most of the old lodging-house districts, forcing their residents to seek shelter in other poor sections of the city. Obliterating the skid rows did not end homelessness, however. The "new homeless" who began to appear in the late 1970s were much younger, more likely to be racial minorities and women, and more numerous and visible than their skid row predecessors. The homeless population continued to expand during the deep recession of the early 1980s, but as with the sudden upsurge of tramps a century before, their numbers did not fall off that much once prosperity returned. Instead, by the beginning of the twenty-first century, these "street people" seemed to have become a permanent part of the postindustrial order. The reappearance of highly visible, mass homelessness encouraged some political leaders to advocate a return to the punitive tactics of the past in dealing with the down-and-out. In the 1990s, for example, a number of cities passed "quality of life" ordinances that allowed the police to arrest homeless individuals for trivial offenses. To some extent, local governments provided food and shelter to persons on the street, but to an even greater degree than had been true in the industrial era, private organizations of concerned citizens remained the most important source of assistance to the homeless.

In the postindustrial era, as throughout most of American history, the causes of homelessness are intertwined with many aspects of society that affect domiciled citizens as well. These include unemployment and a changing job structure, the lack of affordable housing for the poor, inadequate health care provisions, and the lack of family support. The negative consequences of divorce or desertion and of abusive spouses have emerged as particularly important causes of homelessness among women, who now make up a larger proportion of the homeless population than at any time since the Civil War. Historically, the line between the homeless and the working poor has always been a porous one, and there continues to be much movement back and forth between the two groups. Homelessness remains a serious problem because, in many ways, it has always been an integral part of a society riven with many inequalities.

Kenneth L. Kusmer

See also: Charity Organization Societies; Deserving/Undeserving Poor; Dust Bowl Migration; Economic Depression; Food Banks; Housing Policy; Poor Laws; Poorhouse/Almshouse; Relief; Salvation Army; Urban Poverty; Urban Renewal; Vagrancy Laws/Settlement Laws/Residency Requirements

References and Further Reading

Beard, Rick, ed. 1987. *On Being Homeless: Historical Perspectives*. New York: Museum of the City of New York.

Hoch, Charles, and Robert A. Slayton. 1989. *New Homeless and Old: Community and the Skid Row Hotel*. Philadelphia: Temple University Press.

Kusmer, Kenneth L. 2001. *Down and Out, on the Road: The Homeless in American History*. New York: Oxford University Press.

Liebow, Elliot. 1993. *Tell Them Who I Am: The Lives of Homeless Women*. New York: Free Press.

Snow, David A., and Leon Anderson. 1993. *Down on Their Luck: A Study of Homeless Street People*. Berkeley and Los Angeles: University of California Press.

Solenberger, Alice Willard. 1914. *One Thousand Homeless Men*. New York: Survey Associates.

Homophobia

Homophobia is a form of oppression that is aimed against lesbians and gay men. Homophobic myths conceal the fact that many homosexuals can be found among the poor. In fact, the social science data suggest that some specific groups of lesbians and gay men are overrepresented among the poor. Lesbians and gay men are sometimes neglected or badly served by social welfare programs, and homosexuals are particularly vulnerable to the moralistic and religious orientation of emerging public policies.

Opponents of lesbian and gay rights often argue that lesbians and gays constitute a wealthy elite and that they therefore do not need protection from discrimination. One study, however, found that after controlling for education, age, and other relevant factors, gay men earned between 11 and 27 percent less than similar heterosexual men (Badgett 1997, 69). A random poll of voters conducted in 1992 found that lesbians tend to be overrepresented among the very poor and underrepresented in the highest income group (Badgett 1997, 68). Another recent study found that partnered gay men earn substantially less than married men and that lesbians earn more than heterosexual women. Partnered lesbians and gay men are less likely than married heterosexual couples to own a home. Within the home-owner group itself, however, lesbian and gay men are better off; the homes belonging to homosexuals tended to be more expensive than the ones owned by heterosexuals (Black et al. 2000, 152–153).

Many different factors seem to be producing these conditions. Gay men often seek out a supportive cultural milieu. Generally, they tend to prioritize migration to the urban areas that have vibrant gay male communities over career advancement. They may, therefore, be confronted with more-constrained job opportunities and a higher cost of living than heterosexual men from the same class background and age cohort. Biological families continue to play a pivotal role in the reproduction of economic class. Teenagers and young adults often depend upon their parents for college tuition; access to family-based career networks; financial gifts, personal loans, and entrepreneurial investment capital; and wedding gifts, home purchase capital, and estate inheritance. Gay men and lesbians are often excluded from their biological family because of their parents' homophobia and thus are at a distinct disadvantage in this respect. "Family-wage" ideology—the notion that the best-paying jobs should be reserved for married male workers because they are the ones who ought to be supporting their families—may be working in tandem with homophobia. Child rearing by lesbian and gay parents is significant, even if the rate of child rearing is less than among married heterosexuals. Although 59 percent of married heterosexuals have at least one dependent child, 21 percent of lesbian households and 5 percent of gay male households do so as well (Black et al. 2000, 150). Yet despite their responsibility for children, lesbian and gay employees do not receive a family wage. Many Americans believe that homosexuals should not raise children; other Americans believe that lesbians and gay men are not interested in having families. Employers may be influenced by these views and therefore may be overlooking the fact that many of their homosexual employees are actually supporting dependents in their households.

They may presume that heterosexual men, and married heterosexual men in particular, are the only employees who need to earn a family wage.

The data also suggest that sexuality, gender, and class work together in a complex manner. Given the fact that men typically earn more than equally qualified women, one would expect to find that gay male couples typically earn even more than heterosexual couples, since the effect of the gender gap would be doubled in a two-male household. Once the gender gap is taken into account, it is particularly striking that heterosexual couples appear to be better off than gay male couples. The gay men and lesbians in the survey samples also tend to be better educated than their heterosexual counterparts. Further research is needed to find out whether this is actually the case or whether homosexuality is more accurately reported among individuals with higher educational credentials.

Finally, the survey data suggest that income and wealth disparities may be more pronounced within the lesbian and gay male communities than in the population as a whole. Lesbians and gay men are located in every economic class and in every poverty program. But the small number of homosexuals who do belong to the home-owner group seem to be extraordinarily well off. The fact that child rearing is less common among the wealthiest homosexuals than among the wealthiest heterosexuals probably contributes to this difference. It may also be the case that poor and middle-class gay men are exposed to the most costly forms of homophobia. Perhaps the wealthiest gay men are using their symbolic and material capital to "purchase" better protection from discrimination and to locate themselves in more-supportive employment and wealth-generating environments. The wealthiest lesbians may be benefiting from "mommy tracking." Heterosexual women holding professional and managerial positions are often less valued as employees than their male counterparts because it is assumed that they will put a greater emphasis on meeting their family's needs than on their careers. Because lesbians are constructed in homophobic ideology as nonmothers, however, employers might assume that professional and managerial lesbians have no caregiving burdens whatsoever and that they are therefore better suited than their heterosexual women colleagues for career advancement.

The presence of a significant number of lesbians and gays in poverty programs tends to be ignored by social policymakers. Poor homosexuals were certainly overlooked when welfare reformers decided to promote heterosexual marriage and abstinence education for teens as a solution to poverty. Lesbian mothers have special needs. The courts often refuse to grant them custody of their children solely because of their sexuality. Some lesbian mothers are fleeing former male partners who reacted in a violent and abusive manner when they revealed their sexual orientation. The poverty programs and the child welfare system, however, have not taken adequate steps to address these issues. The rapid integration of religious institutions into the welfare system during the 1990s will probably result in homophobic discrimination and exclusion for poor homosexuals, since many of the faith-based organizations that are winning service delivery contracts believe that homosexuality is a moral wrong.

Although the homosexual community has done much to stop the sexual transmission of the HIV virus, gay men—and especially men of color who engage in same-sex activity—remain strongly overrepresented among the people with AIDS (PWAs). With the introduction of new drug therapies, AIDS has been transformed from an acute disease into a manageable chronic condition. Today, PWAs need protection from discrimination as well as access to medication, Medicaid, nursing homes, and hospices. But they also require much more flexible health care policies that support the emerging day treatment and home health care programs. The AIDS Coalition to Unleash Power (ACT-UP), the gay male–led anti-AIDS protest organization, has also changed the face of public health politics by inventing patient-oriented direct action. This form of protest has served as a model for breast cancer activists and has introduced much more democratic accountability into the areas of medical research and public health policy.

Anna Marie Smith

See also: Christian Fundamentalism; Family Wage; Gender Discrimination in the Labor Market; Health Policy; Heteronormativity; Welfare Policy/Welfare Reform

References and Further Reading

Badgett, Lee. 1997. "Beyond Biased Samples: Challenging the Myths on the Economic Status of Lesbians and Gay Men." In *Homo Economics: Capitalism, Community, and Lesbian and Gay Life*, ed. Amy Gluckman and Betsy Reed, 65–72. New York: Routledge.

Black, Dan, Gary Gates, Seth Sanders, and Lowell Taylor. 2000. "Demographics of the Gay and Lesbian Population in the United States: Evidence from Available Systematic Data Sources." *Demography* 37, no. 2: 139–154.

Cohen, Cathy. 1999. *The Boundaries of Blackness: AIDS and the Breakdown of Black Politics*. Chicago: University of Chicago Press.

D'Emilio, John. 1993. "Capitalism and Gay Identity." In *The Lesbian and Gay Studies Reader*, ed. Henry Abelove, Michèle Aina Barale, and David Halperin, 467–478. New York: Routledge.

Lehr, Valerie. 1999. *Queer Family Values: Debunking the Myth of the Nuclear Family*. Philadelphia: Temple University Press.

Housing Policy

Housing policy comprises a broad array of programs designed to promote home ownership and make affordable housing available to low-income families, and measures to assure access to and prevent discrimination against racial minorities. Because shelter is the largest aspect of the household budget for the vast majority of people in the United States, housing policy affects a huge number and variety of people across the socioeconomic spectrum. Indeed, the most sizable and widespread government housing benefits have historically gone to all home owners, regardless of income, in the form of government mortgage guarantees and tax deductions for mortgage interest. Nevertheless, the most visible—and controversial—aspect of American housing policy has been that aimed at increasing the supply of affordable housing for the poor. These programs have been plagued by a combination of resistance to government "interference" in the private housing market, politically charged accusations that public housing advocates have "socialist" leanings, and, most troubling of all, deep-seated racial animosity that makes the United States a nation, especially in the area of housing, profoundly segregated by race as well as class.

Although building regulations date back to the colonial era, the first significant efforts at American housing policy began during the Progressive Era in the early decades of the 1900s. At the time, and with few exceptions, most policymakers viewed construction of decent housing for the poor as a task for private enterprise, but reformers attempted to increase the quality of housing through regulation. During the 1930s, the New Deal witnessed the establishment of the bifurcated housing policy still in place today: mortgage guarantees for middle- and upper-classes and small amounts of funding for publicly owned housing for the poor. Despite constant attack and chronic underfunding, efforts to construct public housing and improve poor people's access to decent housing increased through the Great Society of the 1960s. Since 1970, housing policy has been marked by a consistent decline in government support for public housing combined with inconsistent support for other housing programs that serve the poor.

Although the housing problems of the poor had been well-known for decades, the nineteenth century witnessed few significant policy innovations. Reform societies focused primarily on the moral health of the poor. In 1854, the Association for the Improvement of the Condition of the Poor produced the first "model tenement," based on the principle that decent housing could and should be provided through the private market and make a profit. For the rest of the century, reformers promoted the model tenement, but these efforts produced only a small amount of housing for the poor.

In the last decades of the nineteenth century, several cities passed tenement laws in an effort to establish minimal health standards and prevent overcrowding, but government regulation remained ineffective throughout these years. Jacob Riis's *How the Other Half Lives*, published in 1890, increased public demands for government action. Progressive reformers like Jane Addams and Lawrence Veiller lobbied for greater regulation of city tenements. Chicago, New York, and other cities created tenement commissions to investigate complaints about inadequate housing. Although reformers in the Progressive Era realized that the lack of affordable housing was in part a supply problem, they focused in particular on the moral and health hazards of bad housing. Reformers continued to rely on the private market to produce housing for the poor and did not push for government support for housing construction.

The other major housing policy in the early 1900s was the city beautiful movement. Led by urban elites concerned about the increasing squalor in large cities, the movement sought to bring order to the city through the demolition of tenements and factories and the creation of wide boulevards and public buildings. The production of affordable housing was not a significant focus of this movement, but it did result in the destruction of thousands of units of rundown, but affordable, housing.

World War I provided the impetus for a short-lived expansion of government-sponsored housing. To meet the needs of the war production workers, Congress created the U.S. Housing Corporation in 1917. Business leaders argued that home ownership for the working class was the solution to labor problems, while urban planners and reformers focused on community building. In one year, the agency built more than 16,000 mostly single-family homes and several dozen complete communities. The armistice in 1918, however, brought a swift attack on government housing production that resulted in its cessation; political opponents, playing on the postwar Red Scare, launched congressional investigations into the "socialist" influence of the program.

During the 1920s, housing reformers in New York began to experiment with government support for housing production. New York's Housing Act of 1926 created the Limited Dividend Housing Program, which provided eminent domain powers (the right to acquire land for development or related uses for public purposes) and tax exemptions to private developers who agreed to limit rents in the housing. Several limited dividend projects were built in New York City, but this program did not attract much support elsewhere in the nation.

Central to the emergence of a modern national housing policy was Herbert Hoover during his term as secretary of commerce (1921–1928) under Presidents Warren G. Harding and Calvin Coolidge. Through his support for professional, voluntary, and commercial housing organizations, Hoover increased the focus on home ownership as the answer to Americans' housing problems. Hoover's early advocacy of zoning, planning, and building standards was instrumental in the development of modern, large-scale suburban communities. Like other businessmen, Hoover saw individual home ownership as a bulwark against socialism and as a means to secure economic growth. He supported the nationalization of the home-construction industry and the growth of the home-furnishing industry. The housing programs of the New Deal, particularly the Federal Housing Administration (FHA), built upon this legacy.

Modern American housing policy was created during the New Deal administration of President Franklin D. Roosevelt. The dramatic increase in foreclosures and homelessness during the Great Depression opened the door for government intervention in the housing market. Housing reformers like Catherine Bauer argued that achieving adequate housing for the working class required government subsidy. In 1933, the housing emergency, combined with the desire to increase employment, spurred Congress to include public housing in the legislation creating the Public Works Administration (PWA). Over the next four years, the agency built or funded the construction of 25,000 units of housing. These developments were noted for their success in nurturing community and in attracting moderate-income residents.

Although many of President Roosevelt's advisers recommended a large-scale program for the construction of public housing, he was reluctant to commit significant amounts of funding to such a project. Instead, he proposed the FHA, a government insurance agency that would support home construction for the middle class by guaranteeing private mortgages and making home ownership more affordable. By nationalizing the mortgage market, decreasing the required down payment for home purchases, and increasing the amortization period, the FHA expanded access to home ownership to the middle class and parts of the working class. The organization received widespread public and political support and quickly became the centerpiece of federal housing policy.

Despite Roosevelt's reluctance, liberals continued to push for the construction of public housing. Concerned that the PWA was only a temporary measure, they demanded a permanent program. Real estate and other interests violently opposed the program, saying it was communistic. Nevertheless, after heated debate and negotiations that made the program more attractive to the private construction industry, among others, Congress passed the Wagner Public Housing Act in 1937, creating the U.S. Housing Authority, which funded locally developed public housing. Several important restrictions were imposed on the program. Public housing was linked directly to slum clearance: The law required one substandard unit to be demolished for each new unit constructed. The legislation also imposed strict cost ceilings on the housing produced. These restrictions had serious long-term implications for the program.

World War II resulted in the expansion of the public housing program, which was linked to providing shelter for war production workers. To increase production, Congress passed the Lanham Act in 1941, authorizing the Federal Works Administration to build projects in defense areas. Despite congressional restrictions, program administrators experimented with new types of architecture, building, and forms of ownership, creating several innovative projects. Federal housing programs were merged in 1942 to create the National Housing Administration (NHA). As war production increased, real estate interests took hold of the program, and the majority of units produced were cheaply constructed, short-term buildings. Over 700,000 units of housing were built during the war, but the majority of them were temporary. Postwar legislation required the NHA to dispose of the permanent units. The majority were sold to the inhabitants or to private developers.

Wartime efforts to control inflation also resulted in the imposition of rent controls by the Office of Price Administration. To protect tenants in war production areas, Congress froze rents at 1942 levels for the remainder of the war. After the conflict ended, many housing activists pressed for the continuation of rent controls. Throughout the late 1940s, rent control was a major political issue. Real estate and conservative interests opposed the continuation of controls, arguing that they stifled the production of affordable housing, while advocates argued that rent controls should continue until housing shortages declined. In a series of legislative acts, Congress granted greater control to states and localities to regulate rents. By the early 1950s, however, only New York had a significant rent control program, reflecting the influence of powerful private-sector opponents.

After the war ended, housing reformers and urban elites formed a coalition to press for permanent federal involvement in housing and urban development. Their efforts resulted in the passage of the Housing Act of 1949, which established the goal of "a decent home for every American," expanded federal support for mortgage insurance through the FHA, set a target of building 135,000 units of public housing a year for six years, and created the urban renewal program. Because of opposition to public housing from real estate interests, it took four years to secure the passage of the act.

The act spurred the production of hundreds of thousands of units of housing, particularly single-family homes in the suburbs. During the 1950s, thousands of units of middle-income housing were built through the urban renewal program. Public housing construction also increased, but it was constantly under attack during the 1950s. Although many smaller cities created successful projects, opposition and corruption inhibited the program in many areas. Citing concerns about its impact on property values, many cities refused to build public housing. Voters in Los Angeles, for example, approved a referendum directing the city not to build any public projects.

More explosive, and often just beneath the surface of rhetoric about socialism and property values, was the volatile mix of racial prejudice, fear, and politics that fueled widespread white opposition to public housing, increasingly viewed as housing for Blacks as post–World War II African American migration to urban centers continued. Federal authorities did little to challenge segregationist norms; during the 1930s and 1940s, most public housing authorities maintained racially segregated projects, and minorities gained access to public housing only after civil rights activists mounted campaigns to eliminate discrimination in housing. Blacks continued to be denied access to private housing, however, particularly in newly developing suburbs, because FHA underwriting guidelines considered African Americans to be adverse influences. The guidelines actively encouraged private lenders to deny mortgages to African Americans and in heavily minority or racially mixed neighborhoods. This practice, known as "redlining" because of the official color coding used to designate undesirable lending areas, effectively denied African Americans access to one of the most substantial and expansive benefits of the U.S. social welfare system. Moreover, because Blacks and other minorities were denied access to private housing, public projects became increasingly minority.

Public housing also became increasingly tied to urban renewal during the 1950s. That program, meant to replace slums with upper-middle-class housing or public amenities, resulted in the demolition of thousands of units of affordable housing and the dislocation of hundreds of thousands of residents. In large cities like New York and Chicago, the displaced residents were overwhelmingly Black and Latino. Although the majority of these tenants were forced to fend for themselves, many found shelter in public housing. Racial change in public housing, coupled with increases in crime in the projects and in the surrounding neighborhoods, contributed to the further marginalization of the program.

By the late 1950s, public housing was criticized from both the right and the left. Catherine Bauer, focusing on the sterile architecture and the negative impact of large projects on surrounding areas, decried the "dreary deadlock of public housing" in an influential article by that title (Bauer 1957). President Dwight D. Eisenhower, never a fan of the program, refused to request appropriations for additional units, and federal allocations decreased dramatically. Despite the fact that the Housing Act of 1949 had called for the construction of 810,000 units by 1956, by 1960, only 250,000 units had been completed. At the same time, supported by federal mortgage insurance and highway building, suburban development continued to increase dramatically. As single-family suburban home ownership became accessible to increasing numbers of white Americans, urban neighborhoods lost their middle-class populations and large proportions of their white working-class populations. In the absence of measures to generate alternative sources of tax revenue, this led to housing decline and abandonment and to increasing pressure on city finances.

The 1960s brought increased attention to the need for affordable housing. The Housing Act of 1961 increased support for the construction of housing for seniors and for public housing and created a new program providing incentives to private developers to build low- and moderate-income housing. President John F. Kennedy also attempted to increase the housing access of African Americans by signing an executive order prohibiting discrimination in some federal housing programs.

President Lyndon B. Johnson's administration created several new initiatives to increase the supply of affordable housing. In 1965, Johnson proposed a rent supplement program, providing subsidies to housing developers in return for their agreement to keep rents below market rates. The Johnson administration also pushed Congress to create the Department of Housing and Urban Development (HUD) to coordinate federal housing and other urban programs. Led by Robert Weaver, the first Black cabinet secretary, HUD initiated several programs to increase the supply of housing. The Model Cities program, an effort to coordinate services and redevelopment in the inner city, also promoted housing development by nonprofit, community-based organizations. The administration also organized several commissions to study methods to decrease the cost of housing and increase housing supply.

The Johnson administration's major housing initiative, the Housing Act of 1968, expanded funding for affordable housing, both for rental and for purchase, and further shifted away from government construction of public housing to private development. Section 235 of the act relaxed FHA income standards and enabled lower-income persons to purchase homes. Section 236 provided subsidies to developers who built rental apartments available to low-income persons. Meant to spur private construction for public purposes, both these programs succeeded in increasing the supply of affordable housing. However, corruption and other management problems in the early 1970s brought about their demise.

During the 1960s and 1970s, housing decline in older American cities increased dramatically. Increased maintenance costs, combined with declining revenues, led many apartment owners to abandon their buildings. The South Bronx became a symbol of the decline of urban society as arson and abandonment created a landscape that some compared to a war zone. Public housing also faced increasing difficulties in this period. An amendment sponsored by Senator Edward Brooke (R-Massachusetts) to the 1968 Housing Act, requiring that rents be capped at 25 percent (later increased to 30 percent) of income, made public housing more affordable but also diminished rental revenue. This, combined with decreasing government subsidies and increasing costs, resulted in lower maintenance. Several housing authorities abandoned some of their oldest and most troubled projects. The 1972 demolition of the Pruitt-Igoe project in Saint Louis, featuring a filmed and widely reproduced implosion of the tall, dreary, warehouse-like structures, became symbolic of the decline in public housing during this era.

In the early 1970s, President Richard M. Nixon's administration, citing housing scandals and budget problems due to inflation, imposed a moratorium on all federal housing programs. The administration argued that the federal government had become too deeply involved in directing housing and urban policy, and it proposed that the major housing programs be consolidated into a block grant to be provided to states and localities. Nixon further argued that the government should focus on increasing the income of the poor instead of expanding the supply of housing. In 1974, Congress passed the Housing and Community Development Act, which adopted most of the president's proposals. The act created the Community Development Block Grant program, which provided funds to states and localities, based on a complicated formula of population, poverty rate, and other criteria. Local governments are required to use these funds to produce housing and other vital services, but unlike the Model Cities program or other efforts of the Great Society, federal oversight is minimal.

The act also increased subsidies to low-income tenants through the Section 8 program. This program provides subsidies to local housing authorities that give poor families housing vouchers that can be used to find housing in the private market. Recipients pay 30 percent of their income for rent, and federal subsidies pay the difference between that amount and the fair market rent. Meant to increase the access of the poor to private housing, the program has replaced public housing as the major source of federal funding for shelter for the poor. Critics have argued that the program does not expand the supply of housing and has led to increased rents in existing housing.

President Jimmy Carter's administration increased funding to modernize aging public housing projects, and low-income housing starts hit their high point in the late 1970s. Carter also used the Housing and Community Development Act of 1977 to increase support for private development of affordable housing. The administration's urban agenda, released in 1978, argued that the federal government could not rebuild American cities and envisioned an expanding role for private enterprise. Budget pressures, however, inhibited the full implementation of these efforts.

Since 1980, federal support for affordable housing has witnessed a consistent decline. Federal expenditures for subsidized housing decreased from $31.5 billion in 1978 to $6 billion by 1989. The only significant initiatives in the decade were the passage of the Low Income Housing Tax Credit, which provided credits to those who invest in affordable housing, and the Stewart B. McKinney Homeless Assistance Act, passed in 1987, which provided funds to states and localities to produce housing for the homeless. These laws have supported the construction of several thousand units of affordable housing.

The 1990s witnessed a further shift in housing policy away from public-sector efforts to reliance on the private sector to produce affordable housing. Initiatives focused primarily on increasing opportunities for low-income people to become home owners. In 1990, Congress created the Housing Opportunities for People Everywhere (HOPE) program, which subsidizes the private construction of home ownership units. The HOPE program also provides funds to local public housing authorities to demolish aging projects and rehabilitate the remaining units, and it gives incentives to sell units to low-income buyers. However, no new public housing construction was funded in this program. This initiative supported the revitalization of many public housing developments, but it also resulted in the demolition of thousands of units of public housing.

In 2002, the congressionally created Millennial Housing Commission released the results of a two-year study of the nation's housing. Although the report celebrated the increasing percentage of home-owning households, the report concluded that housing remains unaffordable to millions of Americans.

Wendell E. Pritchett

See also: African American Migration; Homelessness; *How the Other Half Lives;* Public Works Administration; Racial Segregation; Racism; Tenant Organizing; Urban Renewal; U.S. Department of Housing and Urban Development

References and Further Reading

Bauer, Catherine. 1957. "The Dreary Deadlock of

Public Housing." *Architectural Forum* 106 (May): 140–142.

Bauman, John F., Roger Biles, and Kristin Szylvain, eds. 2000. *From Tenements to the Taylor Homes: In Search of an Urban Housing Policy in Twentieth Century America*. State College: Pennsylvania State University Press.

Boger, Jon, and Judith Wegner, eds. 1996. *Race, Poverty, and American Cities*. Chapel Hill: University of North Carolina Press.

Bratt, Rachel, Chester Hartman, and Ann Meyerson, eds. 1986. *Critical Perspectives on Housing*. Philadelphia: Temple University Press.

Chudacoff, Howard, and Judith Smith. 2001. *The Evolution of Urban Society*. Englewood Cliffs, NJ: Prentice-Hall.

Gelfand, Mark. 1975. *A Nation of Cities: The Federal Government and Urban America*. New York: Oxford University Press.

Hirsch, Arnold. 1983. *Making the Second Ghetto: Chicago, 1940–1960*. Cambridge: Cambridge University Press.

Hirsch, Arnold, and Raymond Mohl, eds. 1993. *Urban Policy in Twentieth Century America*. New Brunswick, NJ: Rutgers University Press.

Photojournalist Jacob Riis's* How the Other Half Lives *portrayed life in the slums of the Lower East Side, a life often scarred by crime, darkness, insecurity, danger, and poverty. Riis's work proved effective in the burgeoning movement for tenement reform. (Library of Congress)

How the Other Half Lives, *Jacob Riis*

In 1890, photographer and journalist Jacob Riis published a work that would open the eyes of his fellow New Yorkers to the abominable conditions under which three-quarters of that city's population were living. *How the Other Half Lives*, a combination of muckraking and photojournalism, portrayed the harshness of life in the slums of the Lower East Side, a life often scarred by crime, darkness, insecurity, danger, and, nearly always, poverty. Riis's specific reform focus, however, was on the physical conditions of the tenement buildings that had become the most widespread form of housing for the poor and working-class masses streaming into the cities in search of employment. Largely thanks to his work in this area, New York's Tenement House Commission was convened in 1884, and his continued struggle to make the better-off of the country see "how the other half lives" continued long after.

Riis's horror at the conditions in the tenements, his disgust at the corruption and greed that allowed landlords to profit so handsomely from the vulnerability of their tenants, and his simultaneous compassion for and critical attitude toward the largely immigrant population of New York's slums were based on his personal experience. Like the 300,000 people crowded into each square mile of the city's worst tenement districts, Riis had come to the United States as a poor immigrant, leaving his native Denmark in search of a livelihood and future. Unlike most of them, Riis did eventually climb out of abject poverty to claim gainful employment and a voice in the public debate about the conditions under which immigrant and other disenfranchised groups were forced to live. He began photographing these conditions—the tenement houses, stale beer halls, sweatshops, and back alleys that comprised the brutal world he had known since coming to America—while working as a police reporter for the *New York Tribune*. This work later formed the basis of *How the Other Half Lives*, known as much for its heartbreaking photographs as for its searing indictment of the New York slums.

The book does betray the prevalence of the racial stereotypes that the largely segregated immigrant communities of the day encountered at every turn. Riis depicted Chinatown as a den of immorality and opium, raising the specter of the "crafty Chinaman" seducing white women into a life of evil. Italians, he claimed disparagingly, were "content to live in a pig-sty" (Riis [1890] 1996, 123, 92). At the same time, Riis's photographs also played into—and helped foster—popular prejudices and stereotypes about the poor as abject, pathetic, slovenly, potentially dangerous, and, above all, alien or "other" in the eyes of his comparatively genteel, native-born white readership. Although presented as raw photojournalism, many of his photographs were staged, with lighting used to emphasize the drabness of living conditions as well as the darker skin tones of his subjects.

For all its sensationalism, however, Riis's documentary did prove effective in the burgeoning movement for tenement reform. In his book and in specially mounted exhibits of the photographs, Riis placed the great blame for the inhumane conditions at the feet of a neglectful government and a better-off citizenry that was in a position to demand reform. He proposed the construction of model tenements that would safely and adequately house the working classes in American cities at rates both profitable and fair. With such measures, he argued, immigrants' behavior and life chances, closely linked to their living environments, would improve, and all New Yorkers, rich and poor, could again begin to respect their city and themselves.

Rebecca K. Root

See also: Housing Policy; Immigrants and Immigration; Picturing Poverty (I); Tenant Organizing; Urban Poverty

References and Further Reading

Riis, Jacob. [1890] 1996. *How the Other Half Lives*. New York: Bedford Books.

———. 1902. *The Battle with the Slum*. New York: Macmillan.

Yochelson, Bonnie. 2001. *Jacob Riis*. London: Phaidon.

Hull House

Hull House was a settlement house located in Chicago's multiethnic West Side. It was founded by friends Ellen Gates Starr and Jane Addams in 1889, and many innovative approaches to supplying community-based social services to the urban poor were pioneered there. It stood at the forefront of the American settlement house movement, which by 1910 included over 400 neighborhood settlements nationwide. The settlements were a response to the dire needs created by rapid urbanization and industrialization in the late nineteenth century. Chief among these were the crises in urban housing, sanitation, and child mortality and the low pay rates and hazardous workplace health and safety conditions that working-class Europeans faced as they immigrated to find employment in U.S. factories and trades.

Hull House flourished until the Depression era and had an impact on many levels. As an experiment in communal living and a close-knit network of support for political activism and progressive ideas, the settlement attracted many talented women and men as residents and volunteers. Most were native born, middle class, and college educated, and many brought professional skills to bear on social problems. Tens of thousands of impoverished people of various ages and nationalities from the neighborhoods of the Nineteenth Ward actively participated in the multifaceted educational and cultural programs Hull House offered. Working-class activists and labor organizers also found in Hull House a friendly sponsor for their enterprises, and intellectuals from many countries visited the settlement. And as Hull House leaders had an increasingly high profile in public affairs, the influence of the settlement widened. It became a clearinghouse for many of the urban and social welfare reforms of the Progressive Era.

Under the prevailing vision of Jane Addams (1860–1935) and the many reformers and activists who were involved in the settlement over the years—including Florence Kelley, Julia Lathrop, Alice Hamilton, Sophonisba Breckinridge, Edith Abbott, Grace Abbott, Alzina Parsons Stevens, and Mary Kenney O'Sullivan—Hull House did much to advance the role of women in social welfare policy and to change public perceptions of poverty and ideas about the best means for its amelioration. Addams's copious popular writings, her leadership in national reform organizations, and her skill as a speaker were particularly effective in changing public opinion. Through her many books and articles (including, most famously, the best-seller *Twenty Years at Hull-House*), she helped encourage a shift in thinking from earlier Victorian models of charity and philanthropy, with their moral concepts of the "deserving" and "undeserving" poor. She also challenged the Social Darwinist notion that poverty was the inevitable result of individualized pathology and a highly stratified laissez-faire economy. She posited instead a new ethical paradigm that emphasized collective responsibility and social justice. In that new model, the causes of socioeconomic inequity were understood to be systemic, and it was ultimately the responsibility of a democratic government to address them. Hull House leaders also had a hand in drafting key pieces of social reform legislation on the state and federal levels. In instituting formal social services, they pushed for standardization and training, monitoring, and protective regulation. Their ideas, and the progressive policies they did much to engender, helped lay the foundation for the modern welfare state.

As the Hull House settlement grew in scope in the 1890s and early twentieth century, it attracted low-income women, men, and children, many of them Irish, Italian, Greek, Russian, Polish, or immigrants from other eastern European regions. Subsequent waves of migration brought Mexicans and some African Americans as well. They took part in myriad social programs and services that were designed to mitigate the suffering of the urban working poor; to lift the spirit, improve the body, and train the mind; and to provide for freedom of expression for political convictions and artistic abilities.

From its original building on Halsted Street, Hull House expanded over the next decades into a large multipurpose complex covering an entire city block. It was an extremely active place. It had a coffee house and a residents' dining room, theater space, gymnasium facilities, a dispensary, classrooms, baths, art studios, and meeting rooms for a variety of men's and women's, boys' and girls' clubs, workingmen's debate groups, and unions. It offered symposia, plays, and musical performances, which were open to the public and to community participation. Hull House leaders challenged city politicians. They lobbied for public art and public space, cleaner alleyways, and garbage removal. Neighborhood women enrolled in parenting, nutrition, home economics, and sewing and dressmaking classes. There was an excellent free kindergarten, day care, and afternoon recreation and arts programs for working parents' children, as well as field trips and summer school sessions that brought urban youth into museums and healthy rural landscapes. Women workers gathered in the Jane Club dormitory. Support for striking garment workers was planned from Hull House, and women bookbinders held their first union meetings under Hull House auspices. Ital-

Exterior view of Hull House. The founders of Hull House were Jane Addams, internationally known social worker, and Ellen Gates Starr. (Bettmann/Corbis)

ian girls and Mexican men studied English, civics, and citizenship with Hull House tutors. Pottery was fired in Hull House kilns. Children could read books in the reading room, an annex of the public library, and tenement mothers could check art prints from Hull House out on loan or get help with an ailing baby. Demonstrations of traditional arts and crafts in the settlement's Labor Museum, art appreciation courses, and art workshops were designed—in keeping with the Christian Socialist ideas of John Ruskin, William Morris, and others—to offer transcendence and to counteract the brutalizing and demoralizing effects of industrialization and assembly-line manufacture.

In developing all these programs and facilities, Hull House leaders built on the precedent of preexisting neighborhood benevolent associations, progressive churches, women's clubs, workingwomen's organizations, and activist groups such as the Illinois Woman's Alliance. From the beginning, their concern was directed at all the working poor, but they were especially attuned, in a maternalist fashion, to championing the plight of women and children. The first major Hull House program was a kindergarten, and well-baby workshops became a regular feature. Many of the efforts of Hull House activists were directed at curbing child labor and limiting the working hours of women. They also advocated unionization for women (who were then largely excluded from the trade unions that represented men in skilled positions) and a fair or living wage. Their unflagging support for protective labor legislation sometimes put them at odds with the very workingwomen they sought to help, since factory women viewed these measures as limitations upon their right to work and to serve the immediate needs of their families. Patrician attitudes toward vice, leisure, alcohol consumption, and the sex industry also brought Hull House activists into conflict with working-class mores. Despite real changes in visions of poverty, many Hull House reforms involved the imposition of middle-class values upon working-class people. In addition, ethnic women were largely excluded from pathways to leadership within the settlement house and from its higher policymaking echelons.

In developing tools to combat poverty, Hull House residents were in the forefront in the use of new techniques in social science research as well as in the establishment of the fields of social work, occupational health and safety, and workplace inspection. *Hull-House Maps and Papers* (1895), a collaborative work by early residents of Hull House, was a landmark publication and the first of many social survey studies that would be conducted in the Nineteenth Ward. Residents and their students conducted house-to-house censuses, casework, and field observations to assemble data that demonstrated variety and trends in ethnicity, occupation, health, languages, skills, and residential patterns among the area's poor. This data was in turn used as evidence of the need for remedial action.

Of importance also was the role of many Hull House activists as public administrators and as founders and leaders of major social change organizations—including the Women's Trade Union League (WTUL), the National Consumers League (NCL), the National Committee on Child Labor, the National Association for the Advancement of Colored People, and the Progressive Party—as well as their part in shaping some of the key developments in social welfare policy and public health. Hull House resident Florence Kelley became the first chief factory inspector of Illinois and was later head of the NCL. Child welfare advocate Julia Lathrop inspected county-run institutions for the mentally ill, orphaned, homeless, and sick in Illinois and helped found the Chicago Juvenile Court before she became the first director of the U.S. Children's Bureau in 1911. Lathrop drafted the Sheppard-Towner Infancy and Maternity Protection Act (passed in 1921), and her friend Grace Abbott did much to implement it. Abbott in turn helped shape the Social Security Act of 1935, especially the Aid to Dependent Children, and was also a backer of the Fair Labor Standards Act (1938). Many of these reformers' long dedication to the ideas of regulated protection of women and of women's special vulnerability to impoverishment led them to oppose fellow feminists in their campaign for an Equal Rights Amendment. Meanwhile, in Chicago, physician Alice Hamilton pioneered the study of infectious and industrial diseases among the poor, especially the toxic effects of what she termed the "dangerous" trades. Sophonisba Breckinridge and her close colleague Edith Abbott founded the School of Social Service Administration at the University of Chicago and the influential *Social Service Review*.

Many of the functions of Hull House were supplanted in time by the professionalization of social work, new realities in fund-raising, and the operation of government agencies. Almost all of the original Hull House complex was demolished with the construction of the campus of the University of Illinois at Chicago. The original Hull House building on Halsted Street was preserved and is now a university-run museum, with exhibitions, conferences, and programs. The Jane Addams Hull-House Association continues to function as a community-based social service agency in the Chicago area, now serving a primarily African American clientele.

Barbara Bair

See also: Child Labor; Child Welfare; Employment and Training; *Hull-House Maps and Papers;* Immigrants and Immigration; Juvenile Delinquency;

Maternalist Policy; Progressive Era and 1920s; *Social Service Review;* Social Work; Trade/Industrial Unions; *Twenty Years at Hull-House;* Urban Poverty

References and Further Reading

Addams, Jane. [1910] 1999. *Twenty Years at Hull-House*. Edited with an introduction by Victoria Bissell Brown. Boston: Bedford/St. Martin's Press.

Bryan, Mary Lynn McCree, and Allen Davis, eds. 1990. *One Hundred Years at Hull-House*. Bloomington: Indiana University Press.

Hull House, Residents of. [1895] 1970. *Hull-House Maps and Papers*. New York: Arno Press.

Jane Addams Hull-House Association, Chicago. Web site. http://www.hullhouse.org/.

Jane Addams Hull-House Museum. "Urban Experience in Chicago: Hull-House and Its Neighborhoods, 1889–1963."

Johnson, Mary Ann, ed. 1989. *The Many Faces of Hull-House: The Photographs of Wallace Kirkland*. Urbana: University of Illinois Press.

Schultz, Rima Lunin, and Adele Hast, eds. 2001. *Women Building Chicago, 1790–1990: A Biographical Dictionary*. Bloomington: Indiana University Press.

Hull-House Maps and Papers

Hull-House Maps and Papers (HHMP) was a groundbreaking text published in 1895 by the residents of Hull House, led by Jane Addams and Florence Kelley. They described and measured group patterns associated with immigrants, working conditions, specific laborers, labor unions, social settlements, and the function of art in the community. Women's moral agency was central to their use of social science to improve democracy and the lives of the disenfranchised.

Charles Booth's seventeen-volume study *Life and Labour of the People in London* (1892–1902) served as the model for *HHMP. HHMP,* in turn, became the model for studies of African American communities. Isabel Eaton, a young Quaker who had published a chapter in *HHMP,* helped make this connection through her association with W. E. B. Du Bois on *The Philadelphia Negro* (1899). Other African American scholar-activists, notably Monroe Work and Richard R. Wright Jr., were inspired by this latter book to map life in other African American communities.

Hull House residents continued to map cultural, social, political, and demographic information in their neighborhood for the next forty years. As the neighborhood was increasingly studied (for example, by occupations, family size, housing, milk quality, food use, and epidemiology), the findings were charted and hung on the walls of Hull House for the neighbors to see and discuss.

The mapping of social and demographic characteristics of a population within a geographical area became the core methodology of sociologists at the University of Chicago during the 1920s and 1930s. Acknowledgment that this methodological technique was associated with Hull House residents is singularly lacking in academic sociology. The Hull House residents' empirical studies also helped establish the major topics for academic sociology from the 1890s until the present.

The use of mapping by Hull House residents was radically different from its scholarly use by white male sociologists of the Chicago school. The academics' maps revealed the lives of the people of the neighborhood to an audience of experts and decision makers. The Hull House maps revealed to the people of the neighborhood that their lifestyles had patterns and implications that could be used to make more-informed decisions about community issues and interests. Repeatedly, the Hull House residents and neighbors initiated major social changes as a result of this information; for example, they worked to establish the eight-hour day, the minimum wage, and the elimination of child labor. They also worked in numerous social movements, for labor unions, women's suffrage, and arts and crafts.

Mary Jo Deegan

See also: Hull House; Poverty Research; Settlement Houses

References and Further Reading

Booth, Charles. 1892–1902. *The Life and Labour of the People in London*. 17 vols. London: Macmillan.

Deegan, Mary Jo. 1988. *Jane Addams and the Men of the Chicago School, 1892–1920*. New Brunswick, NJ: Transaction Books.

———. 2002. *Race, Hull-House, and the University of Chicago*. Westport, CT: Praeger.

Du Bois, W. E. B. [1899] 1967. *The Philadelphia Negro: A Social Study. Together with a Special Report on Domestic Service by Isabel Eaton*. New York: Benjamin Blom.

Hull House, Residents of. 1895. *Hull-House Maps and Papers*. New York: Crowell.

Hunger

Hunger is the cutting edge of poverty, its most urgent and immediate hardship. An observer impressed with the obvious abundance and widespread waste that characterize the American food system might easily assume that hunger is rare in the overnourished United States. In fact, however, because official poverty income thresholds are derived from the cost of a minimally adequate diet, virtually all households with incomes below or near the poverty thresholds are at risk of hunger unless they are receiving significant food assistance. A long dispute over the measurement, and indeed the measurability, of hunger in America has been substantially resolved in the last decade with the creation of the Household Food Security Survey administered annually by the Economic Research Service of the U.S. Department of Agriculture. The most recent such survey found 33.6 million Americans living in food-insecure households; about a third of these were categorized as "food-insecure with hunger." Although hunger-related programs are on the whole less controversial than welfare and are therefore less visible to the general public, hunger has elicited relatively large investments by governments at the federal, state, and local levels. More than a dozen federal programs currently address hunger, and hunger-specific outlays are a sizable portion of overall antipoverty expenditures. In 1996, for example, the last year that the Aid to Families with Dependent Children (AFDC) program provided an entitlement to cash assistance for dependent children and their caregivers, federal outlays for food assistance programs totaled about one and a half times the combined federal and state expenditures for AFDC. In fact, food stamp spending alone exceeded AFDC spending by several billion dollars. Hunger has also evoked extensive activity in the voluntary sector; it has prompted the creation of an extensive network of private charitable food assistance programs and has become a primary focus of both policy advocacy and grassroots organizing. In short, hunger in America is a significant social issue with its own set of institutions, organizations, measurements, activities, and public policies, a separate sphere within the larger arena of poverty.

Hunger has always been a part of the American experience. Game shortages and crop failures plagued Native American civilizations, and severe deprivation troubled the early settlements of European colonists. Colonial poor laws, following the English model, set amounts of relief in terms of the cost of food and fuel or provided these items directly, in kind. Municipal soup houses appeared in the coastal cities of the new republic, supplied in part from the stores of the almshouses. But hunger did not become a public issue, an outrage and a scandal, until the abundance of American agriculture and the malfunctions of the market made the means for the relief of hunger obvious to all. During the Great Depression of the 1930s, enormous farm surpluses threatened the profitability of agriculture and placed the issue of hunger firmly in the context of waste and overproduction: the paradox of want amid plenty. The contradiction became irresistible and resulted in public action when large food surpluses accumulated in government hands.

Under the early Depression-era administration of President Herbert Hoover, huge purchases of wheat by the Federal Farm Board failed to stem the downward spiral of grain prices but succeeded in evoking impassioned pleas for release of the wheat to feed the unemployed. Eventually, Congress donated millions of bushels of Farm Board wheat to the Red Cross for relief. In the early years of the New Deal, the threat of bumper crops in the cotton and corn-hog markets led to dramatic efforts by the Agricultural Adjustment Administration to forestall price-depressing surpluses by plowing under standing cotton and slaughtering millions of unripe piglets. The resulting waste evoked a public outcry that was quieted only by the creation of a high-profile alphabet agency—as the major relief agencies came to be known—charged with "resolving the paradox of want amid plenty" by purchasing farmer's surpluses and distributing them to people on relief (Poppendieck 1986, xii). The Federal Surplus Relief Corporation and its successor, the Federal Surplus Commodities Corporation, pioneered the nation's food assistance programs: surplus commodity distribution, food stamps, and school meals. Little effort was made, however, to establish minimum standards for the food programs; with the problem defined as the "paradox of want amid waste," the programs were doing their job if some of the food that would otherwise go to waste reached some of the people who would otherwise go hungry. Meanwhile, the donation of foods that had been removed from the market in order to help support prices became an essential tool in the management of farm income.

When World War II eclipsed the relief activities of the New Deal, hunger slipped from public view. The food assistance activities of the alphabet agencies were quietly transferred to the Department of Agriculture. As war eliminated the surpluses, food distribution activities were cut back, and costs were transferred to the state and county governments. The popular food stamp program was terminated altogether, and county participation in commodity distribution was made a local option. In food assistance, the legacy of New Deal policy and politics was a set of programs administered by the Department of Agriculture, overseen by the Agriculture Committees of the Congress, and not available at all in many of the nation's poorest counties. Even when a food stamp program was re-created in the early 1960s at the insistence of President John F. Kennedy, it was severely constrained by the agricultural establishment's prioritizing of farm-income enhancement.

Hunger became an issue once again in the late 1960s, but this time, in the aftermath of the civil rights movement, hunger was defined as a failure of the federal government to protect the rights of poor and hungry Americans. A dramatic "rediscovery" of hunger occurred when a team of U.S. senators took a tour of the back roads of the Mississippi Delta, where they encountered hunger in its starkest and most visible forms. Hunger was on the nightly news. A Physicians Task Force dispatched to Mississippi by the Field Foundation confirmed the senators' reports. Almost overnight, hunger became a national issue, and a series of high-profile investigations was undertaken, revealing a food assistance safety net full of holes. Food programs reached far too few of those in need, they provided far too little assistance to those they reached, and they failed to embody standards of equity or protect basic rights of participants.

In the wake of these revelations, a process of expansion and reform was undertaken that gradually undid the New Deal legacy and created rights to food assistance. Food stamps were extended to every county in the nation. Eligibility and benefit levels were linked to a standard, albeit meager, of nutritional adequacy and were made uniform across the nation. The purchase requirement was eliminated so that the stamps were distributed free of charge, making food stamps an entitlement. The School Breakfast, Special Supplemental Nutrition for Women, Infants, and Children (WIC), and Child Care Feeding programs were created. The School Lunch and Summer Food Service programs were expanded. Administration remained in the Department of Agriculture, but the programs were transferred from the old agricultural marketing agencies to a new office focused on the needs of consumers. In Congress, first the Senate and later the House created select committees dealing with hunger, food, and nutrition. Federal spending on food assistance grew dramatically.

The transformation of federal food assistance was at once a product of the efforts of a network of skilled advocates and a spur to its expansion and institutionalization. In Washington, the Food Research and Action Center, the Community Nutrition Institute, the Children's Foundation, Bread for the World, and the Center for Budget and Policy Priorities conducted research and public education, collaborated with members of Congress and their staffs, filed class-action suits against the Department of Agriculture and recalcitrant county and municipal governments, lobbied for legislation, mobilized pressure from the grassroots, and made full and effective use of opportunities for participation in the federal rule-making process that shaped implementation of the programs. Labeled the "antihunger network" or the "hunger lobby," these national-level advocacy groups and their affiliates in state and local hunger coalitions and academic institutes and centers kept hunger on the congressional agenda and on the desks of public officials. By the end of the 1970s, advocates were looking forward to an end to hunger in America, and a new investigation by the Physicians Task Force revealed substantial progress toward that goal.

Hopes for victory over hunger proved short lived, however, as the election of Ronald Reagan brought a significant cutback in federal programs assisting low-income people in the midst of a severe recession. One result was a marked increase in the number of people seeking help from local food shelves and food pantries, mostly small, informal operations run by churches, civic associations, and labor unions. Meanwhile, the spread of homelessness generated rising demand for meals at soup kitchens. When the mayors of several large cities, caught between declining revenues and escalating needs, began talking about a "hunger emergency," the concept caught on, and new "emergency food providers"—soup kitchens and food pantries—began springing up in large numbers. Hunger became a public issue once again, but this time the prevailing discourse defined it as an "emergency," a temporary aberration that would soon subside. Once again an agricultural surplus, this time of dairy products, prompted large-scale federal donations, inciting the establishment of yet another round of pantries to handle the cheese distributions. The creation of new pantries and kitchens was further facilitated by the development of food banking, the creation of large warehouse-style food storage operations that receive food donations from both government sources and the private grocery industry and then redistribute them to frontline providers. Food banking was quickly supplemented by food rescue, the process of collecting and distributing prepared foods donated by school, hospital, and government cafeterias, restaurants, hotels, and food vendors at sporting and other public events. Within a decade, an extensive and well-organized charitable food network had emerged, led by America's Second Harvest on the food-banking side and Food Chain for food rescue and claiming more than 50,000 affiliated organizations and agencies. In 2001, Food Chain and America's Second Harvest merged into a single national organization.

The proliferation of emergency food programs provided many well-fed Americans with easy and convenient ways to do something about hunger. Walkathons and canned-good drives became common; churches, synagogues, and temples of all faiths established food donation opportunities embedded in religious ritual and practice. Boy Scouts and letter carriers undertook large-scale national food drives. A donated can of food became part of the price of admission to everything from rock concerts to presidential inaugural balls. All of this activity, however, may have served to obscure the reduction of entitlements to food through public programs—serious cutbacks in both child nutrition and food stamp programs, culminating in the massive reductions in food stamp eligibility and benefits that were part of the 1996 Personal Responsibility and Work Opportunities Reconciliation Act (welfare reform). As the end of welfare was implemented, local kitchens and pantries across the nation began reporting increases in demand despite an improving economy. The arrival of recession accelerated this process, leaving the emergency food system counting numbers of people turned away empty-handed in addition to numbers of people supplied with aid. Projected local, state, and federal budget deficits have the charitable food sector bracing for another escalation of need. The emergency definition has faded as programs have aged and institutionalized, but the private, charitable model continues to dominate public perceptions: hunger as an opportunity for private virtue rather than hunger as a symptom of public policy failure.

This balance may be shifting once again, however, as charitable food providers themselves become integrated into the policy advocacy project through collaboration among the major national organizations active in both arenas. Increasingly, food pantry and soup kitchen personnel are being enlisted to bring their expertise and credibility to bear on public policy issues. It remains to be seen whether the potential for a social movement to demand a real end to hunger in America, long the dream of antihunger activists, will be realized. It seems fairly certain, however, that antihunger activism, and thus the hunger issue, will continue to play an important role in the politics of poverty in America.

Janet E. Poppendieck

See also: Antihunger Coalitions; Center on Budget and Policy Priorities; Charity; Citizens' Crusade against Poverty (CCAP); Economic Depression; Food Banks; Food Stamps; Homelessness; New Deal Farm Policy; Nutrition and Food Assistance; Poverty Law; Welfare Policy/Welfare Reform

References and Further Reading

Berry, Jeffrey. 1984. *Feeding Hungry People*. New Brunswick, NJ: Rutgers University Press.

Eisinger, Peter. 1998. *Toward an End to Hunger in America*. Washington, DC: Brookings Institution.

Kotz, Nick. 1969. *Let Them Eat Promises: The Politics of Hunger in America*. Englewood Cliffs, NJ: Prentice-Hall.

Maney, Ardith. 1989. *Still Hungry after All These Years: Food Assistance Policy from Kennedy to Reagan*. New York: Greenwood Press.

Nord, Mark, Margaret Andrews, and Steven Carlson. 2002. *Household Food Security in the United States, 2001*. Washington, DC: U.S. Department of Agriculture.

Poppendieck, Janet. 1986. *Breadlines Knee Deep in Wheat: Food Assistance in the Great Depression*. New Brunswick, NJ: Rutgers University Press.

———. 1998. *Sweet Charity? Emergency Food and the End of Entitlement*. New York: Viking.

Riches, Graham, ed. 1997. *First World Hunger: Food Security and Welfare Politics*. New York: St. Martin's Press.

Schwartz-Nobel, Loretta. 2002. *Growing Up Empty: The Hunger Epidemic in America*. New York: HarperCollins.

Hunter, Robert

See Poverty, Statistical Measure of; *Poverty*; Poverty Line; Poverty Research

Immigrants and Immigration

The vast majority of immigrants entering the United States during the last two centuries left their home countries because of poverty and continued to live in poverty long after their arrival in the United States. Poor immigrants, arriving in the United States from nearly every country in the world, have brought with them a diversity of racial identities, work experiences, levels of education, and expectations of life in their new home. These factors, combined with the timing and place of arrival of an immigrant group, have shaped—and often hindered—immigrants' placement in the economy and social life of the United States.

In spite of the diverse profiles of different immigrant groups and the differing circumstances of their arrival and integration into U.S. society, there are important similarities among immigrant groups' strategies for dealing with poverty. From Germans and Scots in the mid-nineteenth century to Dominicans and Albanians in the twenty-first century, immigrants have quickly established both formal and informal networks to help more-recent arrivals find housing and employment. In addition, immigrant groups have organized mutual benefit societies to provide social and economic support to members during hard times following a death in the family, the onset of disability, or the loss of a job. Outside of immigrant communities, the institutions available to recent immigrants have varied, sometimes speeding and sometimes deterring immigrant groups' incorporation into the polity and the economy. During the century before World War II, for example, local machine politicians promised certain immigrant groups patronage jobs and other forms of economic and social protection in exchange for electoral support, in effect offering politics as a path to assimilation and mobility for individuals in those groups. Likewise during this period, unions offered membership to workers from some immigrant groups while excluding those from others, in effect improving the wages and job security for workers from some immigrant groups while also nurturing leadership among them.

Poor immigrants' single most important resource upon arrival in the United States has always been other immigrants—typically members of the same national group, often friends or relatives of the new arrivals—who can offer temporary housing, assistance with finding housing, and contacts for seeking employment. Building on such informal networks, immigrants since the nineteenth century have settled in communities that frequently become known by the name of the group's country of origin. San Francisco's Chinatown, Philadelphia's Germantown, and New York's Little Italy were all well-established neighborhoods by 1900; more recently—and especially since the opening up of immigration laws in 1965—communities called "Little India," "Little Odessa," and "*El Barrio*" have made a permanent mark on the maps of many American cities. In such communities, poor immigrants can pool resources for housing, share information about jobs, provide a ready market for entrepreneurs in the community who provide goods from the home country, and function without needing to speak English.

One of the most enduring strategies of immigrants facing marginalization in the U.S. economy is the development of an "immigrant enclave" or an "ethnic niche" in the larger local economy. Long before these terms were coined by postwar social scientists, entrepreneurial members of different national groups, usually motivated by discrimination in the primary labor sector, fought to gain an economic foothold in the United States by starting their own businesses. Seeking out a gap to fill in the local economy, entrepreneurial immigrants would hire compatriots to work in their business and would help finance the entry of friends and family into the same business. The example of Chinese immigrants' participation in the laundry industry highlights the historic origins of some stereotypes about immigrants in the labor market: Even in the early twentieth century, the majority of Chinese workers listed in New York's manuscript census reported that they worked in laundries. More recently, a variety of other immigrant groups have forged enduring and often-prosperous ties to particular industries, creating new ethnic niches (and new stereotypes): Indians in the motel industry, Pakistanis in the mini-mart industry, Koreans and Dominicans in the corner-grocery industry. However, most immigrants in the United States have not managed to acquire their own businesses. Even among those groups that have established an economic enclave—such as the Chinese laundry or the Indian motel—the majority of individuals work for wages, many outside of the relatively protected niche established by a few of their compatriots. In addition to the classic model of the small business ethnic niche, certain immigrant groups have achieved predominance in certain industries, not as owners but as workers, sometimes to the point that stereotypes arise associating the group with a particular sector of the economy. The mid-nineteenth century, for instance, had the stereotype of the Irish maid; in the early twentieth century, the garment industry in New York City was populated mostly by Jewish and then Puerto Rican women, and many midwestern steelworkers and meatpackers were immigrants from Poland or elsewhere in eastern Europe; and throughout the twentieth century, "farmhands" were stereotypically Mexican.

Immigrants who arrive in the United States as single men or women have only their own fortunes to consider when looking for work; without dependents, a period of unemployment or a layoff may be difficult but is not disastrous. For poor immigrant families, however, loss of wages, especially those of a primary wage earner, could be perilous for the health and well-being of the family, especially its children. For these immigrants, then—indeed, for all families living on the brink of poverty—the "family economy" is key to survival. In the past, when it was less common for women with children to work outside the home (and still today, among some immigrant groups for whom it is the norm for women to stay home with children), women found ways to generate income while staying at home. Taking in boarders is one way that women managed to add to the family income without working outside the home. Even in tiny apartments already bursting with the activities of many children and perhaps additional members of an extended family, women would set aside a room—most often the more private and formal front room of a tenement apartment, for instance—to rent to one or more boarders, usually members of the same immigrant group. For the price of a week's or a month's rent, a woman would pro-

Hungarian immigrant family hoeing beets in Corunna, Michigan, 1917. Many immigrants entering the United States during the past two centuries left their home countries because of poverty and continued to live in poverty long after their arrival in the United States. (Library of Congress)

vide a certain number of meals for the boarder, cooking in a kitchen that often had become a bedroom and living room for her family in order to make way for the renter.

Taking in sewing or embroidery piecework is another way that many immigrant women—from Russian Jews in the nineteenth century to Puerto Ricans in the 1950s and 1960s—earned an income from home. Women would accept sewing work, paid by the piece, as private subcontractors to small-scale clothing manufacturers or distributors of crocheted and embroidered handiwork, providing these businesses with low-cost, off-site labor. They were paid very poorly for their work, but the benefit was that women could work for wages while caring for children at home and could often count on children (especially girls) to do some of the piecework as well.

Children have, throughout time, contributed in various ways to the family economy. In the late nineteenth and early twentieth centuries in New York's teeming immigrant neighborhoods, children would be charged with going out each day to collect wood scraps and discarded bits of coal for cooking and heating their families' apartments. Sometimes children also peddled goods such as fruit or other items that they would purchase and resell on the street for a small profit.

Increasingly throughout the twentieth century, and especially during and after World War II, some immigrant women with children were enticed into the labor force by higher wages and the promise of job security, primarily taking jobs in factories but also taking service jobs in department stores, laundries, hospitals, and restaurants. Women developed informal child care networks in their communities in order to manage their lives as workers and as parents. Women who worked outside the home would arrange to have a family member, friend, or neighbor look after their children, paying in cash or in kind (food or clothing for instance, if the woman worked in a restaurant or a shop).

Poor immigrant workers throughout American history have weathered the insecurities of work in the formal economy—layoffs, periods of unemployment during economic downturns, and a general marginalization that relegates them to the secondary workforce—in part through participation in various sectors of the informal economy. At the turn of the twentieth century in New York City's immigrant-populated Five Points district, vendors plied their wares on sidewalks and streets in their native languages and in heavily accented English, hoping to earn enough to pay the rent. All across New York at the turn of the twenty-first century, immigrant vendors engage in similar occupations, some formally licensed by the city and others—those who pack up their goods and flee at the sight of a police officer—unlicensed. So-called Gypsy cab drivers (drivers of unlicensed cabs), nearly all of them immigrants, occupy another prominent place in New York's modern informal economy. On the other side of the law, some immigrants have also participated in a variety of criminal activities as an economic survival strategy. In Harlem in the 1920s and 1930s, for instance, immigrants from Jamaica, Barbados, and other parts of the anglophone Caribbean vied with Puerto Ricans, Italians, and African Americans for a place in the lucrative numbers racket. Immigrants from all corners of the world—Russia, Italy, China, the Dominican Republic—have been implicated, at various times since the nineteenth century, in drug-dealing rings and other criminal operations within the context of highly structured gangs (now commonly referred to by the Italian-origin term "Mafia") organized on the basis of national origins, although frequently different Mafias have cooperated across national-group lines. By about 1880, a number of Chinese gangs, or "fighting tongs," had sprung up in Chinese immigrant communities in California and New York City, revolving around the business of illegal gambling and opium importation. At about the same time, Italian gangs dealing in extortion, bootlegging, and other illegal businesses laid the foundation for the infamous Italian Mafia in the United States.

The majority of immigrants, however, have sought out legal, community-based forms of organization to weather the strains of poverty. Since the nineteenth century, immigrants in the United States (and nonimmigrants as well) have organized mutual benefit societies as a source of economic security. Structured around the simple idea of pooling members' resources through a small weekly or monthly contribution, such societies provide members with a system of informal insurance against the financial strains of illness, accident, or death of a wage earner. Such societies often served the additional function of cultural guardianship, adorning themselves with names that reflected a spirit of patriotism or nostalgia for the homeland, such as the Hijos de Borinquen (Sons of Puerto Rico), or the Association of the Sons of Poland. Some mutual benefit societies were organized, like guilds, around a particular trade or occupation, and some recruited members from a particular town or region of the home country; others were more inclusive. Many immigrant mutual benefit societies, particularly those operating in the nineteenth and early twentieth centuries, did not permit women to join or required women to participate through a "women's auxiliary" branch whose activities were often limited to the social functions of the organization. Women would organize benefit dances and concerts, for instance. Women's subordination in these immigrant organizations reflected their general subordination in public life. Moreover, because men tended to be the primary or sole breadwinners in this era, it was they who held the responsibility of organizing financial security. The institution of the mutual benefit society persisted among immigrant communities even after New Deal social welfare legislation created an economic safety net for legal immigrants and U.S. citizens alike.

For certain immigrants arriving in the United States before the mid-1920s (when laws restricting immigration dramatically reduced the number of new immigrants entering the country), another key strategy of economic survival was incorporation into local machine politics. Democratic machine politicians in New York City brokered the first enduring alliance with an ethnic group with Irish immigrants in the 1830s and 1840s. Naturalized immigrants gave their votes to local political bosses in exchange for patronage jobs, Christmas turkeys, and the assurance of regular police protection and garbage pickup. As the origins of immigrants began to shift to eastern and southern Europe during the late nineteenth century, machine politicians differentiated electoral rewards available to different immigrant groups. Whereas patronage jobs and party positions were extended to many Irish immigrants, for example, local machines tended to offer only services—sanitation, kerosene, the holiday turkey—to Slavic and Italian immigrants. Despite differences in the relationships among immigrant groups and local political machines, for more than a century the boss-immigrant relationship was a powerful source of economic security for European immigrants in cities like Boston, Chicago, and New York.

Beginning in the twentieth century, unions were another crucial source of both political incorporation and economic security for some immigrants. The craft-based American Federation of Labor discriminated against immigrants from southern and eastern Europe and campaigned for the exclusion of the Chinese and other Asians. But during the early decades of the twentieth century, emerging industrial unions in coal, steel, and textiles organized some southern and eastern European workers; during the 1930s, the Congress of Industrial Organizations (CIO) gained significant power from immigrant and second-generation membership in these unions as well as in the unions of newly organizing sectors, such as auto manufacture. However, the economic benefits and protections of unionization were not readily available to all immigrants even after the rise of the CIO. Unions were weak or did not form in the sectors in which many Puerto Rican, Mexican, and Asian workers were employed: in agriculture and service work before the 1960s and in domestic work today. Where unions did exist, race discrimination often resulted in the exclusion of many Latina/o and Asian immigrants, as well as of U.S.-born Blacks, in the decades prior to enactment of the Civil Rights Act. More recent immigrants from Asia and Latin America have not been incorporated or assisted by unions due to the overall decline of union organization and to antiunion federal policies.

For immigrants who arrived in the United States after the liberalization of immigration law in 1965, the welfare state provided a safety net that had not existed for previous generations of immigrants. Available to documented immigrants, though sometimes only after a period of years, many programs of the welfare state attenuated some of the effects of low wage, nonunion work. However, the public charge provision of immigration law impedes immigrants' access to the public assistance programs of the welfare state. Moreover, late-twentieth-century federal immigration and welfare reforms, along with California's effort to restrict immigrants' access to certain health and welfare services, have foreclosed participation by many recent immigrants in such key poverty-mitigating programs of the welfare state as food stamps and Temporary Assistance for Needy Families (formerly Aid to Families with Dependent Children).

At the dawn of the twenty-first century, immigrants in the increasingly globalized U.S. economy have developed some new strategies for dealing with poverty and economic strain. For immigrants entering the United States after 1965, the advent of relatively inexpensive transportation and communication technologies, among other factors, has allowed migrants to retain more-continuous transnational ties to their home countries. The transnational linkages maintained by many of today's immigrants can help them deal with poverty by, for instance, facilitating their return to the home country during economic downturns in the United States (at least to the extent permitted by immigration and naturalization policy). Although the novelty of transnational experiences among immigrants is open to question—previous immigrants also retained ties to their homelands and often engaged in "circular migration," that is, migration back and forth between their homelands and the United States—and while globalization exacts a harsh price from poor immigrants in the United States and elsewhere, today's immigrants are creatively adapting technology and globalizing culture to soldier on, working toward a better future for their children in spite of their poverty.

Lorrin R. Thomas

See also: Asian Americans; Asian Law Caucus/Asian Law Alliance; Citizenship; Domestic Work; Immigration Policy; Informal Economy; Latino/as; Mutual Aid; Puerto Rican Migration; Social Security Act of 1935; Trade/Industrial Unions; Welfare Policy/Welfare Reform

References and Further Reading

Bodnar, John. 1985. *The Transplanted: A History of Immigrants in Urban America*. Bloomington: Indiana University Press.

Foner, Nancy. 2001. *New Immigrants of New York*. New York: Columbia University Press.

Handlin, Oscar. 1959. *Boston's Immigrants*. Cambridge, MA: Harvard University Press.

Morawska, Ewa. 1985. *For Bread with Butter: The Life-Worlds of East Central Europeans in Johnstown, Pennsylvania, 1890–1940*. New York: Cambridge University Press.

Ortiz, Altagracia, ed. 1996. *Puerto Rican Women and Work: Bridges in Transnational Labor*. Philadelphia: Temple University Press.

Sanchez, George. 1993. *Becoming Mexican-American: Ethnicity, Culture, and Identity in Chicano Los Angeles, 1900–1945*. New York: Oxford University Press.

Takaki, Ronald. 1989. *Strangers from a Different Shore: A History of Asian Americans*. Boston: Little, Brown.

Immigration Policy

Federal and state policies regulating the status and rights of immigrants have had a tremendous impact on the lives and livelihoods of immigrants—especially poor and nonwhite immigrants—in the United States. Many of these laws, implemented during more than two centuries of immigration to the United States, have curtailed immigrants' economic rights and social welfare; many have been motivated by racism or by a more general nativism. The first policy regulating immigrants in the United States was enacted by Congress in 1790, limiting naturalized citizenship to "free white persons" only. The Treaty of Guadalupe Hidalgo in 1848 moderated the impact of the 1790 law on some Mexicans, and following the Civil War, the Naturalization Law of 1870 permitted naturalization of Africans. But naturalization restrictions continued to bar from citizenship nonwhite groups for whom specific exception was not made—primarily Asians—until the 1940s, when geopolitical concerns began to prompt changes. During the late 1940s, certain Chinese were permitted to naturalize; then, in a comprehensive policy reversal in 1952, the McCarran-Walter Act lifted the racial bar to naturalized citizenship.

Naturalization policy was the primary immigration policy until the second half of the nineteenth century. In 1855, a naturalization law granted automatic naturalization to immigrant women who married male citizens and automatically conferred citizenship on children born abroad to male citizens. During the Civil War, Congress adopted the first federal policy affecting the admission of foreign-born people to the United States when it enacted the Act to Encourage Immigration. A wartime measure to beef up the labor supply, this was the first and last liberal immigration measure for a century.

Beginning in the 1870s, under pressure from popular agitation, Congress legislated restrictions on the entry of people it considered "undesirable" and "unassimilable." In 1875, the Page Law prohibited the entry of Chinese "prostitutes"—a term deployed to choke off the immigration of Chinese women who were not married before they arrived. In 1882, the Chinese Exclusion Act ended the immigration of most Chinese, especially laborers. Responding to nativist opposition to immigration from eastern and southern Europe, in 1884 the Foran Act barred the immigration of contract laborers—that is, of southern and eastern Europeans whom steamship companies and heavy industry had recruited to immigrate with promises of employment and housing. In 1908, the so-called Gentleman's Agreement with Japan curbed the migration of Japanese workers, and in 1917, the Asiatic Barred Zone Act stiffened anti-Asian restrictions on immigration. In 1921, and then again in 1924, the National Origins Act ended Japanese immigration altogether and set tight quotas on the entry of immigrants from ethnic and nationality groups based on those groups' percentage of the U.S. population in 1890, when the numbers of eastern and southern Europeans had not reached their high point.

Naturalization law continued to reinforce the racist nativism of developing immigration policy. The 1907 naturalization law revoked the citizenship of U.S.-born women who married aliens, even if they never left U.S. soil. The 1922 Cable Act repealed this provision, but only for U.S. citizen women who married men from countries whose subjects were eligible for citizenship. U.S. women who married "aliens ineligible for citizenship" (67 Public Law 346)—namely, Asian men—lost their U.S. citizenship. The National Origins Act compounded these disabilities by forbidding Asian immigrant men who already were in the United States from bringing their wives to join them. Naturalization measures had a particularly acute effect on family formation, in turn constraining the development of "family economies" for some Asian immigrant men and depriving them of the support they might have had in old age from a next generation.

During the first half of the twentieth century, many states and localities reinforced nativist and racist immigration and naturalization policies with local measures restricting the rights of nonnaturalized immigrants to own or lease property, to obtain licenses for certain commercial activities, and to participate in many professions, including law, medicine, architecture, and engineering. These restrictions impeded opportunities for immigrants to achieve even a modicum of economic security.

California was the first state to institute what became known as "alien land laws." As increasing numbers of immigrants from Japan settled in California around the turn of the twentieth century (an increase spurred by the Chinese Exclusion Act of 1882), white Californians and their representatives in the state legislature became increasingly hostile toward these groups, many of whom were buying land in order to farm. Legislative debates to restrict aliens' ownership of land began in 1907 and resulted in a state law forbidding ownership of land by "aliens ineligible for citizenship" in 1913. In response to Japanese landowners' accommodation to the original law—transferring land titles to their American-born children, for instance—the California legislature passed a more encompassing law in 1923 making it illegal for aliens to "acquire, possess, enjoy, use, cultivate, occupy and transfer" property (Takaki 1989, 205). Several other states in the West and the Southwest adopted alien land laws in the 1920s and 1930s; more states followed suit in the era of anti-Japanese sentiment that reached its apex during World War II. In the decades between World War I and World War II, many states and municipalities also passed similar legislation regulating aliens' rights to obtain licenses for hunting and fishing; many also excluded aliens from public works jobs. In 1948, a U.S. Supreme Court decision deemed the California law unconstitutional. Some other states' restrictive laws were also abolished in the postwar years, but several states have yet to officially abolish their alien land laws.

Although states and localities continued to restrict nonnaturalized immigrants' economic rights during the World War II era, ranchers and agricultural employers in the southwestern United States were beginning to lobby for policies that would facilitate the legal immigration of seasonal workers, largely from Mexico. Such businesses depended on temporary migrants for cheap labor and sought the establishment of short-term contracts for manual labor that would attract from Mexico large numbers of workers who would not become permanent immigrants. In 1942, the U.S. and Mexican governments cooperated to institute a guest-worker program—the Bracero Program—that, until its demise in 1964, admitted farmworkers under a classification of "foreign laborers" rather than as immigrants. The short-term contracts offered the braceros a guaranteed place to live and a specified wage, but the contracts were often a losing proposition for the workers: The work was hard, the pay was poor, and the living arrangements often established what were effectively relations of debt peonage between worker and employer, whereby the laborers were forced to pay (or had portions of their pay withheld) for housing and sometimes food and other goods at noncompetitive rates that left them with little or nothing to save. Thus, although the Bracero Program and similar contract-labor programs that recruited Puerto Ricans and other seasonal workers to U.S. industry were touted as systems that protected the interests of workers by guaranteeing employers' obligation to them, the benefits to immigrants have been marginal.

The passage of the 1965 Hart-Celler Act, abolishing the discriminatory national origins quotas established in the 1920s, marked a shift in the national attitude toward immigration that was partly inspired by the emphasis of the 1964 Civil Rights Act (and of the movement that pushed for that legislation) on racial justice and opposition to discrimination. The 1965 law was a departure from the previous postwar immigration policy as it had been articulated in the 1952 McCarran-Walter Act, which affirmed restrictionist policy (although the 1952 law did, finally, remove the denial of admission based on race that had been in place since 1790). In one important way, however, the Hart-Celler Act had a negative impact on some of the poorest immigrants entering the United States: It established, for the first time, annual ceilings on immigration from Western Hemisphere countries, spurring a massive increase in the number of illegal—and overwhelmingly impoverished—immigrants from Mexico, the Caribbean, and Central America. Lack of documentation for these immigrants translated to a higher likelihood that they would find only sub-minimum-wage work and to a lack of entitlement (in the absence of a legal Social Security number) to federal benefits like Aid to Families with Dependent Children (AFDC), food stamps, Supplemental Security Income (SSI), and unemployment insurance.

By the late 1970s, Congress began to view the rise in illegal immigration as a significant problem, and it established the Select Commission on Immigration and Refugee Policy. This commission's most important initiative affecting the lives of poor immigrants was the 1980 Refugee Act, which allowed people fleeing their home country due to persecution to enter the United States under a separate and more liberal admissions system. Although this new law opened doors for many immigrants fleeing oppressive regimes in various parts of the world, it also set in motion a new and, according to many, unjust hierarchy of opportunity among immigrants, not just in terms of access to the United States but in terms of benefits and federal support once in the United States. Whereas Cuban and Vietnamese immigrants in the 1980s—fleeing governments opposed by the United States—were readily granted refugee status and became eligible not just for welfare benefits but also for low-interest loans, immigrants fleeing extreme poverty and political violence in countries like Haiti, El Salvador, and Guatemala—whose governments supported U.S. interests—were denied refugee status. Many such immigrants have entered the United States as "illegals" and have little hope of gaining the civil and economic protections conferred on their more fortunate counterparts who are officially deemed "refugees."

Social policies passed at both the state and federal levels during the mid-1990s cemented the distinctions between documented and undocumented immigrants, placing "illegals" at an even greater disadvantage. At the state level, California led the way—as it had at the beginning of the century—in the effort to pass restrictive policies to deter immigration in the state, particularly illegal immigration. In 1994, a 59 percent majority of California residents ratified Proposition 187, a controversial ballot initiative that would deny undocumented immigrants and their children access to most health, education, and welfare benefits controlled by the state. Although Proposition 187 was eventually jettisoned after a series of court challenges deemed it an unconstitutional regulation of immigration, support for the initiative demonstrated how widespread was the disapproval for public spending on undocumented immigrants in California. It also signaled an increasing concern at the national level about the cost of supporting noncitizen immigrants who had become "public charges" because of age, unemployment, or disability.

The sweeping welfare reforms enacted in 1996 included a number of provisions restricting access of immigrants—both legal and illegal—to federal welfare benefits. Restrictions applying to undocumented immigrants paralleled those in California's Proposition 187: These immigrants were declared ineligible for virtually every federal health and welfare provision except for emergency medical care. The 1996 welfare law also cut off access to social welfare programs for many documented, "legal" immigrants. Restrictive provisions included a five-year ban on nonnaturalized immigrant eligibility for welfare; federal permission for states to withhold benefits from all immigrants; the requirement that an immigrant have ten years of Social Security employment before being eligible for key programs; and outright prohibitions on immigrant eligibility for other programs. Although a pro-immigration lobby managed to reverse some of these restrictions in 1997, at least for documented immigrants who were in the United States before the 1996 law was enacted, the trends in immigration policy in the 1990s—and the public opinion behind those trends—reveal immigrants' precarious access to a "safety net" in the United States.

Lorrin R. Thomas

See also: Asian Americans; Bracero Program; Citizenship; Dillingham Commission; Immigrants and Immigration; Latino/as; Refugee Policy; Social Security Act of 1935; Welfare Policy/Welfare Reform

References and Further Reading

Gimpel, James G., and James R. Edwards. 1999. *The Congressional Politics of Immigration Reform*. Boston: Allyn and Bacon.

Haney-Lopez, Ian. 1996. *White by Law: The Legal Construction of Race*. New York: New York University Press.

Kurthen, Hermann, Jurgen Fijalkowski, and Gert G. Wagner, eds. 1998. *Citizenship and the Welfare State in Germany and the United States: Welfare Policies and Immigrants' Citizenship*. Stamford, CT: Jai Press.

Takaki, Ronald. 1989. *Strangers from a Different Shore: A History of Asian Americans*. Boston: Little, Brown.

Ueeda, Reed. 1994. *Postwar Immigrant America: A Social History*. Boston: St. Martin's Press.

Income and Wage Inequality

Inequality is higher in the United States than in any other developed country, and in recent decades it has been rising at a faster rate than in any country except Great Britain. Rising inequality is especially notable given that it defies expectations. Since the late 1920s, upper-income shares had been declining, or at least holding steady. Moreover, according to what is known as the Kuznets hypothesis (after economist Simon Kuznets), inequality was thought to follow an inverted *U* shape, rising initially with industrial development and then falling as the gains of development become more widely shared through, among other things, universal education and democracy (Kuznets 1955).

Until the 1970s, this seemed about right. First, available data, which were primarily for white men, indicated a decline in the wage gap between skill groups as the supply of high-skill groups—the high school educated in the 1910s and 1920s and the college educated in the 1940s and later—generally outpaced demand (Goldin and Katz 2001). Second, social movements fought for new redistributive institutions both during the period of great economic insecurity in the 1930s and during the period of great economic prosperity in the 1960s. New legislation (1) allowed a fairer distribution of economic rewards between employers and workers (for example, via collective bargaining and the minimum wage), (2) established a social safety net (such programs as unemployment insurance and Social Security), and (3) incorporated previously excluded workers into the mainstream of the economy (for example, through antidiscrimination and affirmative action programs). As a result, wages became more evenly distributed across skill and class as well as across other kinds of divisions, such as gender and race.

Several more contingent factors were also important. First, the Great Depression wiped out large concentrations of capital income (Piketty and Saez 2003). Second, the world wars boosted industrial production and imposed price controls, increasing demand at the bottom and reining in wages at the top. Finally, the strong economic growth of the immediate post–World War II period was helped along by the relative weakness of war-torn Europe. These economic shocks and geopolitical conditions suggest that technological advances and democratic deepening may be necessary but not sufficient explanations of changes in inequality.

Putting the pieces of the inequality puzzle together becomes even less straightforward in the post-1960s period, when the trend in inequality took everyone by surprise by reversing course and climbing, in many cases, to prewar levels. Nearly all forms of economic inequality began to rise in either the 1970s or the 1980s, the major exception being gender inequality. Although standard indices of income inequality, such as the Gini coefficient, shot up, further exploration revealed several unique aspects of the "new" wage inequality (Levy and Murnane 1992).

First, the spread between high and low wages grew *within* groups—within racial groups (that is, *among* Blacks and *among* whites), within gender groups, within education groups, and so on. The dispersion of wages was so pervasive that it is unlikely that a temporary mismatch in relative supply and demand was the only or entire story. In fact, the largest influx into the labor force came from women, yet their relative wages *increased*. Second, real inflation-adjusted wages actually declined for significant shares of the workforce, most dramatically for less-educated men but also for the median male worker. Finally, the compensation of those at the very top of the income distribution—in the top 1 percent—skyrocketed, as did the income of top executives.

Once again, external shocks, long-term developmental dynamics, and institutional reconfigurations each play a role in explaining these new dynamics. In the early 1970s, the Vietnam War and surging oil prices combined with increasing international competition and technological change (for example, the automation of factory jobs) to send the U.S. economy into a tailspin of increasing inflation and unemployment and declining output and productivity growth (Piore and Sabel 1984). The 1970s downturn was used to justify free-market experimentation on a grand scale: Industries were deregulated, unions were crushed, jobs were outsourced, investors gained dominance, and the minimum wage fell to historic lows. The net result was a decisive upward redistribution of income. Although it was hoped that the fruits of restructuring and the computer revolution would eventually "trickle down," the low unemployment and high growth and high productivity of the late 1990s boom did not last long enough to reduce levels of *income* inequality, though it did reduce some forms of *wage* inequality by lifting wages at the bottom, at least temporarily (DeNavas-Walt and Cleveland 2002).

It might be tempting to conclude that the main form of inequality today is between class or skill groups. Although it is true that gender and racial inequality have declined and that increasing inequality within these groups is compelling, the decline in *attention* to gender and racial inequality is misplaced. They each continue to be high in absolute terms and continue to follow relatively separate dynamics, both from each other and from class inequality (McCall 2001). For example, we see persistent wage discrimination against women with caregiving responsibilities, persistent gaps in wealth and proximity to high-quality schools and jobs between racial groups, and persistent concentrations of women and racial minorities in the lowest-wage jobs. This makes a more wide-ranging and integrated analysis of contemporary wage and income inequality both important and challenging.

Leslie McCall

See also: Economic Theories; Economic/Fiscal Policy; Labor Markets; Wealth, Distribution/Concentration

References and Further Reading

DeNavas-Walt, Carmen, and Robert Cleveland. 2002. *Money Income in the United States: 2001*. U.S. Census Bureau Current Population Reports P60–128. Washington, DC: GPO.

Goldin, Claudia, and Lawrence Katz. 2001. "Decreasing (and Then Increasing) Inequality in America: A Tale of Two Half-Centuries." In *The Causes and Consequences of Increasing Inequality*, ed. F. Welch, 37–82. Chicago: University of Chicago Press.

Kuznets, Simon. 1955. "Economic Growth and Economic Inequality." *American Economic Review* 45: 1028.

Levy, Frank, and Richard Murnane. 1992. "U.S. Earnings Levels and Earnings Inequality: A Review of Recent Trends and Proposed Explanations." *Journal of Economic Literature* 30, no. 3: 1333–1381.

McCall, Leslie. 2001. *Complex Inequality: Gender, Class, and Race in the New Economy*. New York: Routledge.

Piketty, Thomas, and Emmanuel Saez. 2003. "Income Inequality in the United States: 1911–1998." *Quarterly Journal of Economics* 117: 1–39.

Piore, Michael, and Charles Sabel. 1984. *The Second Industrial Divide: Possibilities for Prosperity*. New York: Basic Books.

Income-Maintenance Policy

See Aid to Families with Dependent Children (ADC/AFDC); Earned Income Tax Credit (EITC); General Assistance; Relief; Social Security; Supplemental Security Income

Indentured Servitude

Indentured servitude was an economic institution of the British American colonies that was created to lure a large supply of labor from the Old World to the New. Within a decade of the establishment of the Virginia colony in the early 1600s, the abundance of land and the absence of the substantial, low-cost workforce the colonists saw as necessary to exploit the economic potential of that land led them to embrace the concept of indentured servitude. In exchange for the costs of the transatlantic voyage, a citizen of Europe could sign an "indenture," a contract essentially selling his or her labor for a fixed number of years to a colonial landholder. At the end of this term, generally between four and seven years, the servant would be freed and could then pursue an independent existence on a small grant of land (if this was part of the contract), on the western frontier (if he or she could survive the dangers inherent to this prospect), or (quite frequently) on the margins of colonial society. By most estimates, between one-half and three-quarters of all white immigrants to the American colonies in the seventeenth century came as indentured servants.

At first, most indentured servants fit a profile: Most were male, between the ages of fifteen and twenty-five, single, traveling alone, and English. Later, as economic opportunities expanded in England, indentured servants came more often from Scotland, Ireland, Wales, and Germany. However, there was always a mix of the skilled and unskilled, the literate and illiterate, women, children, convicts, paupers, and adventure-seeking members of the Old World middle class intent on finding new opportunities in the colonies. Their destinations varied as well, with fewer going to New England and the "middle colonies" and far more destined for the southern mainland colonies and the English West Indies. Most entered upon their indenture voluntarily,

I hereby assign & convey to James Madison President
-ted States the within named servant, John, otherwise called John [illegible]
during the remaining term of his service [illegible] the 11th day of [illegible]
for the consideration of two hundred and [illegible] one Dollars [illegible]
last past when he was delivered to the said James. Witness [illegible]
this 19th day of April 1809. at Monticello in Virginia.

Sales contract between Thomas Jefferson and James Madison for an indentured servant's remaining term, April 19, 1809. President Thomas Jefferson (1743–1826) wrote this contract for the sale of the remainder of the term of service of an indentured servant, John Freeman, to President James Madison (1751–1836). Both Jefferson and Madison were the owners of many slaves, but neither possessed claims to many indentured servants. The servant in question was probably a free black man, with a special skill as an artisan, who would have been of particular value to Madison, because he was expanding his plantation house. (Library of Congress, Carter G. Woodson Collection) though large numbers did not: English citizens convicted of capital crimes were sometimes sold into indentured servitude as an alternative to the death sentence, indebted citizens were sent to work off their debts, and orphans and "vagrants" were rounded up off the streets of England and forced into servitude. Children were especially valuable as indentured servants, since they were required to maintain their servitude until they reached adulthood at age twenty-one. In all, several hundred thousand indentured servants immigrated to the British colonies.

The experience of indentured servitude was probably as varied as its demographics. Some indentured servants enjoyed decent treatment by their employers and had good prospects for establishing small farms after gaining their freedom. On the other hand, historical records indicate that this was not the case for many others. Indentured servants were often beaten, the women were often raped, and intolerable living conditions spelled the death of nearly half of all indentured servants within the first two years of service. Indentured servants had no voting rights and could not travel, sell or buy goods, or marry without the permission of their masters. However, unlike the slaves who would eventually replace them, indentured servants did enjoy legal recognition as individuals and therefore had the right to sue and give testimony. Furthermore, they were granted the full rights of free men upon termination of their contract, with the important caveat that voting rights for men were contingent upon land ownership. Yet the fact that the masters always possessed the power to hire out or sell their indentured servants, even if this meant separating families, blurred the distinction between servant and slave. Also, many masters found ways of extending the period of servitude by utilizing a legal system structured to severely punish those who sought to escape their masters or who failed to meet the master's demands. As earlier waves of indentured servants gained their freedom, freedmen and freedwomen were increasingly seen as a threat to the interests of the landed class, creating incentives for even harsher conditions, longer terms of servitude, and fewer rights for indentured servants.

Eventually, indentured servants were replaced by slaves. In every colony that adopted slavery, indentured servitude had preceded it. A number of scholars of early America have suggested that indentured servitude, which treated individuals primarily as property, paved the way for slavery in important respects. Many of the first Blacks brought to the colonies were indentured servants, and, during a transitional period, white and Black indentured servants simultaneously filled the colonial labor pool. The relative expense of indentured servitude compared to slavery, and the racist rationale applied toward the new African workers, rapidly ended the large-scale use of indentured servants in favor of wholesale slavery. Although very limited use of indentured servitude continued in the former colonies even after the American Revolution, the abolition of slavery in the British sugar colonies in the early nineteenth century led to a renewal of the use of indentured servitude there, as well as in parts of South America. The institution finally died out there in 1917, marking three centuries of indentured servitude in the Americas.

The importance of indentured servitude in shaping U.S. political roots and the structure of U.S. society has often been overlooked. Though most believe America was "born free" (as French writer Alexis de Tocqueville put it in his renowned observations of *Democracy in America*) and without the class divisions that plagued the Old World, the truth is that colonial America was built upon a clear class hierarchy consisting of a class of landed elites, an intermediate class of freed servants, and a large population of bound laborers—the indentured servants. As more indentured servants gained their freedom only to discover they had far less opportunity than they had anticipated, tension mounted between the masters and their old servants, sometimes breaking out into open rebellion, as in Bacon's Rebellion of 1670. Slavery inserted a new underclass into the system and fundamentally reshaped society, for earlier class divisions now appeared to be less important than racial ones. Poor whites were convinced they had more in common with the wealthy whites than with the Black slaves, and this perception allowed the colonists to convince their former servants to ally with them against the slave class. This early schism between the poorest whites and Blacks would shape the structure and perception of society in the United States for centuries to come.

Rebecca K. Root

See also: Slavery

References and Further Reading

Galenson, David. 1981. *White Servitude in Colonial America: An Economic Analysis*. Cambridge: Cambridge University Press.

Morgan, Edmund. 1975. *American Slavery, American Freedom: The Ordeal of Colonial Virginia*. New York: Norton.

Van Der Zee, John. 1985. *Bound Over: Indentured Servitude and American Conscience*. New York: Simon and Schuster.

Industrial Areas Foundation (IAF)

The Industrial Areas Foundation (IAF) is the nation's oldest and largest community organizing network working to build power for low-income communities. The network was founded in 1940 by Saul Alinsky, and today "Industrial Areas Foundation" is the name both of the institute that provides organizers and training services to local affiliates and of the network to which all affiliates belong. The IAF has contracts with approximately sixty-five American groups and works with sister networks in the United Kingdom and South Africa. Local IAF organizations work together at the statewide level in a number of states, most notably Texas, and often coordinate training and strategy at regional levels.

Influenced by the union organizing movement of the 1930s, Alinsky sought to build the power of workers where they lived, that is, in the neighborhoods around factories, hence the name "industrial areas." He formed his first group, the Back of the Yards Neighborhood Council in Chicago, by working with established churches and neighborhood associations. He then established the IAF to help spread community organizing to other parts of the country, working in white ethnic and Black communities. Alinsky and the IAF became widely known for using militant tactics to win better services and a share of power for poor neighborhoods. Alinsky elaborated his organizing tactics, and his brand of democratic populism more generally, in *Rules for Radicals* (Alinsky [1971] 1989).

Upon Alinsky's death in 1972, the IAF underwent a significant transformation. Alinsky's successor as IAF director, Ed Chambers, moved to systematize the training of organizers and pushed the IAF, which had long focused on material self-interest, to take people's values more seriously as a foundation for organizing (Reitzes and Reitzes 1987, 92–100). The most prominent developments came through the work of IAF organizer Ernesto Cortes Jr. in Texas. Cortes built Communities Organized for Public Service (COPS) in San Antonio in the early 1970s by working with a network of Catholic parishes serving Mexican Americans. COPS emerged as arguably the most powerful community organization in the country, and it permanently altered power relationships in the city. COPS has garnered over $1 billion in public and private funds for an extensive array of projects in its neighborhoods: affordable housing, job training, after-school programs, health clinics, and street and drainage projects, among others (Warren 2001).

The IAF emerged from the 1970s with a distinctive model for community organizing. Local groups are constituted by institutions (for example, congregations), engage faith traditions to motivate and frame action, and focus on the development of indigenous leaders, often women, drawn from the member institutions. The IAF refers to this model as "broad-based," but others use the term "faith-based" (sometimes "congregation-based") in light of the predominant role of faith institutions and values in the organizing approach.

With this model, the IAF has developed multi-issue organizations that are highly participatory, persist over the years, often draw leaders together across different racial and socioeconomic groupings, and increasingly take in full metropolitan areas. IAF groups have initiated a number of innovative policies to address the needs of poor and working-class communities: East Brooklyn Congregations launched Nehemiah Homes, which became a national model for affordable housing; BUILD in Baltimore was a key player in the nation's first living-wage campaign; COPS and its sister group Metro Alliance initiated the Project QUEST job training program in San Antonio; and the Texas statewide IAF network built the Alliance Schools, the nation's largest school reform project based upon parent and community organizing.

Mark R. Warren

See also: Association of Community Organizations for Reform Now (ACORN); Community Organizing; Community-Based Organizations; Living-Wage Campaigns

References and Further Reading

Alinsky, Saul. [1971] 1989. *Rules for Radicals*. New York: Vintage Books.

Horwitt, Sanford. 1989. *Let Them Call Me Rebel: Saul Alinsky, His Life and Legacy*. New York: Vintage Books.

Reitzes, Donald C., and Dietrich C. Reitzes. 1987. *The Alinsky Legacy: Alive and Kicking*. Greenwich, CT: JAI Press.

Warren, Mark R. 2001. *Dry Bones Rattling: Community Building to Revitalize American Democracy*. Princeton: Princeton University Press.

Industrialization

Industrialization is the rapid growth of the manufacturing sector, an event that traces its origins to the early nineteenth century. This shift toward goods made in factories and by machines generally raised incomes and expanded choices for Americans. For those employed in industry, whether native born or immigrant, real wages rose impressively over the nineteenth century. Yet industrialization did bring poverty to some as it encouraged migration to the cities and exposed workers and their families to unemployment, injury, and disease. It also distributed wages and opportunities unequally: For example, women and children were among the earliest industrial workers, but by the early twentieth century, their presence had shriveled, especially in the new mass-production industries. Both African Americans and women experienced discrimination when they sought the better-paying jobs available in American factories.

Before the nineteenth century, most American goods were made in households or small shops or mills by individuals who possessed various levels of skills. Although some urban craftsmen may have earned substantial incomes, most were quite poor. Probated estates from the time of the American Revolution reveal craftsmen as among the least wealthy of white Americans. But they enjoyed a certain independence as they crafted goods from the raw material to the finished product.

Industrialization altered the way goods were made. First, it involved breaking the manufacturing process down into tasks and assigning people to tasks instead of having individuals fashion an entire product. This enabled manufacturers to hire the less skilled, notably women and children, to do the simplest tasks while having the more skilled, usually men, concentrate upon the most demanding jobs. Second, wherever possible, manufacturers introduced machines to increase the quantity of goods produced and to save labor. As markets grew, the numbers of workers multiplied.

The explosion of the manufacturing sector created a tremendous demand for labor, which could not be met simply by recruiting men from the countryside. Initially, manufacturers turned to women and children, who were willing to work for much lower wages than their fathers and brothers. Later, the manufacturers hired immigrants, who were overwhelmingly male, to labor in American industry. Most of these workers toiled in cities, where manufacturers sought ready access to supplies, labor, and markets.

Historians and economists have disagreed about the impact of industrialization and of the quickened pace of immigration and urbanization that accompanied it. Historians tend to be negative in their assessment of industrialization, highlighting the loss of artisanal skill and independence, which surely happened to some workers. They note that wages were low and that a reserve army of unemployed loitered outside the factory gates hoping to underbid the workers within. Much, perhaps most, of the working class lived on the edge of poverty. Unemployment, unknown on the farm, became common. Industrial accidents were distressingly frequent, and compensation for injury or death was woefully inadequate. The costs of occupational diseases were borne solely by the worker. For women, African Americans, and immigrants, industrialization brought pervasive discrimination.

Economists tend to be much more positive. They note that the migration to factories from the countryside and from abroad was voluntary. Although depressions could bring wage cuts, when viewed over the long haul, wages rose markedly for all identifiable groups: men, women, African Americans, and immigrants. Factory work offered an alternative to other, more poorly paying jobs for women in the antebellum period and drove up women's wages from roughly a quarter to better than a half that of men's wages (Goldin 1990, 63–66). Similarly, when compared to their opportunities in the Old World, employment in American factories was a decided improvement for immigrants. Chronically short of labor, the United States offered both high wages and opportunity.

What was the impact of industrialization upon the well-being of its participants? American industrial wages were high compared to those of other nations, and they rose more than 1 percent annually (Margo 2000, 224). These increases over a century meant that the material position of workers in industry must have improved. Statistics from the period show high rates of saving, no doubt necessitated by the absence of meaningful government safety nets. The most commonly cited figures show that manufacturing and mining incomes exceeded the national average for all workers by more than 10 percent on the eve of the Civil War and by 25 percent by the end of the nineteenth century (Gallman 1972, 53). Industrialization also widened the choices of goods available. Indeed, it encouraged escalating consumption, since the real prices of manufactured goods fell dramatically.

Although the primary beneficiaries of these gains would be native-born white males, immigrants, women, and African Americans were employed in industry as well. Immigrants fared the best of these three groups, since they migrated to the rapidly growing industrial centers and readily found jobs. By the end of the nineteenth century, perhaps one-third of all manufacturing workers were foreign born. To be sure, they faced discrimination, and they could not expect to climb to the highest rungs of the occupational ladders. After adjusting for worker and industry characteristics, a large study of workers at the turn of the century found that those from northern and western Europe earned about 2 percent, or 20 cents, less a week than the native born, whereas those from southern and eastern Europe earned 8 percent, or $1.07, less (McGouldrick and Tannen 1977, 734).

Over the course of the nineteenth century,

Boys working at a West Virginia glass factory, 1908. (Library of Congress)

women became a smaller proportion of the manufacturing labor force. In 1840, women accounted for some 40 percent of the labor force; by 1890, this percentage had halved. To a considerable extent, their exodus was voluntary, and most people believed that married women should not work outside of the home. But some of this decline was due to the fact that the industries associated with women, such as textiles and clothing, grew rapidly before the Civil War and failed to keep pace after the war. Employment was highly sex segregated: Men dominated the most dynamic and the highest-paying industries of the late nineteenth century. Earning slightly more than half as much as men, most women were more than happy to leave the factory upon marriage and never return. Some did not have that option, and with comparatively low wages and almost no opportunity for advancement, they lived on the edge of subsistence.

Like women, African Americans were not extensively employed in industry before World War I. Not only did they face discrimination, but some 90 percent of Blacks lived in the heavily agricultural South. Racial segregation prevailed, with African Americans dominant in the tobacco, iron and steel, and lumber industries, while whites held most of the jobs in the textile industry. Although they worked in different industries, unskilled Blacks and whites made about the same wages. But here as with women, advancement up the occupational ladder was well nigh impossible. For African American men with families, in the postbellum South, work in the cotton fields was a better choice than work in the factories (Wright 1986, 185).

Although the trend may have been toward long-term improvements in income and consumption, workers could and did face short but intense periods of rising unemployment, lagging wages, and escalating costs for the necessities of life. In the late 1840s and early 1850s, for example, an influx of immigrants combined with a slowing economy and soaring food prices and rents brought genuine hardship. Some workers saw their skills eroded by the division of labor and mechanization, although the process of technological unemployment was not nearly as rapid in the nineteenth century as it would be in the late twentieth. Moreover, the construction, repair, and operation of machinery required new skills. Mechanization did reduce the demand for genuinely raw, unskilled labor, especially in the later period when the application of steam power and electric motors eliminated much of the backbreaking toil associated with industrialization.

Quickening industrialization coincided with rising death rates in the United States. Abundant evidence exists to show that mortality rose in the second and third decades of the nineteenth century. In this period, many, perhaps most, Americans were stunted or wasted; that is, they did not absorb enough calories to achieve optimal heights and weights. Although some of this may have been due to inadequate diets, most experts argue that the main explanation is to be found in the caloric demands of factory work, especially to fight off infectious air- and water-borne diseases (Steckel 1991, 36–41). By bringing people together in factories, and especially in urban factories, industrialization facilitated the spread of such highly contagious diseases as cholera, yellow fever, typhus, and smallpox. The decline in death rates that began in the last third of the nineteenth century appears to have been due to advances in public health and the construction of urban water and sewer systems.

The primary impact of industrialization upon poverty was to reduce its incidence. Although the yardstick used to measure poverty is subjective, informed estimates show that poverty declined markedly over the course of the nineteenth century. Both by offering good jobs and by providing goods at ever-lower prices, industrialization contributed to that decline. The exceptions to this generalization are those who faced rampant discrimination: married women, African Americans, and southern and eastern Europeans.

Industrialization could and did lead to poverty for some workers and their families, even as many benefited from improved wages and jobs. The greater use of machines with more power meant that work became more dangerous, and the numbers of industrial accidents had soared by the late nineteenth century. Those who were hurt in such accidents could expect little if any compensation from their employers, for companies employed a number of legal stratagems to avoid payouts. This was remedied to some extent with the development of workmen's compensation laws in the early twentieth century. Occupational diseases, such as brown lung for textile workers, shortened careers and life expectancies. Since most families depended overwhelmingly upon the income of the primary breadwinner, incapacitating illness or death could bring widespread misery.

Unemployment was a common event in the nineteenth century, if somewhat more episodic and less long-lasting than unemployment today. Machines broke down, business slowed, the economy went into depression, and organizing workers went on strike; firms adjusted by laying off workers. Workers who lived in cities could not turn to traditional methods of getting by. They could not go to the garden, fish, or hunt. They might find day labor, but hard times tended to result in a tight job market for all. The opportunities for wives and children to work diminished with advanced industrialization as outwork, such as sewing shirts and weaving hats, became mechanized. One of the casualties of industrialization was a certain independence from the market.

Diane Lindstrom

See also: Child Labor; Economic Depression; Globalization and Deindustrialization; Sweatshop; Trade/Industrial Unions

References and Further Reading

Gallman, Robert E. 1972. "The Pace and Pattern of Economic Growth." In *American Economic Growth*, ed. Lance Davis, Richard A. Easterlin, William N. Parker, Dorothy S. Brady, Albert Fishlow, Robert E. Gallman, Stanley Lebergott, et al., 15–60. New York: Harper and Row.

Goldin, Claudia. 1990. *Understanding the Gender Gap*. New York: Oxford University Press.

Margo, Robert A. 2000. "The Labor Force in the Nineteenth Century." In *The Cambridge Economic History of the United States*, vol. 2, *The Long Nineteenth Century*, ed. Stanley L. Engerman and Robert E. Gallman, 207–244. Cambridge: Cambridge University Press.

McGouldrick, Paul F., and Michael B. Tannen. 1977. "Did American Manufacturers Discriminate against Immigrants before 1914?" *Journal of Economic History* 37, no. 3: 723–746.

Steckel, Richard H. 1991. "Stature and Living Standards in the United States." In *Historical Factors in Long Run Growth*. Working paper no. 24. Cambridge, MA: National Bureau of Economic Research.

Williamson, Jeffrey G. 1997. *Industrialization, Inequality, and Economic Growth*. Cheltenham, UK: Edward Elgar.

Wright, Gavin. 1986. *Old South, New South*. New York: Basic Books.

Informal Economy

"Informal," "black," "underground," or "shadow" economy are all terms for economic activity that—for various reasons—operates outside the reach of government or other regulatory agencies and thus is unofficially and in large part illegally exempt from taxation, labor law, official safety regulations, and the like. This includes paid work involving the production and sale of goods and services that are unregistered by or hidden from the government in order to avoid taxes, Social Security costs, or labor laws but that are legal in all other respects. Paid informal work also includes all legitimate activities where payments received by individuals are not declared to the authorities. The informal economy also encompasses work in illegal activities, such as prostitution, the manufacture and sale of illicit goods, and drug peddling. Overall, then, what makes these varied enterprises part of the informal economy is that they involve evasion of both direct and indirect taxes, Social Security fraud where the officially unemployed are working while claiming benefits, and avoidance of labor legislation, such as employers' insurance contributions, minimum-wage agreements, or certain safety and other standards in the workplace. These activities are often accomplished by hiring labor off the books, subcontracting work to small firms, or asking the self-employed to work for below-minimum wages (Williams and Windebank 1998, 4). Moreover, because much of what takes place is hidden from official view, there are many myths about this type of employment, particularly concerning its growth in advanced countries such as the United States, and about its participants, who are stereotypically characterized as the unemployed, the impoverished, women, immigrants, and ethnic minorities in low-income communities. Although these groups are indeed heavily represented in the informal economy, a great deal of the activity in this sector is actually conducted by employed white men supplementing income from their "regular" jobs. In addition, some analysts argue that unregulated work has become an increasingly integral dimension of global capitalism.

Manuel Castells and Alejandro Portes demonstrated the impact of alternative or informal income-generating activities characterized by one central feature: "[I]t is unregulated by the institutions of society, in a legal and social environment" (1989, 12). As a result of the absence of institutional regulations, standard work processes are ignored, changed, or amended. For example, labor may be clandestine, undeclared, paid at less than the minimum wage, or employed under circumstances that society's norms would not otherwise allow. Informal employment often does not adhere to institutional regulations that involve land use zoning, safety standards, hazardous or toxic dumping in the workplace, and other health-related work issues.

Three primary debates drive most of the research on informal employment and help us better understand the origins and nature of this alternative economic activity and the participation of immigrants, ethnic and racial minorities, women, and other marginalized groups in this form of employment: formalization, informalization, and marginality theses.

The formalization thesis argues that as economies become more developed or advanced, informal employment declines, eventually disappearing. This notion is rooted in dichotomies between "first" and "third" worlds. Third world countries are defined in this thesis as economically underdeveloped vis-à-vis their more "advanced," industrialized, technologically driven first world counterparts. According to this thesis, informality exists in developing countries and is part and parcel of their "backwardness," which will eventually disappear as economic advancement and modernization occur. Immigrants, especially those coming from third world or undeveloped countries, export their economic activities, including informal employment. Proponents of this argument use this rationale to explain the preponderance of informal activities in countries such as the United States, Canada, and other advanced economies, in effect treating the informal economy as a temporary third world holdover in otherwise modern first world economies.

On the other hand, the informalization thesis argues that advanced economies are witnessing a growth of informal economic activity for reasons having to do with economic restructuring and globalization. For example, Saskia Sassen (2000) argues that the very development that is occurring in advanced and developing economies is causing a growth of informality. A combination of growing inequality in earnings and growing inequality in profits among different sectors of the urban economy has promoted informalization of an array of economic activities: For example, manufacturers turn to contracting out or to sweatshop labor in order to reduce labor costs and remain competitive. She argues that informal employment is a structured outcome of current trends in advanced economies (Sassen 2000, 7). As a result of restructuring and other economic, social, and political fissures, informal employment has increased in visibility, stature, and number of participants. Informalization is embedded in the structure of the current economic system and is particularly manifest in large cities, where informalization emerges as a set of flexible maximizing strategies employed by individuals, firms, consumers, and producers in a context of growing inequality in earnings and in profit-making capabilities.

Finally, the marginality thesis states that immigrants, women, ethnic minorities, and other vulnerable groups participate in informal employment at higher rates because their status is peripheral, disadvantaged, and outside the margins of formal economic activity. Are immigrants (and racial and ethnic minorities) more prone to informal employment? According to an extensive review of the literature on informal employment (Williams and Windebank 1998), they are. However, this conclusion is mostly based on U.S. research on this topic, the vast majority of it concerning the extent to which immigrant and minority populations engage in informal employment and the type of paid activities making up informal employment. Most work on this topic focuses on low-paid, labor-intensive, nonunionized, and exploitative occupations in poorer areas with high concentrations of immigrants, ethnic minorities, or both (see Fernandez-Kelly and Garcia 1989; Sassen 1989; Stepick 1989). As a result of this focus, informal employment is closely associated with immigrants and minorities. One should be cautious, however, in attributing all, or even a majority, of informal employment to immigrants and racial and ethnic minorities. Informal employment also includes work in white-collar, pink-collar, and blue-collar industries in which nonminority and nonimmigrant groups participate in large numbers.

Even among immigrants and ethnic minorities, further delineation of these two groups is needed to better assess their participation in informal employment. For example, it is important to distinguish among immigrants of different origins and with different legal statuses when assessing their employment opportunities. Naturalized legal immigrants have an experience in the U.S. labor market that is qualitatively different from that of unauthorized immigrants who entered the country without inspection and from those who overstayed their student or tourist visas. Unauthorized immigrants in the United States, by virtue of their tenuous status, participate in informal employment at higher rates than do authorized immigrants.

Excluded from formal employment by the lack of proper documentation, unauthorized immigrants have little choice but to engage in informal employment as a means of generating income. As a result, the most visible forms of informal economic activity are replete with immigrant participants, ostensibly immigrants without proper documents. However, not all unauthorized immigrants partake in informal work. Many employers in the formal sector pay little attention to federal regulations and may not adhere to the strict statutes governing new hires and the required documents needed to finalize employment. In addition, unauthorized immigrants can seek fraudulent documents or use someone else's documents to obtain formal employment. In 1996 (the last time the U.S. Census Bureau estimated the size of the unauthorized population), it was estimated that there were 5 million immigrants without documents in the United States, with approximately half coming from Mexico, and slightly less than half being concentrated in California (U.S. Immigration and Naturalization Service 2002). Although obviously engaged to a greater extent in informal activity than other groups, immigrants also participate in other forms of marginal, formal sector employment, such as flexible or contingent work.

Are the poor, particularly those who are unemployed, more prone to participate in informal employment activities? The primary connection of informality to the poor is through alleged cases of benefit fraud committed by so-called welfare cheats—women and men who claim benefits while also employed in an underground activity so that earnings and taxes are not reported to a government agency. Or, similarly, those without work as a result of structural economic changes—such as a recession—might turn to informal employment as a buffer or alternative to unemployment. Most analyses of poor people participating in informal employment assume that a significant percentage of the officially unemployed are in reality working off the books, being paid in tax-free cash. However, according to Colin Williams and Jan Windebank (1998, 50), participants in informal employment are not usually the jobless, nor are participants doing it as a survival strategy as a result of economic exclusion or unemployment. Instead, their review of research in this area shows that the unemployed find it more difficult than the employed to augment their incomes through informal employment. Rather, working in informal jobs is primarily a strategy to accumulate extra resources for those who already have a job. The vast majority of studies find that the employed tend to engage in more autonomous, nonroutine, and rewarding informal jobs than do the unemployed, who undertake lower-paid and more routine, exploitative, and monotonous informal employment (Williams and Windebank 1998, 52). Here, they suggest a segmented informal market in which employed workers get the better informal jobs while unemployed workers get the worse informal jobs.

The literature concerning the participation of the unemployed or the poor in informal employment therefore suggests that informal employment is concentrated among those who already have a formal occupation and who find relatively well-paid informal employment. These workers get side jobs, for example, if they are in the construction industry and a neighbor fancies their skills and hires them for a "weekend" job repairing or refurbishing the neighbor's home. Other examples include repairmen who will do side jobs, often conducted on a self-employed basis, for a fee below market but clearly profitable. On the other hand, the unemployed or poor generally engage in relatively low-paid organized informal employment, which tends to be more exploitative, more dangerous, and more poorly paid. As a result, the unemployed and the poor do not disproportionately participate in or gain from informal employment, and such employment should not necessarily be considered a reliable survival strategy.

What is the gender division of informal employment? According to Williams and Windebank (1998, 66), studies on informal employment indicate that men constitute the majority of the informal labor force. Of course, exceptions to this general rule exist: In many regions and in occupations such as care work and domestic work, women are participating in larger numbers than men. What is clear is that when women do participate in informal employment, they work primarily in highly exploitative jobs and they are more likely to be poorly paid. In contrast, men tend to be engaged in the higher-paid and more autonomous forms of informal employment (Williams and Windebank 1998, 80), such as construction, repair, and landscaping.

Other important gender factors similarly constrain and aid both genders in their participation in informal employment. For example, women participate in informal employment on a part-time basis mostly because of their domestic roles and household responsibility constraints. Furthermore, their motivation is more economic, based upon the desire to generate extra income to help the family get by during lean times. According to Williams and Windebank (1998, 80), for men, informal employment is more irregular but is more likely to be full-time, and it is often undertaken for the purpose of earning spare cash for socializing and for differentiating themselves from the domestic sphere and women. Therefore, a clear gender segmentation of the informal labor market is evident, in terms of the work undertaken, motivations, pay, and the types of men and women who undertake this line of work.

Abel Valenzuela Jr.

See also: Day Labor; Domestic Work; Labor Markets; Unemployment

References and Further Reading

Castells, Manuel, and Alejandro Portes. 1989. "World Underneath: The Origins, Dynamics, and Effects of the Informal Economy." In *The Informal Economy: Studies in Advanced and Less Developed Countries*, ed. Alejandro Portes, Manuel Castells, and Lauren A. Benton, 11–37. Baltimore: Johns Hopkins University Press.

Fernandez-Kelly, Maria Patricia, and Ana M. Garcia. 1989. "Informalization at the Core: Hispanic Women, Homework, and the Advanced Capitalist State." In *The Informal Economy: Studies in Advanced and Less Developed Countries*, ed. Alejandro Portes, Manuel Castells, and Lauren A. Benton, 247–264. Baltimore: Johns Hopkins University Press.

Portes, Alejandro, Manuel Castells, and Lauren A. Benton, ed. 1989. *Informal Economy: Studies in Advanced and Less Developed Countries*. Baltimore: Johns Hopkins University Press.

Sassen, Saskia. 1989. "New York City's Informal Economy." In *The Informal Economy: Studies in Advanced and Less Developed Countries*, ed. Alejandro Portes, Manuel Castells, and Lauren A. Benton, 60–77. Baltimore: Johns Hopkins University Press.

———. 2000. "Informalization: Imported through Immigration or a Feature of Advanced Economies?" *Working USA*, March-April.

Stepick, Alex. 1989. "Miami's Two Informal Sectors." In *The Informal Economy: Studies in Advanced and Less Developed Countries*, ed. Alejandro Portes, Manuel Castells, and Lauren A. Benton, 111–131. Baltimore: Johns Hopkins University Press.

U.S. Immigration and Naturalization Service. 2002.

Statistical Yearbook of the Immigration and Naturalization Service, 2000. Washington, DC: GPO.
Williams, Colin, and Jan Windebank. 1998. *Informal Employment in the Advanced Economies: Implications for Work and Welfare*. New York: Routledge.

Institutionalization

See Crime Policy; Mental Health Policy; Orphanages; Poorhouse/Almshouse

Islam

The religion of Islam in the United States influences poverty and social welfare through the moral and spiritual dimensions of its teachings and programs sponsored by mosques. Of the 5 million to 7 million Muslims in the United States, 29 percent are African American; 29 percent are South Asian American; 20 percent are Arab American; and 22 percent are "others," mainly Africans, Southeast Asians, Bosnians, and Hispanics and Latinos (Bagby, Perle, and Frohle 2001). Recognizing the diversity of American Muslims, this entry will draw its examples primarily from the African American Muslim community.

The Moral and Spiritual Dimensions of Islam

The simplicity of Islam's Five Pillars has been attractive to people from all class strata, especially the poor. In the first pillar, a Muslim convert begins by publicly reciting the creed, or *shahadah:* "There is one God, Allah, and Muhammad is his prophet." By adhering to a schedule of five formal prayers, or *salat,* from sunrise to evening, that person fulfills the second pillar and begins to develop an Islamic or God consciousness and an internal discipline. The deep compassion of Islam is found in the third pillar, which requires believers to give 2.5 percent of their annual savings to the poor each year. What is often called the charity, or *zakat,* is given to the mosque for distribution to poor people in the neighborhood. Muslims can also make voluntary contributions, called *sadaqa,* for the maintenance of the mosque, the salary of the imam, and other charitable efforts. The fourth pillar, fasting during the lunar month of Ramadan, also contributes to the development of internal discipline. From sunrise until sunset, a Muslim abstains from food, drink, and sexual pleasures. At the end of the thirty-day fast, the first official holiday celebration of Islam, Id al-Fitr, takes place. Gifts are exchanged, and everyone, including the poor, are invited to a feast at the local mosque. The fifth and final pillar, the *hajj,* or pilgrimage to Mecca, should take place at least once in a lifetime if a Muslim can afford it. During the *hajj,* all pilgrims wear a similar white garb, removing all status symbols and class distinctions. The second holiday, Id al-Adha, takes place at the end of the annual *hajj* period; sheep are slaughtered, and the excess meat is passed out to the poor.

The Five Pillars have built within Islam's doctrines and rituals a strong concern for the poor, beginning with the requirement of charity, or the "poor tax," and the feeding of poor people during its two major holiday celebrations. However, Islam also moves beyond charitable acts by also emphasizing the development of the internal discipline that is required by five daily prayers and fasting for thirty days. As Max Weber argued and as numerous studies have shown, the development of a disciplined moral life can lead poor people out of poverty, given the right conditions and opportunities. Islam's most important contribution to the discussion of poverty and social welfare concerns the formation of a disciplined life as a way out of poverty.

Besides the Five Pillars, the Qur'an and the deeds and sayings, or *hadith,* of the Prophet Muhammad and his four senior companions form the moral basis for Islam and Islamic law.

Muhammad's loss of both parents by the age of six reinforced Islam's concern for "widows and orphans," the most vulnerable and least fortunate people in pre-Islamic Arabia. Muhammad taught that when Muslims serve the needs of their fellow human beings, they are also serving God. The teachings of Islam also support strong and stable families.

In his farewell speech, the Prophet said that Muslims should treat each other as "brothers and sisters" and that they should not practice "usury" (charging interest on money that is loaned). There is an incipient type of socialism within Islam, where the practice is that Muslims do not charge interest on loans to fellow Muslims. However, an interest payment can be charged on loans to non-Muslims. This socialistic emphasis in Islam has made the religion open to social welfare programs for the poor.

Social Service Programs Sponsored by African American Mosques

A national field survey of 130 predominantly African American mosques examined the types of community outreach programs sponsored by these mosques, including their cooperation with social service agencies. Almost all of the community outreach programs in the study, which are directly sponsored by the mosques themselves or in cooperation with other social agencies or organizations, have an impact upon families in poor neighborhoods. The data showed that 67 percent of the mosques sponsor programs directly to deal with community problems, while 75 percent of them work with other social agencies on issues affecting their communities. The largest direct program (found in 74 percent of the mosques studied) is the requirement of *zakat*, charity to the poor or to those in need and one of the Five Pillars of Islam. *Zakat* constitutes 2.5 percent of one's annual savings. It is given to the mosque, and the imam distributes the charity. Thirty-nine percent of the mosques sponsor their own food or clothing banks for the poor; 82 percent of the imams provide counseling to their members and the community, and marital concerns account for 52 percent of such counseling. One of the unusual programs that Muslim mosques offer provides temporary housing for the homeless, especially ex-offenders (31 percent). Almost all mosques will provide temporary shelter for travelers and visitors; the physical space of a mosque includes a room or place for overnight guests (Mamiya 2002, 40–43).

Since alcohol and drugs are strongly forbidden by Islamic law, Muslims are generally inclined to participate actively in programs against substance abuse. Thirty-eight percent of the mosques sponsor their own programs, such as Muslims Anonymous or Alcoholics Anonymous groups, and 59 percent of them cooperate with other community agencies and organizations in programs against substance abuse. Similarly, the Islamic ethic of self-defense enables African American Muslim congregations to become more actively involved than Black churches in programs of Neighborhood Watch and security patrols against criminal activity (16 percent) and in working with street gangs and troubled youth (33 percent). It is not unusual to hear an African American imam talk about "cleaning up" the neighborhood around the mosque to rid the area of drug dealers, prostitutes, and petty criminals. Part of the task of cleaning up may involve carrying arms or using strong-arm tactics, which most Christian clergy are not prepared to do. These programs of antidrug and anticrime activities have a direct impact on the quality of life in poor neighborhoods (Mamiya 2002, 43–44).

Perhaps the strongest connection that African American Muslims have with poor families is that many of them are poor themselves, or at least one step away from poverty. In the survey, the imams were asked to give estimates of the economic background of their congregations. They estimated that 36 percent of their most active members had annual incomes below $20,000 and that the majority of their members

(53 percent) were in the working class or the lower-middle income bracket, between $20,000 and $34,000. Only 11 percent of their members had incomes higher than $35,000 (Mamiya 2002, 43–44).

Another problem area that has affected many poor Black families concerns the extremely high rates of incarceration of African American men (49 percent of male prisoners nationwide) and women (52 percent of female prisoners). With America's inmate population at 2.1 million and the number of incarcerated African Americans at more than 1 million, Muslim groups have responded strongly in their ministry to prisoners and ex-offenders. The survey indicated that 90 percent of the mosques have prison ministries in place, with 88 percent of them visiting prisons on a sustained basis, and 79 percent holding special programs at prisons during Muslim holidays. Thirty-eight percent of the imams also worked as prison chaplains. Counseling (at 41 percent of mosques), meetings for ex-offenders (21 percent), and participation in a halfway house (13 percent) constitute the other activities carried out by mosques (Mamiya 2002, 44–46).

Lawrence H. Mamiya

See also: African American Migration; African Americans; Black Churches; Crime Policy; Nation of Islam

References and Further Reading

Bagby, Ihsan, Paul Perle, and Brian Frohle. 2001. *The Mosque Study in America: A National Portrait.* Washington, DC: Council on American Islamic Relations.

Haddad, Yvonne Yazbeck, ed. 1991. *The Muslims of America*. New York: Oxford University Press.

Mamiya, Lawrence H. 2002. "Faith-Based Institutions and Family Support Services among African American Muslim Masjids and Black Churches." In *Journey Inward Journey Outward: ITC/Faith Factor Project 2000 Study of Black Religious Life*, ed. Joseph Troutman, 20–60. Special book edition of Project 2000. Spring. Atlanta: Journal of the Interdenominational Theological Center.

Smith, Jane I. 1999. *Islam in America*. New York: Columbia University Press.

Turner, Richard B. 1997. *Islam in the African American Experience*. Bloomington: Indiana University Press.

Job Corps

See Employment and Training; Employment Policy; War on Poverty

Job Creation

See Employment and Training; Employment Policy; Labor Markets; Works Progress Administration (WPA)

Johnson, Lyndon Baines

See Liberalism; War on Poverty

Judaism

Jewish social welfare in the United States has provided a complex array of institutions and social services directed at relief of Jewish poverty, assistance to Jewish immigrants, and preservation of Jewish culture for what has emerged as the largest, most stable, and wealthiest Jewish community in the world. Over time, Jewish philanthropy has evolved from meeting the material needs of a poor population to providing a broader array of social services and cultural activities not specifically focused on poverty. Jewish social services have become one facet of the heterogeneous, public-private social service network that characterized the late-twentieth-century U.S. welfare system.

Jewish charity is deeply embedded in the religious texts and communal traditions of ancient Judaism. The concept of *tzedakah*, which can be alternately translated from Hebrew into "charity" or "justice," developed from social legislation in Hebrew scripture that stipulated a number of practices to provide food for the impoverished. Subsequent Jewish scholars made central the link between charity and righteousness in the eyes of God. The medieval philosopher Moses Maimonides detailed eight levels of *tzedakah*, with the most noble being the provision of help that promotes eventual self-reliance among recipients. Jewish charity also urged avoiding humiliation of the recipient—an injunction that in the early-twentieth-century United States made Jewish charities comparatively more generous to their clients than other religious or secular agencies.

American Jewish charity is traced to the Stuyvesant Pledge of 1654. The twenty-three Jews in New Amsterdam, the Dutch colony that is now New York City, were on the verge of expulsion by Governor Peter Stuyvesant of the Dutch West India Company. Jewish shareholders in the company appealed to its directors, who forced Stuyvesant to relent, on the condition that the "indigent among [the Jews] shall not become a burden on the Company or the public, but shall be maintained at the expense of the Jewish nation" (quoted in Goldin 1976, 5). Self-help in the face of anti-Semitism became a central characteristic of Jewish charity.

By the mid-nineteenth century, an increasingly prosperous German Jewish immigrant community had created a welter of charitable agencies in the United States, particularly in New York, that had evolved into community-wide organizations rather than retaining close associations with a particular synagogue. Typically, Jewish communities sponsored a general welfare society to provide monetary relief to the impoverished, orphanages for Jewish children, homes for the Jewish elderly, a number of educational institutions, and a hospital. Hospitals in particular served as a key point of pride for the Jewish community, but they also underscored the tension between the forces of anti-Semitism and the tradition of Jewish self-help: One prime motive for creating Jewish hospitals was that other hospitals often refused to train or hire Jewish doctors.

A new wave of immigration beginning in the late nineteenth century strained Jewish communal resources. Russian Jews fleeing the pogroms that began in Russia in 1881 chose the United States as one of their prime destinations. The American Jewish population stood at 250,000 in 1880, but would soon absorb over 1.6 million new immigrants from Eastern Europe. Fearful of an anti-Semitic backlash, some in the Jewish community protested the influx of poor Russian Jews, but the community soon mobilized to create institutions that would help the new immigrants settle and assimilate into America.

What may have seemed like a homogeneous Jewish population when viewed by native-born Protestants at the turn of the century was in reality deeply divided by national origin, sectarian allegiance, and political conflict. The split was deepest between the more established and wealthier German Jewish community (the Yahudim), who often were adherents of more theologically liberal Reform Judaism, and the immigrant, poorer, and more Orthodox Russian Jews (the Yidn). It was reflected in a pattern of charitable interaction in which Yahudim controlled the welfare institutions that serviced a largely Yidn clientele. Yidn recipients, accustomed to a more intimate relationship with charity in their Russian villages, resented the seemingly impersonal and imperious attitudes of Yahudim charities. Such resentment, as well as a desire for the social recognition that charitable giving granted, led to the development of parallel Yahudim and Yidn welfare institutions in many cities.

The imposition of immigration restrictions in the United States following World War I reduced immigrant influence in the American Jewish community and began a process of assimilation that produced a more homogeneous Jewish population. The stabilization and increasing wealth of the community began to prompt questions in the 1920s as to the function of distinctively Jewish charity, particularly in light of the gradual expansion of such public welfare programs as mothers' pensions. Jewish welfare agencies began to discuss shifting their emphasis from charity to "constructive programs" in recreation or cultural activities. The increasing professionalization of social work and the mounting interest in Freudian psychology, influential in Jewish welfare agencies, prompted an interest in the emotional, rather than the financial, problems of the Jewish community.

The Great Depression, however, was a fundamental challenge to this centuries-old system that had prided itself on ethnic self-help. Mass unemployment overwhelmed the capacities of all charities, including Jewish agencies, which had to dispense with their "constructive" programs in order to deal with the poor. Isaac Rubinow, an influential advocate of publicly funded Social Security, declared that the Stuyvesant Pledge was more myth than reality and that Jewish poverty was part and parcel of American poverty and should be dealt with by public institutions. Though this viewpoint was resisted by many charitable leaders, the New Deal paved the way for an expanding government role in welfare provision, a reality that private charity would have to reconcile itself to.

With the advent of public welfare and the professionalization of social work in the 1930s and 1940s, some within the Jewish community began to ask what distinguished Jewish charity from nonsectarian or public relief. In this, Jewish social services mirrored general developments in American social welfare. There were, however, distinctive aspects. An emphasis on self-help had inspired free-loan programs in Jewish agencies that provided business aid to small entrepreneurs, and the development of vocational counseling services that helped locate jobs for Jewish workers who faced discrimination. The Holocaust and the founding of Israel in 1948 also energized Jewish philanthropy and defined a new set of needs that spurred increased philanthropic activity even as American Jews became more prosperous as a group. Maintaining Jewish institutions for the sake of Judaism became an increasingly important element of Jewish philanthropy. Resettling Jewish refugees, first from postwar Europe, then from Russia in the 1970s, was one outgrowth of this commitment.

Most commentators in the post–World War II period, though, observed the growing similarity of Jewish and secular social services, particularly as Jewish philanthropy focused less on charity and more on broader community needs. Jewish poverty remained an issue, but it was largely confined to the elderly. The increasing number of Jewish elderly led to a reorientation of institutional programs toward care for the chronically ill, with supporting social services aimed at allowing the elderly to remain in their own homes for as long as possible. Government rules allowed public funds such as Old Age Assistance and later Medicare to be used at religious institutions, and by the end of the twentieth century, these programs often provided the majority of such institutions' funds. At the same time, the number of children in Jewish orphanages dropped sharply, and many institutions were closed or changed to child psychiatric homes.

The prosperity of the Jewish population was evident in its increasing suburbanization after World War II. The shift to the suburbs left many urban Jewish institutions such as hospitals serving an inner-city clientele that, reflecting broader demographic patterns, was less likely to be Jewish and more likely to be African American or Hispanic. Jews by and large had supported the liberal welfare state of the midcentury, but as welfare became more and more associated with people of color, some rifts began to emerge. Tensions between Jewish and Black communities rose during the 1960s, and led some Jews to question their support for the welfare state. Moreover, increasing concerns about the vitality of the Jewish community (given high rates of divorce and intermarriage) and the survival of Israel following the 1967 war helped raise ethnic consciousness among Jews and led to calls for more community investment in Jewish culture and education, evidenced in the boom in the construction of Jewish community centers between 1960 and 1980.

Though Jewish charity became less and less focused on poverty per se in the late twentieth century, it remained entwined in questions about the communal role of charity and its relationship to the government. In the 1970s, Jewish agencies took advantage of increasing government "purchase of service," or contracting out, to fund counseling programs, work training, foster care and adoption, health care, and care for the elderly. This practice made them vulnerable, like many nonprofits, to social service cutbacks in the 1980s, at the same time that charities were being urged by some conservatives to take responsibility for the poor away from the government. Some Jewish conservatives have welcomed the opportunity for Jewish voluntary institutions to play an increased role in "faith-based" social service provision, but leaders of most mainstream Jewish charities have protested decreasing government commitments to social welfare.

Andrew Morris

See also: Mutual Aid; Philanthropy; Social Work; Voluntarism

References and Further Reading

Avrunin, William. 1957. "Jewish Social Services," *Social Work Year Book*. Washington, DC: National Association of Social Workers.

Bernstein, Philip. 1983. *To Dwell in Unity: The Jewish Federation Movement since 1960*. Philadelphia: Jewish Publication Society of America.

Dollinger, Marc. 2000. *Quest for Inclusion: Jews and Liberalism in Modern America*. Princeton: Princeton University Press.

Goldin, Milton. 1976. *Why They Give: American Jews and Their Philanthropies*. New York: Macmillan.

Kosmin, Barry A., and Paul Ritterband. 1991. *Contemporary Jewish Philanthropy in America*. Savage, MD: Rowman and Littlefield.

Morris, Robert, and Michael Freund. 1966. *Trends and Issues in Jewish Social Welfare in the United States, 1899–1952*. Philadelphia: Jewish Publication Society of America.

The Jungle, *Upton Sinclair*

For seven weeks in 1904, Upton Sinclair lived and examined firsthand life in the stockyards of Chicago; his horror at the conditions he found there led him to write his best-known novel, *The Jungle*, a devastating portrayal of a world of desperate poverty, shocking corruption, unsanitary factories, hopelessness, and suffering.

First serialized in the socialist *Appeal to Reason* in 1905 and then released in novel form in 1906, *The Jungle* is, on one level, a gut-wrenching story of a Lithuanian family brutalized by the wage slavery that destroyed so many families and lives in the early twentieth century. However, it is also a classic of muckraking and of the American realist school of literature. Muckrakers seek to bring to light the dirty secrets of companies such as those of the Beef Trust—the doctoring of spoiled meats, the unsanitary factory conditions, the cruelty of low wages and inhumane treatment for employees. American realists sought to baldly tell the story of the Industrial Revolution with the voice of the common people. Despite critics' charges of sentimentality and a sometimes overly propagandistic and didactic tone, *The Jungle*'s legacy in muckraking and as realist literature has been profound. Moreover, Sinclair's exposure of the reprehensible behavior of the Beef Trust was a significant factor in bringing about the Pure Food and Drug Act and the Meat Inspection Act of 1906.

Meat inspectors examine hogs at the Swift & Company packinghouse in Chicago, ca. 1900. Both hygiene and labor conditions within the meatpacking industry came under close scrutiny by so-called muckraking journalists, and were memorably featured in Upton Sinclair's* The Jungle. *Such reports helped bring about the passage of the 1906 Federal Meat Inspection Act. (Corbis)

Beyond this, however, the novel also operates as an ideological argument; it depicts the failure and inherent injustices of capitalism and points the way toward an ultimate triumph for the poor via the socialist struggle. Sinclair, born in 1878 to a poor family descended from the southern aristocracy, was concerned throughout his life with the struggles of the destitute and with the contrasts of life at the extremes of the social spectrum. He converted to socialism in 1904, and the impact of his ideological commitment to the movement is obvious in *The Jungle*, in which the only ray of hope comes when the main character, Jurgis Rudkus, undergoes his own conversion to socialism and in the process rediscovers his self-respect and the resilience of the human spirit when given hope.

Sinclair's politics infuriated many, yet his portrayal of the meatpacking industry spurred many to outrage and then reform. The impact of *The Jungle* reverberated in policy and politics, as Sinclair challenged the American public to address fundamental questions raised by capitalism.

Rebecca K. Root

See also: Industrialization; Progressive Era and 1920s

References and Further Reading

Barrett, James. 1987. *Work and Community in the Jungle: Chicago's Packinghouse Workers, 1894–1922*. Urbana: University of Illinois.

Mookerjee, R. N. 1988. *Art for Social Justice: The Major Novels of Upton Sinclair*. Metuchen, NJ: Scarecrow Press.

Juvenile Delinquency

Though the term "juvenile delinquency," meaning the antisocial behavior of youth, is of modern vintage, Americans have tried to identify and control wayward children since the colonial era. Efforts to curtail such behavior have been linked in every era both to cultural elites' fears of social instability and to their desire to realize chosen cultural ideals. More specifically, elites' campaigns against juvenile delinquency assumed that some families lacked the capacity to inculcate habits of moral responsibility in their dependents and that a welfare state must control *and* rehabilitate youthful miscreants when families could not. American policymakers and social reformers usually viewed the children of the poor as those most prone to delinquency and most in need of therapeutic intervention by the state. Biases about race, ethnicity, religion, and gender intersected with perceptions of class to shape policies on juvenile delinquency. Successive generations of socially anxious elites complained that existing programs failed to contain youthful deviance, provoking new and expensive rounds of reform. Though the parents of poor children attempted to shape state controls to their own interests, they had limited ability to do so.

The precursor to modern law and policy on juvenile delinquency was the "stubborn child" law, a statute passed by the Massachusetts Bay Colony in 1646 making it a capital offense for any boy to disobey his father or mother. The significance of this law does not lie in the severity of the punishment it prescribed, for there is little evidence of children being put to death for filial disobedience. Rather, the "stubborn child" law, which emerged in a decade of religious and political dissent, codified normative and deviant moral behaviors for parents and children (or heads of household and unrelated servants and slaves) and created a legal framework for the community's regulation of children. It established in America the permeable boundaries between family and state and the state's interest in moral and social control.

The modern juvenile justice system was inaugurated in the 1820s with the opening of Houses of Refuge in Boston, New York City, and Philadelphia. All were founded by social elites who believed that Irish immigration, the growth of the factory system, and urbanization were producing profound social dislocations, including pauperism and juvenile delinquency. The reformers believed themselves to be among God's elect, yet they favored secular and "rational" methods for rehabilitating wayward children. Indeed, the legislation authorizing the private refuges established key principles of modern juvenile justice: a distinction between adult and juvenile offenders, reliance on indeterminate sentences to ensure youthful rehabilitation, and a broadening of the category of delinquent children to include not only lawbreakers but also the incorrigible and neglected. Subsequent court cases upheld the right of the state to separate children from "unworthy" parents, against the wishes of the latter. The inmates of the early refuges were usually poor Irish Catholics, but Philadelphia also established a refuge for "colored" juvenile delinquents. Female inmates were usually disciplined for presumed sexual immorality.

For the remainder of the nineteenth century, state governments supported a variety of moral interventions that built on the underlying assumptions of the Houses of Refuge, though the houses themselves were discredited as overly punitive. Responding to sharpening class tensions, reformers and state officials invented a legal concept of juvenile delinquency that justified the incarceration of children, especially the children of poor immigrants. These social elites declared that impoverished families were cradles of criminal behavior, yet they insisted that children could be rehabilitated by early intervention. Their most important innovation was the state reformatory, designed to turn boys and girls of the so-called dangerous classes into reliable workers and citizens. States gave the new public institutions jurisdiction over criminal as well as noncriminal juvenile delinquents and permitted the incarceration of children without due process.

1936 poster promoting planned housing as a method to deter juvenile delinquency, showing silhouettes of a child stealing a piece of fruit and a child involved in armed robbery. (Library of Congress)

Efforts to control juvenile delinquency intensified during the Progressive Era as elites hastened to resolve social and economic conflicts provoked by the emergence of the United States as a global industrial power. Government officials, social reformers, and social welfare professionals complained that juvenile delinquency was on the rise because poor, immigrant, and nonwhite parents were ignorant of children's needs in a modern industrial society. Cultural elites were especially alarmed by evidence of sexual immorality among disadvantaged adolescent girls. Illinois initiated the most significant reforms of the era: juvenile courts and systems for probation and parole. Juvenile courts favored, at least in principle, a socialized jurisprudence that identified adjudication as the first step in a complex program of diagnosis and treatment. Judges and probation officers in the juvenile system questioned the efficacy of incarceration, yet they enhanced state authority by devising surveillance methods that reached poor and immigrant children at home, school, work, and play.

Progressive reformers sought to anchor innovations in juvenile justice in social scientific knowledge. They often turned to mental health professionals for insights into the mental conflicts that were thought to contribute to delinquency.

By the 1920s, many juvenile courts were turning to child guidance clinics for help in diagnosing and treating juvenile delinquents. This partnership was relatively weak, however. Over time, professionals in child guidance clinics shifted their practices to middle-class children, whose problems seemed less severe than those of the poor delinquents referred by the courts.

Beginning in the 1930s, many poor communities developed delinquency-prevention programs, enlisting help from neighborhood leaders and local organizations. During the 1960s, community-based programs proliferated, some attempting prevention *and* rehabilitation. Federal support for the programs was challenged by ethnic activists who argued that Washington, D.C., was engaging in a form of domestic colonialism. Judges in juvenile courts, police officials, and correctional administrators also challenged the community-based programs, claiming they failed to reduce juvenile crime.

After the 1960s, most states passed laws that separated criminal and noncriminal juveniles and specified different levels of rights and, sometimes, different treatment for the two classes of offenders. Since the 1980s, debates over juvenile delinquency have been dominated by social conservatives, who favor deterrence and punishment for juvenile criminals, including their transfer to adult courts and prisons. Conservatives offer uncompromising definitions of normative and deviant behavior while questioning the extent to which poverty contributes to juvenile delinquency.

Ruth M. Alexander

See also: Adolescent Pregnancy; Child Welfare; Child-Saving; Crime Policy; Feminization of Poverty; Maternalism; Orphanages; Social Surveys; Welfare State

References and Further Reading

Alexander, Ruth M. 1995. *The "Girl Problem": Female Sexual Delinquency in New York, 1900–1930*. Ithaca, NY: Cornell University Press.

Getis, Victoria. 2000. *The Juvenile Court and the Progressives*. Urbana: University of Illinois Press.

Krisberg, Barry, and James F. Austin. 1993. *Reinventing Juvenile Justice*. Newbury Park, CA: Sage.

Sutton, John R. 1988. *Stubborn Children: Controlling Delinquency in the United States, 1640–1981*. Berkeley and Los Angeles: University of California Press.

Kerner Commission Report

The Kerner Commission Report, the product of the 1967 Commission on Civil Disorders, is an eclectic document combining liberal and moderate analyses of the causes and remedies for the widespread urban violence in the late 1960s. Rejecting conservative interpretations blaming revolutionary conspiracies, the report blamed "white racism" for the increasingly violent confrontations between America's "two nations," prescribed a broad reform agenda, but shied away from a structural analysis of urban poverty. President Lyndon B. Johnson appointed the Commission on Civil Disorders in July 1967, after rebellions in Newark and Detroit climaxed four summers of violence that left 130 dead. Governor Otto Kerner of Illinois presided over a liberal-moderate collection of eight public officials, a corporate leader, a labor leader, and a civil rights leader (only two of the commission's members were Black). The commission's report, issued in March 1968, was "a catalogue of ills and a list of reforms" rather than a coherent analysis or popularly accessible challenge to political and economic power (Boesel and Rossi 1971, 256). Yet the commission did push the boundaries of liberalism, recommending more than Johnson or Congress could accept. Commission members heeded Johnson's initial call for an attack on "conditions that breed despair . . . ignorance, discrimination, slums, poverty, disease, not enough jobs." And they challenged Johnson's assumptions that riots were the crimes of a "violent few" and that police deserved respect from "all Americans" (*Report* 1968, 538–541).

Despite its willingness to challenge conventional wisdom, the Kerner Commission was under continual pressure to produce a moderate—and moderating—report. Robert Shellow, a social psychologist, coordinated survey research in twenty-three cities for the commission. When researchers drafted "Harvest of American Racism"—noting a "truly revolutionary spirit" among rioters—administrators appointed by Johnson fired Shellow and 120 researchers. Mayor John Lindsay of New York, who led a liberal faction on the commission, was unhappy with the "wishy-washy" tone of the report written by staff lawyers. He inserted a hard-hitting "Summary" in the beginning (Boesel and Rossi 1971, 255). "White racism is essentially responsible for the explosive mixture" that produced postwar ghettos, it read, indicting racist *institutions* as well as racist *attitudes* (*Report* 1968, 1–2). In part because of such forceful sentiments, the book was an instant best seller.

The eclectic report's catalogue of the riots' causes included discrimination, mass migrations, manufacturing decline, low Black self-esteem, and (central but rarely mentioned), "indiscriminate and excessive" police violence. Despite allegations of riot conspiracies hatched in antipoverty offices, the commissioners found that antipoverty workers, ministers, and community activists acted as "counter-rioters." In a glaring omission, they ignored the Vietnam War and its disproportionately high Black casualty rates, yet they noted that half of Newark's rioters denied that America was worth defending in a "world war." "Rioters" were typically young Black men: better educated than nonrioters, politically aware but disaffected, frustrated by unemployment and job discrimination—not simple criminals. Their grievances were widely shared: "Police practices" and unemployment came first, then "inadequate education," ineffective political structures, and inadequate federal poverty and welfare programs. Still, biased toward social psychology, the commission spoke of "the frustrations of powerlessness" more than of disempowering institutions (*Report* 1968, passim).

Locally, the commission recommended more funding and more citizen participation in community action agencies and "neighborhood action task forces" to press grievances. Nationally, they advocated new taxes and reforms in education, employment (2 million new jobs), welfare (subsidies for poor workers and poverty-line benefits for mothers receiving Aid to Families with Dependent Children), and housing (desegregation and 6 million new units). Johnson refused to comment on a report that he found divisive and legislatively unrealistic, and Congress was increasingly focusing on "law and order." Yet the commission helped spawn a larger body of analytically sharper empirical research challenging the nation, the police, and, ultimately, the commission itself.

Thomas F. Jackson

See also: African Americans; Poverty Research; Racial Segregation; Racism; Urban Poverty; War on Poverty

References and Further Reading

Boesel, David, and Peter H. Rossi, eds. 1971. *Cities under Siege*. New York: Basic Books.

Fogelson, Robert M. 1971. *Violence as Protest: A Study of Riots and Ghettos*. Garden City, NY: Doubleday.

Report of the National Advisory Commission on Civil Disorders. 1968. New York: Bantam.

King, Martin Luther, Jr.

See Civil Rights Movement; Poor People's Campaign